Hindus
of
the
Himalayas:
Ethnography and Change

Berkeley, Los Angeles, London

Hindus

of

the

Himalayas:

Ethnography and Change

BY GERALD D. BERREMAN

UNIVERSITY OF CALIFORNIA PRESS *1972*

UNIVERSITY OF CALIFORNIA PRESS
BERKELEY AND LOS ANGELES, CALIFORNIA
UNIVERSITY OF CALIFORNIA PRESS, LIMITED
LONDON, ENGLAND
© 1963, 1972 BY THE REGENTS OF THE UNIVERSITY OF CALIFORNIA
SECOND EDITION, REVISED AND ENLARGED, 1972
ISBN: 0-520-01423-5 (CLOTH)
0-520-02035-9 (PAPER)
LIBRARY OF CONGRESS CATALOG CARD NUMBER: 73-156468
PRINTED IN THE UNITED STATES OF AMERICA

To My Mother and Father
Sevilla and Joel Berreman

PREFACE TO THE
SECOND EDITION

The decision to reissue *Hindus of the Himalayas* in this form grew both from my restudy of Sirkanda a decade after the initial research, and from my colleagues' suggestions that the book be made more readily accessible to students and others by being issued in paperback.

I have left the text, comprising the ethnography (Introduction through Chapter 10, Conclusion), as it was orginally, except for minor editing. It now has a Prologue, "Behind Many Masks: Ethnography and Impression Management," and an epilogue, "Sirkanda Ten Years Later." The first of these additions was published as a Monograph of the Society for Applied Anthropology (Monograph No. 4), under the title *Behind Many Masks: Ethnography and Impression Management in a Himalayan Hill Village*. Here its Foreword by Robert J. Smith, and the brief Conclusions, have been omitted for the sake of brevity. It has been added to the book because it is a frank account of the conditions under which the research reported in the rest of the book was done. It gives additional and, I think, crucial insight into the bases for the ethnographic descriptions and analyses it precedes. I say "crucial," because I believe firmly that ethnography cannot be understood independently of the experience which produces it. Just as I felt obliged to be thorough and candid in presenting my research findings, so I have felt obliged to be thorough and candid about how I did that research. If fault be found with the former, it is the result of the latter.

Written from an "interactionist" perspective (cf. Blumer, 1969), "Behind Many Masks" emphasizes the problems for research generated by the conflicting interests of the various castes and by their divergent cultures and life-styles, because even in small and isolated Sirkanda, social heterogeneity loomed as a major obstacle to my rapport and my understanding, just as it does to the people's relationships with one another.

The final chapter, "Sirkanda Ten Years Later," is just what its title implies. I returned in 1968–1969 and sought to discover what changes and what continuities were to be found. I was struck by the impact my return had upon Sirkanda people and upon myself, and in this chapter I try, in part, to convey the human qualities of that impact. Utilizing, in general, the ethnographic headings of the preceding parts of the book, I then describe and try to account for the state of the village ten years later. A major topic of the chapter is a description and analysis of a truly remarkable personage—Kalmu the miracle-worker, whom I had known as a 13-year-old goatherd of blacksmith caste and who then became the vehicle of a powerful god, renowned far beyond Bhatbair. I view his career not only as a religious phenomenon, but as a manifestation of social mobility. The discussion turns from him to others who have been socially mobile in—and out of—Sirkanda. Trends in the village and in the region are the focus of the chapter; drawing implications for the country at large is its ultimate aim.

In making these additions, in order to economize on space, I have deleted the appendices which were in the first edition. I did so with some regret, because they comprised amplified descriptions of facets of culture and social organization that are only touched upon in the text and that are not elsewhere described in the ethnographic literature. However, they are primarily of interest to the specialist, and anyone who is interested can still consult them in the first edition. The Appendices were: I: Gods Worshipped in Sirkanda, II: Calendrical Rites in Sirkanda, III: Life Cycle Rites in Sirkanda—all giving detailed accounts of their respective topics—and IV: Sirkanda Kin Terms, a comprehensive chart of the terminology of address and reference of some 83 categories of kinfolk.

References to literature cited in the original text have not been up-dated except where an unpublished work cited has since been published. To do more would have required resetting the entire book. Therefore, a chapter-by-chapter supplementary bibliography has been added in which are listed significant and relevant works which have come to my attention during 1963–1971.

Twenty-eight photographs accompanied the original text, all taken in 1957–58. Eight photographs (numbers 29–36) have been added in this edition. All were taken in 1968–1969, except number 32, of Kalmu herding his goats in 1958. All photographs now follow page 196.

The Acknowledgements, written in 1963, cite the sources of financial support for the original research and write-up. The 1968–1969 research was financed by a Fulbright–Hays Fellowship for Advanced Research, with supplementary funds from the National Institutes of Mental Health, Behavioral Sciences Research Branch, and the Center for South and Southeast Asian Studies of the University of California, Berkeley. I appreciate this support.

It is impossible to give adequate recognition to the individuals whose support, moral and material, have contributed to the book. Because they are all friends, and because the research means much to me, they are close to my heart. I have thanked those who contributed to the initial research in my Acknowledgements of 1963. Now I would like to give their due to those who were kind and helpful in 1968–1969.

In India, Mr. C. S. Ramakrishnan, of the U. S. Educational Foundation, was helpful far beyond the call of duty on all matters of an official nature and on others as well. I am grateful too, to Professor M. N. Srinivas and his colleagues in the Department of Sociology, University of Delhi, where I was designated an Honorary Visiting Professor and was granted many courtesies during the research period.

Those who were in the vicinity of the research were those I depended upon most heavily and interacted with most frequently. Mr. Harilal Dhingra, my friend, teacher, and assistant in Dehra Dun, and occasional companion in Sirkanda, contributed immeasurably to the success of the enterprise. Dr. Lucile F. Newman (University of California, San Francisco) and Dr. J. Michael Mahar (University of Arizona), were engaged in research in Dehra Dun and Saharanpur Districts, respectively. They exchanged ideas, information and research site visits with me, and their presence together with their families provided good company, good times, and moral support for myself and my family. I want to thank again, after a decade, Mr. M. Basir and Mr. and Mrs. J. Suvanto and their families, and to thank Mr. and Mrs. Caldwell Smith and the staff of the Dehra Dun Language School, Mr. and Mrs. Amar Singh whose house we shared, and Mr. and Mrs. S. Lebocq, all of whom were helpful friends.

As I thanked my wife and daughter, Evelyn and Janet, for their company, help and fortitude ten years ago, I do so again and add thanks to my younger daughter and son, Lynn and Wayne, who were born after the previous research. I was glad to have them along and to be able to introduce them to my friends in Sirkanda while reintroducing Evelyn and Janet. They added interest and pleasure to the year, and they bore its very real hardships and occasional crises with equanimity and (usually) with good humor.

My ultimate thanks go again to the people of Sirkanda. I have learned much from them and have benefitted in many ways from our unlikely friendship. I wish I believed that the benefits were mutual. I do not, for while I provided them with some momentary diversion and perhaps some amusing or even valued memories, I could not help them directly with the chronic or acute problems of their lives. I can only hope that this book, by portraying them respectfully, sympathetically and realistically to others—as I have tried to do—will reach and influence those with power to affect their lives, and so repay in part the debt I owe them. That debt is heaviest to Safri and to Ratan Singh, who gave friendship without thought of gain.

Berkeley
January, 1971

Acknowledgments

This book is based upon research first reported in my dissertation, presented to the faculty of the Graduate School of Cornell University, in September, 1959. I am grateful to Professor Morris E. Opler for his interest and suggestions in supervising the preparation of the dissertation and for his encouragement thereafter to revise and publish it. Others who provided helpful advice include Professors Allan R. Holmberg, Lauriston Sharp, Robert J. Smith, and Robin M. Williams. Mr. J. Michael Mahar and Professor S. C. Dube gave liberally of helpful counsel before the research was undertaken. Mr. A. C. Chandola reviewed linguistic and other materials in the course of the final revision. Mr. James M. Sebring checked census figures and numerous bibliographic references and helped in proofreading. To all these people I am grateful.

The Ford Foundation, through its Foreign Area Training Fellowship program, financed nearly three years of work which led to the dissertation, including 15 months in India during 1957–1958, and six months of analysis and writing following the research. Library research and substantial rewriting in the preparation of this book were supported by a University of California Summer Faculty Research Fellowship and by part-time research appointments with the Himalayan Border Countries Research Project and the South Asia Village Studies Project in the Center for South Asia Studies of the Institute of International Studies, University of California, Berkeley. Dr. Joan V. Bondurant, then chairman of the Center for South Asia Studies, Dr. Leo E.

Rose, head of the Himalayan Border Countries Research Project, and Dr. William L. Rowe, my colleague in the South Asia Village Studies Project, have been encouraging and helpful in this research. The Department of Anthropology at the University of California, Berkeley, has been coöperative in accommodating to my part-time research appointments. I wish to thank all of these individuals and institutions for their material and moral support.

My family and I are indebted to many people who were kind and helpful to us in India, especially to Mr. and Mrs. James Alter, Mr. and Mrs. Leon Elliott, Mr. and Mrs. T. D. Fordham, and Mr. and Mrs. J. Suvanto and their families, all of whom were friends in need. In my research I benefited greatly from the assistance of Mr. A. P. Sharma and Mr. M. Basir. Mr. Basir's unfailing interest and untiring efficiency were important factors in the success of the research.

I am immeasurably indebted to my wife, Evelyn, who bore with good humor the difficulties of life under trying circumstances; who managed our household, cared for our small daughter in health and illness, and typed untold hundreds of pages of reference material and notes—all while I was preoccupied with research and most of the time while I was physically absent. Our daughter, Janet, shared without complaint the unstable life of the field anthropologist's family and the crises, maladies, and discomforts inherent therein (and several not inherent therein). Few families are called upon to endure what they endured, and they did so with a grace deserving of respect and my deepest gratitude.

Finally, I am grateful to the people of Sirkanda, without whose trust, friendship, and forbearance the research would have been impossible. In particular I appreciate the kindness and understanding of my friends, Alam Singh and Safri.

Contents

MAPS

PHOTOGRAPHS

He who thinks on Himachal, though he should not behold him, is greater than he who performs all worship in Kashi. In a hundred ages of the gods I could not tell thee of the glories of Himachal. As the dew is dried up by the morning sun, so are the sins of mankind by the sight of Himachal.

SKANDA PURANA

PROLOGUE:
BEHIND MANY MASKS;
ETHNOGRAPHY AND IMPRESSION
MANAGEMENT *

Ethnographers have all too rarely made explicit the methods by which the information reported in their descriptive and analytical works was derived. Even less frequently have they attempted systematic descriptions of those aspects of the field experience which fall outside of a conventional definition of method, but which are crucial to the research and its results. The potential field worker in any given area often has to rely for advance information about many of the practical problems of his craft upon the occasional verbal anecdotes of his predecessors or the equally random remarks included in ethnographic prefaces. To the person facing field work for the first time, the dearth of such information may appear to be the result of a conviction, among those who know, that experience can be the only teacher. Alternatively, he may suspect ethnographers of having established a conspiracy of silence on these matters. When he himself becomes a bona fide ethnographer he may join that conspiracy inadvertently, or he may feel obligated to join it not only to protect the secrets of ethnography, but to protect himself. As a result of the rules of the game which kept others from communicating their experience to him, he may feel that his own difficulties of morale and rapport, his own compromises between the ideal and the necessary, were unique, and perhaps signs of weakness or incompetence. Consequently, these are concealed or minimized. More acceptable aspects of the field experience such as those relating to formal research methods, health hazards, transportation facilities and useful equipment suffice to answer the queries of the curious. This is in large measure a matter of maintaining the proper "front" (see below) before an audience made up not only of the uninitiated, but in many cases of other ethnographers as well.

As a result of this pattern "Elenore Bowen" shared the plight of many an anthropological neophyte when, according to her fictionalized account she arrived in West Africa girded for field work with her professors' formulae for success:

Always walk in cheap tennis shoes; the water runs out more quickly, [and] You'll need more tables than you think (Bowen, 1954, pp. 3-4).

This prologue is not an exposition of research methods or field techniques in the usual sense. It is a description of some aspects of my field research, analyzed from a particular point of view. As such, it is an attempt to portray some features of that human experience which is field work, and some of the implications of its being human experience for ethnography as a scientific endeavor. It is not intended as a model for others to follow. It tells what happened, what I did, why I did it and with what apparent effect. As in all field work, the choices were not always mine and the results were frequently unanticipated. But the choices and results have proved instructive. I hope that this account will add depth to the ethnographic study which follows by conveying the methods and circumstances which led to it.

INTRODUCTION

Every ethnographer, when he reaches the field, is faced immediately with accounting for himself before the people he proposes to learn to know. Only when this has been accomplished can he proceed to his avowed task of seeking to understand and interpret the way of life of those people. The second of these endeavors is more frequently discussed in anthropological literature than the first, although the success of the enterprise depends as largely upon one as the other. Both tasks, in common with all social interaction, involve the control and interpretation of impressions, in this case those conveyed by the ethnographer and his subjects to one another. Impressions are derived from a complex of observations and inferences drawn from what people do as well as what they say both in public, i.e., when they know they are being watched, and in private, i.e., when they think they are not being watched. Attempts to convey a desired impression of one's self and to interpret accurately the behavior and attitudes of others are an inherent part of any social interaction, and they are crucial to ethnographic research.

My research in a tightly closed and highly stratified society can serve as a case study from which to analyze some of the problems and consequences inherent in the interaction of ethnographer and subjects. Special emphasis will be placed upon the differential effects of the ethnographer's identification with high-status and low-status groups in the community.

THE SETTING

The research upon which this account is based took place in and around Sirkanda, a peasant village of the lower Himalayas of North India. Its residents, like those of the entire lower Himalayan area from Kashmir through Nepal, are known as *Paharis* (of the mountains). The village is small, containing some 384 individuals during the year of my residence there in 1957–1958, and it is relatively isolated, situated as it is in rugged hills accessible only on foot and nine miles from the nearest road and bus service.

Strangers in the area are few and readily identifiable by dress and speech. People who are so identified are avoided or discouraged from remaining long in the vicinity. To escape such a reception, a person must be able to identify himself as a member of a familiar group through kinship ties, caste (*jati*) ties and/or community affiliation. Since the first two are ascribed characteristics, the only hope an outsider has of achieving acceptance is by establishing residence and, through social interaction, acquiring the status of a community-dweller; a slow process at best.

The reluctance of Sirkanda villagers and their neighbors to accept strangers is attested to by the experience of those outsiders who have dealt with them. In 1957 a new teacher was assigned to the Sirkanda school. He was a Pahari from an area some fifty miles distant. Despite his Pahari background and consequent familiarity with the language and customs of the local people, he complained after four months in the village that his reception had been less than cordial:

I have taught in several schools in the valley and people have always been friendly to me. They have invited me to their homes for meals, have sent gifts of grain and vegetables with their children, and have tried to make me feel at home. I have been here four months now with almost no social contact aside from my students. No one has asked me to eat with him; no one has sent me so much as a grain of millet; no one had asked me to sit and talk with him; no one has even asked me who I am or whether I have a family. They ignore me.

He fared better than the teacher in another village of the area who had to give up after three months during which he and his proposed school were totally boycotted.

Among the forestry officers whose duty it is to make periodic rounds in these hills, villagers' lack of hospitality is proverbial. They claim that here a man has to carry his own food, water, and bedroll because he cannot count on villagers to offer these necessities to him on his travels. Community development and establishment of credit cooperatives, two governmental programs in the area, have been unsuccessful largely because of their advocates' inability to establish rapport with the people. My assistant, who had worked for more than a year in an anthropological research project in a village of the plains, was constantly baffled at the reticence and lack of hospitality of villagers. As he said:

In Kalapur, when you walked through the village, men would hail you and invite you to sit and talk with them. Whether or not they really wanted you to do so, they at least invited you out of common courtesy. Here they just go inside or turn their backs when they see you coming.

The reasons for such reticence are not far to seek. Contacts with outsiders have been limited largely to contacts with policemen and tax collectors—two of the lowest forms of life in the Pahari taxonomy. Such officials are despised and feared not only because they make trouble for villagers in the line of duty, but because they also extort bribes on the threat of causing further trouble and often seem to take advantage of their official positions to vent their aggressions on these vulnerable people. Since India's independence, spheres of governmental responsibility have extended to include stringent supervision of greatly extended national forest lands, rationing of certain goods, establishment of a variety of development programs, etc. The grounds for interfering in village affairs have multiplied as the variety of officials has proliferated. Any stranger, therefore, may be a government agent, and as such he is potentially troublesome and even dangerous.

Villagers' fears on this score are not groundless. Aside from the unjust exploitation which such agents are reputed to employ in their activities, there are many illegal or semilegal activities carried on by villagers which could be grounds for punishment and are easily used as grounds for extortion. In Sirkanda, national forest lands and products have been illegally appropriated by villagers, taxable land has been underreported, liquor is brewed and sold illicitly, women have been illegally sold, guns have gone unlicensed, adulterated milk is sold to outside merchants, children are often married below the legal age, men have fled the army or escaped from jail, property has been illegally acquired from fleeing Muslims at the time of partition. Any of these and similar real and imagined infractions may be objects of a stranger's curiosity and therefore are reasons for discouraging his presence in the village.

Paharis are thought by people of the plains to be ritually, spiritually, and morally inferior. They are suspected of witchcraft and evil magic. In addition they are considered naive bumpkins—the hillbilly stereotype of other cultures. Paharis try to avoid interaction with those who hold these stereotypes. Alien Brahmins may seek to discredit their Pahari counterparts by finding evidence of their unorthodoxy; alien traders may seek to relieve them of their hard-earned cash or produce by sharp business practices; scoundrels may seek to waylay or abduct village women; thieves may come to steal their worldly possessions; lawyers or their cohorts may seek evidence for trumped-up legal proceedings which a poor Pahari could not hope to counteract in court; Christian missionaries may hope to infringe on their religious beliefs and practices. Strangers are therefore suspected of having ulterior motives even if they are not associated with the government.

The only way to feel sure that such dangers do not inhere in a person is to know who he is, and to know this he must fit somewhere into the known social system. Only then is he subject to effective local controls so that if he transgresses, or betrays a trust, he can be brought to account. The person who is beyond control is beyond trust and is best hurried on his way. This is, therefore, a relatively closed society. Interaction with strangers is kept to a minimum; the information furnished them is scanty and stereotyped. Access to such a society is difficult for an outsider.

Within this closed society there is rigid stratification into a number of hereditary, ranked, endogamous groups—castes—comprising two large divisions: the high or twice-born castes and the low or untouchable castes. The high castes, Rajputs and Brahmins, are land-owning agriculturalists who are dominant in numbers, comprising ninety per cent of the population. They are dominant in economic wherewithal, in that they own most of the land and animals, while the other castes depend on them for their livelihood. They are dominant in political power, for both traditional and new official means of control are in their hands. They dominate in ritual status as twice-born, ritually clean castes while all other castes are untouchable (*achut*). In most villages, as in Sirkanda, Rajputs outnumber Brahmins and so are locally dominant, but the ritual and social distance between them is not great and the economic difference is usually nil (Srinivas, 1959).

The low castes, whose members are artisans, are disadvantaged in each respect that the high castes are advantaged. They are dependent upon the high castes for their livelihood and are subject to the will of the high castes in almost every way. Ideally their relationship to the high castes is one of respect, deference, and obedience. In return high-caste members are supposed to be paternalistic. In practice there is a good deal of tension in the relationship, and it is held stable largely by considerations of relative power (Berreman, 1960a).

In addition there are nonhierarchical cleavages within the high castes and within the low castes based upon kinship ties (lineage and sib lines being paramount) and informal cliques and factions. As a result of these factors the community is divided within itself. While there is consensus on some things, there is disagreement on others. Acceptance by one element of the community does not imply acceptance by the whole community and it frequently, in fact, precludes it.

The Research

It was into this community that my interpreter-assistant and I walked, unannounced, one rainy day in September, 1957, hoping to engage in ethnographic research. On our initial visit we asked only to camp there while we visited a number of surrounding villages. We were introduced by a note from a non-Pahari wholesaler of the nearest market town who had long bought the surplus agricultural produce of villagers and had, as it turned out, through sharp practices of an obscure nature, acquired land in the village. He asked that the villagers treat the strangers as "our people" and extend all hospitality to them. As might have been expected, our benefactor was not beloved in the village and it was more in spite of his intercession than on account of it that we ultimately managed to do a year's research in the village.

The note was addressed to a high-caste man who proved to be one of the most suspicious people of the village; the head of a household recently victorious in a nine-year court battle over land brought against the household by virtually the entire village; the leader of a much-resented but powerful minority faction. That he gave us an unenthusiastic reception was a blow to our morale but probably a boon to our chances of being tolerated in the village.

The interpreter-assistant who accompanied me was a young Brahmin of plains origin who had previously worked in a similar capacity for a large research project carried out in the plains village of Kalapur. I shall hereafter refer to him as Sharma.

For the first three months of our stay in the village, most of our time was spent keeping house and attempting to establish rapport, both of which were carried out under trying circumstances.

According to their later reports to us, villagers at first assumed that we were missionaries, a species which had not previously invaded this locality but which was well known. Several villagers had sold milk in Mussoorie, a hill station sixteen miles distant that is frequented by missionaries. When we failed to meddle in religious matters or to show surprise at local rituals, this suspicion gradually faded. We had anticipated this interpretation of our motives and so were careful not to show undue interest in religion as a topic of conversation. We purposely used Hindu rather than areligious forms of greeting in our initial contacts to avoid being identified as missionaries. As a topic for polite and, we hoped, neutral conversation, we chose agriculture. It seemed timely too, as the fall harvest season began not long after our arrival in the village. Partly as a result of this choice of conversational fare, suspicion arose that we were government agents sent to reassess the land for taxation purposes, based on the greater-than-previously-reported productivity of the land. Alternatively, we were suspect of being investigators seeking to find the extent of land use in unauthorized areas following the nationalization of the surrounding uncultivated lands. My physical appearance was little comfort to villagers harboring these suspicions. One man commented that "Anyone can look like a foreigner if he wears the right clothes." Gradually these fears too disappeared, but others arose.

One person suggested that our genealogical inquiries might be preliminary to a military draft of the young men. The most steadfast opponent of our presence hinted darkly at the machinations of foreign spies—a vaguely understood but actively feared type of villain. Nearly four months had passed before overt suspicion of this sort was substantially dissipated, although, of course, some people had been convinced of the innocence of our motives relatively early and others remained suspicious throughout our stay.

One incident nearly four months after our first visit to the village proved to be a turning point in quelling overt opposition to our activities in the village. We were talking one afternoon to the local Brahmin priest. He had proved to be a reluctant informant, apparently because of his fear of alienating powerful and suspicious Rajputs whose caste-fellows outnumbered his own by more than thirty to one in the village (his was the only Brahmin household as compared to 37 Rajput households in Sirkanda), and in whose good graces it was necessary for him to remain for many reasons. However, he was basically friendly. Encouraged by our increasing rapport in the village at large, by his own feelings of affinity with my Brahmin assistant, Sharma, and by the privacy of his secluded threshing platform as a talking place, he had volunteered to discuss his family tree with us. Midway in our discussion, one of the most influential and hostile of the Rajputs came upon us—probably intentionally—and sat down with us. The Brahmin immediately became self-conscious and uncommunicative but it was too late to conceal the topic of our conversation. The Rajput soon interrupted, asking why the Brahmin was telling us these things and inquiring in a challenging way what possible use the information could be to an American scholar. He implied, with heavy irony, that we had ulterior motives. The interview was obviously ended and by this time a small crowd of onlookers had gathered. Since a satisfactory answer was evidently demanded and since most members of the audience were not among the people we knew best, I took the opportunity to answer fully.

I explained that prior to 1947, India had been a subject nation of little interest to the rest of the world. In the unlikely event that the United States or any other country wanted to negotiate regarding matters Indian, its representatives had merely to deal with the British who spoke for India. Indians were of no importance to us, for they were a subject people. They, in turn, had no need to know that America existed as, indeed, few did. Then in 1947, after a long struggle, India had become independent; a nation of proud people who handled their own affairs and participated in the United Nations and in all spheres of international relations on a par with Britain and the United States. Indians for the first time spoke for themselves. At once it became essential for Indians and Americans to know one another. Consequently

India sent hundreds of students to America, among other places, and we sent students such as myself to India. We had worked at learning their language and we also wanted to learn their means of livelihood, social customs, religion, etc., so that we could deal with them intelligently and justly, just as their students were similarly studying in and about America. Fortunately I had an Indian acquaintance, then studying a rural community in Utah, whom I could cite as a case comparable to my own. I pointed out that Indian and American scholars had studied Indian cities, towns and villages of the plains so that their ways were well known, but that heretofore the five million Paharis—residents of some of the richest, most beautiful, historically and religiously most significant parts of India—had been overlooked. I emphasized that Paharis would play an increasing role in the development of India and that if they were to assume the responsibilities and derive the advantages available to them it was essential that they be better known to their countrymen and to the world. My research was billed as an effort in this direction.

I would like to be able to report that on the basis of this stirring speech I was borne aloft triumphantly through the village, thereafter being treated as a fellow villager by one and all. Needless to say, this did not happen. My questioner was, however, evidently favorably impressed, or at least felt compelled to act as though he were before the audience of his village-mates. He responded by saying that he would welcome me in his house any time and would discuss fully any matters of interest to me. He also offered to supply me with a number of artifacts to take to America as exhibits of Pahari ingenuity. I might add, anticlimactically, that in fact he never gave me information beyond his reactions to the weather, and that the Brahmin, evidently shaken by his experience, was never again as informative as he had been immediately prior to this incident.[1]

The Rajput challenger, however, ceased to be hostile whereas formerly he had been a focus of opposition to my presence. General rapport in the village improved markedly and the stigma attached to talking with me and my interpreter almost disappeared. One notable aftereffect was that my photographic opportunities, theretofore restricted to scenery, small children, and adolescent boys in self-conscious poses, suddenly expanded to include a wide range of economic, ritual, and social occasions as well as people of all castes, ages, and both sexes. Photography itself soon became a valuable means of obtaining rapport as photographs came into demand.

The degree to which I was allowed or requested to take photographs, in fact, proved to be a fairly accurate indicator of rapport. One of the more gratifying incidents of my research in Sirkanda occurred at an annual regional fair some eight months after the research had begun. Soon after I arrived at the fair a group of gaily dressed young women of various villages had agreed to be photographed when a Brahmin man, a stranger to me, stormed up and ordered them to refuse. An elderly and highly respected Rajput woman of Sirkanda had been watching the proceedings and was obviously irritated by the fact and manner of the intervention. She stepped to the center of the group of girls, eyeing the Brahmin evenly, and said, "Please take my photograph." I did so, the Brahmin left, and my photography was in demand exceeding the film supply throughout the fair.

The incident described above, in which the Rajput challenged my interviewing of the Brahmin priest, came out favorably partly because of the context in which it occurred. For one thing, it occurred late enough so that many people knew me and my assistant. Having no specific cause for doubting our motives, they were ready to believe us if we made a convincing case. Also, there was a sizeable audience to the event. My explanation was a response to a challenge by a high-status villager and the challenger accepted it gracefully. It was the first time that many of these people had been present when I talked at any length and my statement was put with a good deal of feeling, which fact they recognized. It was essentially an appeal for their confidence and cooperation in a task they knew was difficult and which I obviously considered important. They were not incapable of empathy.[2] As one man had said earlier, "You may be a foreigner and we only poor villagers, but when we get to know you we will judge you as a man among other men; not as a foreigner." With time, most of the villagers demonstrated the validity of his comment by treating me as an individual on the basis of their experience with me, rather than as the stereotyped outsider or white man.

Most important, my statement placed the listeners in a position of accepting what I said or denying their own importance as people and as citizens—it appealed to their pride. They have strong inferiority feelings relative to non-Paharis which account in large measure for their hostility, and my presence as defined in this statement counteracted these feelings. It was especially effective in response to the Rajput who put the challenge; a man with an acute, and to many aggravating, need for public recognition of his importance. He had gained some eminence by opposing my work; he now evidently gained some by eliciting a full explanation from me and magnanimously accepting it.

Although I remained an alien and was never made to feel that my presence in the village was actively desired by most of its members, I was thereafter tolerated with considerable indulgence. I became established as a resident of Sirkanda, albeit a peculiar one, and no one tried to get me to leave. I have heard strangers en route to or from further mountain areas inquire of Sirkanda villagers as to my identity, presuming that I was out of earshot or could not understand, and be left to ponder the succinct reply, "He lives here."

Other, less spectacular rapport-inducing devices were employed. Unattached men in the village were considered, not unjustly in light of past experience and Pahari morality, a threat to village womanhood. This fear with regard to my assistant and myself was appreciably diminished when our wives and children visited the village and when a few villagers had been guests at our house in town where our families normally resided. We won some good will by providing a few simple remedies for common village ailments. One of the most effective means of attracting villagers to our abode in the village during this period was a battery radio which we brought in; the first to operate in this area. It was an endless source of diversion to villagers and attracted a regular audience, as well as being a focal attraction for visiting relatives and friends from other villages.

At first, reportedly, there had been considerable speculation in the village as to why two people of such conspicuously different backgrounds as Sharma and myself had appeared on the scene as a team if, as we claimed, we were not sent by the government or a missionary organization. The plausibility of our story was enhanced when Sharma made it clear to villagers that he was my bona fide employee who received payment in cash for his services.

Villagers never ceased to wonder, as I sometimes did myself, why I had chosen this particular area and village for my research. I explained this in terms of its relative accessibility for a hill area, the hospitality and perspicacity of Sirkanda people, the reputation Sirkanda had acquired in the area for being a "good village," and my own favorable impression of it based on familiarity with a number of similar villages. The most satisfactory explanation was that my presence there was largely chance, i.e., fate. Everyone agreed that this was the real reason. Villagers pointed out that when the potter makes a thousand identical cups, each has a unique destiny. Similarly, each man has a predetermined course of life and it was my fate to come to Sirkanda. When I gave an American coin to a villager, similar comment was precipitated. Of all the American coins only one was destined to rest in Sirkanda and this was it. What greater proof of the power of fate could there be than that the coin had, like myself, found its way to this small and remote village.

All of our claims of motive and status were put to the test by villagers once they realized that we planned to remain in Sirkanda and to associate with them. Sharma's claim to Brahmin status was carefully checked: extensive inquiry was made about his family and their origins; his behavior was closely watched; his family home was inspected by villagers on trips to town. Only then were villagers satisfied that he was what he claimed to be. When all of the claims upon which they could check proved to be accurate, villagers were evidently encouraged to believe also those claims which could not be verified.

That suspicions as to our motives were eventually allayed did not mean we therefore could learn what we wanted to learn in the village. It meant only that villagers knew in a general way what they were willing to let us learn; what impressions they would like us to receive. The range of allowable knowledge was far greater than that granted a stranger, far less than that shared by villagers. Although at the time I did not realize it, we were to be told those things which would give a favorable impression to a trustworthy plains Brahmin. Other facts would be suppressed and, if discovered, would be discovered in spite of the villagers' best efforts at concealment, often as a result of conversation with some disaffected individual of low esteem in the village. Our informants were primarily high-caste villagers intent on impressing us with their near conformity to the standards of behavior and belief of high-caste plainsmen. Low-caste people were respectful and reticent before us, primarily, as it turned out, because one of us was a Brahmin and we were closely identified with the powerful high-caste villagers.

Three months were spent almost exclusively in building rapport, in establishing ourselves as trustworthy, harmless, sympathetic, and interested observers of village life. In this time we held countless conversations, most of them dealing with the weather and other timely and innocuous topics. A good deal of useful ethnographic information was acquired in the process, but in many areas its accuracy proved to be wanting. Better information was acquired by observation than by inquiry in this period. We found cause for satisfaction during this frustrating and, from the point of view of research results, relatively fruitless time in the fact that we were winning the confidence of a good many people which we hoped would pay off more tangibly later. When the last open opponent of our endeavor evidently had been convinced of our purity of motive in the incident described above, we felt that we could begin our data collecting in earnest.

Until this time we had done all of our own housekeeping, cooking, dishwashing, carrying of water and firewood. These activities gave us opportunity to meet people in a natural setting and to be busy in a period when rapport was not good enough to allow us to devote full time to research. As rapport improved we found our household chores too time-consuming for optimal research. We attempted to find assistance in the village but, unable to do so, we added as a third member of our team a 17-year-old boy who was of low-caste plains origin but had lived most of his life in the hill station of Mussoorie and was conversant with Pahari ways and the Pahari language. His role was that of servant and he assumed full responsibility for our housekeeping in the village. His informal contacts with some of the younger villagers were a research asset and his low-caste origin was not overlooked in the village, but otherwise he had little direct effect on our relations with villagers. His contribution to the research was primarily in the extreme reliability of his work and his circumspection in relations with villagers.

At this point of apparent promise for productive research, Sharma, the interpreter-assistant, became ill and it was evident that he would be unable to return to our work in the village for some time. Under the circumstances this was a disheartening blow. It plunged my morale to its lowest ebb in the fifteen months of my stay in India, none of which could be described as exhilarating. I cannot here go into the details of the causes for this condition of morale: the pervasive health anxiety with which anyone is likely to be afflicted when he takes an 18-month-old child to the field in India, especially if, as in this case, he is away from and inaccessible to his family a good share of the time; the difficulties of maintaining a household in town and carrying on research in an isolated village; the constant and frustrating parrying with petty officials who are in positions to cause all kinds of difficulty and delay; the virtual lack of social contact outside of one's family, employees, and the villagers among whom one works; the feeling of being merely tolerated by those among whom one works and upon whom one is dependent for most of his social interaction. In such circumstances research is likely to become the primary motivat-

ing principle and its progress looms large in one's world view. Therefore, to lose an assistant whose presence I deemed essential to the research, when I was on the threshold of tangible progress after a long
period of preparation, was a discouraging blow. I shall not soon forget the anxiety I felt during the five-hour trek to the village alone
after learning of Sharma's illness and incapacity. To await his re-
covery would have been to waste the best months for research because
his illness came at the beginning of the winter slack season when
people would, for the first time since my arrival, have ample time to
sit and talk. In two months the spring harvest and planting season
would begin and many potential informants would be too busy and
tired to talk.

After a period alone in the village, I realized that I could not work
effectively without assistance because of my inadequate knowledge of
the language. Although I dreaded the task of selecting and then introducing a new and inexperienced assistant into the village, this
seemed to be a necessary step to preserve the continuity of the research.
My hope and intention was to utilize a substitute only until Sharma
would be able to work again. Not wishing to spend too much time
looking for a substitute, and with qualified people extremely scarce, I
employed with many misgivings and on a trial basis the first reasonably promising prospect who appeared. Happily, he proved to be an
exceptionally able, willing, and interested worker. He differed from
Sharma in at least three important respects: age, religion, and experience. Mohammed, as he will hereafter be called, was a middle-aged
Muslim and a retired school teacher who had no familiarity with
anthropological research.

These facts proved to have advantageous as well as disadvantageous
aspects. I was able to guide him more easily in his work and to interact more directly with villagers than had been the case with Sharma
simply because he realized his inexperience, accepted suggestions readily, and was interested in helping me to know and communicate directly with villagers, rather than in demonstrating his efficiency as a
researcher and his indispensability as an interpreter. As a result of
his age he received a certain amount of respect. As a Muslim he was
able to establish excellent rapport with the low castes but not with
the high or twice-born castes. Perhaps most importantly, he had no
ego-involvement in the data. He was interested and objective in viewing the culture in which we were working, whereas Sharma had been
self-conscious and anxious to avoid giving an unflattering view of

Hinduism and of village life to an American in this unorthodox (to him often shockingly so) example of a Hindu village. Moreover, the Brahmin, almost inevitably, had his own status to maintain before the high castes of the village while the Muslim was under no such obligation.

Since it seemed probable that Sharma would return to work after a few weeks, I decided to make the best of the situation and utilize Mohammed in ways that would make the most use of his advantages and minimize his disadvantages, for he was strong where Sharma had been weak, and vice versa. While high-caste people were suspicious of Mohammed on the basis of his religion, low-caste people were more at ease in his presence than they had been with Sharma. Furthermore, low-caste people proved to be more informative than high-caste people on most subjects. I therefore planned to utilize this assistant to get data about low castes and from them to get as much general ethnographic data as possible. I was counting on the return of Sharma to enable me to return to the high castes and my original endeavor to secure information from and about them. However, after several weeks it became evident that Sharma could not return to work in the village. By then we were beginning to get a good deal of ethnographic material with the promise of much more. In addition to remarkably good rapport with the low castes (greater than that Sharma and I had had with anyone in the village) we were also winning the confidence of some high-caste people. In view of these circumstances I felt encouraged to continue with Mohammed and to broaden our contacts in the village in the remaining months of research.

I had not anticipated the full implications for research of the differences in status of my associates, Sharma and Mohammed. For example, villagers had early determined that Sharma neither ate meat nor drank liquor. As a result we were barely aware that these things were done by villagers. Not long after Mohammed's arrival villagers found that he indulged in both and that I could be induced to do so. Thereafter we became aware of frequent meat and liquor parties, often of an inter-caste nature. We found that these were important social occasions; occasions from which outsiders were usually rigidly excluded. Rapport increased notably when it became known that locally distilled liquor was occasionally served at our house. As rapport improved, we were more frequently included in such informal occasions. Our access to information of many kinds increased proportionately.

Mohammed's age put him virtually above the suspicion which Sharma had had to overcome regarding possible interest in local women.

Mohammed's association with me in my by then generally trusted status, precluded undue suspicion of missionary intent or governmental affiliation. Probably his most important characteristic with regard to rapport was his religion. As a Muslim he was, like me, a ritually polluted individual, especially since he was assumed to have eaten beef. For most purposes he and I were untouchables, albeit respected for our presumed wealth and knowledge.

With this description as background, the differential effects which my association with these two men had on the research can be analyzed. In discussing this topic special attention will be given to the implications of the status of each of them for the impressions we gave to villagers and received from them. Some of the more general problems of research in a tightly closed and highly stratified system will also be considered.

ANALYSIS

Erving Goffman, in *The Presentation of Self in Everyday Life,* has devised a description and analysis of social interaction in terms of the means by which people seek to control the impressions others receive of them. He has suggested that this "dramaturgical" approach is a widely applicable perspective for the analysis of social systems. In this scheme social interaction is analyzed "from the point of view of impression management."

We find a team of performers who cooperate to present to an audience a given definition of the situation. This will include the conception of [one's] own team of [one's] audience and assumptions concerning the ethos that is to be maintained by rules of politeness and decorum. We often find a division into back region, where the performance of a routine is prepared, and front region, where the performance is presented. Access to these regions is controlled in order to prevent the audience from seeing backstage and to prevent outsiders from coming into a performance that is not addressed to them. Among members of the team we find that familiarity prevails, solidarity is likely to develop, and that secrets that could give the show away are shared and kept (Goffman, 1959, p. 238).

The ethnographic research endeavor may be viewed as a system involving the social interaction of ethnographer and subjects. Considered as a basic feature of social interaction, therefore, impression management is of methodological as well as substantive significance to ethnographers.

The ethnographer comes to his subjects as an unknown, generally unexpected, and often unwanted intruder. Their impressions of him will determine the kinds and validity of data to which he will be able to gain access, and hence the degree of sucess of his work. The ethnographer and his subjects are both performers and audience to one another. They have to judge one anothers' motives and other attributes on the basis of short intensive contact and then decide what definition of themselves and the surrounding situation they want to project; what they will reveal and what they will conceal and how best to do it. Each will attempt to convey to the other the impression that will best serve his interests as he sees them.

The bases for evaluation by an audience are not entirely those which the performer intends or can control.

Knowing that the individual is likely to present himself in a light that is favorable to him, the [audience] may divide what they witness into two parts; a part that is relatively easy for the individual to manipulate at will, being chiefly his verbal assertions, and a part in regard to which he seems to have little concern or control, being chiefly derived from the expressions he gives off. The [audience] may then use what are considered to be the ungovernable aspects of his expressive behavior as a check upon the validity of what is conveyed by the governable aspects (Goffman, 1959, p. 7).

In their awareness of this, performers attempt to keep the back region out of the range of the audience's perception; to control the performance insofar as possible, preferably to an extent unrealized by the audience. The audience will attempt to glimpse the back region in order to gain new insights into the nature of the performance and the performers.

An ethnographer is usually evaluated by himself and his colleagues on the basis of his insights into the back region of the performance of his subjects. His subjects are evaluated by their fellows on the basis of the degree to which they protect the secrets of their team and successfully project the image of the team that is acceptable to the group for front-region presentation. It is probably often thought that this presentation will also satisfy the ethnographer. The ethnographer is likely to evaluate his subjects on the amount of back-region information they reveal to him, while he is evaluated by them on his tact in not intruding unnecessarily into the back region and, as rapport improves, on his trustworthiness as one who will not reveal back-region secrets. These are likely to be mutually contradictory bases of evaluation. Rapport establishment is largely a matter of threading among them so as to win admittance to the back region of the subjects' performance without alienating them. This is sometimes sought through admission to the subjects' team; it is more often gained through acceptance as a neutral confidant.

The impressions that ethnographer and subjects seek to project to one another are, therefore, those felt to be favorable to the accomplishment of their respective goals: the ethnographer seeks access to back-region information; the subjects seek to protect their secrets since these represent a threat to the public image they wish to maintain. Neither can succeed perfectly.

Front and Back Regions

One must assume that the ethnographer's integrity as a scientist will insure the confidential nature of his findings about the individuals he studies. Those individuals, however, are unlikely to make such an assumption and, in fact, often make a contrary one. While I think it practically and ethically sound for the ethnographer to make known his intention to learn about the way of life of the people he plans to study, I believe it to be ethically unnecessary and methodologically unsound to make known his specific hypotheses, and in many cases even his areas of interest. To take his informants into his confidence regarding these may well preclude the possibility of acquiring much information essential to the main goal of understanding their way of life. I think here of my own interest in the highly charged sphere of intercaste relations, where admission of the interest to certain persons or groups would have been inimical to the research effort.

Participant observation, as a form of social interaction, always involves impression management. Therefore, as a research technique it inevitably entails some secrecy and some dissimulation on the level of interpersonal relations. If the researcher feels morally constrained to avoid any form of dissimulation or secrecy he will have to forego most of the insights that can be acquired through knowledge of those parts of his informants' lives that they attempt to conceal from him. With time, a researcher may be allowed to view parts of what was formerly the back region of his informants' performance, but few ethnographers can aspire to full acceptance into the informants' team in view of the temporary nature of their residence and their status as aliens. In a society where ascription is the only way to full acceptance, this is a virtual impossibility.

If the ethnographer does not gain access to back-region information he will have to content himself with an "official view" derived from public sources publicly approved, and his research interests will have to be sharply limited. An out for those sensitive on this point may be, of course, to do the research as it must be done but to use the findings only with the explicit approval of the subjects. In any case, the ethnographer will be presenting himself in certain ways to his informants during the research and concealing other aspects of himself from them. They will be doing the same. This is inherent in all social interaction.

Teams and Roles

Impression management in ethnographic research is often an exhausting, nerve-wracking effort on both sides, especially in the early phases of contact. Ethnographers may recognize themselves and their informants in this description:

Whether the character that is being presented is sober or carefree, of high station or low, the individual who performs the character will be seen for what he largely is, a solitary player involved in a harried concern for his production. Behind many masks and many characters, each performer tends to wear a single look, a naked unsocialized look, a look of concentration, a look of one who is privately engaged in a difficult and treacherous task (Goffman, 1959, p. 235).[3]

The task is especially difficult and treacherous when the cultural gap between participants and audience is great. Then the impression that a given action will convey cannot always be predicted; audience reaction is hard to read and performance significance is hard to judge. Misinterpretation occurs frequently and sometimes disastrously in such circumstances. Anyone who has been in an alien culture can cite *faux pas* resulting from such misinterpretation. Inadvertent disrespect is a common type. Although no vivid example occurred in the research being reported here, largely due to an exaggerated caution about this, the author experienced such a misinterpretation in the course of research among the Aleuts. He once amused local children by drawing cartoon faces on the steamy windows of the village store. These were seen by an adult who interpreted them as insulting caricatures of Aleuts, although they were in reality generalized cartoons, totally innocuous in intent, and he reacted bitterly. He saw them in the light of unhappy past experience with arrogant non-Aleuts. Strained relations resulting from this incident could well have halted research had it not occurred late in the research effort, after most villagers had been convinced of the ethnographer's good intentions and friendly attitude.

In a tightly closed and highly stratified society the difficulty of impression management is compounded. In a closed society the outsider may be prevented from viewing the activities of its members almost completely. The front region is small and admittance to any aspect of the performance is extremely difficult to obtain. Pronounced stratification makes for many teams, many performances, many back regions (one for each performance group, as well as for each audience), and considerable anxiety lest one group be indiscreet in revealing the "secrets" its members know of other groups.

In Sirkanda the ethnographic team consisted of the anthropologist, an interpreter-assistant and, as a peripheral member for part of the time, a houseboy. This was a team in that it constituted

. . . a set of individuals whose intimate cooperation is required if a given projected definition of the situation is to be maintained (Goffman, 1959, p. 104).

Villagers considered it to be a team. In their eyes the actions of each member reflected on the others.

THE ETHNOGRAPHER

The initial response to an ethnographer by his subjects is probably always an attempt to identify him in familiar terms; to identify him as the performer of a familiar role. The impressions he makes will determine how he is identified.

In Sirkanda several roles were known or known of, under which strangers might appear, and each—missionary, tax collector or other government agent, spy—was for a time attributed to our ethnographic team by some or all villagers as being our real, i.e., back-region role. None of these was a suitable role for accomplishing our purposes and it was only by consistently behaving in ways inconsistent with these roles that we ultimately established a novel role for ourselves: that of scholars eager to learn what knowledgeable villagers could teach us about Pahari culture. I drew heavily on the familiar role of student, and my associates on the familiar role of employee or "servant." Foreign origin was an important aspect of my status, for I was a "sahib" and an "untouchable"; a person of relative wealth and influence but of ritually impure origin and habits.

For me the former was a more distressing status than the latter, but an equally inevitable one. I was always referred to as "the sahib" by villagers, although I succeeded in getting them not to address me as such. Goffman comments on the differences between terms of address and terms of reference in this context noting that

> . . . in the presence of the audience, the performers tend to use a favorable form of address to them. . . . Sometimes members of the audience are referred to [in their absence] not even by a slighting name but by a code title which assimilates them fully to an abstract category (Goffman, 1959, pp. 172–173).
> Perhaps the cruelest term of all is found in situations where an individual asks to be called by a familiar term to his face, and this is tolerantly done, but in his absence he is referred to by a formal term (Ibid., p. 174).

Had I been alone in the village I would have had a relatively free hand in attempting to determine whom I associated with, so long as I did not infringe too freely on village backstage life or on matters of ritual purity. However, since I was in almost constant association with an assistant whose performance was closely tied to my own, my status and his were interdependent. The definition of ourselves which we cooperated in projecting had to correspond to known and observable facts and clues about ourselves and our purposes. Since to villagers my assistant was more conventional and hence comprehensible as a person than I, it was largely from him that impressions were derived which determined our status. It is for this reason that the characteristics of the interpreter-assistant were of crucial significance to the research effort.

THE BRAHMIN ASSISTANT

Sharma, the Brahmin assistant, was able to establish himself before villagers as a friendly, tactful and trustworthy young man. As such he was well-liked by high-caste villagers and was respected by all. Once his plains Brahmin status had been verified, it affected the tenor of all his relationships, and consequently of the ethnographic team's relations with villagers. The effects of these relationships on the research derived from his own attempts at impression management as a performer before several audiences, and from the attempts by villagers to control his impressions of them.

Most importantly, Sharma was a Brahmin of the plains. As such, he felt obliged to convey an acceptable definition of himself in this role to the villagers among whom he worked and to the ethnographer for whom he worked. Before villagers he was obliged to refrain from extensive informal contacts with his caste inferiors. He was expected to refuse to participate in such defiling activities as consumption of meat and liquor, and was in general expected to exemplify the virtues of his status. He was, in this context, acting as the sole local representative of plains Brahmins, a group with which he was closely identified by himself and by villagers.

In the presence of the ethnographer he joined a larger team, or reference group, of high-caste Indian Hindus. In this role he wished to convey a definition of Hinduism that would reflect well on its practitioners in the eyes of the foreigner. When possible he demonstrated an enlightened, sophisticated, democratic Hinduism quite unlike that indigenous to the village. Since, as a Hindu, he considered himself a teammate of villagers, he felt obliged to convey to the ethnographer an impression of village affairs that was not too greatly at variance with the notion of Hinduism which he wished to convey. He was, therefore, reluctant to discuss matters which might contradict the impression he had fostered—especially high-caste religious practices and inter-caste relations, the areas of most flagrant deviation (from his point of view) from the Hindu ideal. He tended, probably unconsciously, to color his accounts and structure our interactions with villagers to bias the impressions I received in this direction. On behalf of the ethnographic team, he was intent upon winning the villagers' acceptance and confidence, a fact which colored his accounts of us to them. His skill at impression management was evidenced by the rapport he achieved with both the ethnographer and the villagers, and by the fact that I, as ethnographer, was largely unaware of his manipulation of impressions until later when I had access to information without his management.

THE VILLAGE TEAM

Villagers, too, had particular definitions of themselves that they wished to convey to the ethnographic team determined, to a large extent, by their interpretation of the nature and motives of this team. With a Brahmin in an important position on the team, low-caste people were reluctant to have close contact with it. High-caste people, on the other hand, were eager to demonstrate the validity of their claims to high-caste status before this patently high-status outsider.

Pahari Brahmins and Rajputs (the high castes of this area) customarily do many things that are unacceptable in high-caste plains circles. As a result they are denied the esteem of such people. The appellations "Pahari Brahmin" and "Pahari Rajput" are often used in derision by people of the plains. Among other unorthodox activities, these Paharis sacrifice animals, eat meat, drink liquor, are unfamiliar with the scriptures, largely ignore the great gods of Hinduism, consult diviners and shamans, fail to observe many of the ceremonies and ritual restrictions deemed necessary by high-caste plainsmen, take a bride price in marriage, marry widows, are not infrequently polygynous (and in some areas are polyandrous), occasionally marry across caste lines, share wives among brothers, "sell" women to men of dubious character from the plains. In order favorably to impress a plains Brahmin they must conceal these activities insofar as possible, and this they indeed do. Just as Sharma wished to convey an impression of enlightened Hinduism to the ethnographer, villagers wished to convey their idea of enlightened Hinduism to Sharma. The two aims were complementary. Both resulted in projection of an exaggerated impression of religious orthodoxy. This exaggeration of behavior, indicating adherence to the "officially accredited values of the society," is a feature characteristic of impression management before outsiders (cf. Goffman, 1959, p. 35).[4]

Impression management of this kind is especially difficult when the intended audience, as in the case of the ethnographic team, has a known or suspected interest in the detection of back-region attitudes and behaviors, and when it is in intimate association with the performers.

Virtually the entire village of Sirkanda was at first a back region for the ethnographic team; a great deal of the conventional behavior therein was back-region behavior. Attempts were made by villagers to avoid "inopportune intrusions" which Goffman describes as follows:

When an outsider accidentally enters a region in which a performance is being given, or when a member of the audience inadvertently enters the backstage, the intruder is likely to catch those present *flagrante delicto*. Through no one's intention, the person present in the region may find that they have patently been witnessed in activity that is quite incompatible with the impression that they are, for wider social reasons, under obligation to maintain to the intruder (Goffman, 1959, p. 209).

When, for instance, an opportunity arose for the ethnographic team to move from a buffalo shed on the periphery of the village to a house in its center, villagers' desire to maintain a modicum of overt hospitality wavered before their covert alarm until an untouchable was induced to place an objection before the potential intruders. The objection had the desired effect although it was immediately repudiated by its high-caste instigators, who blamed it upon the irresponsible meddling of a mere untouchable. They thus assured the continued privacy of the village while maintaining their front of hospitality. The untouchable who voiced the objection had been coerced and bribed with liquor to do so. He later commented that villagers had said that people, and especially women, would be inhibited in the performance of their daily rounds if strangers were to be continuously in their midst; that is, the backstage would be exposed to the audience.

Before the ethnographic team the village at this time presented an apparently united front. Villagers of all castes cooperated not only in concealing things inimical to the high-caste performance, but also those thought to reflect adversely on the people as a whole. For example, an intra-caste dispute among untouchables came to a head at a high-caste wedding where the disputants were serving as musicians. While the disputants were presenting their case to an informal council of high-caste guests which had convened one afternoon, a heated argument erupted. It was suppressed and the council disbanded with the explicit warning that the ethnographer would hear and think ill of the village.

During this period of the research, untouchables were usually relegated to an unobtrusive secondary role, largely in the back region. With a Brahmin on the ethnographic team and with high-caste people as our associates, low-caste villagers were disinclined to associate with us, much less to reveal backstage information. We were in their view associates of the high-caste team and as such were people to be treated cautiously and respectfully. High-caste villagers could not reveal such information to us either because we were, in their view, members of the plains Brahmin team and a source of potential discredit to high-caste Paharis.

Ethnographic information that was acquired in this context was largely of a sort considered innocuous by villagers—observations about the weather and current events, agricultural techniques, etc. Much of it was distorted. For example, our initial genealogies omitted all reference to plural wives; accounts of marriage and other ritual events were sketchy and largely in conformance with the villagers' conception of plains orthodoxy. Some of the information was false. Most of it was inaccessible. The back region was large and carefully guarded. Yet relations between the ethnographic team and the village were relatively congenial.

THE MUSLIM ASSISTANT

When after four months the Brahmin assistant was replaced by a Muslim, there were important consequences for the villagers' conception of the ethnographic team and consequently for their performance before that team. The progress and results of the research reflected these changes.

Mohammed, the Muslim assistant, was respected for his age and learning, liked for his congeniality and wit, but doomed to untouchable status by his religion. This did not disturb him. As an educated and not particularly religious Muslim he had little personal involvement in the caste hierarchy of the village and little vested interest in the ethnographer's impression of village Hinduism. As an individual he was objective and interested but concerned more with projecting to villagers a favorable view of the ethnographic team than any particular image of his personal status. As a performer he played a less prominent role than his predecessor. This was reflected in his interpreting. Sharma had preferred to interpret virtually all statements and to direct the course of conversation to keep from offending villagers (and embarrassing himself) by treading on dangerous ground. Mohammed was anxious that communication between ethnographer and subjects be as direct as possible; that conversation be as undirected as possible except when particular topics were being pursued. Consequently interpreting occurred only as necessary; ethnographer and subjects determined the direction of conversation.

As an audience, the Muslim's effect on the village performance was drastically different from the effect of the Brahmin. High-caste people did not wish to associate openly with a Muslim, for he was by definition ritually impure. He was in no sense their fellow team member as the Brahmin had been; he was in some respects almost as alien as was the ethnographer himself. Consequently, high-caste villagers' behavior became correct but distant: informal conversations and visitations decreased in frequency; the ethnographer was told in private by some high-caste villagers that they could no longer associate closely with him.

Low-caste people, on the other hand, became less inhibited than formerly was the case. When by experimentation they found that the Muslim was apparently oblivious to caste, these people began to be friendly. In the vacuum of social interaction left by withdrawal of the high castes, they were not rebuffed. The effect was circular and soon the ethnographer's dwelling became identified as primarily a low-caste area.

Not all high-caste people were alienated, but most preferred to talk in their own homes, with low castes excluded, rather than in the ethnographer's house. Some would visit the ethnographer only when they had been assured that no low-caste villagers would be present.

In these circumstances the village no longer presented the aspect of
a unified team. Now it became clear that the village was divided. From
the point of view of the high castes there were at least two teams: low
and high castes. The former feared the power of the latter; the latter
feared the revelation of back-region secrets that might be given by the
former. From the point of view of low castes there seem to have been
at least three teams: high castes, "our caste" and (other) low castes.
High castes were feared and resented; other low castes were to some
extent competitors for status before outsiders. Competition took the
form of conflicting claims as to the type and nature of interaction with
one another, each caste claiming to treat as inferiors (or sometimes as
equals) others who, in turn, claimed equal or superior status. Actually,
in the context of the closed village a good deal of interaction took
place among low castes with few status considerations.

LOW CASTE TEAMS

The position of low castes—the untouchables—was an interesting
one relative to the village team and its performance. Untouchables
were in a position such that they might easily admit an audience to
backstage village secrets. They were members of the village team per-
force, but they were uneasy and not fully trusted members. Goffman
has appropriately stated that:

One overall objective of any team is to sustain the definition of the situation that its performance fosters. This will involve the over-communication
of some facts and the under-communication of others. Given the fragility
and the required expressive coherence of the reality that is dramatized by a
performance, there are usually facts which, if attention is drawn to them
during the performance, would discredit, disrupt, or make useless the impression that the performance fosters. These facts may be said to provide
"destructive information." A basic problem for many performances, then, is
that of information control; the audience must not acquire destructive information about the situation that is being defined for them. In other words,
a team must be able to keep its secrets and have its secrets kept (Goffman,
1959, p. 141).

In Sirkanda, low-caste people are in a position to know high-caste
secrets because all villagers are in almost constant contact with one
another; they have little privacy. Castes are not separated physically,
socially, or ritually to the extent that they are in many areas. Low-
caste and high-caste cultures, including back-region behavior, proved
to be very similar among these hill people (cf. Berreman, 1960b). But,

for low-caste people the back region—the part that is to be concealed
—is much smaller than for high-caste people. They do not feel obligated to protect village secrets to the extent that high-caste people do
simply because their prestige and position are not at stake. They do
not share, or are not heavily committed to, the "common official values" which high-caste people affect before outsiders. High-caste men, for
example, were careful to conceal the fact that, in this society, brothers
have sexual access to one another's wives. However, a low-caste man
who had listed for the ethnographer the name and village of origin of
the women of his family, including his wife and his brothers' wives,
was not embarrassed to remark, when asked which was his wife, that
"They are all like wives to me." A more striking contrast was evidenced in attitudes toward village religious behavior. After some time,
low-caste people encouraged the ethnographer to attend their household religious observances wherein possessed dancing and animal sacrifice occurred. High-caste villagers did not want the ethnographer to
be present at their own performances of the same rituals. Some of them
also objected to my presence at the low-caste functions and exerted
pressure to have me excluded. The reason was apparently that high-
caste people felt such behavior, if known outside, would jeopardize
their claims to high status. High-caste people, recognizing that village
culture was essentially the same in all castes and that I was aware of
this, felt their position threatened by the performance of the low-
castes. Low-caste people had no such status to maintain.

Low-caste people, unlike their high-caste village-mates, had little
prestige stake in outsiders' conceptions of the Pahari way of life. They
were not competing with plains people for status nor seeking acceptance by them to the extent that the high castes were. People assume
the worst about untouchables so they have little to gain by concealment. This is not to say that there is no patricular definition of their
situation that untouchables try to project, or that it takes no effort to
perpetuate it; the lowest-status group in Sirkanda, for instance, has
tried to suppress its reputation for prostitution by giving up some of
the activities associated with it. But the range of such back-region
secrets among low castes is limited in comparison to that among high
castes. It does not extend to Pahari practices as such, but instead is
limited primarily to those few practices crucial to their status competition with other low castes in the village and, even more importantly,
to negative attitudes toward the high castes—attitudes which must be
concealed in view of the power structure of the society.

Goffman notes that

. . . to the degree that the teammates and their colleagues form a complete social community which offers each performer a place and a source of moral support . . . , to that degree it would seem that performers can protect themselves from doubt and guilt and practice any kind of deception (Goffman, 1959, pp. 214–215).

It is because, in this highly stratified society, moral support and rewards are allotted on the basis of caste that high-caste performers cannot trust their low-caste colleagues to sustain the performance—to practice the deception—voluntarily. Low-caste people resent their inferior position and the disadvantages which inhere in it (cf. Berreman, 1960a). Not only are they uncommitted to the village performance which is largely a high-caste performance; they are in private often committed to discrediting some aspects of this performance. Both of these are facts of which the ethnographer must be aware. As a result of them, if low-caste members feel they can do so in safety, they are not reluctant to reveal information about village life which embarrasses high-caste villagers. They may also, of course, manufacture information intended to discredit their caste superiors, just as the latter may purposely purvey false information to justify their treatment of low castes. The ethnographer must be constantly alert to the likelihood of such deceptions, using cross checks, independent observation and the like for verification. Eventually he can identify reliable informants and the subjects upon which particular informants or categories of informants are likely to be unreliable.

That high-caste people recognize the vulnerability of their performance and are anxious about it is revealed in their suspicion and resentment of low-caste association with outsiders, such as the ethnographic team. Anyone who associates too freely with such outsiders is suspected of telling too much, but only low-caste villagers are suspected of telling those facts which will seriously jeopardize the status of the dominant high castes. The suspicion that low castes are not entirely to be trusted to keep up the front is therefore not paranoia on the part of those they may reveal; it is a real danger. On the other hand, high-caste members encourage association between strangers and low castes by sending the latter to appraise strangers who come to the village and, if possible, to send them on their way. By so doing high castes avoid the risks of being embarrassed or polluted by the aliens. At the same time they increase low-caste opportunities for outside contact, acquisition of new ideas, etc., and they thereby increase their own anxieties about low-caste behavior and attitudes. They are apparently more willing to face this anxiety than to risk initial personal contact with strangers. As a result, some low-caste people are more at ease with strangers and more knowledgeable about them and their thought patterns, than are most high-caste people.

Since they are not willing to extend to low castes the status, power, and material rewards which would bring them into the high-caste team or commit them to the high-caste performance, high castes rely heavily on threats of economic and physical sanctions to keep their subordinates in line and their secrets, which these people know, concealed from outsiders. To the extent that low-caste people do sustain the performance they are evidently responding to their fear of high-caste reprisals more than to an internalized commitment to the performance.

HIGH CASTE TEAMS

Even high-caste villagers do not present a united front or consistent performance on all matters. Bride-price marriage, for example, is traditional in these hills and until recent times only poverty accounted for failure to pay for a bride. To high-caste people of the plains bride-price marriage is reprehensible; a dowry is always demanded. This attitude has had its effect in the hills so that Paharis, and especially those of high caste, not infrequently forego the bride price in a wedding. There was an interesting division of expressed attitude among high-caste villagers in Sirkanda on this matter. Although there was no consistent difference among families in practice, some claimed that their families would never accept or demand a bride price while others claimed that their families would never give or take a bride without an accompanying bride price. I was unsuccessful in attempting to account for this difference in terms of the economic, educational, or other readily apparent characteristics of those concerned. I finally realized that it was largely a function of the relationship of the particular informant to me and my assistant and, more specifically, the impression the informant wished to convey to us. Many wanted to convey a picture of plains orthodoxy and, not realizing that we knew otherwise, or hoping that we would think their families were exceptions, they tailored their accounts of the marriage transaction to fit this. A few, notably some of the older men of the Rajput landowning caste, wanted to convey their conception of the proper Pahari tradition, perhaps in view of the fact that they knew we were aware of their practice of bride-price marriage and that to conceal it was by then useless. They expressed disapproval of dowry marriage and disclaimed willingness to be parties to such arrangements. They explained that as Rajputs they would not take charity (as a Brahmin would) and would insist on paying for anything they got, including a wife; conversely they would require payment for their daughters, because one does not give charity to other Rajputs. Moreover, gift brides die young and do not produce heirs, they asserted. Some villagers were more frank than either of the above groups when they got to know us, and described quite freely the specific circumstances under which bride price and dowry were and were not included in recent marriage transactions.

On at least one occasion highly controversial information was revealed by a Rajput because of an erroneous assumption on his part that others in his caste had been telling the ethnographer the story in a manner uncomplimentary to himself. Early in the research I learned that the village had been riven by a legal battle over land begun some twenty years previously, and although I knew in a general way who and what was involved, I had not ascertained the details. One evening the proudest, most suspicious and tight-lipped of the members of the winning faction appeared unexpectedly at my house, lantern in hand, and without introduction proceeded to recount the nine-year legal battle blow-by-blow. He was evidently attempting to counteract information which he presumed the losing faction had given me. I was subsequently able to check his version with several other versions from both sides in order to reconstruct approximately the factors involved in this complex and emotionally loaded episode.

Thus, high-caste members are not entirely free of suspicion and doubt regarding the extent to which they can rely upon their teammates to sustain their performance. Even among high castes there are different performances which various groups try to project to one another and occasionally to outsiders. Lines of differential performance and impression management among them most often follow kin group and caste affiliation. These high-caste performance teams are usually factional groups in the village, competing and disputing with one another. They often attempt to disparage one another within the high-caste context by such means as questioning purity of ancestry. The head of the largest family in Sirkanda, a member of one of the two large Rajput sibs of the village, expressed doubt that the other large sib, to which his wife (the mother of his five adult sons) belonged, was actually and legitimately a Rajput sib. This was a recurrent theme. Often cleavages between high-caste groups involved long-standing disputes over land and/or women.

High-caste performance teams also differed from one another in the age, sex, education, and outside experience of their members. Groups so defined can be described as performance teams because they differ in the definitions of their own and the village situation which they attempt to project to various audiences. Rarely, however, do they desert the high-caste team before outsiders or low castes, the two most crucial audiences.

The same kinds of statements can be made about particular low castes, although the low castes as a group rarely cooperate to put on a team performance. Usually, each low caste sustains its own performance, attempting to substantiate its claims to status relative to other low castes adjacent in the hierarchy.

TEAM DYNAMICS

Until Mohammed became my assistant, I was identified and treated by villagers as marginally allied with the high-caste team because of my association with Sharma. With the arrival of Mohammed this identification ceased. Before long he and I became identified more closely with low-caste villagers. Since low-caste people speak frankly about village "secrets" and many other topics only when they do not fear high-caste detection and reprisal (i.e., only before a low-caste audience), the change in assistants enabled me for the first time to gain access to their knowledge. The cultures of low and high castes are similar in this area. The part of the culture that constituted a back region, and that was therefore inaccessible to the ethnographic team, was smaller among low castes than among high castes. As a result, more could be found out that pertained to both groups from the former than from the latter.

The threat of the loss of high-caste sanctions persisted as a deterrent to free communication between the ethnographic team and the low castes, but its effectiveness diminished as some low-caste individuals came to trust us and to take us into their confidence. Even those low-caste people who became willing to talk freely to us often took elaborate precautions to assure that no high-caste listeners were around. The ethnographer's house consisted of three connecting rooms, one of which was at all times occupied by two or more buffaloes. The buffaloes were usually tended by female members of the family of their high-caste owners. Low-caste informants frequently inspected this room to verify that no one might be listening, and on occasion they even circled the house to check on possible eavesdroppers.

In a sense, these informants became members of a team including the ethnographer whose purpose it was to convince others that they were engaging in innocuous conversation and radio-listening, when in fact they might be discussing village customs and secrets of various sorts. In this situation, "team collusion" became an established pattern. Goffman designates by this term

. . . any collusive communication which is carefully conveyed in such a way as to cause no threat to the illusion that is being fostered for the audience (Goffman, 1959, p. 177).

Collusion within the ethnographer's team took the form of signals to indicate when a topic of conversation should be terminated or an invitation declined. Collusion was detectable within groups of informants, one of whom might stifle a comment to the ethnographer in response to a meaningful and imperfectly concealed glance from a colleague. Collusion between ethnographer and informants was exemplified by one low-caste man who requested that the ethnographer tell him an English word by which to indicate that he suspected someone might be overhearing or likely to overhear our conversation, and hence that we should alter the topic of conversation or that his subsequent remarks should be ignored. Double meanings were useful for this purpose. The ethnographer's housemates were buffalo cows and in colloquial speech the term for buffalo cow may be used in unflattering reference to a woman (these facts, naturally, formed the basis for many weak jokes at the ethnographer's expense). Informants might comment that the "buffaloes" were in the next room, or were restless, to indicate that women were tending the buffaloes and hence were likely to be eavesdropping.

The presence of Mohammed did not affect our relationships with high-caste villagers in an entirely negative way from the standpoint of data collection. In his presence high-caste people did not feel compelled to live up to the plains Brahmin standards to which Sharma's presence inspired them. The wealthiest Brahmin in the area, for example, had remarked to Sharma and me that while some high-caste Paharis might eat meat and drink liquor, as we had probably heard, he himself never touched these defiling items. Later, when everyone knew that Mohammed and I knew about and participated in the consumption of these things among high-caste villagers, the same Brahmin shared with us a boiled leg of goat and a quart of liquor which he brought as a gift. He had been uninformative about his family to Sharma and insisted that Paharis were conventional in all respects,

but he once fed Mohammed and me at his home without concealing
the fact that he had three wives. There were, however, facts which he
could no more reveal to Mohammed than to Sharma. He would have
been disconcerted, to say the least, had he known that we knew of his
youthful activities as a member of a notorious woman-selling gang
and that he had spent some time in prison as a consequence.

Thus, although low-caste people were our best informants, as confidence in the trustworthiness of the ethnographic team grew some
members of every village group took us into their confidence and
discussed secrets which other members of the same groups would not
have revealed. As a rule, and not surprisingly, people did not reveal
facts or secrets which directly contradicted the impressions they wished
to convey of themselves or members of their households. Many kinds
of back-region secrets were revealed only by people who were not
members of the groups whose secrets they were reporting.

Data, Secrets, and Confidence

As rapport increased and back-region information accumulated it
became possible for the ethnographic team to accomplish useful research on a broader scale—to understand formerly incomprehensible
activities and attitudes; to relate previously disparate facts, to make
more sensible inquiries, to cross-check and verify information. The
effect was cumulative. As we learned more, more information became
accessible. By being interested, uncritical, circumspect, and meticulous
about maintaining their trust, we won villagers' confidence. For example, high-caste people who avoided close contact with Mohammed in
the village visited his home in town and even ate with him, with the
plea that he tell no one in the village. No one ever discovered these
indiscretions, and those who committed them were not unapprecia-
tive. Contrary to villagers' early fears, no missionaries, policemen, tax
officers, or other outsiders came to Sirkanda as a result of what we
learned there. We tried to show our increasing knowledge in greater
comprehension of our environment, rather than by repetition of items
of information. As we learned more, concealment from us decreased
because we were apparently already aware of, and largely indifferent
to, many of the facts about which villagers were most self-conscious
or secretive. We took for granted things some villagers supposed were
"dark secrets" (i.e., things contrary to the impression they hoped to
convey to us) and far from our knowledge (cf. Goffman, 1959, p. 141).
When we had asked, in genealogical inquiry, what a man's wife's name
was, we always got one name. When we later found that polygyny was

not uncommon we asked first how many wives a man had and thereby got accurate information. Most villagers were unaware that our interests went beyond formal genealogical records, economic techniques and ritual observances. Many secrets were revealed largely because of the apparent casualness of our interest in them, and because villagers had become accustomed to our presence in the village so that we were not considered to be as critical an audience as had once been the case.

Some of the most revealing instances of social interaction occurred between people who were apparently oblivious to the fact that the ethnographer was present. Frequently this was a temporary lapse. A performance for the ethnographer would be abandoned as tension, conviviality, concentration on a topic of conversation, or some other intensification of interaction occurred among the participants. Such instances of preoccupation with one another were conspicuous by the fact that attitudes were expressed or information divulged that would normally be suppressed. The breach in the performance would sometimes be followed immediately, or after some time, by embarrassment, apology, or anxious efforts to counteract its presumed effect on the ethnographer's view of the village or of those involved in the incident. Minor instances of the same phenomenon were frequent sources of insight into the functioning of the society, and sources of confirmation or contradiction of informants' data.

The accuracy of information on back-region subjects could often be checked through informants who would not have intentionally revealed it, by bringing the subject up naturally in conversation as though it were a matter of general information. That is, it was defined by the ethnographer as no longer restricted to the back region of the performance to which he was audience.

Some "secrets," however, could not be adequately verified simply because to do so would precipitate difficulty for all concerned, especially for those who would be suspected of revealing the secrets. Such secrets ranged from gossip about various past transgressions and indiscretions by particular families or individuals, to the fact that villagers of all castes were reported to eat occasionally the flesh of animals such as deer and goats found freshly dead or killed in the forest. One low-caste man told me there were secrets he could not reveal until I had my pack on my back and was leaving the village permanently. He was afraid that some intimation of my knowledge might leak out and he would be punished as the only one who would have revealed the damaging information. After I had said my final farewells this man journeyed sixteen miles to my home in town, primarily, to be

sure, to get some utensils I had offered him, but p;
some incidents which he had been afraid to tell or even
my residence in the village and which he would not t
ence of my assistant or any other person. These incid
primarily with the sensitive area of inter-caste and oth
behavior among powerful members of the community.

To this man, as well as to other low-caste friends, the ethnographer
had become what Goffman refers to as a "confidant," one who is located outside of the team and who participates ". . . only vicariously
in back and front region activity" (Goffman, 1959, p. 159). In this
role I had access to a range of information not often accessible to
those who came from outside the group. Where group membership is
by ascription this seems to be the only feasible role for which the
ethnographer may strive.

Certain secrets remained too dark to be told even by those who
trusted us most. The village remained a team, united in its performance, with regard to some practices or beliefs which were too damaging to all (or to certain powerful high-caste people) to permit their
revelation to an outsider. Obviously, like the perfect crime, most of
these remain unknown. Indications of a few of them were received,
however. For example, one old dispute which resulted in a factional
split among Rajputs would have escaped me had not an old man referred to it briefly, bitterly, and inadvertently. Despite my best efforts
I learned nothing about it beyond his chance remark that it involved
a man and woman of the disputing sibs seen talking and laughing
together at the water source some generations ago. Even the most
willing informants would only say that "Those people are all dead
now so it doesn't matter."

I learned that some Paharis occasionally sacrifice a buffalo to their
gods, but that this has never occurred in Sirkanda. I was convinced
that this was the case when considerable inquiry and observation
seemed to verify it. Then, shortly before my final departure, a dog de-
posited the embarrassing evidence of such a sacrifice—the neatly-severed
head of a buffalo calf—on the main village trail shortly before I
chanced by. Villagers of all castes refused to discuss the matter in
which all were obviously implicated. My one opportunity for a candid
explanation occurred at the moment of discovery when I asked a child
at my heels which god the buffalo had been sacrificed to. A reply
seemed imminent until his elder, a few steps back on the trail, caught
up and silenced the discussion as well as all chance for future fruitful

nquiry on the subject. Villagers thought that to plains people this would seem akin to cow-killing, the greatest sin of all, and so it had to be rigorously concealed.

The sacrifice had evidently occurred during my absence from the village.

If an individual is to give expression to ideal standards during his performance, then he will have to forego or conceal action which is inconsistent with these standards. When this inappropriate conduct is itself satisfying in some way, as is often the case, then one commonly finds it indulged in secretly, in this way the performer is able to forego his cake and eat it too (Goffman, 1959, p. 41).

It was six months after my arrival before animal sacrifices and attendant rituals were performed in my presence, although they had been performed in my absence or without my knowledge throughout my residence in the village. Likewise, it was not until after Sharma left that I witnessed drinking and meat-eating parties in the village.

Since I left the village for two or three days every week or so, there was an opportunity for essential and enjoyable back-region activity to be carried on quite freely in my absence, and this opportunity was not neglected. In fact, it probably made my research in the village much more bearable to villagers than if I had been there constantly. It was largely the threat to their privacy that motivated villagers to make sure that I did not take up residence in the center of the village (as described above), but continued instead to live on its periphery. No doubt one of the most anxiety-producing situations known to man is to make public that which he considers to be private, back-region behavior.

Impression Management in Response to Research

During my presence in the village, high-caste people appeared to be always playing to the low-caste audience, as well as to their outside reference group of high-caste plains people. In front of the low castes their effort was to appear as undivided as possible in matters relating to that audience, primarily in matters considered necessary to maintain their status relative to the low castes. In front of the outside reference group they tried to appear as conventional as possible, at least in their conception of high-caste plains conventionality.

There was little difficulty in maintaining the high-caste front relative to low castes when only villagers were involved. When outsiders appeared, however, the front was jeopardized to the extent that the strangers might fail to play the role of the caste group to which they belonged. Thus, there was fear that government officials of high caste might come and mingle too freely with untouchables, or that officials of untouchable caste might come and expect or demand to mix with high castes. These fears were activated by the presence, as members of the ethnographic team, of Sharma and Mohammed respectively. Alleviation of the fears was a gradual process. It was feared that from contacts with the aliens, untouchables might get disturbing notions about their own status. Government advocacy of the abolition of untouchability and official promotion of an equalitarian ideal intensified these fears. The village council president was willing to conform to government rules and eat with other council presidents and government officials of unknown caste at District headquarters, but he would not do so in the village or in the presence of villagers lest it set a dangerous precedent and lower his status in the eyes of others. More immediate than the fear of status loss or of the introduction of upsetting alien ideas to untouchables was the well-founded fear that potentially harmful or embarrassing back-region information about the village would leak to outsiders—notably the ethnographic team—from the low castes, as discussed above.

The performances of each team described here were aimed toward particular audiences. Therefore "audience segregation" was essential to the performers.

By audience segregation the individual ensures that those before whom he plays one of his parts will not be the same individuals before whom he plays a different part in another setting (Goffman, 1959, p. 49).

Probably there is no more revealing or embarrassing situation, in Sirkanda or elsewhere, than when two audiences for whom different performances are appropriate are present at the same performance. An example was the incident described above, wherein a hostile Rajput joined and thereby effectively terminated an interview between the ethnographer and a local Brahmin.

Audience segregation on the part of villagers was manifested in the fact that their behavior differed before Sharma and Mohammed; that it differed in my presence and in my absence; and that it also differed when they confronted us alone and in groups. The performance of low-caste people was different in the presence of the ethnographic team (when the team included Mohammed) and in the presence of high-caste people, the former apparently approximating their behavior among their fellows (i.e., their behavior when in front of us, whether as individuals or in groups, was consistent and contrasted sharply to their behavior before us in the presence of high-caste villagers). The greatest difference was in their expressions of resentment against the high castes before us and their fellows, as contrasted to their usual inhibition of such expressions or any hint thereof before high castes.

Exceptions occasionally occurred, some apparently stimulated in part by the presence of the ethnographer. One of the most memorable examples occurred when a young Rajput man of relatively low personal and familial prestige brought his axe to be sharpened by the blacksmith, who happened to be listening to the ethnographer's radio. The blacksmith took the axe, inspected it with obvious distaste and announced:

This axe is worth eight annas (10 cents). My file is worth 15 rupees (three dollars). It would spoil my valuable file to sharpen this worthless axe. Go find a flat rock and sharpen it yourself.

Further feeble entreaties brought nothing but refusal from the blacksmith, and the Rajput left, presumably in search of a flat rock. This was unusual, but not unprecedented behavior for a blacksmith. It would not have been tried with a more prestigious or cantankerous Rajput or with a valuable client. It probably would not have happened in this case had the ethnographer not been present to inhibit, by his presence, any retaliation.

Such sallies occasionally occur away from the presence of an outsider. They are long remembered, fondly by low-caste people and resentfully by high-caste people, although they do not always result in immediate overt retaliation.

Low-caste people occasionally expressed reluctance to become too closely identified with the ethnographer. They realized that I would be there a relatively short time, so any advantages they might derive from my company would be small and transitory compared to the retribution which envious or suspicious high-caste villagers could exact from them over a lifetime. One or two high-caste people expressed similar sentiments.

Some high-caste people behaved differently in our presence than in front of low-caste villagers. As has been mentioned, they would eat with me and with Mohammed in town, but few would do so in the village; they would never do so in the presence of low-caste people. In our presence some of them expressed bitterness toward low castes that they would not have expressed to low-caste people unless greatly angered. A few expressed to us privately a willingness to interact more freely with low-caste people than was possible in the village situation, or respect for individual low-caste members that would not have been acceptable to their caste-fellows.

Impression Management in Pursuit of Research

Finally, my own behavior was tailored for my village audience. I carefully and, I think successfully, concealed the range of my interests and their intensity in some matters—such as inter-caste relations. I refrained from going where I was not wanted, even when I could have gone without being challenged and when I very much wanted to go. One instance occurred when I decided not to move into the proffered house in the center of the village. As another example, I never attended a village funeral. On the two occasions upon which I could have done so, I found that there was considerable anxiety lest my presence upset guests from other villages, though Sirkanda villagers claimed they would welcome my presence. There was evident relief when I stayed home.

In the village I concealed the extent of my note-taking, doing most of it at night or in private. I felt free to take notes openly before only a few key informants, and then only after I had known them for a considerable time. I recorded some kinds of detailed information, such as genealogies and crop yields, in the presence of all informants when I found that I could do so without inhibiting responses appreciably. This, too, took time and circumspection. Some subjects, such as ceremonial activities, could be freely recorded before some informants and not at all before others. I discarded my plans to use scheduled interviews and questionnaires because I thought they would do more harm in terms of rapport than good in terms of data collection, in view of village attitudes and my relationship with villagers. I never took photographs without permission. I concealed such alien practices as my use of toilet paper—a habit for which foreigners are frequently criticized in India. I took up smoking as a step to increase rapport. I simulated a liking for millet chapaties and the burning pepper and pumpkin or potato mixture which makes up much of the Pahari diet. Even more heroically, I concealed my distaste for the powerful home-distilled liquor, the consumption of which marked every party and celebration. Such dissimulations were aimed at improving rapport and they were worth the trouble. In this behavior a front was maintained in order to sustain a particular definition of my situation; a definition which I thought would increase my access to village backstage life, thereby contributing to the ultimate goal of understanding the lifeways of these people.

CONCLUSION

In such a society as this the ethnographer is inevitably an outsider and never becomes otherwise. He is judged by those among whom he works on the basis of his own characteristics and those of his associates. He becomes identified with those social groups among his subjects to which he gains access. The nature of his data is largely determined by his identity as seen by his subjects. Polite acceptance and even friendship do not always mean that access will be granted to the confidential regions of the life of those who extend it. The stranger will be excluded from a large and vital area if he is seen as one who will not safeguard secrets, and especially if he is identified as a member of one of those groups from which the secrets are being kept.

Sharma was a high-caste plainsman and consequently identified with very important groups in the village, groups rigorously excluded from large areas of the life of both high-caste and low-caste villagers. As such he could likely never have achieved the kind of relationship to villagers which would have resulted in access to much of the life of Sirkanda. Access to that information was essential to the ethnographer because it constituted a large proportion of all village attitudes and behaviors. Mohammed was able to gain substantial rapport with the low castes. In view of the attitudes of villagers and the social composition and power structure of the village, the low castes were the only feasible source of information which high-caste villagers considered to be embarrassing, damaging or secret. They were a reasonably satisfactory source of such information about the entire village because all castes were in such close contact that they had few secrets from one another and did not differ greatly in culture. This is not to say that the information obtained was complete or totally accurate, but only to assert that it was much more so than would have been the case had Sharma been my assistant throughout the research.

Thus, there is more than one "team" which makes up Sirkanda; more than one definition of the village situation is presented or may be presented to the outsider. As the ethnographer gains access to information from people in different social groups and in different situations he is likely to become increasingly aware of this.

The question of whether the performance, definition or impression fostered by one group is more real or true than that put forth by another, or whether a planned impression is more or less true than the backstage behavior behind it, is not a fruitful one for argument. All are essential to an understanding of the social interaction being observed.

Note ON HINDI TERMS

English equivalents have in most instances been substituted for Hindi and Pahari terms. Where pertinent, the Hindi or Pahari word has been included in parentheses. Where a Hindi or Pahari term has seemed more appropriate than an English one, it has been italicized and defined (if it is not defined by context) in its first appearance. Such words have been written as nearly phonetically as possible, according to Sirkanda pronunciation, in Roman script, with long vowels (‾) and nasalization (~) indicated in their first appearance. Retroflex consonants have been indicated by capitalization in their first appearance. Pluralization has usually been indicated as in English with a final "s" rather than as in Hindi. Some words which appear frequently in English writings are spelled in the conventional manner rather than phonetically, especially if they are proper nouns.

Place names of villages within the immediate vicinity of Sirkanda and all personal names of individuals (except those in the Acknowledgments) are pseudonyms. "Sirkanda" is not the name of a real village, though it is the name of a well-known Pahari temple dedicated to Devi, the most important goddess in the village described here. The employment of pseudonyms is done for protection of privacy rather than for concealment. Anyone who set about it could easily locate "Sirkanda."

INTRODUCTION

In India, as in peasant.societies elsewhere, the village community has been found by many anthropologists to be the most manageable unit for ethnological research. As a result of their experience no one would now be likely to assert that the village is isolated, independent, or unchanging, or that it can be studied meaningfully without reference to its past and its extensions into other communities, towns, and urban centers. In fact, dependence upon market towns or urban areas is inherent in most definitions of peasant communities. Redfield, for example, describes the peasant as a "rural native whose long established order of life takes important account of the city. The account that the peasant takes of the city or town is economic, political and moral" (Redfield, 1957, p. 31).

Although no peasant village can be understood in isolation, it can serve as a useful focus for research. A village, with its extensions into the surrounding region, constitutes a functioning segment of rural Indian society of a size amenable to anthropological research techniques. Although no village is representative of rural India as a whole, any village properly understood represents in a general way villages of a particular type and area. Dube has commented that "what we need today is a series of studies of village communities from different parts of the country covering the many divergent patterns of organization and ethos. Until this is done our picture of social systems in rural India will remain vague and inadequate" (Dube, 1955, pp. 6 f.). Only then will we be able to assess the validity of generalizations already set forth on the subject. The present study is, among other things, a contribution in this direction.

The research reported here was in the nature of a community study carried out from September, 1957, through August, 1958, in and around Sirkanda,[1] a village of the lower Himalayas of western Uttar Pradesh, India.

The aims of the study were three: (1) to provide an ethnographic community study in an important and previously unreported culture area of India; (2) to analyze the functioning and interrelationship of kin, caste, and community ties in a Hindu society known to be differently organized in some significant respects than those of the adjacent and well-known plains; and (3) to study the effects of recent governmental programs and other outside contacts on a relatively isolated and conservative Indian community.

The area selected for the research was the hill region near the town of Dehra Dun. It was chosen over other, equally promising hill regions because of ease of access, availability of competent medical care, and adequate housing in nearby Dehra Dun—features lacking in many hill areas but important in view of my plan to take my wife and infant daughter. Other factors were that I had an advance contact with a potential interpreter in the town of Dehra Dun and that town, as district headquarters and an educational center, had useful libraries and other documentary resources. The particular locality and community were chosen as suitable in terms of the combined requirements of the type of community to be investigated, the plan of the research, and the necessity of remaining within a reasonable distance of the facilities of Dehra Dun.

In selecting a site for the research, I visited some 25 villages over a period of two months, both in the hills and in the Dehra Dun valley bordering the hills. Sirkanda, a village ten air miles from Dehra Dun, was attractive in that it was large for a hill village, was fairly isolated but accessible, had a caste distribution typical of the area, and had no apparent important atypical features. During the period of research I lived most of the time in Sirkanda and simultaneously maintained a house in Dehra Dun or, for the last four months, in the nearby hill town of Mussoorie. Except on visits to the village, my family occupied the house in town. My characteristic routine during the research period was to spend four or five days in the village followed by two days in town. This provided a weekly opportunity to type notes, consult library resources and official records, secure supplies, and get needed rest.

In addition to my residence in Sirkanda, I had fairly extensive contacts with other hill villages in the immediate area. I passed through other villages and intermediary markets en route to and from Sirkanda, and I paid occasional visits to surrounding villages, often in the company of Sirkanda villagers. Contrasting hill regions were observed in two treks, one from Simla to Chakrata, a 110-mile trip in Himachal Pradesh and Jaunsar-Bawar, to the west. The other was from Mussoorie east to Tehri, a 40-mile trip through the heart of the culture area represented by the people of Sirkanda. From these contacts and similar ones in the Dehra Dun valley, I gained a first-hand perspective on the place of Sirkanda in its own culture area and its relation to neighboring ones.

Living conditions in the village were primitive even by local standards—a fact which led me to reject the idea of moving my family there on a full-time basis. Except for a period of about four months when I owned an unreliable jeep and could drive by a devious route to within five miles of the village, access from Dehra Dun was by a foot trail nine miles beyond the end of a bus line. The last five-mile distance to the village was along a mountain trail climbing 2,700 feet. Access from Mussoorie, location of my "town house" for the last four months, was by a relatively level, but in places extremely rough, trail of 16 miles. My village house consisted of three small connecting rooms, one of which was occupied continuously by two to four water buffalo, and all of which were inferior to those inhabited by most villagers. The only food consistently available in the village was grain, milk, sugar, and tea. The source of water was one-fourth of a mile distant over a rocky trail. In short, Sirkanda was not suitable for protracted family living by outsiders.

Throughout the research the services of an interpreter were utilized. The language of the people is the Central dialect of the language group known as Pahari. This is related to Hindi, and most villagers knew Hindi well. I knew elementary Hindi and was able to carry on ordinary conversation and to comprehend much of what was being said by informants. However, for research purposes an assistant conversant with the language was needed. Two interpreters worked with me consecutively.

Problems of the research, especially as it was affected by the contrasting personal and social characteristics of these two men, have been the subject of a short monograph (see Prologue). Suffice it to say here that villagers were at first suspicious of us and our motives. The nature of the rapport we established and consequently of the information we obtained was heavily influenced by the villagers' perceptions of us. The first interpreter, a young Brahmin, was helpful in establishing friendly relations but, partly because of his status as a Brahmin of plains origin, he inhibited people in their presentation of themselves to us. Villagers are self-conscious about many of their religious and social practices, which are unorthodox and even defiling by plains standards. They were anxious to conceal these from the young Brahmin in order to secure his respect. When it unexpectedly became necessary to find a replacement as interpreter, a retired Muslim schoolteacher was employed. Although his religion prevented him from achieving close friendship with most high-caste villagers, he won remarkably good rapport with villagers of low caste who, in any case, were the best informants. Moreover, neither he nor the villagers felt compelled to impress one another with their status or ritual purity. This led to more candid information and observation among all groups than had been possible when the Brahmin was present.

The primary sources of data were Sirkanda villagers themselves. Initially they were, as a result of their suspicions, an unreliable source, and many of the data obtained were in the nature of half-truths. In the beginning there was consistent suppression of many kinds of information, especially that which the villagers felt reflected adversely on their status as Hindus, and that which they believed might result in additional taxation, legal proceedings, or other governmental interference. Thus their subjects of conversation with me were limited to the weather, agricultural techniques, and similarly innocuous topics. Gradually we won their confidence and they gave information more freely. A few individuals remained suspicious and uncommunicative throughout the period of research; others became friendly but not informative; some became both friendly and informative. In virtually all instances, however, it was possible to check information with two or more informants. Most villagers were at least occasional informants.

Low-caste people were freer with most kinds of information than were high-caste people, apparently because they had a smaller stake in the impressions others received of them and because they did not feel threatened by the anthropologist and his interpreter. Low-caste villagers contributed a relatively large amount of information per capita, but this was compensated for by the greater numbers of high-caste informants. Information was always obtained from or checked by those in a position to know whereof they spoke on a particular topic. In the year of research there was an opportunity to observe many events at first hand. However, some of those to be described, and especially some religious and ceremonial activities, did not occur in my presence. Descriptions of such events were obtained from people who had participated in them.

Information was obtained primarily from observation and through informal interviews, both directed and undirected. Interviews were conducted wherever and whenever the occasion arose—in my house or yard, at the houses of villagers, in the shops, at places of work of artisans, in the fields, at the water source, on the trails, and so on. Generally several people were present at once, contributing information and attitudes and inhibiting one another's contributions. Such interviews were not recorded on the spot. At the first opportunity they were recorded in private. The approach could not be called participant observation because real participation was a virtual impossibility in most contexts. My interpreter and I were outsiders. Our participation was limited largely to informal social situations, and even there we were usually in the role of guests, invited or uninvited.

As time passed villagers became interested in our work and accustomed to our queries, and some were willing to have interviews recorded in their presence. This was done in the unreliable privacy of my village house. Some objective and largely quantitative types of data were gathered, notebook in hand, from all the villagers or from a cross-section. These included genealogical and census materials, economic data, and the like. Scheduled interviews had been drawn up to get at attitudes toward the outside world and related matters, but they were discarded. I felt, on the basis of experience in informal interviewing and in collecting genealogical and other information, that these would do more harm in terms of rapport than good in terms of reliable data. More was to be gained, I believed, by getting this information informally than by drawing attention (and inevitably, suspicion) to my interests by attempting a survey approach. This is an unusually closed society, whose members are accustomed to concealing and protecting themselves from the outside world. Data obtained by survey techniques on matters about which villagers are sensitive would, in all probability, have been of little value except as a kind of projective test, and any attempt to secure such data would have jeopardized further research efforts.

The difficulty of obtaining reliable data is reflected in the quality of the official statistical sources of information presumably available on the village. There are such records as voting lists, birth and death records, census lists, school enrollment lists, livestock census, land records, and tax records, which provide neat statistical summaries. However, much of the information is inaccurate. On the current voting list, for example, 142 names appear accompanied by the person's age and name of father or husband. Among these are three people who appear twice, at least eight who are incorrectly identified, seven who

are unidentified, and at least two who appear also on the voting list
of a neighboring village. The list includes a mixture of full-time and
part-time residents and people who no longer reside in the village,
while some individuals in each of these categories are missing from the
list. Ages given are at best rough approximations. The village livestock census was conducted by a forestry officer, who was reported to
have looked at the cattle in the yards of one or two houses and multiplied by his guess as to the number of houses in the village. Land
records are more accurate, since they are based on measurements, but
they are inadequate to show current land distribution because informal
division of land has long gone unrecorded. The man responsible for
recording births and deaths in Sirkanda lives in another village and
misses many births and cases of infant and child mortality. Even the
school enrollment record which is kept in the village includes four
students whom the teacher has never seen (these are excluded from all
discussions and calculations with regard to the school in later chapters).
The record fails to list six students who attend regularly.

In view of the difficulties faced by those responsible for keeping
records both in terms of the reliability of their informants and the
pressure from their superiors, it is remarkable that they do as well as
they do. But documentary records are less useful sources of data for
research than might be expected. Each type of record has its own
specific types of limitations. Reliance upon such records is misleading
unless their limitations are recognized.

Literature dealing with Central Pahari-speaking people is extremely
scarce. The earliest account, and an indispensable one, is G. W. Traill's
"Statistical Sketch of Kamaon" (1828). E. T. Atkinson's three-volume
work, *The Himalayan Districts of the North-Western Provinces of
India* (1882–1886), is a comprehensive and accurate report on the area
and the people. It is the only such source, and most subsequent accounts rely heavily upon it. To these two insightful civil servants we
owe most of what we know of these people. G. A. Grierson in the
Linguistic Survey of India (Vol. IX, 1916) provides invaluable linguistic and historical data. E. S. Oakley's *Holy Himalaya* (1905) also
contains interesting material. Other useful works are the District
Gazetteers of Dehra Dun, British Garhwal, and Almora (the latter two
largely revisions of pertinent sections of Atkinson's volumes) by H. G.
Walton (1911a; 1910; 1911b), the *Historical and Statistical Memoir
of Dehra Dun* by G. R. C. Williams (1874), and to a lesser extent the
District Gazetteer of Naini Tal by H. R. Nevill (1904).

An informative informal description by one who knew the people
well is that of "Mr. Wilson of Mussoorie," contained in *A Summer*

Ramble in the Himalayas, edited by Wilson under the nom de plume of "the Mountaineer" (1860, pp. 121–232). Useful works by local historians are: *Garhwal, Ancient and Modern,* by P. R. Bahadur (1916), *History of Garhwal* (in Hindi) by H. K. Raturi (1928), and *Kumaon* (in Hindi) by R. Sankrityayana (1958). L. D. Joshi (1929) compiled a valuable account of customary law—primarily family law—in the Central Pahari area, and V. A. Stowell (1907) contributed a source book on land tenures.

With the exception of a brief appendix to the Gazetteer of British Garhwal, none of the above deals specifically with Tehri Garhwal, the administrative unit immediately adjacent, and for many purposes most relevant, to Sirkanda. The books cited do, however, deal with closely related peoples in neighboring Garhwal and the Kumaon districts to the east.

The Pahari area is populated by five million Indo-Aryan speaking Hindus. It is famous as the location of some of the most important Hindu shrines, as the setting for widely known religious epics, as a traditional region of retreat for religious figures, and as the site of many points of historic interest. It is the home of the men who made up the Garhwal Rifles, who won fame in two World Wars. It is the location of "hill stations," where thousands of people from all over North India go annually to escape the summer heat, and where state and national governments and international political conferences have met. It is the source of an increasing variety of natural resources. Yet it has remained a virtual blank on the ethnographic map and is ignored by most of those who write about North Indian culture and society.

The situation has changed little since 1935, when S. D. Pant noted that, "The Himalayas have for many years constituted a subject of such profound and unique interest, and have attracted so distinguished a company of explorers and investigators, that it seems all but incredible that no adequate scientific account of the human geography and social economy of the Himalayans has yet been written" (Pant, 1935, p. 9). Pant himself has provided the first exception to this dearth of scientific work in the area with his book, *The Social Economy of the Himalayans,* a valuable general survey of Almora and Naini Tal districts focusing upon the economy of the Paharis and Bhotiyas. This is the only contemporary study conducted even partially among Central Pahari-speaking peoples.

The only Himalayan hill people to have attracted the attention of Indian anthropologists or sociologists are the polyandrous residents of Jaunsar-Bawar, a small area in Dehra Dun District inhabited by

Western Pahari-speaking people. Evidently attracted by unusual marital customs and related features which have led to characterization of the society as "a fossil of the age of the *Mahabharata*" (Munshi, 1955, p. i), D. N. Majumdar and his students, notably R. N. Saksena, have done some work in that region (Majumdar, 1944; Saksena, 1955).

Recently short reports of village studies carried out in hill tracts farther to the west, in Chamba and Kulu, have appeared, by W. H. Newell (1955) and C. Rosser (1955), respectively. The area is certain to receive further attention.

The present study is, therefore, the first community study or ethnography attempted in the Central Pahari area, and one of very few studies of any kind that have dealt with Himalayan hill people. Because of this it has seemed worthwhile to include in this account a good deal of ethnographic material which could have been omitted if it were available elsewhere. There is no independent documentation for much that is presented here. Without documentation and cultural context, the reader would be faced with the problem which faced the researcher in the initial phases of his work—he might fail to see existing relationships and he might assume nonexistent ones. The reader familiar with India would be especially likely to jump to erroneous conclusions about the degree of similarity or difference between the community described here and other Indian communities with which he might be acquainted. This would be likely to prejudice his estimate of the credibility and applicability of the generalizations, analyses, and conclusions presented. Intelligent appraisal can follow only from data presented in cultural context. For this reason I have tried to present some of the empirical data upon which these generalizations, analyses, and conclusions are based.

The aims of this book, then, are both ethnographic and analytic: the description of an example of a heretofore undescribed culture; the analysis of social organization in a uniquely organized caste society; and the analysis of reactions to planned and unplanned change in a remote and unsophisticated village. These aims have been important in determining the content and manner of presentation of the materials to follow.

1 THE SETTING

The lower Himalayas from western Kashmir to eastern Nepal are populated by peoples sharing common and distinct cultural, linguistic, and historical traditions. This study deals primarily with the inhabitants of Sirkanda, one village in this broad culture area, and with their neighbors and relatives in nearby villages. Sirkanda lies in the Himalayan foothills bordering Dehra Dun and Tehri Garhwal districts in Uttar Pradesh, India, 125 air miles north and slightly east of Delhi, and 85 miles southwest of the Tibetan border. It is about ten air miles northeast of Dehra Dun, a large town situated in a valley at the foot of the Himalayan range, and seven miles east of Mussoorie, a British-built hill station on the crest of the first ridge of the Himalayas north of Dehra Dun. Distances in this region are deceptive because the terrain is rugged and mountainous. The only means of travel within the area is by mountain trails which average at least double the air-mile distances. There are adults in Sirkanda who have never visited Dehra Dun.

NATURAL FEATURES

The Kumaon Himalaya or Himalaya West comprises the central portion of the mountainous expanse from Kashmir to Darjeeling. It constitutes the northernmost part of the Indian state of Uttar Pradesh and is bordered on the east by Nepal, on the north by Tibet and on the west by the state of Himachal Pradesh.[1] It rises abruptly from the

Gangetic plain at scarcely 1,000 feet above sea level to the perpetual snows of the passes into Tibet at 16,000 to 18,000 feet and the peaks of Bandarpunch, Trisul, Nanda Devi, and others reaching 20,000 to 25,000 feet. The main axis of the high or snowy Himalayan range is an arc from Kashmir in the northwest, through and beyond Nepal in the east. The region of interest here comprises the lower and outer ranges known as the Sub-Himalayas, and specifically those portions of the Kumaon Himalaya lying predominately below 10,000 feet and often called the Kumaon hills.

Topographically the Kumaon hill area is one of mountains and rivers. Since the mountains are geologically young they are precipitous and rocky. The valleys are steep and narrow, the streams and rivers are swift, and in the rainy season they become rushing torrents. The mountainous area is separated from the plains to the south by barren, rocky talus slopes below which is a strip of forest and marshland.

Along part of their length the Himalayas are paralleled a few miles to the south by remnants of the ancient Siwalik range. Between these ranges lie narrow valleys such as that of Dehra Dun, bordering the Himalayan foothills for 45 miles and separated from the Gangetic plain by the low but rugged Siwalik hills. Here, as in popular usage in the area, "the valley" will be used to refer to the Dehra Dun valley, some of the eastern portion of which is visible from Sirkanda. The valley is about 2,000 feet above sea level, while the Gangetic plain beyond the Siwaliks is not over 1,000 feet in elevation. It is the latter plain that is here termed "the plains," in accordance with local usage.

Throughout the Himalayas, population density is restricted by the terrain. Prime requisites for occupation by the agriculturists who inhabit these mountains are topsoil that can be terraced and a steady water supply. Alluvial fans, gradual slopes, or broad valleys are exceptionally favorable spots for habitation. Most of the population is found in valleys and on the lower slopes of the mountains below an elevation of 6,000 feet.

The Kumaon Himalaya lies across 30° north latitude and is therefore within the Temperate Zone not far from the tropics. Climate is influenced by the high Himalayas to the north and the Gangetic plain to the south. Three seasons are recognized and terminologically distinguished by the inhabitants: winter, hot season or summer, and rainy season. Winter lasts from mid-October to mid-February and is characterized by clear, cool weather, followed by colder weather and some precipitation in December, January, and February. Temperature varies with altitude, so that even during the coldest period little snow falls below the 6,000-foot level while considerable falls above that level. In Sirkanda for about a month in winter, temperatures often fall slightly below freezing at night, but they usually rise considerably during the day. Summer begins in mid-February and extends through the middle of June. In March and April localized storms occur. By mid-April the hot, dry season is at hand and lasts until the monsoon breaks in the latter half of June. Rains continue to come frequently and heavily and temperatures remain fairly high until mid-September, when temperatures begin to drop and rains cease. Annual rainfall varies greatly, with the outer range of mountains catching the heaviest precipitation as the clouds move in from the plains. Annual rainfall in Mussoorie averages around 80 inches, while other hill locations report rainfall of 40 to 100 inches per year. Vegetation is profoundly influenced by altitude and rainfall.

Generally the slopes which face northward are more thickly wooded than the southward slopes, as in the former the sun's rays only slant across the surface, and the moisture is retained in the soil for a longer period. With the decrease in elevation a gradual change in the composition of the forest is observed. . . . The slopes above the Kali . . . present an excellent epitome of this plant variation. One passes from the *shisham* (*Dalbergia sissoo*) and *sal* (*Shorea robusta*) in the river beds, through oak and rhododendron on the high hills, to firs, birch, and box on the still higher central ridges. (Pant, 1935, p. 37)

The fauna is varied and includes deer, goats, pigs, monkeys, foxes, jackals, porcupines, bears, leopards, and an occasional tiger. A wide variety of birds is to be found, including native wild chickens. The streams abound in Indian trout. The wild life and terrain of the Kumaon hills have been vividly depicted in the well-known works of Jim Corbett (1946), while the fauna has been described in detail by Atkinson (1884a, pp. 1–266).

ADMINISTRATIVE HISTORY

The western half of the Kumaon Himalaya is known as Garhwal —the country of fortresses—after the large stone structures found scattered through the region. It comprises the present districts of Garhwal, Tehri Garhwal, and the Himalayan hill area of Dehra Dun District exclusive of Jaunsar-Bawar (see map 1). Almora and Naini Tal districts to the east are often called the "Kumaon districts" when contrasted to Garhwal. In the Hindu scriptures Garhwal is referred to as Kedarkhand. Kedarkhand is important in Hindu religion and mythology as the place of origin of the two sacred rivers Ganges and Jumna and as the site of famous places of pilgrimage including Hardwar, Rishikesh, Kedarnath, Badrinath, Jamnotri, and Gangotri.

> *Rishis* [sages] and ascetics in large numbers resorted to its silent valleys for purposes of meditation or the instruction of their disciples. The final scene of the life of the five heroes of the *Mahabharata* was enacted amid its mountains and many place-names in the Alaknanda valley still recall the memory of BhimSen and his brothers. Garhwal may still claim to be the holy land of India: its valleys are full of ancient temples and there is scarcely a ridge from which the wonderful spectacle of the snowy range is visible without its humble shrine. Every year thousands of pilgrims from all parts of India make their laborious way on foot along the *via sacra* of Badrinath. (Bahadur, 1916, p. ii)

Little is known of the early history of Garhwal and the surrounding areas either through written sources or local tradition.

> Up to the time of Ajaiya Pala [about A.D. 1358] Garhwal was divided amongst a number of petty Rajas. Every glen or hill, as formerly was the case in the highlands of Scotland, was subject to its own chiefs who have left no record behind except the moss-covered walls of their strongholds. And although Ajaiya Pala is credited with having reduced fifty-two of these petty chiefs under his own rule, we may well suppose that he was only the first of his line to aim at more than a local supremacy, and that to his successors is due the extension of the Garhwal power over the Dun, Bisahir, and the tract now known as Tihri or foreign Garhwal. (Atkinson, 1884a, pp. 526–527)

For the end of the sixteenth century and later, more precise records and dates are available. Then Garhwal appeared as an independent kingdom at its greatest recorded extent. It remained thus until 1803–1805, when the Garhwal Raja, Pradhuman Shah, was defeated and killed in battle by invading Nepalese armies which pushed westward, extending Nepalese suzerainty to the Sutlej River. Although the Nepalese acquired a reputation for harsh, exploitative rule which reportedly led to mass emigration out of the hills, their eleven-year rule left few imprints in relatively inaccessible localities such as Sirkanda.

The British defeated the Nepalese in 1815 and, in taking control from them, divided Garhwal into its present parts. The eastern half, comprising 5,629 square miles, was placed under direct British rule and was thenceforth known as British Garhwal or simply Garhwal. For administrative purposes it was included with the districts of Naini Tal and Almora, to its east, to form the Kumaon Division. The Dehra Dun valley and adjacent hills in the southwestern corner of Garhwal and the hill tract called Jaunsar-Bawar west of Garhwal were annexed

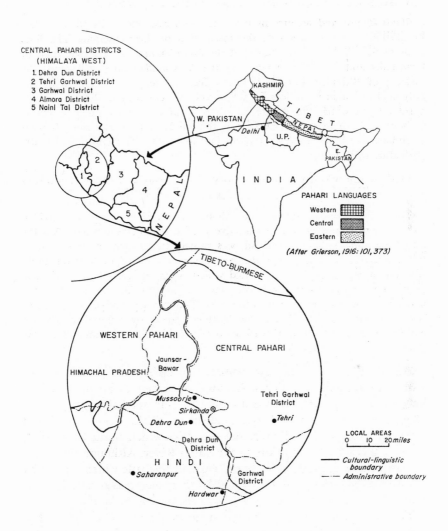

Map 1. Linguistic and administrative environs of Sirkanda. Partly adapted from Grierson (1916), pp. 101, 373.

to Saharanpur District, which was already under direct British rule.
Later the annexed sections became Dehra Dun District. The remaining
large portion of Garhwal, comprising 4,200 square miles between
British Garhwal and Dehra Dun District, was ceded to Sudershan Shah,
the son of the last of the Garhwal Rajas (who had died in the Nepalese
war). This section, called Tehri Garhwal, remained an independent
princely state under succeeding rajas until Indian Independence (1947),
when, after some delay, it was incorporated into Uttar Pradesh. Since
Independence these areas have remained administratively separated
as districts in Uttar Pradesh but are, of course, under a common law.
Throughout the period of recorded history, the inhabitants of Garhwal
have retained their social and cultural ties despite administrative
division of the area.

The People and Their History

The people of the Sub-Himalayan hills from western Kashmir to
eastern Nepal are referred to by the generic term *Pahari* (of the mountains). While not a particularly precise term, it is a useful one and is
recognized throughout North India. Two major ancestral stocks are
generally believed to have contributed to the present Pahari population. One, often assumed to have been an early, indigenous group,
now appears as the *Dōm* or low castes. The other, described as an
Indo-Aryan speaking group, is presumably more recent and of Central
Asian origin. Its descendants, called *Khāsa* or *Khāsīya,* comprise the
present high castes of the hills. The term "Khasiya" is used by the
people in the region of this study, while "Khasa" is more frequent in
the literature about Paharis. Throughout this account, the *Bhōtīya,*
a Mongoloid, Tibeto-Burmese speaking, and culturally distinct people
of the higher Himalayas are excluded from the discussion except where
specific reference is made to them.

Both Khasas and Doms are often described as internally relatively
undifferentiated. Khasas are divided into Brahmin and Rajput groups,
but interaction is more intimate between them than is usual on the
plains. Even intermarriage is tolerated. Doms are divided into several
endogamous groups ranked relative to one another and associated
with occupational specialties. However, occupational specialization is
remarkably variable, and many accounts describe them as formerly
less differentiated. One might speculate that at one time there were
two relatively homogeneous groups, the dominant, agricultural Khasas
and the dependent, depressed artisan or service group known as Doms.
These were probably groups of different ethnic affinities, but they

could have been status groups originating from a common source. Internal differentiation within each may have resulted from subsequent contacts with plains peoples—perhaps immigrants to the hills. As a result of such contacts Khasas took the names and other status characteristics of Brahmins and Rajputs, or in some areas they may all have become "Rajputs" while the immigrants from the plains were Brahmins. Meanwhile Doms may have subdivided according to occupational specialty as a result of high-caste expectations or their own adoption of plains attitudes, or as a result of an influx of artisans from the plains. Around Sirkanda it seems not improbable that the caste of drummer-tailor-basketmakers (*Bājgī*) may be descended from the archetypical "Doms" while the other specialties (such as blacksmiths) were derived from immigrant groups or possibly from specialization within the old Dom group (such as weavers). This, like the widespread assertion that Doms preceded Khasas, is speculation and should be interpreted as nothing more. With present evidence no better can be done. We can safely say only that the origins and affinities of contemporary Pahari castes and occupational groups are largely unknown, and that this fact has stimulated conjecture. Such conjecture has centered most heavily on the Khasas, who are dominant in numbers, wealth, and status and about whom some historical information is at hand.

Khasas

"Sanskrit literature contains frequent references to a tribe whose name is usually spelt Khaśa, with variants such as Khasa, Khasha, and Khaśira. The earlier we trace notices regarding them, the further northwest we find them" (Grierson, 1916, p. 2). They appear frequently in the *Puranas* (ancient Hindu literature), and they figure prominently in the *Mahabharata*.

We gather that according to the most ancient Indian authorities in the extreme north-west of India, on the Hindu Kush and the mountainous tracts to the south, and in the Western Panjab there was a group of tribes one of which was called Khasa, which were looked upon as Kshatriyas of Aryan origin. These spoke a language closely allied to Sanskrit. . . . They were considered to have lost their claim to consideration as Aryans, and to have become Mlèchchhas, or barbarians, owing to their non-observance of the rules for eating and drinking observed by the Sanskritic peoples of India. These Khasas were a warlike tribe, and were well known to classical writers, who noted, as their special home, the Indian Caucasus of Pliny. . . .
It is probable that they once occupied an important position in Central Asia, and the Kashgar of Chitral were named after them. They were closely

connected with the group of tribes nicknamed "Piśàchas" or "cannibals" by Indian writers, and before the sixth century they were stated to speak the same language as the people of Balkh. At the same period they had apparently penetrated along the southern slope of the Himalaya as far east as Nepal, and in the twelfth century they certainly occupied in considerable force the hills to the south, south-west and south-east of Kashmir.

At the present day their descendants, and the tribes who claim descent from them, occupy a much wider area. (Grierson, 1916, pp. 7–8)

The languages of the hill regions, like the peoples, are termed Pahari.

The word "Pahari" means "of or belonging to the mountains," and is specially applied to the groups of languages spoken in the sub-Himalayan hills extending from Bhadrawah, north of the Panjab, to the eastern parts of Nepal. To its North and East various Himalayan Tibeto-Burman languages are spoken. To its west there are Aryan languages connected with Kashmiri and Western Panjabi, and to its south it has the Aryan languages of the Panjab and the Gangetic plain, viz.:—in order from West to East, Panjabi, Western Hindi, Eastern Hindi and Bihari.

The Pahari languages fall into three main groups. In the extreme East there is Khas-Kura or Eastern Pahari, commonly called Naipali, the Aryan language spoken in Nepal. Next, in Kumaon and Garhwal, we have the Central Pahari language, Kumauni and Garhwali. Finally in the West we have the Western Pahari languages spoken in Jaunsar-Bawar, the Simla Hill States, Kulu, Mandi and Suket, Chamba, and Western Kashmir. (Grierson, 1916, p. 1)

"It is a remarkable fact that, although Pahari has little connexion with the Panjabi, Western and Eastern Hindi, and Bihari spoken immediately to its south, it shows manifold traces of intimate relationship with the languages of Rajputana" (Grierson, 1916, p. 2). There is general agreement that the relationship between the Pahari and Rajasthani languages is attributable to the movement of peoples, notably the Gurjaras, between these two areas.

The earliest immigrants [into the Pahari tract] of whom we have any historical information were the Khasas, . . . They were followed by the Gurjaras, a tribe who invaded India about the sixth century A.D. and occupied the same tract, then known as Sapadalaksha. At that time, they [like the Khasas] spoke an Aryan, but not necessarily Indo-Aryan language. Of these Gurjaras the bulk followed pastoral pursuits and became merged in and identified with the preceding Khasa population. Others were fighting men, and were identified by the Brahmans [priestly class] with Kshatriyas [warrior class]. In this guise they invaded Eastern Rajputana from Sapadalaksha and, possibly, Western Rajputana from Sindh, and founded, as Rajputs, the great Rajput states of Rajputana. (Grierson, 1916, p. 14)

Vincent Smith, quoted by Grierson, differs in his explanation of the sequence in this relationship, but not in the fact of the relationship:

The Gujars, etc., of the lower Himalayas who now speak forms of Rajasthani are in large measure of the same stock as many Rajput clans in Rajputana, the Panjab and the United Provinces; . . . their ancestors emigrated from Rajputana *after* they had acquired the Rajasthani speech; and . . . the most likely time for such emigration is the ninth century, when the Gurjara-Rajput power dominated all northern and northwestern India . . . (Grierson, 1916, p. 12; emphasis added)

In either case ". . . it is plain that down even to the days of late Musalman dominion the tie between Sapadalaksha [the Western Pahari-speaking areas] and Rajputana was never broken. And this, in my opinion, satisfactorily explains the fact of the close connexion between the Pahari languages and Rajasthani" (Grierson, 1916, p. 13).

The Khasas were apparently among those participating in the large movements of Aryan-speaking peoples into India. Therefore it is probable that they entered between 1500 and 1000 B.C. from the northwest. There is not universal agreement among scholars that this was the route followed or even that there was large-scale immigration then. F. E. Pargiter concludes from his research that "tradition or myth indicates that the Ailas (or Aryans) entered India from the mid-Himalayan region, and its attitude towards the N. W. frontier lends no support to any invasion from that quarter" (Pargiter, 1922, p. 299). Thus he believes that entry was from Tibet through Garhwal into India. Probably archaeology can best resolve this question.

It is evident that the Khasas have been in the Sub-Himalayan hills for a very long time. It is also true that there has been a continuing immigration of people from the plains who have become absorbed into the hill population. Grierson notes that the Gujars not only emigrated from the hills to the plains, but

. . . there was a constant reflux of emigration on the part of the Gujar-Rajputs from Rajputana and the neighbouring parts of India. These re-immigrants became, as befitted their Kshatriya station, the rulers of the country and today most of the chiefs and princes of the old Sapadalaksha trace their descent from Rajputs of the plains. The re-immigration was increased by the oppression of the Mughul rule in India proper, and there are historical notices of tribe after tribe, and leader after leader, abandoning their established seats in Rajputana and seeking refuge from Musalman oppression in the hills from which they had originally issued to conquer the Gangetic valley. (Grierson, 1916, pp. 14 f.)

Other non-Pahari people from the plains adjacent to the Himalayas also frequently sought refuge in the hills and became merged with the hill population.

Contact has long existed between Paharis and Tibeto-Burmese speaking peoples, often referred to as Bhotiyas or Tibetans, who occupy the higher Himalayas bordering the Pahari region along its northern periphery. In border areas physical and cultural intermingling occurs. In the Western and Central Pahari regions such admixture has been minimal, while to the east, especially in Nepal, it has occurred to a much greater extent.

The physical appearance of the high-caste Paharis of the Central and Western hills is often described in idealized fashion, as in these words of a contemporary anthropologist:

> The Khasas are usually tall, handsome, fair-complexioned (rosy or sallow), possess a long head, vertical forehead, fine or leptorhine nose, hazel eyes with a sprinkling of blue, curly hair and other features well-cut and proportioned. The women are also comparatively tall, slender, graceful, of a very attractive appearance and of extremely gay disposition. (Majumdar, 1944, p. 110)

The number of exceptions to such a description probably exceeds the examples, and the range in physical types overlaps greatly with that found in the Gangetic plain. However, there is perhaps a statistically significant tendency in the direction suggested by Majumdar. Some observers claim to find physical differences among contiguous populations of high-caste Paharis. Thus R. N. Saksena's description of the Khasas of Jaunsar-Bawar: "Their physical features, fair complexion, tall stature, aquiline nose and well-defined features of the face easily distinguish them from their neighbours, the Garhwalis" (Saksena, 1955, p. 9). Such statements are based on stereotypes rather than observation.

The Khasas have often been referred to as a "tribal" people. This term has not been defined in such a way as to include satisfactorily the diverse groups it is often used to designate nor to exclude many of the diverse groups it excludes. However, in India it usually refers to peoples who are not Hindus or Muslims or followers of other major religions, who do not have caste organization, or who practice a more primitive economy than that of most Indian communities.

Whatever their origin, the Khasas of today cannot be considered a tribal people by any of these criteria. They certainly are not aborigines as that term is used in India to denote non-Hindu "original sons of the soil," who live in a "primitive state of existence."

The great mass of the population in Kumaon and Garhwal profess a belief little differing from the orthodox Hinduism of the plains. . . . All their feelings and prejudices are so strongly imbued with the peculiar spirit of Hinduism that although their social habits and religious belief are often repugnant to those who strictly observe the orthodox ceremonial usages of Hinduism, it is impossible for any one that knows them to consider the Khasas to be other than Hindus. There are several facts connected with their history that show, whatever their origin may have been, the Khasas have for centuries been under the influence of the Brahmanical priesthood. (Atkinson, 1884a, p. 269)

Their unorthodox practice of Hinduism is well-known and long-recognized. Grierson refers to the Laws of Manu: "Looking at the Khasas from the Brahmanical point of view, he says (X, 22) that Khasas are the offspring of outcaste Kshatriyas, and again (X, 44) . . . he says that [among other tribes, the] Khasas are those who became outcaste through having neglected their religious duties . . ." (Grierson, 1916, p. 5). "Even in the most orthodox writings the Khasas are looked on more as heretical members of the great Aryan family than as outcaste aborigines, and . . . from a very early period they have been recognized as an important tribe in Upper India" (Atkinson, 1884a, p. 283).

Today the Khasas universally define themselves as Hindus who are in some respects culturally distinct from others of their religion and caste. This they attribute primarily to the rigors of life in the hills. They display no pan-Khasa unity beyond recognition of the term and certain cultural similarities. Recently there has been some pressure in the Western Pahari area to form a separate hill state, but that is a post-Independence phenomenon of educated hill men.

It is worth noting that in many areas, including that of this research and Jaunsar-Bawar to the northwest, only Rajputs (*Kshatriyas*) refer to themselves as Khasiya or Khasa. Brahmins, though apparently of the same stock, do not there admit to the designation. In fact the term Khasa refers historically to a Kshatriya group. However, Majumdar (1944, p. 110) notes that "the Khasas or the Khasiyas who constitute the high caste people of the cis-Himalayan region are either Rajput or Brahmin. . . ." "Khasiya Brahmans" are referred to by Atkinson (1886, p. 430), who states that, "Nearly ninety per cent of the Brahmans in Kumaon belong to the Khasiya race and are so classed by the people themselves. . . ." "Khas-Brahmins" are found throughout the Pahari regions both as landowning and tilling agriculturists, like the Rajputs, and as priests. Atkinson (1884a, p. 734) remarks that these Brahmins really have no title to the name Brahmin, evidently reserving legitimate application of the term to Brahmins of plains origin. In any event,

Pahari Brahmins are indistinguishable from Rajputs in most respects.
Even caste distinctions between the two are not as rigid as in most of
India. It is likely that the division into Rajput and Brahmin castes
occurred after the Khasas moved into India and not before the earliest
references to them. Brahmin disavowal of the Khasa appellation may
well relate to its association with defiled, or at least very unorthodox,
Hindus.

Some Rajput Paharis deny that they are Khasas on grounds that
they are of plains origin. They say the term refers to degraded people
who are not really Rajputs, and they claim higher status for themselves. No such people reside in or around Sirkanda, and it is impossible to assess the accuracy of their claims to plains origin. Probably
some are of more recent plains ancestry than avowed Khasas, but
others may well have adopted this claim as a means to status enhancement.

Doms

The second large population group of the Sub-Himalayan region
is that of the alleged predecessors of the Khasa, commonly called Dom.
Little or nothing is known of the history of these people. They are
often described as having occupied the region at the time the Aryan
invasions occurred, and having then been pushed back, subjugated,
and assigned to their rigidly inferior social status by the conquering
Aryans. For this reason they are sometimes included in accounts of
aborigines. Majumdar (1944, p. 110) has suggested that the Aryans may
have brought the Doms with them when they entered India. Whether
they are related in any way other than by name to Doms of the plains
is unknown.

Doms are the low-caste groups of the Himalayan area.

In the hills and in the Dun they comprise all classes who do menial and
more or less degrading duties such as are performed by separate occupational
castes in the plains. They are a depressed race, seldom cultivate and practically never own land. (Walton, 1911a, p. 97)

"They have for ages been the slaves of the Khasiyas and been thought
less of than the cattle . . ." (Atkinson, 1884a, p. 370). They are the
"serfs of the Khasiya race in Kumaon, Garhwal and along the hills to
the westward as far as the Indus valley" (Atkinson, 1886, p. 443). They
constitute the artisan class and in fact are also collectively referred to
as *Shilpkār* (artisan). They are untouchable (*achūt*) whether they be
blacksmith, carpenter, musician, shoemaker, weaver, tailor, basketmaker, or whatever. Fifteen to thirty castes of Doms are found in

various parts of the Kumaon hills (Atkinson, 1886, pp. 444 f.; Bahadur, 1916, pp. 101 f.; Raturi, 1928, pp. 196 ff.). Some of these may be wholly or partly derived from equivalent castes of the plains who have emigrated to the hills, while others are old indigenous groups or groups derived from internal differentiation of the Doms.

Doms have had no distinct language in history or tradition, and their religious and social beliefs and practices appear to be continuous with those of the higher castes. Whatever their cultural heritage may have been, it is now merged with that of the Khasiyas so that traces of their separate origin, if any, can no longer be identified. Many writers attribute the unorthodox religious and social practices of high-caste Paharis to their contact with Doms, but there is no evidence to support this explanation. At least one writer attributes the origin of the worship of Shiva, one of the great gods of modern Hinduism, to the aboriginal low-caste Paharis (Bahadur, 1916, pp. 73, 122).

Aside from occupational and status differences, the most widely remarked distinctive feature of Doms is their physical appearance. The stereotypes regarding Doms are essentially those regarding low castes and "aborigines" or "Dravidians" elsewhere in India. Majumdar (1944, p. xvi) refers to them as ". . . a dark-skinned, short-statured, flat-nosed people who 'scourge the eastern districts of the province.'" Atkinson (1884a, p. 370) notes their "exceedingly dark complexion." In the Central and Western Pahari regions with which the writer is familiar, these are physical stereotypes based on a grain of truth, but little more. It is impossible for Paharis or others to distinguish Doms from high-caste people accurately and consistently on the basis of physiognomy alone. Majumdar is the only physical anthropologist to have worked among Paharis. The results of his measurements show minor physical differences between Khasas and Doms (Majumdar, 1944, pp. 181 ff.). Genetic admixture between the groups has largely eliminated the physical differences that may once have existed.

Census materials indicate that high-caste people outnumber Doms ten to one in Tehri Garhwal District. This is almost exactly the ratio in Jaunsar-Bawar to the west and in thirty villages related to Sirkanda by marriage ties, although particular villages sometimes show wide deviation from this average.

Language

The people of Sirkanda speak the language termed "Central Pahari" by Grierson, a language which includes the local dialects of the lower Himalayas between the Nepalese border and the Punjab, except for Jaunsar-Bawar, where Western Pahari is spoken. Very likely field studies would demonstrate extension of this language well into western Nepal, without sharp demarcation between it and Eastern Pahari. Grierson recognizes two component languages, Kumauni and Garhwali, and he refers to several subdialects of Garhwali including "Gangapariya" (language of the country beyond the Ganges) or Tehri Garhwali, which, with some variations, is evidently that spoken in Sirkanda and surrounding villages. Estimating the total number of speakers of these languages is difficult because of the nature of records available and because of the lack of accurate definition of the linguistic designations. Grierson gave the Pahari-speaking population of India, excluding the large but undetermined number of speakers of Eastern Pahari in Nepal, as 2,067,514 in 1891. Of these over half, 1,107,612, were recorded as speaking Central Pahari, and over half of the Central Pahari speakers, 670,824, were recorded as speaking Garhwali. The 1931 census is the most recent one for which reasonably complete figures on Pahari speakers are available. At that time slightly over 4,200,000 Pahari speakers were reported in India, distributed in significant numbers from Muzaffarabad District in Kashmir (164,000) on the west to the Nepal border on the east, with some Nepali or Eastern Pahari speakers in Darjeeling. A total of 1,725,000, all in the Kumaon hills of Uttar Pradesh, spoke Central Pahari. Whether or not this figure included some 300,000 in Tehri Garhwal is unclear.

The 1951 census of India shows just over 4,500,000 residents of the "Western Himalayan Sub-Region" exclusive of Jammu and Kashmir. This area plus Jammu and Kashmir, which contains well over 600,000 Pahari speakers, corresponds approximately to the Pahari-speaking area of India, though it would include a few Tibeto-Burmese speakers and the non-Pahari residents of several hill stations. We may estimate, therefore, that there are now around 5,000,000 Pahari speakers in India, over one-third of whom would be classed with Sirkanda residents as Central Pahari speakers by Grierson and about 1,000,000 of whom he would classify as Garhwali speakers (cf. volumes of Census of India listed in the Selective Bibliography). There is no information upon which to base an estimate of Pahari speakers in Nepal.

Grierson estimated speakers of Tehri Garhwali at 240,281. In the 1951 census, 408,000 speakers of Garhwali, presumably Tehri Garhwali, were reported out of a total population of 412,000 in Tehri Garhwal. However, the administrative boundary probably does not correspond to a significant linguistic boundary on its eastern border.

Since culture and language are to a large extent correlated in these hill regions, an idea of the population of the culture area represented by the subjects of this study can be derived from the above figures. From this can be inferred something of the representativeness of what will follow.

Our discussion turns now from the culture area of which this study is broadly representative to the specific location of the research.

SIRKANDA VILLAGE

Northeast of Dehra Dun lies a hill area roughly triangular in shape and seven miles on each side, known as *BhatbaiR* (sheep den) in recognition of its use by Bhotiyas of the higher Himalayas as a winter pasture for their sheep (see map 2). This region comprises primarily a single spur of mountains projecting southwest from the first ridge of the Himalayas. It lies within Dehra Dun District but is bordered on the north and east by Tehri Garhwal District, the crest of the Mussoorie Hills forming the northern boundary and the Bandal River forming the eastern. To the south and west it is bordered by the Dehra Dun valley and the Baldi River. Bhatbair has a total population of around 1,700 people living in about 10 villages and at least 15 smaller settlements. These have been combined, for administrative convenience, into seven revenue villages including Sirkanda. This is now the official definition of "Bhatbair."

In local usage the term "Bhatbair" has not been very precise. It is sometimes used by Sirkanda villagers to refer to the immediate Pahari area familiar to them and almost entirely within a four-mile radius of Sirkanda, including the side of the ridge facing them to the east, in Tehri Garhwal. This larger region forms a relatively independent economic and social unit of about 60 villages and settlements with a total population of almost 5,000. In another publication (Berreman, 1960b) I have referred to this larger area as "Bhatbair" for convenience. In the present account I will use the term in its more restricted sense, closely approximating the official definition. The larger area can simply be designated Bhatbair and vicinity.

Probably the earliest historical reference to Bhatbair is that by Williams (1874, pp. 92 ff.), who refers to a "Rajpoot Princess Ranee Kurnavutee" who had a palace near the present site of Dehra Dun before the arrival of the town's founder Guru Ram Rae (that is, before 1700). "Under her fostering care the valley smiled, and many flourishing villages sprang up such as . . . [among others] Bhat Beer. . . ." Although he has confused the name of a local region and administrative

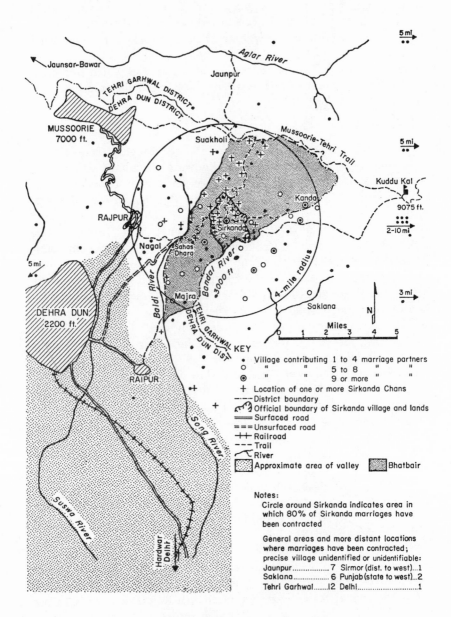

Map 2. Sirkanda marriage network and chans.

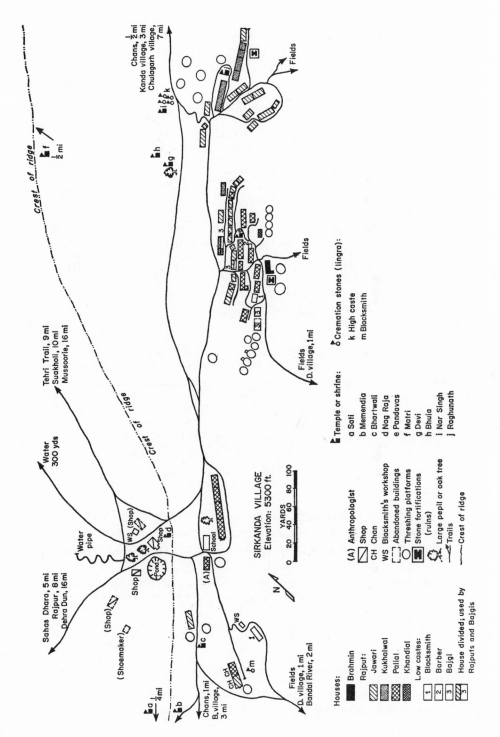

unit containing several villages with that of a single village, there can
be little doubt that the reference is to the area of which we are speaking.

For some time before the Nepalese conquest in 1804 and the British
conquest in 1815, Sirkanda was included with the rest of Bhatbair,
the Dehra Dun valley, Tehri Garhwal, and Garhwal as part of the
kingdom of the Garhwal Raja. Villagers retain a good deal of pride in
this raja as contrasted to other rajas, albeit they can also recount his
tyranny and injustices. There are several tales told which relate his
special interest in the tall, powerful, and honest residents of Sirkanda
and the recognition given them in his court. In the later days of the
Garhwal Rajas, Sirkanda was one of five villages located on this spur
of hills. According to villagers these five and adjacent lands were listed
in the Raja's records as being the revenue responsibility of Matthu, a
hill Brahmin of Kanda, one of the five villages. As *sayana,* or tax collector of the villages, he was allowed to keep a considerable portion of
his collections after turning over an annual sum to the Raja. Bhatbair
was apparently

one of those curious *taluqs* or clusters of several villages, so prevalent in the
. . . hills, which are cultivated by a numerous community of zamindars
[landowners], all enjoying separate and independent proprietary right but
at the same time all bound together by joint responsibility for the revenue
assessed on the whole *mahal.* (Walton, 1911a, p. 109)

Each taluq (called *khat* in Jaunsar-Bawar and some other Pahari areas)
was under a sayana who collected land revenue for the Raja from the
landholders in each component village. At one time the landowners
may have been individually responsible directly to the Raja for
revenue, as was the case over most of the Kumaon Himalaya (cf. Stowell,
1907, p. iv; Baden-Powell, 1892, II, p. 313). Whether cultivators were
individually or collectively responsible for revenue, ultimate rights in
the land were vested in the Raja, who not only collected revenue but
was free to alienate any land in his dominion to his own purposes—
most often to cede it to people he wished to reward. When this occurred, former owners suddenly became tenants (cf. Stowell, 1907, pp.
ix, 1–6, 31 f.).

When the British took over in 1815, Bhatbair was joined administratively with the Dehra Dun valley. Due to the accident that it is a very
small hill tract in a district made up primarily of people of the plains,
special conditions in Bhatbair have been ignored in the various revenue
settlements. For revenue purposes Bhatbair villages have usually been
treated like villages of the valley. Initially the revenue settlement for

Bhatbair was probably made with the sayana, Matthu. There was much vacillation in the policies of early revenue officers dealing with Dehra Dun District, some favoring development of a landed aristocracy and acting accordingly, and others favoring owner-cultivators (cf. Williams, 1874, pp. 200 ff.). However, under the British a Rajput of Kanda is said to have become headman of Bhatbair, which had come to include seven villages. He wielded considerable influence with the British, and is credited with having pressed for the rights of cultivators and having influenced the government finally to allot proprietary rights to the lands in Bhatbair in equal portions to the principal cultivating families, who thereafter paid reduced taxes directly to the British through a local tax collector. Matthu and his descendants then lost all connection with the lands they did not cultivate.

At that time Sirkanda had 16 high-caste cultivating families. Cultivated village lands were divided into 16 equal parts, and equal portions of each type of land and of land in each area were assigned to each of the 16 families. As new land came under cultivation, it too was divided in this fashion. In continuation of local tradition, uncultivated lands, trails, and certain open places in the village settlement area were deemed to be the common property of the village. This allotment, with alterations resulting from family division, inheritance, and purchase, has remained to the present. This system is referred to as the *"bhāichāra"* (custom of brothers) system of land tenure, a British introduction to the area which Sirkanda people compare most favorably with the landlord-tenancy system retained until Independence in nearby Tehri Garhwal under the Raja.

Another portion of Bhatbair and lands west of it had been granted by the Raja to the Sikh religious leader who founded Dehra Dun. He exacted rent from the people living on this land, people who had until that time been owner-cultivators. The British honored his proprietorship, and his successors continued to enjoy this revenue until well after Independence; in fact, they still hold rights to some of the land. Sirkanda lay outside this estate, though some Sirkanda-owned lands did not.

Independence was never an important issue in Sirkanda, as the British government was looked upon without disfavor. No government is really approved of by these people, but according to them the British government was not meddlesome and was preferable to that of the Raja. After Independence there were revisions in administrative procedures and in taxation policies and other laws affecting Sirkanda. The forests and other uncultivated lands adjacent to the village, which provide a substantial part of the means of livelihood in the hills and which formerly could be utilized quite freely, were nationalized. Access to their products and the right to cultivate previously uncultivated lands were sharply curtailed. This was the most resented and probably least obeyed of the many unpopular post-Independence reforms in these hills. Other innovations, such as village *panchayat* (council) rule, community development work, and attempts to set up village credit coöperatives, were largely ignored or actively opposed. Where the appearance of conformity seemed desirable it was provided, but nothing more. The government-supported village school, established in 1950, met with a somewhat more favorable reception. The role of the government and reactions to it will be discussed in detail in chapter 9.

Sirkanda is populated by Paharis who identify themselves as such and more specifically as Garhwalis. In this book the generic term "Pahari" will be used to refer to them in preference to the more specific term "Garhwali," except where a contrast is intended. This is done simply because that is the term most used by the people themselves and by their neighbors on the plains and because on present evidence it seems to be a more defensible term culturally and linguistically than "Garhwali." There is no intention of minimizing differences among Pahari areas, most of which have yet to be studied. Sirkanda is representative of the following areas, in order of decreasing cultural homogeneity: Tehri Garhwal, Garhwal, the Central Pahari area, and the Pahari area.

The people of Sirkanda are closely attached culturally, linguistically, and historically to their relatives in Tehri Garhwal, though for 150 years they have been administratively separated as a result of British rule. Theirs is one of the three largest villages within Bhatbair. It is situated on the crest of the spur of mountains comprising Bhatbair, 5,300 feet above sea level, facing southeast, 2,300 feet above the Bandal River which separates it from Tehri Garhwal at a distance of one mile, and 3,100 feet above Dehra Dun, which is ten miles to the southwest.

The history of Sirkanda is vague in the minds of its residents and is unrecorded elsewhere. Two large stone fortifications in the village overlook the steep valley of the Bandal and face the hills of Tehri Garhwal. They are thirty feet square and constructed of stones so large and heavy that it is believed no modern mortals could have placed them. According to village tradition they have been in place for many millennia, and were built in a former age when men were nine yards tall, lived for a thousand years, and were supremely intelligent. The use of the structures is unknown, though they are thought to have been either houses or forts. Bricks and charcoal have been found around them in recent excavations for housebuilding. Such fortifications occur throughout Garhwal and are responsible for its name. Fifty-two major forts are frequently cited in descriptions of Garhwal (Sirkanda's not among them) including one in the Dehra Dun valley. They are thought by historians to be the work of the various petty rajas who ruled small independent states in these hills before the seventeenth century. One writer attributes them to the pre-Aryan indigenes (Bahadur, 1916, p. 70).

Local tradition states that Kedarkhand or Garhwal, of which Bhatbair is a part, was first occupied in modern times by hermits, ascetics, and sages who were attracted by the serenity and beauty of the area to spend their meditative years there seeking enlightenment. The springs which provide water for many of the villages, including that for Sirkanda, are thought to have been created by sages who did so miraculously in order to provide water at their stopping places. Villagers say that some of these ascetics failed to keep to the spiritual life, married, produced children, and so populated these hill regions.

In view of Williams' mention of Bhatbair as having been in existence before 1700, it is probable that Sirkanda has existed for at least 300 years. Villagers' estimates run to 1,000 years. Among its current residents there is general agreement that Sirkanda was founded by the ancestors of its single Brahmin family, who came from Genogi, a village in Tehri Garhwal, a long day's trek east of Sirkanda. The Brahmin family soon thereafter brought a family of barber caste from the valley below to provide them with agricultural labor and barbering service. Since barbers are not a caste indigenous to this section of the hills, their functions are performed by other low castes in neighboring villages. These were, then, the first two families in Sirkanda. Thereafter the Khasiya Rajputs, who today form 87 per cent of the village population, came in. Each of the two largest Rajput sibs in Sirkanda claims to have preceded the other.[2] Both are said to have come from villages to the east, in Tehri Garhwal. The drum-playing Bajgi family's ancestors also came from Tehri, shortly after the Rajputs. The blacksmith family was the most recent arrival, having come from a village 35 trail miles to the northeast, in Tehri Garhwal, about 90 years ago.

It is thought by all villagers that their ancestors came ultimately from "Kumaon," the present Almora and Naini Tal districts adjacent to Nepal. From there they moved to Tehri Garhwal, probably to escape political and economic difficulties, and then on to Sirkanda to find new land or to escape the pressures of local rajas. Their origin prior to Kumaon is unknown, though some believe their ancestors must have come there from the plains—perhaps to escape the Moghul rulers—while others claim they have always lived in the hills. High-caste villagers bear the names of sibs and phratries (gōtras) found on the

plains. This may reflect plains origin or merely adoption of names of
Rajputs who fled the plains to live among the hill-residing Khasiyas.
Both explanations may be correct in view of the nature of plains-hills
contacts. Two and perhaps three of the four Sirkanda Rajput sib names
are among those listed by Tod in his *Annals and Antiquities of
Rajast'han* (1829, p. 120) as being among the "eighty-four mercantile
tribes" of Rajasthan: "Pilliwal," "Khandailwal," "Kakulea," corresponding to *Paliāl, Khandiāl,* and *Kukhalwāl*(?) in Sirkanda. Two and
possibly three (*JawāRi,* Palial[?], Khandial) appear among the 116
Rajput groups listed by Raturi (1928, pp. 167 ff.) for Garhwal. Possibly one (Palial) appears among 102 listed by Bahadur (1916, pp. 96 ff.).
The Brahmin family of Sirkanda does not belong to any of the 68
Brahmin subgroups listed by Bahadur. The barber is of plains origin.
Bajgis and blacksmiths both are populous groups in Garhwal and ap-
pear among the 15 to 30 Pahari Dom groups listed by Bahadur and
Raturi, respectively.

In physical appearance Sirkanda villagers differ little from plains
people. There is perhaps a tendency toward lighter complexion and
narrower features among the high-caste hill peoples, but individual
variation virtually obscures this. Much more distinctive are cultural
traits, and these are often mistaken by other Indians for racial traits.
Paharis are noted by people of the Dehra Dun valley and the plains
for their peculiarities of speech and dress and for general rusticity,
much as are hillbillies in America. They are also known for honesty
and bravery:

Honesty and valour are possessed in ample measure by the Khasas. Their
honesty is beyond question. A verbal bargain is seldom repudiated and theft
is almost unknown. . . . The military exploits of the Khasas in modern
times are enshrined in the records of the 39th Royal Garhwal Rifles, and
we find that the descendants of the ancient Khasas [reported in the *Mahabharata*] are endued with great courage, unyielding and obstinate in battle.
(Joshi, 1929, pp. 23 f.) [3]

As a group, Paharis are readily identifiable outside their own area
by their dress, speech, and manners. The badge of the Garhwali man
is a black cap and cane. Now the "fit pajama" (tight from the knee
down), shirt, dark vest, and black coat are in vogue for special occasions, with a wool blanket as wrap. *Dhōti* (loincloth), loose pajama,
shorts or abbreviated loincloth, shirt, and sometimes coat or vest are
daily wear. Formerly a cap, a small loincloth secured by a string, and,
for cold weather, a blanket held in place with wooden skewers sufficed.
Women are noted for their massive silver jewelry, and the large gold

nose ornaments of married women. They do not wear the red mark at the part of the hair which designates the married woman of the adjacent plains, nor do they wear the red beauty spot on their forehead. Their hair is usually braided in one piece down the back, extended by a black or colored artificial hairpiece. The calves of their legs are generally decorated with tattoos. Men and women alike often have tattoos on hands and arms. Women's dress consists of a colorful print skirt, a long black fitted jacket (or sometimes a shirt and vest), and invariably a head scarf. In earlier times they wore a long, loose blanket-like garment, the fitted jacket, and the head scarf. They are not secluded in *purdāh* as are many high-caste plains women. To one familiar with the area it is possible to determine quite precisely the locality from which a Pahari woman comes by observing the details of her dress and jewelry (Berreman, 1960b). Regarding Pahari dress, Traill's comment is as applicable today as it was in 1828:

It may be observed, generally, of the hill people, that they are extremely indifferent in regard to the state of their every-day apparel, and continue to wear their clothes till reduced to mere shreds and tatters, but on holydays and festivals, individuals of either sex prefer absenting themselves from the festivities, to appearing in a worn out garment. (Traill, 1828, p. 212)

Sirkanda is strategically located in the sense that it is at the junction of two important trails. Several villages of Bhatbair and the adjacent section of Tehri Garhwal are accessible to Dehra Dun only via one of these trails, and the other is a good and frequently used pack trail built in 1914 by the Tehri Raja to enable his subjects to bypass the toll-tax collectors of Mussoorie on their way to and from the markets of the valley. This trail is still a trade route of some importance. It connects valley markets with the heavily used trade and pilgrimage route between Mussoorie and Tehri, nine trail miles from Sirkanda.

Until recent years these trails were used by Paharis exclusively for foot traffic. Governmental employees and some traders used pack animals on them. Today some of the more prosperous high-caste families of Sirkanda and other villages utilize horses or mules for transporting goods. However, goods of all types, from grain to roofing materials, are still carried primarily by people—men carrying the loads on their backs and shoulders, women balancing the burdens on their heads.

Since 1930 a motor road has connected Mussoorie to the valley, but this does not directly affect Sirkanda villagers because it lies in a different direction. Before 1930, Rajpur, which is a small town seven miles north of Dehra Dun at the foot of the mountains (seven miles

south of Mussoorie and nine trail miles west of Sirkanda), was the end
of the road. Today there is frequent and inexpensive bus service from
Rajpur to Dehra Dun, a facility used by Sirkanda villagers which cuts
the walk to Dehra Dun from sixteen to nine miles. Recently a motor-
able road has been built into Sahas Dhara, a small market and place of
pilgrimage five miles from Sirkanda on the trail to Dehra Dun. So far
its use has been limited largely to the trucks of a limestone quarrying
company for whom it was built, and there is no bus service on it. Occasionally villagers can hire empty trucks belonging to the quarrying
company to carry heavy loads for them from Dehra Dun to this point.

The village has features in common with others of the Sub-Himalayan
area, and is reasonably typical of those in Tehri Garhwal. Like most
Pahari villages and unlike many villages bordering the hills in the
Dehra Dun valley, Sirkanda is nucleated, with its terraced lands oc-
cupying the steep surrounding hillsides. Some two-hundred acres of
terraced, cultivated lands lie below and beside the village, while 1,200
acres of uncultivated forest and scrub land administratively attached
to Sirkanda surround the cultivated and occupied area. The village
houses are scattered for almost half a mile along the southeast contour
of a hillside overlooking the mountains and valleys of Tehri Garhwal
and part of the Dehra Dun valley. There are nearly sixty of the characteristic stone houses with gabled slate, thatch, or corrugated iron
roofs supported by heavy wooden beams. Most of them are two-storied
with an outside stone stairway and a narrow, shelflike porch extending
the length of the house at the second floor level. Open, arched verandas
with ornamentally carved columns occupy the center of the upper level,
with closed rooms on either end and often in back as well. The rooms
are entered by doorways off the veranda and have small, barred windows for ventilation and light. Verandas, doors and windows open on
the front, which is almost invariably the downhill side. The backs, and
often the ends, of houses are entirely closed. The family occupies the
second floor, its animals the first.

Part or all of the ceiling is boarded over to provide a storage garret,
reached by a ladder. Here are kept boards and implements. Every family
has the necessary agricultural implements or tools of its trade. Two
families have phonographs, one in operating condition. The Bajgis
have their drums and harmonium plus a sewing machine and iron
used in tailoring. In general, high-caste houses are larger and better
equipped than others. Wealth is to some extent reflected in the house
and its contents, but the difference between houses of the well-off and
of the poor is not as great as in most non-Pahari areas. This is partly

because differences in wealth are less, but is also due to consumption patterns which inhibit conspicuous display of wealth.

Household furnishings are few and simple. One or two of the inner rooms contain hearths for cooking. Brass and iron cooking utensils, a wooden churn, wooden vessels for storage of liquids, and large baskets and wooden cupboards for storage of dry goods are also found in these rooms. Pottery vessels are used hardly at all because none are made in this area, transportation is difficult, and they break easily. Light is given by small oil lamps. Many houses have string cots, the typical Indian bed, but this is a relatively recent innovation and there are never enough to go around. Bedding consists of quilts, blankets, and rugs which are used on the floor if beds are not available. People usually sit or squat on the dung-plastered floor, but small wooden slabs and pieces of leather or animal pelts may also be used for this purpose and are always offered guests. Every house has its water smoking pipe for the use of all its members and guests.

Circular threshing platforms and adjacent storehouses surround the village, which is composed of three main settlement areas, the southern-most being a recent addition and the site of the school. Two small shops and a blacksmith's workshop are out of sight of the village, over a ridge and at the junction of the main trails leading into Sirkanda. The trail leading to the village water supply goes past them, and nearby is a rain pond which is dry half the year. Smaller trails emanate in all directions from the village to the fields and to neighboring houses and villages. The trails are for the most part rough, steep, and often dangerous. Every year mules, horses, and cattle plunge off, and oc-casionally men suffer this fate. Travel is difficult and casual visitors are a rarity.

Although fields surround the village, there are no irrigated lands near Sirkanda. The village water supply is a small but reliable spring one-fourth to one-third of a mile from the village on the opposite and uncultivable side of the ridge. The spring's proverbial purity and re-liability apparently compensate for its inconvenience, though an el-derly wife of Sirkanda was once heard to mutter, as she lifted her heavy water pot to her head and prepared to negotiate again the difficult trail to the village: "I'd like to set fire to the beard of the man that founded this village here." Villagers want to pipe the water into the village, but the ridge forms a barrier. As a result of one abortive attempt to improve the situation, a small pipe brings water somewhat closer to the village but this water is considered inferior and is used mainly for animals.

Sirkanda is primarily a crop-raising village with an important secondary investment in animal husbandry. Normally it produces more grain than its residents eat in a year, and famine is virtually unknown. Since the establishment of the hill station and military cantonment of Mussoorie in 1829–1835, a six-hour trek from Sirkanda (and only half that from some Sirkanda cattle sheds), and with the growth of Dehra Dun and adjacent areas, milk-selling has been a profitable enterprise with which Sirkanda villagers supplement the traditional agriculture. The introduction of potatoes as a cash crop in the hills above Sirkanda has afforded further income and additional traffic past the village.

The poverty of Paharis is proverbial, but this reputation is based on their frugality, the simple clothing and equipment they possess by plains standards, and their inelegant and unvaried diet wherein coarse millets substitute for rice. They do not share the precarious life of many plains people in food-deficit areas. They have sufficient lands, regular rainfall, and a tradition of maintaining the productivity of their fields by crop rotation and fertilizers, so that they have a consistently adequate food supply.

Not all Sirkanda lands are near the village, and not all people known as Sirkanda villagers live in Sirkanda. As population has increased, new lands have been opened up and cultivated on the hills north and south of the village. Today villagers cultivate land up to eight trail miles north and seven trail miles south of Sirkanda, on the same spur of hills, at altitudes ranging from 7,000 feet to 2,000 feet above sea level. In order to tend fields and livestock at these distances, it is necessary to build dwellings near them. Such field houses or cattle sheds are called *chāns*. A chan is defined in terms of location and construction. It is never in a village, though it may be very near one. It is generally only one story high, unpartitioned, and is less finished inside than a house (*ghar*). Usually livestock are quartered in the chan among its human inhabitants, whereas in a house livestock are always kept downstairs or in an adjoining, but partitioned, room. Eleven of the 71 Sirkanda-owned dwellings outside of Sirkanda qualify as "houses" rather than "chans" on the basis of location or construction. Chans are occupied by their owners during planting and harvest times, and some members of the family live year-round in many of the chans or migrate seasonally between low-altitude winter chans and high-altitude summer chans. Formerly chans were only temporary dwellings, but, as they have been improved and as families have grown, many have become permanent. The 71 Sirkanda chans and second houses are owned by a total of 45 joint families and are to be found in 31 distinct locations (see map 2). In most cases the village affiliation of chan dwellers is strong, and they are readily identified as Sirkanda villagers by themselves, by Sirkanda people, and by residents of other villages and chans. This in spite of the facts that they no longer reside in the village, that other villages may intervene between them and Sirkanda, and that they may be surrounded by the chans of other villages. While some Sirkanda chans are at considerable distances from Sirkanda, chans of other villages may be found adjacent to Sirkanda. On the other hand, some Sirkanda chans are so close to the village that a nonvillager might not distinguish them from village houses. This makes village census reporting and land records a complex and difficult matter. The problem is solved in official reports by ignoring it. For administrative purposes village membership is assigned by geographical proximity, based on administrative boundaries.

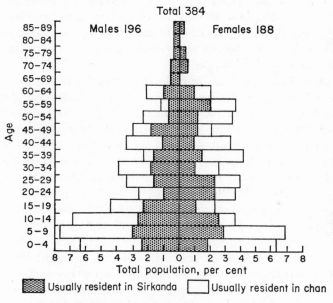

Fig. 1. Sirkanda population pyramid, 1958.

Of a total Sirkanda population of 384, only 178 people are usually resident in Sirkanda, 43 stay there at regular intervals to work land, and 163 rarely or never reside there (though 38 of these occupy chans close enough to afford almost daily contact). On festive or ceremonial occasions many people who normally live away return temporarily to the village. Women move from chans to the village to have their babies, and elderly people usually return to live their final years in the village.

Chan sites may develop into village sites, and in fact this is a means by which new villages are often formed. Residence in a cluster of chans can gradually lead to new village affiliation. The former chan status of many present-day villages is revealed in the village names. In some of these locations part of the residents consider themselves residents of that village, while others maintain their ties to some antecedent village affiliation. About one-fifth of the living persons (excluding married daughters) recorded in Sirkanda genealogical materials as having been born of Sirkanda families are no longer considered to be affiliated with Sirkanda, though their origin is remembered. Nearly all these people now live in locations once considered to be chans. There are undoubtedly others who have been forgotten or are no longer even mentioned in this context. People who belong to joint families with a dwelling in the settlement area of Sirkanda are considered by all to be Sirkanda villagers regardless of where they live. Anyone who separates from his joint family, taking a chan and the lands near it as his share of the property and giving up all rights in the village, may cease to be considered a village member; certainly his children will not be considered members of the ancestral village.

Other important extra-village ties are those of marriage. Over 80 per cent of Sirkanda marriages take place outside the village; that is, the bride comes from or goes to an alien village. This makes for close ties and contacts with almost 100 villages; most of the ties are with villages within 8 trail miles of Sirkanda, and virtually all are with Garhwali villages (see map 2).

Immigration or emigration of men is rare. One Bajgi has come to live in Sirkanda in the past 25 years. Other immigrants are the five agricultural servants who are considered, and who consider themselves, to be temporary residents. In addition there is a shopkeeper from Rajpur who spends considerable time in his shop near the village. In recent years a schoolteacher and periodically a Village Level Worker and Economic Coöperative Supervisor, all government employees, have lived in the village school. In the past ten years one man has emigrated to an urban area, and another joined him during 1957. Most villagers who have left the village have returned. A few have disappeared.

Garhwali villages are so constituted that no one village is likely to have the range of castes necessary to provide the occupational variety required for maintenance of community life. This brings about further intervillage ties of economic and ritual interdependence, to say nothing of the social ties of an intra-caste, intervillage nature. All such factors make an area such as Bhatbair (combined with an equally large adjoining area in Tehri Garhwal) a more nearly self-contained economic, social, and religious unit than the village.

Sirkanda is predominantly a Rajput village; 87 per cent of its members are of this caste. The one Brahmin family adds another 3 per cent, making 90 per cent of the village of high caste. The 10 per cent who are of the Dom castes include two households of blacksmiths, one of barbers, and four of musician-tailors (Bajgis). The proportion of high castes to low castes is almost identical to that found throughout Bhatbair and Tehri Garhwal. However, particular villages may be predominantly or even exclusively Brahmin. In some, relatively large proportions of low-caste people are found, while in many, few or no low-caste people live.

In population Sirkanda is above the average for Tehri Garhwal villages. In caste composition it is not unusual. It is as representative of Tehri Garhwal villages as one village could be expected to be except that it is somewhat less isolated than most, and in the past 150 years its administrative history has been at variance with the Tehri Garhwal norm and similar to that of British Garhwal and other districts under direct British rule. The effects of its relative lack of isolation and its subjection to British rule have been less than might be expected because of its distance from Dehra Dun, the difficulty of access to that administrative center, Sirkanda's insignificance in the view of administrators, and the fact that its members' attention and identification have been directed throughout its history primarily toward the northeast—into Tehri Garhwal.

2   THE ECONOMIC CONTEXT

The subsistence base in Sirkanda, as in most Indian villages, is agriculture. Of second importance and closely related to agriculture is animal husbandry. Both of these activities are primarily the province of high-caste villagers but are open to and practiced by some members of all castes. The functional unit in these as in almost all economic matters is the joint family, often referred to as the household (*chūlā*, cooking hearth). Goods are produced, distributed, and consumed primarily by the household unit, and any relevant economic decisions are made there. In Sirkanda there are 45 such household units or joint families, averaging eight or nine individuals each but ranging in membership from one to twenty-five. The household is ideally a patrilocal extended family under the leadership of the eldest active male. In practice we find that 32 (71 per cent) of the households in Sirkanda are of this type, including seven which consist of only a nuclear family and one parent of the husband. Thirteen (29 per cent) consist of strictly nuclear family units. Eighty-four per cent of the population lives in extended family groups. Nonagricultural castes and families tend to be divided into more and smaller independent units than are agriculturists.

Improved land and livestock, the main forms of capital in this area, are owned and manipulated by the joint family, and their products are shared within it. Ideally the joint family occupies one large house with separate rooms for each nuclear family when they are in the village, and shares one or more chans when they are out. In reality some families own more than one house in Sirkanda, so that all their members do not live under one roof, while others are crowded with more than one nuclear family per room. Nearly all have chans, many of which are almost continuously occupied by some nuclear families of the household. Members of the joint family who live under a single roof eat from the same cooking fire (the literal meaning of chula), and all members, regardless of living arrangements, eat from the same store of food.

LAND

Since agriculture is the basis of livelihood in Sirkanda, land is of utmost importance. At least one popular Pahari song concerns a hero who fought to the death rather than lose land which was rightfully his. Sirkanda families own 298 acres of cultivated land, according to records of the village accountant. These include 176 acres in the immediate vicinity of the village and 122 acres in outlying areas, tended from chans or other houses. As previously noted, about half the current village population usually lives in the 71 Sirkanda chans and other houses in 31 separate locations extending over fifteen trail miles north and south of the village settlement area (see map 2). Some idea of the fragmentation of village lands can be gathered from the following figures. Two hundred and five acres are recorded as cultivated "Sirkanda lands." [1] The land is officially divided into 745 separate plots varying in size from less than one-tenth of an acre to seven acres. These figures are based on long-standing recorded divisions of land. In reality the plots have been subdivided into smaller parts as the old extended families have broken up. Today there are 1,144 separate land claims recorded for the 745 plots, and unrecorded but recognized divisions probably bring the number of separately cultivated plots to nearly 1,500.

Cultivated land is categorized by villagers in several ways relevant to its productivity. Probably the most important distinction is between land which is irrigated and that which is not. Most Sirkanda land is unirrigated. Only three acres out of 205 are recorded as being irrigated and hence unusually valuable. Sirkanda-owned land in lower-lying areas is often irrigated. While records for these lands were unobtainable, crop yields for rice indicate that 16 Sirkanda households own 25 to 30 acres of such valuable land, while 29 households own none. Some Bhatbair villages are located in the river valley and have considerably more irrigated land. Another valuable type of land is that at higher altitudes and on north slopes suitable for growing potatoes. Twenty-one Sirkanda families have such lands, totaling around 15 acres.

Although irrigated land and potato land are the most valuable, neither is necessary for livelihood. The traditional economy of Sirkanda is based upon dry-land grain agriculture, and dietary staples are grown on dry lands in amounts exceeding consumption rates.

Villagers recognize and terminologically distinguish several types of land other than those based on irrigation. The two most important of these classifications are by soil type and exposure to the sun. The best soil is classed as "loamy," while inferior soil is "rocky." Fields on the sunny (generally south) side of slopes are preferred. Fields on the shady (north) slope, called "place of moisture," are considered less productive of the staple crops. Consequently they are chosen for cultivation when no more sunny-side slopes are available, although some villages are so situated that all their fields are of this type. For certain crops, such as potatoes, and in exceptionally dry seasons shady fields are superior. All Sirkanda lands near the village are on the sunny slope, and more than half are on loamy soil. Fields are also classified in terms of terrain; level ones are preferred to those on slopes. All Sirkanda lands near the village are on slopes and are, of necessity, terraced. Vertical stone walls three to eight feet high follow the contour of the hills to retain the soil of these terraces. Entire hillsides of scores of acres are so terraced. Fields located below the village, as are most Sirkanda fields, are considered preferable to those above the village because of the greater ease of carrying fertilizer to them.

As a result of constant fertilization of fields with animal manure and the burned and raw stalks of harvested crops, combined with systematic crop rotation, most fields produce consistently good crops. Certain distant fields which are too inaccessible for easy fertilization are simply used until they become exhausted, after which they are left, permanently or until they have regained their vitality.

Land ownership by households shows the expectable caste-based variation. The ten per cent of the population who make up the low castes own only two per cent of the land. In the days of the Garhwal Raja's dominion, low castes were not allowed to own land or houses at all. This was the situation in nearby Tehri Garhwal until after Independence in 1947. In Sirkanda it ceased to be the rule when the British took over in 1815, but it has continued to influence practice in this area to the present. It was possible under the Raja for high-caste landowners in the village to grant land or buildings to low-caste members for use rent-free, and land was regularly granted as a reward for services or to enable a service-caste family to make a living in the village and provide their services to villagers. However, the tenant was not allowed to sell or rent the land, and at his death or at the owner's discretion the property reverted to the owner. During British rule each of the low-caste families of Sirkanda managed to get some such lands recorded in their names.

Brief reference has already been made to the history of land tenures in Bhatbair. The pattern of land ownership which exists today in Sirkanda dates from the early days of British rule, when the bhaichara system of land allotment in equal portions to cultivating families was established. At the time there were sixteen cultivating households in Sirkanda, one family of Brahmins and the others of Rajputs. The sixteen divisions of cultivated land averaged about eleven acres each. As new lands came under cultivation they were similarly apportioned. Since that time, as lands have been divided, bought, and sold, they have retained the designation of the caste or sib of the original owner as *patti Brahmin* (Brahmin section), *patti Palial* (Palial Rajput section), and so on, for identification purposes. Uncultivated lands were held by the village in common.

Under the bhaichara system low-caste members did not get shares in village lands, but they were assigned the small plots that had been previously granted them by the high castes or that were subsequently given to them. In this fashion the blacksmiths, for example, acquired slightly over two acres. Half this land had been granted by the village tax-free; that is, it remained in the names of former owners, who continued to pay its taxes. The other half had been given to the blacksmiths outright. The lands given outright were not assigned by name but instead were recorded as having been allotted to "blacksmiths." Later a friendly village accountant recorded all this land in the individual names of the blacksmith owners, thus protecting their interests. The other low castes were granted land in similar fashion, so that the barber family had nearly 1½ acres and the Bajgi family had nearly 3 acres. Virtually all low-caste lands are on steep, rocky, unproductive soil, some of such poor quality that it is hardly worth cultivating and would be spurned by high-caste agriculturists. This reflects the nature of high-caste generosity to the service castes.

Under this system there are said to have been only two classes of landowners in Sirkanda, in contrast to the many types recognized elsewhere: (1) the original sixteen owners, who paid the government tax on the land they acquired under the bhaichara division, and cultivated it or let it out as they wished; (2) those who cultivated lands not allotted to them under the bhaichara system and to which they therefore did not have title. In Sirkanda most agriculturists were in the former category, although some families who had more land than they could use let part of it out to those who had too little from their bhaichara shares to support their enlarged families. Under bhaichara these non-owning cultivators (tenants or *kachcha khaikars,* cf. Stowell, 1907, p. ix) paid the amount of the taxes to the owners but in most cases paid no rental beyond that amount. This is in striking contrast to lands not included under bhaichara, such as some in Bhatbair that were owned by the Sikh founder of Dehra Dun and his successors. In such cases the landlord collected an amount several times the government tax and kept all except the tax money for himself.

With Independence bhaichara lands went to the cultivators. Non-cultivating owners were reimbursed by the government in the amount of ten years' tax on the land they were to relinquish. Nonowner cultivating tenants were assessed an amount equal to ten years' tax on the land they occupied and then were recorded as its owners. Each owner thereafter paid the taxes on his own land, direct to the government. Taxation on owner-cultivated lands in Sirkanda has become slightly higher since Independence (from around Rs. 1.50 per acre before to Rs. 1.75 after).[2] For non-bhaichara land, the cultivators' taxes have greatly decreased since Independence because the landlord middleman has been eliminated. This decrease in the affected portions of Bhatbair and nearby Tehri Garhwal has been from about Rs. 4.50 to Rs. 1.75 per acre. The precise amount of tax is a function of the quality of the land as recorded by the government. In an official threefold categorization of Sirkanda-owned lands, none around Sirkanda is of first quality, and most is third and therefore least heavily taxed.

Under bhaichara, when a joint family dissolved, land was to be divided equally among sons and each son's portion was to be divided equally among his sons if they separated. These "ancestral fractional shares" were to be officially recorded at the time of division. Each holder would then pay his share of the taxes, depending upon the proportion of village lands he held. In practice the division was generally done informally and went unrecorded; hence the chaotic state of land records at present. Today three families—two of the Rajputs and the one Brahmin family—retain their original $\frac{1}{16}$ portion of village lands undivided. This retention has been possible because the families have remained relatively small. Consequently they are among the best-off of villagers. In 1958 the Brahmin family was preparing to divide its lands among three brothers, so that only two of the original shares would remain intact. Some bhaichara portions have been divided into four or more parts, though often these have been supplemented (in at least one case to an extent exceeding the original share) by lands subsequently purchased outside the village.

Land is the basis of livelihood, and those who control it, primarily the high castes, control the economy. Ownership of land, and especially of good land, is highly correlated with wealth. It is not, however, sufficient in itself to ensure wealth. There must also be manpower to work the land. Land that is unused is of no benefit to anyone. One of the wealthiest families in Sirkanda at present—the possessors of one of the original undivided shares of village lands—was poverty-stricken two generations ago when the sole member of the family was a teen-age boy who could not work the land properly and so had to hire out as a servant to others to make a living. Years later, when he and a son were both able to farm and to hire a servant as well, he made profitable use of the same lands. Acquisition of extra wives, servants, and adopted sons are means used to increase the labor force in a household and thereby to derive more benefit from the land.

Although there is variation in wealth and land ownership by family and by caste, there are no big landholders in the sense of the "zamindars" of the plains, and there are no tenant farmers in Sirkanda. Sirkanda agriculturists are owner-cultivators; they live by their own work on their own lands. The biggest landholding recorded in Sirkanda is 20.4 acres, owned by a joint family of 22 individuals (nine adults, thirteen children below 16 years of age). The smallest holding by an agricultural family (that is, one of high caste, though some of the low-caste families own none) is 2.3 acres, supporting six people (two adults, four children). The average size of recorded holdings in the agricultural castes is 4.5 acres per eight- or nine-member joint family. Most agricultural families have about one-half acre per adult, counting two children as equivalent to one adult. Some have less, and the most prosperous have one acre per adult.

There is little rental or sharecropping of lands in Sirkanda. One man has a share in some lands owned by his wife's relatives in a distant village. Another lets out on shares some lands he owns that are too far away for him to look after. One man, whose lands were too scattered for him to look after, effected a mutually advantageous exchange of lands with another farmer so that lands of each were somewhat consolidated. Occasionally some elderly or dependent person who cannot tend his or her land will rent it out to others on a share basis, as one Sirkanda widow does. Others sell land they can no longer work. More commonly, the owner gives the land to whoever is slated to inherit it and joins that household for the remainder of his lifetime. Several instances of the latter arrangement are in evidence in Sirkanda.

Until Independence it was possible for any agriculturist to extend his holdings by cultivating previously uncultivated land. The primary requisite was labor—it is hard and time-consuming work to clear and terrace new land. The availability of land prevented the pressure on land common in much of North India. An expanding Pahari agricultural family in this area could usually, with effort, expand its holdings.

For low castes the story is different. In pre-British times they were prohibited from owning land and from cultivating new land without permission from high-caste villagers. Under the British they were prohibited by informal but effective village sanctions from seeking new lands. They were prevented from becoming economically independent rather than from farming at all. This situation has continued to the present when, as will be discussed in the context of intercaste relations, a blacksmith has been denied access to unused land in Sirkanda by the high-caste village council. Thus, low castes have been kept dependent and poor while both cultivated lands and population have increased.

Throughout the period since 1815, the main settlement of Sirkanda is said to have remained about the same in population. Records of land within the village boundaries show very little change since 1904. However, in this time lands outside the village have come under cultivation or have been purchased until the village cultivates twice as much land as formerly. Also, the lands have been increasingly fragmented. The resident population of Sirkanda has remained about 150 or 175, but the population of Bhatbair and vicinity has doubled or tripled. Additional village population has been drained off to chans and second houses. The number of villages in Bhatbair has doubled since 1815. Chans, which were a rarity then, have been built and fields cleared where there was previously only wilderness. The trend is evident even in the period since Independence with the addition of new lands and new chans in several locations. Within Sirkanda the entire southern section of the village, comprising five houses, is a post-Independence phenomenon. As old houses in the village have become decrepit or crowded, new ones have been built in the new location. New lands have been opened up on the southern periphery of the village surrounding the new houses. It is one of the ironies of the post-Independence era that governmental restrictions have been imposed which discourage expansion of agricultural lands into hitherto uncultivated areas. This is a source of keen resentment among high-caste Paharis of this region because, until Independence, uncultivated lands had been considered the property of the villages nearest them, and available to their members for cultivation. Now they have been made subject to stringent governmental regulation. As one Sirkanda farmer pointed out: "The government asked us to increase crop production to help the nation. When we did so in the only way possible, by opening up new lands, they accused us of infringing on government property and brought a suit against us."

AGRICULTURE

Agriculture is a family enterprise—those who share the hearth share in the work and the harvest. There are two annual crops and harvests which govern the work of villagers and influence the yearly cycle of all activities in Sirkanda. These are "millet harvest" in early winter (mid-September to October) just after the rainy season, and "barley-wheat harvest" in mid-summer (April) before the hot, dry period. These correspond to the *kharīf* and *rabi* harvests of the plains, respectively, but are not called by these terms. Each planting season follows closely after the previous harvest.

Winter Crop

While the millet harvest is in progress, men of each family begin plowing the harvested fields preparatory to planting the principal winter crops, wheat and barley. Stalks of the previous crops are burned and the ashes are plowed into the ground along with manure, which has been spread on the fields. The plow, similar to those used on the plains, is wooden with a wooden moldboard and an iron bit and is pulled by a yoke of bullocks. A week or two after plowing men sow the fields by hand broadcast. Immediately thereafter the fields are again plowed and a leveler is dragged over them. The fields are plowed and seeded between mid-October and the end of November. Ideally, approximately equal proportions of land are devoted to wheat and barley. In reality, wheat, the preferred crop, may be sown in two-thirds of the available 200 acres of land in the vicinity of Sirkanda. *Masūr (Ervum lens)*, a pulse, is also planted at this time but in much smaller quantities.[3] Some land is left fallow. Once planting is completed the main agricultural activity is transporting animal manure and spreading it on the fields. This is done two or three times after planting, at intervals of about a month.

In February and March, over a month before harvest time, the fields that have been left fallow over the winter are plowed for the first time in preparation for planting *janghōra (Oplismenus frumentaceus)*, a millet which is one of the principal crops of the rainy growing season. The plowing continues, twice per field, over a period of six weeks, overlapping with the barley harvest, since barley fields as well as fallow ones will be planted in janghora. Toward the end of March and in early April barley and masur are harvested, and the

fields are plowed after the stubble or stalks have been burned. Wheat
matures shortly after the other winter crops and is harvested in mid-
April. As wheat is harvested threshing begins. This is done by driving
cattle over the grain heads, which have been spread on a hard, dung-
plastered circular threshing floor. The cattle, two to ten in number,
are hitched to a central post and driven around by people of almost
any age and either sex. It is an eight- to ten-hour job to thresh one
batch of about two maunds (160 pounds) of unthreshed grain. Thereafter the grain is winnowed by women in traditional North Indian
fashion with a winnowing tray and the aid of the breeze. Finally ashes
are mixed with the grain "to prevent worms from infesting it." Women
do this by trampling the grain and ashes on a threshing platform. It
is then stored in the home in large baskets sealed with dung-plaster or
in wooden storage boxes. Each family spends about two weeks at
threshing, winnowing, and storing. Since not every family owns a
threshing platform (there are 21 platforms in the village), they are
borrowed for further use as soon as the owners are finished. Such
borrowing occurs freely across sib and caste lines. The chaff is burned
and the straw is saved and stored in tall stacks supported by central
poles or saplings, to be used later as thatch or fodder.

Rainy-Season Crop

Before and during the wheat and barley threshing period, janghora
is planted in the same manner as was wheat the previous season. Con-
currently, the harvested wheat fields are burned over and plowed.
After plowing they are left for about two weeks and then planted with
rainy-season crops other than janghora, primary among which is a
millet called *khōdā* or *mandūā* (*Eleusine coracana*). Janghora and
khoda are the principal rainy-season crops, forming about 75 per cent
of the grain product of the season. They are planted in roughly equal
amounts. At the same time are planted *kūlat* (*Dolichos biflorus*), a
pulse, and *chaulāī* (*Amaranthus polygamous, Amaranthus blitum*), an
amaranth which supplies a grain (forming about 20 per cent of the
grain harvest of this season) and also leaves which are used as vegetables. Other crops of the season include dry and wet rice, taro, pumpkins, beans, corn, ginger, chili, cucumbers, leafy vegetables, and tobacco. Wet rice is planted at this time in seedbeds in areas where
irrigation is possible. At the beginning of the rains (late June) wet
rice is transplanted from seedbeds to irrigated fields, and chili plants
are transplanted to Sirkanda gardens from irrigated seedbeds elsewhere.

The fields are manured during the rainy season just as they were in the winter. From shortly after the rains begin, in July, until the first of September, harrowing, followed by weeding of the fields, is a full-time job. First the fields are harrowed from one to three times each with a long-toothed harrow pulled by bullocks. This has the effect of thinning the fields, which were purposely overseeded to prevent erosion and uprooting of the seedlings by the heavy rains. It is also alleged to kill weeds, the belief being that grain withstands the disturbance better than weeds do. Some incidental transplanting may be done at the same time to even out plant distribution in the fields. Thereafter the fields are repeatedly and painstakingly weeded by hand by the entire families, using small pick-like tools. By the first of September weeding is no longer necessary, and the harvest begins in late September. First janghora, corn, and beans are harvested, followed in about two weeks by khoda, chaulai, kulat, and the rainy-season crops. The harvest continues to the end of October. Threshing of the millets extends throughout October and overlaps with plowing and sowing for the winter crops.

Maximizing Productivity

In the planting of crops there is an ideal pattern of crop rotation said to enhance the productivity of the soil. The sequence in an individual field is as follows: (1) barley, followed by (2) janghora or dry rice, followed by (3) wheat, followed by (4) khoda, followed by (1) barley, and so on. Although the sequence is not adhered to religiously, it is a traditional pattern that is approximated by most farmers in Sirkanda. Periodically crops not included in the rotating sequence are planted in some of the fields. Any field that appears to be losing its vitality as evidenced by smaller crops is left fallow for a season or two. The above pattern applies only to fertilized fields. Those which cannot be adequately fertilized or are poor to begin with are left fallow every other season. Often entire hillsides are planted in a single crop and are rotated in the same sequence, a result of informal consultation among the various people who own the many plots involved. Crop rotation is practiced in most Pahari areas but in different patterns (cf. Stowell, 1907, p. 11; Walton, 1910, pp. 26 ff.; 1911a, p. 55; Pant, 1935, pp. 136 ff.).

Few fields can be irrigated in this terrain. Stowell reported in 1907 (p. 9) that only 3 per cent of all cultivated land in Garhwal was irrigated, and 8 per cent in Almora. Only three of the 205 acres within Sirkanda's boundaries are irrigated, plus 25 to 30 of the 93 acres which lie outside of Sirkanda and are owned by Sirkanda people. These 25 to 30 irrigated acres are nearly all low, flat lands bordering the valley.

Irrigation of fields in these hills is an engineering feat of considerable complexity. Water is obtained from streams or springs which are blocked with stone dams at distances varying from a few hundred yards to more than a mile upstream from the fields to be watered. From the dams narrow channels are constructed following the contour of the land at sufficient gradient to keep a steady flow of water. Where these canals skirt bare rock cliffs or bridge small ravines, they are made of wood lined with clay and are held in place by wooden or stone supports wedged in crevices. The canals empty into the highest of the fields to be irrigated, and outlets are so arranged as to provide maximum subsequent use of the water in lower fields. Irrigation canals are built and maintained coöperatively by those who use them—usually high-caste people of a single village.

The nature and extent of cultivation of some crops is limited by the type of land available; that is, irrigated lands are necessary for wet rice; shady, loamy lands are required for potatoes. Another important factor is animal molestation. Corn is grown only in small quantities and in fields adjacent to the village because bears and porcupines destroy more distant stands. Potatoes are grown only in the vicinity of chans in most areas because wild pigs destroy unsupervised fields. Monkeys menace several crops. No specific measures are taken to ward off these pests other than to plant their favorite crops where they are unlikely to come and, occasionally, to build a shelter near a field where someone can stay or a dog can be tied to scare off the marauders. Persistent animal pests may be ambushed and shot.

Thus far only the "practical" means by which agriculture is carried out and good crops are ensured have been discussed. To enhance success there are also supernatural means, ranging from an annual ceremony to deities who influence crops and weather (described in Appendix IB) to beliefs as to the appropriate day of the week for beginning planting and harvest. Ceremonials and beliefs of this nature are not extensive and seem to be of decreasing importance, perhaps reflecting the relatively reliable and adequate nature of Pahari agriculture. Difficulties with crops are usually treated, as are illness, financial reversal, or other adversities, as manifestations of the displeasure of specific household or village deities. These matters will be discussed in the following chapter.

Cash Crops

Growing crops primarily for sale is a relatively recent innovation in the village. The most important such crop now is potatoes. Several varieties with different growing seasons are cultivated, so that some are in the ground at almost any time of year. Potatoes are grown in chan locations north of Sirkanda and usually above it in altitude. Less than half of the villagers own land suitable for this crop.

Other cash crops grown on Sirkanda-owned lands include ginger, onions, garlic, koreander, and the surpluses of wheat, rice, and taro.

Preparation and Consumption of Food

Year-around daily staples eaten in Sirkanda are the millets janghora and khoda (mandua). Wheat and barley are often mixed with the latter variety of millet. In addition, dāl (pulses) and vegetables, primarily taro and potatoes, are eaten regularly.

Grain must, of course, be milled before use. Normally milling is done at intervals after harvest so that an adequate supply is on hand for use, but at any one time most of the stored grain is unmilled. Two water-powered mills are patronized, payment in flour being made to their owners at each milling. The mills are four and five miles distant in opposite directions, the farther and more patronized being en route to points in the valley and owned by a member of a Sirkanda Rajput household. In addition, some families have small stone hand mills which are used occasionally. The daily supply of rice and janghora is husked each morning in a stone mortar with a long wooden pestle. There are several community mortars in convenient locations around the village and individual ones at several houses. Pounding in them is regular early-morning women's work.

Cooking is done by women in an inner room of the house, over a small wood fire in an open, dung-plastered stone fireplace. Brass and iron utensils are utilized as in the plains, and the style of cooking is similar to that in the plains.

Two large meals and one or two small ones are prepared daily. At 6:30 or 7:00 A.M., about an hour after rising, there is a light meal consisting of leftover chapāties (unleavened bread) eaten with salt and chilis or milk or one of several milk products. Between 10:30 A.M. and noon a large meal is prepared consisting of janghora boiled in water and served with boiled dal. Boiled vegetables (potatoes, taro, pumpkin), and occasionally curds, may also be served. At 4:00 to 7:00 P.M. another light meal may be served, consisting of leftovers from the noon or previous evening's meal. This meal is sometimes omitted. Between 8:00 and 10:00 P.M., one to two hours before retiring, another complete meal is prepared. This consists of chapaties made of khoda, often mixed with wheat or barley, and a vegetable mixture, usually of potatoes or taro cooked with spices and chilis. Water and rarely milk or buttermilk are drunk after each meal. This fare is considered very plain and inferior to that which is served guests, in which the chapaties are made of wheat, rice is substituted for janghora, and milk, *ghee* (clarified butter), and other fancier foods are served. Paharis are self-conscious about their food before outsiders and frequently make depre-catory remarks about the poverty of Paharis and Pahari food. "Jang-hora is Pahari *basmati* [the finest grade of rice]," is a frequent wry comment in Sirkanda.

When guests are present tea is served regardless of time of day, though it is rarely used otherwise. Ceremonial feasts are elaborations of the daily fare with a variety of pulses, ghee, curds, vegetables, pickles, sweetened rice, and *halwā* (a sweet dish) generally added to it. In any case the food is almost exclusively of locally grown products, so that cash expenditures on food are minimal.

ANIMAL HUSBANDRY

Second to crops in the economy of Sirkanda is livestock. A man's first investment after land is in livestock. Most important of his animals are his bullocks or oxen which pull the plow. The usual way to desig-nate how much land a man owns is by how many oxen he uses to till it. In Sirkanda there are twenty-five "two-bullock" (one-plow) house-holds, twelve "four-bullock" households, three "six-bullock" house-holds, and one "eight-bullock" household. A total of 124 bullocks are owned by 41 households—a sizable investment in view of the fact that a good pair of oxen are worth 250 to 350 rupees. No family owns more oxen than it uses, and any that are not in good condition are quickly sold.

Almost equally important are cows and buffaloes. These are kept for their two valuable products, milk and manure. Animal manure is considered necessary for agriculture and is often sufficient reason for keeping an animal. Milk is a cash product. Most of it is sold to shop-keepers in the form of milk, butter, ghee (clarified butter), or a boiled-down solid product used in the making of sweets. Relatively small amounts are used in the village.

Most cows and many buffaloes are kept at chans and are moved seasonally from low altitudes in winter to higher altitudes in summer. This protects them from climatic extremes. It also gives them an optimal diet, and brings them close to the milk markets of Dehra Dun or smaller, closer markets in the valley during the winter, and to Mussoorie (with its big milk trade during the vacation season) or closer hill markets in the summer. Sirkanda villagers own about 725 cows worth Rs. 70 to 150 each, and 140 buffaloes worth Rs. 250 to

400 each. Buffaloes are more valuable as milk producers than cows, but are harder to care for since they are too heavy and awkward to be allowed out to pasture or to get water in this rugged terrain.

In the markets buffalo milk is generally preferred to that of cows, but in the village cow's milk is often preferred. It is admitted that buffalo milk is "better for the body" and makes men virile (any appreciative wife or lover will feed her man buffalo milk and its products frequently), but it does not help the brain. One villager commented that, "If you drink too much buffalo milk you will get buffalo wisdom," that is, stupidity. The difference in quality of milk from these two sources is locally ascribed to diet—a cow has a more varied diet since it grazes for itself, and therefore its milk is superior. On the same basis goat's milk, though it is not used (see below), is better than that of cows, and woman's milk is best of all.

Buffaloes are occasionally killed as offerings to gods in Bhatbair. Their flesh is said to be eaten only by people of the shoemaker caste, but there is some evidence that others, even in Sirkanda, may occasionally eat buffalo meat. The sanctity of cows is as strongly felt in the hills as in the plains, and they are never killed nor is their meat eaten.

About 350 goats and 10 sheep are kept by a total of 24 families in Sirkanda. They are raised primarily for sale in the markets, where they bring Rs. 15 to 30 each. In a year 10 to 20 goats may be sold by a single household. In addition, their manure is considered more valuable as fertilizer than that of other animals. Their flesh is eaten in the village—usually after they have been used as religious sacrifices. In the entire village not over 20 or 30 goats are used yearly for sacrifice. Occasionally a goat is killed solely for eating, but this fact is not readily admitted. Villagers imply that a sacrifice may sometimes be an excuse to eat meat, but in no case is meat eaten as part of a regular meal. Instead, it is treated as a special feast and is generally consumed with liquor. Goat's milk is not used. The proffered explanation for this is that one cannot take the milk of an animal whose flesh he eats, nor vice versa, because an animal that gives milk is in some respects like a mother. This is also a reason for not eating buffalo meat.

Horses and mules are used as beasts of burden and for human transportation. There are now 15 horses and two mules in the village, owned by 16 of the larger high-caste households and representing an investment of Rs. 200 to 1,000 each. They are a relatively recent innovation in the village; previously all loads were carried by the men and women of the village.

It is worth noting that livestock, like land, is predominantly high-caste property. The 10 per cent of the population that is of low caste owns 2 per cent of the cattle, 5 per cent of the bullocks, 6 per cent of the buffaloes, and 8 per cent of the goats. They, more than many of the high-caste families, find it worthwhile to supplement their income by goat breeding, because they need the money and have the time to devote to this activity. They own no horses or mules.

Other Economic Activities

No animal fodder as such is grown by villagers. The straw of grains is often kept for use when other fodder gets scarce, but the major dependence is upon wild grasses and leaves collected daily the year around, green or dry as the season permits. This is a major occupation for women of the village. In addition, all animals except buffaloes are pastured daily, and all of these except horses and mules are attended at all times. No one goes to the forests to shepherd animals without bringing in a headload of fodder or firewood. In the months of May and June grass fires are lit by villagers in order to burn over the hillsides and ensure a superior grass crop after the rains. These fires—the bane of the government forestry officers—dot the hills during this season. Often, and not surprisingly, they leave burned chans, and occasionally dead livestock, in their wake.

For two or three months before the rains the year-round activity of wood collecting is intensified in order to prepare a stockpile of dry fuel for the rainy season. It is the availability of wood for fuel which makes possible the extensive manuring of fields, in contrast to the plains custom and necessity of utilizing all manure for fuel.

Housebuilding and repair are winter and summer activities. Considerable frantic roof repair takes place after the rains begin, revealing its need. Agricultural terraces and stone fences are built and repaired when the need arises and when other work permits, especially before and after the rains, which do considerable damage to terraced fields and retaining walls.

The agricultural slack season comes in December and January, when only daily routine work and building has to be done. During this time men engage in minor activities such as rope-making and repairing equipment and houses, and the whole family contributes to yarn-making, knitting, and the like in idle moments. Somewhat the same situation exists in the midst of the rains.

Beekeeping is an incidental enterprise conducted by many households in the village and in chans. A small hole on the outside wall of a house leads to a cubical space about a foot square in the wall with a removable board at the back of the space, inside the house. Wild bees nest in this space. Twice a year (in April and October) the bees are smoked out and the honey is removed and sold in the markets. Hunting and gathering play a very small part in the Sirkanda economy. Although most high-caste households own guns, they are used primarily to frighten or kill marauding animals. Occasionally native wild chickens, partridges, wild pigs, wild goats, or deer are shot for meat. If a freshly killed prey of some carnivorous animal is found it is eaten by villagers, though they admit it reluctantly if at all. Fish are obtained from the rivers by low-caste people of villages near the rivers who net them to sell, or by young men of Sirkanda who make a picnic excursion of the fishing and a party of the ensuing feast. In late summer several varieties of wild berries and wild apricots and peaches may be collected. Except for the apricots, which are sold in urban markets, there is relatively little enthusiasm for these products.

Production and Income

Crops and livestock provide the high castes with most of their livelihood. Estimated annual crop yields were obtained in detail for 20 (just over half) of the high-caste households. The estimates indicated that almost 150 per cent of the household's annual grain needs were produced in the fields during a good year. An average household (eight or nine persons) consumes about 50 to 60 maunds (4,000 to 4,800 pounds) of grain per year and produces 75 to 90 maunds.[4] Each harvest is customarily stored and used throughout the year for subsistence and for payments to artisans and priests. The surplus is sold only when the succeeding harvest is in. Sale of surplus grain and cash crops together were reported to yield about Rs. 600 in a good year for a nine-member family. This would amount to around Rs. 20,000 for the whole village.

The main source of cash and credit is dairy products. Estimates of milk production and sale in 39 households indicated an annual cash income of around Rs. 800 per family from this source. Total yearly cash expenditures for a nine-member family were roughly calculated at Rs. 1,000.[5] Thus total income was estimated to exceed total expenditure by an average of Rs. 400 (equal to about 27 maunds of grain) per family per year among land- and cattle-owning families. The estimates are extremely rough, and it seems probable that both income and expenditures are exaggerated. Moreover, the sample is slightly biased in favor of the more prosperous joint families. The estimates indicate relative orders of magnitude rather than precise quantities. There is a range, with some families exceeding the average and others falling well below it. Some years bring larger or smaller than average crops, greater or smaller expenditures, on family and village levels. Some families spend more than the average on ceremonies and other approved means of conspicuous consumption, while others economize. There are significant caste differences, with the service castes having considerably less to live on than the landowning castes. Low-caste incomes are discussed below under the description of their occupational specialties. These figures do serve to suggest, however, the relative prosperity of this village compared to many Indian villages. Moreover, they check with separate inquiries, such as that into the village accountant's official estimates of crop yields per acre multiplied by acreage planted.

Only one "famine" year is recalled by Sirkanda residents, and it occurred some fifteen years previous to the research. Crops were insufficient to meet food requirements that year, and a number of families had to go to Dehra Dun to buy grain. The significant fact is that they were able to buy it; no one went hungry, and no one went deeply in debt.

It is apparent that some families will accumulate wealth under these conditions. In Sirkanda, when income exceeds that which is necessary for family welfare and livelihood, a man first sees to his lands and then to his livestock. If these are sufficient he is most likely to use his money for house- or chan-building. If these too are sufficient he may buy household utensils and jewelry. Beyond this, with the simple needs of life in the hills met, extra money is stored in concealment or part of it is loaned on interest (15 to 25 per cent) to other villagers or reliable acquaintances. Money is never kept in banks. At least six Sirkanda families regularly or occasionally lend money. These include the three families who retain their original undivided lands and three others with higher than average land-to-person ratios. The wealthiest man of the group is variously estimated to have Rs. 8,000 to Rs. 50,000, the latter doubtless a greatly exaggerated estimate. Borrowing is done to finance such major outlays as marriage (which averages from Rs. 2,000 to 3,000 for a son and, depending upon the type of marriage, from nothing to Rs. 1,500 for a daughter); house construction (which ranges from Rs. 2,000 to 4,000); purchase of animals, purchase of land, costs of legal cases. Several Sirkanda families have been chronically in debt from such expenditures in recent years, but the relative wealth of families shifts with time. Thus, of the four wealthiest families in the village, two have become so recently—one in the generation just past, the other since Independence. Both of the others have increased their wealth during the past generation. Several other families are said to be less well off than in previous generations. This type of shift has in all cases but one been linked with a change in the man-land ratio. The more land per man, up to a point, the more wealth is accrued. With too little manpower, even land is useless, and in one of these cases wealth came when a man finally acquired a son and a servant to help him work his more than ample lands. In one case sudden wealth came from an unexpected windfall in the form of money acquired by questionable means from fleeing Muslims at the time of the partition of India and Pakistan.

There are few people in or out of the hills who will not attest to the poverty of Paharis. As applied to Sirkanda and neighboring villages this stereotype is a fiction, based largely upon the simple material possessions and hard work that characterize Pahari life. While it is true that by plains standards Paharis do not acquire great wealth and that what wealth they do acquire is not displayed, it is also true that they do not live the marginal existence led by many of their plains brethren, nor have they faced periodic famines and droughts as have people of Bihar and Bengal.

Trade and Markets

Neither Sirkanda nor the interdependent and relatively isolated group of villages which make up Bhatbair and the adjacent area in Tehri Garhwal are entirely self-sufficient. They are and perhaps always have been dependent upon larger centers. This relationship is an important prerequisite for classifying these Pahari villages as an example of peasant society. A peasant society is one composed primarily of people who make their living by agriculture and who live in symbiotic interdependence with market towns or urban areas though living away from them (cf. Kroeber, 1948, p. 284; Redfield, 1957, pp. 31 ff.).

The peasant has some product which the city consumes, and there are products of the city—metal tools, guns, patent medicines, or electric flashlights—which the peasant takes from the manufacturers in the city. Since the coming of money into the world, the peasant village has come in great degree to define its economic affairs in terms of this measure. (Redfield, 1957, pp. 31 f.)

Having been included in the "economic nexus of civilized society," the peasant is imbued with "a spirit of pecuniary advantage" (ibid.).

The dependence of Sirkanda peasants on urban centers is increasing. Sixty years ago one trip per year to a major market sufficed to exchange the agricultural surplus directly or indirectly for major items not locally available, and to transact necessary business with official agents of authority. Several trips to intermediary markets and occasional visits from peddlers provided those items needing more frequent replenishment, such as salt, sugar, and glass bangles. As transportation has improved, urban areas such as Dehra Dun have increased their direct influence on the village. Some men go every month, and most go several times a year. Those living in chans may go weekly or oftener because they are close to town and have milk products to sell. Intermediary markets are visited with proportionately increased frequency. The range of products sought and of agencies providing them has increased in the area as money has become more readily available. Milk and agricultural surpluses are sold to get money to buy an increasing array of goods, to pay taxes and court costs, and even to pay village artisans.

Reliance upon products and services deriving from urban areas is therefore a traditional feature of the Sirkanda economy which is becoming more prominent. Today the urban economy reaches into the village in many ways.

There are two shops in Sirkanda. One is owned and operated by a large household of Rajputs in Sirkanda. It sells mostly staples such as cigarettes, matches, kerosene, cooking oil, sugar, salt, spices, and tea to villagers, and hot tea to passing travelers, on a cash basis. The other is operated by a merchant from Rajpur, who was asked to come by a group of villagers who did not want to trade in the other shop because of personal rivalries. He has run this shop for some 25 years.[6] His trade includes selling staples, often on credit, but his main business is buying some of the villagers' produce, notably the solidified milk product, pumpkins, apricots, lemons, and anything else he can resell in Dehra Dun at a profit.

Lower prices and greater selection encourage villagers to buy at larger centers except in emergencies. Likewise, they can sell their produce to greater advantage in market towns. Dehra Dun and Mussoorie are the large trading centers, but smaller, closer ones are frequently patronized. Suakholi, ten miles from Sirkanda and six from Mussoorie on the Mussoorie-Tehri trail, is much used by hillmen throughout this area. Similarly Sahas Dhara, Nagal, and Rajpur are traditional markets below Sirkanda, five to nine miles away. Supplies for such special occasions as marriage, and items not produced locally, such as salt, sugar, oil, jewelry, trinkets, cloth, utensils, and some tools, are often obtained from these places. In each market are particular merchants with whom Sirkanda farmers regularly trade. The relationship becomes somewhat personal, so that villagers may stay overnight in the trader's shop when they visit town even if they have no business to transact with the shopkeeper. The shopkeeper may also serve as an informal adviser on matters unfamiliar to the villagers.

Itinerant peddlers come through Sirkanda selling bangles and other small items of decoration and convenience two or three times a year. One who came and stayed three days while I was in the village sold trinkets worth seven maunds (560 pounds) of grain, for a gross of about Rs. 100 and a profit of at least Rs. 70, in Sirkanda alone. Even with an extra rented mule, he had to make a return trip to carry off his proceeds. Interestingly enough, he arrived shortly after the annual fair at which the people had already spent a good deal of money, much of it on items which this very peddler had been selling at the fair.

The annual fair (taulū) of Bhatbair is held a few miles from Sirkanda and is by far the most important event of its kind for the residents of Bhatbair, but it is too provincial to attract outsiders other than two or three merchants. Other fairs attended by Sirkanda villagers are those held annually at Rajpur, Mussoorie, and at a well-known temple on the Mussoorie-Tehri trail. At all of these there is ample opportunity to spend money on tea, refreshments, sweets, trinkets, entertainment, liquor, and women. A number of Sirkanda villagers set up concessions at the annual Bhatbair fair, but aside from the Ferris wheel operated by Bajgis of Sirkanda and a nearby village, these rarely show much of a profit. The profiteers are the two or three outside merchants who sell trinkets, the clandestine sellers of liquor, and perhaps some of those who sell sweets, which are the medium of exchange for obtaining sexual favors from women, one of the major activities of this fair. The inexperience of the amateur village entrepreneurs who set up booths at this fair generally dooms them to financial failure. They join the spirit and activities of the festival and forget to collect cash for their wares or are distracted from their shop-tending by other activities, while their stores are good-naturedly depleted.

The Jajmani System

A number of essential activities in the village, especially those requiring particular skills or knowledge, are performed by specialists. Most of these occupations are thought of as caste monopolies, and the arrangements for work and payment are standardized in some form of traditional exchange, known widely in North India as the jajmānī system (cf. W. H. Wiser, 1936; Beidelman, 1959; Berreman, 1962b, in which part of the following has appeared).

When Sirkanda villagers use the term jajmān they refer to one kind of exchange: that of the Brahmin's ritual services to his clients (jajmans) in exchange for traditional "gifts" paid in grain or other goods. This is in accordance with widespread usage of the term among villagers in North India and with its etymological meaning: one who asks another to perform worship and offers a gift to him in return.

Sirkanda villagers also understand, though they do not themselves normally use, the term jajman to refer to the traditional arrangement whereby an artisan serves the needs of an agriculturist in his specialty. In this relationship the artisan or service caste member is paid a fixed portion of grain at each harvest, the amount depending upon the size of the household or landholding of the agriculturist and the type of service performed.

The Pahari term which Sirkanda villagers normally use in reference to an artisan's clients, parallel to their use of "jajman" in reference to a Brahmin's clients, is *gaikh,* one who purchases the service of another. Ideally the relationship between artisan and gaikh is a permanent one with standard traditional payments, but in practice there is a good deal of shifting, especially where there is more than one local artisan available.

A third kind of traditional economic exchange in the village is that of service among artisans. This is not usually included in either the term "jajman" or "gaikh" by villagers. Blacksmiths, for example, see to the ironwork needs of the local drummers, who in return drum for the blacksmiths as needed. Agreements to this sort of exchange are about as stable as those in the gaikh arrangement.

Finally, many services are performed, and have been traditionally performed, on a piecework or daily wage basis, with cash or grain used for payment. These include the sporadic services of ceremonial cooks, stonemasons, wood turners, and others, who are not resident in or near most villages, as are blacksmiths and drummers. They include also the nontraditional or non-caste–specific activities performed by local artisans. Tailoring and basketmaking, for example, are in this village done by drummers. Payment for these services is on a piecework basis.

Any low-caste person may be called upon to help a high-caste villager in emergency jobs or in tasks which the high-caste person is unable or unwilling to do himself. Most often the high-caste person calls upon one of the artisans who serve him, that is, for whom he is a client. The low-caste person cannot refuse to help without a good reason such as physical incapacity or an urgent prior commitment to another client. Otherwise he risks economic or physical sanctions. This is not the case with either Brahmin-jajman relations or intraservice caste relations.

Although each caste in and around Sirkanda is identified with a particular occupational role, there is considerable flexibility in the system.

Important in the jajmani or gaikh system is the fact that service castes, unlike Brahmins, have a difficult time maintaining a monopoly on their services and often have no other reliable source of income such as farming. The traditional occupation of each caste may remain caste-specific, but its members' livelihood may depend largely or entirely on specialties which are not restricted to a single caste. Under conditions of necessity or even convenience, many occupations are interchangeable among low castes. Occasionally a high-caste person will perform an artisan's work. Therefore, if an artisan quits working for a client there are others, even outside his caste, who can and will take his place.

Another feature of significance in economic organization is the absolutely small number of individuals who make up each local artisan caste group, often only one nuclear family or two closely related and recently separated families. Probably partly as a result of this fact the artisan castes are not very cohesive groups. Unlike the high castes, they have little or nothing in the way of group organization and discipline beyond local kin-connected groups. Moreover, in many areas, as population has increased, so has access to bazaar-made goods. Agriculturists have become less dependent upon artisans' services and less inclined to make full payment to them. There is increasing competition among artisans for a decreasingly remunerative clientele. As a result there is considerable friction among them. In Sirkanda the local blacksmith and drummer castes are both divided within themselves between two competing and often hostile brothers, neither able to make an adequate living at his traditional occupation and therefore supplementing it by brewing illicit liquor, raising goats, practicing medicine and divination, tailoring, or carrying on agriculture if he has land. Thus gaikh relationships are unstable, with much jockeying for the better-paying clients on the one hand, and for the better-performing artisans on the other. The effect of this situation is shown by the fact that only among service castes do brothers frequently dissolve the joint family and divide the common patrimony.

Exploitation in the sense of arbitrary and self-seeking control over the behavior of others is characteristic of the relationship of agriculturists to artisans in Sirkanda. While many clients are responsible individuals who do not often overtly exercise their power over the low castes, still, as in the village of Karimpur described by the Wisers, "let there be any move toward independence or even indifference among them, and the paternal touch becomes a strangle-hold" (C. V. and W. H. Wiser, 1951, p. 18).

Exploitation is not characteristic of the ritual relationships between

Brahmins and their clients, nor in the exchange of services among the artisan castes. The reason for this pattern seems to lie largely in the distribution of power—the control that local castes exert relative to one another.

In Sirkanda low castes are dependent upon high castes for livelihood —almost absolutely so. Moreover, they have little leverage on the high castes because of the absence of caste cohesion among themselves and the absence of caste monopolies on the essential goods and services which they provide for the high castes. The high castes, in contrast, are generally well organized and able to present a united front to the artisans of any local area. Moreover, potential clients are sufficiently restricted in numbers, and villages are sufficiently isolated from one another, that village artisans often find it difficult if not impossible to seek new clients. In the village context, therefore, they subsist at the discretion of their high-caste patrons.

Low-caste people who have become agriculturists no longer dependent upon their craft skills are, like Brahmins, free of obligation to, and potential exploitation by, other agriculturists. They have in most cases moved out of their traditional villages to nonvillage locations where they do not have to deal frequently with the high castes and where they perform most of their own labor.

In the exchange of services among low castes in Sirkanda there is no opportunity for exploitation, since none controls the livelihood of others nor performs unique and essential services.

A feature of the artisan-gaikh relationship that should not be overlooked is the part played by high-caste clients in the work of the low-caste artisan. A scene repeated daily for several months during the building season of the writer's year in Sirkanda took place at the construction site of the Brahmin family's imposing new house. The two carpenter-masons were engaged in their skilled but relatively leisurely work of placing and mortaring stones, making window frames, or carving columns. Meanwhile the Brahmins, women and men, struggled with immense loads of stone from the quarrying place ¾ mile distant. They quarried the stone, dug, transported, and mixed mortar clay, felled and transported trees, carried corrugated iron sheeting from the valley, handed stones up to the masons (who might airily reject any particular stone), and generally did all the heavy, dirty work of the construction. Their exhausted and begrimed countenances were in striking contrast to those of the masons, who often sat and waited for more materials to be brought. Lesser manifestations of the same phenomenon were to be seen when Rajputs operated the bellows or wielded the sledge under the direction of the blacksmith on jobs too pressing or too big for him to handle alone. Rajputs were also to be seen sewing buttons on their newly made shirts while the tailor worked on more complicated phases of his craft in order to get a rush order finished.

No incongruity was seen in these aspects of the gaikh relationship, and they did not embarrass those involved. The superior skill of the artisan in his specialty was recognized, and his client got the most for his money by arranging to let the artisan concentrate on the skilled aspects of his work. The low-castes were still expected to respond at once without remuneration, when not otherwise employed, to a call for assistance in thatching a roof, mixing tobacco and molasses, killing a goat, plastering a floor, carrying a load, or assisting in other ways when a high-caste member needed help. The high castes' relative ritual and social status was never ignored or compromised.

OCCUPATIONAL SPECIALTIES

In Sirkanda four castes of specialists are represented: Brahmins, the high-caste priests, and three low-caste artisan groups: blacksmiths (Lōhār), barbers (Nāī), and drummer-tailors (Bājgī). Each of these groups is tied in some form of the jajmani or gaikh arrangement to exclusively agricultural families in the village, and usually to other specialist families as well. If there is more than one household which follows a particular specialty in the village, each normally has its own circle of traditional clients, just as each agricultural household has its own fields. In each instance the household remains the important economic unit. The proceeds of traditional specialties, like those of agriculture, are shared within the household. The economic roles of the occupational specialists will be considered in turn.

Brahmins

Sirkanda Brahmins are primarily agriculturists, most of whose economic pursuits are indistinguishable from those of Rajputs. Their income from agriculture is equivalent to that of the more prosperous Rajputs. Priestly work is done only by Jairam, one of three brothers in the family, and it does not interfere with his agricultural work. In his own words and in obvious reference to his competitor, a Brahmin from Tehri Garhwal who gets most of the high-caste business from Sirkanda, "Some Brahmins haven't anything else to do but spend all of their time gallivanting around doing their priestly work. I am too busy for that."

Jairam officiates at weddings, funerals, and various ceremonies in

Sirkanda but usually only when his competitor is not available or needs assistance, or when a request comes from low-caste people, whom his competitor will not serve. He is too close to people in Sirkanda to be held in awe or any great respect. The Tehri Brahmin from fifteen miles away is used whenever possible and is considered to be the family priest by most Rajputs of Sirkanda. He is credited with more priestly learning than Jairam, and his rates are higher. He serves a restricted clientele of high-caste people who can afford him. Either Brahmin is paid for the work he does, for example, around Rs. 20 for a wedding or funeral, Rs. 1 to 5 for simple ceremonies. These Brahmins are also the recipients of occasional extra charity on certain religious days and occasions when people want to acquire merit in this manner. The two Brahmins refer to those families they serve regularly as their "jajman." They can depend upon being called to serve any ritual needs these families may have and to receive charity as well as payment from them. However, neither Brahmin is the hereditary priest or *purōhit* for Sirkanda people in the true sense of the term.

The traditional Sirkanda Brahmin or purohit is Tula, who lives in another village two hours' walk from Sirkanda. All Sirkanda families as well as those in several neighboring villages are in his jajman—the traditional, hereditary client-practitioner relationship. The office has been in his family for many generations and continues in full force although Tula, like his father before him, practices very little and allegedly knows even less of priestly duties. Some generations back his family were highly regarded in Bhatbair as learned priests. Now they are not so regarded and make no pretense in this direction, limiting their priestly participation to minor roles in ceremonies, to astrology, and so on. Nevertheless, as traditional priest or purohit in this and surrounding villages, Tula attends and is given the purohit's charity and payment at every marriage, funeral, or other important ceremonial event and at every occasion calling for the granting of charity to Brahmins. Thus he receives many times the amounts that the officiating Brahmins do. He is given due honor and respect as the traditional and rightful recipient. As a result he is one of the wealthiest men in the area, with three houses, three wives, much land, and many children, some of whom have married into prominent families of Garhwali Brahmin ancestry in Dehru Dun. He is also the only obese Pahari I have ever seen and is addressed and referred to almost exclusively as "mōtā Brahmin" (fat Brahmin). The jajmani system has worked to his advantage.

The term jajman is used loosely by all three of the above-mentioned

Brahmins to refer to the people they regularly serve (as, "Family X is in my jajman"). However, only Tula has the long-standing, hereditary relationship with its system of traditional payment that is generally associated with the term "jajman."

Artisans

All the artisan (shilpkār) castes in Sirkanda, commonly referred to as Doms, depend upon their crafts for their living and are to some extent prevented from acquiring other means of livelihood. An artisan's clients are referred to as his *gaikh* or, commonly, simply "farmer" (*kisān*), terms which are roughly parallel in usage to the Brahmin's use of "jajman." "Jajman" is also used sometimes by the artisans, though it is not thought to be entirely appropriate. The artisan is known as the "worker" (*kām karnewālā*) by his clients. The client usually pays the artisan who works for him a fixed amount of grain at each harvest, that is, twice a year. There is not the rigidly hereditary association between worker and client reported for the plains (W. H. Wiser, 1936). However, no farmer will be denied service by an artisan if he demands it. Threat of physical punishment can be used if necessary, with the backing of the rest of the high-caste majority. The artisan may use more subtle pressures, such as inferior or slow service, to encourage prompt and adequate payment by a delinquent client. If an artisan does not perform satisfactorily, his clients may patronize another craftsman in the same or a nearby village.

BLACKSMITHS

The blacksmith's main job is making and repairing iron tools, horseshoes, bells, occasional religious images, and so on. Agricultural implements, axes, and grass knives make up most of the blacksmith's work. Today there are two blacksmiths, brothers, who work and live separately in separate households. One of the two has 20 households in his clientele, including "all the big people"—those who pay regularly and well—in Sirkanda and nearby villages. He prides himself on having maneuvered himself into the favor of the more desirable customers by personal charm rather than superior work. His brother has 29 of the "lesser" households including 12 in Sirkanda and 17 in neighboring villages. Though he recognizes the inferiority of his clientele to his brother's, he philosophizes that "God will provide for all." Some other households patronize blacksmiths near their chans and only occasionally utilize one of the Sirkanda ones, on a job-payment basis. Neither of the Sirkanda blacksmiths is kept very busy by his work, and it provides only a marginal income. When the father of these two men was the village smith he had a good income; he is said to have loaned money to Rajputs, and to have left a cash nestegg when he died. Now the business is divided in half. Moreover, the smiths claim that payment has fallen off as people have come to use ready-made tools from the bazaar more frequently and as households have increased in membership or split up. Where formerly there was one household there are now often two or three, or membership has doubled or tripled, while the members continue to pay a total of only one household's traditional payment. Meanwhile other households have passed out of existence or have moved to chans, so that their business is lost. Equally important is the fact that formerly grants of grain, livestock, or even land, as well as clothing, tobacco, tools, and so on, were given to all the low-castes as gratuities. Now these things are rarely given. The attitude of the higher-castes has ceased to be as paternalistic as it was in former days—partly, according to the high-caste people, because the low-castes do not now conform to the submissive role expected in a paternalistic relationship.

The blacksmiths are the poorest of Sirkanda villagers and are the only ones aside from two Bajgis who now own virtually no land, having sold what little remained of their holdings some time ago when the extended family divided. Payment for their traditional work is in five-seer (ten-pound) measures of grain. At each harvest they are supposed to get two to three measures from each two-oxen household they serve, three from four-oxen households, and four measures from a six- or eight-oxen household. This scale is not rigidly adhered to, and the blacksmiths claim that they are consistently underpaid. They get a total of 16 to 18 maunds of grain per year—about half their minimum requirement for livelihood. One of the blacksmiths supplements his income by distilling and selling home-made liquor—a brisk business yielding 25 to 35 maunds of grain per year. The other has tried cloth-selling and other schemes to augment his income, all unsuccessful largely because of his illiteracy and softheartedness, which have prevented him from recording and collecting debts or refusing credit. He now makes ends meet by raising goats, from which he nets 25 maunds of grain per year. He also does odd jobs around the village and generally remains on such good terms with all villagers that free meals and occasional gifts come his way.

Blacksmiths live a marginal existence, their income barely exceeding the requirements for livelihood. However, they do not fear starvation because they know that other villagers will not allow them to go hungry if they are really in need so long as they continue to perform their functions in the village without offending their caste superiors. Such assistance comes bit by bit as needed rather than in an advance, security-providing amount. Opportunities exist for blacksmiths to work where large-scale stone-quarrying operations are in progress some six to ten miles away. There a cousin of the Sirkanda blacksmiths makes up to Rs. 20 per day blacksmithing. When asked about this, one Sirkanda blacksmith commented that such work, while profitable, is uncertain. Here he has lifetime security which he would lose if he left, and the stone quarry might close down at any time. Moreover, he says, "I've never worked in my life." The latter point has a large element of truth. No one in Sirkanda leads a life as leisurely as that of the blacksmiths. This man volunteers that if he worked harder he could make more money right in Sirkanda—by getting work from customers in nearby villages and doing it promptly and well. He attributes his father's prosperity partly to his industry.

BARBER

The Sirkanda barber is a descendant of a barber brought from the valley at the time of the founding of the village. Elsewhere in this area the barber's functions are performed by other low-caste members, usually Bajgis and sometimes blacksmiths. When the Sirkanda barber left the village for three years once, his duties were taken over by one of the blacksmiths. Whoever performs the barber's functions receives annual payment of four seers (eight pounds) of grain at each harvest for each bewhiskered man in each household and two seers per whiskerless boy in each household he serves. At this rate the Sirkanda barber gets about 25 maunds (2,000 pounds) of grain per year for his small family from his rather extensive practice, including all of Sirkanda and several neighboring settlements. This meets his subsistence requirement for grain. In addition he receives payment for his traditional ritual services at weddings, funerals, initial hair-cutting ceremonies, and one annual festival day, ranging from Rs. 20 to a few annas (one anna = ⅛ of one rupee) each. This barber owns some lands in Sirkanda and more land and bullocks in the village of relatives in the valley, which give him a modest but comfortable income beyond that of his barbering.

BAJGIS

The work of Bajgis in Sirkanda is varied. With the exception of barbering, they perform the functions common to their caste in most Pahari villages: drum-playing, tailoring, and basketmaking.

Of these activities, only drum-playing is done in the traditional artisan-gaikh relationship. It is done for the entire village by two households working jointly. They play drums at all ceremonies and festivals. In return for their drumming each village household gives the drummers 16 seers (32 pounds) of grain at each harvest and occasional other gratuities in the form of grain. This income is divided between the two households who do this work in Sirkanda. Formerly it was one household, but the two brothers have divided their property. Since the drumming requires a team of two, they have retained this as a joint enterprise and they divide the proceeds. In former days Bajgi women danced on special occasions as part of the caste's traditional duties, but they have given up this defiling practice.

Tailoring is an important activity of the Bajgi caste—so much so that Bajgis are commonly referred to as *Darzi* (tailors), whether or not they follow this profession. In Sirkanda tailoring is done on a piecework basis for cash or its grain equivalent. Rates range from six rupees for a coat down to six annas for a cap. One man does all the tailoring in Sirkanda, and the payment is kept in his household, one of the two drum-playing households. This arrangement was the basis for a major but short-lived dispute when the household which shares the proceeds of the drumming activity demanded, but did not get, half the income from tailoring as well.

Baskets are made on a similar basis at rates ranging from three rupees for a large grain-storage basket down to four annas for a small basket or winnowing tray. Three Bajgi households make baskets.

In addition, one of the two non-drum–playing Bajgis makes and sells liquor. The other, an immigrant of some twenty-five years' residence in Sirkanda, lives entirely on his income as a practitioner of a kind of curative magic. The two large, drum-playing households own land and bullocks, which provide a substantial addition to their other income. They get about 18 maunds of grain apiece annually for drumming, about one-third of their grain requirements. They make another 12 maunds in their other specialized work, 20 maunds from milk, goats, and so on, and 40 maunds from their fields. They are therefore reasonably well off. The two smaller households, who have no land and no income from drumming, are about as poor as the blacksmiths.

Blacksmiths and Bajgis exchange traditional services in lieu of payment. The barber is, however, paid in grain by all who have it and in cash equivalent by those (like the blacksmiths) who do not.

NONRESIDENT SPECIALISTS

A number of Pahari occupational specialists contribute to the Sirkanda economy, although they do not reside in the village. All of these described below are represented within the eight-trail-mile (four-air-

mile) radius which is the area of face-to-face social and economic interaction for Sirkanda villagers.

Sarōlā is the name of a subcaste of Brahmins who specialize in cooking for Brahmins and Rajputs on ceremonial occasions. They are
ritually superior to other Brahmins and therefore pure enough that
anyone can eat from their hands. Payment is Rs. 16 to 20 for the job
or R. 1 per maund (80 pounds) of food cooked—whichever is greater
—plus their board and shelter while the job lasts. In addition they get
a traditional payment of 2½ seers of gūr (sugar) and R. 1 at the time of
the ceremonial lighting of the cooking fire.

Sōnārs are makers of silver and gold jewelry. In these hills there are
two castes of these goldsmiths—one equivalent to Rajputs in every way,
the other a Dom caste equivalent to blacksmiths and carpenters. The
Rajput goldsmiths are called "Sonar" as an occupational term, just as
are Dom goldsmiths, but they are Rajputs and intermarry freely with
other Rajputs. Similarly Dom goldsmiths intermarry freely with blacksmiths and carpenters, with whom they are included under the broader
occupational classification, Mistrī. Most of the Sonars of this area are
of the Rajput group, and they include some of the wealthiest of Paharis.
They are paid in cash or grain by the job. They have shops in towns
such as Mussoorie and in small trading centers such as Suakholi. Some
travel from village to village taking orders and doing their work as they
go.

Carpenter-masons (BaRhāi) intermarry with blacksmiths and Dom
goldsmiths, but their occupational specialty is usually handed down
patrilineally. They make wooden tools and utensils and construct
houses. In Sirkanda most men make their own wooden tools, but carpenters are called in to build houses. Carpenters live in the village
while they work, receiving their food and shelter plus Rs. 4 per day.
They may also be paid by the job, for example, Rs. 80 for sawing out
100 boards. There is occupational specialization among carpenters;
some, called Rengālda, produce lathe-turned wooden containers and
churns which are sold by volume. There is no traditional economic
relationship of Sirkanda households with carpenters, though certain
ones are usually called in because of their skill and proximity.

Khōlīs are weavers of wool blankets and heavy wool cloth. Formerly
their work was more in demand than it is today because their cloth was
used for coats and they were virtually the only source for blankets and
cloaks. Now cloth from the bazaar is much used and the Kholis' main
trade is in a distinctive type of blanket used as a wrap. They are paid
a piece rate, an arm and hand length of loom width being the unit and
costing Rs. 2.50 if the customer furnishes the wool.

There are several terms for people whose profession is singing and

dancing. The only Paharis of this profession in Bhatbair are called
Bēdā. One family of this caste has long been associated with Bhatbair,
and, though they have moved from their traditional home in a village
in the heart of Bhatbair, they still live within walking distance in a
Pahari village bordering the valley. They (two men and one or two
women) visit Sirkanda and other Bhatbair villages about once a year,
staying three or four days in each village and going from house to house
entertaining with songs and dances. For this they receive 2 to 4 seers
of grain from each house. People of this caste are thought to possess
unusual spiritual powers. They were formerly the performers of the
rope-sliding feat, a spectacular form of worship which, when performed,
brought them a large lump sum of cash and goods as well as a great
deal of honor (Berreman, 1961). Since Beda women dance and sing,
they are thought of as prostitutes. Today the Bedas are primarily agriculturists and are trying to give up their hereditary occupation and
the stigma attached to it. They have ceased to give evening command
performances while in the village, apparently because these were linked
to prostitution. Instead they perform only in the daytime at each house
and they give a public performance in the evening in one place. According to the present practitioners of the trade they would give it up
altogether as, indeed, they intend to, if it were not for pressure from
their father to carry on in the family tradition.

Mōchīs or *Chamārs* are shoemakers and removers of dead animals.
They are not indigenous to this Pahari region, although farther back
in Tehri Garhwal there are local people of this caste. Those who live
and work near Bhatbair come from the Kangra valley, a Pahari area
some 150 miles to the west. They have been in the region for 20 or 30
years or more. Before they came, villagers assert, people here went barefoot, as many of them do yet. They remain culturally distinct and are
readily identifiable by dress, house type, and speech, although not by
physical type. Their work is more defiling and their caste rank lower
than that of any other group in these hills. They sell shoes by the pair,
or by an arrangement in which a household gives them 5 seers of grain
per harvest in return for which they provide all the shoes needed in
that household at R. 1 per pair. In addition they are called to remove
any large domestic animal which dies. In return they keep the skin and
give the owner a pair of shoes unless the animal is a cow or an ox, in
which case the owner takes nothing. A few years ago a family of this
caste moved to the outskirts of Sirkanda but found it unprofitable and
moved on to Sahas Dhara, a larger center below.

In addition there are ten to fifteen other Garhwali service castes,
most of them never seen in Sirkanda. Some, such as rope bridge-makers,
may be called upon if a special need arises.

Several important occupations are not closely or rigidly bound to caste. Farming is foremost among these, as evidenced by the fact that currently some members of every caste in Bhatbair make a substantial part of their living by farming.

Special occupations in this caste-neutral category are primarily those associated with divining, curing, and dealing with the supernatural. Whatever their caste, practitioners of these arts are paid in cash or grain for their work. One Bajgi in Sirkanda makes his entire living from his work as a practitioner of curing through exorcising spirits. Another makes some income as a diviner. Specialists in the treatment of various maladies (chickenpox, mumps, boils, snakebite) are found among all castes. Jairam, the Sirkanda Brahmin, carries on a brisk business in simple Vedic medical practice, that is, curing based on ancient Hindu prescriptions. Shamans are found in several villages in and near Bhatbair and are frequently consulted to learn the cause of difficulties besetting families or individuals. In the process a god enters the shaman's body, speaks through his mouth, and provides the desired information. The shaman, who may be of any caste, is paid a small fee for each consultation. *Pūjarīs* specialize in the worship of household gods, playing drums and reciting praise of these gods to induce them to dance in the bodies of the worshipers and frequently to speak through them. These practitioners come from all castes, with a tendency toward the lower castes. They too are paid by the job.

There is no Pahari Vaishya or merchant caste. Shopkeepers and peddlers come from the plains, from Tibet and Nepal, and from all Pahari castes. Of three Pahari tradesmen in Bhatbair, two are Rajputs and one is a Brahmin. As mentioned previously, a Sirkanda blacksmith tried his hand at selling cloth throughout the region for several years, and people of all castes may become temporary shopkeepers at the annual fair.

SERVANTS

Some high-caste agriculturists of Sirkanda employ servants to help tend their fields and livestock. Those who do the hiring are people who have more land, or land in more scattered locations, than the men in the family can handle. In a small family with considerable land a good servant pays his way many times over.

Servants live with their employers and are paid a small amount monthly (Rs. 10 to 30). Because of their close association with their employers they are chosen from high castes to avoid problems of ritual pollution. Thus, of the three permanent servants in Sirkanda, two are Rajputs and one a Brahmin—all Paharis, two from Nepal and one from Tehri-Garhwal. Servants are given responsibilities equivalent to those of a family member, often being left for long periods to look after a chan, and frequently one of its owner's wives and her children as well. A lifelong servant is generally given land and a house as a reward for faithful service. The oldest resident of Sirkanda is the widow of a man whose father came to Sirkanda as a servant and remained there after having thus acquired lands.

Temporary servants in the person of carpenter-masons engaged in house construction, or indebted high-caste men (often relatives of their employers) working as laborers, are generally to be found in the village during the winter housebuilding season. As many as eight of these were resident in the village at once during 1957–1958.

Occupational Variation

Occupational variation within caste is found throughout India (cf. J. M. Mahar, 1958; Sharma, 1961). Paharis are tolerant and flexible in this respect. As mentioned above, in addition to the traditionally caste-neutral occupation of agriculture, there are a variety of magical-medical practitioners of all castes, Rajput goldsmiths, merchants of blacksmith, Rajput, and Brahmin castes, and high-caste agricultural servants. Barber functions are shared among several low-caste groups. In general, low castes share the artisan occupations, and not uncommonly a member of one low caste will be found doing the work of another, especially where economy demands it and population does not provide the appropriate caste specialist. Thus either blacksmiths or drummers may serve as barbers, either may serve as tailors, and it is not unheard-of for a blacksmith to play drums. Such occupational flexibility is characteristic of caste and economic organization in the hills. Just as status differences among Dom groups are somewhat ambiguous, so are their occupational specializations. For both purposes, Doms are often treated by the high castes as an undifferentiated group.

Even high castes perform the work of artisans on occasion. They exhibit many of the skills of artisans while assisting them in their work in order to hurry things along or to save payment. Since there was no carpenter in Sirkanda, Rajputs and Brahmins did their own routine carpentry, calling in an outside specialist only for major building jobs or tasks requiring unusual skill. In addition high-caste people are not entirely barred from becoming professional artisans. An example that has already been mentioned is that of the Rajput goldsmiths. An example on the individual level is that of a skilled carpenter of Bhatbair who is a Rajput and is accepted as such in every respect, although he makes his living in precisely the fashion of low-caste carpenters and in their company. Another highly respected Rajput of Sirkanda worked for a Vaishya shopkeeper as a servant in the trading village of Nagal.

Outside Employment

Residents of Sirkanda and Bhatbair have not been attracted in large numbers to outside employment. Most of those who have, have been gone only a short time. A frequent pattern of adolescent male behavior is running away from the village. Boys often go to the plains to wander around, see the sights, engage in sporadic employment, and in a few months return to remain in the village. At least this has been the pattern until the present. Perhaps with improved preparation through the village school and increased job opportunities outside, the high return rate will decrease.

Six recent cases of the kind concerned boys 13 to 15 years of age. Two, a Brahmin and a Rajput, ran away together to Delhi, where they worked for three months in a tea stall washing dishes and delivering tea at Rs. 15 per month plus board and room. They came back after they had had enough of city life and had been unable to find more inspiring or remunerative labor. As one said, "You could spend all your life washing glasses in a tea stall and never get anywhere." A blacksmith boy had run away to Dehra Dun twice, staying three or four months each time and working once in a tea stall and once in an embroidery shop, at Rs. 15 per month. One boy was taken by an employer from Dehra Dun to Naini Tal, 100 miles to the southeast, where he worked as a kitchen boy for seven months before coming home. Another worked in a dairy south of Delhi for five months and then returned. Two boys left during the winter of 1957–1958 and had not yet been heard from seven months later. More than once people from neighboring villages came through Sirkanda in quest of runaway sons. At least five older men in Sirkanda recounted similar youthful adventures. That not all return is indicated by the fact that three or four men were listed in the genealogical survey as having disappeared from the village in their youth and having never been heard from again.

Needless to say, such short-lived escapades result in little economic gain for those involved, and by the time worried relatives have gone to look for and bring back the truants, as is frequently done, the financial loss to the household is appreciable.

Not all outside employment is of this youthful and transitory nature. One young Sirkanda Rajput left the village as a result of a family dispute (there is nearly always some such motivating incident), and got a

job in a textile mill in an industrial suburb of Delhi. He has been at
it six years, has been promoted, and has no intention of leaving the
job. He occasionally visits Sirkanda, but does not keep in close touch
with his family and sends little or nothing in the way of financial aid—
partly because he spends most of what he makes (Rs. 120 per month)
and partly because the family dispute has alienated him from his
household. In the minds of villagers, he is the single example of a
local boy who has made good on the outside. Another young man left
the village early in the period of my residence to join the millworker.
He got a job at Rs. 70 per month at which he was still working a year
later, and he gave no indications of quitting. He had hoped to send
money home but had as yet failed to make enough to enable him to do
so. His departure—in secrecy—worked a real hardship on his family,
as he was one of only two adult males available to work the land upon
which ten people depended for livelihood.

One Rajput had left the village several years previously to escape
some outside creditors, and ended up running a tea stall for over two
years in Kalsi, a town in the Dehra Dun valley 20 miles to the west.
He returned at the urging of relatives, stayed three years, and again
left for an unknown destination. Two Sirkanda Rajput men had been
in the army during World War II, though neither left India. Both
returned to the village after demobilization. One, however, neglected
to procure a discharge and was later picked up and forced to return
to the army where he is today, having served about ten years in two
periods. Both these men sent money to their families sufficient to contribute substantially to the support of their dependents, though in both
cases they and others felt that economic as well as emotional ties
would have been better served by their presence in the village. Several
other men of Bhatbair, but outside Sirkanda, served in World War II,
including men of Rajput, blacksmith, carpenter, and shoemaker castes.
A carpenter and a shoemaker who work for Sirkanda families had each
served several years in both the African and Pacific theaters of operations, one with American and the other with British troops. All these
men were able to make sufficient income so that their families did not
suffer. One deceased Sirkanda Rajput served in World War I, as did a
Rajput shopkeeper from a nearby village.

Dehra Dun is not an industrial city and does not offer many employment opportunities for people who are uneducated, as are most
Paharis of this region. This situation probably contributes to the low
rate of outside employment. Two educated young men of villages on
the edge of Bhatbair near Dehra Dun (a Brahmin and a Rajput whose
wives are from Sirkanda) have gotten jobs in that city—one with a

small government ordnance factory employing primarily skilled personnel, and the other with the office staff of a limestone quarrying company which operates near Bhatbair. Both make about Rs. 100 per month and live at home, so that they contribute a substantial amount to supplement the agricultural income of their families.

The total number of Paharis in the ordnance factory is only ten or twelve, and the others are all from a neighboring region in Tehri Garhwal. The husband of another Sirkanda woman who lives in the Bhatbair village nearest Dehra Dun has become wealthy as a result of having been given the contract to maintain the Rajpur canal, which supplies much of the water used in Dehra Dun.

One Sirkanda Rajput moved to Sahas Dhara, a small trading center and site of a popular religious shrine five miles below Sirkanda, where he made his living for many years as a shopkeeper and where he is now retired. A Sirkanda-born blacksmith makes his living in the same place, largely from the work he gets from commercial limestone quarries in the area.

These make up the sum total of Sirkanda men, plus a sampling of others from Bhatbair, who have engaged in outside employment. The importance of such employment to village economy is small, though possibly it presages things to come. To the present, no Sirkanda villager has relatives resident in Dehra Dun. No Sirkanda couple or larger family unit has migrated from the village to a larger center. One of the men who was in the army took his wife with him for a period of about six months and then brought her back to Sirkanda. The man who recently went to work in the cloth mill sent without success for his wife, but would not come back after her. Rarely is outside employment considered more than a temporary activity. Rarely is the type of employment available spoken of by others with approval or admiration. Nearly every person who has left the Bhatbair area to work has done so surreptitiously and without advance warning. Other aspects and implications of these defections, and of outside experiences and contacts in general, will be discussed in chapter 9.

ILLEGAL ECONOMIC ACTIVITIES

Liquor is manufactured independently by two men in Sirkanda, a Bajgi and a blacksmith. In other villages other castes engage in this activity, but most are nonagricultural castes, probably because they have more time to devote to such side-line enterprises and more need for the additional income. Since to sell untaxed liquor is illegal, there is an element of risk, and therefore of secrecy. Usually the distilling apparatus is so designed as to be easily and quickly disassembled, and always it is well concealed. Any particular distillery may close down suddenly and indefinitely if the owner fears detection by outside authorities, whose approach is usually, of course, relayed well in advance. Detection can lead to fine and imprisonment or demands for large bribes. The liquor is made by soaking any of several grains in sugar and water for about a week, and then distilling it. The product has a high alcohol content. It is drunk for effect rather than taste and is in constant demand at R. 1 per bottle. No celebration is complete without liquor. Liquor manufacture and selling is a profitable business, especially at festival times, when the demand generally exceeds the supply.

Marijuana is also produced in the village. Its addicts mix it with locally grown tobacco and smoke it to produce a euphoric effect. Its sale is illegal, and the two or three Sirkanda men who use it prepare their own or buy it illegally from neighboring villagers.

Another much publicized and criticized illegal activity of hillmen is the traffic in women. Although its prevalence has been exaggerated and it is evidently on the decrease, it has at times been an important activity among certain people of all castes. The procedure is simple: Pahari women of any caste but especially of the low castes, and almost invariably married women, who are unhappy with the hard and simple life of the hills and who have heard and have been convinced of the luxuries and pleasures of plains life, are helped by a Pahari, often of their acquaintance, to travel to Dehra Dun or some other center. There they are turned over as wife to a contact man. The woman may live as the wife or concubine of this person permanently or temporarily, she may be turned over to someone else seeking a wife or concubine, or she may be utilized in prostitution. The Pahari's profit in the transaction is in the initial payment made by the man who received the woman to the one who delivered her. One transaction may net the "abductor" several hundred or a thousand rupees, which is clear profit, as the wronged husband is unable to collect compensation unless he can find the person who was responsible, effect his arrest, and press court action. Occasionally a husband or other family member may coöperate in the transaction.

Sisters and wives of people now living in Sirkanda have been subject to this experience. One Bajgi woman currently resident in Sirkanda had been abducted and sold in her youth, but she returned after a few years. More commonly such women are not heard from again. Tula, the hereditary Brahmin of the village, was one of a trio, together with a Rajput and a Bajgi, who carried on this traffic some 25 years ago. They were apprehended, convicted, and imprisoned. Only Tula returned, one man having died in prison and the other having escaped and disappeared. Tula's priestly standing seems to have been unaffected by the incident. The men of one whole Rajput household in the village were at one time actively engaged in this trade; several were eventually caught, and others left the region to escape prosecution. Several Sirkanda men have occasionally profited from participation in such transactions, as recently as the past ten years. Most of these were not members of a professional gang, as were Tula and the household mentioned above, but rather were men who took advantage of an opportunity when it arose. Several factional disputes in Sirkanda can be traced to incidents of this nature.

Throughout North India the hills are thought of as a source of prostitutes, sought after for their beauty and lack of inhibition. Paharis and plains people alike assert the truth of this statement, at least as applied to the states bordering the hills. This is not to say that there are prostitutes in abundance in the hill areas, but rather that many prostitutes come originally from the area. Apparently the process described above accounts for the transportation of a good number of women to the plains. The custom of "bride-price" marriage in the hills facilitates such transactions, as it is customary to take money for women in perfectly valid marriage arrangements. It is not uncommon for men from the plains to come to the hills looking for brides from poor families who may not be too inquisitive or particular about their credentials. Some of these men are genuine seekers of wives. At least two low-caste Sirkanda women are today in distant places as the wives of such men, and are apparently happy. Some men have less noble motives. On the other hand prostitution is not despised by the lowest castes, from which these girls (at least those who are heard from again) usually come. It is an occupation providing a good income by Pahari standards and it has a certain glamour as compared with village life, because of its association with an urban setting. While not marriageable, these girls are not outcastes, and they visit their homes occasionally. A famous prostitute of Dehra Dun is the sister-in-law of two Sirkanda Bajgis, and prostitutes of Mussoorie and Dehra Dun who come from villages in the vicinity of Bhatbair are known and patronized, at a discount, by Sirkanda men.

DIVISION OF LABOR BY SEX

Paharis work hard to make their living and in return they are able to lead a fairly secure existence. Men, women, and children above the age of about eight years all make their contribution to family economy. The men are the heads of the families and make the decisions in economic matters. Men do all the plowing and other cultivation of fields that is done with animals. They also generally sow the fields. Men market the produce and do the family's trading. They deal with all outsiders and outside agencies, though women, too, participate in buying from peddlers. Men see to the construction and repair of houses and fields; they make and maintain household equipment.

Women cook and care for children. They collect most of the fodder for animals and, with the children, tend the animals most of the time. They take care of the manure, dry it, store it, and are primarily responsible for seeing that the fields are fertilized with it. They carry most of the water for the family and animals. They winnow the grain after it is threshed and prepare it for storage. When the time comes, they prepare the food for cooking. They do unskilled labor in assisting the men in constructing houses, terracing fields, and clearing land.

Men, women, and children all take part in weeding crops, harvesting, and threshing, though men are often engaged in plowing by the time the harvesting and threshing are well under way, and so they participate relatively little in them. Everyone collects firewood. All spin wool into yarn and knit yarn into garments in their free moments.

In the artisan and priestly castes men do the specialized work and women perform nearly the same tasks as do women in exclusively agricultural families. In the tailoring and basketmaking castes they may occasionally help their menfolk do some of the stitching or weaving.

One of the most striking features of Pahari life is how hard the women, in particular, work. Even a person who has been accustomed to plains villages, where women, especially those of the lower castes, are far from idle, cannot help being struck by this feature of Pahari life. Women are almost constantly at work carrying headloads of fodder, firewood, manure, water, grain, flour, and, in building season, rocks and clay—often herding cattle or goats at the same time. They are frequently gone from the village most of the day collecting grass, leaves, or firewood and tending animals in the forest. On moonlit nights at harvest time they often come out to work after the evening meal, from ten to one at night. They are rarely idle. Men too work hard, but the winter and rainy seasons are periods of relative inactivity, and in all seasons except plowing and planting they spend some time sitting, talking, and smoking. Children from an early age help their mothers, engage in herding goats or cattle, look after younger children, bring water, fodder, and firewood, and in the specialist castes learn the traditional trade.

Coöperative Labor

Most work in Sirkanda is done on a family basis or with hired assistance. There is, however, a tradition of coöperative group labor within the community which cuts across lines of kinship and caste. Such voluntary help (called *madat dēnā,* to give help) is undertaken when someone announces that he needs help on a task. On the appointed day all those who are free to do so assemble at the place of work. The only people likely not to participate or to be asked to participate are those who have had a dispute with the person to be helped or with others closely identified with him. The principal occasion for coöperative labor is the transplanting of rice. Occasionally weeding of rice or of other rainy-season crops is done coöperatively. Special songs, vigorous, rhythmic, and heroic in theme, are sung by those who participate in such coöperative agricultural work. Whenever there is a great deal of carrying to be done over considerable distances, coöperative labor may be employed, as when wood, slate, or sheet iron is to be brought for house construction. Roof beams are lifted into place on a new house in this coöperative manner. After the work is completed the "host" serves some refreshment, but no formal obligation to repay is incurred.

Village property, such as the water supply and the trails, are repaired coöperatively when their condition demands. Since Independence there has been a tendency to feel that the government should look after the trails. Governmental attempts at enlisting the voluntary coöperative labor of villagers have met with little or no success, the common complaint being that the government servants who make the requests are paid employees, so they should do the work rather than asking villagers to do it. "What right has a salaried official to ask for voluntary work from others?" "Pay us sixty rupees a month and we'll do voluntary labor willingly." This attitude relates to a larger area of attitudes toward the government to be discussed in chapter 9.

Inheritance

Property is normally passed down within the patrilocal extended family in this area. When a man dies his property goes to his sons as a group. If his wife is living it stays in her custody until her

death or remarriage, at which time it goes to his sons. If a man leaves
no sons and designates no son surrogate, his nearest male relatives
(in order: brothers, father's brothers, father's brother's sons) take their
place in the line of inheritance. This is at variance with Hindu law,
according to Joshi, but it is in accordance with Khasa customary
law:

> The distinct feature of Khasa agnatic succession is that the inheritance
> does not go to an individual, but to a group, which may consist of the male
> descendants of the *propositus* himself or of those of one of his ascendants.
> There is no rule of the nearer agnate excluding the more remote such as is
> found in Hindu law. The sons of a deceased brother take the share which
> their father would have received if he had been alive when the inheritance
> opens. . . . The distinction between undivided brothers or between full
> blood and half blood . . . has no place in Khasa customary law. . . . The
> rules of inheritance are based on the theory that agnates alone are entitled
> to the estate left by a deceased person, and that the ancestral land held by
> a person who has no male descendants reverts to the immediate parent stock
> and is distributable accordingly. (Joshi, 1929, pp. 296 f.)

If there is no son, an adopted son, a daughter's son, or a son-in-law
can be designated to substitute for a son, both in inheritance of property
and in performance of the father's funeral rites. In each of these cases
the heir must come to live in the house of the one from whom he will
inherit (Berreman, 1962e). A son-in-law who assumes this function
lives with his wife's father and is known as a "house son-in-law." Actually the inheritance in such a case remains in the hands of the woman
and ultimately passes on to her sons (or lacking sons, to her lineage
mates) unless a bequest has been made to her husband. However, the
husband has use of the land during his lifetime. This status is embarrassing for the son-in-law in a patrilocal society, but it is sufficiently
advantageous to all concerned that it occurs quite often. Since sib
membership is patrilineal, this arrangement often results in a transfer
of property to another sib. Houses and land in Sirkanda have been
transferred in this manner to sibs other than those in which they were
originally held.[7] If no lineage claimants exist, property reverts to the
village, not the caste. A woman's jewelry is treated as her husband's
property for purposes of inheritance.

Incorporeal property such as jajman or gaikh clients and the hereditary title of *mūkhīā*—a village leader—is inherited similarly.
Where, as with a hereditary title, there is a single, discrete entity to
be passed along, it goes to the eldest son. Where no son is left, incorporeal property, like other property, may go to a near male agnate
or may be assigned to the husband of a daughter who lives in her

father's house, and thence to the daughter's son, or it may go directly to a daughter's son who comes to live in his mother's father's house. Thus the Sirkanda barber inherited his clients from his mother's father. As with corporeal property, the arrangement often results in transfer of the property to another sib.

In this patrilocal society the levirate is practiced: a wife is inherited by her husband's eldest surviving brother or equivalent relative. At least, first claim to her is so inherited and the decision as to whether she will become his real wife, or the wife of another brother, or not, is left to him. If she wishes to marry a nonfamily member (as she often does) she is generally allowed to do so but, unless she runs away (as she also often does) or receives special permission, payment has to be made by the new husband to the family of the deceased husband. When a woman leaves or is left by her husband, her children generally remain with their father's family. In this way property is kept in the patrilocal extended family.

3 THE RELIGIOUS CONTEXT: THE SUPERNATURAL

Most Paharis are Hindus, as evidenced by their own profession of faith and by application of any realistic definition of that term to observation of the behavior they exhibit and the beliefs they profess relating to the supernatural world.[1] D. N. Majumdar (1944, pp. 139 ff.) supports this statement in his discussion of the people of Jaunsar-Bawar: "The Khasas are Hindus; their customary rites in temples, the manner and mode of offering sacrifices . . . periodical festivals . . . all indicate their Hindu origin . . ."

They are not orthodox Hindus. That is, they are not highly Sanskritized or Brahmanical in that they do not adhere closely to written prescriptions and proscriptions of post-Vedic Hinduism (cf. Srinivas, 1952, p. 30; 1956). This unorthodoxy is evidently confusing to many who are familiar with Khasas. Majumdar, a few pages beyond the above-quoted passage wherein he verifies the Hinduism of the Khasas, says:

While the Khasas claim to be Hindus . . . their social life as well as their beliefs and practices connected with their religion do not identify them with the Hindus of the plains. They re-marry their widows, practise levirate, sororate and polyandry, recognize divorce as legal, while inter-marriage between the various Khasa groups is not tabooed and children born of such marriages do not suffer any social stigma. While they worship Hindu gods and goddesses, they have a partiality for ancestor spirits, queer and fantastic demons and gods and for the worship of stones, weapons, dyed rags and symbols. The sun, the moon and the constellations are their gods. (Majumdar, 1944, p. 150)

Paharis themselves are well aware of these deviations from high-caste orthodoxy of the plains, and in fact they often actively try to emulate plains rituals in order to raise their status in the eyes of other Hindus. That their unorthodoxy makes them any the less Hindu is contradicted by a comparison of their own traditions, practices, and beliefs with the range of equivalent traits among village Hindus elsewhere in India (cf. Cohn, 1954, pp. 174 ff.; Dube, 1955, pp. 88 ff.; Lewis, 1958, pp. 197 ff., 249 ff.; P. M. Mahar, 1957, 1960; Marriott, 1955a; Opler, 1958; Planalp, 1956; Srinivas, 1952).

Hinduism in Sirkanda shares virtually all of its forms with that in the rest of Bhatbair, most of its forms with that in Tehri Garhwal, many with that in other Himalayan hill areas, some with that in North India, and fewer with all-India Hinduism.

In this context it is useful to utilize the concept of "spread" of Hinduism and the terms "local Hinduism," "regional Hinduism," and "national Hinduism" (Srinivas, 1952, p. 213). "Spread" refers to the area (horizontal spread) or social groupings in an area (vertical spread) within which traits associated with Hinduism are distributed. ". . . As the area of spread decreases, the number of ritual or cultural forms shared in common increases, as the area increases, the common forms decrease" (Srinivas, 1952, pp. 213 f.).

Morgan (1953, pp. 3 ff.) notes that Hinduism is "ethnic rather than creedal," pointing out the difficulty in distinguishing its essential features in view of its tremendous diversity. Dube indicates something of this diversity and the complexity of beliefs which make up village Hinduism:

A text-book knowledge of the religious lore of India, and an acquaintance with her ancient classics and their modern expositions will hardly give us a true picture of the actual religious beliefs, thoughts, feelings and practices of the people now living in the countryside. A classification of their religious beliefs and rituals is not an easy task. Folklore and myths, religious teachings of saint-poets, and contacts with persons having knowledge of scriptures and popular religious books have all influenced their religious ideology, and consequently their religion is a mixture of animism, animatism and polytheism, with the occasional appearance of monotheism also. To these must be added a living faith in spirits, ghosts, demons, witches and magic. The complex of all these diverse factors constitutes the picture of the supernatural world as it is understood by the people in the countryside. Tenets of classical Hinduism having an all-India spread are mingled with the regional religious beliefs and forms of worship current among the Hindus of the [particular area].

Several cults and worships of a purely local nature add further to the complexity of the beliefs and ritual system of the community. A wide variety of cults is observed by the family, some by the village as a whole; and still others by individual caste groups. (Dube, 1955, p. 88)

Despite its diversity, there is a basic unity to Hinduism by which it may be recognized. Morgan (1953, pp. 6 f.) identifies this as lying in "common scripture, common deities, common ideals, common beliefs, and common practices." Srinivas makes a similar statement and then characterizes the elements of Hinduism according to their spread. He describes all-India Hinduism as "chiefly Sanskritic" in contrast to the more limited spread of most non-Sanskritic elements in regional and local Hinduism. By "Sanskritic," Srinivas means those elements of all-India Hinduism which are recorded in the classic religious literature and are often called Brahmanical or post-Vedic Hinduism by other writers. They are frequently identified as the "great tradition" of Hinduism, while local, regional, and even universal Hindu beliefs and practices which are not included in the "literate religious tradition" are identified as the "little tradition" (Redfield, 1955; Marriott, 1955a).

It is apparent to any student of village religious practices and beliefs that there is a considerable body of non-Sanskritic elements of all-India spread (cf. Berreman, 1961b). Care must be taken not to confuse "little tradition" with "local spread." Many elements of "little tradition" as conventionally defined are regional, national, or greater in extent.

In this chapter religion will be presented in terms of beliefs and practices regarding the supernatural as they were observed and reported in and around Sirkanda. Part of the purpose is to illustrate one variety of the genus village Hinduism. Another is to point out specific examples of the great and little traditions as they manifest themselves in this village and to throw some light on the relevance and limitations of these concepts in the village context. In so doing, the evidence for and the nature of Sanskritization, or change from adherence to the elements of the little tradition to recognition and practice of the elements of the literary tradition of Hinduism will be mentioned. The more immediate purpose, as in the preceding chapters, will be to furnish prefatory material for the discussion of social organization to follow, and to illustrate the functions of kinship, caste, and community ties in the religious sphere of life.

RELIGIOUS BELIEFS

The supernatural is almost as pervasive in the minds of Sirkanda villagers as is the natural, though to an observer it may be less readily apparent. Difficulty of any kind—crop failure, ailing animals, economic reversal, mysterious loss of property, persistent family troubles, disease, sterility, stillbirth, hysteria, death—is attributed ultimately to fate and more immediately to the machination of one or another of a host of supernatural beings. A sizable amount of time, effort, and money is invested in activities designed to influence these beings to tread lightly on the people of Sirkanda. Most of these activities are carried on at the joint-family level, some at the community level, and, in this area, practically none at the caste level.

The supernatural beings who affect humans range from capricious sprites, malevolent ghosts, and ancestral spirits to household, village, and regional gods. On another level is a general belief in inevitable fate (*mūkadar, bhāg*) controlled by a remote, impersonal, and ultimately supreme deity, *Bhagwān* or *Narāyan*. This deity is neither personified nor worshiped. To it is attributed almost any event or circumstance worthy of notice and beyond immediate human control. Such comments as "It is God's will," "God only knows," and "It is in the hands of God," are frequently made by villagers. There is no effective means by which to deal with Bhagwan or his manifestation in fate, although villagers may occasionally direct an appeal for mercy or help to him in a general way, as "God help me." Nevertheless there is lively interest and activity in influencing events by propitiating the many specific deities and other supernatural beings which are thought to control or influence daily life. When the inconsistency which an outsider may see, between belief in inevitable fate and simultaneous efforts to influence or control events, is pointed out to villagers their answers are vague but not defensive because their belief is not threatened. Such inconsistencies are considered irrelevant. One informant affirmed that fate is inevitable, that Bhagwan controls fate and cannot be influenced, but that worship of specific deities is still necessary "because gods are closely associated with fate." And there the matter rests. Evidently it is through gods that fate is accomplished.

The effects of predestined and unalterable fate are everywhere apparent. To demonstrate its importance a villager pointed out that a potter makes many pots that look alike, and yet each has a different subsequent history. That is fate. Similarly, men are born essentially alike but no two lead the same life. The classic example was that of myself. "There are millions of Americans and none of them have ever heard of this small and distant village. There are thousands of villages in India to which no American has ever come. Now you have come to live here. Is not that evidence enough of fate?" Death, disease, disability, poverty, wealth, beauty, travel, marriage—all are attributed to fate or God's will. Weather too is predetermined. Yet these are pre-

cisely the things which villagers seek to control through their worship
of various gods. Late in the dry season I asked a villager when it would
rain. His characteristic reply was: "I do not sit with Bhagwan, nor am
I his brother." But before the week was out he was one of many who
participated in a ceremony calculated to please specific deities who
control the weather and thereby to bring rain. Of course, since everything is controlled by fate, my informant could retreat to the argument
that it was the villagers' fate to carry out such worship with the preordained results.

Closely allied to belief in fate is the belief in reincarnation. It is
believed that the present condition of any being is largely determined
by his deeds in previous lives. "As you sow, so will you reap." Present
deeds influence fate after death and in future lives, but they have no
effect on the present life. An informant commented on the point,

> Fate in life is determined before birth and nothing can alter it. If a man
> has given much gold in charity in a previous life he will in the next life
> be a raja, if he has given grain he will be a money-lender, if he has taught
> others he will be a great leader like Nehru, if he has killed a female or
> thirsty wild animal he will be a leper or blind, if he was a slanderer he
> will be an idiot, if he did not give *ritu dān* [seasonal charity—man's obliga-
> tion to have sexual relations with his wife after her menses each month]
> he will starve sexually.

Disappointments are nearly always rationalized in terms of fate as
determined by misdeeds in previous lives. A Brahmin from the village
nearest to Sirkanda had such an explanation for the nagging, unat-
tractive wife with whom he had been saddled. When his friends asked
him why he was so unfortunate he reflected at length and finally reported that in a previous life he had been a crow and his wife a camel
on whose back he had sat, pecking and worrying her. Now it was her
turn to get revenge. His friends urged him to leave her, but he replied
that he could not as this was his fate and it could not be escaped by
running away.

Low-caste status is always attributed to misdeeds in previous lives,
while people who commit misdeeds in the present are thought to be
ensuring punishment in future lives. The idea of life after death (and
particularly the time between death and reincarnation) is a vague and
confused one to villagers. Many have no systematic conception of what
occurs, and others hold firmly to mutually contradictory views. But all
agree that acts in this life determine the nature of the next life. Punishment for misdeeds may include a long period after death in which
the soul wanders in suffering as a ghost before finding a body in

which to be reborn. Then it may be reborn as a crawling worm or insect, or in an undesirable human condition. A good life is rewarded by rapid transit of the soul to another body so that the cycle of 184 births through which it must pass may be quickly accomplished and the ultimate goal attained—heaven or, according to learned Brahmins, unity with the infinite. The new body will be, in such cases, one that is desirable: if animal, a bird that can fly and enjoy itself; if human, of a high caste, in a pleasant locale with access to good food. Light skin color, beauty, health, wealth, many sons, and happiness are also considered rewards.

Station of birth is, therefore, no accident. A low-caste informant who had probably pondered the matter more than most Sirkanda people, explained:

America and England are pleasant places where everyone is wealthy and comfortable. To deserve such good fortune the citizens of these countries must have been very pious Hindus in their previous lives. On the other hand, in those countries people do many evil things in their lifetimes. They eat meat, especially beef, they eat eggs, they kill people in great wars. It is a very sinful life. After death they must be punished by being reborn in filth, poverty and sorrow—namely, as low-caste people in India.

He felt that this must certainly be the case, though he admitted the circularity of the sequence and had not solved the problem of how one could escape the circle.

The same informant considered birth as a Pahari to be punishment, partly evident in the hard work, poor food, and primitive living conditions which Paharis must endure. Another reason was also given: since nothing in life is chance—all is part of the larger design called fate— to be born in circumstances where sin punishable by low birth is inevitable is in itself a punishment. Thus, to be born a Pahari, where the sin of taking the life of animals in sacrifice is part of regular religious practice demanded by local deities, is not an accident; it is an indirect kind of punishment in that it will lead to further punishment in future lives. God or fate uses it as an excuse for further punishment. The informant referred to this as an "excuse of fate." Perhaps it is consideration of such factors that accounts for the widespread Pahari joke, "When we Paharis die we are reborn on the plains as donkeys." This logic might also explain the peculiar fate of Americans as deduced by the informant. Awareness of punishment in future lives does not lead Paharis to give up animal sacrifice, nor would it prevent them from behaving like other wicked Americans were they to be reborn in America. It is all fate and cannot be altered. Paharis accept their fate philosophically. A blacksmith who had learned from a Brahmin who read his horoscope, that he had been a raja in his previous life and was destined to be a merchant in the next shrugged when asked what he thought of the prospect, and said simply, "I am adaptable."

After a birth a Brahmin is called to read the horoscope of the newborn. This tells with perfect accuracy all that has befallen an individual in past lives and all that will befall him in the present and future lives. Everything pertaining to the individual's past and future is there to be read. Where inaccuracies occur the Brahmin is either incompetent or misinformed. The latter is most often the explanation, as accuracy depends upon precise reporting of time of birth. As the villagers point out, in a community with no clock this is a difficult feat.

Deeds in life which lead to punishment in future lives include failing to give charity, physically hurting others, exploiting others or taking their property, and taking to evil ways—robbery, killing, stealing, cheating, lying, covetousness. Breaking caste rules was not included by informants. Upon inquiry, low-caste informants held that this is a social, not a spiritual, matter, and is to be enforced by man, not God. This is in contrast to traditional Hindu doctrines of caste duty and destiny, doctrines which high-caste people profess. All groups relegated rules regarding incest, exogamy, endogamy, and other sexual behavior to the secular realm.

The things Pahari men aspire for in life regardless of caste include: sufficient money to satisfy wants and a surplus to lend out on interest, good land, good crops, good cattle, hard-working and obedient sons, and profit in whatever transactions are entered into. Stories and anecdotes illustrating the importance of good deeds to reap desired rewards in future lives and, conversely, the dire consequences of evildoing in this life, are many, vivid, and well-known in Sirkanda.

It is within this general context of belief in an impersonal, allpowerful supernatural force called Bhagwan, evidenced in unalterable fate, that other beliefs regarding the supernatural are held in Sirkanda. This is in conformance with the great tradition of Hinduism.

In everyday life in Sirkanda people think about and deal with religion in terms of immediate problems of their welfare and that of their families. The supernatural agents who are closely involved in these matters are personal, personified beings whose behavior influences and can be influenced by people. The effective social unit for dealing with most of these beings is the household. As in economic activity, so in religious worship, the extended family is the most significant element of social organization.

Village religious life in Sirkanda, as elsewhere in India, is primarily concerned with the maintenance of proper relations with supernatural beings who have power over the members of the family and of the village. Their displeasure is easily aroused by neglect and is quickly evident in the several kinds of difficulties, notably illness, which beset their negligent worshipers. Fortunately, they can usually be placated. Their form, origin, and affinities are of less significance to villagers than are their effects and the means to placate them. Some of these beings are gods or goddesses which affect the entire village, or which affect only particular households. Others are ancestral spirits. Other categories of powerful supernaturals are ghosts and sprites. Some of the gods can be traced to the great gods of Hinduism, but others cannot. Some spirits are ghosts of dead relatives or of known types of individuals, while others cannot be traced to specific people or to people at all. These facts are of interest, and are often known, but are of little immediate relevance to the villager. All such beings are active forces which must be recognized and dealt with in specified and often similar ways, or else their subjects will suffer well-known and dreaded consequences.

Before describing the patterns of worship and the exorcism of these beings, it will be well to comment briefly on the phenomena usually described as supernatural possession. Possession is a common occurrence in Sirkanda in the cause, diagnosis, and alleviation of difficulties of many kinds. But it is not a uniform process. Its nature varies with the type of supernatural being involved.

A shaman voluntarily induces his personal familiar spirit to possess him and speak through him to his clients. He does this by chanting certain phrases, playing a drum, and performing other acts pleasing to the spirit. When the spirit leaves it does so without ill effect. Its good will is maintained by the shaman's worship.

Anyone may be possessed by a household deity attracted by the drumming of pujaris during worship of a household god. Such possession results in the deity's dancing in the worshiper's body, and sometimes in his speaking through the worshiper. No one knows who will be possessed, but possession is expected to result from the activities of the pujaris on these occasions.

At village-wide worship, individuals often become possessed by village gods, just as they do by household gods in household worship. Generally the person whom a particular god will possess is known as the traditional vehicle through which that god dances and, more rarely, talks.

In all the above cases the god is attracted by drumming, the rhythm of which induces him to engage in the pleasurable activity of dancing.

One god, *Mēmendīa,* possesses people unexpectedly and then calls for music to dance by. A god's presence is indicated by the behavior of the one he possesses—especially by trembling, rolling of the eyes or fixed staring, insensitivity to touch or pain, incomprehensible speech, and generally uncontrolled behavior. Once a god is present, he is honored with incense, gestures of devotion, and so on.

Such possession is described by a phrase meaning that a god has "come to the head" of his devotee. It is never harmful to the one possessed, and the deity leaves voluntarily. In fact, the possessed person is said to be immune to pain or lasting harm inflicted while he or she is possessed. Gods do harm individuals, but not as a result of possession. A god who is angry will possess his victims only briefly in order to tell them what they must do to appease his anger and to relieve themselves of his punishment.

Harmful possession is of a different order, described as "adherence" of a ghost. It occurs unexpectedly. Usually it can be terminated only by strenuous exorcism by a specialist. Ghosts are not worshiped. Only by forcing the ghost to leave can the harmful effects of such possession be alleviated. The fact of ghost possession is indicated by the harmful effects of the possession—great pain or other inner torment, illness, misfortune, barrenness, stillbirths, mental derangement, physical impairment, or even death. Ghost possession usually follows severe stress on the individual. Calamity, frightening illness, the death of a friend or relative, interpersonal strife, and physical exhaustion immediately preceded cases of such possession in Sirkanda. Possession is a satisfactory explanation or excuse for almost any behavior. The one possessed is an object of solicitude rather than condemnation. Possession therefore appears to be a psychological mechanism used to alleviate stress, to explain otherwise incomprehensible and often taboo behavior. While women are more often subject to this kind of possession than men, it is by no means limited to women.

Some spirits can harm people without possessing them, merely by "striking" them. In the case of one type of sprite, such harm is not malicious nor intended, but once it has occurred it is irreparable. Its only symptom is the harm done, usually a sudden physical, sensory, or mental incapacity.

PATTERN OF WORSHIP

The details of worship of various supernatural beings in Sirkanda vary. There is, however, a basic pattern underlying most worship in the village. In order to make subsequent descriptions clear and variations more obvious, the general pattern of worship will be presented. In outline it bears many similarities to worship by plains villagers.

Most supernatural beings make their presence felt by imposing difficulties or troubles upon people—usually disease or death to people or animals, and sometimes other troubles such as hysteria, faithless spouses, sterility, poor crops, dry cows, financial loss, or mysterious disappearance of belongings. "Above all a prevailing health anxiety is suggested by the data regarding ghost and spirit possession" (Opler, 1958, p. 566). In such cases the householder usually repairs at once to his favorite shaman (bāki), or sometimes to a less prominent practitioner, to find out what is causing the trouble (cf. Berreman, 1964). The only supernaturals regularly worshiped without illness or other difficulty as a signal that worship is demanded, and therefore without the advice of a shaman or other practitioner, are village gods (to be defined below). Such worship follows the pattern to be described here except that consultation with the shaman is omitted. It is relatively infrequent as compared to the worship recommended by shamans, which occurs somewhere in the village every few weeks.

A shaman is a man who may be of any caste and who is devoted to a particular deity for whom he acts as medium in the diagnosis of difficulties. It is from this practice that the shaman makes his living. He generally holds regular sessions which his clients attend. First he conducts a short pūjā (ceremony), and to the beat of a small drum he sings mantrās (prayers or incantations) in honor of the god to whom he is personally devoted. Gradually, as the god takes possession of him, the shaman becomes impervious to pain, often demonstrating this by touching red-hot metal or by some similar action. The god when in complete charge speaks and acts in the body of the shaman. The god then singles out the various waiting clients one at a time and tells each what troubles he has had and what the cause is, that is, what supernatural being has been tormenting him, and what should be done to alleviate the trouble. The god may also identify human thieves or other culprits and point out objects that have deleterious magical effects. If the victim is not satisfied with the diagnosis he will merely say "The god knows better than I," and go elsewhere for advice until he finds a shaman who seems to have a more accurate god.

The treatment recommended by a shaman is almost invariably performance of a puja in honor of the offending supernatural being, or exorcism if it is a ghost. In cases of theft the shaman will merely identify the guilty party. In cases of magical affliction he may identify the offending object and recommend its removal. Treatment may also be a pilgrimage or other specific action designed to please the god. In some very difficult afflictions, such as apparently incurable insanity, an impossible recommendation may be made, such as sacrifice of a cow which, as Hindus, these people cannot carry out. The necessary puja is usually a stereotyped one for the particular deity to be honored. Sometimes the shaman may have specific recommendations as to how, when, or where the worship should be conducted. The shaman's main functions are to identify the cause of the trouble and to specify what action must be taken to alleviate it or to contact the being responsible in order to hear his demands. From then on the family of the victim takes steps to carry out the shaman's recommendations, for which special practitioners are required. In this respect the Pahari shaman differs from the shaman of the plains reported by Opler (1958) and by Planalp (1956). The plains shaman, with the help of his personal spirit, induces a god or spirit which has entered the body of its victim to make known its demands. Among Paharis the shaman does not take part in exorcism or in ceremonies in which the god speaks through its victim and is ultimately appeased. The Pahari shaman is primarily a diagnostician who is able to call upon his personal god at will, become possessed by him, and then diagnose the difficulties of his clients through the wisdom of the god. The Pahari sequence is virtually identical with the shamanism of a Mysore village reported by Harper (1957, pp. 268 ff.).

Some exorcists of ghosts (not bakis) function in a fashion similar to that of the plains shamans in that they perform both the diagnosis and exorcism, sometimes with the help of their own god. However, such practitioners are less frequently consulted and their advice is less valued. As often as not a shaman is consulted first, and he may direct his client to one of these practitioners to perform the exorcism. Malevolent ghosts are quite distinct from gods and ancestors and will be described later. The discussion which follows applies to gods and ancestors only.

Sometimes worship of a god or ancestor is held without first consulting a shaman. A less powerful diviner may be consulted because he is more easily available or has a reputation for accuracy. Occasionally no specialist is consulted at all, when the victims feel certain they know which god is responsible for their difficulty, either because of experience with similar past affliction or because of an unfulfilled vow. Worship may also be held to fulfill a vow before trouble has come to compel its performance.

Vows are often made to gods and are a frequent antecedent to worship. If a puja or other propitiatory act which has been recommended by a shaman cannot be performed at once for reasons of economy or conflicting obligations, a vow may be taken to perform it within a certain period. The vow has the same efficacy as performance of the puja itself provided that it is fulfilled. Trouble of any kind may be met by such a vow even, in some cases, without a shaman's advice. Whether or not a shaman is consulted, the vow itself is made without the services of a specialist.

In order to carry out the pujas, most of which are undertaken on the advice of a shaman, one or more often two practitioners who specialize in performing worship for particular gods or classes of gods must be called. These pujaris (or a pujari and his assistant) arrange and perform the puja at the request of the family who is to sponsor it.[2] The purpose of the puja is to ensure that the god is pleased or at least has a chance to possess one of his victims, dance in the victim's body, and through that person make known any further demands. It is a family member, never a specialist, who becomes possessed during the performance. These specialists may be of any caste, but usually they come from the low castes. They play percussion accompaniment for the dancing that is a part of every such performance and that brings the god to possess his worshipers. In fact, particular types of pujaris are known by the term for the kind of drum they play, which in turn is determined by the god they worship. For some village gods, Brahmin priests act as pujaris in that they perform the worship, and low-caste people merely play the drums for dancing.

The ceremonial proceedings in such worship are in three major parts: the dance, the puja, and the offering. The entire sequence usually takes place before the shrine of the deity to whom it is dedicated, which is either in the house or somewhere in or around the village.

Preparing the shrine is a simple process because, though it is neglected in the months or years intervening between occasions of worship, it is so simple as to require little arranging. The shrine generally consists of one to four simple iron tridents (tirsūl) of varying shapes, about eight inches in height, made by the local blacksmith. These are placed in a niche in the wall of an inner room if the shrine is a household one, or at the base of a large stone or in a stone enclosure if it is outdoors. During the ceremonies the shrine is illuminated by a small oil lamp, and often a container of grain and a few coins are placed by it. Sometimes a small bag filled with rice and coins is hung near the shrine. Such accouterments are in the nature of offerings to the deity.

The first stage of worship is the dance (kālrātrā, literally "black night" or "night for Kali"). It is intended to attract the gods or ancestors who like to dance and who can do so in the bodies of humans.

This in itself is pleasing to the gods. It also induces them to speak and air their complaints and demands if they wish to do so. Usually dancing occurs during an evening and again the following day. The puja to one god requires seventeen dances over a period of nine days.

A kalratra or dance begins late in the evening of the appointed day, when householders, onlookers, and specialists assemble by the shrine. The pujaris begin to play their instruments, and one of them chants or sings sacred mantras (prayers or incantations) honoring the deity. During this time the god in whose honor the worship is being held, and often other gods and ancestral spirits as well, come and gradually possess people. The room is filled with onlookers, smoke, and heat, and it reverberates with the compelling rhythm of the drums. Gradually one or more members of the household and sometimes others as well begin to move in time to the drums, then to jerk, shout, and finally to dance, first gently and then wildly as they become possessed by a god. This period is called "awakening." The possessed person is honored with incense and religious gestures and is fed boiled rice because he or she is a manifestation of the god at that time. The dancing continues, with occasional breaks for smoking and talking, far into the night. Some people dance who are not possessed, or, if so, only temporarily. The same god may possess several people in sequence in one evening.

Village gods are worshiped outdoors, usually at the dancing ground adjacent to the *Pāndavas'* temple (to be discussed below), but sometimes near *Dēvī's* temple. At that time any village god or gods may possess individual villagers. Household gods do not possess people on these occasions. In contrast to the nature of possession by household gods, there is one particular individual whom each village god usually possesses. Most often village gods utilize the state of possession merely to dance, but they may speak if they wish to.

After the god has danced his fill, usually on the last night of the kalratra, he may leave or may choose to speak. If the latter, the dancer becomes immobile, speaks unintelligibly ("It sounds like English," asserted one informant), and then begins to answer questions put to him. This stage is simply called "questioning." The god tells the cause of his anger and the action necessary by the victimized household to appease that anger. Usually he demands a goat or other sacrifice, but sometimes he asks for a more elaborate puja. The god also gives advice, solves dilemmas, and issues warnings and ultimatums. When he is through, he so states, the drums of the pujaris beat briefly, the god departs, and the session is over. The possessed person shows no after-effects and does not remember the period of possession, although I noted that some showed a remarkable ability to recall the number and subject matter of photographs taken during possession.

Shortly after the god has left, the pujari and the victimized members perform a short ceremony or puja in the god's honor, and then make an offering. The offering to be made, usually a young male goat, is placed before the shrine and rice is thrown on its back by the household members as the pujari chants mantras. When the goat shakes itself, this is taken as evidence that the god has accepted the offering. Thereupon the animal is taken outside and beheaded—usually but not always by some low-caste person, as high-caste people consider this somewhat defiling and prefer not to do it. Then a foot and the head of the animal and some delicacies such as bread and sweet rice are placed before the shrine as offerings for the god. Afterwards the pujari takes these items along with his fee of Rs. 1.25. The rest of the animal is divided among the participating householders and observers.

The efficacy of worshiping gods to combat difficulties is not doubted by most villagers, and many cases of miraculous results are cited in support of their belief. One teen-age boy professed disbelief until his father, sick with pneumonia, began to breathe more easily as soon as the practitioner began his mantras. In the boy's words, "I never believed until I saw it work on my father. A dying man was saved by mantras to the god. That is proof." Another informant replied to my question as to the effect of such a puja in his household: "Of course it worked. We satisfied the god's every demand, didn't we?" On the occasion of an elaborate and difficult puja, an informant commented: "Why not go to all this trouble? It gets results. Gods are like lawyers; the more you give them, the more they will do in your behalf."

The intended result of these observances is to alleviate difficulties attributed to deities, or in the case of worship of some village gods, to ensure their continued good will. An important latent function is that of providing entertainment, relaxation, and social intercourse for the spectators. At the same time they reinforce ties of kinship and village solidarity. There are few recreational activities for these hard-working, isolated people, and the occurrence of a puja of some sort every few weeks is a welcome break in routine. It is also one of the few occasions upon which there is widespread involvement in a common activity. Every such event involves participation of a group of kinfolk or of the entire village, and it plays to a full house of all castes including a large proportion of women and children who have less access to varied experience and entertainment than do men. The behavior of the audiences at such exercises is very similar to that of cinema audiences in the big towns of the valley. They smoke, talk, wander in and out, and generally enjoy the show.

More than once informants implied that a particular puja was held by someone (not of their own household) largely as an excuse to kill a goat and have a feast. Generally when a puja is to be held people lay in a supply of liquor, the perennial accompaniment of meat at Sirkanda "parties." A kalratra for village gods, as distinguished from household gods, is largely a social and recreational occasion for participants and spectators alike, and only occasionally does a god seize the opportunity to talk or make demands of villagers. More often the gods merely enjoy this opportunity to dance, and many of the dancers participate without benefit of supernatural possession.

The nature of worship of the gods honored in most of these pujas is definitely placative. It consists of efforts to appease angry deities, to cater to their cravings for worship and sacrifice.

The truth is that popular religion in these hills is a worship of fear. . . . When famine and pestilence stalks abroad, village temples are crowded and promises of oblations are made; if the evil be averted these promises are fulfilled, if not the deity is frequently abused and his shrine is neglected. The efforts of all are directed to appease the malevolence of these spirits who are supposed to lie in wait to take advantage of any error willingly or unwillingly committed. . . . (Atkinson, 1884a, p. 839)

Villagers themselves sometimes describe their worship as motivated by fear. One man asserted, "If a god can do no harm, it has no power and need not be worshiped." Another commented, "All gods are bad, but *Nār Singh* and *Agornāth* are the most terrible of all." Most gods are feared for the power they have to punish men who incur their wrath. The exceptions are certain village gods, to be discussed below. Even they have the power to punish, but they are primarily benevolent. The prevalence of disease, untimely death, and unpredictable misfortune stands as a constant reminder of this power. Fear of gods is continually reinforced by attribution to them, especially by shamans and diviners, of almost every misfortune that occurs. If a god whose worship depends on fear fails to make his power felt by punishing people, he is rarely or never worshiped and is soon forgotten. Anxiety is maintained by the fact that misfortune often strikes where it is least expected. However, though fear is an important motive, it is not helpless fear. Gods do not punish randomly or capriciously. They punish when punishment is due. The offense is generally unintended and is often unknown or unrecognized, but a shaman can usually detect it. Most often the offense has been that of neglecting the god—failing to worship adequately. The offense may have been one against the god or against one of his devotees; the essential thing is that the god has interpreted it as an action or oversight deserving of punishment. The victim is not helpless. In fact, he has at his disposal extremely effective means of appeasement, which are sometimes difficult and often expensive, but are rarely beyond the realm of possibility. The efficacy of these means is attested by the many spectacular successes people recall, the routine reliance upon them, and the readily available alternative explanations for apparent failures.

Therefore, Sirkanda villagers do not lead a life dominated by helpless terror of the gods they worship. Observation of worship reveals a range in individual attitudes from relative indifference to enthusiasm, from apprehension to confidence. It seems that gods are treated much as are powerful people. They are feared insofar as it is well known that their anger can lead to serious consequences. On the other hand, it is known that the means to prevent or assuage their anger are at hand and are often easily put into play, as is not often the case in dealing with powerful secular forces. The prevailing attitude is one of respectful awareness of what are conceived to be the realities of life in a world where ultimate powers are in the hands of divine beings, whose anger is easily and often unwittingly aroused, but whose demands are communicated to their subjects and can usually be met. Worship is the means by which these dangerous beings are controlled.

Gods

By far the most active class of supernatural beings in Sirkanda are the gods and goddesses (devtā, devī) or, as they are sometimes referred to in English, the godlings. Gods indigenous to Sirkanda are referred to in the village as ghar kā devtā (household gods) or kul devtā (family gods) and are thereby distinguished from gods of other villages and other regions. Any god to which local people are devoted is isht devtā. These terms are used loosely and often interchangeably in the village. However, an analytic distinction can be drawn to categorize deities in Sirkanda as household gods and village gods. Household gods will here be defined as those gods worshiped consistently by the members of a particular household as a group, usually within the house, where the shrines are kept, and not worshiped jointly with the members of other households, nor with the aid of Brahmin priests. Devotion to these gods is passed down in the lineage. Village gods are those gods worshiped jointly by all or nearly all villagers at some central shrine called a temple (mandir) in or near the village. The worship is usually

under the supervision of a local Brahmin priest. One worships these
particular village gods because he is a Sirkanda villager. Other differences between these two categories of gods will be mentioned in the
course of discussion of each class. This dichotomy is not commonly, if
at all, noticed by villagers, though it is evident to the observer of religious behavior in the village. Neither is it a rigid distinction. Some
household gods have gradually shifted to become essentially village
gods. Some village gods have been adopted as household gods by one or
two families. Occasionally particular households worship village gods
individually at their village shrines. Certain village gods are not worshiped by every household. Some household gods in Sirkanda are village gods in other areas, and vice versa. A distinction is, however, useful for purposes of presentation. In the beginning it is usually the god
himself, speaking through a shaman or some other person, who directs
the type of shrine and worship to be given him.

Household Gods

Six major household gods are worshiped in Sirkanda homes: *Nār
Singh, Manglīā, Gaurīl, Nāg Rājā, Agornāth,* and *Dhagbairū.*[3] Each
of these gods is worshiped by certain households and not by others.
Thus, of the 45 Sirkanda households, 41, none of whom are Brahmins
or Bajgis, worship Nar Singh; 28, all Rajputs, worship Manglia; 13 (1
Brahmin, 7 Rajputs, 1 blacksmith, and 4 Bajgis) worship Gauril; 13,
all Rajputs, worship Nag Raja; 3, all Bajgis, worship Agornath; 2
Rajput households worship Dhagbairu. These gods appear in villages
throughout the area. Not every village contains households worshiping
each of them, and some have households worshiping other gods, but
the pattern is the same and none of these deities is unique to a particular village. Every household which worships one of these gods,
except some of those worshiping Nar Singh and Nag Raja, has a
shrine, called "god's place," dedicated to that god, and usually the
shrine is inside the house. In those houses worshiping more than one
god, which includes all but five of the 45 in Sirkanda, separate shrines
are kept for each god. When joint families divide, each new household
unit sets up its own shrines to the family gods.

Household gods are the most acutely feared gods worshiped in
Sirkanda. They are worshiped as long as, and to the extent that, they
demonstrate their power and interest by tormenting household members and placing demands upon them. Each is usually worshiped in
ceremonies directed exclusively to him and calculated to alleviate
trouble attributed to him by a shaman. The god has generally been
displeased by neglect of worship or unfulfilled vows. However, trouble

may also stem from a plea to the god by one of his devotees who wishes to inflict harm. A god can be induced, by worship, sacrifice, or vows, to attack one's enemy if the enemy is either a nonworshiper or a less faithful worshiper of that god. The victim learns the cause of his trouble by consulting a shaman. To alleviate the attack, the victim must worship the god. If he is not already a devotee of the god, he must worship that god in some house where there is a shrine—and generally no other household wants to become involved with the god's wrath—or else he must set up a shrine of his own, in his own house. Then he becomes the god's devotee and must continue to worship him because the god thereafter frequents his house.

Three recent cases were reported in Sirkanda, in each of which a wife found that her husband was having illicit sexual relations with another woman. Thereupon the aggrieved wife verbally abused the other woman in public. In response to this abuse the other woman set her household god's wrath upon the wife. A puja to that god therefore had to be performed in the house of the wife, and her husband thereby acquired a new household god. In another case a policeman was set upon by the god of a household whose members he had apprehended for selling diluted milk. He had to worship their god, thereby acquiring him as a household god, and to reimburse them. These examples, in addition to their relevance to an understanding of village religion, provide an interesting indication of attitudes on sex and interpersonal relations (to be discussed in chapter 5).

The most common source of a new god in a household is a bride, who usually comes from another village. Her household god frequently goes or is sent with the girl to her new home and protects her interests there. Such a god is known as *mathwā dēvtā*, as distinguished from the *ghar kā dēvtā* that already frequents the household. If the bride is mistreated in her new home or if her family is slighted at the wedding or in subsequent situations, the god will attack the family of the groom. This may happen at any time after marriage. Then it is necessary for the groom's family to placate the god by worship. If the god is one not already worshiped in the house, a new shrine must be set up for him and thereafter he is a household god, although at kalratra he will usually possess only the bride and will voice his demands through her. Later he may possess her daughters-in-law or other female relatives.

A household god may also be acquired if a shaman diagnoses some misfortune as the work of a god who has not previously been worshiped or even known in the household he has attacked, and who is not acting on behalf or at the bidding of a worshiper. The god simply demands attention and utilizes this means to acquire it. In any event, the result is the same in that the god must be worshiped to be appeased. He then acquires a shrine, bringing occasional trouble and demanding occasional worship.

Therefore, although most of the household gods currently worshiped in Sirkanda have been in the families of their worshipers for several generations, the acquisition of new gods is not an unusual event. Several informants remembered when their families began to worship current household gods. Likewise, as interest in old gods is lost, they lose significance and are finally forgotten. When new houses are built or families separate, the members will not bother to devote shrines to ineffectual gods, while in the old family home those shrines may be ignored. Some Sirkanda villagers remember that their immediate ancestors worshiped none or only some of the present gods, but most are unable to specify which ones were worshiped previously.

A special household ceremony is performed to protect a new house and its occupants from alien gods and spirits. It is similar in purpose to the village-protection rite to be mentioned below, but it protects the household group rather than the village. It is called literally, "house pot." In the ceremony an all-night puja is performed in which a pot containing certain sacred items is sealed into the house wall, where it remains to protect the household from disease, accident, violent death, financial reversal, and crop failure.

Other ceremonies associated with the house and household members are those performed by carpenters when they place doorframes and the ornamental archways in a new house, and those performed by Brahmins to purify a house after pollution by violent death or by occupation by low-caste people, anthropologists, and the like. All assure the future well-being of those who occupy the dwelling, and inhibit the depredations of alien supernaturals. The only occasion upon which Brahmin priests regularly participate in worship of household gods is during the marriage ceremony, when the good will of the gods is secured by invoking a brief blessing.

Village Gods

There are seven shrines in Sirkanda devoted to what are here termed village gods. All are in the immediate vicinity of Sirkanda, the most distant being that to *Mātrī* a half-mile away on the crest of the hill which dominates the village (map 3).

All village gods are worshiped at village temples (mandir) rather than in the home, and usually a Brahmin conducts the worship rather than a low-caste pujari. Village gods are distinguished from household gods primarily by this greater honor and by the fact that their relevance and worship is not household-specific. Some may have begun as household gods, but they have not remained as such. All village gods can be and occasionally are worshiped by all or nearly all villagers. A few households, lineages, or sibs are partial to certain village gods and not to others, but there is not the pattern of household devotion or non-devotion found with household gods. Several temples are identified with particular lineages whose members are temple keepers, maintaining the temple, supervising worship there, and receiving offerings on behalf of the god, but worship at a village temple is not private or limited to particular households.

Worship of village gods does not follow a uniform pattern to the extent found among household gods, though the same elements of worship occur—kalratra, puja, sacrifice. The worship of village gods tends not to be as specific or mutually exclusive as that of household gods. Often several village gods are worshiped together in a single ceremony. Each village god possesses some villager at ceremonies in his honor and often at other village-wide ceremonies. Most village gods possess the same individual each time they appear. When that individual dies they usually shift to another member of the same lineage, sib, or clan, but sometimes they shift even to another caste. The god's possession of an individual is thought to be auspicious for the whole village, not merely or even especially for that individual's lineage or household as in the case of household gods. Village gods speak to their worshipers less frequently than household gods and torment them less, usually being content to dance occasionally in their bodies.

Village gods can inflict troubles on their worshipers, but they are less cantankerous and hence less feared than household gods. Worship of them does not depend upon fear of the consequences of failure to worship to the extent that is true of household gods. While most village gods are sometimes worshiped to alleviate specific difficulties which according to a shaman's diagnosis they have imposed or can counteract, they are often worshiped simply to maintain the *status quo* of village life. Thus, they figure in periodic worship and that performed in stereotyped situations, as well as in worship indicated by a shaman's diagnosis. Finally, they are more permanent than household gods in the village pantheon. Household gods come and go; village gods rarely do so, partly because they are not so dependent on a shaman's advice for their continued relevance to village life, and partly because they enjoy village-wide interest and support which is less fickle and less subject to alteration by happenstance and petty disagreements.

As with worship of other supernatural beings, worship of village gods is influenced by shamans because they can attribute difficulty to these gods. However, most troubles are attributed to household gods—perhaps because most difficulties strike household units—and so shamans are less vital in trends of worship of village gods.

Among village gods there are differences of form and function that are worth pointing out and using as classificatory criteria.[4] The classification used here is arbitrary, its recommendation being that it permits orderly presentation and comparison. Two village gods, *Mēmendīā* and *Bhartwālī*, are comparable to household gods in several respects, and so they can be grouped to form a class of "household-like" village gods, on the borderline between these two categories, just as Nar Singh and Nag Raja are household gods bearing similarities to village gods. These two village gods are worshiped to avoid or counteract difficulties which they may inflict on the village. Like household gods they are respected to the extent that they are thought capable of inflicting punishment. Bhartwali is said by some to be *Bharat*, described in the *Ramayana* as the brother of Ram, who is an incarnation of Vishnu. The temple keeper for Bhartwali is the local Brahmin priest. Memendia, like several village gods, has no specific temple keeper.

A similar god is *Raghunāth*, the only god to whom a real temple building is dedicated in the village. He is worshiped by all village brides and grooms, at the time of their wedding, under the supervision of a Brahmin priest and with the aid of the Rajput temple keeper whose family built the temple three or four generations ago. The god is also worshiped by the entire village at the crop ceremony and at almost any ceremony honoring village gods. Like the paramount gods described below, he is likely to dance in the body of a particular person—in his case a Rajput woman—at village-wide kalratras. In addition, Raghunath inflicts punishment on particular households. Two Rajput households worship him at the temple in a fashion and under circumstances similar to those under which a household god is worshiped. He is the most dangerous village god and is among the most powerful. It appears that he is becoming one of the paramount gods of the village. A few villagers identify him with Shiva, but in the region he is usually identified as the grandfather of Ram, an incarnation of Vishnu. Another of Vishnu's incarnations (*Pārasū Rām*) is said to be separately depicted in the Raghunath temple. *Bhairū*, a god associated with Shiva, is also said to be represented in this temple.

One village god, *Lhēsānīā*, is specific to an age group, children. He is associated with the coming of spring and is honored at that time by children. He is not feared because he does not inflict punishment.

Two village gods are primarily associated with agriculture, crops, and weather. These are Matri, evidently a form of mother goddess, and *Bhūiā*, god of the soil. They are worshiped to ensure success in agriculture, often in ceremonies including offerings to both of them as well as to Devi or other village gods.

Two village gods, *Dēvī* and the Pandavas, are paramount in Sirkanda, in that they are distinctly more highly regarded by most villagers than are other gods. They are worshiped on a wide variety of occasions for many purposes, and their worship is of more general interest than that of other gods. Together they receive village-wide worship at most important ceremonies. They are appealed to in times of village-wide trouble and are honored to ensure success or good fortune in the village. They are thought of primarily as protectors who deserve honor rather than tormentors who must be placated. These gods are thought to take a special interest in Sirkanda and its people, and to have had a particularly intimate association with it in the past. Consequently, the villagers feel closely identified with them. Part of being a Sirkanda villager, as distinguished from being a member of another village, is this identification which cuts across all other divisions within the village. At the same time, these gods' relationships to individuals and families in the village are usually not as specific and personal as those of household gods. They are, to a greater extent than other gods, identified with the welfare of the entire village. In some contexts they are even identified with broader entities such as the residents of Bhatbair, or Paharis, or even mankind. They are more closely identifiable with "all-India Hinduism" than are most gods of this region.

Devi is a local version of the Hindu mother goddess, *Dūrgā*. A temple to her, 15 miles to the northeast, is the most important temple in western Tehri Garhwal. She is honored in a small temple in Sirkanda as a sort of village patroness. She dances in the body of a village woman at nearly all occasions of worship of village gods and assumes special significance in ceremonies having to do with the crops and weather. Such ceremonies are carried out at her temple. She therefore forms something of a link between "agricultural" and "paramount" village gods. She traditionally possesses the barber's wife at public ceremonies. The barber's family now worships her as a household god, in their home.

Sītala Dēvī, the smallpox goddess of the plains, is known to Sirkanda villagers, but no shrine or worship in her honor is found in the area, perhaps because smallpox is rare and of little interest to people in these hills. Apparently she is assimilated with Devi in the minds of villagers.

The most honored deities or complex of deities in Sirkanda, and as

important as Devi in Bhatbair and the surrounding Pahari area, are
the five Pandava brothers and their common wife *Draupadi* (locally
Drōptī), whose story is told in the Hindu religious epic *Mahabharata*
where they are described as having lived in these very hills. Every
village of the area has its shrine to the Pandavas. Adjacent to this shrine
is the village's ceremonial center, a small open area called *māDān*
(in Hindi, *maidān*, field) but frequently described by village folk
etymology as *mānān* from the verb "to please," "because that is where
we please the gods." Here most village dances and public ceremonies
are held and here all village gods take the opportunity to dance in the
bodies of their worshipers, but the Pandavas are the gods most directly
honored at the madan. The Pandavas' puja is the most important village ceremony. It comprises part of almost all village religious activities,
including the all-important village protection and boundary rite known
as *Mundkīlē*. This ceremony is devoted to worship of the Pandavas
and a number of other village gods, prominent among whom is Devi.
Its immediate aim is to protect the village as an entity by excluding
malevolent ghosts and alien gods from its boundaries. (Described in
detail in Appendix IB, first edition.) It is usually financed by village
subscription, though in some circumstances a well-to-do family may
sponsor it. In any case participation and benefit is village-wide. Although most village gods play a part in the ceremony, it is considered
by villagers to be primarily for the Pandavas. In it we find evidence of
the interrelation of village gods and of their distinctness from household gods. Household gods do not appear during this ceremony. In
face, they do not appear at all during worship of village gods, although
the reverse occasionally happens. Not infrequently one household god
appears during the worship of another, just as village gods appear at
one another's pujas.

A god of importance comparable to Devi and the Pandavas in this
area, but not in Sirkanda village, is *Mahāsū*. This god, often identified
as *Mahādēv* or Shiva, but distinct from Shiva in the minds of most
villagers, is the paramount god in some neighboring villages (cf. Saksena, 1955, pp. 40 ff.). Mahadev, whether equated to Mahasu or not, is
consistently identified with Shiva, and like Mahasu is a major god in
the area. He is worshiped in a number of ceremonies, the most elaborate
of which is the spectacular rope-sliding feat peculiar to the Himalayas
and known as *bēdāRat* (cf. Berreman, 1961). When this is performed
in the region, Sirkanda villagers attend and seek the blessing of the
god (and his wife *Pārbatī*), even though they do not worship him.

It is important to note that there is wide variation among villagers in interpretation, practice, and reported practice in all ceremonies, the more so the more complex they are. The ceremonial sequence, number of sacrifices, and alleged objectives are not consistent. This variation was especially evident in the Mundkile ceremony, where even the participants differed in their explanations of what was going on (cf. Marriott, 1955a).

Pilgrimage

Pilgrimages are frequently undertaken for reasons similar to those motivating worship of village or household gods. A person suffers from some trouble or disease such as, in one recent case, weeping ulcers. A shaman is consulted and advises the sufferer to worship at a particular holy place, in this case Kedarnath. The person vows to do so and sacrifices a goat to his god, whereupon he recovers. At the first opportunity he undertakes the journey to fulfill the vow. People also go merely to see the temple or to give charity there in order to attain credit toward the next life. A number of middle-aged high-caste men of Sirkanda have been on pilgrimages to Hardwar, Kedarnath, Badrinath, and a few to distant Gaya. At least one woman and one low-caste man have been to Badrinath. Many tales of the wonders of these holy places and the miracles which regularly occur at them are current in the village as the result of reports brought back by pilgrims or traveling ascetics and priests. The fewer villagers who have seen a place, the more numerous and amazing are the stories. Many villagers—about twenty-five men—have been to Hardwar to bathe in the Ganges or attend funeral rites, and there is relatively little lore about it, but there are many stories of the wonders of remote Kedarnath.

Equally current, among low-caste people, are the stories of discrimination, disappointment, and denial of access to these places experienced by their caste-fellows who have made the trip, despite official denial of such practices. The one village blacksmith who had gone to Kedarnath nonplussed the priests by his presence (fellow pilgrims had complained) and was not allowed access to the temple. Eventually he was shown the temple padlock and told to worship that.

Closer and less prominent temples such as that to Devi at Kuddu Kal and several in nearby sections of the valley are occasionally visited in order to fulfill vows or contribute charity. Caste discrimination at these, as in fact at the Raghunath temple in Sirkanda, is as strict as at the large and famous shrines. Post-Independence laws and pronouncements regarding nondiscrimination in access to temples have been unenforced and totally ignored in this part of India.

Gods of the Great Tradition

Concepts and deities contained in the great religious literature of India are known to Sirkanda villagers as a result of their own traditions and of outside contacts. Traveling priests and ascetics occasionally stop in the village and recite religious works and stories. Residents of the village occasionally attend religious celebrations such as *Ram Lila,* the annual dramatization of the religious epic, *Ramayana,* which is held in towns and villages of the valley. They also attend fairs, moving pictures, and ceremonies held in the larger centers. Much of the knowledge so acquired does not readily penetrate into the daily thought and action of these people because of the imperfect manner in which it is communicated and the alien context in which it is acquired. Among Paharis, plains (*dēsī*) beliefs and practices are often considered sophisticated and even worthy of emulation, but, as they are observed in casual contacts with plains people, they usually seem alien and inapplicable to the Pahari context. More potent sources of such knowledge are the local schoolteacher, villagers who have gone to school outside the village, and especially practicing Pahari Brahmins, all of whom communicate plains Hinduism in a Pahari idiom.

There are devout and learned Brahmins in Tehri Garhwal, among them Har Nam, who counts most high-caste Sirkanda households among his clients. Such Brahmins read standard Sanskritic Hindu literature and utilize the standard procedures described therein in their ceremonial duties. In some areas they have reportedly contributed to a high degree of emulation of plains Hinduism. Har Nam, on his visits to Sirkanda, is without doubt the most vocal advocate of plains Hinduism in the village. The influence of such people in Sirkanda has been insufficient to alter significantly many of the basic beliefs or practices of villagers, but they have not been without effect. Superficial familiarity with certain deities and concepts identifiable with the "great tradition" but alien to the hills has resulted from the influence of these Brahmins, among others. Its superficiality is indicated by the fact that many of these deities and concepts are not integrated into the religious life of the village or region.

On the other hand, some aspects of the great tradition are an old and integral part of Pahari Hinduism. The story of the *Mahabharata,* including especially the Pandava brothers and their wife, their allies, and their enemies, is an example. The god Shiva, relatively recent in Hinduism but now universal, may even have originated as a Pahari god. Belief in fate and reincarnation, practice of certain annual and life cycle ceremonies, and many other religious features could extend this list. Many of these great traditional elements are as old as Pahari culture, which like all cultures is constantly changing and adding elements. In any case they confirm the Hinduism of these people and their ancestors, but they do not alter the fact of its regional distinctiveness nor the significance of its deviations from plains orthodoxy.

Beliefs and knowledge of such aspects of the great tradition as cosmology and the origin of man and the universe vary with the experience of individuals. Broadly they conform to ideas held by village Hindus elsewhere in India. Some village Brahmins have read or heard religious works and the explanations given therein. People who have attended schools have heard the teachers' explanations, which are likewise based upon the great tradition, with a smattering of Western science. Everyone has heard Brahmins or others give various explanations along these lines. Most villagers, however, simply have no consistent or fixed opinions on these subjects. If asked they will repeat stories they have heard which are widespread in India, such as that the earth was created when an egg broke in half forming the earth from one half and the sky from the other, and that the earth is held on the horns of an ox. The problem is apparently not relevant to most villagers.

It is possible to identify among the deities of local significance in Sirkanda evidence of relationship to prominent gods in the literary tradition of Hinduism. These relationships are often vague, sometimes not extending beyond the similarity of name or form. To many villagers such relationships are largely or totally unknown, while to others, though known, they are ignored or their significance is virtually nil. To educated people and especially to practicing priests these relationships are known and often magnified. The trend toward emulation of plains Hindus and the attendant self-consciousness about local tradition on the part of educated people leads to the adoption of explanations for local beliefs and practices in terms of all-India and regional Hinduism where these probably did not previously exist and are unrecognized by most of the people.

Four or five high-caste families in Sirkanda are alleged to own copies of one or more classic religious works, but they read these rarely if at all and none of them holds regular readings or worship. No Sirkanda family has religious pictures or objects other than shrines to local gods. The traditional Brahmin or purohit for the village (who lives in another village) does possess religious pictures representing gods of the great literary tradition, but he pays little attention to them or to their meaning.

The effect of educated Brahmins is greatest in the conspicuous aspects of plains Hinduism—in getting villagers to Sanskritize their cere-

monies, particularly the marriage ceremony, and to observe some of
the periodic all-India festivals. At the same time they have achieved
some success in getting these Paharis to conceal some of their more
flagrantly non-Sanskritic practices from outsiders, by communicating
to them most of the responses and behaviors necessary to gain the approval of plains Hindus. There is a general self-conscious reluctance
among many Paharis, especially those of high caste, to discuss their
ritual and religious practices, their marital regulations, and so on, and
a tendency to present these as being closer to Hindu orthodoxy than
they actually are. Here acceptability by high-caste non-Paharis and
educated Paharis has been a major goal, and sophisticated Brahmins
have been among its most active advocates. They have attempted to
counteract the derisive connotation which the term "Pahari" and especially "Pahari Brahmin" holds for many non-Pahari Hindus. It is
toward the same goal that educated and prominent Paharis are striving
when they recall and extol the sacred heritage of the high-caste hill
people of this area. For these purposes conspicuous aspects of practice
are more important than subtle aspects of belief. The religious and
social changes in Sirkanda have been in the direction of the efforts of
those who wish to bring about more of these outward changes.

Crooke refers to the all-India spread of this process:

If the chief of a forest tribe becomes for the sake of respectability an
orthodox Hindu, he brings with him his tribal or village god, who becomes
an incarnation of Vishnu or a manifestation of Siva. If a village shrine gains
a reputation for miraculous cures of spirit diseases . . . by and by a Brahman
or an ascetic takes possession of it as a working concern, and develops it according to orthodox rule. (Crooke, 1926, p. 28)

Srinivas (1956) is among those who have made the same point:

Each region has its own body of folklore about the heroes of the Ramayana
and Mahabharata and not infrequently, epic incidents and characters are
related to outstanding features of local geography. And in every part of India
are to be found Brahmins who worship the local deities which preside over
epidemics, cattle, children's lives, and crops, besides the great gods of all-
India Hinduism. . . . Throughout Indian history Sanskritic Hinduism has
absorbed local and folk elements and their presence makes easier the further
absorption of similar elements. The absorption is done in such a way that
there is a continuity between the folk and the theological or philosophical
levels, and this makes possible both the gradual transformation of the folk
layer as well as the "vulgarization" of the theological layer. (Srinivas, 1956,
p. 494)

Here some of the apparent ties between beliefs and practices in Sirkanda as compared to those found over part or all of India and in the

literary tradition will be mentioned. The village gods of Sirkanda show closer affinities to gods of the great tradition than do household gods, and so they will be discussed first in this context.

The Bhartwali shrine in Sirkanda is said by some informants to be in honor of *Bharat,* brother of *Rama* in the *Ramayana* epic. *Kali,* who possesses a low-caste woman during kalratras to village gods in Sirkanda, is the same in name as the Kali who is prominent in Hinduism as a deification of femaleness. In Sirkanda she is not so identified. Devi is apparently also a manifestation of the mother goddess and particularly the goddess known as Durga, who is popular in the hills as well as elsewhere. She is represented by Sirkanda informants as riding a tiger, the characteristic vehicle of Durga.

Raghunath is identified by some in Sirkanda as Mahasu or Mahadev, generally described as other names for Shiva, one of the three great gods of Hinduism. In Kumaon, Raghunath is identified as Vishnu, another of this trinity (Atkinson, 1884a, p. 813). In Sirkanda this deity is associated with Parasu Ram, an incarnation of Vishnu whose image is in the Raghunath temple. Shiva as represented in prominent temples is occasionally worshiped by Sirkanda people, and the commemoration of his birth is one of the Hindu festivals recognized in Sirkanda. Some historians of Garhwal believe that Shiva as an all-India deity originated in the beliefs of the aboriginal inhabitants of this area. (Cf. Bahadur, 1916, pp. 73 f.) These are deities worshiped in Sirkanda which are directly identifiable with gods of the great literary tradition.

Two household gods have tenuous ties of this type: Nar Singh is the name of an incarnation of Vishnu, and temples are devoted to him in Garhwal. In Sirkanda, however, he is a household god. As such he is found throughout this region and is also reported for the hill region of Chamba (Crooke, 1926, p. 201). Nag Raja, the snake king, has a Shiva temple dedicated to him elsewhere in Garhwal (Atkinson, 1884a, p. 811). ". . . We have numerous traces of Naga worship in these hills, but now chiefly connected with the special cult of Vishnu or [less frequently] Siva" (Atkinson, 1884a, p. 835). Worship of this deity is non-Brahmanical in origin and is thought to have derived from the religion of the Nagas, a non-Aryan tribe of uncertain affinities and wide spread who have apparently long been displaced to the east or have been absorbed in the later populations in Garhwal (cf. Atkinson, 1884a, pp. 373 f.; Crooke, 1926, pp. 383 ff.). In Sirkanda, Nag Raja is a household, or at most a village, god.

Paharis are generally described as Shiva worshipers, but in Sirkanda deities identifiable with Vishnu are more prominent. To Sirkanda residents, however, these affiliations are irrelevant and largely unknown.

To them each is a deity in its own right, and none overshadows household gods in their relevance to daily life.

Notwithstanding the number and importance of the more orthodox forms of Vishnu and Siva in this portion of the Himalaya the non-Brahmanical deities . . . have far more worshippers and are more constantly addressed. . . . The common resort in times of trouble or distress is Goril . . . and the other village gods. (Atkinson, 1884a, p. 839)

The general belief of Sirkanda villagers relative to the great tradition of Hinduism, and the essence of their responses to inquiries designed to bring out relationships between their brand of village Hinduism and all-India Hinduism, were summed up by an informant who said, "The learned people know all those things, we don't. They don't concern us."

The term "village gods" or "local gods" as applied to Indian villages should not be interpreted as meaning that these gods are unique to the particular village in which they are found. As a matter of fact, like most other traits of culture they generally occur over cultural-linguistic regions of fairly broad extent. Those that originate in a single village, say as a deified ancestor, are likely to spread to others as their fame spreads and as they accompany brides to other villages, until eventually their origin is forgotten or in dispute. Most of the non-Sanskritized deities, village and household, worshiped in Sirkanda are of this superlocal character. "Goril . . . if we judge from his general repute and the number of temples to his name, is the most popular of all deities worshipped by the lower classes in Kumaon" (Atkinson, 1884a, p. 821). A birth story recorded by Atkinson for Gauril is different but vaguely similar to that told in Sirkanda. Kali, who is a manifestation of the "mother goddess" in great traditional Hinduism and is associated with the Pandavas in Sirkanda, is reported by Atkinson (1884a, pp. 821 ff.) in that story as the mother of "Goril." This relationship did not appear in my Sirkanda materials. *Kalua,* brother of Gardevi and associate of Gauril in Sirkanda, is the name of an independent deity who, according to Atkinson, originated in a village in Garhwal as the spirit of a murdered man, and *Masān* (Appendix I), is identified as a demon who inhabits cremation grounds. Bhuia is well known in villages throughout northern India as the "tutelary god of fields and boundaries, . . . a beneficent deity who does not as a rule force his worship on anyone by possessing them or injuring them or their crops" (Atkinson, 1884a, p. 825; cf. Crooke, 1926, pp. 87, 92).

Mahasu is a name applied to a group of four regional deities in Jaunsar-Bawar adjacent to Garhwal (Saksena, 1955, pp. 40 ff.; Atkinson,

1884a, pp. 836 ff.). As mentioned above, the same term refers to a single deity sometimes equated to Shiva in Sirkanda. Reference has already been made to various regional interpretations of Nar Singh and Nag Raja. Devi shows similar variation. Such similarities, variations, discrepancies, and identities could be repeated many times over for the other deities of Sirkanda, and in fact for those of villages throughout India.

Caste and Deities

Religious belief and practice do not vary significantly by caste in Sirkanda. No caste gods, as such, are worshiped. Low castes do not engage in unique worship or hold beliefs that offer a clue to their presumed early cultural distinctiveness from the higher castes. In this Sirkanda differs markedly from plains villages, where caste differences in religious practice are pronounced (cf. P. M. Mahar, 1957; Cohn, 1954, pp. 174 ff.; Planalp, 1956). Perhaps the absence of caste distinctions in Sirkanda's religion can be largely attributed to the relative lack of physical and social isolation of castes. We have noted, however, that certain gods tend to be identified with certain castes in Sirkanda. Informants point out that such distinctions are most likely to appear during village dances, when certain gods tend to possess members of certain castes. Thus, Bhartwali, if he were to appear, would allegedly possess a Brahmin, Memendia would possess a Rajput (though he has on occasion possessed members of all castes). A blacksmith (Lohar) would be possessed by a god called *Kaluāl Lōhār* if it appeared, and a Bajgi would be possessed by Kali Das. In practice in Sirkanda the last of these appears regularly, the first two rarely, and Kalual Lohar not at all.

One low-caste informant commented that the gods do not recognize caste distinctions and they never punish people for breaking caste rules. As he said, "If gods were caste-conscious would Devi, who is such an important deity, possess the barber's wife?" The fact that high castes are apparently somewhat more aware of Sanskritic belief and ritual than low castes seems to be a result of their greater contacts with education and educated people rather than of any caste heritage of belief.

Caste discrimination in worship has been mentioned in the discussion of pilgrimages. Discrimination occurs in the village temples as well as in distant ones. At festivals and marriages low-caste members receive their blessings indirectly from the Brahmin, who flicks the vermilion paste onto some object as, for example, the drum of a Bajgi, and it is then applied to the Bajgis' foreheads by the owner of the drum.

Low castes perform the same ceremonies and worship as high castes, but they do so separately or indirectly so as not to pollute the high-caste worshipers. They stand outside the temple to worship Raghunath, but they worship him as devoutly as do Brahmins or Rajputs.

Ancestors

The spirits of deceased people may evolve into gods as was reportedly the case with Kalua in Kumaon mentioned above, with Happy Eye in Kishan Garhi (Marriott, 1955a, pp. 212 f.), and Ghatal Deo in Rampur (Lewis, 1958, pp. 204 f.). In Sirkanda such spirits occur in a form closely resembling household gods in behavior and demands. Some of these might conceivably become minor gods—the first step in "universalization" or elevation to super-local status (cf. Marriott, 1955a, pp. 207 ff.).

Such spirits occur in Sirkanda as *rati*, the spirit of a deceased male who returns to torment his former household, and *hanthiā*, the spirit of a female. These beings are identified by shamans and are worshiped as household deities by the households they afflict (Appendix IC, first ed.). The difference is that only one household worships each of these, and generally after a generation or two they are dropped.

In Sirkanda there are currently thirteen of these ancestor spirits which afflict a total of eleven households, nine of which are Rajputs, one a barber, and one a Bajgi. Eight of the spirits are female. The relationship of these to living household members is as follows: four, and possibly five, are wives who do not want to be forgotten by their living husbands, two are mothers, and one is a co-wife. Of the five male spirits, three are father's younger brothers, one is a father, and one a brother, of current householders. They are worshiped in a manner very similar to that for household gods, and under similar circumstances.

An ancestral spirit that has virtually become a devi or goddess and is, in fact, sometimes referred to by that term, is that of a village wife who committed *sati* (immolation on husband's funeral pyre). After the event no stone or monument was erected in her honor. People of the village gradually forgot about her noble act and failed to honor her. After some time the family of the woman began to suffer with boils and fevers, and their cows went dry. A shaman diagnosed the trouble as being due to neglect of the sati. Therefore the householders built a shrine to the shaman's specifications. This shrine is now the place of worship for the sati spirit or devi. So far its use has been limited almost entirely to the Rajput sib of the household who built the shrine, but it has extended within the sib beyond that particular household and lineage. It seems a likely candidate for a village goddess.

All recent ancestors in each household are worshiped in an annual ceremony (*kanāgat*, Appendix II, first edition), even though they have in no way afflicted their survivors.

GHOSTS

A variety of ghosts or malevolent spirits inhabit the countryside, unassociated with any one family or even any one village. They are usually the wandering spirits of deceased people who are wont to attack living people with results ranging from death to luckless fishing. In general these ghosts (*bhūts*) or demons (*shetānths*) attack at night and in dark places. Strange or unaccountable sounds, rock slides, and the like are attributed to them. None inhabit Sirkanda, but some are known to inhabit deep, jungle-covered ravines on trails leading into Sirkanda. Whistling, lights, and dislodged stones attributed to them are frequently encountered at night. Fear of them tends to keep people from traveling at night.

The worst of the ghosts come to people and enter their bodies because they are miserable disembodied souls seeking a body in which to dwell. Others are jealous of human beings, or merely cantankerous. However, possession by a ghost differs from that by a god or ancestor. The term for ghost possession is *bhūt lag gēā* (ghost has adhered) or *chat patānā* (to cause torment as evidenced by trembling), as contrasted to "*sir ā gēā*" (has come to a head) for possession by a god. Ghost possession is qualitatively different from possession by a god. Once a ghost has "caught hold" it will usually not leave unless forced out by exorcism. During the time it is in possession, it causes illness, unusual behavior, and even death. Insensitivity to pain is the usual diagnostic symptom of possession by a ghost. Other afflictions are: eyes rolled back, fever, inability to talk coherently, melancholia, some sensory disability or aphasia, catatonic adherence to a particular posture, illness, barrenness, or repeated stillbirths. Sometimes these afflictions may prove incurable because the ghost cannot be exorcised. Inexplicable sudden death is often attributed to ghosts. The very fact of possession by a ghost is harmful to the one possessed. A god, in contrast, bothers his victim without possessing him. He possesses only to dance or to speak. He does so temporarily without harm to the one possessed, and he leaves voluntarily.

Ghosts do not attack as punishment for misdeeds or oversights, and they are not usually propitiated. They are avoided by means of charms, magical acts, or use of objects inimical to them. Once possession has occurred, they are driven out with the help of a professional exorcist who knows what will send them away. A few require sacrifice as ransom before departing, but this is not considered to be propitiatory sacrifice in the sense of an offering such as is given to the gods. People simply pay off an evil spirit. There is no feeling of guilt or laxity, as they cannot avoid such spirits by worship in advance.

Usually a shaman diagnoses possession by a ghost and refers the patient to an expert in exorcism. Practitioners who exorcise ghosts can often do so simply by chanting appropriate mantras and placing a sacred mark on the victim's forehead. The ghost cannot face such sacredness and must leave. Some ghosts leave under physical duress such as the application of a scorpion plant to the body, a mild beating, or blessed grain thrown in the face of its victim. Some require very complex rites of exorcism. Some can be exorcised only at certain places, for example, by running water, at a cremation ground, at a crossroads where a goat's or sheep's head has been buried. Some can be warded off by specific objects, words, or written formulas. Iron, black color, and scorpion plant are anathema to most ghosts.

In appearance and effect as well as susceptibility to various types of exorcism, ghosts vary. All or nearly all have backward-turned feet and long fangs if they have human form. Some take the form of snakes or other animals; one looks like a white pillar, another like a bright light. They are adept at disguise. Some are prone to attack women, one attacks new mothers, another attacks men wearing blankets. Cremation grounds are populated by many ghosts—those of the recently dead, those which torment the souls of the dead, and those which feed on corpses. It is often remarked in Sirkanda that it is really ghosts rather than flames which consume the corpse.

Special precautions are taken at cremation to ensure that nothing of the body remains for ghosts to use or torment sexually or otherwise, and to ensure that the spirit of the deceased will not be bothered by other ghosts. The spirit of a dead person wanders for at least thirteen days after cremation. No matter how well-loved the person was in life, his spirit is feared in the village until after the thirteenth-day ceremony, which allows it to settle in some body or at least to pass into a less restless condition. A new mother and infant are especially vulnerable to the jealous ghosts of women who died in childbirth. As protection, mothers carry iron sickles and black blankets when they go out and leave scorpion plant and the sickle by their child or in the doorway when they are at home.

In discussing ghosts of the dead and ancestors, it is worth noting that the dead who return to torment the living are those who are thought to have reason to be angry or jealous. They are usually those who died prematurely or are improperly mourned. A deceased wife torments her successor; a person who died prematurely, jealously torments the living; a woman who died in childbirth attacks young mothers; a father whose sons failed to give proper charity on his behalf at his funeral suffers in the afterlife and therefore plagues his sons; a man whose family neglected to perform the thirteenth-day ceremony after death cannot enter a new life, and so disturbs his family; a woman who brought honor to her family by immolating herself on her husband's funeral pyre torments her neglectful descendants.

Ghosts are often categorized terminologically by their origin. Thus *chūRail* is the ghost of a woman who died in childbirth, and *shāiad* is the ghost of a Muslim. Eight named ghosts plus a number of unnamed ones were described by Sirkanda men. Some of these are well known in other areas. Crooke (1926, pp. 134, 171), for example, describes *"churel"* and *"shahid"* on the plains, corresponding to the two types mentioned immediately above. Others are doubtless of very limited distribution.

SPRITES

One category of supernatural beings differs from others in that their effects on people are harmful but not malicious. These are the *mātrīyā* (matris) or sprites associated with the goddess Matri, mentioned above and representing the ghosts of little girls. They live around the shrine dedicated to Matri, atop the hill overlooking Sirkanda, and their affinity to her may be based primarily on that (Appendix IB, first ed.). Sirkanda villagers think of them as a band of fast-moving, invisible, playful fairies who occasionally leave their normal abode on the hilltop to flit about over the countryside like a flock of birds or a swarm of insects. If a person happens to get in their way while they are traveling or cavorting, he will be struck with fatal or debilitating maladies such as insanity, blindness, deafness, muteness, or aphasia of various sorts. Sudden occurrences of such disabilities, without warning symptoms, are often attributed to these beings. The effects are considered incurable, but the sprites have not inflicted them as punishment, nor is it done in anger or spite. It is simply an inevitable result of happening into the midst of matris at play. The matris are capricious and without malice. They strike people in passing rather than possessing them. Therefore, they cannot be propitiated or exorcised. They are a hazard to human beings—one that cannot be anticipated, avoided, or cured.

"He just got in the way of the matris; it was his fate," is the way their afflictions are explained. Fortunately, the chances that one will be struck by them are slim, for like lightning and wild animals they strike rarely and over an area so large as to make direct contact with them unlikely. Perhaps one out of each thousand Bhatbair residents has been struck by matris.

Their nature and activities are very similar to those of the *acheri* or fairies described by Traill. "These reside on the tops of mountains, but descend at dusk to hold their revels in more convenient spots. To fall in with the train, at the time, is fatal . . . : they occasionally also molest those who may cross the sites of their abodes during the day . . ." (Traill, 1828, p. 221; cf. Oakley, 1905, pp. 212 f.).

It should be remembered that the categories of supernatural beings, such as sprites, ghosts, household gods, and village gods, as well as the subdivisions of these categories, are not entirely distinct and in practice constitute a continuum or spectrum of intergrading types of supernatural beings with similarities running through all. When informants recount memorable or recent instances of the machinations of supernatural beings, they often jump from one type to another and back again without pause, explanation, or even identification of the type of supernatural responsible. On the other hand, inquiry can usually produce such identification.

Supernatural Functionaries

In a world beset by such a variety of supernatural troublemakers there are a variety of professional people whose job it is to deal with them. In Bhatbair these can be categorized according to the functions they perform, as priests, temple keepers, shamans, pujaris, diviners, exorcists, and curers. These categories are not necessarily mutually exclusive.

Priests maintain the system of Hinduism in ways prescribed in the great tradition. It is they who help people achieve a favorable afterlife and rebirth. Their primary responsibility is the long-range welfare of their clients. They perform the annual ceremonies and life-cycle rites as well as many special ceremonies. In addition they perform pujas to village gods, and they practice astrology and some forms of divination based on written prescriptions of Hinduism. They are the local experts on the great tradition, though their beliefs and daily practices in Bhatbair do not differ materially from those of other castes.

Temple keepers maintain particular shrines to honor gods, receive gifts on their behalf, and often lead or assist in their worship.

The other supernatural functionaries deal with the exigencies of daily life relative to the supernatural. Their primary responsibility is the immediate welfare of their clients in this life. The shaman who diagnoses difficulties through the offices of his own personal deity, and the pujari who performs worship for household gods and plays drums to let the gods dance, have been discussed sufficiently above so that no elaboration is required here (cf. Berreman, 1964). These two types of functionaries enable people to find out what deities are troubling them and how to appease them. The pujaris help in satisfying the deities' demands.

With regard to gods worshiped locally we can say that Brahmin priests are to village gods as pujaris are to household gods; that is, they perform comparable functions. By the same token, temple keepers are to the gods of their temples as household heads are to the gods of their households; they maintain the shrines and supervise the worship, though often specialists actually perform the worship.

Aside from these there are a variety of specialists in several kinds of supernatural activities. These practitioners range from the lowliest shoemakers to Brahmins, but there is a heavy predominance of low castes. Their methods vary with their specialties, their place of origin, and in some cases their personal predilections. Although the specialties are not hereditary, the practitioner usually derives the necessary knowledge and skill from a parent or other relative who practiced before him and taught him the necessary lore.

In Sirkanda there are two such practitioners, both Bajgis. Each represents a common type of practitioner in the area. One is a diviner. He performs much the same function as a shaman in that he diagnoses trouble and divines the past and future, but he is without the shaman's personal god as his source of information. In this practice he uses at least two techniques of gaining insight, one involving a system of counting grains of rice brought to him by a client, and the other a system of reading significance in patterns of drawn lines. The second Sirkanda practitioner is an exorciser of ghosts and spirits. This man is credited with several impressive successes. He is especially adept at exorcism of ghosts which cause stillbirths. One of his techniques is that of *jhārā tārā karnā* (to do brushing away of evil), a term applied to the magic used to treat cases of spiritually caused diseases and other difficulties. He is sometimes called to diagnose and treat a patient assumed to be possessed by a ghost. More often he is called as a result of diagnosis by a shaman in order to carry out exorcism.

There are many other practitioners of similar arts in neighboring areas. In a distant but accessible village lives a Nepalese Rajput exorciser of considerable renown and spectacular methods who brings ghosts physically into his clients' terrified presence in their natural form and habitat (at the cremation grounds) and browbeats them into submission to his will. Like well-known specialists in many cultures, his services do not come cheaply and he is therefore a last resort in most cases of ghost possession.

All these practitioners serve over a wide geographical area, and their practice is a direct reflection of their reputation for success. Rarely are their services as highly valued in their own villages as in distant ones —an instance of the general rule in these hills that respect for a practitioner who deals with the supernatural varies inversely with physical (and sometimes social) proximity to him. Typical is the Sirkanda Bajgi exorciser, one of the few of his profession able to make a living without supplementing his income by following a trade, making liquor, or engaging in agriculture. He is patently in great demand in other villages and lives as well as many other villagers, but he is rarely consulted in Sirkanda. A villager summed up local opinion when asked his estimate of this practitioner's skill: "If he were any good would he live here in poverty as he does?" Another commented, "Everyone has to make a living; some work, some beg, some steal; he does exorcising." Similar attitudes are expressed regarding the local Brahmin priest as compared to more distant and hence more respected priests.

Diseases are usually considered to be supernaturally caused. Diagnosis is most often performed by a shaman, who recomends the appropriate type of practitioner and treatment. As we have seen, shamanism is a major focus of religion in Sirkanda. Some common diseases are thought to be amenable to direct treatment either with herbs and diets or with incantation by minor specialists. Those who treat such diseases tend to specialize in certain diseases or groups of diseases. Other practitioners, like the Sirkanda Brahmin, will treat almost any ailment. Afflictions characterized by some external, visible symptom such as sores or swelling (for example, boils, gout, mumps, chicken pox, sore eyes, snakebite, and spider bite) are usually treated by the class of specialists called *jhārnēwālā* (practitioner of *jhārnā*, stroking or brushing). In Bhatbair there is a specialist for each of the above-named ailments, and for most of them there is a specialist in Sirkanda itself. Such practitioners may be men of any caste who perform this duty when called upon but do not make a major occupation of it. Treatment varies with the disease, but in general it involves recitation of appropriate mantras by the practitioner while he repeatedly touches the afflicted member and the ground (or water, lump of sugar, animal, or other object) alternately with a hawk's feather, thus transferring the trouble from the patient to the ground or object. Smallpox is rare in the area, but if it occurred would be treated by worshiping the deity to whose displeasure it was attributed, probably Devi.

As previously noted, the Sirkanda Brahmin practices elementary Vedic medicine. In this practice he follows a book of instructions, based upon Hindu religious works, which directs the practitioner in herbal, dietary, and hot and cold treatments, as well as others. He also practices jharna.

General debility or lingering illness may be treated by giving charity to relieve the misery. The treatment, under the direction of a Brahmin, is called "weighing." It is a rather elaborate process the essence of which is that the patient is balanced in a large scales against a counterweight of several items, primary among which is grain. A puja is performed, the counterweight goes to the Brahmin as charity, and thereafter the ill-ness is cured.

Occasionally Vedic doctors in Mussoorie or Dehra Dun are consulted to set bones or prescribe for diseases such as tuberculosis, malaria, venereal disease, chronic dysentery, general weakness, and male sexual difficulties. Women rarely go outside the village for treatment. In serious or lingering cases a variety of treatments and practitioners may be tried. Some minor ailments are treated in the home without the ad-vice of specialists, either with traditional folk remedies or with local interpretations of Vedic prescriptions.

Spell-Casting, Witchcraft, and Evil Eye

Some practitioners of curative magic and occasionally others have learned to cast spells (*jāddū*) into people that will cause either slow suffering and eventual death or sudden death, depending upon the type of spell. The latter is more difficult and the method is a closely guarded secret, while the former is well known. The same practitioners are proficient in the process of *lautanā*, "to send back" or counteract jaddu, whereby the evil spell can be removed and returned to the sender or put in some harmless place. Such practitioners are supported by the god *Bhairū*. A goat is sacrificed to the god as part of the prepa-ration for sending or counteracting a spell. There have been Bajgi, Rajput, and Brahmin practitioners of this magic in Sirkanda. In ad-dition, there is a lesser form of jaddu which takes the form of practical jokes which inconvenience or make ridiculous their victims. This type is especially common among Bajgis, who use it to interfere with the drum-playing of their rivals.

Casting of spells and counterspells is a very precise and difficult art. Slight mistakes in the ritual can result in the death of the practitioner, and instances are readily cited. In one local case the magically treated pot by which the spell was to be conveyed turned upon the errant spell-caster who had prepared it and dispatched him with a blow on the skull. Similarly, misuse can be the doom of the practitioner, according to a belief that fatal jaddu must be used only on those who deserve death. It is often stated that anyone who learns this art has to pledge his teacher never to use it irresponsibly under pain of dire punishment. One death and a case of affliction with leprosy in the family of Tula, the traditional Brahmin of Sirkanda, are attributed to injudicious, impulsive use of fatal jaddu by a member of that family on an innocent Bajgi victim.

Jaddu is accomplished by a combination of imitative and contagious magic. A flour-and-water image of the intended victim is prepared and placed in a pot along with various rare and esoteric, magically treated items. Incantations are recited over this, and pulses (legumes) are thrown over the image as its intended fate is spelled out. Then the pot is secretly buried in the home of the intended victim, who begins to suffer the consequences. The source of the victim's trouble is usually diagnosed for him by a shaman. Then a practitioner—preferably the one who cast the spell in the first place—is called in at considerable expense to nullify the spell by a special performance with a similar container, or redirect it by finding the buried container so that it can be reburied elsewhere.

A related technique of spell-casting is magically sending flour and water images of the victim and of a sheep (the latter as an offering "to the art of jaddu") to the victim after magical preparation similar to that exercised upon the pot in the above description. The images are made to walk in upon the victim by force of magic, whereupon he is expected to drop dead of fright. This spell can be counteracted by a practitioner if the victim survives long enough to summon one.

Mantras can theoretically be recited by a practitioner over the nail and hair clippings of a potential victim to drive him insane by jaddu, but fear of this danger is not sufficient to motivate Sirkanda people to conceal clippings. Shamans rarely designate clippings as the source of a person's trouble; ghost possession or contact with matris are the usual diagnoses of such symptoms. Nail and hair clippings automatically cause bad dreams if left in a house and will cause creaking roof beams if placed among the rafters of a house. In such cases a shaman can diagnose the trouble and specify where the offending objects can be found.

Dāg, witchcraft, is practiced secretly by certain women. Other hill areas, including Jaunpur and Jaunsar-Bawar, are thought to abound in witches, so that girls are not sent there as wives or taken from there without careful advance investigation. Three of five Sirkanda girls who were married in Jaunpur died early, allegedly as a result of witchcraft. There has never been a witch in Sirkanda and there are no witches in Bhatbair now, according to Sirkanda people, though there are reported to have been some who came as brides from time to time in the distant past. The nearest witch now lives in a village on the farthest periphery of the area within which Sirkanda people regularly marry. Witchcraft is associated with people who are different, and hence mysterious and therefore dangerous. Witchcraft is a reason for staying away from alien people and areas and for avoiding unnecessary interaction, especially marriage, with distant and unknown people.

Witches are very covetous. They insidiously destroy any person, animal, or object which they admire. They can disguise themselves as cats or other animals to gain access to the homes of their victims. There they may measure the victim with a thread or eat his liver or replace it with another object without leaving a trace. As a result the victim, whether human or animal, will die a miserable death. Sometimes shoemakers report that dead cattle are found to have had no liver—a sure sign of dag. There is no countermagic for this dread practice.

The "evil eye" (nazar lagnā, to look covetously) is well known over North India and bears some superficial resemblance to dag. In Sirkanda, as elsewhere, the evil eye consists of a covetous, greedy, admiring, or envious look cast by certain persons at any person, animal, or object. The result is that the object of the evil eye is harmed—the child or adult becomes weak or sickly, the cow goes dry, the artifact breaks. The possessor of the evil eye is usually unaware of the effect he produces. Not all people possess the evil eye, and those who do cannot control it. It is not restricted to any particular type of person. A shaman generally diagnoses the trouble. Specialists prescribe amulets or short ceremonies to dispel its effects. However, it is not very much feared in this area, and is rarely blamed for trouble. There is not, as a result of this belief, reluctance to have a child admired or complimented in any way, as is often the case in the plains. Neither are such precautions as eye-blackening commonly used to protect children. As one informant said,

If we have many children we don't fear evil eye at all. If we have only one or two we fear it and we protect the child by giving extra charity and, if necessary, with amulets. We like to have our children admired and we don't think admiration increases the likelihood of evil eye. It is counteracted by charity and charms, not by disguise.

A somewhat related concept is that of *dūr lakshinī,* a person of evil portent. The term refers especially to a person who utters curses or dire predictions which have a tendency to come true. If a person uses a common curse such as "I hope you fall and skin your knees," and it comes true regularly, he is referred to by this term and is feared.

Certain social relationships into which people enter prove to be inherently fortunate or unfortunate. Most frequently, marriage is of this nature. Some marriages bring a marked change in the luck or fortune of a family. The change is attributed to the new relationship and more particularly to the bride since, in this patrilocal society, she is the new element in the situation. There are many examples of Sirkanda households whose luck changed from bad to good or good to bad immediately after a marriage. Bad luck is attributed to misread or mismatched horoscopes of the married couple because, if properly read, the horoscopes would have predicted the difficulty and the marriage would not have been performed.

Similarly the birth of a particular child may prove lucky or unlucky to a family. Children born under one astrological condition (*mūl*) are so dangerous to their parents that they are usually adopted by others, and they may even prove to be harbingers of bad luck to their foster parents.

There is in Sirkanda a whole series of auspicious and inauspicious omens, days, acts, and objects with corroborative stories about people who have felt their effects or narrowly missed feeling their effects. These need not be enumerated here. Some of the portents are based on religious writings and are known primarily by the Brahmins who consult religious works and astrological tables to detect them. Others are known to diviners and similar practitioners. Many are the common knowledge of every villager.

4 THE RELIGIOUS CONTEXT: CALENDRICAL AND LIFE-CYCLE CEREMONIES

A number of recurrent ceremonies in which household and village gods play important roles have been mentioned. In this chapter two cyclical patterns of ceremonial observance will be discussed. The first of these is the annual cycle of festivals, and the second is the lifetime cycle of rites of passage—the ritual observance of changes in status of the individual. No attempt will be made to describe these observances in the vast detail that would be necessary in order to reproduce them. Rather, their main outlines, the social composition of groups which participate in them, and their points of difference and similarity in comparison with equivalent ceremonies of all-India Hinduism will be described.

It will be noted that no daily cycle of ritual or worship is described for Sirkanda. There is no tradition of such practice in this village among the members of any caste, although in other areas of the hills high-caste people do perform daily ceremonies much like those observed by some plains groups (cf. Atkinson, 1884b, p. 65). In Sirkanda one middle-aged Rajput who has had eight years of schooling and operates the village shop is the only person who lays claim to any such practice, and he says only a brief prayer at the time of lighting his lamp in the evening. A few high-caste households possess religious books but do not read them regularly. There is little in the way of private, individual worship of any sort in the village.

Calendrical ceremonies in Sirkanda are observed by all or nearly all community members, but specific ceremonial activities which make up the calendrical observances are carried out primarily within the household. Life-cycle ceremonies are performed by the kin group (usually the lineage) but are carried out in the household with household members playing the most important roles. The household therefore is the basic ritual unit.

Annual Ceremonial Cycle

Twelve ritual observances or religious ceremonies are celebrated annually in Sirkanda.

Nine of these (numbers 4–12 in table 1) are local manifestations of widespread Hindu festivals, two of which (numbers 5 and 12) are given little more than lip service in Sirkanda. Another (number 9) is observed in a manner very different from its observance on the plains. Three festivals (numbers 1, 2, and 3) are apparently of only regional significance.

This sequence can be compared with the calendrical ceremonies reported for various villages of the plains: 12 are reported for the Chamar caste of Senapur (Cohn, 1954, pp. 200 ff.), and 35 are recorded for the entire village of Senapur (Planalp, 1956, pp. 249 ff.). Nineteen each are reported for Kishan Garhi (Marriott, 1955a, pp. 191 ff.) and Rampur (Lewis, 1958, pp. 197 ff.).

Marriott notes that half the festivals of Kishan Garhi are identifiable with those of the great tradition. In making this comparison he makes certain qualifications that must be borne in mind. These apply equally well to other North Indian Hindu villages, including Sirkanda.

. . . The presumption that the festivals of Kishan Garhi are approximately identical with those of the great tradition needs to be qualified in at least four ways. These four qualifications bring us to confront the little tradition of Kishan Garhi.

First, there are four festivals which have no evident Sanskritic rationales. . . . Second, those festivals of Kishan Garhi which do have Sanskritic rationales represent only a small selection of the total annual cycle of festivals which finds sanction in the great tradition. . . . Third, between the festivals of Kishan Garhi and those sanctioned by the great tradition, connections are often loosened, confused, or mistaken because of a multiplicity of competing meanings for each special day within the great tradition itself. . . . Accustomed to an interminable variety of over-lapping Sanskritic mythology, villagers have ceased to be much concerned with distinguishing the "right" great-traditional explanation of a festival from such Sanskritic-sounding and possibly newly invented ones as may be convenient.

Fourth, behind their Sanskritic names and multiple great-traditional rationales, the festivals of Kishan Garhi contain much ritual which has no evident connection with the great tradition. (Marriott, 1955a, pp. 193 ff.)

Srinivas has pointed out regional variety in festivals:

Festivals such as the Dasara, Deepavali, and Holi have no doubt certain common features all over the country, but they have also important regional peculiarities. In the case of some festivals only the name is common all over India and everything else is different—the same name connotes different things to peoples in different regions. (Srinivas, 1956, p. 494)

TABLE 1

CALENDRICAL CEREMONIES IN SIRKANDA [a]

Name	Meaning	Month
1. Phūl Dālnā	Flower placing; rite of spring	Chait (March–April)
2. Pōprīā Sākrānt	First of month when poppers (type of bread) are eaten; children's god worshiped	Baisāk (April–May)
3. GhōRlīā Sākrānt	First of month when image of wild goat is eaten	Jēt (May–June)
(Taulū)	(Secular fair, following spring harvest)	Jēt (May–June)
4. Rakrī	Wrist charms	Bhādo (August–September)
5. Jēnem Āshtmī Barat	Krishna's birthday fast	Bhādo (August–September)
6. Kanāgat	Worship of household dead	Asōj (September–October)
7. Naurātrā	Nine nights (worship of Durga)	Asōj (September–October)
8. Gāōjīmān	Cow honoring	Kātik (October–November)
9. Pahārī Diwālī	Festival of lights; follows fall harvest, one month after plains Diwali	Māgsīr (November–December)
10. Kicherī Sākrānt	First of month when rice and dal mixture is eaten	Mau (January–February)
11. Panchmī Basant	Spring fifth	Mau (January–February)
12. Shiv Rātrī Barat	Shiva's (birthday) night fast	Phāgun (February–March)

[a] For descriptions of these ceremonies, see Appendix II, first edition.

Marriott's first point has been applied to Sirkanda in the discussion above, and his third and fourth points will be elaborated in the descriptions to follow. The second point, that the festivals in any particular locality are but a small sample of the universe of Hindu festivals, can be documented here. Of the thirteen major festivals of Hindu religion listed by Hindu scholars in Morgan's book, three are celebrated in Sirkanda as compared to seven in Kishan Garhi (Morgan, 1953, p. 423; Marriott, 1955a, p. 194). "Of the 35 presumably all-Indian Hindu festivals listed by Swami Sivananda only 9 occur in Kishan Garhi" (Marriott, 1955a, p. 194), and only seven occur in Sirkanda (Sivananda, 1947, pp. 1–57). In comparing local with regional festivals we note that among the twelve annual festivals of Sirkanda are nine of the nineteen festivals of Rampur, seven of the nineteen at Kishan Garhi, nine of the thirty-five calendrical festivals at Senapur, and five of the twelve among Senapur Chamars. Obviously some of these are North Indian regional festivals or festivals which, like Kanagat, are practically universal in Indian Hinduism, but are not included in the literary "great tradition."

Sirkanda is within the broad culture area of North India but more specifically in that of the sub-Himalayan hills. It would therefore be expected to share religious observance with other people of the area. Atkinson reports a variety of local, regional, and all-India ceremonial and festival observances which occur among hill people of Garhwal and Kumaon, totaling over 60 (Atkinson, 1884a, pp. 847–874). Ten of these are among Sirkanda's twelve, leaving only two Sirkanda observances of such limited significance or distribution that they are not reported for neighboring regions of the same cultural-linguistic area.

The outstanding feature of Sirkanda's ceremonial cycle is its basic similarity to that of other Indian villages. Its greatest differences seem to lie in its sparseness and the weakness of its ties to the great tradition, even where great-traditional affinities can be detected.

Conspicuous by their absence in Sirkanda are the great festivals of the plains, *Holi*, and *Dashera*. Occasionally Sirkanda villagers witness such festivals in towns or trading villages in the valley. The Ram Lila, a dramatic presentation of the *Ramayana* preceding Dashera, is attended in valley villages by a few Sirkanda villagers, and Holi can hardly be avoided by any who may be traveling outside the hills on that day. Such events are, however, regarded as alien, just as are similarly recognized Sikh and Muslim festivals.

The social composition of participating groups in calendrical ceremonies in Sirkanda can be briefly indicated here, although descriptions of the nature of the ceremonies is confined to Appendix II, first ed.

In all but one ceremony, the ceremonial observance takes place primarily within the household unit, by household members. The exception, Nauratra (number 7 on the list in table 1), is celebrated by a village dance and worship of Devi. There is similar worship on Diwali (number 9), accompanied by household worship and worship by all devotees of one god, Nag Raja. All village children together worship the children's god on Popria Sakrant (number 2), and there is household worship as well on that occasion. On all other calendrical ceremonies household units worship separately.

Jenem Ashtmi Barat (number 5) and Shiv Ratri Barat (number 12), the two fasts, honoring Vishnu and Shiva respectively, are observed by only a few of the more sophisticated (educated, high-caste) families, who fast in accordance with plains custom. On the other ceremonial occasions there is enthusiastic participation by nearly everyone, on a household basis.

Brahmins are prominently involved as priests in three of the ceremonies, Rakri, Kanagat, and Kicheri Sakrant, and less prominently in two others, Navratra and Diwali. In the first they tie wrist bands on household members and receive charity in return. In the third they are the recipients of charity given for general merit but not in return for any specific service. In the last two they perform worship to village gods on behalf of the village.

Bajgis, as drummers, are prominent in all three Sakrants, and in the celebration of Panchmi Basant, for which they play their drums and receive gifts of sugar, grain, or cooked food in return. They perform similar service for like remuneration on other periodic and life-cycle ceremonial occasions.

Finally, the barber is the main religious functionary on Panchmi Basant, when he performs a simple ceremony welcoming spring.

In the rest of the ceremonial observances cited here, the family performs its own ritual functions without assistance.

One annual secular event is important in Sirkanda. This is the fair (taulū) held in the middle of Jēt (May–June), on a hilltop in the center of Bhatbair about four miles from Sirkanda. It is widely attended by Bhatbair residents including many people from Sirkanda, but attracts no non-Paharis other than two or three merchants. This fair corresponds in its temporal relationship to the spring harvest, precisely as Diwali, the greatest annual festival of Sirkanda, does in its relationship to autumn harvest. Both occur just after the hard work is over. The fair bears many resemblances to Diwali, but the resemblances are not related to religion, for it is not a religious event. As on Diwali, there is general blossoming out in good clothes, accompanied by gaiety, sociability, dancing, singing, drinking, and general lowering of inhibitions. The fair and Diwali are the two big holidays in the hills, and they are anticipated with equal relish. Only an occasional wedding matches them in public appeal. They may well be derived from the two non-Brahmanical but "really popular festivals . . . held at the two harvests," mentioned by Atkinson (1884b, p. 64).

Three other fairs are attended regularly by some Sirkanda people. All have some religious significance that is vague or unimportant to villagers. One is held at the Kuddu Kal temple in mid-*AsāRh* (June–July), one is at Mussoorie in early *Asōj* (September), and the third is at Rajpur in mid-*Baisāk* (April–May). The first two are primarily Pahari fairs, and the last is heavily attended by Paharis. Sirkanda people do not care to attend festivities of non-Paharis simply because they feel out of place.

LIFE-CYCLE CEREMONIES

Three events in the lives of all individuals in Sirkanda are reinforced by the family and community with ritual performances. These are: birth, marriage, and death. In addition high-caste males are admitted as adult members of their caste in the sacred thread ceremony, generally associated with marriage. These rituals are universal in Hindu India. Those in Sirkanda, like those in villages throughout India, show certain differences from, as well as resemblances to, the rites prescribed in the literature of the great traditions of Hinduism. In Sirkanda they are based on written prescriptions used in the area by Pahari Brahmin priests.

Birth and Childhood

Birth ceremonies in Sirkanda are much like those in the plains. The birth of a son is announced by distributing sugar lumps to friends and relatives on the day of birth. A girl's birth is not formally proclaimed. The first ceremony in the child's life is that of *das sōtan*—the tenth day after birth. On this day a Brahmin is called to prepare the child's horoscope, a process which may take many days, during which time he lives at the house of his client. The Brahmin gives the child a name at this time, but he is not known by this name. Many people do not know the names written in their own horoscopes or those of their children. In the first weeks, months, and years a child acquires names given by its parents or other family members. One informant had five such names. Literate men often later adopt yet another name for signatures which, in contrast to their village name, is usually a conventional

Sanskritic Hindu name. One man ridiculed a current trend toward fancy Sanskritic names: "If you call a jackal 'lion,' it is still a jackal."

One year after birth a Brahmin conducts a ceremony, the "taste of boiled rice," which is supposed to be at the time of first giving the child solid food. Boys have their first haircut during a ceremony performed by a Brahmin and a barber, held on the third, fifth, or seventh birthday, depending upon the Brahmin's reading of the horoscope.

Special ceremonies related to birth include those performed to bring about conception in childless couples, and those held to eliminate the danger which two new mothers (those who have given birth in the same month) pose to one another if they are in contact.[1]

Marriage

Marriage in any Hindu family is a complex process. Lewis distinguishes five major phases in what he terms the "marriage cycle" of Rampur, and within these he notes twenty distinct "ceremonial steps" (Lewis, 1958, pp. 157–190). He also distinguishes two less frequent types of marriage, and remarriage of a deserted woman.

In Sirkanda there is greater variation in marriage practices than is described or implied for Rampur. Ceremonies are used in Sirkanda to celebrate only the first marriage of a woman—about 65 per cent of all unions established. Until the post-Independence era at least one-third of initial marriages of high-caste women were unmarked by ceremonies simply because of the expense and effort involved. Marriages without ceremonies still occur, but less frequently. Thus, among the residents of Sirkanda no more than 50 per cent of current high-caste unions were marked by wedding ceremonies. Among low castes the proportion is considerably smaller. Among the 50 per cent of all marriages which were marked by ceremony, there have been three major varieties of ceremony: (1) the traditional Pahari wedding (biā), a manifestation of regional tradition, (2) the traditional Hindu wedding of the plains modified by bride price and related practices, called takō-ka biā (money marriage) or paisā (money) wedding, (3) the traditional plains wedding complete with dowry, called kanniādān (daughter charity) or pūn (gift) wedding. The first of these was the only type of wedding ceremony performed in Sirkanda until five or ten years before Indian Independence, but it has since been dropped altogether. In it, as in all Pahari weddings but unlike plains weddings, the groom's family takes the initiative in arranging the marriage. A unique feature of the traditional Pahari marriage is that the final ceremonies are conducted at the home of the groom. In the other forms of marriage in this area, as in the plains, the ceremonies occur in the bride's house.

The plains-type dowry marriage has long occurred among educated and wealthy Paharis of neighboring areas, but it has occurred in Sirkanda only since shortly before Independence. The second type, a syncretism, is an equally recent innovation and is currently the most frequently used. The latter two types, and particularly the orthodox plains Hindu dowry marriage, are indicative of the trend toward emulation of plains culture (Sanskritization) advocated by educated Paharis.[2] The percentage of initial marriages unmarked by ceremony has dropped in recent years, but has not disappeared.

At weddings a considerable number of interested people participate —in preparation, caring for guests, assisting the ceremonial cooks and the priest, assisting the principals in the wedding, and so on. The people involved in order of decreasing intensity of involvement are: the extended-family members, the lineage, the kindred (including people outside the lineage who are recognized as relatives of the bride or groom), and often friends, especially sib-fellows and caste-fellows in the village. The kindred comes nearer to visibility as a group at this time than at any other.

DOWRY AND BRIDE PRICE

The traditional form of Pahari marriage involves a bride price; that is, the family of the groom pays an agreed-upon sum in cash to the family of the bride. In the early 1900's this amount was generally under Rs. 50; by World War II it had risen to between Rs. 200 and 400; and now it varies from Rs. 500 to 1,500 with an average around Rs. 1,000. In addition to the bride price the groom's family spends around Rs. 1,000 on food and other materials for a good-sized wedding, Rs. 750 on jewelry and other gifts, and Rs. 250 for the services of specialists and other miscellaneous expenses. The bride's family spends an equal amount on entertaining guests (about Rs. 1,000) and perhaps another Rs. 500 on clothing, dowry, gifts, and so on. Therefore, the bride price is used in the marriage by the bride's family. Rarely is any profit realized. If no bride price is given, as is the case with some well-to-do families, the expenses on both sides are about equal. A dowry is nearly always given by the bride's family to the couple, but in bride-price marriages it is a token gift only.

Everyone knows that bride-price marriage is contrary to high-caste plains custom.[3] Therefore there is considerable striving toward dowry marriages on the part of some of those who can afford it. The Brahmin who performs most high-caste ceremonies is a vociferous advocate of such marriages. Prestige is the goal of these ceremonies. Statements such as the following from a well-to-do Rajput are common: "We don't like bride-price marriage. How can you sell a daughter you love?" Or another: "You can't enjoy money you receive for a daughter." Usually this is merely repetition of platitudes, as both the men quoted had given and received bride price in their day. On the other hand, there are many families who will not give or take a bride without payment and are proud of it. As one Rajput elder said, "It is not proper for Rajputs to accept charity. Only a Brahmin can do that. When we take a girl, we pay for her." There is also a widespread belief that dowry brides do not live nor produce children. It is only in the past fifteen years that a real trend toward dowry marriages has begun even among families who can afford them. Still at least 80 per cent of all marriages include a bride price. Sometimes when no bride price is given, the groom's family promises to bear all the wedding expenses. If so, it is a case of the bride's family trying to have the cake and eat it too. In at least one recent situation a dowry marriage was held but a bride price was demanded later.

In former days it was common among all castes to effect a bride-price transaction without ceremony of any kind beyond agreement between the families. Meals might be exchanged at the time of agreement and of bringing the bride. A puja to the household god was frequently included. Thus the expenses of marriage ceremonies were avoided. The practice still exists, especially among the lower castes. Joshi cites a legal case in which validity of a Pahari marriage was sought to be proved on grounds that the bride was delivered to her husband, those who brought her were feasted, and a puja was performed. Although this failed in the courts where Pahari custom was unrecognized, Joshi asserts that even these three acts are not required for a valid marriage under Khasa customary law. "The payment of bride-price and formal entry as wife in the husband's house are enough for the purpose" (Joshi, 1929, p. 40).

SECOND MARRIAGE

Some families of all castes now have Sanskritized marriage rituals. Second or subsequent marriages of women, and often of men, have always been effected without ceremony. Usually a divorced woman's parents are then paid the bride price and they pass it on to her former husband, though occasionally direct payment is made to the husband. In the case of widow remarriage, a universal practice in this area, payment is generally made to the first husband's family if the widow marries outside it, unless she elopes.

Second marriages for men may be carried out with ceremonies just like the first if it is the bride's first marriage and especially if the man is young and has no children. Such marriages are most often bride-price marriages because a girl's family who wants a big dowry marriage will usually find an unmarried husband for their daughter. Moreover, many second marriages are contracted to produce children, and a bride price is considered more likely to bring that result.

Elopement and inheritance of a wife from a brother are both publicly recognized forms of marriage wherein ceremony and payment are avoided, though payment is exacted by the aggrieved husband in an elopement if possible. Poor families of all castes often effect marriage without ceremony or payment simply by common agreement.

Divorce proceedings will be discussed in chapter 5.

Sacred Thread

Rajput and Brahmin males are initiated into adulthood with the ceremony of investiture with the sacred thread (*jainū* or *bartbhandan*) indicating their spiritual rebirth (cf. Atkinson, 1884b, pp. 92 ff.). They are then said to be "twice born" and therefore are possessed of the knowledge necessary to an adult man of high caste. The ceremony is evidently of relatively recent origin in these hills, adopted along with Sanskritic marriage forms in an effort toward plains emulation or Sanskritization. Normally this ceremony takes place in the groom's village as part of the pre-marriage ceremonies. If a man is not married and is an adult, or if he has not gone through a marriage ceremony, he may call for the sacred thread ceremony at any time after he is about 20 years old.

Death Ceremonies

Ceremonies surrounding death are as complex as those surrounding marriage (Appendix IIIC, first ed.). It is believed in Sirkanda, as in Hindu India generally, that a person's life after death will be greatly influenced by the amount of charity that he has given in this life and that is given in the ceremonies associated with his death. Specifically it is thought that only what has been given in life and at these ceremonies will be available to the spirit for livelihood in the afterlife. Sirkanda villagers tell an eye-witness account of a woman who came back to life shortly after death and begged that more charity be given, since she had found that there was nothing for her to live on and no comforts in the other world because of her niggardliness in life. Therefore a person who has no descendants upon whom he can depend to carry out the death ceremonies properly will usually sponsor pujas and give the necessary charity in advance. This charity is given to the traditional village Brahmin or purohit, although in Sirkanda the ceremonies are performed by more learned Brahmins. The persons involved in the mourning and ritual pollution which follows a death are primarily the male lineage members—those who trace descent to a common ancestor—and to a lesser extent the local sib members and those closely associated with them, that is, the clan, for wives of these people play a minor role. The eldest son or an equivalent male relative (sometimes an adopted son) performs the duties of chief mourner. During the ceremonies the Brahmin performs pujas, directs the chief mourner in his duties, and receives charity. The barber provides leaf packets used in the ceremony, prepares the pipe for the Brahmin's use, and prepares the leaf plates for the feast at the end of the mourning period.

Widows are not restricted in activity or dress, as they often are on the plains. An unremarried widow does not, however, take an active part in birth or marriage ceremonies. Also, she does not wear gold nose ornaments (the symbols of marriage) for at least a year after her husband's death or until she remarries, whichever comes first. Widow remarriage is universal here except when the widow is elderly.

If a villager dies far from home the postdeath ceremonies are performed in his village home. A married woman's death is observed only in the village of her husband and by the family of her husband. Her family of origin takes no part in it except as observers if they are in the same village.

Children, and often unmarried adolescents, who die are buried without ceremony in unmarked graves near the village. Strangers who die in the vicinity are usually buried rather than cremated so that proof of death can be established if necessary later. Adults who die of epidemic diseases are buried and then exhumed and cremated after the epidemic has passed, usually three to six months later.

Kin, Caste, and Community in Religion and Ceremonies

The household, comprising the joint family, is the most significant social unit in religious matters in Sirkanda.[4] Deities and other supernatural beings generally attack the household and must be dealt with by its members collectively. This is true even when only a single member feels the wrath of the gods, since they remain with the household once they have entered it. The worship of household gods is the most frequent expression of religious behavior in the village. Life-cycle rites are likewise observed in the household unit, generally with participation by local sib fellows, their spouses, and adopted sons (that is, the clan); other villagers are observers or guests at best. Local lineage is most significant in death ceremonies for a man, and the local clan runs a close second. For a woman the corresponding groups are the husband's local lineage and the clan. The kindred looms large in marriage. Most annual festivals are performed in household groups. There are special ceremonies for the well-being of the household. Lineage, clan, kindred, and sib are significant in such household ceremonies in that order.

No specific caste deities are worshiped in this village, although certain ones tend in fact to be associated with certain castes. Household observances, whether worship or life-cycle rites, remain within the caste in that those primarily concerned are relatives, and all relatives are caste fellows. For castes separated by little social or ritual distance, attendance at ceremonies extends across caste boundaries, as, for example, between Rajputs and Brahmins, or between barbers, blacksmiths, and carpenters. Members of ritually and socially more distant castes are not often explicitly barred from attendance, but they are barred from participation in many activities, such as group eating, which are central to the celebration and which would be polluting to, or polluted by, these castes. Usually there is no desire for cross-caste participation in such ceremonies, as was made explicit by a low-caste informant who commented that, "There is no enjoyment for me at a Rajput wedding. We can only have fun at weddings in our own caste."

There are no caste festivals or holidays among the castes represented in Sirkanda. Caste enters the religious and ceremonial picture primarily in the caste-specific roles of participants, as in the barber's duties in life-cycle rites, the Bajgi's role in worship of deities and certain annual and life-cycle ceremonies, the carpenter's ritual function in blessing the doorways of a new house, and the Brahmin's priestly role.

Caste differences in religious belief and usage are virtually absent— a notable contrast to the situation reported for other parts of India. Where they do occur in Sirkanda, they represent differences in education, wealth, and enforced restrictions on low-caste behavior more than differences in beliefs or aspirations. Educated people know more of the Sanskritic tradition than do others, and they tend to be of the high castes, but uneducated Brahmins and Rajputs differ little from Doms in their knowledge and beliefs. Even among Brahmins there is little concern with ritual observance or daily worship. They maintain ritual distance from lower castes as do Rajputs and some of the low castes, but their ritual life does not differ significantly from that of other castes. Diet of high-caste members and Doms differs not at all except as dictated by differential income. Bathing is as foreign to most Brahmins as to Bajgis.

The lack of caste differential in such matters is apparently attributable in part to the frequent and intense interaction among members of all castes in Sirkanda. In such villages the entire population is largely isolated from frequent contact with people other than their fellow villagers. Since most castes are very small in numbers, their daily social interaction must be largely with members of other castes. No caste remains isolated from any other. The various castes have more in common and interact more frequently than would groups separated by greater social barriers or with caste communities of their own, and consequently they have less opportunity to maintain differences in beliefs and practices (cf. Berreman, 1960b).

The community is the unit which observes some annual festivals, notably Diwali. It is also the traditional unit for observance of agricultural ceremonies and worship of the village gods. Two specifically village-directed ceremonies are the Mundkile village-protection ceremony and the rope-sliding event to alleviate village and regional troubles.

Supervillage observances are limited to annual regional fairs and the rope-sliding ceremony. In Bhatbair the one such fair is evidently secular in nature, while those in larger centers often have religious meaning.

Religion is thus an important feature at every level in Sirkanda. Its place is similar to that of religion in other Indian villages. Opler's summary statement applies as well to Sirkanda as it does to Senapur, the plains village of which it was written:

> To live a very full and estimable life, a villager has to participate in the religious round. Religion justifies the existence of his line, the tie between his ancestors and his sons. It holds his kin together in family rituals. It provides travel, adventure, and new experience and connects his village with others. . . . The presence of the protective godlings of the village strengthens group consciousness. The agricultural rites, the worship of the disease goddesses, and the life-cycle ceremonies awake courage and hope in areas of life where uncertainty and anxiety are most prevalent. (Opler, 1959b, p. 226)

BRAHMINS AND SHAMANS

One of the most striking features of traditional religious organization in Sirkanda and vicinity is the strategic importance of the shaman (baki) (cf. Berreman, 1964). In the sphere of religion he is a "cultural policy maker," to use Singer's term (Singer, 1955, p. 30)—a cultural "gatekeeper." He is a man, who may be of any caste, whose prestige and power are dependent upon success in his practice of diagnosing supernaturally caused difficulties through the use of a personal deity who

provides the insights and information, using the practitioner as a vehicle. He is the key man in virtually every instance of traditional religious worship. He determines which supernatural being is to be
worshiped or placated, be it household, village, regional, or all-India
Hindu god, or be it ancestor, ghost, spirit, or witch. He often determines
which puja will be performed, which sacrifices will be offered, which
pilgrimages undertaken, which new gods will be worshiped, and, in the
long run, which ones will fall by the wayside. Styles and fads of worship, means of correcting troubles and treating disease, are largely in
the shaman's hands. Certain lesser practitioners share a part of these
important functions. To be sure, such people work within their culture and are probably largely unaware of their key importance. They
may well be unaware of the extent to which they could manipulate
their clients if they wished. This does not alter the fact of their crucial
role. Traditionally they have undoubtedly been the most important
individuals in influencing the nature of religious practice.

Brahmins have played an important but less significant religious
role from the point of view of dynamics of culture in the traditional
setting. They operate primarily within rigidly prescribed limits of
ritual with little opportunity for initiative or innovation despite their
high status. When they are called and what they will do are often
prescribed by a shaman. They are, in fact, ritual technicians or engi-
neers. The shaman makes most of the decisions and therefore is the
policy maker.

Plains emulation has been effectively advocated by some Pahari
Brahmins, but these advocates have been priests with a plains orientation seeking to establish or enlarge their clientele, not traditional family priests or purohits whose clientele is fixed and assured. It seems
likely that the change would come about more quickly in this area if
it were advocated by shamans. Shamans could diagnose difficulties of
all types as being attributable to failure to conform to plains religious
and social standards. They could presumably prescribe Sanskritic
worship of great traditional gods in many circumstances and people
would be likely to follow their advice.

However, shamans, being uneducated and with a stake in the traditional Pahari religious system, have remained traditional in their
attitudes and consequently have impeded plains emulation in the
religious sphere. They have nothing to gain and everything to lose by
emulation of plains Hindu orthodoxy, for that orthodoxy undermines
their religious roles. They therefore generally use their considerable
influence to encourage adherence to traditional religious usages and to
stave off plains emulation.

Family priests (purohits), with their assured clientele and their status in the traditional Pahari religious system are in much the same position. They, too, stand to lose by plains emulation, since villagers would come to depend upon other priests more learned in plains Hinduism. Plains emulation, therefore, threatens the purohit, as it does the shaman, with loss of religious importance and ultimately of income. For other Brahmin priests, however, the reverse is evidently true; it is a means to economic and status enhancement (cf. Berreman, 1964). Plains emulation offers new clients and prestige to priests who have few clients or no traditional clientele and who have learned plains Hinduism.

Increasing contacts with plains people have led many Paharis—especially those with education, and these are mostly from the high castes—to adopt high-caste people of the plains as a reference group in many contexts. With this aspiration for plains emulation they come to demand services which the purohit and shaman cannot provide. Sophisticated, ambitious priests actively compete for clients in this sphere, whereas they could not—at least not so overtly—in the traditional situation. As a result, in recent times some Pahari Brahmins have been cast in the role of religious innovators or policy makers. Relative to them, shamans and purohits have been religious conservatives. The effect of the changes advocated by these enterprising atraditional Brahmins in any given locality is more spectacular and perhaps of more fundamental structural significance in Pahari religion than that effected by shamans in the traditional setting over a comparable time span. It involves new religious and social conceptions, whereas the influence of shamans has been felt primarily in introducing variations on traditional Pahari religious themes and in invoking sanctions on individuals and groups. The sanctions can even be invoked against Brahmin priests, who have traditionally consulted shamans as avidly as anyone else. It can be argued that through use of such sanctions shamans in the long run have had the potential for structural effect as great as that of atraditional Brahmins. It can also be argued that priests who advocate plains emulation are often merely reflecting or accommodating to a trend among sophisticated Paharis rather than initiating it.

That shamans have not become a powerful elite in their own right is perhaps partly attributable to the openness of their profession. Being neither hereditary nor caste-bound, it is highly competitive. There are many such practitioners and they are approached by their clients on a very pragmatic basis, success being the criterion for patronage. There is no traditional practitioner-client arrangement comparable to the jajmani system. Thus the clientele shifts easily, public opinion is a limiting factor, and no shaman has a monopoly on the market. Shamans do have in common their opposition to plains emulation.

Competition among atraditional Brahmin priests is tempered by jajmani-like loyalties on the part of their clients, whom they in fact refer to as "jajmans." Such Brahmins share a vested interest in the advocacy of plains emulation.

PLAINS–PAHARI RELIGIOUS DIFFERENCES

In discussing religious life in Sirkanda emphasis has been placed on its essential similarity to that found in other Indian villages, and particularly those of the Gangetic plain. Implicit throughout, however, has been an emphasis upon differences, upon the unique aspects of Hinduism as it is practiced in Sirkanda. Such differences have been, for the most part, differences common to the region—differences which help define the Sub-Himalayan region as a distinct culture area, that define the Central Pahari-speaking peoples as a subcultural group, that distinguish the residents of Tehri Garhwal or even Bhatbair from their neighbors. The differences have been most frequently differences of emphasis rather than differences of kind. Paharis do not do many things that are unknown on the plains nor are many plains practices entirely foreign to them, but they do more of some things and less of others and that is where the real difference lies.

As has been noted above, perhaps the most striking religious differences are those relating to caste. In Sirkanda there is remarkably little variation in religious belief and practice from caste to caste, whereas in the plains caste differences are prominent features of village religion. In Sirkanda, Brahmins and Bajgis carry out very similar rituals, observe the same festivals, and express virtually the same beliefs. They have distinct ritual functions and are characterized by the expectable differences in ritual purity, but they do not possess significantly different religious subcultures.

The Brahmin perhaps plays a less crucial role in religion here than on the plains. There are fewer events requiring his presence. There is apparently a more important and complex system of non-Brahmanical practitioners—of shamans, diviners, pujaris, exorcists, curers, and so on, than among most plains groups. The services of these practitioners are available to, and in demand by, all castes, whereas in the plains they are often caste-specific (cf. P. M. Mahar, 1957).

There is a casualness about matters of ritual purity, marriage regulations, and similar religion-based social practices, which is not characteristic of high-caste plains groups.

Gods of the literate tradition of Hinduism are less widely recognized and less honored in this area than in the plains. Similarly there is less observance of the ceremonies and festivals of all-India spread than is common in the plains. Rituals that are observed are adapted to local convenience and taste to a degree perhaps exceeding that in most areas. This is especially noticeable in the celebration of Diwali and in marriage ceremonies. There is virtually no daily or private worship. However, the people have a lively interest in religion and do not lack for ceremonies arranged to appease their traditional gods. Worship is aimed at controlling powerful and dangerous supernatural beings who plague them. Such worship is a group matter rather than an individual one—a family or village undertaking. Probably the most distinctive aspect of worship is the incorporation of animal sacrifice as an integral part of virtually every ceremony. The life of an animal is required to please Pahari gods. The gods must also be given the opportunity to dance in the bodies of their devotees if they are to remain favorably disposed.

In a low-caste plains community such beliefs and practices would not seem unusual. The striking feature is that Sirkanda and other Pahari villages are predominately high-caste communities which closely resemble low-caste communities of other areas in the religious life of their members. It is for this reason that Paharis are considered ritually inferior by their plains-dwelling caste-fellows. And it is for this reason that plains emulation or Sanskritization is becoming increasingly evident among informed Paharis, who more and more frequently come into contact with critical plainsmen in positions of authority or influence.

SIRKANDA AND THE GREAT TRADITION

The discussion of religion has demonstrated that Sirkanda is within the range of variation of other Hindu villages in the practice of Hinduism. While it has perhaps less in the way of all-India Hinduism than many Indian villages—especially in comparison to other largely high-caste villages of the plains of northern India—it is not atypical in this respect in comparison to other Pahari villages. This leads to the observation that, while elements of the all-India Hindu tradition as represented in sacred writings and India-wide precepts and practices are prominent enough in the village to make it recognizably and undeniably a part of that tradition, a large proportion of village religious traits do not fit into that tradition. To suppose that these other traits are purely local would be, however, fallacious. Many are characteristic of villages throughout all or much of Hindu India. Others are characteristic of Pahari villages. "Regional Hinduism" is perhaps the best term to apply to those traits of less than all-India spread, since "local Hinduism" is likely to imply that the traits referred to are unique to the village or small locality, when in reality they are to be found over a fairly large cultural area (cf. Cohn and Marriott, 1958).[5] Finally, there are purely local elements—if not in pattern at least in specific content. Such terms as "local," "regional," and "national" Hinduism are merely labels along a continuum. There are no sharp boundaries and the continuum is a moving one.

The terms "great tradition" and "little tradition" present further difficulties. They imply considerably more than simply geographical, cultural, or social "spread." The "great tradition" generally denotes the "literate religious tradition" (Marriott, 1955a, p. 191). However, it is often used in the context of "all-India Hinduism" in discussions of Indian religion. Conversely, the "little tradition" is generally implicitly defined as the nonliterate, vernacular religious tradition but is often used as though it meant local Hinduism. In India these are two entirely different dimensions. In village India it is possible to identify literate religious traditions based upon the great religious writings and embodying the philosophical foundations of the religion. These can be contrasted, as Marriott has done, with the folk practices and beliefs which have not (or not yet) been incorporated into the literate tradition. However, the nonliterate tradition includes many elements which are as widespread geographically as elements of the literate tradition. Some of these folk elements may be more widespread than many literate ones in terms of the population which understands or practices them. In discussing traits of village Hinduism it is useful, therefore, to discuss spread in terms of geography, culture, social organization, and so on, as well as to attempt to apply the literate-nonliterate or great-little tradition dichotomy.

It should be clear that Sirkanda is not unique in its deviation from the literate tradition as evidenced in the religious beliefs and practices of its members. Researchers have found similar circumstances in other Indian villages (for example, Opler, 1958, pp. 553 f.).

Historically, it is suggested by many writers from the time of Manu, the Hindu lawgiver, to the present, that Paharis of the high castes (that is, Khasas) came from a culture that was once more highly Sanskritized than at present, but which fell away from the practices and beliefs that define this term. The decline is attributed to a combination of the exigencies of life in the hills and the intimate contact which the Khasas are supposed to have had with the subjugated indigenes and their "inferior" religion. It is interesting to note the extent to which local historians credit the lowly Doms, who were presumably so readily overpowered by the Khasas, with having altered or even revolutionized the way of life and religion of these allegedly pristine Hindus. Another view is that these high-caste hill people represent a relatively untouched and unchanged survival of antediluvian Aryan culture. It seems probable that in reality the Paharis are the product of mixture between the early Khasas and Doms (if indeed they were different cultural groups) and more recent immigrants. Pahari religion, like the rest of their culture, is the product of gradual change in an area of relative isolation where they have been out of direct contact with many of the influences important in shaping Hinduism on the plains. Beliefs and practices have been influenced by their cultural heritage and by contacts with peoples of the plains and the higher Himalayas.

There is an increasing trend toward religious change on the model of high-caste plains Hinduism at all caste levels in and around Sirkanda. There has long been awareness of plains ways through contacts with educated Brahmins, merchants, government officials, and others knowledgeable in the great traditions of Hinduism. Recently with improved means of communication, increased movement of people between the hills and plains, more easily available schooling, and increased financial capabilities, this awareness has increased, resulting in an active tendency toward emulation. The motivation is simply to be respected by plains people, for Paharis increasingly feel the effects of their unorthodox religious and social practices as a result of their increasing contacts with people adhering to plains values, especially with people in positions of authority or influence. Paharis are considered to be rustic, degraded Hindus by most plainsmen. Plains Brahmins and Rajputs often reject the caste status claims of their Pahari caste-fellows, largely because of their unorthodoxy. By adopting some of the symbols of plains culture, Paharis hope to improve their status in the eyes of the plains people. Instrumental in this change have been those Paharis who have had the most extensive and intensive exposure to orthodox plains viewpoints and who feel their status most threatened by invidious comparisons. These are the high castes and especially the Brahmins. They have been active in effecting the most obvious changes in this trend: Sanskritization of marriage customs, adoption of other Sanskritic rituals and festivals, and attribution of

Sanskritic interpretations to traditional Pahari religious beliefs and practices. The trend is similar to the process of Sanskritization or status emulation widely documented among tribal and low-caste groups elsewhere in India.

Few Paharis have adopted the modern values and ideas associated with education, urban living, and cash economy that have been adopted by some plains people—especially those of the higher castes—and that have been termed "Westernization" by Srinivas (1956; cf. Cohn, 1955). The reasons are very similar to those which account for the fact that, when high castes adopt modern aspirations and values, low-caste plains groups adopt Sanskritic behaviors formerly denied them rather than following the high castes in the new life. These groups have differential experience and different reference groups—in short, different sources of values and aspirations. High-caste people of the plains have benefited from the results of increased educational and employment opportunities in the new context, while Paharis, like low castes of the plains, have benefited less. In fact, the latter groups have had little opportunity even to learn the modern, Western culture within which such benefits can be realized. It is a basic axiom of reference group theory that, if one group is to identify with another so that its members adopt the outlook, and judge themselves by the standards, of the other group, there must be both knowledge of the identification group and some perceived similarity or equivalence to it (Merton and Kitt, 1950, p. 61). Among many high-caste plains people, travel, education, and employment have resulted in familiarity with modern ways and competence in them which make possible perceived similarities and subsequent identification with extra-traditional groups. Adoption of new values and aspirations to the relative neglect of traditional Sanskritic values and aspirations has followed.

Meanwhile Paharis, like low-caste groups of the plains, have lacked equivalent facilities and experience for acquiring the knowledge and competence prerequisite to adoption of nontraditional reference groups. In Sirkanda cultural, physical, and intellectual isolation have in all castes militated against adoption of new alien reference groups to any significant extent. Plains people have long served as something of a reference group for Paharis and have long been known to them. Increased contact has resulted in increased knowledge of their viewpoints. This, combined with increased wealth, has enabled Paharis to push toward higher status in their eyes by emulating them. Since Pahari experience has been for the most part with plains people who advocate a traditional Hindu world view, emulation has been in this direction. For low-caste plains people the enabling feature for upward mobility has been decreased downward pressure from the high castes, as well as increased financial capability and social justice. For both the Paharis and the plains low castes, it is the high castes of the plains in their traditional role who form the reference groups, for they are sufficiently known, understood, and envied for the other groups to identify with them and seek to emulate them. From the Pahari point of view, modern, urban, or Westernized society is simply too alien to be emulated. Traditional plains culture is a familiar and increasingly attainable reference point.

There has been little caste differential in the "plainsward mobility" of Paharis. This is partly because of the cross-caste cultural homogeneity of Paharis of this area and the fact that there has been relatively little difference from caste to caste in opportunity to acquire outside reference groups. High castes have had only slightly better opportunities for education and close contact with educated Brahmins than have low castes. Low castes have had as much or more per capita outside contact as they travel to trade and procure the tools and materials of their trades. High castes have had significantly greater financial capability to carry out Sanskritization by performing expensive rituals under the supervision of educated Brahmins, and it is in this respect that high and low castes differ most. But due to the intensive nature of intercaste interaction in the Pahari context, low castes have been fully aware of the practices of their caste superiors and follow them insofar as they are financially able. It could perhaps be asserted that low castes emulate their high-caste neighbors while the latter are emulating a plains model. If so, the time lag is so short as to be unnoticeable; it is as if both were emulating the plains model. Both groups are explicit in attributing their practices to the plains model.

Another factor in the cross-caste nature of Pahari Sanskritization may be the fact that high castes have not felt a threat of imminently successful low-caste upward mobility. They have therefore not felt the necessity of seeking Westernization as an alternative source of hierarchical supremacy, a motivation for Westernization suggested by Gould (1961a).

Therefore, while the picture of changing caste status on the plains is often one of the low castes moving up in the Sanskritic caste-status hierarchy as the higher, more advantaged castes move out of this hierarchy into a non-Sanskritic milieu, in Sirkanda the picture is of the entire Pahari community attempting to move toward the ways of their plains reference group while castes within the community retain their relative status positions. This is not to deny some cases of new non-Sanskritic aspirations in Sirkanda. Neither is it to deny ambitions of upward mobility and competitive scrambling for status among the lower castes in this area. These occur, for example, among the Bajgis, whose women have given up dancing for the public in order to raise their status, and among the Bedas, who, in the present generation, would like to follow suit. It can be asserted, however, that the dominant trend is a society-wide movement toward what is viewed as the religious context of the plains in order to win the respect of members of that dominant group.

5 KIN GROUPS AND KINSHIP

Previous chapters have described the relationship of men to their natural environment in Sirkanda and to the supernatural world which impinges upon them. This and the following three chapters will describe and analyze the interrelationships among people in and around Sirkanda. An attempt will be made to describe and distinguish ideal patterns of social behavior as expressed by informants and actual patterns of behavior as observed and reported. Similarly, an attempt will be made to distinguish between what is believed and done, and what people would like outsiders to think is believed and done (cf. Berreman, 1962c).

Here, as in preceding chapters, the way of life of the residents of this village and the culture area it represents is compared with that of villages in other parts of India.

From the point of view of social life, the whole of the cis-Himalayan region behaves as a culture area, as there is a homogeneous social code to which both the higher and lower groups subscribe. . . . But the hill culture differs from that of the plains and all cultures that surround them. . . . (Majumdar, 1944, p. 139)

It will become evident that basic similarities accompany important differences, and it is essential that these be presented for comparative purposes. A basic aim, throughout this account, is to throw light on the role of kin groups, castes, and community organization in the lives of the people under discussion.

Basically Sirkanda shares the social structure of Hindu Indian society. Family, caste, and community are the most significant social units.

The discussion will begin with the extended family or household, the economically coöperating residential kin group and the most intimate, immediate social unit in Sirkanda. From the residential kin group the discussion will proceed to its extensions in consanguineal and affinal kin groups, to castes, and finally to the community and its extensions. It is impossible to understand the functioning of Sirkanda society at any of these levels without reference to the others. The system is an interdependent one which does not operate on independent subcircuits. Choice of family as a starting point for presentation is, therefore, largely arbitrary and perhaps stems from an inductive bias.

A further qualification should be inserted. In Sirkanda, as in most Indian villages, there are differences in internal social organization among various castes. They are less in the Pahari area than in many others and by comparison they may seem almost insignificant, but they do exist. Since 87 per cent of the population of Sirkanda is of one caste—Rajputs—more reliable data were obtained regarding that caste than any other. However, caste differences were a special focus of the research and were sought out whenever possible. Such differences as were revealed have been reported here. Differences not mentioned did not exist or were not obtained in investigation aimed at detecting them.

FAMILY

As the Wisers (1951, p. 160) have commented, "no villager thinks of himself apart from his family." Ideally the basic residential, social, religious, and economic unit in Sirkanda is the patrilocal extended family. This consists of a man, his wife, his sons, and their wives and children plus any unmarried daughters. In Sirkanda this unit is supposed to occupy a house, preferably with a separate sleeping room for each nuclear family consisting of man, wife, and children. It is an economic unit which includes fathers, sons, and brothers and their wives and unmarried daughters, and therefore may be termed a "joint family." All members share in the family occupation and in the product obtained. All eat from the same hearth—a distinguishing feature recognized by the people themselves, who refer to this family unit or household as the chula (cooking hearth). The eldest active male is the family head and bears final responsibility and authority for family well-being. The wife of the eldest male, whether he is living or not, is the head of the female component (wives and unmarried daughters) of the household in domestic matters. She becomes the titular head of the household upon her husband's death if there are no brothers to take over, but generally a son acts in her stead. Within the component nuclear families the age and sex hierarchy is the same.

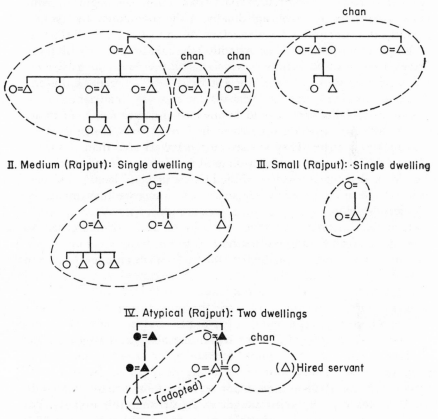

I. Largest household in Sirkanda (Rajput): Four dwellings

II. Medium (Rajput): Single dwelling

III. Small (Rajput): Single dwelling

IV. Atypical (Rajput): Two dwellings

(△) Hired servant

▲ deceased ancestor   △ living household member

Fig. 2. Household composition and residence. Residence in a single dwelling is indicated by a broken line.

In Sirkanda there are several types of deviation from this ideal pattern (see fig. 2). As has been mentioned previously, most households (37 of 45, or 82 per cent) own houses or chans outside of Sirkanda. Twenty-five of these joint families, 55 per cent of those in the village, are continually or usually split into two or more residential units because of regular occupancy of chans or second houses away from the village. Therefore, in over half the joint families the basic family economic unit is not a residential unit, as villagers say it ideally should be. The extended family may become permanently divided, and more distant households may sever connections with the village. As has been noted, approximately one-fifth of the living adult males who appear in Sirkanda genealogical materials do not appear as members of Sirkanda households at present. They have severed village and joint-family ties.

Between one-third and one-fourth of the family units (13 of 45, or 29 per cent) consist only of a nuclear family or a single individual. Seven more consist only of a nuclear family and a parent of the husband (a "minimal extended family"). In these 20 small family units there are 99 individuals, while among the 25 larger family units are the remaining 285 Sirkanda residents. Thus, over one-third of all Sirkanda residents live in family units much smaller than the ideal. Ten of the large units are fraternal joint families, consisting of brothers and their dependents, while 15 include one or both of an elder man-wife couple and their sons, daughters-in-law, unmarried daughters, and grandchildren.

Household membership ranges from 1 to 25 individuals with an average between 8 and 9. Thirteen households have 10 or over; thirteen have 5 or under. Household membership spans four generations in 1 case, three generations in 25 cases, two generations in 14 cases, and one generation in 5 cases. In only 4 cases have real brothers divided into separate households. In 1 case the only half-brothers currently in the village without a living father did so, and in 2 cases father-son divisions have occurred. In the latter instances the sons with their fathers' approval took advantage of chances for adoption into heirless families. Half-brothers quite consistently divide their father's property upon his death and establish separate joint-family households. Real brothers of the same mother rarely divide joint property, but the relatively landless low castes do so more frequently than the high castes. Of the four current cases, two are in low-caste families—the only low-caste brothers, with father deceased, in Sirkanda—while only two are in the high castes, of twelve possibilities in that group.

One of the most prominent differences between high and low castes in Sirkanda is in joint family size and composition. Not only do low-caste brothers usually divide their property when their father dies whereas high-caste brothers retain it intact, but low-caste people characteristically live in smaller joint family units. This is indicated in table 2. The differences are perhaps attributable more to economic conditions than to caste. All three of the low-caste extended family households are dependent in large part on agriculture, while none of the low-caste nuclear households has land to till. Agriculture requires many hands to make it productive, and it will feed many mouths. Two low-caste brothers, each the head of a good-sized extended family, have divided their lands and clients, but they perform one economic function jointly where teamwork is requisite, namely drumming. Thus it seems that larger joint families are usually retained when it is advantageous or necessary to do so, and they break down more readily when they perform no useful or necessary function.

TABLE 2

SIRKANDA POPULATION BY FAMILY TYPES

| | Households | | Population | |
	Extended families	Nuclear families	Extended families	Nuclear families
High castes	30	9	306	40
Low castes	3	4	22	16

Division of a household generally takes place among first cousins (brothers' sons). In no current cases do such first cousins belong to the same household unless their parents are living. Thus, the division of the extended family into smaller units occurs quite consistently after the third generation; that is, brothers do not often divide their father's property, but when the brothers die their offspring (first cousins) do divide it. This conforms to the ideal pattern.

It is worth noting in this connection that in nine of the 13 nuclear family household units there is no other nuclear family related to the household head more closely than at the first cousin level, the level at which division of the family is to be expected. Therefore, in only four cases can the nuclear family be called a voluntarily or prematurely segmented social and economic unit. Two of these households are those of blacksmith brothers and one is that of a Rajput who moved to his wife's house to acquire her inheritance. In the other nine cases, segmentation has resulted from necessity brought about either by differential birth and death rates or by the custom of dividing property in the third generation. Likewise, only one of the seven minimal extended families is minimal by choice. One Rajput household head expressed a common attitude:

These days in some of the families when boys become young men and are married they think of breaking away from the joint family. In my family my younger brother and I never thought of separating. Of course, now that our father is dead we don't know how things will take shape. But we like the joint family system. I sometimes feel overburdened being in charge of such a big family, but the household work, agricultural work, and tending the cattle is done very smoothly as there are enough people to take care of it all. If there are only two or three people in a family they just don't know how to take care of all of the agricultural and other work. They don't know where to leave their children when they go to work in the fields or to bring firewood and grass.

In the above figures on household size and composition I have included "polygamous families" with nuclear families. A polygamous family is made up of more than one nuclear family linked by a common spouse (Murdock, 1949, p. 2). In Sirkanda these are polygynous —multiple wives and a single husband—and generally with only two wives. Murdock calls both extended and polygamous families "composite" families, as distinguished from nuclear ones (Murdock, 1949, pp. 23 ff.). I have lumped the polygynous and nuclear types simply because in Sirkanda only a man-woman or man-women combination is a family. A man and woman are potentially an independent family unit; an additional wife is not. An additional wife does not alter the family make-up in the same sense that another nuclear family does. In any event, there are currently twelve polygynous families in Sirkanda, ten of which are included in larger joint families. Of these ten, two have only a dependent parent in addition. The other two constitute households in themselves. All are Rajputs and are therefore landholding families. Seven of these families occupy two separate houses, and five families occupy single houses. Size of the extended family is apparently the most important factor influencing the living arrangement in the polygynous families. A small family often has to separate wives into different locations in order to occupy outlying dwellings, whereas larger families send out an entire nuclear unit. In all five cases in which the polygynous family constitutes virtually the entire family unit, the co-wives and their children occupy separate dwellings. In all five cases in which they occupy a single house the extended family is large enough to tend its chans with other nuclear units. This leaves two cases in which wives are separated purely out of choice—a frequently cited means of minimizing co-wife friction.

MARRIAGE REGULATIONS

The nuclear family is established as a result of marriage customs described in the preceding chapter. Joshi summarizes the traits of Khasa marriage which distinguish it from Brahamanical Hindu marriage: existence of levirate, marriage as a secular transaction involving bride price, religious ceremony unessential for marriage, marriage dissolvable by mutual consent, remarriage of widows and divorcees recognized, sacred thread ceremony not deemed essential. These are characteristics of traditional marriage in Sirkanda. The religious ceremony and sacred thread ceremony are gaining prominence with the increasing trend toward Sanskritization (Joshi, 1929, pp. 50 f.). Here I will use the term "marriage" very loosely to designate any instance in which a man and woman live openly together so that any child born of the woman will be acknowledged to be that of the man as well.

As has been indicated, the ideal marriage is one between a previously unmarried man and woman with appropriate and compatible genealogical and astrological credentials. It is arranged by the parents of the principals without their direct participation and at the initiative of the groom's family.

In order to understand marriage regulations it will be necessary to jump ahead of the discussion and comment briefly upon two important social units more inclusive than the family. The largest of these is the caste or *jāt* (*jātī* in Hindi), which has frequently been mentioned in earlier chapters and which functions much as it does over the rest of India. It is the endogamous unit—the unit within which marriages should always be contracted. In fact, its extent may be defined by the extent of marriage ties. The other unit relevant to marriage is also called jat or jati by villagers but is here termed sib (cf. Lowie, 1947, p. 111; Murdock, 1949, p. 47). This is a subgroup of the caste and is composed of assumed consanguineal relatives. It is exogamous—its members are not potential mates.[1] Neither, according to the rules followed in this area, are people potential mates if their mothers (or, ideally, other maternal ancestors for several generations back) are of the same sib. Caste is virtually universal in India, while sibs occur primarily among the higher castes. In Sirkanda the low castes claim to have a sib structure, although their sibs are somewhat less consistently and uniformly defined than those of the high castes. Another feature of marriage in Sirkanda, as in most of India, is that it is normally patrilocal—the bride goes to live at the home of her husband and his family.

In practice it is found that these rules are followed quite rigidly in first marriages, arranged by the parents with the advice of Brahmins. The rules are less consistently obeyed in subsequent marriages, which are often informally contracted, and may even omit bride-price.

A total of 471 marriages were recorded in genealogical materials collected in Sirkanda—390 high-caste and 81 low-caste marriages. Of this number, 300 were marriages of village men (that is, sons of the village) and 143 of these were marriages of men who are living and currently identified as Sirkanda villagers.[2] For most purposes the 300 total is most useful in that it is large and is associated with accurate data. Data on village women's marriages, except those on location of spouse's village, are not complete enough to warrant their use.

Multiple Marriages

Ninety-six of 300 unions, 32 per cent, were second or subsequent marriages. These were almost evenly divided between polygynous unions and nonpolygynous or sequential unions (that is, in which first wife died or left before the second marriage). It is probable that in this accounting the number of nonpolygynous plural marriages are underreported because there is a tendency to overlook first wives, especially if they were childless and either left or died early in marriage. This is indicated by the fact that in the figures for living Sirkanda men such cases outnumber polygynous ones by one-third, while in the total figures there is a slight preponderance of polygynous marriages. It therefore seems likely that around 40 per cent of all marital unions are second or subsequent ones for the man. Polygynous marriages consistently form about 15 per cent of all unions.

Polygyny involving more than two wives is rare. Only four cases are reported in the genealogical materials, although it is likely that some cases stemming from inheritance of additional wives have gone unreported. Polygyny and nonpolygynous plural marriages have occurred in all castes represented in Sirkanda. No significant caste differences appear, but there is a tendency toward more polygyny among the high castes than among the low castes. This tendency may relate to the greater usefulness of extra wives in agricultural households than in others and the fact that extra wives can evidently pay their way in labor more effectively in agriculture than in the specialized occupations.

Since the people of the area are widely reputed in India to be polygamous, some special inquiry was directed toward determining the extent and nature of such marital arrangements. In the process some detailed information about marriage in general was obtained. I have already indicated that polyandry is not at all practiced here as it is in neighboring Jaunsar-Bawar. In the discussion of intrafamily relations it will become evident, however, that there is not as much difference as might be expected in the sexual arrangements within the family in these two areas (cf. Berreman, 1962a).

I have shown in the above discussion that polygynous unions are permitted and occur with a frequency of about 15 per cent. Twelve established polygynous families and one *de facto* case on the verge of public recognition were observed in some detail in Sirkanda. They were the total current cases wherein all the principals were alive and participating in the marriage. All were Rajputs.

Reasons given for polygyny in particular cases were four: (1) to produce children when the first wife has been barren, (2) to help with the work, (3) for "pleasure," (4) inheritance of an additional wife from a deceased brother.

In eight cases of polygyny in Sirkanda the first two reasons were given in combination. The work contributed by the second wife was stressed in each of these cases, but sterility of the first wife was apparently the primary motivation. In one of the cases the woman herself asked that another wife be brought for these two reasons, and it was her father who made the necessary arrangements to secure a distant classificatory sister as her co-wife. In another case the husband was inclined to repeated marriages—he had had four previous wives—but had produced no children and claimed to need two women at a time to take care of the work.

One villager commented,

A wife is a valuable asset here. Here the wife takes care of her husband in many ways, and she does much of the work of the household. Therefore, two wives are better than one. In your country and in the plains the husband has to support the woman, so a second wife is a hardship and a luxury.

Atkinson (1886, p. 255) says that in Garhwal "the custom probably arose from the great difficulty there was in cultivating the large amount of waste land available. Wives were procured to help in field work. . . ."

In three cases in Sirkanda "pleasure" was given as the reason for taking a second wife; that is, there was no question of need for more workers or more children in the family. In two cases wives were inherited from elder brothers. In one of these cases a man inherited two wives from his brother and already had one of his own. He had not declared that the widows were his wives, though in fact they were, and one of the inherited wives had borne a son by him. It was expected that the relationship would soon be publicly acknowledged, especially in view of the fact that one of the inherited wives had moved from her deceased husband's house to that of his brother shortly before my departure. In two additional cases a man got his second wife from a living brother. In one case the husband acquiesced when his wife declared her intention to leave and expressed her desire to marry her husband's brother. In the other case the man simply took over the wife of his younger brother, lived with her and his first wife in a chan, and fathered a son by her. After the birth of the son and an announcement by the household head (a still older brother), she became publicly known as his wife. At that time the younger brother was promised a new wife.

Fifteen of the 27 women in these polygynous marriages were virgins (that is, previously unmarried) at marriage. The twelve nonvirgins included the five procured from brothers (three inherited, two taken) and seven divorcees. There is a significant difference in the incidence of virgin brides among first, as compared to second, wives in these polygynous unions. Ten first wives were virgins and three were nonvirgins, while five second wives were virgins and nine were nonvirgins. Although three cases of inheritance account for three of the nonvirgin second wives, there is still a marked tendency to accept previously married brides as second wives and to reject them as first wives. There is also a preference for marrying a virgin daughter to a single man.

In 22 of the 27 marriages in these 13 families, bride-price payment was made at the time of marriage either to the bride's family or to a former husband, while in only one case, a first marriage, was a dowry given instead. The remaining four cases were those of wives obtained from a brother and involved no exchange of money.

Marriage ceremonies were performed in seven of the 13 initial marriages which established families destined to become polygynous. All seven were among the 10 with virgin brides. This conforms to the village ratio: about 50 per cent of all marriages have been without benefit of ceremony, and ceremonies are performed only when the bride is previously unmarried.

Second marriages are less often ceremonialized than first ones. Of the 14 second marriages (that is, those which made the family polygynous), only two were ceremonialized, and both of these were among the five such marriages which involved virgin brides. Intervals between marriages ranged from two to 20 years. In six marriages the co-wives normally shared a house or chan as residence, and in seven marriages they were separated.[3]

Three of the thirteen instances of polygyny were sororal—sisters married to the same man. Two pairs of co-wives were real sisters and the other pair were classificatory sisters (daughters of first cousins related through the male line).

Levirate, or inheritance of wives from a brother, is standard procedure here. Either an elder or younger brother may inherit at the discretion of the household head, who is usually the eldest surviving brother. Although no preference for junior levirate was expressed in Sirkanda, it is most frequent, probably because elder brothers tend to die first. If an outsider wishes to marry the widow, he must secure permission and reimburse her husband's family. This, too, is frequently done. Elopement is another frequent means by which a widow marries the man of her choice. A boy who has been betrothed and then dies may be replaced by his brother to fulfill the marital contract. There is no evidence of the systematic practice of sororate, wherein a deceased woman is replaced by her single sister in the marital union. Two or three isolated instances occur in the data. Similarly, there are isolated instances of brothers marrying women who are sisters, but this is an unusual arrangement neither encouraged nor discouraged.

In this society it is important to contract proper marriages for one's children. Once this has been done, regardless of what may happen subsequently, the honor of the family is intact. Danger of an intercaste or intra-sib union is precluded because a proper match has been made. If, later, a proscribed alliance develops, the individuals involved will take the blame; the family has done its duty. This explains the fact that no deviations from rules of caste endogamy and sib exogamy were found or reported for first marriages in Sirkanda. Maintenance of family honor is also offered as an explanation for early marriage. Early marriage prevents the disgrace of an unwed mother or nonvirginal bride because no girl old enough for childbearing or adult sex activity is unwed. That she may have relations with various men and perhaps even bear children by them in the absence of her husband is irrelevant—she is a properly married woman. Virginity at first marriage is important, while sex behavior thereafter is unimportant. As one man put it, "We disobey the law [which sets the minimum marriage age for girls at fourteen], but we protect our honor." As a result, unwed pregnant girls are a rarity. When they are found out they are immediately married to their lover if possible, or to one of their sisters' husbands, or to some boy whose family is willing —usually a family hard pressed to find a bride for financial or other reasons. Unwed mothers are virtually unknown. The nearest approach to unwed motherhood that can be cited in the village is the occasional un-rewed widow who bears a child, to the consternation of her family.

First marriages for women, as described in the preceding chapter, are likely to be accompanied by ceremony and public acclaim. Subsequent marriages for women are contracted without ceremony and receive little attention, though they do receive public recognition and approval. Second marriages for men are less likely to be ceremonialized than first ones. In second marriages which run counter to rules of endogamy or exogamy, and in other "love marriages," the couple usually elopes or the woman comes secretly to the home of her new husband and the marriage is accepted by others as a *fait accompli*. Numerous cases of this kind have occurred among all castes. They are frequent bases for disputes, sometimes resulting in long-standing factional splits involving considerable numbers of people.

Endogamy

Paharis have a reputation for disregarding the rules of caste endogamy and other orthodox Hindu marriage regulations. My data indicate that in this region the reputation is undeserved so far as initial marriages are concerned but finds corroboration in subsequent marriages. While no deviations occurred among first marriages in Sirkanda, some did occur in second or subsequent marriages. The numbers of such deviations are not large, but the fact that they exist is important.

In Sirkanda there is at present one established and recognized intercaste union—that of a Rajput man and a Brahmin woman who eloped. The woman came to the man's village and took up residence with him, and he then reimbursed her former husband, a Brahmin. The only long-range effect in Sirkanda was estrangement between the Rajput husband and his brothers, who resented his bringing a Brahmin woman into the family. To this day his elder brother will not let the Brahmin woman into his house, nor allow her to address him as "husband's elder brother." In the woman's village the Brahmins were angry but did nothing beyond lodging a prompt protest and threatening to punish physically the Rajput who took this woman. There is a similarly accepted union of a Brahmin man and a Rajput woman in another Bhatbair village.

A second case involving a Rajput man and a Brahmin woman in a neighboring village was terminated by public pressure after a council met and directed that the woman be returned to her former husband and the abductor pay a fine (which he avoided by leaving the village). A child had been conceived in this union, and there was talk of inducing an abortion. However, when the father left and the woman settled back with her former husband the idea was dropped. The child was born and was accepted as a Brahmin—as the offspring of the man and wife in whose household it was born—despite its well-known and undoubted parentage. The Rajput involved was a well-known "loafer" or philanderer who had left more than one wife and had established unions with several women, including a low-caste woman. Moreover, he had taken the Brahmin woman far away, to Delhi, on the strength of promises which were never fulfilled. He failed to provide for her properly and allegedly mistreated her and sold her jewelry for his own profit. Had he been a stable member of the community, it is likely that little sentiment would have been aroused over the incident. Normally feeling does not run high in such cases. As a Brahmin commented in the council meeting to resolve this case, "There is not much difference between Rajputs and Brahmins, so it doesn't matter very much anyway." On the other hand a Rajput was apparently incensed and made the comment, "A Brahmin woman is like a mother to Rajputs." The latter attitude is evidently a statement of ideal rather than actual behavior.

Unions across high- and low-caste lines meet with greater public disapproval. They are nearly always unions of high-caste men with low-caste women; the reverse is violently condemned and could not be continued if it were known. In Sirkanda two Rajput men have taken low-caste wives from outside the village—one of barber caste and one of a charcoal-making group. Both unions were terminated under public pressure when the facts became known. One Rajput man related to a Sirkanda family but resident in a neighboring village took three low-caste wives, a weaver, a carpenter, and a blacksmith, and lived with all three at once. In the case of the last of these the couple underwent a ceremony at the insistence of the girl's parents, for she had not been previously married. A Brahmin was found to perform it, but no one other than the girl's relatives attended. The man remained with these three wives throughout his life but was ostracized by his own caste. His one son is of the caste of his mother but has inherited the property of his father. A life-long Rajput-weaver union existed in a nearby village, and in another village a Rajput had three blacksmith wives. Both the blacksmiths and Bajgis of Sirkanda trace their ancestry to high-caste male ancestors, a Rajput and a Brahmin, respectively, who married women of low caste with the result that their children were assigned to the same caste as their mothers. Whether this ancestry is fact or fancy, it is believed and indicates the possibility of such unions and their results.

An extreme case of intercaste marriage in Bhatbair involved the elopement of a boy of shoemaker caste and a Brahmin girl—the lowest and highest castes and the reverse of the expected sex-caste affiliation. This was a universally disapproved case. When such a union is hypothesized to villagers in a question, the questioner is promptly assured that the result would be death to the man or perhaps to both partners, and lifelong ostracism should either survive. In reality, the couple ran off to Dehra Dun, where they lived together for some time. There fellow shoemakers finally put pressure on the boy to return the girl to her people, and he too went home. Now both live in their respective villages, unmarriageable but otherwise unimpeded in carrying on their normal lives. Rumor has it that they are still in love and perhaps in surreptitious contact and that they have no desire to remarry even were this allowed.

Among the low castes, blacksmiths and carpenters form a single endogamous group while weavers and the immigrant Sirkanda barbers are separated from them and from one another by little social or ritual distance. These groups intermarry frequently and without public disapproval (see discussion of "Relations Among Low Castes" in chap. 7).

Bajgis and shoemakers stay within their respective castes more consistently as they are more distant from one another and from the above group than are the castes within the above group. Exceptions cutting across these lines probably occur with about the same frequency and results as the above-listed high-caste deviations. No examples of exceptions were found in Bhatbair, where only a small sample of low-caste marriages could be obtained because of their small numbers.

Married women of any caste may be "sold" to outsiders, as described in the section on "Illegal Economic Activities" in chapter 2. In such cases caste is not a significant consideration. There are Sirkanda women who have been married in this way to plains merchants (*Banias*), Nepalese Rajput military officers, and a Sikh religious leader. There is no caste in Bhatbair whose women have not on occasion been involved in such transactions, though all, and especially the high castes, are careful to conceal the fact. In terms of frequency, more low-caste women have been sold. Usually the woman's family and her husband lack prior knowledge and do not consent, although one Rajput husband apparently connived in such a transaction in order to make way for a new wife for himself. Among the low castes an unmarried girl is occasionally "sold" by her parents to outsiders in this fashion. Two such instances were recorded as initial marriages in Sirkanda. These were two of 32 recorded marriages of low-caste village girls, so the practice is not especially rare.

One current case of cross-caste marriage exists in Sirkanda and three others have been reported in recent years, constituting a total of about 1 per cent of all unions. Marriage of women to non-Paharis would not raise this above 2 per cent at the maximum. Of the local intercaste unions only Rajput-Brahmin and some inter-low-caste marriages survived public disapproval. In all reported cases marriages which crossed the boundary between high and low castes resulted either in ostracism of the high-caste partner by his caste-fellows or dissolution of the marriage under public pressure. No union would be allowed to persist between a high-caste woman and a low-caste man, and none would be openly attempted in the area. There is an explicit tradition that, while intercaste marriage is not permissible, if it does in fact occur and if it is repeated for seven generations, a new caste is formed and recognized. No example of this was known, and the mechanics of its operation were hazy in the minds of villagers. Normally the children of an intercaste union belong to the caste of the lower-caste parent, usually the mother.

Before closing this discussion of rules of endogamy it may be relevant to mention that the most popular Pahari song in Sirkanda during 1957–1958 glorified an intercaste elopement and widow remarriage. This song, sung primarily by young people as they worked in the jungle, had several versions. In essence, it was the story of a young widow of weaver caste who was directed by her own and her husband's family to remain in the family of her deceased husband. Unable to face the prospect of such a lonely life, she eloped to the plains with a Brahmin man. Tracked down by her relatives, the couple were taken to court, where the magistrate ruled in favor of the couple, saying that it was their right to do as they felt best. He fined the relatives for causing such inconvenience to all concerned. The couple went off to live happily ever after, but not before the woman's relatives had secured a measure of revenge by branding her on the forehead with a red-hot coin. The song is allegedly based on a true story of recent origin in a neighboring area of Tehri Garhwal. It was popular with all castes, and the heroine was known affectionately to all by her pet name.

Thus, marriage across caste lines is not abhorred in this society to the extent that it is in many areas of India. Rules of endogamy are not rigidly adhered to, but they are not violated as frequently as the Pahari reputation would lead one to expect.[4] Intercaste marriage is tolerated if it is not the initial marriage and if the castes of the individuals involved are of the same general economic and social level. As will become evident in later discussion, this is one aspect of a generally looser definition of appropriate caste behavior in the hills as compared to the plains.

Exogamy

Besides caste endogamy, marriages are also regulated by sib exogamy. In this region no person is allowed to marry within his own sib or that of his mother. To do so would be to commit incest, since it would be to marry classificatory siblings or other relatives. All of the mother's sib is included within the kindred (discussed below). Children of mother's siblings (real and classificatory) are classified as siblings of ego, even though they are of different sib affiliation, just as are children of father's siblings. In addition, among the high castes the sibs of direct female ancestors are supposed to be excluded from eligibility for marriage for five to ten generations back, as reported variously by Brahmin informants, who are the ultimate authorities on such matters. This is evidently an expression of the Hindu *sapindā* rule of exogamy prohibiting marriage within the bilaterally defined kindred:

> The marriage rules as regards *Sapinda* relationship or consanguinity define that a man should not marry a girl who is related to him through a common male ancestor up to the 7th generation in the father's line and up to the 5th generation in the mother's line. Different law books give different rules. (Karve, 1953, p. 55)

Unfortunately in Sirkanda sib affiliation of village wives proved to be a difficult and unreliable type of data to obtain for generations preceding the present, although marriage does not alter a woman's sib affiliation. However, the village contains two large and two smaller Rajput sibs. The data on these are good and throw light on the matter of inter-sib marriage arrangements, since these sibs can and do intermarry frequently in the village. Fifty-three Rajput marriages between people of the sibs found in Sirkanda were recorded, and they revealed no cases of marriage within own or mother's sib on first or subsequent marriages.[5] Four cases of marriage into paternal grandmother's sib occurred. One of these four was a first marriage, and two comprised an instance of sororal polygyny. This indicates that the effective exogamous units are own and mother's sib only, and accords with information given by Joshi (1929, p. 75) and with the testimony of uneducated Rajput informants, who mentioned only these as prohibited groups.

A single instance of intra-sib marriage was reported. The wife of a Sirkanda Rajput left him shortly after marriage to live as wife of a man in another village who stood in the relationship of father's brother's son's son to her and was therefore her sib-fellow and nephew. Since this was a second marriage, objection was mild and the union has endured. Probably the fact that the relationship was not particularly close and that the woman was not older than the man added to its acceptability. No other instances of marriages within incest boundaries appeared. Perhaps this is partly because when they occur among the most distant prohibited relationships they are not as conspicuous as the more frequently reported intercaste marriages. However, these data and the expressed attitudes of villagers suggest that rules of exogamy are less frequently broken than rules of endogamy in this society.

Marriage Networks

There is no rule of village exogamy in this area such as is reported for other parts of North India, including nearby Jaunsar-Bawar (Saksena, 1955, p. 28; Berreman, 1962d). Neither is there any reluctance to give and take brides in the same village as is true, for example, among the Noniyas of Senapur (Rowe, 1960b). As will be mentioned again, high-caste sibs in Sirkanda may derive from formerly exogamous community affiliation, but this does not affect the present situation in and around Sirkanda. In this region, if a man and woman of the same caste are not within one another's kindred, if they are of different sibs and their mothers are of different sibs, they are potential mates regardless of village membership. Local exogamy often results from the fact that these conditions cannot be met within the village, but this is local exogamy in effect, not in intent. Local exogamy occurs in all castes of Sirkanda except Rajputs, because all but they are single-sib local segments of castes. Some Bhatbair villages are entirely single-sib villages, and hence their members must marry outside the village.

Of 471 recorded marriages contracted by Sirkanda people, 377 were Rajput marriages, and of these 77, or 20 per cent, were contracted within the village.[6] The remaining 394 Sirkanda marriages were contracted with people of 92 identified villages and four general areas at greater distances—roughly 400 marriages in 100 localities (see map 2). The numbers ranged from 45 marriages in one village (Kanda) to one each in 36 villages. Thirty per cent of these marriages were contracted in seven villages, and 80 per cent were contracted in 50 villages (including the seven just mentioned but excluding Sirkanda), all within a four air-mile radius of the village, that is, eight trail miles, an easy half-day's trip. This leaves 20 per cent of the nonvillage marriages spread over 42 villages and four broader areas up to 18 air miles distant (about 35 trail miles, a two-day trip each way). Thus, of all Sirkanda marriages, 83 per cent are within a radius of four air miles. Sixteen per cent (all Rajput marriages) are within Sirkanda itself.[7] A villager remarked, "On the plains it is easy to travel, and people there go great distances for brides. Here it is very difficult to get around so we have to find ours closer to our own village. It is as hard to go one mile here as it is to go five miles in the plains on foot, and many places there they can go by motor bus or at least by cart."

Virtually all Sirkanda marriages are contracted in Pahari villages, although non-Pahari villages are well-known and easily accessible within five air miles of the village, in the valley en route to Dehra Dun. Marriages at distances this great or greater comprise 17 per cent of all village unions, but they are all in Tehri Garhwal, which is culturally more similar, though physically less accessible, than the valley. The only exceptions in Sirkanda have been six barber-caste marriages and the sale of two low-caste women to outsiders.[8]

Caste differences in distribution of spouses' villages revealed differential extent in marriage networks (cf. Rowe, 1960b) in the various castes. Eighty-five per cent of high-caste marriages occurred within the four-mile radius, and 73 per cent of Bajgi, 53 per cent of blacksmith, and 35 per cent of barber marriages were that close. This is a direct reflection of the relative population of these groups and of the outside origin of the barbers. The fewer the potential mates for a group in the area, the farther they have to go to find mates. The overwhelming majority of Bhatbair residents are Rajputs and Brahmins. Likewise, individual villages reflect their caste and sib composition in the frequency of intermarriage with Sirkanda villagers. One village provided 45 mates, all Rajputs, while another provided 14 mates, 12 of low castes, and two Brahmins. There were no discernible patterned differences between distribution of bride-giving and bride-taking villages; that is, giving and taking of brides appeared to occur randomly among villages in the marriage networks of each caste, except where sib exogamy prevented it.

The marriage network of each caste roughly defines the limits of its informal social interaction outside the village. Most visiting is done with relatives, and most relatives outside the village are affines. However, the village community remains the social unit of most frequent and important interaction. It is not surpassed, even among low castes (as is the case among Senapur Noniyas) by the intervillage marriage network. Low-caste people of Sirkanda have not experienced the newfound freedom of the Noniyas and, even if they had, demography and topography might have precluded development of transcendent social and political functions characteristic of the marriage network of Senapur (cf. Rowe, 1960b, p. 310). Sirkanda villagers are still closely tied to the multi-caste village dominated by the local Rajputs.

New Wives for Old

Divorce and remarriage are frequent among the people of Sirkanda, although perhaps not so common as in Jaunsar-Bawar, where Majumdar (1944, p. 162) reports that barrenness results in divorce and Saksena (1955, p. 36) reports that the "slightest disloyalty or the slightest slip" on the part of a wife may result in divorce.[9]

A couple who do not get along well together or who have specific grievances either on their own part or that of their families—for example, the wife refusing to stay with her husband, or the husband's family refusing to make good the bride price—may go through a procedure called *chūt,* divorce, which breaks the marriage bond. Either party may initiate this action. In such cases an *ad hoc* panchayat, or council, of friends of both parties acts as intermediary to achieve a satisfactory settlement. A written agreement is signed by the father of the wife and by the husband or his father. The agreement specifies the amount to be paid by the family of the wife and states that thereafter the parties are to be free of mutual obligation. In addition, a sum is paid to the panchayat. If the girl plans to live with someone else, that man may pay the former husband's family either directly or indirectly. One such formal dissolution occurred in a Rajput family in the year 1957–1958.

A much more common type of divorce, and virtually the only type among low castes, occurs when a wife goes to her parents' home or to another man and refuses to return, or a husband sends her home. In the former case the husband will try to exact reimbursement but may not be successful, especially if the wife runs some distance away. Village or caste panchayats may intervene to secure a just settlement in such cases. In any elopement the panchayat is called by the family with which the girl was affiliated at the time (usually the husband's family, but sometimes the bride's parents), as they are the aggrieved party.

Threats of running away or unannounced short-term retreats to the home village are used by women to secure better treatment from their husbands. Husbands may deprive errant wives of things they want (trinkets, new clothes, attendance at a fair) or physically punish them. No accurate data were obtained on frequency with which the husband, as compared to the wife, instigated divorce, but it appears to be about equal. Although precise data are lacking, it seems likely that at least 20 per cent of all marriages are dissolved by formal or informal divorce. This estimate is based primarily on figures for high castes. Unlike the plains situation, where low-caste divorce is frequent but high-caste divorce is infrequent or concealed, there are no apparent differences in divorce rates among the various hill castes. Divorce is taken as a matter of course.

Causes of divorce are many and complex. Failure to fulfill the formal and informal obligations of marriage are overt reasons given for divorce. Among reasons given in specific instances were: nonpayment of bride price, nonvirginity of allegedly virginal bride, mental or physical defect in one partner, bride's failure to perform her duties in the house, bride's inability to get along with in-laws, bride's refusal to stay in the household or refusal to return after postmarriage visit to her home, husband's mistreatment of wife, husband's failure to provide adequately for wife, husband's departure from village leaving wife stranded there, father-in-law's molestation of bride, and persistent adultery or philandering on part of wife or husband. Occasional adultery is not normally a ground for divorce and is, in fact, expected. However, when it is practiced openly, when lasting attachments are made, when a person acquires a reputation for excessive indulgence—especially if it involves cross-caste relations—or when a person neglects his or her spouse in favor of a lover, divorce is likely to follow. If either partner falls in love with someone else, he or she is likely to leave or purposely bring about divorce. In at least one case in Sirkanda a wife left when her husband took a second wife, although his intent had been to establish a polygynous relationship. A Brahmin man in a nearby village lost his first wife, a Brahmin, when he brought in a Rajput woman as second wife. Remarriage after divorce is almost universal. Some men and women have had a succession of marriages. One Sirkanda man voluntarily parted with three successive wives. One nineteen-year-old girl is living with her third successive husband, a young Sirkanda man. On the other hand, one village daughter in Sirkanda has returned home after a particularly unhappy marriage, resolved to live out her life in the large extended family of her parents and brothers and never to remarry.

Remarriage after a spouse's death is expected. High-caste plains customs in this regard are known but not envied. This is one instance in which orthodox, Sanskritic custom is not emulated. Even educated Pahari Brahmins do not press for it, saying that in these hills it is impractical to keep dependent widows unmarried. There is no reluctance to discuss the subject and no inferiority feeling about it, as there is about some non-Sanskritic practices. One Rajput man said,

> Forbidding widow remarriage is a stupid custom. What is a widow to do with herself if she does not remarry? She is a burden to her family and to herself. Anyway, it would not work here. Every man needs a woman and every woman needs a man. If our widows didn't remarry we would have dependent widows and unmarried men who couldn't do all of their work in the village. It is taken care of easily because the woman often goes to her husband's brother.

If a widow remarries outside her husband's family, she usually gives up her rights to her husband's property, though her children by him will receive it when they reach maturity, even if she keeps them with her. Occasionally a widow remains in her husband's house and remains a clan member, even though she does not become the wife of one of his brothers. Rarely such a woman will take a husband from outside the family and yet remain in the house. As in the unusual case of a matrilocal initial marriage, this occurs only if there are no eligible men in the family and most often when there are no other adults in the family at all. The new husband then becomes a member of the clan of his new wife and her former husband. He is derisively said to have "gone to sit" at the woman's house, and he is likely to be ridiculed if he is an outsider in the village. The arrangement is advantageous if the woman has property from her first husband which she can in this way retain and still be remarried. One such case had occurred in a Sirkanda chan in recent years.

ADOPTION

Having children, and especially sons, is very important in Sirkanda families, as it is throughout Hindu India. The son not only helps with the work and carries on the family line but inherits the father's property and performs the necessary rites associated with the death and postdeath welfare of his parents. If no son is born to a man he often designates his son-in-law to fulfill these roles. The son-in-law must then come to live in the father's house, and he manages the lands of his deceased father-in-law, ultimately passing them on to his sons by this wife, or to an adopted son. If he has no sons, the land does not revert to others in his lineage, but stays in the lineage of his wife.

If a man has no son or daughter, he may designate some other relative to be his heir and to perform the death rites. More often, however, he will adopt a son. Girls are not adopted. There are currently four cases of adoption in Sirkanda. An adopted son is usually a relative who stands to gain more in the way of property by the adoption than if he stayed with his real parents. Often he is a daughter's son. He may be a boy born under an inauspicious asterism, an orphan or semi-orphan, or one of many brothers in a poor family. Like marriage, adoption does not alter sib affiliation, but it does alter clan identification. Adoption is frequently resented by relatives of the adopter, who would inherit his property were it not for the adopted heir. Sometimes a family offers a son for adoption, especially when he is near adulthood already, for purely mercenary reasons: they hope to get additional property into the family.

Adoption is publicly recognized but is informally effected without ceremony. The adopted child simply comes to live with the adopting family, and it is announced that this boy will inherit the property of his new father. From that time on the boy is treated as a son by his new parents. "An adopted son is just like a real son to his father. He serves and honors his father even more than a real son would. Since a foster father has no other sons, he showers more affection on the adopted boy than he would if he had several of his own. He won't adopt a boy he doesn't like." If adoption occurs in childhood, the boy grows up in the family as a son. If, as is often the case, adoption occurs later in life —after the foster parents have given up all hope of offspring of their own—the boy moves into the household of his new parents even if he is already married. He begins to share in that economic unit and ceases to share in that of his real father. The parents by adoption will make wedding arrangements and payments if the boy is unmarried or takes a second wife. In such cases the boy may be entitled to claim inheritance from his real parents as well as the foster ones. Adoption is generally arranged with an advance understanding on this matter, and usually the boy surrenders his claim to his real parents' property.

Sometimes an orphaned or otherwise disadvantaged child, usually a relative, is taken into a family where there are already several children. There is less interest in such a child, probably because he is thrust upon the family and will perform no important function for it, and often he is exploited and deprived in comparison to the real offspring of the family. Two current instances of this type were found among Sirkanda families.

CHILD REARING

An important function of the family is, of course, child rearing. Children are usually carefully cared for. If there are already four or more in the family, a child may tend to suffer from neglect. Infant mortality rates are high, but accurate data are unavailable. Three children two years of age or under died out of 31 in the village during 1957–1958. One of five born during the year died shortly after birth. Two families reported twice as many births as living children; some others had had few or no infant deaths. Probably infant and child mortality runs over 20 per cent.

Children are not given solid foods until a year after birth. They continue to nurse until another child is born, and sporadically thereafter. Occasionally a youngest child may be allowed to suck for six years or longer.

The atmosphere of child rearing is indulgent and permissive. The child is allowed to handle anything within reach, and its parents or relatives and friends are usually around the house, sitting on the floor where the child can crawl over them as it pleases and where they can show it whatever attention it demands. Almost anything a small child does is accepted. No special effort is made to encourage the child to walk. Toilet training is gradual and not intensive; the mother or a sibling simply begins taking the child out of the living area of the house when defecation or urination seems imminent, and accidents are tolerated without comment for at least three years. The small child, until it can walk competently, spends most of the time in the house or on the hip of an elder sibling. Since dwelling rooms are on the second story, doorways and verandas are barricaded with boards to protect the infant from falling. Often the child is tied around the waist with a leash attached to a bedpost. In most extended families someone, often an elderly person, is always around to look after the child, and this is cited as an advantage of the extended family system. In families where there is no extra person about to watch the child, it may simply be locked in the house when the parents have to be away to work in the fields or forest. One infant was burned to death in 1957 when it rolled into the fireplace after having been left alone while its parents were working in the fields. As children grow old enough to get about easily and to take care of themselves, they are free to roam the village with siblings or other children, though they are encouraged to stay near the house when unaccompanied.

About half the boys resident in the village and an occasional girl attend the local school with varying degrees of regularity from age 6 to 11 or 12. The children who attend are those whose parents want them to, and this is largely a matter of whether they are needed to help with the household work. By age 8 to 12 boys begin to accompany their fathers in their work, while girls continue to help their mothers. By age 14 a girl is ready to live with her husband, whom she has married 1 to 3 years earlier. Ideally she should have her first menstruation in her husband's household, but some marry considerably later. A boy is ready to take a wife by 16 or 17, though some do not do so until later.

Throughout childhood the child is rarely disciplined. He is reprimanded, commanded, and threatened, but these words are not often enforced by physical means, and the child soon learns this. Lackadaisical compliance is the typical reaction to adult direction. The child is generally in the company of other children but is rarely excluded from adult company. There is little a child cannot see and attempt to imitate, although sex activity is (not very successfully) concealed from children. Caste consciousness and discrimination are learned from childhood through instructions received, references overheard, and behavior observed. However, caste barriers do not enter into children's interaction among themselves until after puberty. One case of mutual "puppy love" during my stay in the village was between a 15-year-old blacksmith boy and the 14-year-old daughter of the village headman, a Rajput and the wealthiest man in the village. During this period the girl became engaged to her future husband, but this did not dismay her nor her friend. Their relationship was concealed from adults but not for reasons of caste.

INTRAFAMILY RELATIONS

Patterns of interaction among members of the patrilocal extended family depend in large part upon interplay of age, sex, and relationship roles. Males take precedence over females, age over youth, consanguineal over affinal relationship.

As has been stated, the eldest active male is the household head. This man is in the relationship of father or elder brother to other adult males in the family. He is responsible for all decisions in the family, and his is the final authority, whether it be in matters of allocating lands to crops, performing worship, or arranging a marriage. The father is not always the authoritarian family head as ideally described. He may hesitate to rebuke an adult son. The father of one young Sirkanda man was disturbed at his son's continual absence from home in pursuit of an illicit love affair in another village. He was not doing his share of the family work (they were Bajgis). But the father had not the courage to face the boy on the matter. Finally he went to the husband of his son's lover and complained to him that his wife was ruining the boy and taking his money, and that the affair must stop. The husband, who had known of the affair but had not interfered (probably because his wife was getting material rewards for her service), then spoke to the young man and told him to leave the woman alone. It worked, for a time at least, with a minimum of hard feeling and no intrafamily tension in the Sirkanda family.

In most instances the family head acts on family matters after consulting with other males and often his wife as well, but this is not necessary nor prescribed. When an old man becomes senile or inactive or when he dies, he is replaced by the next in line. If conflict occurs over succession, the joint family is likely to divide. An old and inactive man tends to be ignored or actively resented by other family members and he himself often resents their attitudes toward him, so that everyone looks forward to his death. Old men, like old women, find occupation around the house in caring for children or doing domestic tasks. After the death of the household head his widow may be referred to as the head, but in reality the authority usually passes to the next eldest male if he is an adult.

Among brothers in a family, age takes precedence. Younger brothers are expected to obey and respect their elders. This rule applies to parallel cousins (father's brother's sons) as well as to real brothers. Sisters are expected to respect and obey brothers regardless of relative age, though of course they often care for and wield authority over much younger brothers in childhood. Among sisters, age takes precedence. The mother has the honor and respect of sons and daughters. She retains authority over daughters till they marry, and loses authority over sons as they reach maturity.

Before proceeding further it will be well to emphasize that Pahari women of all castes enjoy a degree of freedom unknown among any but the low-caste women of the plains. They work alone or in groups without male accompaniment. They come and go as they please around the village and talk to whomever they please except strangers. They are not restricted to separate living quarters, and they are not subject to *purdāh* (seclusion). Therefore in the ensuing discussion, their subordination to men must be recognized as subordination within a context of relative freedom. It is not the same order of subordination found among many plains groups. One indication of this is the ease with which divorce and remarriage are effected and the freedom allowed women in sexual matters. If a woman is unhappy she can always turn elsewhere or go home.

The relationship between the patrilineal family and the wives who have joined it from outside is ideally one of a cohesive group taking in a stranger. The bride comes in to be critically appraised by the extant in-group. She must prove herself by her good works. The new wife finds herself at the bottom of a well-established hierarchy. She often does not know her husband, and in any event his loyalties and responsibilities are first to the family. She is under the direct authority of her mother-in-law and the wives of her husband's elder brothers. She must show obedience, respect, and deference to all of her elders. She shows respect by never using the names of the males and elder females in the family, by never smoking in their presence or laughing to their faces. Often she is accepted and even comforted by all or most of the women in the household. Sometimes she is not. Her fate in this respect is in the unpredictable hands of others, and therefore it is an uncertain and potentially unpleasant one. Consequently the tears of a bride at leaving her family of origin are not entirely conventional. As time passes and a wife proves her value as a contributing member of the family through her industry and skill and especially by producing children, her position becomes increasingly secure. As younger sisters-in-law come in, her authority increases. She learns which family members are her friends and which are not; to whom she can turn for consolation and from whom she must keep her secrets. Often a woman's husband becomes her strongest ally and will mediate on her behalf if necessary. The husband's younger brothers are traditionally her friends, and often it is only with them that a young wife is able to establish an easy, informal friendship. There is something of the "joking relationship" between these two that is traditional over much of North India. Sisters-in-law may become friends and so may other village wives, especially if they have previous ties, as when they are related to one another or are from the same village. In such cases a woman may receive moral support outside the family, but her loyalties and responsibilities must remain with her husband's family. This is true even when her own family lives in the same village. In such a case a woman is in frequent interaction with her family of origin, but she must be careful not to let such interaction interfere with her responsibilities to her husband's family.

One day in Sirkanda a young village wife who lived a stone's throw from her parents' house stopped to talk to her mother. The mother and she requested that she be photographed with her infant daughter. When I offered to do so at once, they quickly declined, saying that the girl's mother-in-law had sent her to collect fodder and would not like it if she delayed to be photographed at her mother's request. I was advised to come to the mother-in-law some time and offer to take the photograph without mentioning this prior arrangement.

A woman's natal household gods may intervene in her behalf if she is mistreated by her husband's family. If worst comes to worst, it is relatively easy for her to escape to her home or to another potential husband. This happens frequently in the village, though usually a girl's parents return her to her husband, often after a conference with her husband's family. In happier circumstances a wife from outside the village can expect to visit her home about once a year for a few days or weeks and can expect to see relatives and friends from her own village occasionally on visits.

In visits to her village of origin, among her parents and siblings and childhood friends, a woman is very free and relaxed. She is under the authority of parents and brothers, but it is normally an indulgent authority. She has few responsibilities at home. Her brothers' wives do the work, and she is the guest of honor. There is no one to watch her moves and report or criticize her behavior. She is more likely to joke, talk, or flirt with men and dance if a dance is held, than in her husband's village. Often she uses the opportunity to carry on clandestine love affairs with the men of the village whom she knew in her youth. There is something of the "double standard of morality" for a woman in the house of her parents and that of her in-laws, which is more pronounced in Jaunsar-Bawar, where Majumdar reports: "A woman has two standards of morality to conform to, one in her parents' house, the other in her husband's. In her parents' house she is allowed every kind of liberty and licence and nothing is an offence unless specifically prohibited" (Majumdar, 1944, p. 163; cf. Saksena, 1955, p. 36).

Marriage is an important event in a man's life, too, but it is not as potentially traumatic as it is for a woman. He remains in his own family and village where there are friends and allies on every side as contrasted to the strangers and critics who usually greet a bride. A man's social situation changes relatively little. That his responsibilities are somewhat increased is recognized in the vows he makes at marriage. A village joke runs to the effect that an unmarried man is a free man, he can run about as he pleases "on two legs"; a married man is like a quadruped, he must spend most of his time foraging for food; a man with children is like the eight-legged spider, he must weave a net and be ever ready at its center to seize any food that comes his way.

A husband who visits his wife's home is in the position of all in-laws. He is the honored and respected guest, but neither he nor his hosts are likely to feel at ease and the visit is usually made as short as possible. Of course, in many instances, the husband and his in-laws know one another well and may visit frequently and easily, but the ideal pattern is one of respect and distance. Most visiting outside the village is with affinal relatives, especially the wife's brothers. When a man's in-laws live in his own village, he is often on close terms with them and frequently visits with, and works with, his father-in-law and brothers-in-law. However, an element of mutual respect is maintained.

The relationship of wife to husband is ideally one of devotion, service, and respect. The husband is referred to by his wife as *mālik*, owner, or simply "man." He makes the decisions and gives the orders, though in reality a wife may exercise as much influence as their personalities allow, and the henpecked husband is a familiar concept.

A woman shows her respect and devotion by catering to and anticipating her husband's wishes. When he comes back from a trip or from working, even if she is tired herself, a wife will massage his limbs with oil, feed him, prepare his pipe for him, and make him comfortable. She will not refuse his sexual advances and afterwards will "replenish his virility" by feeding him ghee and other milk products. She will bear and care for his children, keep his house, cook his meals, and do the necessary household work in the fields and forest. In the words of an informant,

A wife should have three qualities: (1) she should be beautiful, (2) she should keep the house in order, (3) she should be able to cook good food when guests come. When she has none of these qualities it is very sad; she cannot expect much from her husband, and he may leave her. My wife has no such virtues, but I cannot leave her. The chains of flesh are too strong— I love my children.

As has been noted in the section on death ceremonies, widows are not expected to retire from public life as is the ideal among high-caste plains groups. Pahari widows mourn their husbands during the thirteen-day mourning period, and many do so for a year. They take off their nose ring and do not wear it again until they have remarried or until they no longer wish to display their respectful grief for the dead husband. The practice of sati, wherein a wife threw herself in anguish upon her husband's funeral pyre, was popular among high castes in the plains in the seventeenth and eighteenth centuries, but was apparently never widely practiced in this area, perhaps partly because a widow here had no unpleasant future to dread. One sati did occur, however, in Sirkanda a few generations ago, and at least two popular Pahari songs celebrate the stories of brave men whose wives destroyed themselves after their husbands' deaths. In general, the Pahari attitude is that a wife should respect, honor, and obey her husband in life but that she has little obligation to him after the ceremonies immediately following death.

In return for his wife's fealty, a husband is expected to provide for her physical well-being, and is supposed to fulfill his obligation to have sexual intercourse with her at least once a month, and preferably oftener, as a woman is believed to have seven times the sexual energies that a man has.

If a man has regular sex relations with his wife, she will be happy and do anything for him. If he neglects her for a while she gets suspicious and restless and may start an argument and accuse him of loving another. Divorce is always due to a man's failure to satisfy his wife in this way. If he kept her satisfied she would never look elsewhere and would have eyes for no one but him.

Also, a husband may go out of his way to intercede for his wife in intrafamily matters, to see that she has a chance to visit her family periodically, and to provide her with things she wants or take her to some fair or market outside the village occasionally.

When a man has more than one wife he usually takes the second with the approval, and sometimes with the encouragement, of the first. If the wives are sisters it is expected that trouble between them will automatically be at a minimum. If not, they may live in separate dwellings, one in the village and one in a chan. In former days they more frequently lived together, as chans were fewer, less productive, and more isolated than today and were therefore less suitable for year-round occupation. Whatever the arrangement, polygyny is a potentially explosive situation. The first wife is traditionally the dominant one, and her attitude toward the second is much like that of a mother-in-law or elder sister-in-law toward a younger brother's wife. Skill and tact may win more power to a second wife, but tradition is on the side of the first. The first wife is especially likely to be jealous or vindictive if the second wife has been taken to make up for her own failure to bear children, for in such a situation she may feel threatened. The mother of a man's children is likely to take precedence over other wives in the eyes of both the husband and the extended family. However, wives are usually separated if they do not get along together, and many who live together do so congenially. They may even coöperate to press demands on their common husband. A husband must always be careful not to favor one wife conspicuously over the other. One man commented in this context, "If you get two cups of tea from the teapot and I get only one I will naturally be jealous. So it is with wives sharing a husband." If a co-wife feels neglected she will react just as does a single wife who suspects her husband of having another lover. She will sulk, do her work poorly or not at all, and try to provoke an argument in which to express her charges against her husband. If he is unable or unwilling to make amends, she may run away.

The relationship between a wife and her husband's brothers is one of considerable sexual freedom. Though polyandry is publicly ridiculed and abhorred by people in this area, covert sexual relationships within the family are not greatly divergent from those among fraternally polyandrous families such as those of Jaunsar-Bawar (cf. Berreman, 1962a). Paharis are well aware of standard Hindu attitudes on polyandry and familial sexual freedom, so that these practices are generally concealed from outsiders. Despite such precautions, they have attained a reputation for deviation from orthodox Hindu behavior. A change toward orthodoxy or modernity in both attitudes and behavior is taking place as some of the younger and educated people object to traditional patterns of intrafamily sexual behavior and make their feelings known.

The traditional view here is that a wife's sexuality may be freely used not only by her husband but by his brothers as well. One low-caste elder drew laughter from listeners when, in providing genealogical materials, he listed his brothers' wives as his own in addition to his own wives. His response was, "What's the difference? They are all like wives to me." In discussing the matter other informants said, "A woman would never refuse herself to her husband's brother because he is in the same relationship as her husband and she would not like to create discord in the family."

An elder brother has the right to make sexual use of his younger brothers' wives. Younger brothers do the same so long as the age difference is not too great. There is no quarreling or jealousy on this score. It is their right, and they are expected to do it. They don't do it in the husband's presence. They wait till he has gone out, if only to fetch water, and then approach his wife. The wife will yield readily if she likes the brother, but even if she doesn't he can insist. If she is angry she may tell the man's wife, and the wife will scold him for forcing himself on the unwilling woman. Usually such things are kept secret only from the wife who may be jealous. A brother should not be jealous on these grounds. If a woman wishes she may send her sister-in-law on errands in order that she may have access to the girl's husband.

A woman is obligated to satisfy her husband's sexual wants and her husband always takes precedence, but she should not deny the requests of his brothers either. Informants were incredulous that relations between a man and his brother's wife could be expected to lead to divorce, if discovered, in some cultures. A husband has no justifiable grounds for complaint if his wife has relations with his brothers as long as he is given precedence and is not denied his own sexual rights and as long as the relations are carried on discreetly, away from the house or in his absence. In reality husbands do occasionally complain on this score. If a man's brother is overly attentive to the man's wife he may abuse the brother by saying, "You have been eating my feces" —a circumlocution which serves as a warning to the brother to pay less attention to his sister-in-law.

If a wife is suspected of extrafamilial affairs or is going to work in the jungle where such liaisons can easily be made, her mother-in-law or elder sister-in-law may send one of her husband's brothers—often an unmarried one—to accompany her or to work in the same area. This protects the wife from the advances of nonfamily members and encourages relationships between her and her brother-in-law. "It protects our wives' honor from men outside the family." It is assumed that every wife has at least occasional relations with her husband's brothers, and this is a typical way in which boys are initiated into adult sexual activities.

Such freedom does not cross generational lines, and if it did it would be considered a serious and reprehensible deviation. Generation is an important boundary in all sex relations. This is reflected in the prejudice against relations between a very young man and a much older sister-in-law. Brothers' and parallel cousins' wives are available as partners; wives of sons, of brother's sons, of father's brothers are not. The kinship terminology for a younger brother's wife, who is available sexually, and for a son's wife, who is not, is the same, but this fact apparently does not bear on the current behavioral situation. One case was reported in Sirkanda in which a man made advances to his daughter-in-law, but she was promptly recalled to her parents' home and was not returned to her husband. A middle-aged and much-married man who took as wife the wife of his young classificatory uncle was widely criticized for crossing the generational boundary.

Great sexual freedom is practiced outside the extended family by both men and women. It is assumed to be virtually a foregone conclusion that if a man and woman meet alone in the jungle, intercourse will ensue. The nature of the terrain and of the work engaged in by both men and women make such meetings, planned or not, frequent. Clandestine liaisons occur regularly, often with the connivance of the female age-mates of the woman. There are well-known signals and other means of arranging these. Few women are considered unapproachable in such matters, and it is thought to be unlikely that any woman would refuse an insistent request. As in the case of the Lepchas, ". . . casual sexual relationships are so unimportant emotionally . . . that few women would think it worth while making a fuss" (Gorer, 1938, p. 160). While villagers may overestimate the frequency of casual sexual contacts, it seems likely that most men and women of the same general age and caste status in the village, outside of the exogamous sibs, have had relations with one another. Some lasting liaisons have been established. Instances of cross-caste and in-sib relationships are also known.

The difference between all such relations and those between brothers and their wives is that in the former cases legitimate grounds for complaint exist, whereas within the family there is no such sanction. If a husband wishes to press a charge of persistent adultery outside the family he can usually win the support of the community to bring about divorce, punishment, or a promise to desist. Even a wife may be supported in presenting such a charge. A similar charge against a brother would be laughed off or hushed up in the family as mere bickering.

In line with the shift toward adoption of plains behavior and San-skritization in general, there is apparently a tendency away from the pattern of sharing a wife's sexuality among brothers. Some high-caste families, perhaps under the influence of the outside Brahmin who per-forms their rituals and is the most vocal advocate of Sanskritization in the village, express an orthodox Hindu view on this matter. They state that an elder brother's wife should be respected like a mother, a younger brother's wife should be treated like a sister or daughter. This view is found in association with disapproval of bride price (also a Sanskritic attitude), but both are often practiced by their detractors. One young man in the village was quite upset by the fact that his wife had lived openly, for over a year, with his elder brother in a chan. When she returned to the family house to bear her husband's brother's child, to be known officially as her husband's child, intrafamily tension grew until the young wife suddenly discarded her nose-ring (symbolic of marriage) and ran away to her own village. It was later found that she was possessed by a ghost who impelled her to take this action, and she nearly died of its affliction before she was brought back to her husband's village, where the ghost was exorcised. After she gave birth the problem was solved by a familial announcement that the baby was the elder brother's. Thenceforth the baby's parents were considered man and wife and a new wife was to be procured for the dispossessed younger brother. It was largely at the insistence of the younger brother that this solution was reached.

The relationship among nuclear families in the joint family is above all a combination of the various specific relationships mentioned above. Nuclear families or larger subdivisions of the extended family are the units which remain together when the extended family breaks up. Despite the frequency of divorce, there is a unity within the nuclear family which in some cases is stronger than that which runs through the extended family. The break-up of extended families follows mutual agreement among the separating units that they can get along better separately than they could together. Most often the break-up is among cousins (sons of brothers) and is blamed on their wives. It is said that wives drive a wedge between brothers (classificatory as well as "real" brothers). A wife complains to her husband that she and he are doing more than their fair share of work in the family and perhaps that other nuclear units are expending more than their share of the in-come. Behind this is often sister-in-law jealousy, and particularly re-sentment of the domination of an elder sister-in-law. The husband finally becomes convinced or willing and expresses his desire to separate.

Eventually a division may be effected. Wives are often blamed for what is really fraternal strife. Brothers are supposed to get along with one another harmoniously and to respect their elders. Therefore, if they cannot get along in the joint family, it is socially more acceptable to blame their strife on disputing wives who, as outsiders, do not reflect on the family reputation as directly as do brothers.

Division of the joint family may thus be brought about by disputes among brothers or cousins, though for sake of appearance it may be attributed to friction among wives. The Brahmin family in Sirkanda was on the verge of dividing its lands into three parts in 1958, as a result of the feeling by each of the three Brahmin brothers that he was contributing more than his share and getting less in the joint economic arrangement. This split was to occur despite the fact that their elderly mother was still living. As a first step in the dissolution of this joint family, the fields were being marked off into three equal parts and a large house containing three separate dwelling units was being built to replace the less spacious one the joint family had shared. In this instance the old house furnished part of the materials for the new one. In other cases the old house has remained in use by one of the new family units, has been given to a Dom for occupancy, or has been abandoned. As has been pointed out, low-caste brothers more frequently divide their property than do those of high castes. This difference is evidently related to their occupations. In the agricultural high castes land can best be worked by large joint families, but the occupations of artisans can be efficiently performed by smaller family units.

While Sirkanda and its component extended families have increased in population, there has apparently been no commensurate increase in the frequency of breakdowns into smaller family economic units as is reported for other parts of India. Some informants, in fact, reported that proportionately fewer splits occur now than in former days; that joint families have become larger rather than smaller. This trend, which is not in the direction one might expect, is attributed to the fact that in former days the entire joint family occupied a single house where its members, and particularly the wives, were constantly in contact with one another and disputes were frequent. Disputes led to disintegration of the joint family because disputing groups within it could only avoid conflict by moving out, and moving out meant setting up a new household. Few families had chans in those days, and chans were isolated and surrounded by relatively little cultivated land, so that they were not suitable for year-round living. Now most families have chans or second houses. There are several chans at most locations, and the lands have been developed so that year-round occupancy is possible and even necessary in terms of the crops and animals to be cared for. Many nuclear family units are now separated from others within the same joint family. They thus avoid the friction that is inevitable in the close daily contact of a shared dwelling. With less frequent disputes and with the possibility that a disgruntled nuclear family can live in another dwelling, there is less pressure to divide family property. The joint family remains intact as an economic unit while it no longer remains a residential unit.

Between half-siblings of polygynous marriages there is often no love lost. This probably reflects the relationship between the co-wives who were their mothers. Such rivalry is common knowledge among villagers and finds expression in folklore. Frequently in adult life the dislike takes the form of merely ignoring the half-sibling or having little or nothing to do with him. Sometimes it takes the form of continual disputing or unfriendly rivalry. In one family in Sirkanda it is the basis for a four-generational factional split. In most of the reported cases half-brothers have divided their father's property into separate economic units after his death.

LINEAGE

The patrilocal extended family is the most important social, economic, and ritual unit in most phases of life in Sirkanda. There are, however, more inclusive kin groups which are relevant in certain contexts. The smallest of these may best be termed the "lineage"—a consanguineal kin group that traces common descent through known ancestors, in this case male ancestors and therefore a patrilineal group (see fig. 3). In practice in Sirkanda this unit usually excludes married sisters and daughters and includes wives of the male lineage members. As such it resembles a "compromise kin group" in Murdock's formulation, combining unilineal descent with residential unity, so that lineage members who live away from the group are excluded from it and nonlineage members who live with the group are included in it. I will here refer to this unit in Sirkanda as the lineage because the unilinear rule of descent is paramount; lineage ties do not disappear in fact or theory at marriage. This is indicated by the fact that women are accepted heartily as lineage members when they visit their parents' homes. Lineages, as segments of sibs, are strictly exogamous. A woman has sex relations with her husband's brothers, real and classificatory, but never with people of her own lineage or sib. When a woman is widowed or divorced she either marries her husband's brother or is accepted back into her parents' household, where subsequent marriages are arranged with reference to her parents' lineage and sib rather than that of her husband, that is, for considerations of exogamy. The lineage of her erstwhile husband is disregarded except that it is reimbursed if she leaves voluntarily. It should be remembered, however, that residence, in combination with lineage, is important in daily life. As long

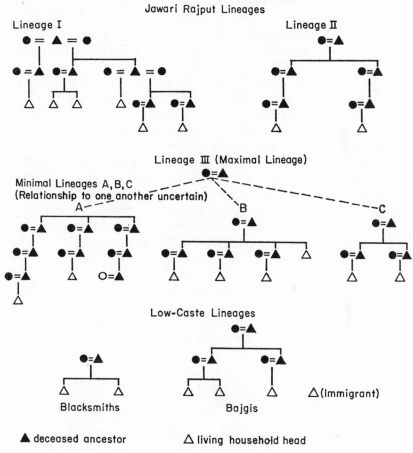

Fig. 3. Sample lineage structures.

as a woman's husband lives, she participates in the ritual, social, and economic activities of his lineage and sib. If she dies, her funeral is performed by her husband's family, not her family of origin. But she retains her identification with her lineage of origin. In short, she becomes a member of her husband's clan, the compromise kin group determined by descent, residential unity, and social integration (Murdock, 1949, p. 68) but not of his sib.

The lineage is termed *khāndān* locally, and its component households are called "hearths." In Sirkanda there are few households which do not belong to lineages containing several households. As generations pass, lineage connections in the larger village castes grow dim and eventually are forgotten as subsidiary divisions assume lineage proportions. The male Sirkanda members of each caste except Rajputs —the Brahmins, blacksmiths, barbers, and all of the Bajgis except the immigrant one—belong to single lineages as well as single sibs within their respective castes. There are at least nine Rajput lineages.

Three of the Rajput lineages in Sirkanda are named. They have acquired the names of honored ancestors from whom their members trace common descent. One of these lineages is well-known for its devotion to the worship of the Pandavas and for the special attention the Pandavas show its members in return. Corroborative stories are told of this relationship. In two of these lineages the common descent of members can be accurately traced. In the third there are three named sublineages or minimal lineages within which common descent is easily traced but between which the relationship has grown hazy. If the names persist and the relationship of the sublineages is forgotten, the sublineages may be elevated to lineage status and the present lineage would then become a kind of sub-sib and might conceivably assume sib significance, just as sibs (*jatis,* see discussion below) may have succeeded gotras as sib units in this area. At present the three sublineages together resemble a maximal lineage in that together they are considered a lineage relative to others, while each of the three component sublineages is considered to be a lineage relative to the other two.

Four other Rajput lineages are distinct, while the remaining two are known to be related to one another but have drifted apart as the ties of relationship have been forgotten. None of these is a named lineage.

The typical lineage contains three or four households. The largest contains eleven, but it is the one which is now reduced in reality to three sublineages. The largest intact lineage has seven component households. Beyond the household it is the members of the lineage unit who are most likely to participate actively in the life-cycle ceremonies of their members. They tend to support one another in social situations, to worship the same gods, and, of course, to honor the same ancestors. In short, they share a feeling of common identification and a somewhat more homogeneous culture than occurs across lineage lines, though less homogeneous than that within the extended family. There is also a tendency toward residential proximity within the lineage, based apparently on common origin. The lineage has inherited from people who once held property in common, and it is part of this property upon which houses have been built. Factions tend to follow lineage lines, but here the exceptions almost equal the examples in their frequency.

KINDRED

Not all the people significantly related to one another in Sirkanda are related through the male line. There is a circle of kinfolk recognized as relatives of the individual, who are related to him through either one or the other parent, that is, bilaterally. They will be termed the kindred, following Murdock (1949, pp. 46, 56, 61). The kindred form a group only from the point of view of the individual to whom all are related. They do not comprise a self-conscious identification group. The kindred's common interest is focused specifically on an individual who ties it together on certain occasions, notably life-cycle ceremonies. Such bilateral relationship is widely recognized in Northern India. The common name for the kindred is sapinda, mentioned above (p. 158) in the discussion of marriage regulations. Although this term is not commonly used in Sirkanda, the concept is prevalent.

Those who are born of one body are *Sapinda*. A child is a *Sapinda* of his father and mother. He is also the *Sapinda* of his father's brothers, sisters, father and grand-father as also of his mother's brothers and sisters, father and grand-father. He is Sapinda to his cousins (father's sister's children, mother's sister's children, father's brother's children and mother's brother's children) as he shares with them common body-particles either from his mother's side or from his father's side. In this meaning of the word *Pinda,* a common kinship of blood is established with both the father's and mother's side. (Karve, 1953, p. 55)

As has been noted, one cannot marry within the sapinda group, though its boundaries are variously defined even for this important function. In other situations the kindred is variable in its extent and inclusiveness. As in its function of regulating choice of marriage partner, the function of the kindred in ceremonial activities is parallel to that described by Murdock (1949, pp. 56 f.) for American society where ". . . its members are collectively called 'kinfolk' or 'relations,' [and] it includes that group of near kinsmen who may be expected to be present and participate on important ceremonial occasions such as weddings, christenings, funerals. . . ." Kindred serve many of the

same functions as lineage members, and in fact by definition kindred
membership overlaps greatly with that patrilineal group. Participation
of kindred in ceremonial functions is likely to be less intensive than
that of the lineage simply because kindred are residentially separated
and include relatives whose relationship to one another is traditionally
one of mutual respect and even avoidance. They do not identify themselves as a group. Kindred are not bound by diffuse, interconnected
group ties. It is in this crucial respect that the kindred differs from the
lineage group, which is closely bound by ties of consanguinity and common identification to which any particular individual is incidental.

SIB

Above the lineage in degree of assumed patrilineal relationship
is the sib (jat or more often jati in local parlance). In this named kin
group, relationship in the patrilineal line is assumed but cannot be
traced. It is the effective exogamous unit within the caste, and it extends across village boundaries. It occurs most prominently among
Brahmins and Rajputs. Judging by sib names and local tradition, some
sib names may have derived from a former place of residence of the
group—indicating, perhaps, that local exogamy was there the rule. If
some sibs did originate in this way, local exogamy ceased to be the rule
when people emigrated from the villages in which it was practiced to
new localities, such as Sirkanda, where people of other villages or areas
settled. The other migrants were potential mates because they were
from other villages, and their common residence in Sirkanda was
deemed irrelevant for marriage purposes. That is, the ancestral villages of some Sirkanda Rajputs may have been exogamous. If so, when
they settled in the present location, they may have excluded from
marriageability their former village affiliates but not the members of
their new local group. In that way, former village affiliation would
have become important so that the names of those villages were used
to identify the exogamous group (hence sib). Other groups evidently
carried their sib names with them from the plains or adopted those of
plains groups. The latter explanation seems the most probable in light
of available evidence.

As has been mentioned in chapter 1, some 116 Rajput sibs have been
listed for Garhwal. These include three of the four found in Sirkanda
(Raturi, 1928, pp. 167 ff.). The names of these three (Jawari, Palial,
Khandial) are attributed in that listing to the names of the villages in
which their ancestors settled. Whether the sib got its name from the
village or vice versa is a moot question. The village name was likely

derived from its early settlers or founders, though it may then have been adopted by subsequent immigrants. Tod (1829, p. 120) lists "eighty-four mercantile tribes" of Rajasthan among which are "Pilliwal," "Khandailwal," and "Kakulea," which are apparently three of the Rajput sib names of Sirkanda. He suggests that the Palial (Pilliwal, Palliwal) group originated in Palli, the great commercial market of western Rajasthan. "A community of Brahmins then held Palli in grant . . . whence comes a numerous class, termed Palliwal, who follow mercantile pursuits" (Tod, 1829, p. 700). Bahadur (1916) mentions a "Pyal" Rajput group (an alternative pronunciation, according to a Sirkanda informant) which is said to have come to Garhwal from Delhi. This could well be the same group or a branch of it. Villagers themselves retain no traditions on the matter beyond assertions that their people came from various locations in the Kumaon Hills to the east and that sib names indicate the village of origin. The sib names of two village wives were said to be the names of their villages of origin in Garhwal. One village man said, "Jati is named for the place where a member of the caste went and settled. His descendants carry this name." Another attributed it to the name of an ancestral leader who brought his people to some new locality. A glance at the village map (map 3) will show that sibs retain a pattern of residential proximity, though it is not rigidly followed and most villagers are not even aware of it. It probably reflects the fact that sib ancestors settled in one location when they first came to the village as a group, and that this location has remained somewhat intact through patrilineal inheritance of land and houses.

The low castes claim such kin groups and utilize them as exogamous units just as do the high castes. Among low castes the units are apparently of varied origin—some are the jati, gotra, or caste names of alleged high-caste ancestors. Some are the personal names of particular ancestors, and some may be place names. Some may well be lineage names of fairly recent origin. The low castes may often have adopted names in imitation of high-caste practice, as, in fact, Khasiya Rajputs may also have done in earlier days. In any event, the named groups are in effect sibs, and they are referred to as jatis or gotras. Insufficient data were collected on low-caste marriages of any one caste to determine precisely the extent to which their "sibs" are important or to verify their functioning. The data that were collected and the testimony of informants showed no consistent differences at this level between high-caste and low-caste sibs in marriage regulation. Both conform equally well to the definition of sib. Differences are apparently of origin and extent rather than of local functioning.

Since all non-Rajput castes in Sirkanda contain only single lineages (except for the single immigrant Bajgi), they are also made up of single sibs; for example, the local Brahmins are of the Kōtāri sib. Among Rajputs four sibs are represented: Jawari, comprising 20 households and three main lineages, including the one which is in effect three sublineages at present; Palial, comprising 11 households and three lineages; Kukhalwal, comprising five households and two lineages; and Khandial, comprising a single household and lineage. Within these sibs the lineage divisions are sufficiently recent that the tradition of interlineage relationship is strong, strong enough that the term khandan (lineage) is applied to each of the four local Rajput sibs as wholes as well as to their component lineages. A Rajput elder's comment on the subject was typical: "Our Khandan divided seven generations back, but now no one remembers who the people were who divided it." In other contexts people distinguish khandan as lineage from jati as sib. The term *birādarī* (brotherhood) is also used to designate the sib. Among low castes this term is applied to the entire caste group.

The significance of sib groupings is primarily in establishing boundaries of marriage eligibility. Members of the same sib are never potential marriage partners. Neither are people whose mothers were in the same sib. A secondary function is participation in ritual. The entire local sib unit is supposed to observe a degree of ritual pollution after the death of a member, and to a lesser extent the sib functions as does the lineage in other life-cycle ceremonies. Actually, since the group involved in ritual is localized and for some purposes includes wives of sib members, it is perhaps more properly termed the clan. It appears likely that the lineages may eventually replace sibs or clans in these functions, as sib and clan responsibilities in this context seem to be decreasing in importance in the minds of villagers.

Sibs and clans also enter into faction formation. Although there are many factions within sibs, and factions which separate sibs, relatively few cut across sib lines allying members of different sibs against their sib-fellows. That sib identification is still a real factor in the village is indicated by sib loyalties. In reference to the founding of Sirkanda, each of the larger sibs claims precedence. A member of either one is likely to disparage the members of the other, especially to compare them unfavorably in terms of wealth, honesty, or Sanskritization of ritual observances and marriage regulations. An old Jawari, head of the largest household in his sib, said, "We Jawaris were the first Rajputs here. Then those Palials showed up, and our forefathers let them settle here too. We don't know where they came from or who they are. Hell, we don't even know if they're Rajputs—we just took their word for it!" The speaker's wife of 40 years, mother of his five adult sons, is a Palial. There is considerable rivalry between the sibs, as evidenced in all their relationships and recorded in disputes, court cases, and recently in voting patterns in elections of village officers. The divisions are not rigid, but they do show up.

There is no concept of hierarchical ranking of sibs in the village— all are equally prestigeful. Some sibs or larger subcaste groupings outside the village are thought of as more or less prestigeful. Among the Brahmins and low castes prestige of subcastes is often related to occupational specialization. Ceremonial cooks (Sarola) are ritually purer than family priests. Carpenters often consider themselves higher than blacksmiths. Among Rajputs and some Brahmin groups the place of origin is important. Plains groups are more prestigeful than Pahari ones; that is, those admitting the appellation "Khasa" are lower than some of those denying it. Among some low castes prestige is related to alleged high-caste ancestry. These distinctions do not come into play in the village and, except in the case of Sarola Brahmins, they rarely crop up in Bhatbair. With the exception, again, of Sarola Brahmins, they are unimportant in determining marriage relationships within this area, although they do assume significance in some outside arrangements. No evidence of subcaste hypergamy appeared in the research.

CLAN

The clan in Sirkanda is made up basically of the local members of one sib together with their wives.[10] As such it is very closely identified with the sib, and its functioning often cannot readily be distinguished from that of the sib or the lineage. It is an unnamed, overtly unrecognized group which can be of considerable analytic utility. Its core is the local portion of the patrilineal sib. It is distinguished from the sib by the fact that it is a compromise kin group (Murdock, 1949, p. 66), that is, it includes some people on the basis of their local residence who are not tied to it by consanguinity, and it excludes some on the basis of their outside residence who do have consanguineal ties to its members. It includes the wives of local members of the sib, and it excludes their married sisters and daughters. It also excludes sib-fellows of other villages and areas. It functions to include the occasional adopted son who is of another area or another sib, and the rare man who marries into the local sib matrilocally. Conversely, it excludes the local boy of the sib adopted elsewhere and the rare local man of the sib who marries outside and lives in his wife's village.

The third criterion of a clan (in addition to a unilineally related core and residential unity) is social integration. This is a feature of Sirkanda clans which becomes most apparent at times of ceremonial participation. Confusion easily arises at this point, since villagers themselves do not recognize the clan as a group. When describing life-cycle and other ceremonies, they describe the participants as members of the family, lineage, sib, kindred, caste, or community, depending upon the nature of the participation. In their descriptions of sib participation, however, it is often apparent that they are including local members of the sib and their spouses and excluding nonlocal members of the sib, that is, they are describing participation of the clan, as that term is defined by Murdock. Even "lineage" participation often proves to include wives of lineage members and to exclude lineage members who live elsewhere; it includes the most closely associated clan group centering on the lineage, rather than the lineage itself.

The concept of the clan, as distinguished from the sib, provides a consistent explanation for a number of otherwise perplexing features of Pahari social organization. First, of course, is the composition of the groups which participate in ceremonies. While family, kindred, caste, and community are social units which can account for many of the non-unilineally related participants in ceremonies, the clan more succinctly defines the local, socially integrated group centered on a unilineally related sib, but including other individuals, which participates in several kinds of ceremonies.

Second, the clan concept clarifies the complex matter of changes in group affiliation, identification, and inheritance which accompany changes in residence at the times of marriage and adoption (in the relatively rare cases where adoption occurs across sib lines). Without the concept of clan this has proved difficult to understand. Wives, adopted sons, and matrilocally resident men stoutly deny that they have altered their sib affiliations when they go to live among people of another sib. Yet some informants claim that they have done so. Certainly, for some purposes, they have severed ties with their natal groups and have established ties with new groups. To explain this in terms of complex alterations in sib affiliation and responsibilities, as is usually done, is both confusing and inaccurate. Sib ties have not been altered. What has happened is that clan affiliation has changed. The individual has ceased to be a member of one localized clan and has become a member of another. If the relationship is terminated and the person returns to his natal group (as when an adopted son leaves his foster family) or joins yet another group (as when a divorced woman remarries) then clan affiliation is changed again without difficulty. Clan affiliation is as easily changed as is residence, but sib affiliation is inherited and unalterable. This is the affiliation which is important (by delimiting the exogamous group) in determining marriage. Thus, a woman of sib A and clan a who marries a man of sib B becomes a member of clan b when she goes to live with him, but she remains in sib A. She has sexual relations with her brothers-in-law in sib B as well as with her husband, and upon being widowed or divorced she may marry someone else in sib B. If it were claimed that upon marriage she had become a member of sib B, these relationships would be incestuous and therefore prohibited.

When a man dies, the wives of his local sib-fellows participate in the mourning insofar as women participate at all. His married daughters and nieces do not. When a wife dies, her major funeral ceremonies are performed by the clan-fellows she acquired by marriage, including those extending beyond the extended family, but are not performed by her sib-fellows. A *lingrā* stone (see Appendix IIIC), symbolizing that the deceased woman is one with Shiva, is placed with those of the rest of the dead of the local clan group. It is not sent back to rest with those of her sib-fellows. A woman participates in the life-cycle ceremonies of her clan-fellows much more consistently and actively than in those of her sib-fellows. Moreover, an adopted son or a son-in-law resident in his wife's father's house can perform the father's funeral rites and can inherit his property. In this manner property can pass from one sib to another. The lingra stones of adopted sons and resident sons-in-law are placed with those of the family with which they reside. The stones are not sent back to rest with those of their family of origin. This practice, like inheritance by an adopted son, does not depend upon a change in sib affiliation; rather it depends primarily upon place of residence and therefore upon clanship. A sib-fellow, lineally related, is preferred to perform funeral rites and to inherit property, but failing such a person, a clan-fellow can substitute. One who lacks both sib and clan ties (for example, a son-in-law resident in his natal household) is not eligible under normal circumstances. These facts emphasize the social structural importance of the residence group. If funeral participation is described as primarily involving the household, lineage, and clan, with lesser participation by the sib, kindred, caste, and community; if patrilocal marriage is viewed as entailing a change in clan affiliation for the woman, and if adoption and matrilocal residence are viewed as entailing a change in clan affiliation for the man, then these practices are consistent and more readily understood than if one were to assume that there is *no* significant change in group affiliation at marriage or adoption or that sib affiliation is changed at these times.[11]

Therefore, the local compromise kin group, the clan, assumes greater significance in ritual and ceremonial participation (especially that surrounding life-cycle ceremonies) than does the sib. The unilineal

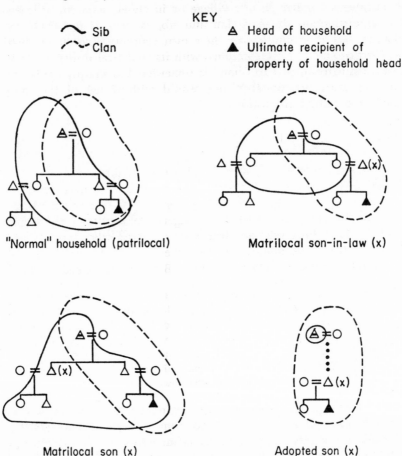

Fig. 4. Sib and clan affiliations in Sirkanda families. From Berreman (1962e).

descent group, the sib, determines eligibility for marriage and is the preferred means for determining inheritance. It is the core around which the clan is formed. Sirkanda villagers lump these analytically distinguishable groups under a single term, jati, which literally refers to the sib. They tend to think of wives as members of their husbands' sibs in the ceremonial context and as members of their natal sibs in most other contexts. They think of adopted sons as members of the family of adoption for purposes of ritual and inheritance, and as members of their natal families for purposes of marriage. In most cases (other than those involving determination of limits of exogamy) they think of the sib in terms of its local membership, that is, those sib members who live in one village or in closely adjacent villages. A clear distinction between clan and sib, as such, is not made by villagers, but it is implicit in their own conceptualization of their social organization. This, combined with its analytical utility, make it worth distinguishing. The "clan" is somewhat less sharply defined— less a corporate group—than one would wish if use of the term "clan" were to be fully justified.

GOTRA (PHRATRY)

The exogamous unit among high castes over much of India is called the gotra. In many areas this unit amounts to a patrilineal sib (cf. Lewis, 1958, p. 23; Dube, 1955, pp. 42 f.). Gotras appear in Sirkanda and are said by educated villagers to derive from the names of twenty-four great religious teachers or ascetics who founded vast lineages whose descendants in the male line retain the name of the founder as the gotra name. A local Brahmin explained:

> Gotras are called by the names of great *rishis* who were founders of the original families. Bharadwaj was a great rishi. Some of his children went into religious work, and their descendants are Bharadwaj Brahmins. Others among his children went into the work of governing, and their descendants are Bharadwaj Rajputs. Jawari [a sib name] was the name of the headman of a group of Bharadwaj Rajputs who came and settled in one place in these hills. Now his descendants are Jawari Bharadwaj Rajputs.

Tod (1829, p. 27) explains gotra origin in a similar way. Others describe Brahmin gotras as deriving from a lineal ancestor's name, while Rajput gotras derive from the name of the religious preceptor (*gūrū*) of a lineal ancestor. In any event, the same gotras are found among both Brahmins and Rajputs in this area, but among no other castes, and remote common ancestry for Brahmins and Rajputs is assumed by some.

On the basis of his research in "Kalapur," a plains village, Hitchcock (1956, pp. 43 ff.) refers to this usage of the term "gotra" as "Brahmanical." "Nothing in our data shows that the *gotra* concept in the Brahmanical sense now has any functional significance for marriage . . ." (*ibid.*, p. 45). However, he reports that it is used in

a second sense (the sense common on the plains) to refer to the sib—
a usage parallel to the Pahari use of the term "jati" as described here.

In Sirkanda the low-caste sibs are sometimes termed "gotra," and
sometimes "jati." Only the high castes have both units consistently
and distinguish them precisely. Even among them "gotra" does not
mean what it means among many plains groups. The term "gotra,"
as Hitchcock's comment would suggest, does not mean the same thing
throughout India to those who use it. "Sometimes a caste is divided
into exogamous groups called Gotra with no further division. Sometimes a caste is divided into exogamous Gotras or endogamous Gotras
with further smaller divisions" (Karve, 1953, p. 118).

In Sirkanda there are two gotras among the Rajputs: *Bhāradwāj*,
which includes the sibs Jawari and Kukhalwal, and *Kāsīb*, which
includes the sibs Palial and Khandial. The Brahmin gotra in Sirkanda
is also Kasib. Each gotra includes many sibs—an estimated 20 to .50
in each gotra—but only two of each are represented among Sirkanda
Rajputs. In addition, there are at least ten other gotras in this
general area.

Both the Sirkanda gotras receive mention by Tod as having been
present in Rajasthan. He refers to an ancient lineage in which, in
the fifteenth recorded generation, nine brothers "'. . . took to the
office of religion, and established the Causika Gotra or *tribe* of
Brahmins.' From the twenty-fourth prince in lineal descent from
Yayat, by the name of Bhardwaja, originated a celebrated sect, who
still bear his name and are the spiritual teachers of several Rajpoot
tribes" (Tod, 1829, p. 27). Rajputs and others took the gotra names
of their priests when they adopted the gotra system (Karve, 1953,
p. 115). This constituted an early step in Brahmanization or Sanskritization.

Gotra, like sib, is an inherited affiliation passed down patrilineally.
Since sibs are subdivisions of gotras, the gotra contains many sibs
but one sib never spans two gotras. Gotras therefore fit the definition
of phratry, wherein ". . . two or more sibs recognize a purely conventional unilinear bond of kinship . . ." (Murdock, 1949, p. 47).
Among Rajputs in Sirkanda this would amount to a moiety division
because there is a division into two phratries. This is fortuitous:
neighboring villages have one, three, or more phratries.

In Sirkanda and the surrounding region, gotra is not now a functional unit in marriage regulations. Joshi (1929, p. 272) states, "The
Khasas have no real *gotras*. Mr. Atkinson noted that they all stated
themselves to belong to the Bharadwaj *gotra*, and had no idea of what
'*gotra*' meant." As a Sirkanda Rajput said, "People must marry in

their own caste and they cannot marry in their own sib or their mother's sib. That is all that matters in marriage. Gotra is just a name, it doesn't mean anything." In this respect these people are not unique, as indicated by Hitchcock in the discussion noted above. Karve reports that among the Rajputs of Rajasthan and among the Kayasthas of Uttar Pradesh, gotras do not seem to have any function in marriage relations (Karve, 1953, pp. 119, 141). On the other hand, ultimate common ancestry in the gotra is admitted. This is consistent with Murdock's point (1949, p. 47) that the larger the kin group, the less likely it is to be exogamous.

Among Sirkanda Rajputs there are six possible sib combinations for marriage within the village based on the division into four sibs. All six have occurred among the 53 marital unions that were recorded as having been contracted among the four village sibs. Of the six possibilities, two are in-gotra combinations and four are cross-gotra combinations, based upon the division of the four sibs into two gotra groups (phratries or moieties). Since the two large sibs are in opposite gotras and since four of the six possible sib combinations in marriage are gross-gotra ones, cross-gotra marriages would be expected to predominate among those contracted within the village. This proves to be true, with 39 of 53 marriages across gotra lines. However, 14 in-gotra marriages were also recorded, virtually all of which were first marriages. This is actually greater than the expectable proportion. Half (5 of 10) of the in-village marriages of members of the smallest sib (Khandial), for example, were in-gotra ones, whereas well under half of all potential mates in the village for these people have been in their own gotra (at present 38 per cent of the village population is in this gotra and out of this sib).

Almost two-thirds (9 of 15) of the in-village marriages of the other small sib (Kukhalwal) were in-gotra ones, although potential mates in the village for these people have been about equally split between the same and opposite gotras (at present 58 per cent of the population is in this gotra and out of this sib). The relatively high rates of in-village and in-gotra marriage in small sibs reflect the larger number of potential mates in the village for members of small sibs (those with small population in the village) as contrasted to members of large sibs.

I do not suggest that in-gotra marriage is preferred. There is a tendency in this direction within the village, but it is not based upon a large enough sample to establish significance, and in any event when extravillage marriages are included it is an even less impressive trend. What I have demonstrated, however, is that gotra does not enter into regulation of marriage contracts in this area. There is no preference for cross-gotra marriages over in-gotra ones. This substantiates verbal testimony. No Sirkanda informant expressed a feeling that gotras should play a part in marriage arrangements, and no case was reported in which they did. Few villagers know their gotras and fewer yet know those of their wives, whereas everyone knows his own sib, and many know the sibs of their wives. Precisely the same situation obtains for Brahmins, except among those who are better-informed because they deal in horoscopes and life-cycle rites where gotras are mentioned. Interestingly enough, the "gotra puja" is an integral part of every Sanskritized Pahari marriage ceremony, which includes most first marriages these days. In this puja, taken directly from the religious prescriptions of the "great tradition," the gotra affiliations of the bride and groom are repeated many times over in the recitation of the sacred verses. The history and honor of the gotras that are being joined by marriage is reiterated. In Sirkanda the gotras so described and honored are sometimes one and the same. This is perplexing to many high-caste non-Paharis who learn of it. However, even the most sophisticated of the Brahmins who function in Bhatbair see no contradiction in the practice. It may be expected that plains emulation will result in the attaching of greater importance to gotra in the future, as has happened among upwardly mobile castes of the plains.

The gotra unit was found to be virtually nonfunctional among Sirkanda Rajputs, in both theory and practice, in every sphere of life. The only suggestive evidence that the gotra is of any importance is the fact of residential proximity of several households of the two sibs comprising the Bharadwaj gotra in the easternmost of the two Sirkanda settlement areas. This is probably the original village site (map 3). If, as is likely, this is more than a chance occurrence, it is not recognized as such in the village and it has no detectable ramifications beyond those of residential proximity found elsewhere in the village. I would speculate that it represents early common association or common origin of the two sibs, so that when they settled here they built houses near one another. More recent building has not followed this pattern and it is not noticeable in other sections of the village, although, as has been noted previously, residential unity of lineages and sibs is found fairly consistently.

Among the lower castes there are apparently no gotras in the sense of phratries such as those found in the high castes. Some claim to have them, but these usually prove to be sibs. Sometimes non-sib names are given in addition to sib names but they are usually lineage names, names of ancestors, names of localities, or subcaste occupational terms and are recognized only over a very limited area by fellow caste-members. Sometimes the names apply to precisely the same group as the sib name, even though they are given as gotra and are distinguished from jati. It is not unlikely that real phratries do exist among some low castes in this area, but none was found in Sirkanda. Such claims are apparently attempts at achieving Sanskritic respectability. Said a Bajgi, "We are just like Rajputs and Brahmins in that respect. We have the same divisions and marriage rules. Some other low castes don't have that, but we do." The high castes do not concur in this: "The low castes have regulations, but they don't have the same kind we do and they are lax about these matters."

KINSHIP

In order to understand the aggregates of related individuals that have been referred to above as kin groups, it is necessary to understand the kinship system, the system of relationships defined in terms of consanguinity and affinity which exists among people. This is codified in the system of terms used by people in addressing and referring to one another. The terms are given in Appendix IV, first edition. In Sirkanda, terms of reference and address are generally identical, although the latter are sometimes contractions of the former (didī jī becomes dijī). The most prominent exceptions are cases in which terms of reference are avoided in address between persons who stand in a relationship of respect or conventional social distance. Sometimes in reference descriptive terminology is used for clarity, especially when a term applies to more than one kind of relative. Specific exceptions are noted below and in Appendix IV, first edition.

In order to characterize Pahari kinship relative to other systems that have been reported, we may refer to the criteria by which kin are classified suggested by Murdock (1949, pp. 100–106).

In Pahari kinship, *generation* is specified with these exceptions: the term for wife (reference) and for junior female affine (address) and that for husband (reference) and young male affine (address), apply in all generations. Terms for father's brothers apply also for spouse's sisters' husbands. *Sex* is specified in all terms. *Affinity* is specified in most terms of reference. That is, consanguineal relatives are not referred to by the same terms as affinal relatives. The primary exception to this is a pattern of equating close affinal relatives within a generation to consanguineal relatives of that generation. A man refers to his wife's brothers' wives as he would to his own sister, and a woman refers to her husband's sisters' husbands as she would to her own brothers. A person's mother's brother is terminologically equated to his father's sister's husband, and his father's brother is equated to his mother's sister's husband. The same equation is made in the grandparental generation. This resembles a moiety distinction. It is elaborated to the point that a man refers to his wife's sisters' husbands as "co-brother" or "half-brother." He addresses and refers to his mother's sisters as "elder mother" or "younger mother," the same terms by which he addresses his father's co-wives. There is a special term of reference for father's co-wives. A woman addresses her husband's brothers' wives as her sisters, although they are distinguished by terms of reference. Her husband's sister's husbands are referred to as her own brothers. Thus, members of one's own patrilineage are equated to affines of one's mother's or spouse's patrilineage, and members of one's mother's or spouse's patrilineage are equated to affines of one's own lineage. This might suggest that there is or was a norm of sororal polygyny or a custom of brothers of one family marrying sisters of another. Both types of marriage occasionally occur, but there is no independent evidence that either has ever been common or preferred. Therefore, we can safely say only that there is a tendency to identify relatives of a single generation terminologically as members of a single household, which potentially they are. It is here that the criterion of affinity is ignored in kinship terminology.

Collaterality, that is, the degree of relationship in the consanguineal line, is ignored except in the distinction between father and father's brothers and in that between mother and mother's sisters. In the latter case the terms are derivatives of that for mother, meaning "elder mother" and "junior mother." Otherwise, merging is the rule. *Bifurcation,* distinguishing whether the connecting relative is male or female, is an important criterion in Pahari kinship. Whether the person who links two relatives is a mother or a father, a brother or a sister, a wife or a husband, is specified terminologically. Relatives linked by sons and by daughters are not distinguished from one another, however. *Polarity,* use of the same kinship term reciprocally by two relatives, is found only in affinal relationships between people of the same generation where the affinal link is in the first descending generation from the relatives using the reciprocal term. *Relative age,* whether the person referred to is elder or younger, is always specified among consanguineal relatives of the same generation. In address, relative age of cousins and siblings is sometimes ignored. Among affinal relatives, it is the relative ages of the connecting relatives that are crucial. For example, whether a wife's brother's wife will be referred to by the term which means elder sister or that for younger sister depends upon whether that woman's husband is an elder or younger brother of ego's wife. Generation always takes precedence over age in determining seniority. An uncle who is younger than his nephew should still be accorded the respect due his generation by the nephew. *Speaker's sex* is not a factor in Pahari kinship, nor is *decedence* (whether the connecting relative between two relatives is living or dead).

Pahari kinship can now be analyzed according to Murdock's typologies of kinship terminology, based primarily upon cousin terms (Murdock, 1949, pp. 223 ff.).

In Sirkanda siblings and all cousins, cross and parallel, related through mother and father, are called by terms which vary only by sex and relative age. The terms are: elder brother or male cousin, *dīda;* younger brother or male cousin, *bhula;* elder sister or female cousin, *didī;* younger sister or female cousin, *bhuli.* The same pattern appears in kin terms recorded for the Western Pahari dialect (Karve, 1953, pp. 98 ff.). This is the standard "Hawaiian" type of cousin terminology in Murdock's classification. Since in Sirkanda this terminology is associated with exogamous patrilineal kin groups, the system conforms by definition to Murdock's "Guinea" type of social organization, and since these groups are patrilocal, it belongs in the "normal Guinea" subtype. Murdock (1949, pp. 225 f.) includes ten criteria in his discussion of types of social organization. These will be briefly presented for Sirkanda: (1) descent: patrilineal; [12] (2) cousin terms: Hawaiian type; (3) residence: patrilocal; (4) clans-demes: groups closely resembling patri-clans are analytically discernible, and demes are absent; (5) other kin groups: bilateral kindreds present; (6) exogamy: patrilineal exogamy and bilateral extension of incest taboos (all second cousins ineligible for marriage, though deviations occur); (7) marriage: polygyny permitted, incidence around 15 per cent; sororal polygyny permitted, incidence around 20 per cent of polygynous marriages; (8) family: patrilocal extended family; (9) aunt terms: bifurcate collateral, that is, separate terms for mother, mother's sister, and father's sister (the mother's sister's terms are, however, derivatives of the mother term, which indicates a tendency toward bifurcate merging, and Karve [1953, pp. 98, 100] reports terms indicating bifurcate collateral terminology for both mother-aunts and daughter-nieces in the Western Pahari language); (10) niece terms: bifurcate merging, that is, one term for daughter and brother's daughter, another for sister's daughter. All these data were obtained from men, but so far as could be determined, the same terminology is used regardless of whether a man or woman is speaking. This conforms to usage elsewhere in North India (cf. Karve, 1953, pp. 99 f., 104).

In a patrilocal, patrilineal society such as this, patrilineal relationship and male relatives would be expected to be more prominent than matrilineal relationship and female relatives. This is true in that the kindred extends farther on the paternal side than on the maternal one. But in accounting for greater refinement of terminological distinctions, residence seems to be a more important factor. Those relatives among whom there is or might be repeated interaction are members of the residential group—the patrilocal extended family. They are the ones among whom the most refined terminological distinctions are made, especially those having to do with relative age. Those who are not in the patrilocal group (mother's brothers) and those who leave it (father's sisters) are in less frequent interaction and are not distinguished as to relative age. Father's brothers are in this group, and mother's sisters potentially could be (in line with the Pahari kinship terminological pattern, they are called by terms indicating that they are). Both of these categories are distinguished by age relative to the connecting relative. Seniority is an important matter to be kept in mind among those who interact frequently, for it has significant behavioral concomitants.

Affinal relatives outside one's own generation are classified under fewer terms than are consanguineal relatives, suggesting the lesser emphasis placed on affinal relatives and the greater social (and in the case of a man, physical) distance between a person and his affinal relatives.

Something has already been said of the behavior of various relatives toward one another. Husbands and wives never address one another by name nor by the term of reference. Rather, teknonymy is generally resorted to ("father of X," "mother of X"). Often a wife is addressed in the household as "girl" (chōrī). In reference by the spouse, gharwālī (one of the house, housewife), or "woman," is used most often for a wife, and mālik (owner), or "man," for a husband. Similarly the terms for mother-in-law and father-in-law are never used in address. They are avoided by teknonymy or other circumlocutions and indirections because they are relationships of respect. All younger relatives or those who wish to show respect add the honorific jī to the relationship terms, especially in address. Minor phonetic changes often accompany this addition. In the table in Appendix IV this information has been omitted except where it always occurs in both reference and address.

There is a tendency in Sirkanda to adopt some kinship terms common among Hindi speakers of the adjacent plains and distinct from Pahari terms. Most often these appear as variants rather than as substitute terms. Those Hindi terms most frequently used simplify or make more symmetrical the terminological structure. Thus the Hindi term *mausa*, husband of an affinally related senior woman (mother's sister's husband, wife's elder sister's husband, husband's elder sister's husband) tends to be used in place of the more complex set of Pahari terms for these rather distant and seldom-seen relatives. In three cases distinct Pahari terms for affines are replaced with Hindi terms derived from the term for the consanguineal relative connecting ego and the affine, making a pair of terms for a man and wife that are identical except in ending. For example, Hindi *pupha* replaces Pahari *mama* as husband of *puphu*. A trend toward consistency seems to explain the changes shown in table 3.

TABLE 3

SOME VARIATIONS IN KINSHIP TERMINOLOGY [a]

Traditional local terms		Newer, Hindi-influenced terms	
es: *dīdi*	esh: *jījā*	es: *dīdi*	esh: *bahēnā*
ys: *bhulī*	ysh: *jawāī*	ys: *bhulī*	ysh: *sālā*
Wife of web: *dīdi*	web: *jēThu*	wife of web: *dīdi*	web: *bahēnā*
Wife of wyb: *bhulī*	wyb: *syālu*	wife of wyb: *bhulī*	wyb: *sālā*

[a] See Appendix IV for meanings of the abbreviations.

USE OF KIN TERMS FOR NON-KIN

In a number of situations kinship terminology is applied outside the kin group.

Most common in this respect is the general tendency to address anyone of roughly one's own age in friendly and respectful greeting by the term "brother" or, in the case of a woman, "sister." This usage occurs often in addressing strangers and is common among Hindi speakers throughout Northern India. "Puphu" (father's sister) may be used respectfully to address any older woman. There is no general practice of referring to fellow villagers (as distinct from members of other villages) by kin terms as is done in the plains. This may reflect the fact that Sirkanda is not an exogamous village, and so all villagers are not thought of as relatives.

In Sirkanda close friendship between two men sometimes results in their consistently addressing and referring to one another's wives as "sister," and treating them as sisters in social relationships. It is then said that the offspring of the two couples would not be potential mates even if sib affiliations and other factors were favorable.

If two women who are close friends have infant sons of approximately the same age they may suckle one another's child. In such cases the children are treated as brothers and will later so address one another. They are referred to as "milk brothers" and are expected to be especially close and mutually attached, much as would real brothers. Probably the sister of each would not be a potential mate for the other, though in the cases recorded they were ineligible on other grounds.

Across caste lines relationship terms are also used in address. A blacksmith in Sirkanda is consistently called "uncle" (mother's brother, *mama*) by high-caste people younger than himself, and his wife is called "aunt" (father's sister, *puphu*). To address a stranger as mother's brother would be an insult implying that one's father has had relations with the stranger's sister. It has no such connotation in this case, however. The blacksmith addresses younger high-caste women as "niece" (sister's daughter, *bahanjī*). He addresses high-caste women of his own age as "sister," and they sometimes address him as "brother," whereas he addresses older women as "father's sister." All these terms used to address high-caste women are terms of respect and honor precluding sexual interest, an important fact for low-caste men's relationship with high-caste women. High-caste men are usually addressed by low-caste people in honorific terms, usually by their caste title (*thākurjī*, landlord; *panditjī*, priest).

Terms of reference across caste lines are never kinship terms. Names, caste names, or occupational terms are used. An elderly person, regardless of caste or relationship, is likely to be addressed and referred to simply as "old man" or "old woman." Descriptive terms are frequently used in reference, as "black man," "white man," "fat man," "tall one," "crippled one."

1. Sirkanda village and neighboring hills. View eastward from the school
(see map 3).

2. Settlement area of Sirkanda. The Brahmins' house in the foreground is being rebuilt by carpenter-masons while two members of the family and two elderly Rajputs watch.

3. The respected head of a prosperous Rajput household. He wears gold earrings to honor a household diety.

4. Wife and mother in a Rajput household. The gold nose ring indicates marrage; the heavy silver necklace was given at her engagement. The other jewelry is simply for "fashion."

5. Three young Rajput girls and a little boy. The eldest girl is approaching marriageable age.

6. These boys, like men, carry loads on their shoulders or backs rather than on their heads as women do. The boy on the left is a Bajgi; the other two are Rajputs. They show physical differences which fit the stereotypes of their castes. Ten years later the one in the center was training to be an auto mechanic.

7. Women such as these Rajputs spend considerable time every day carrying water more than a quarter of a mile from the village spring to their homes.

8. Residents of two good-sized villages farm this terraced hillside. One of the villages is discernable in the lower foreground; the other is near the crest of the hillside on the right.

9. A Rajput harrows his plot of millet on a large terrace early in the rainy season.

10. Children and bullocks here perform the tedious task of threshing wheat.

11. Bringing fodder from the forest is a year-round job for women and children. This Rajput boy is bringing dry fodder in the dry season.

12. Women of all castes devote much of the day to housekeeping. This Rajput woman grinds spices as she watches the children.

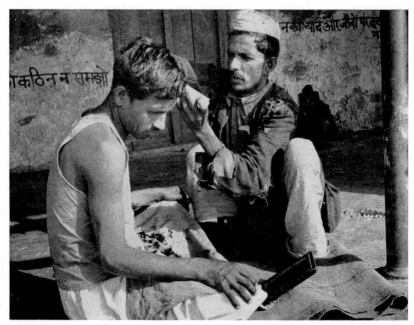

13. The barber is of a caste alien to these hills, but his people have lived in Sirkanda since its founding and have intermarried with Pahari service castes. Here he performs his traditional duty for the village schoolteacher.

14. Sibba, the blacksmith does all the iron work for his clients in return for traditional payments in grain at each harvest. Here he is repairing a grass knife.

15. This Bajgi earns his living by making baskets to order. His relatives are farmers, musicians, and tailors, and one operates an illegal still.

16. A gala wedding party (*barāt*) sets out for the bride's village. In this group the musicians and palanquin bearers are Bajgis while the groom and guests are Rajputs. The groom will walk most of the way because the trail is rough and the way is long, but during the triumphal exit from his village and the entry into the bride's village he will be in the palanquin.

17. The Brahmin priest (book in hand) calls for a recess in the night-long wedding ceremony. It is being performed in a *chan* where the bride's family lives, sharing this room with three buffalo even during the ceremony.

18. While the wedding ceremony is in progress, some of the men amuse themselves by singing and dancing out-of-doors.

19. A feast is part of every major life-cycle rite. Women do not travel to ceremonies but local women eat together, adjacent to their menfolk and the male guests.

20. The annual Pahari fair (*taulū*) of the area is a secular event that is greatly enjoyed, much as are weddings and the religious festival, *Diwālī*. Here gaily dressed men and women take a ride on a Ferris wheel.

21. A Bajgi woman dances while possessed by a household god whose shrine is visible in the rear wall. The *pūjārīs* who have induced the god to dance sit on the right. The female victim of the god's wrath, whose illness has necessitated the ceremony, sits behind the dancer.

22. A Bajgi diviner analyzes the troubles of a Rajput client. In the foreground is a typical water pipe.

23. Taking milk products to market to sell for cash or credit is a regular activity of young men such as these Rajputs. These men's ideas of stylish dress differ considerably. The one on the left is a villager with little experience outside. His companion has been to school in the valley and has acquired a taste for plains styles.

24. Occasionally an outside merchant brings his wares to Sirkanda. Here an itinerant Tibetan bangle seller, his son, and his employee are enjoying a lively market for their goods.

25. The school is a recent and relatively successful source of governmental influence in Sirkanda. Note that two students are spinning wool thread while reciting their lessons.

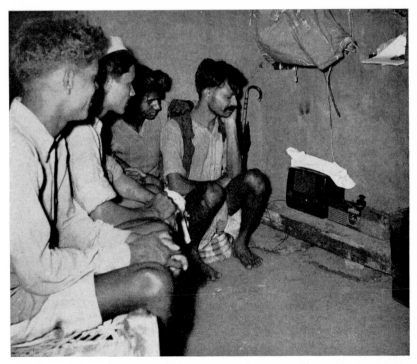

26. An even more recent outside intrusion is All India Radio, brought to Sirkanda for the first time via the anthropologist's radio, shown here. The listeners on the cot are Rajputs, the others are Doms, (Ram Singh on the far left, Sibba on the far right). If a village panchayat house is built, a free radio and loudspeaker will be provided by the government.

27. These members of the older generation of Rajputs look back contentedly on their lives. They have four obedient sons and good land. They do not foresee rapid or unsettling changes in the village, but they do expect young men to take advantage of new opportunities.

28. This young Rajput, Mangal, is considered to be the outstanding pupil in the village school. From a prosperous family, he expects to go to high school and perhaps to college. As a fourth-grader, he is the first member of his family to be educated beyond the first three grades. He would like to get a job "in service," that is, a white-collar job.

29. Puran Singh's tea shop, 1969, with the Devta's dwelling and temple under construction on the knoll behind. Gossipers sit by the shop while a man and little girl drive livestock to the watering place.

30. Buffalo sacrifice at the Mundkile ceremony in Taal.

31. Mangal, the schoolboy grown up (see photograph no. 28), with his favorite wife, visiting her natal village.

31a. Two Bajgi couples dressed for a festival.

32. Kalmu, the Devta-to-be, in 1958, with his goat herd.

33. The Devta in front of his temple.

34a. Devta dancing but not yet in a state of possession.

34b. Devta possessed at the height of his religious role in the Mundkile ceremony at Taal.

35. The Devta and the father of his deceased wife, on the final day of the Mund-kile ceremony when his ritual role was in abeyance.

36. Blacksmiths' songfest on the ethnographer's final visit to Sirkanda, 1969.

6 CASTE

The caste system has probably attracted more attention from sociologists and anthropologists than has any other feature of Indian society. The emphasis is not unwarranted, for it is one of the dominant social and cultural facts of life in India. In this chapter caste will be described as it functions in Sirkanda. Some of the differences and similarities of the Sirkanda system as compared to other examples that have been reported in India and elsewhere will be pointed out.

Caste has been defined variously or not at all by the many writers who have discussed it.[1] Many have been concerned exclusively with India and have therefore dealt with caste in terms so specific as to apply only to India, the area of their interest or experience (for example, Gilbert, 1948, pp. 31 f., and Leach, 1960). Such narrow definitions are useful because caste in India is unique and has distinctive regional variations. The same is true of religion, family organization, economy, and most other phases of life. To understand these things thoroughly it is well to make explicit their unique characteristics. Srinivas emphasizes a prominent and unique aspect of caste in India when he says, "The concept of pollution governs relations between different castes. This concept is absolutely fundamental to the caste system and along with the concepts of *karma* and *dharma* it contributes to make caste the unique institution it is" (Srinivas, 1952, p. 28).

However, to define caste in terms of its uniquely Indian attributes eliminates or at least diminishes its use as a cross-culturally comparable phenomenon (Bailey, 1959; Berreman, 1960a). This in itself is not a criticism. Cultures do have unique traits. I prefer, however, to define caste more broadly in order to include, for purposes of comparison, similar systems of social stratification which occur in other cultures. More is lost, from the point of view of social science (though not, perhaps, from that of Indology) by emphasizing its unique aspects at the expense of comparability than is gained by the added precision.

The definition of castes which will be followed here seems to be valid both in India and elsewhere: *Castes are ranked endogamous divisions of society in which membership is hereditary and permanent.*[2] Implicit in this minimal definition are additional criteria: castes are recognized as groups (i.e., they are usually named); they are in some ways interdependent; barriers to free social intercourse exist between castes; there are cultural differences between castes; there are differential degrees of power and privilege between castes. Associated with caste in many and perhaps all instances is a degree of occupational specialization. While all the members of a caste are not often committed to one line of work, there is a particular occupation or range of occupations which is considered to be appropriate to each caste. Passin (1955, p. 41) notes that among the "untouchable" groups of India, Japan, Korea, and Tibet, ". . . What is particularly striking is the detailed similarity of their occupations. In principle, they were restricted to the despised and menial functions of the community which were, however, essential. Someone had to do them." Occupational specialization may be evidenced in the occupations a caste cannot or does not practice as well as in those it does practice. In India caste groups are specifically characterized by (1) a common traditional occupation and / or a claim to common origin, and (2) a ritual status which must be maintained and which can be defiled by specified types of behavior and contacts with other groups.

The concepts of ritual status and pollution, as mentioned above in the quotation from Srinivas, are important in understanding the functioning of caste in India. Stevenson specifies that ". . . it is from ritual rather than secular status and from group rather than personal status, that the caste system derives it unique consistency and viability." "The ritual status relationship between individuals and groups and between groups of different categories [castes] rest wholly upon behavior-patterns linked with mystical beliefs in general, and mainly upon behavior linked with a particular corpus of beliefs concerning purity and pollution, . . . the Hindu Pollution Concept" (Stevenson, 1954, p. 46).

Indian caste distinctions are explained in terms of elaborate religious, mythological, and historical rationalizations. It is sometimes asserted that as a result of such rationalizations the caste system is made acceptable to all those who are included within it. This may be true, but the implication that therefore all who are included within the system are content with their assigned position in the hierarchy either as individuals or as groups is contradicted by the present research and by the many examples of caste-group mobility and individual aspirations of low-caste people that have been reported (Berreman, 1960a).

In India castes are generally divided into five major hierarchically ranked groupings or levels. The top four of these are the four *varna* or categories described by Manu, the Hindu lawgiver, comprising the three "twice-born" groups (Brahmins or priests, Kshatriya or rulers and warriors, Vaishya or traders and farmers) and the *Shudra* artisans. At the bottom, outside the varna system, are the untouchables. This system is well known and is discussed at length elsewhere (cf. Basham, 1954, pp. 137 ff.; Dube, 1955, pp. 34 ff.). Also well known is the division of these major caste levels into many endogamous regional subgroups, called jati in much of North India, the "castes" of ordinary parlance. The many details of ritual and other barriers restricting social relations between castes have been explained at length by other authors (cf. Srinivas, 1952, pp. 24 ff.; O'Malley, 1932, pp. 1–31). One of the best concise discussions of these matters is that of Stevenson (1954). Recently attention has been directed toward objective and precise determination of caste functions, characteristics, and especially relative status or ranking of castes (cf. Gough, 1959; P. M. Mahar, 1959; and Marriott, 1959, 1960). It is unnecessary to go further into these matters here.

CASTE FUNCTIONS

Caste (jat or jati) is the ultimate extension of the kin group. Its members are considered to be remotely related to one another, and it is the furthest extent of potential or actual affinal kin ties. In fact, the geographical and social limits of a caste may be defined most satisfactorily in terms of the marriage network. As a result, caste functions are in many respects similar to family, sib, clan, and kindred functions, although caste is a less intimate group. It is a unit of social control in that its members or their representatives determine collectively what the membership may and may not do, and what shall be done to enforce these rules. It is the unit of ritual and social equality. It is the endogamous unit, the commensal unit, the unit within which there are no ritual prohibitions on contact and outside of which such prohibitions must, theoretically, be observed. It is an economic unit of importance in that it tends to be the largest competitive unit—the largest unit whose members engage in the same traditional occupation. Caste is an important reference group for its members. Matters of importance to individuals, families, sibs, clans, and kindreds are of some concern to the caste as a whole and are likely to engage the attention of caste-fellows. Ritual and ceremonial occasions reveal this. Cliques and factions show the influence of caste boundaries. People interact socially and ritually with their caste-fellows more often than with members of other castes.

As a result, caste members share a culture which differs slightly from that of other castes. Although caste cultures vary less in Sirkanda than on the plains, differences do become apparent in matters pertaining to traditional occupation, to social organization, to caste preferences in worship, and to interaction with other castes.

CASTE IN THE SUB-HIMALAYAN REGION

There has been no systematic study of Pahari caste organization. There are, however, enough references to the population and customs of the Pahari areas to give a general picture of caste structure there and to verify much of what came to light in Sirkanda. The Pahari caste system is similar to that in other parts of India and is well within the range of regional variations.

All over the cis-Himalayan region, the Simla states, the Doon valley, Kulu and Kangra valleys there exists a hierarchy of social status, though the rigidity of the caste system as in the plains does not exist. The upper class consists of Brahmins and Rajputs (Kshatriyas) . . . the lower strata is composed of innumerable social groups who form the artisan elements in the population of these parts. . . . These suffer from a number of disabilities and are treated as serfs or dependents and thus provide a dual organization of economic classes in these hills. (Majumdar, 1944, pp. 137 f.)

It has been noted before that the component castes of the "upper class," the Khasiyas, are not separated by great social or ritual distance in some Pahari areas and that, in fact, intermarriage between them is not rare. The "lower strata" are called Doms, a term which applies to all the artisan castes of the hills. "The Doms . . . are as far as can be asserted the aborigines of the country. They are found wherever the Khasiyas are found, living with them in a state even now not far removed from serfdom" (Walton, 1910, p. 62). Saksena reports that while the Brahmins and Rajputs of Jaunsar-Bawar form a single endogamous group, "each group among the Doms constitutes a single endogamous group, arranged in hierarchical order" (Saksena, 1955, p. 28).

There can be no doubt that we are dealing with a caste society. It is not as rigid, perhaps, as that found on the plains, but the bases for status evaluation of castes, the barriers limiting contacts between them, and the nature of interaction among them are in general similar to those characteristic of the Hindu caste system throughout India. It cannot be accurately described as a class system, as Majumdar wishes to do, because legitimate individual mobility within the system is impossible.

Most writers attest to the physical and cultural distinctiveness of the Doms as contrasted to the high castes or Khasas. The difference is traced to their alleged separate origins as early aborigines and Indo-Aryan invaders, respectively. These views have been discussed at some length in chapter 1. Whatever may have been the earlier situation, it is evident that these distinctions now exist primarily in the minds of their advocates and to a minor extent if at all in the physical and cultural make-up of the Paharis. Today Khasas and Doms are physically virtually indistinguishable and culturally similar.

There is a homogeneous social code to which both the higher and lower groups subscribe. The disabilities that obtain in these parts among the lower castes in the matter of dress, food and drink, in the restrictions to marriage and inter-dining, are mostly superficial, and they have not affected the social relationships to any appreciable extent. (Majumdar, 1944, p. 139)

Thus Pahari caste stucture is characterized by a twofold division into high-caste groups (Brahmin and Rajput or Khasiya) and low-caste artisan groups (Dom). The latter are accorded the status of untouchables and include most of the occupational groups found among both the clean Shudras and the untouchables of the plains. Within each of these classifications there are status distinctions, but not of the same order as that of the main division. Even intermarriage is tolerated between castes of the same general social and economic level. As will be made clear below, the high-low or pure-polluted caste dichotomy is a striking feature of caste structure in Sirkanda as distinguished from the multiple divisions of the plains. On the other hand, this is not a qualitative difference—plains people too distinguish "clean" castes (the four varnas) from untouchables, and "twice-born" castes (the top three varnas) from those which are not twice-born (the Shudras and untouchables). Cohn (1954, p. 116) notes that, in the plains village he studied, "it would appear that, although the caste system is a graduated hierarchical one, the difference between the Thakurs and all the others is greater than any differences among the low-caste people." Bailey (1957, p. 8) emphasizes the importance of the "line of pollution" between untouchables and others in an Orissa village. Hocart (1950, p. 4) comments on the distinction in Ceylon between the three leading castes or "good people" as ". . . opposed to the 'low-castes,' who comprise fishermen, smiths, washermen, . . . tailors, potters, weavers. . . ." Marriott (1960, pp. 43 ff.) cites comparable systems of caste status ranking in the middle Indus and Bengal delta areas. In much of South India Brahmins, Shudras, and untouchables are the major groupings.

In plains villages the most important division seems to be at least threefold (twice-born, Shudra, untouchable) if not fivefold (Brahmin, Kshatriya, Vaishya, Shudra, untouchable) rather than twofold as in Sirkanda. Also, in the plains there is evidently greater social distance between groups which would in Sirkanda fall within the high- or low-caste divisions. Another difference is that in the hill area there are few ranked subcaste divisions such as those characteristic of plains castes. Among the indigenous hill castes in and around Bhatbair, the subdivisions (sib, gotra) are of equal rank and purity. The only exception is in the superior ritual purity of ceremonial cooks over other Brahmins.

The range of castes in the hills, as in any other particular locality in India, is but a small segment of the total of endogamous castes and subcastes found in India. Ghurye (1952, p. 23) estimates that at the beginning of the nineteenth century there were 500 to 2,000 subcastes in each linguistic area of India. In comparison to the adjacent plains, the absolute number of castes in the Pahari area and in each Pahari village is small. For Garhwal, Raturi (1928, pp. 196 ff.) lists Brahmins, Rajputs, and 30 untouchable castes. Bahadur (1916, pp. 101 f.) lists 15 "professional castes" belonging to the Dom group. It is probable that both these listings of artisans include occupational groups which cannot accurately be described as castes in that they are not endogamous, but the pattern of two high castes and a variety of low, ritually impure artisan castes of roughly comparable status is verified. Conspicuous by their absence in the Pahari region are indigenous Vaishya (members of the merchant caste) and Shudras (clean, but not twice-born, castes, primarily artisans).

CASTE IN SIRKANDA

There are five castes represented in Sirkanda: Brahmins and Rajputs in the twice-born, Khasa category, and blacksmiths, Bajgis (drummers), and barbers in the untouchable, artisan Dom category. Although the barber caste is not an indigenous Pahari caste, the Sirkanda barbers were brought into the village by its Brahmin founders and have therefore been an integral part of Sirkanda since it has existed as a village. Blacksmiths are the most recent immigrant group, having come about 90 years ago. One Bajgi man settled in Sirkanda only 25 years ago, but the other Bajgis are long-time residents. At one time or another, in the past, shoemakers and weavers have lived temporarily in or near the village, but, like the Vaishya merchant who operates one of the village shops, they were never identified by themselves or others as villagers. Within a half-day's walk of Sirkanda are a few other service groups who are occasionally utilized in the village, notably shoemakers, weavers, and carpenters. Traditional caste occupations, occupational deviation, and the role of caste in the local economy have been discussed in chapter 2.

Caste organization in this area is extremely loose and informal. There are no organized caste governments or councils. When an infraction of caste rules occurs in a high caste, a group of male high-caste members may be called together as a council to take action. If so, they discuss the case, listen to any evidence or pleas that are to be given, and come to a decision. They may fine or otherwise punish the offender or, in extreme cases, ostracize him from the caste, that is, outcaste him by refusing to let him take further part in caste functions and refusing to interact socially with him. The only remembered occasions upon which such councils have been called have been for consideration of breaches of rules of caste endogamy. Theoretically they might be called for other cases of disobedience of rules of ritual purity. Often no meeting is called and the offender is merely ostracized by informal agreement.

Generally councils are made up of Rajputs and Brahmins. It is thought proper by both Rajputs and Brahmins to invite representatives of both castes to any meeting that may be held by either of them because they are interdependent as priests and protectors and therefore have common interests.

Members of low castes usually try to settle their problems informally among the individuals or kin groups involved. This course is most frequently taken as numbers are too small to make a caste council feasible, and the members wish to attract as little attention and interference as possible. If agreement cannot be reached on that level, high-caste people will intervene whether requested to do so or not. As the masters and possessors of superior judgment, and as people with a stake in smooth social relations and docility among their subordinates, high castes do not hesitate to assume their traditional authoritarian, paternalistic role even in the internal affairs of low castes. Often a meeting to decide a dispute or punish a misdemeanor involving only low-caste people will be made up entirely of Rajputs and Brahmins. It may even be called by the high castes when the caste involved has no intention of acting in the matter. Individual low-caste people often turn in times of trouble to high-caste patrons—usually people to whom they are committed by employment—who are expected to intercede on their behalf. The dominance of high castes (in this area, Rajputs) is readily apparent in such matters, as they can control the behavior not only of their own caste members, but to a significant extent that of other castes as well.

The real source of day-to-day control within the caste is social pressure applied informally, but often relentlessly, by the group.

CASTE IDENTIFICATION

Caste identification or loyalty is prominent despite the informality of caste organization. It is to be expected that in a caste society in an isolated area caste identification will be strong. From childhood the individual learns that only among caste-fellows is he among equals. He hears the stereotypes about other castes and sees the conventional behavior between castes. He is taught that he cannot deviate from caste rules. If he is of high caste he gradually learns the advantages which accrue to him as a result of his position. If he is of low caste he learns of his dependent status and the sanctions which can be applied to keep him in his place. He learns that to leave the village is to leave all that is familiar, all that provides security. Most people therefore come to accept their position, though not necessarily to like it. Inter-caste conflicts are frequent enough, and rivalries are persistent enough, that other castes are seen as rival groups in many contexts. Sympathy for caste-fellows generally overrides local loyalties. In the interests of village harmony or personal survival, caste loyalties may be suppressed but they do not disappear. Thus, initial inquiry among low-caste people invariably brought the response that in a dispute they would side with their high-caste village-mates against aliens regardless of caste. "Our village must stand together." Later, as they came to trust the inquirer they stated emphatically that their sympathies invariably lay with their caste-fellows regardless of village affiliation. A blacksmith informant said, "If there were a dispute between a blacksmith of some other village and a Sirkanda Rajput my whole sympathy would be with the blacksmith, but I would speak out for the Rajput, if I had to speak, for fear of the punishment of Rajputs. This is always the case. I think it is true of all castes." A Bajgi commented, "If there is an intercaste dispute involving a Bajgi we are on his side whether he is from a neighboring village or from Bombay. If they knew of it, every Bajgi in India would be on his side."

That such attitudes do not seriously affect village stability is largely attributable to the concentration of numbers and power in the high castes. Organized opposition to them is hopeless, and overriding caste loyalties among low castes are restricted largely to private attitudes.

Caste loyalties appear to be somewhat less strong in Rajput-Brahmin relations, where village unity or in-caste factions often override inter-caste rivalry. In a real power struggle, however, a high-caste man can usually count on the support of his caste-fellows, or demand it.

High castes frequently intervene or support one side or the other in inter-low-caste disputes. Low castes try to avoid involvement in inter-high-caste disputes within the village and enter into such disputes across village lines only at the urging of high-caste villagers.

The status identification of low-caste people is recognized by all castes. A radio program devoted to "Harijan uplift" (untouchable uplift) heard on the anthropologist's radio, attracted the immediate attention of low-caste people and was the subject of pointed remarks and jokes by high-caste villagers. "Well, you will soon be a big man, Ram Lal. The government will teach you to read and make you a cabinet minister." Low-caste people are expected to be interested in talk of their position and government efforts to improve it, but not to take it seriously. They are watched closely by high-caste people, and a wrong response or attitude can bring abuse. I described to a group of Rajputs the visit to India of United States Congressman Dr. Singh Saund, and mentioned that he was of Punjabi Indian origin and, according to the papers, had been a blacksmith. My listeners shouted at once for the blacksmith, who was working in his shop. The story was repeated for his benefit, and all expectantly awaited his reaction. Having been put on the spot, he mulled the idea over briefly and then said evenly, "I want to go to America," and returned to his shop.

DOMINANT CASTE

A study of the locally dominant caste and the kind of dominance it enjoys is essential to the understanding of rural society in India. Numerical strength, economic and political power, ritual status and Western education and occupations, are the most important elements of dominance. Usually the different elements of dominance are distributed among different castes in a village. When a caste enjoys all or most of the elements of dominance, it may be said to have decisive dominance. (Srinivas, 1959, p. 15)

Of 384 current residents of Sirkanda, 90 per cent are in the high
castes (87 per cent Rajputs, 3 per cent Brahmins) and 10 per cent
are in the low castes (5 per cent Bajgi, 3 per cent blacksmiths, 2 per
cent barbers). Of 45 households or joint families, 37 are Rajputs, one
Brahmin, two blacksmith, one barber, and four Bajgi. Therefore
Rajputs are numerically the dominant caste in this village.

Rajputs own 94 per cent of the arable land surrounding Sirkanda,
while the Brahmin household owns another 4 per cent, leaving but 2
per cent for the low castes. Similarly the high castes own 97 per cent
of the cows, buffaloes, and oxen, all the horses and mules, and 92 per
cent of the sheep and goats of Sirkanda. Of the livestock, the Brahmin
family owns its proportional share as a larger-than-average high-caste
joint family—about 4 per cent. A Rajput family has the only locally
owned and operated shop, and another Rajput family owns the building in which the outside merchant keeps his shop. Low-caste income
is derived primarily from high-caste villagers in return for services
as artisans. It is therefore apparent that Rajputs are economically
the dominant caste in Sirkanda.

Formal village government and political affiliation count for little
in Sirkanda. However, of the eleven Sirkanda members of the village
council, 10 are Rajputs and one a blacksmith (by law one seat is
reserved for low castes). The president and vice president of the council,
as well as their opponents in the last election and their predecessors,
all are Rajputs. The five Sirkanda members of more inclusive governing bodies (judicial councils) have all been Rajputs, including the
president of one of these councils. The two officers of the Sirkanda
credit coöperative, although they have never had occasion to function,
are Rajputs. In the past various official and semiofficial offices were
given to appointed villagers by the British for administrative purposes. One of these, village accountant, was held by a Rajput; another,
village tax collector (*Lambardār*), was held successively by two Rajputs
of Sirkanda and before that by a Brahmin of a neighboring village. The
hereditary title of Mukhia (a local administrative officer supposed to
be a keeper of the peace) was held in a Rajput family, and a son-in-law
of that family retains the title today.

No official position within the village, except the recently designated
low caste seat on the village council, has been held by other than a
Rajput. A frequent criticism which low-caste people voice against
the village council is that it is dominated by Rajputs and therefore
dispenses "Rajput justice." A blacksmith commented:

> The president of the village council is a Rajput. He was put into office
> by Rajputs. Even if he wanted to be fair to us and help us get some land

to till he could not. There would be too much pressure on him from other Rajputs. So everything he does is for the benefit of Rajputs.

Another low-caste man said:

They run the village to their own advantage. They never think of us. They fine us if we bring a dispute before them and do not fine Rajputs in the same circumstances. Then they use our money for their enjoyment. They prey on our vulnerability.

In the more important realm of traditional leadership and power in the village, Rajputs play the dominant role. When meetings or councils are called to decide disputes or infractions of rules involving villagers, those called are high-caste people, so that Rajputs are always represented and dominate even though their caste-fellows may not be involved in the issue at hand. They combine the traditional roles of landowners, rulers, and protectors of the village, and so they are its leaders.

It is therefore evident that Rajputs are politically the dominant caste in Sirkanda.

Nontraditional education is as yet not a powerful influence in Sirkanda. The village school, established in 1950, is open to, and attended by, all castes. However, of the twelve villagers who went outside Sirkanda for schooling before establishment of the local school or for higher education than that offered in the village, all were Rajputs.

Of Sirkanda villagers only three, all Rajputs, have been in military service. Rajputs have no monopoly on casual outside contacts or temporary sojourns in urban or non-Pahari areas. Members of all castes have had such experience, and low castes, in particular, travel— primarily to get materials for their crafts. However, such travel seems to have relatively little lasting effect. The two villagers who have moved out to take apparently permanent employment in urban areas are both Rajputs. On the whole, then, Rajputs have had greater access to nontraditional education and experience than have other castes in Sirkanda.

Ritually, Rajputs are second to Brahmins in status, but the difference is relatively unimportant in this area. As will become evident, the difference in ritual status is not as great between these two groups as it is in the plains; intermarriage is tolerated (although it is disapproved and occurs infrequently), and a high degree of social intimacy is practiced. Moreover, these two castes are far above the other Pahari castes in ritual status.

Thus Rajputs enjoy nearly all the elements of dominance in Sirkanda and are therefore the possessors of "decisive dominance" as defined by Srinivas. In Sirkanda, as throughout the hills, Rajputs and Brahmins are what Mayer (1958) terms "allied castes" in that they act together on certain occasions, notably in relation to the low castes, to present a united front. There are disputes and jealousies between the two high castes, but they are rarely divided in their relations with the low castes, to whom they appear as a single dominant group.

In some villages of the area Brahmins are approximately equal in numbers to Rajputs, and in a few they outnumber Rajputs. I would estimate the Brahmin population of Bhatbair and vicinity at one-fourth to one-third that of Rajputs. According to the census of 1872, there were 81,000 Brahmins and 152,000 Rajputs in Garhwal (Atkinson, 1886, p. 277; see also table 4 below).

TABLE 4

POPULATION BY CASTE

Sirkanda

Caste		Sibs	Lineages	Households	Individuals Number	Individuals Percentage	
High	Brahmin	1	1	1	11	3	90%
	Rajput	4	11	37	335	87	
Low	Blacksmith	1	1	2	12	3	10%
	Barber	1	1	1	5	2	
	Bajgi	2	2	4	21	5	
	Totals	9	16	45	384	100	

26 Villages Which Each Supplied at Least 1% of Sirkanda Mates [a]

High-caste individuals	4332	(93%)
Low-caste individuals	339	(7%)
Total	4671	

India [b]

Harijans	51,000,000	(13%)
Others	333,000,000	(87%)

Population of Garhwal, 1872 [c]

Brahmins	81,000	(28%)
Rajputs	152,000	(53%)
Doms	52,000	(18%)

[a] Census of India, 1951.
[b] Planning Commission (1958), p. 380.
[c] Atkinson (1886), p. 277.

Relative size of population is decisive in determining which of the two high castes will exercise practical dominance in any given village, because they differ little in the other criteria of dominance. The importance of numbers is as readily apparent to villagers as it is to the outside observer. Even among low castes a frequent rationalization for the power of high-caste villagers is in terms of their superior numbers. A blacksmith described the discrimination practiced by Rajputs in the village against his own caste, and then commented, "The reason Rajputs can do those things is that they outnumber us so much. If blacksmiths were in the majority, the Rajputs would be untouchables." He also recognized the importance of land to power:

Because of our skill at blacksmithing, our ancestors spurned land—they wanted to make their living by their craft. What they did not realize was that people with land are people with power. So now we blacksmiths are suffering the consequences. We are just like servants now. We have to do what the landowners tell us to do. Since we do not grow our own food, we must come begging to them for payment.

Another low-caste man explained:

Caste is a matter of wealth and numbers. A wealthy untouchable can have the District Magistrate and others to his house. A poor untouchable cannot even draw water from the public well. In this village there are many Rajputs, so they can tell the low castes where to sit. If the numbers were reversed they couldn't do this. As an example, there are few shoemakers and sweepers [the lowest castes] in Dehra Dun and they are poor. They are not allowed to touch anyone of higher caste. On the other hand, before partition there were many Muslims in Dehra Dun and many of them were well-to-do. The Muslims were fed and entertained in the homes of high-caste Hindus and vice versa. A Muslim kills the sacred cow and eats its flesh, while a shoemaker merely removes the hide of a dead cow and with it makes shoes for people —a necessary service. But Muslims were numerous and wealthy, so in spite of their defiling practices they were treated well. Shoemakers are few and poor, so they must suffer as untouchables. Such is the nature of caste.

Although Rajputs are the dominant caste they are dependent upon other castes in and around Sirkanda for economic and religious services, as discussed in previous chapters. Before we proceed to an examination of intercaste relationships in these and other contexts, it will be well to consider the important matter of relative ranking of castes.

Caste Ranking in Sirkanda

Determination of the relative rank of castes is not as easy as it might at first appear. To simply ask a person may or may not produce a coherent account of rank order. To ask several people is most likely to produce several rank orders.

Individuals and even groups may be given one rank order in a particular context and a different ranking in another context. . . . What is quite constant is a set of criteria for ranking; what varies is the interpretation given in a specific instance to a particular combination of characteristics. (Mandelbaum, 1955, p. 241)

Recently a good deal of attention has been directed toward this problem. Among the most interesting studies has been Pauline Mahar's use of a multiple scaling technique to get at caste ranking from the point of view of ritual purity and pollution by investigating the "norms relevant to the interactions symbolizing inequality of ritual status in dyadic inter-caste relations" (P. M. Mahar, 1959, p. 128). Through this technique she was able to show quite precisely the relative ranks of 18 of 22 castes in Kalapur and to specify areas of disagreement in caste ranking.

In Sirkanda the situation was less complex than that with which Mahar and most other researchers have worked in Indian villages, in that a relatively small number of castes were to be dealt with. The pattern of intercaste relationships was, however, essentially the same as that found by other researchers. In view of the limited number of informants and castes, I was able to question extensively on this subject and to derive a fairly consistent body of data. In analyzing these data I compared a range of statements of what should be done and what is done with the observations and reports of actual interaction among members of the various castes. As a result, I obtained a quite complete picture of caste as it functions in the village and as it is seen from the various caste levels.

In the research an attempt was made to pay equal attention to "ritual" and "secular" criteria of caste ranking. It soon became evident that "secular status" is significant to caste ranking primarily as it is reflected in "ritual status," but not in and of itself. The two cannot be separated. Traditional occupation, which is an important factor in caste status and might be assumed to be a secular consideration, is in fact not secular. Inherent in it is attribution of ritual status. That is, occupation is accorded ritual significance. A shoemaker or blacksmith is, by the nature of his traditional occupation, ritually impure. If a group gives up or adopts a ritually impure occupation, its ritual status will usually vary accordingly. Thus it was reported that some Bajgis further in Garhwal had, in the absence of available shoemakers and at the insistence of high castes, adopted the occupation of skinning and disposing of dead animals. They had thereupon become untouchable to other Bajgis. On the other hand, a group of Bedas near Bhatbair were trying to raise their status by giving up their traditional occupation of singing and dancing. It is important to keep in mind that ritual status is a group phenomenon. An individual cannot raise his status by changing his occupation, and he is unlikely to lower it in this fashion unless he is ostracized by his own group. The discussion in chapter 2 of caste occupations, occupational variation within castes, and caste-neutral occupations is relevant in this context. It seems likely that occupational variation within castes is more acceptable and has wider limits here than in the plains.

In Sirkanda the details of caste ranking vary with the status level from which the individual views his fellow villagers. In general, ritual and social distance (in one direction) between the caste of an observer and two castes being observed varies inversely with the perceived ritual and social distance between those two castes. However, pattern of ranking is remarkably consistent. In the discussion of caste ranking below, ideal patterns will be presented first and thereafter some of the exceptions and deviations will be mentioned.

Ritually purest of all castes are the Brahmins—traditionally the priestly caste. Regardless of whether or not individuals follow a priestly occupation they are accorded their traditional ritual primacy. Their touch or presence defiles no one. All castes will take water and boiled (*kachchā*) food from them.[3] One group of Brahmins is ritually even purer than other Brahmins. They are the ceremonial cooks (cf. p. 67) who accept kachcha food from no one but their own subcaste-fellows. Brahmins in general take kachcha food from no other caste, will let no other caste enter their cooking and eating area, and when smoking the water pipe will share the wooden pipestem with no other caste.

Rajputs are a close second to Brahmins in ritual status. They are approximately as far from other castes in ritual distance as are Brahmins but are slightly inferior to Brahmins. Brahmins will not accept kachcha food from them, share the wooden pipestem with them, nor let them eat in a Brahmin kitchen. When a Rajput eats in a Brahmin house he rinses the utensils he has used and leaves them outside where they can be cleaned before being used again in the Brahmin household. Rajputs and Brahmins do, however, freely share the brass pipestem or, lacking this, the brass base of the water pipe, and cigarettes. In most situations they interact as equals.

The Brahmins and Rajputs are the two "twice-born," ritually clean castes. From their point of view all other castes are *achūt* (literally "untouchable") or defiling and are referred to as Dom. Distinctions among Doms are known but irrelevant to these high-castes. They will accept from Doms no drink except liquor and no cooked food except parched grain, and potatoes or meat roasted directly on the coals of a fire. Doms must not touch the water pots or other utensils of high-caste people. If they do, the contents are discarded and the utensil, if it is brass (as is usual), is cleaned. If it is of the alloy known as *kansī*, which absorbs pollution easily, it cannot be cleaned and must be discarded. Bodily untouchability is not observed—it is not polluting for a high-caste person to be touched by a Dom. Cohn found the same to be true in Senapur. "When a Thakur uses the term *achut* in reference to a Camar he does not mean that he cannot touch or be touched by him, but rather that he cannot take water or food from him and that the Camar's touch of utensils or of cooked food is defiling" (Cohn, 1954, p. 120).

Doms are not supposed to sit on the same string cot with high-caste people or, in fact, on a string cot at all in the presence of high-caste people. Doms are not allowed to enter or sit in the houses of high castes. When visiting high-caste homes Doms are expected to sit on the narrow porch outside the house or on the steps leading up to the house. On the other hand, high-caste individuals can enter freely into the homes of low-caste people and are given the seat of honor when they do so. Doms cannot share either the pipestem or the base of the water pipe with high-caste people. When smoking in a group they are given only the clay pipe bowl to smoke. They are not allowed to share cigarettes with high-caste people. They cannot worship in the Raghunath temple or the larger temples outside the village. When being blessed by a Brahmin they are not touched by him. Instead he throws a small amount of vermilion substance onto a convenient surface and a Dom applies it to the foreheads of his caste-fellows. Sexual contacts between Dom men and high-caste women are taboo.

When a Dom and a high-caste person meet one another, the Dom is expected to bow or nod and respectfully address the high-caste person with the traditional Pahari greeting, *"Samanī Thākūr"* (greetings, landlord).[4] This is an enforceable rule.

There is thus a great social and ritual barrier between Rajputs and Brahmins, on the one hand, and Doms on the other. Strengthening the barrier, in the minds of villagers, is the traditional occupation associated with each caste. Brahmins are traditionally priests and Rajputs are traditionally administrators and warriors, but both are thought of, in the present context, primarily as landowning agriculturists. The high castes are also thought to be ultimately related in that sons of the great ascetics became Brahmins and Rajputs depending upon their choice of occupation. On the other hand, Doms are identified as artisans—people who work with their hands. A word which is sometimes used in reference to Doms, and which carries the same connotations of pollution and inferiority implied in that term, is shilpkar, artisan. In this category fall the craftsmen and specialists who would be classified as Shudras and untouchables on the plains. The same sorts of disabilities are imposed upon them as upon untouchables of the plains.

The Doms of Sirkanda are blacksmiths, barbers, and Bajgis. Carpenters, weavers, and shoemakers will be included in this discussion, since these groups are continually in contact with Sirkanda villagers and are residents of the area. Mention will also be made of Bedas (the rope sliders and musicians described in previous chapters), who are indigenous to the area and are still in occasional contact with Sirkanda. All these groups are lumped together under the term "Dom" by high-caste villagers, who often assert that "Doms are all alike." A blacksmith remarked, "They [high castes] treat all low castes alike. We are just Doms to them even though there are great differences among low castes." [5] High-caste people know the distinctions among low castes but consider them unimportant and irrelevant, as indeed they are to high-caste people. All low castes are considered by them to be approximately equally polluting.

Blacksmiths and carpenters actually form one endogamous group, although there is a strong tendency for males of the families to remain in one or the other occupational specialty. There are no formal ritual distinctions between them, and for most purposes they can be considered a single caste. Dom goldsmiths also fall in this group. These three occupational specialties are collectively and exclusively termed Mistri. This group and barbers and weavers are roughly equivalent in status and consistently rank above other Dom castes in the ritual hierarchy among Doms. The barbers, being of alien origin, have been in a somewhat anomalous position. They share a common marriage pool with Mistris, although both barbers and Mistris claim ritual superiority and often will not allow one another in their kitchens. Weavers are generally considered to be slightly lower in status than Mistris and they, on their part, claim to be higher. Both observe ritual distance in that they do not normally go into one another's kitchens. Intermarriage is allowed but is not encouraged and is infrequent. Weavers are in nearly all respects equivalent in status to the Sirkanda barbers and, like Mistris, intermarry freely with them. Thus, the barbers form a link between Mistris and weavers. This entire group is of nearly equivalent status, so that a rigid hierarchy cannot be outlined. All claim to be highest; all claim to be polluted by others in the group; all occasionally intermarry.

Below the above-listed group of artisan castes are the Bajgis, musicians who are also tailors and basket weavers and in this area usually perform the functions of barber (although Mistris, too, may perform these duties). Restrictions placed upon Bajgis in their relationships with Mistris are, according to the latter, the same as those Rajputs place on all Doms. In practice, however, the restrictions are not as far-reaching or carefully observed as those between Doms and Rajputs. Bajgis frequently challenge the superiority of Mistris, but if forced to a showdown will concede it. Roughly equivalent in rank to Bajgis are other musician castes such as Beda. The most defiling characteristic of these people is apparently their occupation as musicians and dancers, with the assumed correlate that their women are prostitutes. This interpretation is based both upon observation of caste ranking and upon local explanations, which usually include mention not only of the occupation of Bajgi men but also their women's role as prostitutes. To explain the significance of this in terms of the pollution concept, we might turn to an interesting point made by Stevenson, who distinguishes between "external pollution" and "internal pollution," the latter being much more defiling and difficult to counteract (Stevenson, 1954, p. 52). Stevenson points out that bodily emissions are ritually polluting to Hindus. He speculates that this may explain the fact (true also in Sirkanda) that intercaste sexual congress is much more serious for a woman than for a man. A lower-caste partner defiles a woman permanently and irreparably but affects a man only slightly. Stevenson hypothesizes that, ". . . since in sexual intercourse it is the man who emits the polluting secretion, and the woman who receives it internally, the man is exposed only to external pollution, which can be removed by a bath, whereas the woman is internally polluted [so that she cannot be purified] . . ." (Stevenson, 1954, p. 57). Perhaps the low ritual status of the musician castes might be accounted for by interpreting the sexual availability and assumed prostitution of their women in these terms—their women are continually and irreparably polluted by sexual contacts with members of many castes. More simply, they are occupationally associated with human emissions which are polluting, and therefore they are polluted. Bajgi women in Sirkanda have given up dancing, and the Beda women in this area dance less than formerly in an effort to overcome this stigma.

Lowest among the Dom castes are the shoemakers and skinners of dead animals (Mochis, Chamars). They are often musicians as well. These people are treated by Bajgis and all higher castes much as Doms in general are treated by Rajputs and Brahmins. They are the scapegoats for Bajgis, who are the scapegoats for Mistris, just as all Doms are scapegoats for higher castes. Mochis and Chamars are consistently ranked lower by all castes than other Doms and are reportedly even more restricted in their contacts with high castes. Their rank is apparently due primarily to their uniquely defiling occupation. It is often asserted or suspected by others that they occasionally eat not only dead buffaloes, but even dead cows or oxen. Their alien origin and persistent cultural and residential separateness in the area probably contribute to the great social distance between them and other castes. Much of what Bhatbair people "know" about them is rumor. This added factor makes assessment of their caste status relative to other Doms especially difficult. While they are definitely the lowest of the low castes, it is difficult to determine to what extent high-caste attitudes toward them differ from those toward indigenous Doms in terms of pollution, and to what extent cultural factors are accountable.

Among low castes, then, there are three hierarchically ranked endogamous groups whose ritual status is linked to their traditional occupational specialties: all are artisans and therefore, by Pahari standards, polluted. On this basis alone the clean castes treat them as a group and largely ignore their differences. Among artisans the purest are those who practice only a craft (metalwork, woodworking, weaving, barbering), whose women are not suspected of prostitution, and who do not handle dead animals. Inferior to them are those castes who, in addition to whatever other occupation they may follow, are musicians and whose women are dancers and therefore suspected of prostitution. Lowest of all are those whose work is with dead animals. There is a consistent progression of pollution: All low castes are artisans, those who are also musicians are lower than those who are not, and those who also deal with dead animals are lower than those who do not (see table 5).[6]

The details of this hierarchy differ from those reported by Atkinson for Garhwal and Kumaon. Speaking of the Doms of this area he says:

According to popular estimation, they are divided into four grades, all equally impure and outside ordinary caste life, but furnishing certain distinctions from occupation and the like which bring up the first grade very close to the lower forms of Rajput clans and these again connect with Brahmans, so that no link in the chain of social distinction between the highest and the lowest is wanting. (Atkinson, 1886, p. 444)

Atkinson then lists the four grades or status levels of Doms, starting at the top, as: (1) smiths, carpenter-masons, weavers, and "Khasiyas degraded for caste offences"; (2) basketmakers, wood turners, oil pressers, messengers, miners; (3) leather workers; (4) "vagrant tribes of musicians, dancers, jugglers, acrobats, etc." The differences between that account and the situation in Bhatbair are that the second category is missing in Bhatbair, since wood turners are categorized with other carpenters, and basket makers are musicians. The castes which approximate the third and fourth are reversed in status level. Perhaps the facts that leather workers are not indigenous to the Bhatbair area and that in Garhwal and Kumaon their women are not thought of as prostitutes account for the reversal of their status.

TABLE 5

CASTE RANKING IN SIRKANDA

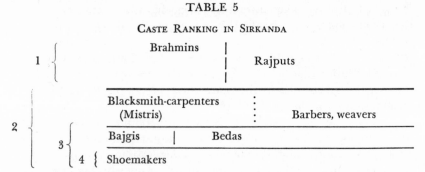

1. Clean castes (twice-born)—landowning agriculturists.
2. Unclean castes (achut)—artisans.
3. Castes in which men play musical instruments and women dance.
4. Castes that handle dead animals and/or scavenge.

In this schematic representation, a solid line indicates strongly enforced prohibition of intermarriage; the broken line indicates ideal prohibition of marriage but rare toleration of it; the dotted line indicates some claims to ritual distance, including marriage restrictions, but little distance in fact. Those caste names which appear on the same horizontal plane are of approximately equal status.

In general, a caste's members may freely engage in any activity less defiling than that appropriate to their caste status or irrelevant to caste status, but not in anything more defiling. Caste terminology is instructive in this context. Mention has already been made of the use of the traditional Pahari greeting as indicating relative status, and that clean castes refer to all the lower castes as "Doms" and consider them "achut." Among low castes the term Dom is resented and is applied only to castes lower than one's own. Blacksmiths refer to Bajgis and shoemakers as Doms but deny that the term is properly applied to themselves. Bajgis, in turn, apply the term only to shoemakers, and shoemakers resent the appellation, preferring a more specific caste term. The government listed all these low-caste groups as "scheduled castes" in the 1951 census. The census taker who came to Sirkanda termed them *Harijans,* Gandhi's term for untouchables— literally "children of god." As one Bajgi said, "In the census they listed all who are not Brahmins or Rajputs as Harijans. Of course that is absurd. There aren't any shoemakers or sweepers in this village, and they are the only real Harijans." Low-caste people resent general terms which lump them with other low castes. They prefer specific occupational terms. Some low-caste groups have alternative terms of reference which they prefer to the usual one. Thus Bajgis often refer to themselves as Darzi or *Aujī* (tailor). Shoemakers are often called Chamar by other castes, but prefer to be called "shoemaker."

CLASS DIFFERENCES

Within castes there are differential advantages and status based in part on wealth. In general, as has been shown previously, high-caste villagers control the wealth of Sirkanda. Wealth correlates positively with caste but is not rigidly bound to it. Although great differences in land ownership and income do not exist among high-caste families, this does not mean that no differences are found. Some families are in debt; others have money to lend. Some are financially better off than they were a few years or generations ago; others have less than formerly. Changes in fortune are a prime topic of gossip in the village. One Rajput family came into a large and unexpected sum of money obtained by dubious means from Muslims at the time of India's partition. They now possess the best house in Sirkanda, display their wealth, and affect airs of superiority—behavior which is repulsive to the entire village. Villagers commented that they are little people who got too much money and do not know how to live with it. "A big person is unchanged by a change in fortune; a small person is overcome with it. Money is like a rainstorm which affects the ocean hardly at all, but makes a mountain stream into a raging torrent that tries to carry away the mountain with it."

Low castes are, on the whole, much less secure financially than are the high castes. However, there are differences among them. At present the blacksmiths and the two small Bajgi households are the poorest villagers. They have no land to cultivate, they own few animals, and their traditional income is scanty. The barber and the two larger Bajgi families are better off. They have animals and some culti-vable land in addition to income from their traditional occupations. They are almost as well off as the poorer Rajputs. The shoemakers of this area are as well off as the Bajgis. They too own land and have a sizable traditional income. Several artisans of the Mistri group who live in areas adjacent to Sirkanda have become very well-to-do, and live in a manner superior to that of Sirkanda Rajputs.

Thus, while "class" differences are correlated with caste status, there are exceptions and there is differential wealth within castes. Such deviations and differences do not affect caste status (that is, ritual purity), but they are relevant to individual status, standard of living, and to interpersonal and intercaste relations. Blacksmith-Bajgi rivalry in Sirkanda is based partly upon the disparity between their traditional ritual status and their present relative economic status (cf. Rowe, 1960a, pp. 70 ff.). According to reports, blacksmiths were formerly relatively well off, and friction between them and the Bajgis was minimal. Sirkanda Brahmins hold their own in the village, despite their small numbers, largely because their wealth backs up their ritual status.

Low castes hesitate to press for their rights partly because of their economic inferiority to, and dependence upon, high castes. A blacksmith said, "We cannot press charges against a Rajput. He and his caste-fellows would pay bribes and hire lawyers such as we could never afford. Twenty Rajputs could raise Rs. 100 by collecting Rs. 5 each. What could two poor blacksmiths do against that?" A Bajgi does not hesitate to press charges against a blacksmith because he knows he can bring at least as much money (and therefore influence) to bear as can the blacksmith.

Although there are well-known differences in income within the village, display of wealth is tightly controlled by custom. To display wealth in disapproved or unconventional ways is to invite public criticism, social pressure, and even open hostility, as has the newly rich Rajput family mentioned above. This is true at all caste levels but especially at the lower levels, where it would be considered not only bad taste but arrogance. The objection is not to living beyond one's means, but to living beyond the approved level of expenditure, which is considerably below the means of a number of families.

Wealth is legitimately displayed among high-caste villagers in expensive weddings and, to a lesser extent, in funerals and other ceremonies, and in the giving of charity to Brahmins. This ritualistic sphere is really the only one in which "conspicuous consumption" is practiced without disapproval. A family's wealth is shown in other ways: in the jewelry worn on special occasions by its women; in large, well-built houses (here the number of ornately carved pillars on the veranda is a publicly recognized criterion of wealth, as is the type of roof, thatch being least expensive, corrugated iron next, and slate most expensive); in the number and quality of cattle owned; in the number and quality of household utensils (brass trays, tumblers, and so on) used; and in the quality of food served in the house. Education of a son outside the village is coming to indicate wealth, but its absence is not a sign of lack of wealth. Wealth cannot be legitimately displayed by low-caste members in the village. Any display would bring prompt and painful sanctions.

For the most part, however, wealth is not displayed even by high castes. Instead, money is stored in concealment or loaned on interest. Clothing, household furnishings, and most other material possessions, as well as the work and other activities of well-to-do families, are not significantly different from those of poor people. Wealth is usually apparent more in spite of its owner's wishes than because of them. There is an effort at nonconspicuous consumption, or perhaps more accurately, conspicuous nonconsumption.

The Wisers have explained an important reason for villagers' reluctance to advertise their wealth—the fear of exploitation by agents of authority, fear of increased taxes, and so on—by paraphrasing village sentiment in these terms:

> In self-protection we have learned to make it almost impossible for anyone to tell who is prospering among us. You may guess, and we may guess. But who is going to tell us if we are right. . . . Some among us are honestly poor. And the rest of us, excepting the affirmed leaders, have learned to make a show of poverty. (C. V. and W. H. Wiser, 1951, p. 159)

The wealthiest man in Sirkanda shows his wealth in no perceptible way except in the very favorable marriages (with educated boys of prominent, well-to-do families) that he has contracted for his daughters. Quality of marriage arrangements in the family is the ultimate criterion of wealth and status within the caste.

The most important factor in "class" or status within the caste besides wealth and the things correlated with it, is Sanskritization. The more a family conforms to Sanskritic orthodoxy in life-cycle ceremonies, the more highly it is thought of. This is not wholly independent of wealth, as Sanskritization is expensive, but it is a somewhat different dimension.

CASTE STEREOTYPES

Associated with conventional criteria of caste ranking in terms of ritual status are a number of caste stereotypes. Rajputs are said by low-caste informants to be proud, haughty, jealous of their power, authoritarian. Brahmins are supposed to be niggardly with their own property and exacting in their demands for charity and service from others. "A Brahmin is never satisfied," is a frequent saying. Low-caste people are considered by high-caste informants to be lazy, impulsive, thoughtless, ignorant, irresponsible, childlike, addicted to music, drink, and narcotics. Low castes are capable of taking advantage of these stereotypes by using them as excuses for behavior that would otherwise be inexcusable. If a Bajgi is found holding a drunken songfest in his home or is away from the village pursuing an illicit love affair while he is supposed to be preparing a set of clothes for a Rajput client, he will be cursed but, after all, "what can be expected of such people?"

Low castes hold particular stereotypes about one another which are shared to varying degrees by high castes. Blacksmiths are considered physically powerful, Bajgis are considered hard-working and clever, and the barber (whose functions are elsewhere performed by Bajgis) is also considered clever. Shoemakers are considered degraded in every respect. (Cf. Oakley, 1905, pp. 260 ff.)

Stereotypes tend to justify the system and perpetuate it. The members of various castes are often said to be suited to that caste and no other by their very nature. To give advantages to low castes would be useless, as they would not be able to make use of them. "Maggots which live in feces cannot live in grain." On the other hand, in Sirkanda as elsewhere, this philosophy is not put to the test by making advantages accessible to low castes. Rather, low castes are actively denied access to advantages which high castes assert they could not use or would not want anyway.

ATTITUDES ABOUT CASTE

Individual attitudes on caste are shaped from earliest childhood by observation of behavior of elders and by direct instruction or admonition. A blacksmith discussed his own feeling toward Bajgis in response to a query following up apparent inconsistencies between his behavior and his statements about caste. He had condemned caste discrimination while stoutly denying that he would treat a lower-caste person as he wished to be treated by Rajputs.

I don't mingle with Bajgis any more than Rajputs mingle with blacksmiths. In my heart I cannot bring myself to do it. My conscience will not let me. I have been taught all my life that they are inferior and unclean. Even if I wanted to, I could not overcome this feeling. Secondly, it is due to the character of their women who become dancers and prostitutes—and the men play drums. Such people cannot be my equals. Finally, there is pressure from other people in my caste and the knowledge of what higher castes would think. If I mixed with Bajgis the high castes would treat me just like a Bajgi, and it would degrade my whole caste. High castes would expect the same behavior from blacksmith women as from Bajgi women. My own caste members would be angry with me.

This particular informant made all the following statements representing a variety of different views: "The high castes treat all low castes alike, even shoemakers." "Caste is an undesirable thing, it divides people and makes for conflict; it should be abolished." "There are really only two castes in the world, men and women; all others are artificial and unnecessary." "I don't mix with Bajgis and shoemakers; I treat those Doms just as Rajputs treat low castes."

Low-caste people's resentment of their own caste position is constantly evident. Equally evident is their need to rationalize their status relative to others. Their thoughts along these lines vary from individual to individual and from time to time. An attitude shared and expressed by several low-caste villagers was stated by one: "Englishmen and Muslims are untouchable because they have an alien religion and they eat beef. This is logical. We are Hindus and we do not eat beef, yet we too are treated as untouchables. This is not proper. We should be accorded higher status."

A blacksmith explained, "Long ago Bajgis used to kill and eat cattle and buffaloes and that is why they are untouchable. Our people never did that, so we should not be called untouchable." This alleged inconsistency in occupation and status is usually rationalized in terms of high-caste numerical and economic dominance. It is commonly also explained in terms of mythology, which takes away some of the sting of the negative associations of low status, usually by providing respectable ancestry for the caste and explaining its decline in terms of unfortunate circumstances. Atkinson notes that in Kumaon "the Doms, like all the others, claim an exalted origin and say that they are the descendants of a Brahman named Gorakhnath and were turned out of caste for eating forbidden food" (Atkinson, 1886, p. 446). The blacksmiths and Bajgis of Sirkanda lay claim to relatively recent but unrecognized Rajput and Brahmin ancestry, respectively.

Q. What is your caste?
A. We are Lohars [blacksmiths]. Sometimes we are called Mistri.
Q. Are you Doms?
A. No, Bajgis and shoemakers are Doms. We are above them. We cannot take water from them.

Q. Someone told me you are Mahar Rajputs.

A. Oh yes, that is true, but people here don't recognize that. We are descended from a Mahar Rajput who lived several generations ago farther up in the hills and who took a blacksmith wife. Since we are his children we are of his caste, but people here call us blacksmiths. There are other such cases. A man should be of the caste of his father, but people don't recognize that when the mother is of low caste.

Similarly, the Chamars of Senapur trace their ancestry to Rajputs or Brahmins (Cohn, 1954, pp. 112 ff.).

Besides rationalizations for the low status of their family or caste, people almost invariably seek rationalizations for individual status; that is, in addition to denying that his caste deserves low status or has always been of low status, a man usually denies that, granted the low status of his caste, he is deserving of having been accorded such caste affiliation or that he is an ordinary low-caste person. The attitude is, "I was meant for greater things." There are many stories of low-caste individuals who were destined for high status because of their good works in previous lives, but through mischance were assigned to life in a low caste. The same people who adhere to claims of un-recognized higher caste status believe (in apparent contradiction) that they have been assigned low status in some almost accidental way. Thus, the blacksmith who gave the above responses on his caste status also recounted the story of his own origin as it had been told him by a Brahmin who read his horoscope.

The pundit read my horoscope and told me my fate and my history. He is always right in these matters. He said that in my previous life I was a wealthy Raja. I was well known for my valour, honor, and piety, and the fairness of my rule. I was destined for a very high rebirth. One time I de-cided to give away a great deal of wealth in charity to my Brahmins. In order to do this I had my servants bake a great many pastries. Instead of filling them with food, I instructed my attendants and servants to stuff them with gold and distribute them to the Brahmins. This was done secretly and was intended as a surprise. This was a very meritorious act. However, my assist-ants and servants were dishonest, and instead of doing as I had instructed they stole the gold and filled the pastries with stones. These were distributed and I was unaware of the deceit. The Brahmins who received them did not tell me because they did not know my intent, so I never found out. Although my intent was pure, I was guilty of putting trust in untrustworthy assistants. Therefore, when I died, I was punished by being born a blacksmith. It is my fate in this life never to succeed in any enterprise and never to acquire or retain wealth. This has proved true. I have tried several schemes to get money and all have failed. When I had some money which I inherited from my father, it was stolen from me on a trip into Dehra Dun. The only way

I can get anything out of money is to spend it at once before I lose it, and that is my policy. In my next life I am destined to be a merchant—perhaps I will do better then.

A Bajgi from another village had a comparable tale. He had been an ascetic destined to become a Raja in the next life. While meditating on the infinite, he had ignored the plight of a cow entangled in the brush. As punishment he was reincarnated as a lowly Dom.

Such stories of deserved but unintentionally provoked punishment apparently account for many instances of low birth. They are disseminated by Brahmins and serve as a means of rationalization and comfort for low-caste people. As such they are effective means of control for the high castes. Whether or to what extent Brahmins are conscious of the usefulness of the stories I did not find out, but their effect is obvious. As will become evident, the high castes in general and the Brahmins in particular have a strong vested interest in the caste system and therefore in keeping the low castes in their place and relatively content.

No informants were found who said, in effect, "I was a scoundrel in a previous life and now I am getting my just desserts." Neither was any caste found whose members said in effect: "We have always done defiling work. This is what we were created to do and we do it. Therefore we are untouchable." These (and particularly the first) seem to be psychologically untenable positions for individuals to accept. On the other hand, high castes readily admitted that they were receiving the deserved rewards of exemplary previous lives.

In Sirkanda, as in Hindu society generally, there appears to be an inherent contradiction between what some would call social structure and culture. That is, according to the concept of dharma (here definable as inherent duty), every member of every caste group is enjoined to behave according to the hereditary station of the caste in the hierarchy. This is an explicit injunction against social mobility in the context of the caste system.

At the same time there is upward mobility among low castes in India. Lipset and Bendix have asserted that

the fact that there is constant striving for upward mobility in the most status-ridden society in the world, adds considerable weight to the hypothesis derived from Veblin, according to which a system of stratification is a fundamental source of mobility motivation in and of itself. Apparently, there are imperatives which prompt men to resist and reject an inferior status and these imperatives persist regardless of the way in which any given society has legitimated inequality. (Lipset and Bendix, 1960, p. 63)

If this statement is correct then a dilemma faces the low-caste person who according to his religion should stay in his place, but according to this "natural law" wants to rise.

In Sirkanda and, I believe, throughout India, this dilemma is often neatly resolved by exactly the mechanisms described above: accepting cast dharma but denying that one's apparent dharma is his real dharma. That is, the individual takes the position that a person should behave according to his caste status but that he or his kin group or jati is not really of the caste or status to which others ascribe him (or them). He is of a higher caste. He aspires to live as a member of his "true" caste in order to fulfill his true dharma. Therefore his mobility aspirations are legitimized and even made imperative. He rationalizes his own mobility aspirations without challenging the system.

The over-all pattern is one of high castes justifying their superior position in terms of myths and religio-philosophical beliefs. Subordinate castes assert their superiority to some castes while rationalizing their inferiority to others, and their consequent mobility aspirations, in terms of unrecognized but deserved higher status and dharma than that accorded them by society.[7]

In Sirkanda expressed resentment about caste was usually put in terms of the way it affects "me" or "my family" or "my caste." It rarely extended to other groups. Even those low-caste individuals most piously opposed to upper-caste abuses were likely to be equally abusive to their caste inferiors. No group admitted to being lower than all others. Even shoemakers would point to sweepers of the plains or to beef-eating Muslims or Christians as being lower than themselves.

Thus, objections to the caste system, as such, were not common. Those voiced in Sirkanda were isolated references apparently derived from the opinions of a previous low-caste schoolteacher or others who had had experience with the *Arya Samaj* (a reform movement), or Gandhian or government views on caste. They did not reflect a consistent objection in the village to the caste system.

This is a feature of intercaste relations common throughout India. Gould (1961a, p. 946) attributes it in large part to "repressed hostility which manifests itself not in the form of rejecting the caste system but in the form of its victims trying to seize control of it and thereby expiate their frustrations on the same battle field where they acquired them." I would suggest that an important factor is simply that all castes are so imbued with the value of hierarchy that none wants to associate with those it considers inferior. Should the caste system be abolished, the opportunity to mingle as equals with superiors would be accompanied by the necessity to mingle as equals with inferiors. The latter would be an especially distasteful prospect to a group whose only claim to status is a tenuous superiority to one or a few degraded groups. To seek to undermine the caste system would be to seek the end of one's own superiority to at least some other groups. To seek to raise the status of one's own caste within the system gives, prom'se of superiority to more groups. The former would put any caste in an ambivalent position relative to its previous status; the latter would bring clear-cut advantage. Above all, the Indian ethos is not one of equality but one of hierarchy, of which caste is the epitome. The upwardly mobile Indian peasant seeks superiority, not equality.

Individuals who are the objects of caste discrimination generally direct their resentment not at the intergroup phenomenon as such, but at the manifestation of it which affects them personally. They resent not caste discrimination, but discrimination directed against themselves. One of the persistent problems of "Harijan uplift" in India is that, once untouchables become educated and can break away from many of the restrictions and disabilities imposed by their traditional caste identification, they tend to disassociate themselves from their caste fellows and (with notable exceptions) contribute nothing to further the cause which was at least part of the reason they were given scholarships or other extra advantages which made possible their rise in status. The former schoolteacher in Sirkanda, who was of blacksmith caste, had been popular among all castes in the village, but was accused by his caste-fellows of having curried favor among high castes and others to his own advantage while ignoring the welfare of his own caste. This pattern is not surprising, nor is it unique to the hills or to India. It occurs in intergroup relations everywhere. The same kinds of accusations are directed toward the "emancipated Negro" of the United States.

However, the pattern seems to be somewhat more acute and general in India, partly, perhaps, because in India intergroup relations are largely carried out on such an intensely personal, individual level.

I sometimes discussed the status of whites, Indians, and Negroes in Africa with urban people of Dehra Dun. There was great indignation about the situation, but it invariably boiled down to the statement, "They treat Indians just like Negroes there—it is a grave injustice." Curiosity about American race relations was of the same quality, in essence: "How does an Indian fare in America? Like a white [as he deserves] or like a Negro?" No one I knew was disturbed about or interested in racial or national discrimination in principle. This attitude reflects the pervasiveness of the theme of hierarchy. People assume there is everywhere a hierarchy in social relations based on inherited status, with attendant discrimination, and they want to be sure that they are at or near the top.

CHANGES IN CASTE

Judging by testimony of informants and by the few available accounts of Pahari castes, caste organization today is not greatly different from what it was 50 or 150 years ago. It seems probable that there has been a tendency to shift from a more consistently dual division of the society into low- and high-caste groups to one in which, while this division has remained paramount, status differences within the two groups have become increasingly pronounced. On the other hand, this may reflect a high-caste conception of the earlier situation (a conception to which the high castes still adhere) as compared to a more realistic appraisal of the present situation. On the high-caste side of the barrier, it seems likely that in earlier days (before increasing outside contact and "Sanskritization") Rajput-Brahmin distinctness was less emphasized. Intermarriage between the groups was reportedly more frequent, and very likely other ritual barriers were much reduced.

Doms were evidently somewhat less differentiated among themselves than at present. Bajgis claim that at one time they and the Mistris were one endogamous group. Under the Raja of Garhwal and more recently in nearby Tehri Garhwal, Doms of all subgroups were legally prohibited from owning land or dwellings outright. They could not own or use eating utensils of a particular alloy. They were prohibited from wearing gold jewelry. Today one still finds an occasional old Dom woman whose marital nose ring is a silver replica of the gold one (now worn by all castes) which was formerly restricted to the high castes. In many areas Doms were prohibited from living within the village. Thus, they were treated as a homogeneous group by the high castes, and the scanty evidence available suggests that they may have considered themselves more nearly as a single group.

Doms claim to have been in former days the recipients of more paternalistic concern by the high castes than at present. They were given land, houses, grain, and gratuities by the high-caste people for whom they worked. The high castes interceded on their behalf and protected their interests from outsiders when necessary. In return the high castes demanded respect and obedience. Physical punishment and economic sanctions were used by high castes to maintain their status.

Now high-caste people complain that the low castes are growing disrespectful and independent. According to high-caste people, the low castes no longer want to live by their traditional occupations. Low-caste people complain that the high castes no longer give them gratuities or even their proper pay, that high castes will not come to their aid when they need help. Each blames the other for having brought about the changes.

Among low castes there has been increased rivalry. Apparently the situation was relatively stable shortly before Independence—or at least it seems to informants to have been so in retrospect. Then the Bajgis, who had rankled under the growing superiority complex of the Mistris, began to press for equality, encouraged by rumors of the Congress political party's platform and their economic superiority and traditional claims of former equality. This has irritated the Mistris, whose status position is shaky at best. Now each group claims superiority, although Bajgis often display deference behavior and are evidently ready to settle for equality. A recent council case resulted when a Bajgi's sarcastic greeting of "Samani Thakur" to a blacksmith was accepted and acknowledged by the blacksmith as though it had been respectfully offered. The Bajgi lodged a complaint at the urging of high-caste villagers. In typical council fashion the Bajgi was fined for thus greeting a low-caste man; the blacksmith was fined an equal amount for accepting the greeting. The council members, all high-caste men who had pressed for the suit in the first place, enjoyed a liquor party from the proceeds—a result which low-caste people not involved in the case claimed was predictable and planned in advance.

In general the trend in behavior associated with caste status is now toward adoption of orthodox Hindu behavior in some contexts. As has been noted in previous chapters, the trend is especially evident in life-cycle and annual ceremonies. In other spheres of life the trend is limited largely to concealing unorthodox practices from potentially critical outsiders, while in some matters there is little or no self-consciousness about such practices. Thus sacrifice of buffaloes, consumption of buffalo meat, and eating of carcasses of recently dead wild animals found in the jungle are carefully guarded secrets. That goats are killed purely for their meat is also denied. Sexual freedom within the caste and sharing of wives among brothers are concealed. Cross-caste and polygynous marriages are not readily admitted. Liquor and meat consumption are admitted with little concern, but excuses are occasionally offered. Widow remarriage and lack of seclusion of women cause no embarrassment at all. There is surprisingly little caste difference in attitudes and behavior on these matters, although low castes cannot afford to carry out Sanskritic rituals to the extent that high castes can. They are somewhat less inhibited about their non-Sanskritic behavior than are the high castes, who have a greater prestige stake and who are also in somewhat closer contact with educated Brahmins and other advocates of Sanskritization. When high-caste Paharis are accused of behavior proscribed in plains Hinduism, especially that involving ritual purity, they often deny the behavior themselves and attribute it to low-caste Paharis.

7 INTERCASTE RELATIONS

Intercaste relations, as practiced and enforced in Sirkanda, differ significantly from ideal norms. Analysis of intercaste behavior as it compares to the normative model will contribute to an understanding of the dynamics of stability and change in the caste system. The previous chapter dealt primarily with caste organization, and with attitudes and behavior which are publicly recognized. The discussion will turn now to the nature of caste and the conduct of intercaste relations as revealed by observation of behavior to which caste is relevant, both behavior which is "relatively easy for the individual to manipulate at will," and that "in regard to which he seems to have little concern or control" (Goffman, 1959, p. 7; cf. Berreman, 1962c). As a result, the functioning of the system will be made more comprehensible.

RELATIONS AMONG HIGH CASTES

As has been noted, intermarriage can and does occur between Rajputs and Brahmins in and around Sirkanda. Although such marriages are disapproved and are never arranged as initial marriages, relatively little indignation is aroused by them once they have occurred. Brahmins engage in considerable informal social interaction with Rajputs, as is inevitable in a village where Brahmins are in such a small minority. This is also the case, however, in nearby villages where the two castes are more evenly distributed. They can be seen sharing freely even the wooden pipestem, although this is verbally denied. Brahmins and Rajputs do not usually distinguish rank by deferential behavior, seating arrangements, greetings, or the like, although an honored Brahmin from outside may receive such deference from Rajputs.

Extramarital sex relations between Brahmins and Rajputs are treated in no appreciably different light than those within each of these castes. The most celebrated beauty of the Sirkanda area was a Brahmin girl of a neighboring village who was sexually available to Rajputs and Brahmins alike. What little critical gossip circulated about her was concerned with the frequency and openness of her contacts, not their intercaste character. In fact, her reputation and the identity of several of her lovers (in Sirkanda all were Rajputs) were revealed to me some time before I learned that she was a Brahmin. Her family voiced no objection, and even her husband kept quiet. The analysis given by villagers was, "He can't say anything—if he did she might leave him and then he would have nothing. It is better to share something good than to lose it altogether."

Relations between Rajputs and Brahmins are not always amicable, and the power distribution between the two groups often comes to light when conflict arises. In Sirkanda Rajput-Brahmin relations have been somewhat strained because, while the Brahmins are said to have been the founders of the village and are one of the more prosperous families, they are far outnumbered not only as a caste but as a sib and lineage, so that they are outnumbered in interfamily and inter-sib disputes as well as in intercaste ones. A dispute over ownership of a valuable tree on the border between Brahmin property and a Rajput family's property created a tense situation in which the Rajput family head threatened the Brahmin with physical punishment if he carried out his stated intent to cut the tree. It was well known by all that the Rajput could make good his threat with the help of sib-fellows if necessary. Cooler heads prevailed when the Brahmin braved the Rajput's threat and felled the tree. Had there not been Rajputs who valued peace over power, the Brahmin would probably not have dared risk such action.

A further irritant in relations between the high castes is that the Rajputs depend upon outside Brahmins for most of their ritual needs but expect the local Brahmin to be available in emergencies, while at the same time they disparage his capabilities in religious matters. The outside Brahmin is respected partly because he restricts his practice to high castes and partly because he devotes full time to his religious duties. The local Brahmin serves the low castes also and spends much of his time on agriculture because he does not get enough high-caste clients to make a living by his traditional occupation alone. It is a circular situation and causes resentment on both sides. Moreover, as a result of daily contact and competition, it is evident to villagers that the local Brahmin is a very ordinary person while the alien Brahmin has an aura of purity, wisdom, and infallibility about him which is perhaps due more to the lack of intimate contact with these Rajputs than to any inherent priestly superiority. The effect of distance is confirmed by the Sirkanda Brahmin, who receives more respect in alien villages than in his own. Any religious practitioner in these hills would confirm the adage that familiarity breeds contempt. Upreti (1894, p. 378) quotes a Pahari proverb to this effect. The relative position of the alien Brahmin is suggested not only by his practice in Sirkanda but by his reception there. He invariably stays at the homes of Rajputs, who compete for the honor, rather than at that of his Sirkanda caste-fellows, and he himself speaks disparagingly of the local Brahmin's abilities and merits.

As a result, the Brahmin family of Sirkanda is somewhat isolated socially from Rajputs, not because of ritual barriers, but because of a combination of circumstances among which ritual differences are minor. However, Tula, the purohit or traditional Brahmin for Sirkanda, participates intimately with Rajputs in every type of interaction including drinking and meat-eating parties. He is also known as a great ladies' man. Important in this context is the fact that Tula retains his position by tradition—he will not lose his clientele because of his behavior. Moreover, in his position he is neither required nor expected to have special knowledge or special virtue. The Sirkanda Brahmin, on the other hand, has a voluntary clientele and risks losing clients or failing to get more if he does not retain what esteem he has in their eyes. Since he is responsible for ceremonies, he is expected to know more than other people and perhaps be more pure than they—expectations which are not verified in daily contact with him in the village. Also, the charity given the village Brahmin can as meritoriously be given to any other Brahmin, whereas Tula receives traditional charity which must go to him or his family regardless of circumstances. As a Bajgi said of the local Brahmin, "He works for Rajputs just like we do; he can't afford to displease them."

Therefore the local Brahmin is sensitive to public opinion. He participated little in Rajput drinking parties. He was extremely reluctant to discuss the village or his work with me if there was a chance others might find out, for fear that villagers would accuse him of divulging secrets and would bring pressure to bear upon him. Similar charges were frequently made against other villagers and were usually ignored or dismissed, but the Brahmin was especially sensitive to them. He was ever aware of his minority status, his vulnerability, and their implications for his place in the village which was, after all, his home.

RELATIONS AMONG LOW CASTES

Among low castes there is also considerable deviation from stated norms. Although blacksmiths and carpenters form an endogamous group, it is not uncommon for one to offer the other only the bowl of his pipe, not the stem, just as though there were a great difference in status between the two. Weavers and barbers keep themselves ritually separated from Mistris in some contexts. There is evidently a reciprocal feeling of superiority among all these groups. On the other hand, marriage is acceptable among them and inter-sex contact is very free. Moreover, unfriendly rivalry among them appears to be at a minimum, partly because not all are represented in the village and so they do not have close contact with one another.

In contrast, Bajgis are said by all the above-listed low-caste groups to be inferior in ritual status. This is made explicit in a number of disabilities imposed on Bajgis. The pipestem is never shared with them. Restrictions on eating and drinking are observed about as carefully as those across the high-low caste boundary. Intermarriage is denied, and no cases were reported. Bajgis often yield the seat of honor to blacksmiths in the presence of outsiders. Bajgis occasionally strike back by proclaiming their own superiority and imposing the same restrictions upon other low castes which those castes inflict on Bajgis. The attitude of the Bajgis is, "If they can do it to us, we can do it to them too." The Bajgis' reaction toward the other groups is often one of resentment that people of approximately their own status should turn against them and affect superiority. In the presence of outsiders, or even of some high-status villagers, blacksmiths assume an air of superiority which is not characteristic of their normal relationship with Bajgis and which is therefore irritating to the latter. Relations between the two groups are not helped by the fact that blacksmiths are less prosperous than Bajgis and yet claim ritual and social superiority. The discrepancy constantly rankles both parties. Evidently the distance between them is neither too great nor too little to discourage rivalry.

Bajgis consistently claim equality even when not claiming superiority. In reality there is considerable freedom of interaction between these groups and also considerable rivalry. Sex relations are frequent, with Bajgi women being more openly pursued by men of the higher status group than blacksmith women are pursued by Bajgi men. Friendship is common across this line, and there is a much greater air of camaraderie in the relations between men of these groups than across the high-low caste boundary. Deference behavior is not practiced between these groups, although both claim to expect it of the other. Cigarettes are shared freely, quite in contrast to blacksmiths' private assurances that this is not done. Despite such evidence of relatively close relations, Bajgis recognize that their claims to equality are unlikely to be recognized and they get small comfort from knowledge that the government of India supports their rights.

Contacts between Mistris and Bajgis, on the one hand, and shoemakers, on the other, are few. The former groups are anxious to disavow any equivalence between themselves and the lowly shoemakers. Geographical and cultural distance prevent much contact, but social and ritual considerations would probably be sufficient in themselves to accomplish the same thing. Shoemakers are the true Doms or Harijans from the point of view of Bajgis, though high castes recognize relatively little status difference between them. With regard to sex contact and social interaction, the relationship between the shoemakers and the Bajgis is comparable to that between Rajputs and Doms.

Shoemakers themselves adjust to their status as aliens who are lowest of the low by keeping away from other people to a considerable extent. They live by themselves, and thereby avoid many of the discriminatory acts directed toward their caste. They retain the cultural distinctiveness derived from their alien origin in the Kangra Valley area far to the west. They cling to their assertions of superiority to sweepers of the plains and to non-Hindus.

HIGH–LOW CASTE RELATIONS

Relationships between high and low castes do not always conform to the ideal patterns of paternalistic control and maintenance of ritual distance by the high castes. The most conspicuous deviations are the examples of intercaste marriage and elopement discussed in chapter 5. Although instances of this type which cross the high-low caste boundary are widely disapproved and result in dissolution of the relationship or ostracism of the high-caste member (who is usually the man) by his caste-fellows, the fact that they occur is significant. Much more common than marriage or elopement are instances of informal liaisons and sex relations between high- and low-caste individuals. Most often high-caste men take advantage of the vulnerability and traditional receptivity of low-caste women. Such situations attract little or no attention and, in fact, are routine. They become the subject of gossip only if they are flagrantly pursued, if a particular union becomes well established, or if a man is openly accused by his wife of indulging too freely in such escapades. Low-caste people overtly accept the situation with a shrug and perhaps a bitter comment: "What can we do about it? We are at their mercy." They harbor strong resentment, however, and express it privately.

Relations between low-caste men and high-caste women are strongly condemned and severely punished if detected by high-caste people. A low-caste informant who had an apparently well-earned reputation as a ladies' man in his own and other low castes commented, "There is plenty of opportunity for sex relations in all castes, but I would not risk an affair with a high-caste woman. I fear for my head." It was universally agreed that a man caught in such a relationship would be beaten, probably to death, or chased out of the village. Low-caste informants asserted that such affairs were occasionally pursued success-fully but that the man involved had to be very sure of the coöperation of the woman because she could easily bring about his downfall by complaining to others, and if the relationship were discovered she might put on a show of indignation and shift the blame to her lover. The man takes most of the risk. A low-caste informant said:

> One of us would approach a Rajput or Brahmin woman only if we were sure she had her eye upon us. It is, after all, the woman who takes the initiative in sexual matters by making her wishes known through looks and signals. Contact would have to be made secretly in a secluded spot unknown to others. If the woman were willing, the relationship might be carried out and continued successfully. If the woman were unwilling and she were a gracious person who wished to avoid trouble, her reaction to such an ap-proach would be to reply, "Brother, you have asked me once and I excuse you. I respect you as my brother, but never ask me again. I am your sister." This would be the end of the matter and no one would ever know. However, if the low-caste man were foolish enough to persist or if the woman were touchy, she might at once go to the men of her family and complain and then the low-caste man would be in grave trouble. For this reason we avoid such dangers.

That such relationships do occur is widely known, although they are concealed by high castes. Their results are less drastic than verbal testimony would lead one to believe, as evidenced by the shoemaker-Brahmin elopement described in chapter 5. A recent case in Sirkanda had been that of a Bajgi man and a Rajput woman, the first of two wives of a prominent Rajput householder. The lovers had evidently been carrying on a secret affair for some time when they were accidentally surprised in the jungle by the village Brahmin. The Brahmin was indifferent or unable to identify the man, who beat a hasty retreat, and he told no one. The Rajput woman was, however, afraid that the Brahmin would spread the word through the village. She revealed her fear in confidence to a trusted friend. Later the two women had a falling out, and the erstwhile friend exposed the illicit relationship to others. The Brahmin, who up to this point had kept his knowledge to himself, corroborated the story. The cuckolded husband did nothing to punish the low-caste man until another Rajput man had occasion to beat the offender for a different reason. At that time the aggrieved husband loudly encouraged the beating and shouted, "Beat him to death!" The end result was that the beaten man and his father went to court and on the basis of testimony by witnesses to the beating, including a Rajput of a rival faction, received a judgment in their favor by which the two Rajput men each had to pay a fine. The husband held his tongue throughout. To admit publicly to having been cuckolded by a Bajgi was apparently harder than to ignore it publicly. His wife continued to be his first wife, and her lover was sufficiently frightened to break off the relationship. This was certainly not the only affair of its kind, but it was the most recent one to have come to public notice.

In intercaste sex relations in Sirkanda, as in Negro-white sex relations in a town of the southern United States reported by Dollard, "It would seem . . . that the taboo falls heaviest on social acknowledgement of such relations rather than on the fact of their occurrence" (Dollard, 1957, p. 151).

Persistent resentment is harbored by low-caste people toward high-caste people in Sirkanda, especially by blacksmiths, the most deprived group in the village. Most of the Bajgis and the barber make an adequate income, have some land and animals of their own to supplement their income, and therefore have less cause for complaint. They share the blacksmiths' resentment of the indignity of their position and the injustice of their treatment, but economic well-being softens their feelings. Only the blacksmiths feel acutely underpaid and underprivileged. They have been blocked by Rajputs in their recent efforts to acquire land in the village. When a strike was described to a blacksmith he responded by saying,

It would never work here. The Rajputs would just beat up the ones who refused to work and throw them out of the village. Then they would find someone else to take their place—at twice the pay if necessary. We are small in numbers and therefore weak. The Rajputs hold the key to the low castes and can manipulate us as they wish, just as you manipulate the radio dial.

Rajputs don't want us to have land because they want us to have to come begging for our grain payment. When we ask for land, they laugh at us. The Bajgis and barber don't join with us in our efforts to get land because they make a good income from their work, and anyway they already have some land. We, on the other hand, have neither land nor a good income from our work. We are alone in our desire to get land, and it seems hopeless.

High- and low-caste men alike affirmed the obedience accorded high-caste men by low-caste men. However, subtle countermeasures were admitted by low-castes and complained of by high-castes. Thus, in performing his craft a blacksmith claimed to do work quickly and well for those who paid him promptly and justly and who treated him civilly (as many, in fact, did) and to do it poorly and slowly for delinquent or arrogant clients. An incident of this nature occurred in the writer's presence. While it conformed to no reported pattern of intercaste behavior, it aroused no comment among witnesses, so it was apparently not out of the range of acceptable behavior. A young Rajput man of a large household known by village artisans as a bad credit risk and not a particularly desirable client, came to the blacksmith with an axe he wanted sharpened. The blacksmith, who was listening to the anthropologist's radio, took the axe, inspected it with evident distaste, and announced, "This axe is worth eight annas. [10 cents]. My file is worth 15 rupees [three dollars]. It would spoil my valuable file to sharpen this worthless axe. Go find a flat rock and sharpen it yourself." Further feeble entreaties brought nothing but refusal from the blacksmith, and the Rajput left, presumably in search of a flat rock.

Needless to say, the blacksmith did not frequently practice this pattern of behavior, as he could not have done it with impunity in other circumstances. He would not have tried it, for instance, with an older or more prestigeful man. However, in an occasional well-chosen situation he could get by with it, and it obviously gave him considerable satisfaction. Members of all low castes relished tales of moral victories by low-castes over high-caste people.

High-caste men do not observe rules of pollution carefully when they go to the larger towns. There they eat in public places with people whose caste they do not know, and even with low-caste people of their own village. They patronize the same prostitutes as are patronized by Doms (and by Brahmins from the plains). They would even eat at the homes of the writer and his Muslim assistant, although they would not eat in their house in the village. A 15-year-old Rajput boy expressed the attitude of most men when he politely refused to share the writer's dinner in the village with the comment, "I would gladly eat if we were elsewhere, but we are in my own village. Here everyone knows my caste and I must be careful what I do. In town no one knows me nor I them, and I do as I please without fear of consequences."

The influence of the caste-equality, anti-discrimination stand of the dominant Congress party in India has been felt even in Sirkanda. The president of the village council occasionally has to attend a meeting or workshop for council presidents in the valley. There he not only hears the official policy of the party to which he nominally belongs but has to practice it by eating with fellow officials and civil servants of all castes. The food is prepared and served by people of unknown (and highly suspect) caste status. He makes no effort to conceal this when he returns to the village, but it does not alter the fact that in the village he is as caste-conscious and discriminatory as anyone else.

Anti-discrimination talk led to the nearest thing to a test case of caste discrimination that has ever occurred in the village—in itself an indication of new or changing attitudes. The blacksmith who holds the village council seat reserved for untouchables planned to brew tea at his home and serve it at a village council meeting which was to be attended by the teacher, village level worker, accountant, tax collector, forestry officer, economic coöperative supervisor, and the anthropologist in addition to the local council members. The blacksmith's intent was to press charges of caste discrimination if anyone refused the tea, and he counted on the outsiders to form an august body of impartial witnesses. He made his intent known only to the teacher, village level worker, and anthropologist. However, when the time came, no tea appeared. The advocate of the test case lamely claimed to have forgotten, but in reality he had apparently not felt like risking the probable consequences of such a defiant act in his vulnerable position.

In discussing caste relations in the village a young Rajput man complained:

I would like to spend more time at your house talking with you and listening to your radio. I would share tea and food with you. I could learn many things and have a good time. But too many low-caste people come there. I do not care so much about that for myself, but people here are very strict. On the plains caste rules are broken frequently and everything is breaking down, but not here. We cannot share food, drink, utensils, or cigarettes with Doms. I must live my life in this village. If I associate with those low people my people will be angry with me. I could be your friend and associate with Doms at your house, but I would lose my friends in the village. There would be no comfort in the friendship of a few Doms when you are gone.

People of all castes denied that there were individual differences in the strictness of caste observance among high-caste individuals. Everyone maintained that in the village all were equally rigid. Observation proved this to be not entirely the case. While most high-caste men shared cigarettes only in their group, a few shared them with low-caste men as well. Some interacted socially with low-caste men regularly; others did so rarely or not at all. Age and position within the family were evidently important factors in this context. Old men and young men were noticeably less concerned with caste rules governing social interaction than were middle-aged men. Middle-aged men (roughly 35 to 55 years of age) were usually also the effective family heads. They were the leaders of their castes. They felt responsible for maintaining the status of their families and their castes. They were the most suspicious of outsiders, the most proud, the most arrogant in their relationship to low castes, the most authoritarian in all their relationships.

In a village of the size and caste composition of Sirkanda, it is almost inevitable that a good deal of informal social interaction will take place across caste lines, including the high-low caste boundary. There are very few low-caste people in a predominantly Rajput village, and the village is isolated from other villages. If low-caste people are to have social life at all, it must be to a large extent with Rajputs. In Sirkanda this is especially true because the two blacksmith households are not on good terms with one another, nor are the three main Bajgi households, because of intrafamilial strife. Moreover, the blacksmiths and Bajgis are on somewhat strained terms, largely because of the claims to higher status held by the blacksmiths and the reality of greater prosperity of the Bajgis. Bajgis have a number of relatives within easy walking distance of the village, and much of their social life is with these caste-fellows. In the village, however, they, like the blacksmiths who have few relatives, must find friends among the Rajputs. The amount of friendly interaction between high and low castes is therefore considerable—evidently more than would be found on the plains and certainly more than one might expect from the expressed attitudes of these groups toward one another and the formal restrictions placed upon interaction between them. That such interaction is allowed by the high castes does not mean that caste status is ambiguous but rather that it is so secure that it is not jeopardized by interaction of this kind.

The place of work of each artisan is a gathering place for men of all castes to sit and talk. The tailor's veranda is rarely without one or more high-caste people watching the craftsman at his work, talking to him and his relatives and to other visitors. The same is true of the blacksmith's workshop, the basketmaker's porch, the sites of house construction, and the carpenters' work areas. The village shops and school serve also as meeting places for informal social interaction across caste boundaries. High-caste houses are the locus of high-caste interaction, but not uncommonly a low-caste person may participate, sitting on the steps or doorsill or standing outside.

Intercaste groups form in various circumstances. Intercaste work groups are common, including both coöperative labor and independent labor performed in groups (as tending goats and gathering wood or fodder). In times of trouble or need, caste boundaries may be subordinated. A Rajput family of Sirkanda owes its prosperity to loans granted it a generation ago by a sympathetic Brahmin when the family was not producing enough to survive. A nearby Brahmin family took in a homeless Rajput widow and her invalid son when they had nowhere to turn. Rajputs did not hesitate to borrow money from a blacksmith two generations ago. When the Brahmins were in need of a place to stay during part of the time their house was being rebuilt in 1958, they stayed with a blacksmith family although they ate separately. Those who have to travel away from the village seek traveling companions, and no caste is excluded from such a group. Intercaste groups often go to town to trade, to do business at government offices, or even to seek entertainment together. In the village and outside, drinking and gambling groups are often intercaste in composition. The famous illicit woman-selling gang of Bhatbair was made up of a Brahmin, a Rajput, and a Bajgi who worked as a team, sharing the risks and profits with little caste distinction.

Perhaps the most frequent occasion for intimate social interaction across caste lines in the village is at drinking parties. There caste barriers are largely ignored. Low-caste people may be invited to a high-caste house where a party is to be held, and there they are allowed to participate fully in it. Of course such parties are held on verandas of houses, not in cooking areas, and boiled food is not served, so it is not potentially a very polluting situation. Although low castes may contribute liquor, they do not furnish the site for such parties. In Sirkanda one blacksmith and one Bajgi are inveterate participants in high-caste drinking parties.

In general, activities which are illegal, overtly disapproved, or non-Sanskritic are much more likely to be intercaste in nature than are

those which are entirely legal, approved, and orthodox. Thus intercaste drinking, meat-eating, dancing, and trips to town are indulged
in often with little regard for caste differences. Even illicit sex activity
may be pursued by intercaste groups who together go to a house of
prostitution or approach low-caste girls outside the village. A Rajput
and blacksmith both told a story on themselves which occurred at
the Pahari fair. The blacksmith was paying for Ferris wheel rides
and sweets for two Muslim girls of easy virtue when the Rajput came
and joined in. Both were confident of their reward until the girls
got off the Ferris wheel and were spirited away by two husky strangers,
to the dismay of the girls' erstwhile benefactors.

Among the most colorful personalities in Sirkanda is a blacksmith
man. His company is sought and enjoyed by all. No party or discussion
is complete without him. His wit and good judgment combine to make
him popular despite his caste status. He is the greatest talker and gossip
in the village. He spreads news and helps formulate opinion. He is
the repository of knowledge not possessed by others; he remembers
things others forget. More than once Rajputs turned to him when
questioned for details of their own genealogies or family histories.
Although in many contexts he plays the role of the joker, his opinion
on serious matters is highly valued but rarely, to his disgust, acknowledged. When unusual circumstances arise, he is often sent forth to
appraise the situation or express village sentiments. Numerous examples could be cited. When a horse trader came to Sirkanda, the
blacksmith was sent to look over the horses and sound out their owner
before high-caste potential customers made an appearance. He passed
judgment on the trader's honesty, his willingness to bargain, and the
value of his horses. As he himself noted, he received no thanks for his
efforts, although several villagers relied heavily on his advice in subsequent purchases.

When the Brahmin family wanted to move a large rock which
they thought endangered their house but which was on village property, Rajputs objected. The blacksmith looked it over, said "This rock
is a hazard to the Brahmin's house and should be moved," and began
to decide the best method of moving it. Soon the Rajputs were helping.
This blacksmith is the usual choice for making contact with and
appraising strangers—a role which a low-caste man can perform well
without committing the village. He is the informal channel for communication with outsiders and sometimes with rival factions. When
the schoolteacher was new, the blacksmith communicated to him village
attitudes on schooling and the role of the teacher. When the anthropologist considered moving into a house in the most crowded section
of the village, the blacksmith was sent to voice the objections of some

influential villagers (stating them as his own), who were thus able to have their opinions voiced while denying any responsibility and, in fact, condemning the blacksmith for inhospitality.

This is not to assert that the blacksmith is the most important man in the village or even that his opinion was decisive in all the above cases. It does, however, point out that one low-caste man, at least, is important far beyond the admission or realization of his caste superiors and far beyond their ideal of the complaisant, subservient, know-nothing Dom. He has achieved importance largely as a result of personal characteristics which override his caste status. It is significant that his importance is not admitted or even realized by most villagers, and his caste status is never forgotten or ignored.

He is apparently an atypical Dom, but he is not beyond the range of permissible behavior in Doms. Some individuals in each of the other Dom castes were to a lesser extent influential in the village.

High-caste jealousy of this blacksmith reveals implicit recognition of his role. He was often accused of not knowing his place, of having big ideas, or of being a troublemaker. His wit was sometimes disparaged by those who could not equal it. His love of liquor, women, music, laughter, and leisure were frequently criticized. That he made fun of himself on these very grounds only served to exasperate his detractors. As he said,

> People here are very jealous. I have to be careful lest I suffer their wrath. Even if I wanted and could afford some comforts and a better house or better clothes I could not have them because Rajputs would accuse me of putting on airs. I must always remain humble to them if I am to survive in this village.

This man frequently mentioned wealthy caste-fellows of his, resident in other villages, who surpass local Rajputs in wealth and sophistication but are still untouchable in their eyes. This he considered to be an example of unreasoning pride on the part of Rajputs. He asserted that they would not tolerate action on the part of low-caste people which they consider inconsistent with caste status.

> I could put these Rajputs to shame by getting a table and serving you with food and drink at my house. They would be envious and angry and after you are gone they would make it hard on me. Therefore I must show that I know my station and not be unduly close to you in public social relationships. They will be jealous when you give me your radio. For that reason I will have to tell them that I bought it from you. They are jealous to see me associating with big people.

On another occasion he remarked upon his relationship with Rajputs:

No matter how friendly a Rajput may be at one time, he will turn against a low-caste person the next time. All are proud and jealous of their caste position. None are true friends to us. They always resent my presence in social situations. They will eat with me in Dehra Dun but never in the village. They will drink liquor with me and often invite me to sit on their veranda to do so. If they are having something dry like parched gram [chick peas], I can eat it with them. If they have something cooked, I am given a separate plate. They are very strict on such matters. I am with them a great deal, but I cannot say they are my true friends. I am always a Dom and they are big people. Here big people mingle with other big people as friends. I call that man truly big who mingles with high and low alike. Such are not to be found in this village.

VESTED INTERESTS IN CASTE

The functioning of the caste system in an Indian village can be assessed on several different levels. From the point of view of the community or of the society as a system, the Indian caste system is remarkably efficient. Ideally, it assures a stable division of labor with a constant supply of specialists in all occupations. In return it provides the individual with an assured occupation, an assured income, and a body of people who share his interests. It provides a religious and philosophical rationale for differences in status and standard of living which minimizes discontent and subversion. It is preordained and static, so that status change is, ideally, impossible. It reduces ambiguity by the recognition of rules and symbols segregating social groups. It minimizes intergroup frictions. It provides stable group identification and affiliation for individuals at all status levels and minimizes the chances of disparity between reference group and membership group and the potentially disintegrative results of such disparity.

Not only does everyone have some place within the Hindu system, but it is significant that every group, from the Brahmin to the Chamar caste, has been somehow integrated into the social and ceremonial round of the community and has been given some opportunity to feel indispensable and proud. (Opler and R. Singh, 1948, p. 496)

That the system has not been completely successful; that change, discontent, and subversion occur in spite of the system, does not belie its relative efficiency as a system. Breakdowns in discipline, changes in caste status, and the like, are either suppressed or rationalized. Rationalizations become part of the system and are not remembered as deviations from it. What these facts do reveal is that there is more to caste than its ideal structure. Human beings are involved, and the effects of the system on the individuals who live in it must be understood if its functioning in reality is to be understood. Despite pious statements to the contrary in India and elsewhere, no group of people has been reported which relishes a life of deprivation and subjection to other groups. That people submit to depressed status does not mean that they feel it is justified nor that they would not like to see it changed, nor, in fact, that they would not do everything in their power to change it if given the opportunity. The rationalizations for caste status which are consistent and convincing to those who benefit from them or are unaffected by them seem much less so to those whose deprivation they are expected to justify or explain. Adherence to a religion or a religious principle may not significantly affect attitudes and behavior to which logic would seem to tie it. It will be well, therefore, to look briefly at caste as it affects people. As John Dollard has said in studying caste and class structure in a town of the southern United States,

We should like to know something not only about the class structure but also about the differential advantages and disadvantages of membership in any particular caste or class; and, in particular, we wish to state these advantages and disadvantages from the standpoint of the types of direct, personal, ultimately organic, gratification derived. (Dollard, 1957, pp. 97 f.)

Following Dollard, I will state the advantages which the caste system in Sirkanda provides for its high-caste participants. Inherent in most of these advantages are disadvantages which automatically fall to the low castes. An effort will be made to point out as well those ways in which low castes may benefit from the caste system. "In using the concept of 'gains' we are not leaving the 'social' plane of perception; we will merely . . . look for a moment at the individuals rather than at the society" (Dollard, 1957, p. 98). In listing gains the three broad categories suggested by Dollard will be used: the economic, sexual, and prestige gains. In addition, a fourth category, here called "ultimate rewards," will be mentioned. Use of Dollard's categorization for this portion of the Sirkanda data is based not upon the pressing of data into alien molds but upon my belief in real similarities in the situations analyzed—a position elaborated in another publication (Berreman, 1960a).

The discussion need not be lengthy because most of the evidence has been presented in this and other chapters. An effort will be made not only to assert that a particular gain is achieved but to show that gain by particular individuals is a result of the caste hierarchy. Although the discussion is based primarily upon Sirkanda data, the same sort of analysis, leading to essentially the same conclusions, could no doubt be made in other Indian villages.

It seems likely that, in villages where caste dominance is less clear-cut than in Sirkanda, our present approach would produce less consistent evidence. An economically deprived high-caste or a wealthy low-caste person might well upset the statements about economic gain, but they would have done so in spite of caste affiliation. Caste affiliation would doubtless still be a force in the expected direction even if it were overcome by other factors. Such a case, looked at from this point of view, would be an interesting study. The obvious conclusion would probably be that caste operates to the best advantage of high castes when their rank is correlated positively with decisive dominance.

Obtaining reliable data on intercaste relations and attitudes is a difficult task. It is especially difficult in India, where any evidently educated or urbanized person is automatically classed by low-caste villagers as a member of the elite regardless of his professed aims and affiliations, and by the high-caste villagers as a potential threat to the *status quo*. The low-caste informant is likely to be wary of saying or doing anything which might conceivably be held against him at a later date. Many high-caste people, on the other hand, are aware of official doctrines of equalitarianism and may respond verbally in ways quite different from those which represent their true feelings on the subject (cf. Berreman, 1962c).

In Sirkanda these were problems in obtaining data, but information was obtained from enough different people and observations were made in so many different situations, that a body of reliable and apparently valid information was obtained. Where inconsistencies occurred, they were often closely linked to situational factors. Responses of both low- and high-caste people varied predictably in the presence of the opposite status group, while responses of some individuals varied predictably in the presence of their caste-fellows. Since these were predictable variations, they apparently did not contaminate the data.

In this discussion the only status distinction to be considered will be that between high and low, or clean and untouchable, castes. This is a valid distinction in the Pahari area, as preceding discussion has shown, in terms of both ritual and secular status attributes. Subsidiary caste distinctions will not be dealt with because in Sirkanda they are minor by comparison and would only serve to provide lesser examples of the points made more clearly in an examination of the major status distinction.

The Economic Gain

It has been pointed out that land is wealth in Sirkanda. The high castes, by restricting land ownership to themselves before British dominion, ensured their own economic dominance. The paramount importance of land is recognized by Sirkanda villagers, as has been illustrated by examples and quotations in previous chapters. It is further illustrated by the history of the struggle which the villagers have waged and are still waging for land. The high-caste villagers considered it a victory when, under the British, the bhaichara land ownership pattern was established, eliminating an intermediary land-lord and giving the cultivators direct ownership of their lands. The low castes considered it an even greater victory when lands formerly allotted to them only for use (that is, they did not own these lands) were assigned by law to their castes and later to them as individuals. Until that time high castes had control over low castes in that lands and dwellings alike were in the names of high-caste owners. An un-ruly, disobedient, or disrespectful artisan was readily dispossessed of house and livelihood. Post-Independence restriction on further de-velopment of uncultivated lands by villagers has brought bitter resent-ment of the government by all castes.

Efforts by low castes to acquire more land have been fought at every turn by the high castes, not because they stand to lose land as a result (they do not), but because they stand to lose a measure of economic dominance. Thus, the village blacksmiths have needed only the support of the village council president or the accountant to put in a request to open up heretofore uncultivated village lands. The council and its president have stated, "If you want land, you will have to leave this village to get it." They have used their influence to prevent the village accountant (a government official alien to the village) from submitting a favorable report on behalf of the black-smiths. In the closest village to Sirkanda a blacksmith had been granted a share of village lands under the British, the only low-caste person of that village who was so fortunate. A few years ago he decided to sell part of this land. Over high-caste protests he sold it to a local, landless Bajgi who was his friend. The high-caste villagers were in-furiated. They retaliated by calling the police, making out a false accusation of theft against the hapless blacksmith, and bribing the police to ensure that he would be punished. As a result he served seven months in jail. As one of his caste-fellows said, "You can't go against the wishes of high-caste people and get away with it around here." Low-caste people occasionally openly accuse Rajputs of "wanting to keep us in slavery," and not wanting to see them economically secure or self-sufficient.

To keep the low castes dependent not only assures greater income for the higher castes; it also assures a ready supply of cheap labor. For, as long as the low castes are dependent for their livelihood upon high castes, the latter can call upon them for all sorts of services, under implicit or explicit threat of economic sanctions. Low-caste members are available to carry loads, thatch houses, pound tobacco, clean up debris, plaster floors, run errands, or help in any work where another person is needed. They also brew liquor, kill animals, and perform other unpleasant, risky, or polluting tasks at high-caste bidding. As long as they are landless or own insufficient land for survival, the high castes can use them almost at will. Thus the high castes have a strong economic interest in maintaining the caste system in its traditional form, which includes economic dominance over the low castes. This is perhaps the key enabling factor in sexual and prestige gains as well.

An economic advantage of the caste system which is specific to Brahmins is their role as recipients of charity—charity which is necessary to ensure a favorable future for the soul of the giver (cf. Weber, 1958, p. 60). This is an India-wide phenomenon and the degree to which individual Brahmins exploit it varies, but it is apparently no accident that the formulators and primary agents of communication of the religio-philosophical tradition are its greatest benefactors. Stories illustrating the necessity of giving ample charity are widely repeated in Sirkanda and elsewhere. Such stories are told primarily by Brahmins and are often included in their professional services of reading the past and future fate of villagers in horoscopes. Villagers often refer to the avariciousness of Brahmins and sarcastically hint at pecuniary motives in their visits or scheduling of ceremonies.

All economic gain is not on the side of the high castes; there are compensatory gains for low castes. Specific gains which accrue to low castes include exclusive access to a number of foods and other goods. Shoemakers, for example, get the carcasses of dead animals, which provide both materials for their trade and meat for consumption. Such advantages are more pronounced on the plains, where diet differs by caste more than it does in Sirkanda. Under the traditional system the low-caste individual was assured of work and of payment for it as long as he did not offend his employer. He also expected and received a paternalistic sort of care and protection much like that accorded the

Negro who knew his place in the American "Old South." These were notable compensations for dependent status. However, they often did not satisfy the low-caste person and were in themselves aspects of the exploitative economic situation perpetuated by the upper castes. They were the kinds of compensations an authoritarian system often offers its subjects.

Srinivas notes in the Mysore village he studied that:

> While the Governments of India and Mysore want to abolish Untouchability, and the Untouchables themselves want to improve their position, the locally dominant caste stands in its way: its members want the Untouchables to supply them with cheap labor and perform degrading tasks. . . . They have the twin sanction of physical force and boycott at their disposal. (Srinivas, 1959, p. 4)

K. Singh found that, out of five frequently cited grounds for conflict leading to tension between landowners and low castes in a plains village, three were directly economic and the two others indirectly so (Singh, 1967, p. 110). Lewis makes much of the economic advantages which accrue to high-caste landlords at the expense of the low castes that serve them in Rampur (Lewis, 1958, pp. 55 ff., especially 79–84). P. M. Mahar (1958), interviewing in a plains village, found that a Rajput elder ". . . disapproves of educational advancement for untouchables not only because of sacred precedent, but also because it will lead to a depletion of the Rajputs' labor supply." She quotes the informant:

> Now the government says all should become one. We are afraid of that. Now we can't get anyone to work for us. If they are all clerks and gentlemen, who will plow our fields? Even now it is hard to get laborers. It used to be you could get a man for five rupees to work for you. Now they ask thirty or forty. (P. M. Mahar, 1958, p. 56)

This reasoning explains in part the emotional reaction by high-caste people in Sirkanda to low-caste attempts to acquire land and achieve economic security. Such attempts are a threat to their own economic dominance and ultimately to their status.

The Sexual Gain

The sexual advantages of high-caste status in Sirkanda are not inconsiderable, but they are less pronounced and are probably less important motives for maintenance of the *status quo* than is the case in many plains areas. The reason is simply that in Sirkanda there is a relatively high degree of permissiveness in matters of extramarital sex relations within and between castes. Men and women rarely lack for variety in sexual partners if that is their desire. On the plains, in contrast, there is close supervision of high-caste women.

This does not, however, alter the basic fact that in Sirkanda the low castes provide a constant source of available women for high-caste men, and the men are not reluctant to make use of this advantage. It is the one relationship in which a man can find a sex partner to whom he owes nothing and from whom he needs fear no trouble. While he may make sexual use of women of his own caste, he will be expected to supply them with trinkets, cigarettes, sweets, or other favors to show his appreciation. He also runs the risk of a fight with an irate husband or his own irate wife. A low-caste woman expects and usually gets no more than a cigarette for her favors; her husband is in no position to exact revenge; the chances of the news reaching the high-caste man's wife are less across caste boundaries than within a caste, and even if it does the wife is unlikely to be particularly upset or able to win sympathy from others if she is. A low-caste woman is not considered a serious threat to a high-caste wife. Such liaisons are expected and are usually lightly dismissed. An example of this attitude is found in the case of a prominent Rajput, whose short-lived liaison with a low-caste girl has become a family joke told by his wife, whereas his liaison with a Rajput widow caused a serious and never-again mentioned family fight. Low-caste men's resentment of free use of their women by high-caste men is suppressed but comes to the surface readily when the subject is discussed out of the hearing of high castes. Low-caste women, too, resent the advantage taken of them by high-caste men.

Relations between low-caste men and high-caste women, when they do occur, are extremely risky for both parties in view of the attitudes of high-caste men. Informants of all castes affirm the dire nature of the punishment which would befall the participants if caught. Exaggerated fear is also revealed in precautions taken by high-caste men to prevent such contacts, for example, often prohibiting their womenfolk from attending intercaste occasions where drinking and dancing occur, such as fairs, celebrations, and so on.

Some idea of the sexual gain enjoyed by high-caste men can be inferred from the fact that eleven recognized unions of some duration between high-caste men and low-caste women were reported for Sirkanda and neighboring villages. Only one recognized union between a low-caste man and a high-caste woman occurred, and it was in a more distant village than any of the others (thus, more unusual, and so reported and remembered more widely). It involved an elopement out of the area, unlike the other eleven, all of which were carried on in Bhatbair. Similarly, casual affairs and extramarital sex relationships were frequently reported between high-caste men and low-caste women, while extremely few cases of the reverse situation were reported.[1] Whether these reports reflect sexual behavior accurately or not (and it is likely that they do), they certainly reflect attitudes accurately.

There is little in the way of compensatory sexual gain for low-caste men in Sirkanda. Looking at the situation from the low-caste woman's point of view, it could be argued that she derives a gain comparable to that of the high-caste man and that the high-caste woman is deprived as is the low-caste man. Actually, the high-caste man has the advantage of choice which the low-caste woman is denied, though both have access to a greater variety of partners than have their spouses. In other areas of India greater freedom of sexual expression is allowed low-caste people within their status group than is allowed high-caste people within theirs, but there is little caste difference on this score in Sirkanda. An economic gain may accrue to low-caste people from the high-caste sexual gain. Occasionally a low-caste woman succeeds in getting money, clothing, or other goods from a high-caste lover, and in at least one instance in a village near Sirkanda the low-caste husband encouraged his wife in an affair that bordered between prostitution and concubinage.

Sexual gain derived by high castes as a result of their status position in the system is frequently implicit in accounts from other areas of India and seems, in fact, to be a universal aspect of caste in India. Majumdar (1944, pp. 175 f.) remarks that Rajput men cannot marry or have social intercourse with Dom women but can have sex relations with them or keep them as mistresses. Lewis (1958, p. 257) notes that ". . . lower-caste women are more vulnerable than the women of other castes to the sexual advances of higher-caste men." Cohn (1955, p. 68) says that "it was a commonplace a generation ago for a *Thakur* man to have sexual relations with a *Camar* woman. This still occurs . . ." Stevenson asserts:

A man may keep as a lover or a concubine a lower status woman, from whose hand he would not take either food or water, without requiring further purification than a bath after contact. A high status woman conducting a liaison with a lower status man, however, would be expelled from her status group. (Stevenson, 1954, p. 57)

A standard joke told in the plains concerns two Chamar women watching the funeral procession of an old landlord. As the body is carried past, one hand falls out from under the shroud and flops about. One

Chamar woman turns to the other and says, "You see, Thakur Singh is dead, but he still beckons to us."

In general the situation conforms to that in Southerntown as reported by Dollard. In this and the following quotations from Dollard, I have substituted the words in brackets: "high-caste" for "white," and "low-caste" for "Negro."

> . . . [High-caste] men, by virtue of their caste position, have access to two classes of women, those of the [high] and [low] castes. The same condition is somewhat true of the [low-caste] women, except that they are rather the objects of the gain than the choosers, though it is a fact that they have some degree of access to [high-caste] men as well as to the men of their own caste. [Low-caste] men and [high-caste] women, on the other hand, are limited to their own castes in sexual choices. (Dollard, 1957, p. 135)

The Prestige Gain

High-caste people gain, by virtue of their caste status alone, deference from others, constant reinforcement of a feeling of superiority, and a permanent scapegoat group in the form of the lower castes.

> The gain here is very simple. It consists in the fact that a member of the [high] caste has an automatic right to demand forms of behavior from [low-caste people] which serve to increase his own self-esteem.
>
> It must always be remembered that in the end this deference is demanded and not merely independently given. (Dollard, 1957, p. 174)

In Sirkanda relative prestige and the attendant symbols conform well to these statements. The honorific greeting accorded the high castes by low castes has been mentioned previously. It is enforced if it is not volunteered. A respectful form of address and reference is always expected from low castes by high castes. The continual inflation of high-caste ego is emphasized not only by verbal adulation but by other symbolic acts. Low castes sit lower than high castes. Normally they also remain outside high-caste houses, squatting on a step or doorsill rather than entering. On the other hand, the high-caste person can enter freely into the house of the low-caste person. Low castes step out of the way when high castes pass on the trail. They perform small services for high-caste members upon demand, including especially those that are inconvenient, risky, dirty, or defiling. They are expected to live in inferior dwellings, use inferior utensils, wear inferior clothes and ornaments, and generally play the role demanded by their inferior status. They must follow the leadership of high-caste people and refrain from pressing complaints. They must accept judgments handed down from the high castes, even in their private affairs, including the punishment or abuse that often accompanies them. They must endure quietly many kinds of impositions upon them, including sexual impositions upon their women. They must often beg payment for their labor and receive it humbly. They must carefully avoid high-caste temples and be ever on their guard not to defile the persons or possessions of high-caste people according to the traditional rules governing intercaste contacts. Powerful sanctions—economic, social, and physical—are at hand to enforce these rules and are not used reluctantly. Gould (1961a, pp. 946, 948) cites examples, from the plains village of Sherupur, of fear of "rule of the lower orders" as high-caste villagers saw their position of respect being undermined.

The whole tenor of intercaste relations is prescribed by custom. The high-caste person is paternalistic, authoritarian. The low-caste person is submissive, subservient. He must not pay undue attention to high-caste women. He should be indulgent and friendly to high-caste children. He is expected to be respectful, agreeable, mildly humorous in the presence of his superiors. He must laugh at jokes at his expense and conceal resentment if he feels it. He must know how to respond with just the right note of humor or self-deprecation when intercaste relations are discussed in a mixed-caste group. A light remark can bring an ominous response.

In Sirkanda the pride of high-caste people is proverbial. They are quick to censure the low-caste person who steps out of line. The rules are known by everyone, but a misjudgment by a low-caste person can lead to a rebuke or physical punishment. When a Rajput asked me the time, using an honorific form of address, a low-caste man made bold to look at his tattoo-watch (a common form of male adornment) and say "4:30 by my watch." The questioner shot back edgily, "Watches sometimes get broken."

In general the impression I gained, not only from my own experience but from that of the schoolteacher and other outsiders in the village, was that, while high-caste villagers feel relatively secure in their prestigeful status position in the village, they feel very insecure in the presence of outsiders, especially non-Paharis. This is doubtless related to self-consciousness about their own unorthodox Hindu practices and their resultant low status in the eyes of plains people, combined with awareness of their relatively simple or primitive living conditions, clothing, and foods. Their insecurity in this context is revealed in self-conscious jokes about their being "wild men" (undomesticated), being destined to be reborn as donkeys on the plains, being readily identifiable in town by their boorish manners and rustic appearance despite efforts to appear cosmopolitan, and the like. Another factor may be their awareness of government efforts to raise the status and living conditions of low-caste people. For these reasons, among others, the high castes show extreme reluctance to have anything to do with outsiders—to feed them, talk to them, or even offer them a seat or a smoke. After he had been in the village three months, the schoolteacher complained that no one had invited him to eat and no high-caste person had even inquired as to his origin or family status. He was himself a Pahari Rajput from a neighboring area. Stories of the suspicious and inhospitable nature of Paharis are many and graphic. To the extent that they are true, they seem to be based largely on a general insecurity in the presence of the status threat posed by strangers. Any stranger is an unknown quantity who may be of low-caste or alien religion and hence defiling. He may be an advocate of intercaste equality and interaction. Worse yet, he might try to put some such ideology into practice, thereby defiling high castes or putting ideas into the minds of low castes. On the other hand, he may be a high-caste Hindu and hence be critical or contemptuous of unorthodox claimants to high status.

Also of fundamental significance is the fact that this is an isolated and relatively closed social system where kin, caste, and community ties are extremely important. Anyone who lacks these familiar ties is outside the system and cannot be placed within it readily if at all. Such a person poses an inherent threat to the community. Therefore, the best way to handle him is to get rid of him, or, if that cannot be done quickly, to ignore him. If he remains he will gradually come to be accepted as an outsider who is resident in the village, tolerated but ignored except in the context of his legitimate function in the village. Fear of outside agents of authority also leads to rejection or avoidance of strangers.

Low-caste people are often more relaxed than are those of high caste in the presence of outsiders. Evidently they have little to fear and nothing to lose in terms of status. They are often used by high-caste people, perhaps for this reason, to deal with strangers. This aggravates intercaste tensions because low-caste people come to know outsiders (the schoolteacher, the village level worker, the anthropologist) better than do high-caste people. They learn more of the ways of outsiders, become accustomed to being with them, and even acquire habits and ideas from them. The high-caste people fear what may be passing between the local untouchables and the potentially threatening outsider, and dread that they will be "found out," ridiculed, and hence lose status. They therefore try to get rid of outsiders if possible, or keep them away from close contacts with villagers.

Middle-aged high-caste men are especially sensitive on this point. Only when they are secure in the knowledge that their status and importance are recognized and properly appreciated do they relax their pose. On the other hand, it is not a matter of consciously striving for prestige and deference. These are considered to be natural and just concomitants of caste status. When infractions of rules of inter-caste relations are brought to the notice of these men, they usually attribute them to outside influence or general deterioration from the golden age of amicable intercaste relations—a period in the indefinite past when the low castes knew their place and the high castes were able to play their paternalistic role to best advantage.

Compensatory gains of low-caste people are few in the social sphere. They strive to maintain status superiority to one or more castes which they consider lower than themselves. Their only direct gain is in relative freedom from ritual and status restrictions. In the hills, this does not result in important advantages for low castes because all castes are relatively unorthodox. In the plains the demands of ritual purity and social distance on high castes are considerably stricter, particularly in such matters as the seclusion of women, continence of widows, abstinence from liquor and meat, and so on. There low castes can ignore these prohibitions while high castes must adhere to them, at least in public. In Sirkanda the primary advantage to low-caste people is in their prerogative to largely ignore prestige considerations in their daily life and live with relative freedom from fear of loss of a respect they do not have.

Ultimate Rewards as Gains

High-caste people feel that they are justified in demanding respect and service from their caste inferiors, as the direct result of their own meritorious acts in previous lives. But the matter does not end there. According to the conventional Hindu view they are destined, by the fact that they play their high-caste role well, to reap further and even more desirable rewards in subsequent lives. In turn, low-caste people can hope to improve their lot by submitting to their fate as disadvantaged people. Weber (1958, p. 122) points out that "the neglect of one's caste duties out of high pretensions unfailingly is disadvantageous in the present or future life." In the orthodox Hindu view, high castes can increase their chances for ultimate rewards by increasing the economic and prestige advantages they seek in this life, while low castes can increase their chances for ultimate rewards by subordinating economic and prestige gains in this life to the cause of pursuing their caste duty, including the serving and honoring of high castes. Thus, immediate and ultimate rewards are consistent in the behavior they require of high-caste people but contradictory in the behavior they require of low-caste people.

In Sirkanda this view is held primarily by educated, high-caste men. Orthodox Hindu views of caste duty, as such, are not held by most villagers. However, it is believed that by living a good life and giving charity a person can enhance his caste status in the next life. The opportunities for low castes in the next life are less than those for high castes simply because the next step for them is not as high as that for high castes. Moreover, the economic advantages possessed by high castes enable them to give more charity at less personal sacrifice than can low castes, thus furthering their prospects for ultimate rewards.

MAINTENANCE OF THE SYSTEM

The caste system is maintained by caste stereotypes and by religio-philosophical beliefs relating to fate and proper behavior. Many vivid stories are told of the wonderful results of living a good life and the dire results of improper behavior. Low- and high-caste status is rationalized and justified, both on caste and individual levels, as described above. More immediately and practically, proper caste behavior is enforced on the low castes by high castes and on all people by their caste-fellows, through social and economic pressure and physical force. The actions of individuals are likely to have results which affect the entire caste. A high-caste person who pollutes himself endangers the status of others of his caste; a low-caste person who angers a high-caste person may bring retribution to his caste. Sanctions are most conspicuously applied, however, across caste lines. A recalcitrant Dom can be readily taken care of through economic pressures (such as non-payment), by physical violence or threats thereof, by expulsion from the village, or by legal action (wherein high castes can control the decisions through superior wealth and judicious use of bribes).

To the present, low castes in Sirkanda have made no concerted effort to break out of their status as a group, nor is it likely that they will do so. Particular castes or individuals have made brief sallies in this direction but nothing more. Relative caste status remains quite stable. A certain flexibility among younger and older high-caste men, combined with a fair degree of realistic tact on the part of low-caste people, has prevented open conflict. Many low-caste members have thought out rationalizations which make acceptance of their status easier. One Bajgi said:

We actually are better off than the high castes in some ways. When they want work done, they have to come ask us and we can refuse if we are too busy. They have to give us grain or money periodically. When we need help in doing our work we get high-caste people to do it and they follow our instructions.

A blacksmith said:

Anyone who serves another is a slave regardless of his position because he does not determine his own action. In that respect we are no worse off than many people who are wealthy and respected. The district magistrate, the schoolteacher, the surveyor—they are servants just as surely as are their peons or we blacksmiths. The district magistrate has a great deal of power. He can collect fines and send people to prison whether they are poor or wealthy, strong or weak. Therefore he is greatly feared. However, even he can do only what the law says. He is not to be feared as a person because he only implements the law. He has no power beyond what the law gives him and he can harm no man who has not disobeyed the law. He can give no punishment not written in the law. Therefore he is just a servant of the law like any other servant of a master. This is true of many positions. All of us who work for others are servants.

The methods which low-caste people adopt in accommodating to their depressed status are similar to those reported by Dollard (1957, p. 253) for Negroes in Southerntown. In Sirkanda the most common reaction is adoption of attitudes of passive accommodation and acceptance of gratifications commensurate with low-caste status. Overt aggression is rare, though not unknown. More characteristic of the plains and particularly of urban areas than of the hills is competition by low-caste members for high-caste values and increased status (cf. Bailey, 1957, pp. 186 ff.; Cohn, 1955; Opler and R. Singh, 1948, p. 476; Rowe, 1960a, pp. 58 ff., 298 ff.). In Sirkanda low-caste members characteristically turn their aggressive impulses toward members of their own group. They are explicitly encouraged in this by high-caste members. Overt aggression by low castes in Sirkanda (fights, cases referred to council action, and even legal suits) is almost exclusively directed toward caste-fellows or members of castes of roughly equivalent status, often with high-caste support.

Tension between high and low castes is not lacking but is usually kept on the covert level. It is based on the dominance of high castes in all spheres of life, which results in differential availability of advantages, primarily economic and prestige advantages. K. Singh, in a study of intercaste tensions in two plains villages, found essentially the same situation as that in Sirkanda, but with overt tensions and resultant conflict evidently considerably further developed. Speaking of these tensions he states:

> With land as the immediate cause, the conflict between the Thakurs and the low castes gradually assumed the character of a struggle for power accentuated further by the democratization of the Panchayats and other legal measures designed to create an equitable social order. Almost entirely, tension in the two villages may be seen in terms of the desire in the low caste people to assert their independence against the landlord class and their inability to do so successfully. (Singh, 1967, p. 108)
>
> The greater the dependence on and interaction with Thakurs, the greater is likely to be the tension exhibited by a low caste. (*Ibid.*, p. 111)

If the low castes are to decrease their dependence in Sirkanda, they must have access to more land. At present this is an issue on which the high castes are in no mood to conciliate and on which the low castes are in no position to press demands.

Caste Trends

Sanskritization in relation to caste has been discussed in chapter 4. There it was noted that a trend toward adoption of the orthodox Hindu usage of the plains is occurring among all castes in Sirkanda as compared to the dual trend toward low-caste Sanskritization and high-caste urbanization (or what might be called "atraditionalism") in the plains reported by Srinivas, Cohn, and others. The high castes of Sirkanda have adopted somewhat more of the orthodox traits than have the low castes, but this difference seems to be more a result of their economic ability than of differential aspirations. In Sirkanda there is relatively little evidence that any one caste is making an organized effort to raise its status in the system. The most conspicuous effort has been that of the Bajgis, whose women have ceased to dance professionally. A similar effort was underway in the Bhatbair Beda caste. The status rivalry, and its behavioral ramifications, among blacksmiths and Bajgis is another approach to mobility, but it lacks organization or consistency, and does not affect other castes.

Therefore, low castes are anxious to rise in status, but they seldom see any way to do it. They feel that they are subject to the will of high castes who would never tolerate infringement upon their superior status. Moreover, the low castes are small in numbers and divided among themselves by the jealousies inherent in a competitive situation, such as that with which households in the same occupational specialty are faced. As Cohn (1955, p. 74) has pointed out, mobility in a caste system must be a group phenomenon. So far, group effort in this direction on the low-caste level has been largely lacking in Sirkanda. Low castes realize that any organized effort to raise their own status, even if it could be undertaken, would meet with bitter and powerful opposition by the high castes. The high castes prefer to deal with low-caste people as dependent individuals. Organized opposition is a much greater threat than individual opposition.

On a broader level, trends in Pahari culture as a whole have brought changes in behavior and perhaps some enhancement in the status of the people of this culture area relative to those of the neighboring plains. This, at least, is the goal of changes in ritual usages among Paharis, and especially among people of high caste. Elsewhere this goal has been referred to as "plainsward mobility" (Berreman, 1961b).

Caste is not a static phenomenon. Not only are relative caste status and the attendant caste rules in constant flux, but the caste system itself assumes new and varying significance under changing circumstances. The accommodations, alterations, and new functions of caste in nontraditional settings have been discussed at some length by several authors (cf. Bose, 1958; Gadgil, 1952, pp. 184 ff.; Niehoff, 1959; Olcott, 1944; O'Malley, 1932, pp. 161 ff.; Ryan, 1953, pp. 307 ff.; Srinivas, 1955a, 1957). In these accounts emphasis is placed upon the functions of caste in the newly relevant political arena. Political consciousness and participation began to spread widely in India only shortly before Independence. Caste has arisen as a vital unit in national and regional, as well as local, politics. In Sirkanda these changes have not yet become apparent. While Sirkanda people have voted both in local and national elections, there has been no caste alignment evident in the elections. The low castes do not see the vote as a means to obtain desired ends. To put up a low-caste candidate never occurred to Sirkanda Doms, and when an outsider suggested it the idea was dismissed as useless and likely to cause trouble. Doms are so outnumbered that their attitude is realistic. They are cynical about the reservation of a seat for untouchables on the village council. While it is good in principle, it is an empty gesture in practice, because one low-caste man has little influence in such a body. Doms are pleased that schooling is equally available to all in the village and that scholarships to higher schools are available for untouchables, but no one plans to make use of the latter provision simply because it is too far from the realities of village life. Therefore, caste has not become a divisive factor in recent years as it reportedly has in other areas. Srinivas, who has discussed the increasingly divisive nature of caste in the villages and the nation, has also emphasized the "bonds opposing the divisiveness of caste," the "links that bind together the members of different castes who inhabit a village or a small local area" (Srinivas, 1955b, pp. 32, 34). In Sirkanda it is true, to a significantly lesser extent than in the villages studied by Lewis and by Srinivas, that caste is ". . . a distinct ethnic group with its own history, traditions, and identifications, and [that] each caste lives in more or less separate quarters in the village" (Lewis, 1958, p. 314). In Sirkanda the numbers of individuals in all castes except Rajputs are too small to function as separate little communities. Nevertheless, in Sirkanda caste per se is divisive—it frequently turns the attention and loyalties of everyone but Rajputs to the world outside the village and toward the caste brotherhood. Caste creates intergroup friction within the village and often prevents common purpose. However, caste organization entails economic and ritual interdependence, and associated with it in the village context is social interdependence. In the following chapter factors contributing to village unity and cohesion will be discussed. These are the factors which override intracaste identification and intercaste friction to make the village community a functioning social, economic, and religious unit within the larger field of its extensions in surrounding villages and its relationship to larger social, economic, and administrative units.

8 THE VILLAGE COMMUNITY

"From time immemorial the village has been a basic and important unit in the organization of Indian social polity" (Dube, 1955, p. 1). As such, villages are useful units for anthropological analysis (cf. Bailey, 1959). In fact, I would maintain that in the area in which this study was carried out, the community is the most relevant manageable unit of analysis if one's aim is to achieve an over-all understanding of the way of life of the people in a limited time. Detailed studies of an entire region would be impossible. Studies of kin and caste groups would be fruitful, but in a different direction.

Like all Indian villages, Pahari villages are not static, isolated, or autonomous. To be understood they must be viewed in historical perspective and in their relationship to other social, political, economic, and religious systems of which they or some of their members are a part. The nature and extent of these larger systems must be determined empirically. "Like any unit in a segmentary social system, the Indian village has to be examined to determine in what respects it stands alone and parallels for its members the advantages and purposes of similar units, and in what respects it combines in various ways with other units to serve wider purposes" (Opler, 1956, p. 10).

SIRKANDA AS A COMMUNITY

Sirkanda is readily identifiable as a village community. It is named, and it is called a village (*gāōn*) by its residents and by others familiar with it. Village affiliation of individuals is widely recognized in this area by people of other villages as well as by fellow villagers. There is village loyalty and, in some contexts, rivalry between villages. There are stereotypes about villages as entities, as in the local saying, "Two things to be wary of are Sirkanda's rocks and Kanda's women." Travelers on the trail invariably inquire as to one another's village of origin and the villages of their departure and destination. People are often identified in conversation by personal name, caste, and village. The villages of origin of brides brought in from outside are long remembered.

As has been mentioned, slightly over half of all Sirkanda villagers (206 of 384) live outside the nucleated settlement area which comprises the village, and yet their affiliation with it—resulting from their origin, family ties, and property owned in the village—is not questioned. The focus of community identification is, therefore, the well-defined nucleated settlement area containing dwellings and surrounded by cultivated lands. People who identify with this settlement rather than with other similar settlements are members of this village. Whether or not they usually live in the settlement, it is the focus of their religious activity and much of their social and economic activity, and it is the location of traditional family lands and dwellings. The village is therefore unquestionably a real, functioning social entity of great importance to its members and to others who come into contact with its members.

Economic and religious functions of the community and its relationship to other communities, towns, and regions in these matters have been presented in chapters 2, 3, and 4. Kinship and caste as they function within and beyond community boundaries and as they affect community organization have been discussed in chapters 5, 6, and 7. In this and the following chapters it will be my purpose to comment further on the village community of Sirkanda as a social and administrative entity. The village will be examined in terms of both its internal organization—the relations of various groups and categories within the village—and its relations with, and inclusion within, entities external to it.

INTERACTION BY AGE AND SEX

Relationships between individuals within kin groups as influenced by age, generation, and sex have been discussed in chapter 5. Age and sex have a similar importance in the relationship of individuals unrelated by kin ties: Males almost always dominate over females; age dominates youth. Women are usually more relaxed and sociable among women than in the presence of men; young peoples' behavior is inhibited by the presence of elders. Women and young people are especially careful of their behavior in the presence of outsiders or members of other villages.

A recurrent situation in which these relationships were clearly manifested was that presented early in the period of this research when the anthropologist wished to secure photographs. Young men were almost invariably willing to be photographed when alone or in the presence of age-mates. In the presence of male elders they would usually await an indication of approval from the elders. With women the situation was even clearer. A young woman would refuse to be photographed if she were in the presence of either men or older women unless she received specific encouragement from them. With a word of encouragement from males or elders (or in their absence) a woman was as eager to be photographed as was a man.

Ideally a male dominates even an older female, but this does not always work out in practice. An elderly woman can persuade a young man to allow his wife to be photographed. At the Bhatbair fair, an intervillage function, a group of gaily dressed young women of various villages agreed to be photographed until a proud, middle-aged, and inebriated Brahmin man stormed up and ordered them to refuse. An elderly, high-status Rajput woman of Sirkanda who knew the photographer, as the Brahmin did not, and who had been observing the proceedings, was obviously irritated by the arrogant intervention. She interceded by stepping to the center of the group of girls. Eyeing the Brahmin evenly, she said, "Please take my photograph." Her age, status, and composure were sufficient to abash the Brahmin, who left, and to encourage the women, who posed willingly for the picture.

Within the village there is great freedom in the relations among men and women. They work, travel, and participate in village functions together. Women do not leave the village in marriage parties or other such functions, but in the village they participate freely. Nowhere is this more evident than in drinking and dancing parties where, especially if outsiders are not present, women often participate with their menfolk. At public feasts women often eat with men. Evidently in villages more remote than Sirkanda such participation is even freer; Sirkanda has felt, to some extent, the effects of plains customs on this score. Such behavior is significant as one aspect of informal community organization.

Freedom in sexual behavior has been discussed in chapter 5, where it was emphasized that both men and women commonly engage in extramarital sexual relations. Men have especially free access to women of lower caste than themselves and to the wives of their brothers. Women visiting in their natal villages are also unusually free. Much of the conversation of young men is devoted to their sexual exploits, a topic upon which immoderate boasting is not uncommon. At fairs and other celebrations sexual activity accompanies drinking and dancing as a source of diversion. An ideal of romantic love pervades the culture, expressed in stories and songs, and realized, with greater frequency than seems usual in most of India, through elopement and extramarital liaisons. Pahari songs generally recount tales of romantic love or of heroism. The most popular type of song can best be described by quoting Traill (1828, p. 219):

> The *Byri*, or *Bhagnaol*, is a species of duet, sung commonly by a male and a female, who respond to each other in extemporary stanzas alternately. The subject has commonly reference to the situation or actual occupation of the parties, clothed in numerous metaphors and similes, drawn chiefly from vegetable products; where the parties are skillful, the *Byri* is made the vehicle of personal praise or satire: this style of singing is highly popular in the *Kamaon* pergunnahs, and it is there a common saying, that no female heart can withstand the seductions of an accomplished *Byri* singer. The measure is slow and plaintive.

The haunting melodies of these songs, as verses are exchanged between young men and women working out of sight but within earshot of one another on the steep, forest-covered hillsides, no passer-by can easily forget. Such singing is a means of maintaining contact and finding reassurance in lonely work in isolated areas, as well as a vehicle for indicating romantic interest and exercising creative wit.

Caste and Community

Caste has been presented in the preceding chapter as a primarily divisive force in the village. However, it is worth emphasizing again that this is only part of the picture. The nature of caste in this area creates economic and religious interdependence in the village. Every local caste is essential to every other, and, to the extent that people depend upon members of other castes within the village, a strong cohesive bond is formed. From such interdependence and from the crucial fact of residential proximity, intercaste social bonds also grow to be effective cohesive forces. There is certain lore about the village, its locale and people, which is shared almost exclusively among villagers without regard to castes and cliques. There are common attitudes on many subjects. There is an essentially common body of religious belief and behavior. These common understandings help tie village members together.

Participation in common enterprises, ownership of common property, and preoccupation with common problems and common antagonisms further bind the community together despite caste, sib, and clique alignments. Community members participate in annual ceremonies, ritual observances, and informal drinking, dancing, and singing parties. Coöperative work on village-owned trails, on the water source, and in certain phases of housebuilding and agriculture also contribute to community identification. Indicative of a degree of village unity and interdependence is ownership by the village in common of large cooking vessels and a few large tools available to all community members as needed. Community government (discussed below) and informal councils are enterprises cutting across divisive loyalties, though they also provide a setting for engaging in disputes. Common loyalties are shared by villagers in their identification of themselves as Sirkanda villagers. They share pride in village history, its former relationship with the Garhwal Raja, and in him and his kingdom.

Common problems and antagonisms are found in uniform dislike of the present government, its programs and personnel. No faction deviates on this matter. Rivalry with other villages and areas, and feelings of strangeness in alien settings, serve also to bind people together before strangers. Village-wide suspicion of outsiders has a similar effect. Certain village secrets are kept by all factions. Caste may have a counterfactional function in that cross-caste antagonisms make for occasional cross-factional alliances within castes, especially in disputes with caste or status implications.

Therefore, in spite of the many cleavages and potential cleavages in the village, there are counterforces which make it a real community —an identification group as well as a membership group. Srinivas (1955b, p. 35) has said that in Mysore, "the village is a community which commands loyalty from all who live in it, irrespective of caste affiliation. Some are first-class members of the village community, and others are second-class members, but all are members." This is true too in Sirkanda. The village is thus enabled to survive as a unity, to maintain conventional understandings about behavior, and to deal with deviants effectively.

VILLAGE EXOGAMY

An outstanding feature of Sirkanda as a community, in contrast to many plains communities, is the absence of village exogamy (Berreman, 1962d; cf. Gould, 1960, 1961b). This is important in community consensus and cohesion in that intravillage marriages create strong ties across cleavages of sib, clan, and clique. Lewis (1958, p. 325) has emphasized the importance of rules of village endogamy and exogamy in the world view of those who live under them; they are "so important that it might be useful to add endogamy and exogamy as crucial universal variables in our models of the folk society and peasant society."

Despite absence of formal exogamy in Sirkanda, in 84 per cent of all marriages the wife comes from outside the village. In the minority castes (that is, all but Rajputs) all wives come from other villages due to sib exogamy. However, the "region whose limits are determined by kinship bonds" is relatively small in the hills as compared with the plains. In Sirkanda, 83 per cent of all spouses come from within four air miles of Sirkanda.

To the extent that Sirkanda marriages are contracted within a small area and with relatively few families, most of whose members are personally known to Sirkanda villagers, Sirkanda presents a contrast to Rampur, as reported by Lewis, and to similar plains villages. The area of "rural cosmopolitanism" surrounding the village, which Lewis found to be so extensive around Rampur, is relatively restricted in the hills. There is a very real "isolationist" and "inward-looking" tendency among residents of Sirkanda and neighboring communities. This isolationism occurs not at the village level, as it would in endogamous villages, but at the level of the immediate cultural area— the area of the marriage network. There is not, therefore, sufficient contrast between exogamous Rampur and nonexogamous Sirkanda to test Lewis' ideas rigorously.

A contrast between Sirkanda and Rampur, which may be partially attributable to the difference in marriage rules, is the apparently greater flexibility, changeability, and ambiguity in factional alignment in Sirkanda (Lewis, 1958, p. 114). This probably stems in part from the incidence of in-village, cross-sib, and hence often cross-faction marriage in Sirkanda. The extreme suspiciousness which Sirkanda residents display toward outsiders may be partly attributable to the relatively small, well-known group of people with whom marriages are contracted and other intercommunity relations occur. However, most differences which appear between villages of the hills and of the plains are more plausibly attributable to other cultural and ecological factors.

CLIQUES AND FACTIONS

The most prominent social units within Sirkanda are those based upon considerations of kin and caste ties. These have been discussed in previous chapters. However, there are other relationships among individuals and groups which are significant to life in the community although they are not coextensive with these units. Primary among these are informal alliances and friendships which go to make up cliques or factions of individuals who tend to help one another in economic and religious undertakings, to interact with one another more frequently than with others in social relations, and to support one another in rivalry or disputes with others in or out of the village.

In Sirkanda these are not powerful, stable, well-delineated factions which consistently oppose one another and command the loyalty of their members, as are those reported by Lewis (1958, p. 114) for Rampur. Rather they are often vague, shifting, uncoördinated groups of people. It therefore seems preferable in most contexts to call such alliances in Sirkanda "cliques" in translation of the villagers' own term, *gutt*. The term "faction" will be used in this presentation to refer to groups involved in disputes. No rigid terminological distinction is advocated here. Friendship groups and other groups distinguishable on grounds other than disputes will be termed cliques. Actively disputing groups will be called factions. Often these groups are the same, in which case context will determine usage.

In Sirkanda such groups are found primarily in the Rajput caste, it being the only group large enough to contain many such alignments, just as it is the only caste large enough to contain several different phratries, sibs, clans, and lineages within the village.[1] However, not all Rajputs are aligned with cliques nor are all non-Rajputs unaligned. Some members of other castes are tied into Rajput cliques, sometimes despite their own efforts to remain neutral. In addition, as has been noted, there are disputes within and among joint families, between castes, and between high- and low-caste groups. Examples of these have been discussed in previous chapters in connection with the social units in which they occur.

In Sirkanda there are no named groups which correspond to cliques. The nearest thing are some kin groups which happen to be coterminus with certain cliques. Most cliques, in fact, are not generally recognized social entities. There are no special social centers or regular occasions for intra-clique interaction. Even informants who wish to coöperate in giving information on this subject and who understand the concept well are hard-pressed to delineate cliques or to name clique members in any but the most obvious alliances. Clique divisions and membership can in many cases only be inferred by observation of interaction in economic, religious, and social contexts. Important sources of data in this respect are patterns of visiting and friendship, and disputes among villagers.

As a result of inquiries along these lines it was found that in Sirkanda cliques tend to follow caste, sib, clan, lineage, and family lines, in order of increasing relevance. The core of a clique is usually a large or well-to-do family, and those influential in the clique are usually family heads. But around this core are other individuals who side with the core group. To consider cliques independently of family and larger social divisions would be to misunderstand them. If they deviate from, or cut across, these boundaries, that fact in itself is important, since it runs against traditional ideals of caste and kin-group unity. Another important dimension was found to be that of age. People of roughly the same age tend to participate on the same level of interaction in inter-clique behavior, while those of other age groups have somewhat independent alignments. Sex is also a factor in that women have their own cliques, apparently somewhat independent of those of their husbands and based upon ties of relationship and common village origin as well as upon jealousies and disputes among themselves. Women, as family and clan members, often follow in the clique alignments of their husbands. The wives of men who are at odds generally also avoid one another unless they have close ties of relationship or common village origin, and sometimes even these ties are subordinated to male factionalization. In this study only male cliques were studied sufficiently to draw many conclusions.

Friendship and Visiting Patterns

One important manifestation of clique membership is that of patterns of friendship and visiting in the village. These are not easily delineated. One villager commented:

There are no special friends here. People talk occasionally to everyone—whoever they meet at the water source, at work, or around the village. They don't talk a lot with anyone outside of their joint family. An exception is the young men of the village, who often sit around and talk together. Certain people avoid one another because of disputes they have had.

There is not the custom, such as is found on the plains, of men sitting in a living area reserved for them and passing time with their friends. There is no area in Pahari houses where men can gather, undisturbed by women and children. Informal visiting by small groups of men (two to four) does occasionally take place on the veranda of the house, but many men rarely participate. Principal locations for social interaction among groups of men are the village shops and the places of work of artisans. These represent "neutral ground," and an individual does not compromise himself by stopping there regardless of who else may be there or may later come. Since everyone is welcome at these places and is, in fact, expected to stop at least briefly if he is passing by, patterns of friendship and clique composition are not as clearly revealed as they would be in individual houses where only friends are welcome. Other informal groups relevant to an understanding of friendship and clique formation are those of men working or traveling together.

On the basis of observations of friendly interaction in Sirkanda, six main cliques were found among Rajputs. One of these consisted of two lineages of the Palial sib, the second consisted of the third lineage in that sib, and the third consisted of most of the members of the largest lineage in the Jawari sib. The fourth and fifth were formerly one clique consisting of another lineage in the Jawari sib, but it has split so that now there are essentially two family isolates. The sixth is another small Jawari clique (see fig. 5). The importance of kin ties in these alliances is obvious. Two of the cliques follow lineage boundaries (one includes two and the other one lineage), and the other four follow family boundaries (in each there are two family cliques within a lineage). In only one case are brothers in different cliques.

In addition to these main groups, there are individuals and groups whose interaction does not reveal any clique alignments or, more importantly, whose interaction spans clique boundaries or makes crossclique groups. Four main factors seem to be basic to such individuals: (1) age ties, (2) affinal ties, (3) ties of geographic proximity, (4) lack of particular kinship ties which would tend to commit the individuals to specific cliques. In the first category, age ties, is the group of young men (20 to 35 years in age) who generally ignore the factional affiliations of their elders and associate quite freely with one another. They even cut across caste barriers to some extent, with a blacksmith and a Bajgi often being included in the group. Children are another such age group. In the second category, affinal ties, are the relationships between men who have married within the village, and their male in-laws. There are several of these relationships, which take the form of frequent informal social interaction at the home of the father- or brother-in-law. In the third category, geographical proximity, fall the friendship and economic and ceremonial coöperation of the occupants to this category is the interaction of neighbors, especially the greater of four chans in a small area ¾ mile distant from the village. Related frequency of interaction among people living within each of the three main settlement areas of Sirkanda than occurs between these sections,

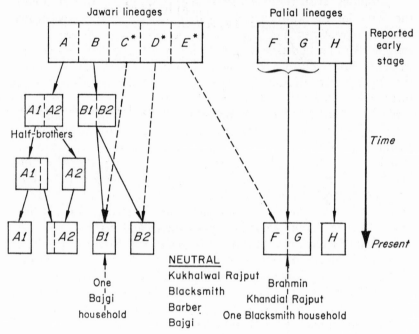

Fig. 5. Principal Rajput cliques through time.

Cliques are enclosed in solid-line boxes. Broken lines indicate lineage boundaries within cliques. Solid arrows indicate development through time. Broken arrows indicate casual alliances. Asterisked lineages are at present small in numbers and largely unaffiliated.

other things being equal. In the last category, lack of kinship ties which commit individuals to cliques, fall the members of three relatively small Jawari Rajput lineages, the members of one small sib in the village (Kukhalwal), and the members of other castes. The remaining Rajput sib, Khandial, consists of one family which is committed by marriage to the first Palial clique listed above.

Clique alignments and deviations from them are evident not only in visiting patterns but in coöperation in ritual and economic undertakings as well. No family, lineage, sib, or clan is large enough to perform an important marriage without outside assistance, and this is usually not available from members of opposing cliques. Drinking parties are another activity in which cliques and clique deviations are readily apparent.

Disputes and Dispute Resolution

Disputes reveal clique divisions sharply. They are, in fact, usually the bases for the avoidance between individuals and groups which becomes stereotyped into clique behavior. A study of disputes, therefore, leads to an understanding not only of what the clique structure is, but of how it got that way, that is, how cliques are formed and how they change through time. In addition, such a study reveals important information about the means and dimensions of social control and conflict resolution in the community.

In discussing disputes a major difficulty is that of deciding relative significance. Disputes of all intensities occur, from the minor irritation that is quickly forgotten to the major power struggle that is remembered for generations. Some disputes bring about formation of cliques or factions; most are symptomatic of already existing factionalization, and some are unrelated to clique affiliation. Here disputes that have aroused strong feelings among the participants and that are apparently associated in some way with clique alignments will be considered. They include all those upon which sufficient relevant information was available for analysis—the recent and the well-remembered. A few occurred during the writer's residence in Sirkanda; most occurred within the previous 10 years; one took place 40 years ago. In all cases, however, relevant and apparently reliable data were obtained from informants who were present at the time of the dispute.

That this is a biased sample is indicated by the fact that of the 32 in-village disputes analyzed, 19 resulted in estrangement of the parties to the dispute although no apparent estrangement had existed previously, and only 13 perpetuated or were symptomatic of old animosities, so far as could be determined. Obviously the latter would be far more frequent than the former in a random sample, but they are less well remembered.

Once a major factional split has occurred, further disputes usually follow at frequent intervals which sustain and often deepen the rift. Disputes without significance either as causes or symptoms of factionalization do not appear here, not because they do not occur, but because they are frequent, usually minor, and not germane to this discussion. In this category would fall most such temporary and recurrent disputes

as those which occur frequently among family members, between individual women in the village, and between village occupational
specialists and the clients they serve.

Fifty-one disputes are analyzed here. Of these, 44 involved Sirkanda
people either as both parties in the dispute (32 cases) or as one party,
the other being from a neighboring village (12 cases). The seven remaining cases involved primarily people of neighboring villages, but
Sirkanda people were involved as relatives, council members, or
witnesses.

The disputes have been analyzed in terms of the nature of the
grievance and the action taken as a result. Grievances were categorized
as follows: (1) sex, arising from illicit sex relations or alienation of
affection; (2) property, arising from conflicting claims to land, houses,
or income; (3) status, arising from nonadherence to caste rules, or
inappropriate caste or intercaste behavior; (4) legal testimony, arising
from a person's refusal to testify for, or his testimony against, another
in a court case in which he was to have appeared as a witness and
in which some connivance had been planned; (5) beating or physical
assault on another (in all cases this occurred as a result of grievances
falling under one of the other categories listed here); (6) wife-stealing
(transporting a woman out of the village for profit rather than for
personal sexual reasons); (7) malpractice of a curing rite.

Actions taken to resolve or win a dispute have been categorized
as follows: (1) threats, avoidance, insults, family division, and so on,
which involved none of the other types of action listed below but which
sometimes eventuated in a *modus vivendi* or solution acceptable to
both; (2) beating or physical assault on another; (3) revenge by committing a like offense, the only such case in this sample being one in
which a man whose wife was regularly having sexual relations with
another man helped steal that man's wife; (4) council (referral to an
ad hoc council of villagers); (5) intervention by gods; (6) intervention
by officials (referral to police, courts, or government officials outside
the village); (7) "frame-up" (revenge by bringing a false legal charge
against an opponent after arranging matters so that he will be found
guilty). An example of the last befell a man whose prosperity was
envied by his caste-fellows. They had once tried unsuccessfully to get
some of his land by bribing the government records officer to testify
that he had acquired the land illegally. Failing in this, they obtained
revenge by hiding liquor in his house and calling the police to say
that he was dealing in illicit liquor.

The frequencies of these types of grievances and the actions taken
are presented in table 6. Not shown in the figures in table 6 is the

fact that beatings, and to a lesser extent all types of action taken in disputes, were preceded and accompanied by threats, avoidance, insults, and so on, and that a fight was always a possibility. As one villager remarked when a crippled man verbally abused another man, "A person should not use abuse unless he is strong enough to fight." Also not shown here is the fact that the council case for woman-stealing was subsequently prosecuted by the government in the courts, but not as a result of action by villagers.

TABLE 6

SIRKANDA DISPUTES BY TYPE AND RESULTANT ACTION

Grievance	Threats, avoidance	Beating	Like offense	Council	Gods	Officials and courts	Frame-up	Totals
Sex	6	5	1	3	2	2	1	20(39%)
Property	8	1	—	—	—	4	1	14(27%)
Status	3	—	—	2	—	—	1	6(12%)
Testimony	3	—	—	—	—	—	—	3 (7%)
Beating	—	—	—	—	—	4	—	4 (8%)
Woman-stealing	2	—	—	1	—	—	—	3 (6%)
Malpractice	—	—	—	1	—	—	—	1 (2%)
Totals	22 (43%)	6 (12%)	1 (2%)	7 (14%)	2 (4%)	10 (20%)	3 (6%)	51 (100%)

These figures and the relationships among them show a number of things about the nature of Sirkanda disputes. Sex and property are the main causes for disputes which get into the public eye and are felt to be important by all concerned. Together they account for two-thirds of all disputes recorded. Sex disputes are consistently resolved in the local context. The two cases that went to court involved obvious breaches of law. Property disputes, on the other hand, go much more frequently to official, outside agencies for resolution. Beatings are usually cause for a lawsuit. The reasons here are very obvious: you do not go to an official, the police, or a court of law unless you have good reason to think you will win your case. These people have found that beating can be easily proved and prosecution is sure, and that in property disputes the law courts often decide cases on the basis of evidence which is ignored in the village context. Consequently, it is worthwhile to take such cases to official agencies. Sex, status, malpractice in curing, failures to keep a promise to testify in court, and

woman-stealing are areas in which court decisions are either unavailable or unlikely to be useful. Woman-stealing, which might seem to
be amenable to court decision, is rarely referred to the courts because
the woman has invariably coöperated so that evidence against the
"abductor" is usually lacking. Those who have engaged in woman-
stealing as a regular business rarely participate in the abduction of
local women, and those who do it only once can always plead innocence
and support their plea by evidence of good character.

Further insight into the nature of appeal to courts is found in
the three "frame-ups." In each case grievances which could not be
successfully brought to a court of law were resolved by manufacturing
a case which could be decided in the courts. The three actual grievances
were an illicit sexual affair, jealousy over property, and anger caused
by low-caste insolence. The grievances manufactured and brought to
court were, respectively, assault and rape, liquor-selling, and theft.
Incidentally, this was the only case of alleged rape known in the area,
and one of the very few allegations of theft.

One other fact worth noting is that the village council is not used
for property disputes. Villagers feel that justice cannot be obtained
because the council is made up of people with heavy vested interests
in local property, who would decide solely in terms of self-interest or
bribes.

Disputes are not submitted for arbitration by courts (in cases of
alleged breaches of legal statutes) or by the village council (in cases
of alleged breaches of custom) unless those who present them are confident that they will win. Often those with grievances are challenged
to take them to court or a council. As one Rajput informant said,
"If there is a legitimate complaint the case will go to a panchayat or
to a court. If not, it is just bickering."

Gods intervened in only two disputes, both hinging on sex. Sex
disputes are the most ambiguous as well as the most frequent kind
of grievance. Gods can give satisfaction to one party when no one else
can. They intervene much more frequently than this analysis indicates, because they often enter a sex dispute between two women
or between family members which never reaches the public eye or
never enters into factional alliances. Likewise gods frequently intervene on behalf of brides from other villages in matters unrelated to
sex.

The functions of various kinds of groups in the village can be made
clearer by investigating the nature of social groups which engage in
various types of disputes and employ various types of action to resolve
them.

Forty of the disputes analyzed here took place between people of the same caste. Thirty-two of these were Rajput disputes, and eight were blacksmith or Bajgi disputes. Eleven were intercaste disputes, three between Rajputs and Brahmins, two between blacksmiths and Bajgis, and six between particular high castes and low castes. These figures are largely a reflection of population and social structure in Sirkanda. There is only one household of Brahmins. Disputes, as defined here, do not occur within households except when they result in a lasting division of the household unit. Bajgis and Lohars are few in numbers, and each of these castes in Sirkanda is composed of a closely related group of people in a single lineage. The eight intra-caste disputes within these two groups are a reflection of the fact that low castes are more likely to divide the household and compete for livelihood than are the other castes. Rajputs are numerous and comprise four different sibs; consequently, most disputes in the village involve them. Most disputes which villagers would describe as inter-sib disputes involve local sib members, and usually wives side with their husbands. Therefore such disputes will here be termed inter-clan disputes.

In the 40 intracaste disputes, 22 were between clans, five were within clans but between lineages, and 15 were within lineages. One dispute involved both inter-clan and interlineage disputants, and another involved both inter-clan and intralineage disputants; hence the disparity in totals.

In table 7, grievances and action taken are tabulated according to their occurrence in intercaste disputes, disputes which are within the caste but between clans (inter-clan), disputes which are within the clan but between lineages (interlineage), and those which are within the lineage (intralineage). This table shows that inter-clan disputes are predominately concerned with alleged sex offenses, while intralineage disputes are most often centered on property. This can be easily explained in retrospect. Only within the lineage is property derived from a common estate, and only there is property held in common by several members of the group. That is where one would expect to find disagreements over property—in its management and division. Intense sexual activity occurs across clan lines because clans are essentially sibs, the exogamous units. Since all legitimate mates are found across sib lines, the potential for this type of dispute among these groups is high. Within the clan, sib, and lineage, wives are quite freely available to their husbands' brothers, real and classificatory, while other women associated with the lineage are exempt by incest rules. Therefore, disputes of this kind are less likely within these largely exogamous units. The sex disputes which did occur within lineages nearly always involved one man's taking over another's wife or carrying on a conspicuous affair with her.

TABLE 7

INCIDENCE OF DISPUTES BY SOCIAL GROUPS INVOLVED [a]

Grievance	Intercaste 11	Inter-clan 22	Interlineage 5	Intralineage 15
Sex	4	11	2	3
Property	2	5*	2*	6
Status	3	—	—	3
Testimony	2	2*	1	1*
Beating	1	2	—	1
Woman-stealing	1	1	—	1
Malpractice	—	1	—	—
Action Taken				
Threats	4	7*	2	10*
Beating	1	4	—	1
Like offense	—	—	—	1
Council	3	3	—	1
Gods	—	1	—	1
Officials	2	5*	3*	1
Frame-up	1	2	—	—

[a] The two totals marked with an asterisk which appear on the same horizontal row include one case in common; for example, in the property disputes, there was one with inter-clan and interlineage disputants, and so it was included in both columns although it was a single dispute. This accounts for the fact that the total number of cases listed here is 53, whereas only 51 cases were analyzed.

Disputes in general are more common among status equals than across status boundaries. Large differences in status are associated with differences in power, so that disputes across status boundaries are infrequently essayed and are likely to be nipped in the bud if begun. Of the six recorded high-caste–low-caste disputes, one involved woman-stealing and included a Brahmin and Rajput as well as a Bajgi among the culprits, so that it was hardly a case of high caste versus low caste. Two of the others involved low-caste insolence, one resulting in a "frame-up" and the other, which involved behavior of children, resulting in threats and verbal abuse. Another was a low-caste grievance against a Brahmin who failed to pay for a cow taken on agreement to purchase. The final two stemmed from a sexual liaison between a low-caste man and an acquiescent Rajput woman. The man was beaten and then took his assailants to court.

The other five intercaste disputes were between castes adjacent in the status hierarchy, and did not differ in type or distribution from what would be expected within castes.

Status disputes occurred either between castes or within lineages. The former were matters of low-caste insolence prosecuted by the high castes. The intralineage status disputes were cases of individuals failing to conform to requirements of caste or family honor. Lineage members, as those most immediately involved, were the group which sought to rectify matters.

Figures on action taken show that lineage solidarity is effective in keeping most intralineage disputes on a verbal level, with a minimum of public display and outside intervention. Beatings, council action, and court cases occurred frequently in inter-clan and intercaste cases. Apparently group controls across these lines are relatively weak.

Physical assault as a means of resolving a difference occurred most often among status equals unrelated to one another, that is, at the inter-sib or inter-clan level. Relatives are reluctant to fight, and low-caste people are reluctant to get themselves into a position where powerful high castes will have an excuse to attack them. The only intercaste beating was the one described above, in which a low-caste sex offender was beaten.

The distribution of cases in which there was resort to outside officials reflects closely the distribution of disputes over property, since it is in property disputes that official agencies are most useful.

When a council is appealed to voluntarily it is almost always as a result of an intercaste dispute. Within the caste, less conspicuous means of arbitration are preferred. Three of the four cases involving single castes (that is, inter-clan) which went to councils were intra-low–caste disputes into which councils intervened without the request of those involved. Low castes try to keep their disputes out of councils, where they say low castes always lose and only the council wins.

"Frame-ups" occurred only in intercaste and inter-clan disputes, probably because such plots are a drastic action, usually resulting in imprisonment, which relatives would rarely inflict on one another.

Clique and Faction Formation

The clique or faction structure revealed by disputes corresponds closely to that shown in friendship and visiting patterns, and explains the formation of current alignments.

The Jawari sib of Rajputs is characterized by several factional splits and antagonisms toward other groups as a result of a number of important disputes. It was allegedly once undivided by major disputes. Then two factions, A and B, split off a few generations ago, as the result of a serious sexual dispute (see fig. 5). Later each of these factions split into two groups along family lines (A1, A2; B1, B2) as a result of property and status disputes. One of these divisions also involved a half-brother relationship, a relationship which quite consistently results in social distance between the parties. Most recently, one family in A1 was alienated from that clique as a result of a status dispute, and so it joined A2, its current alignment. Similar histories could probably be traced for other cliques in the village.

In general there is considerable disputing between the two large sibs in Sirkanda, and they have each acted as factions in and of themselves. Within these groups lineages and sometimes households have formed cliques. The importance of kin ties can be readily seen in the diagram, although they are not equally important in all cliques. Other groups which might prefer to remain neutral tend to become aligned with cliques through friendship, work relationships, affinal relations, proximity, and so on.

In correlating friendship groups with disputant groups it becomes evident that not all friendship groups are antagonistic to one another. Between the Palial cliques there is little or no animosity (H, FG). The same holds for the relationship of B2 to H and FG. These are, therefore, cliques that are on good terms with one another. On the other hand, A1, A2, B1, and B2 are antagonistic to one another, and A1, A2, and B1 are antagonistic to FG and, to a lesser extent, to H. The household comprising clique B1 is generally disliked by everyone in the village except one Bajgi household, with which it is in a patron-like relationship, and lineage C, which has sided with it occasionally. Clique FG is the most generally liked group in the village. It has had few disputes with others and comprises a loose-knit, open group.

The attitudes between cliques are usually related directly to the types and intensity of disputes they have had with one another. The Jawari sib is permeated with jealousy, animosity, and disputes, while the Palial sib is at present relatively congenial. As has been mentioned before, all but the most serious disputes tend to be ignored after one or two generations unless they are reinforced by new ones. Therefore, young men of A1 and A2 associate freely with those of H and FG, and even the youngest man of the isolated and generally disliked clique, B1, has some informal social contact with these groups.

The effects of disputes and factionalization on the community are important and far-reaching. They sometimes seriously affect village cohesion just as they do lineage and clan unity. The complexity of disputes, the means of dealing with them, and their effects may be illustrated by picking two examples and describing them briefly.

CASE I

The most serious dispute in recent history was over land. About the time of World War I the army purchased some Sirkanda lands a little over a mile from the village, to be used as a small summer encampment for Ghurka troops. Two stone houses and some other improvements were made there by the army. For nearly twenty years the camp was often occupied during the summer months. The army was rigidly segregated from the villagers by army orders, with one exception—one village family (A in the diagram of cliques) sold milk to the army and became friendly with its personnel. When the army left in 1932, the milk-selling family bought the desirable army land, complete with its buildings, for a ridiculously small sum. Other villagers were incensed when they found out because many of them had formerly owned shares in the land and they had been given no opportunity to buy their shares back. According to them, the sale should have been publicly announced and all should have had a chance to buy some of the land.

A nine-year legal suit resulted which was eventually won by the milk-selling family (A). Although the law seemed to be on the side of the other villagers, the village accountant, whose records were crucial to the case, was a member of the winning family. Also the army officers had liked that family, had coöperated with them in the sale, and had testified in their behalf in court. The appellants were of the opposite clan (clique FG) but were actively and openly supported by members of a rival faction (B1) in the milk-sellers' clan who hoped to get land, although they had not been among the original owners of the land. It was essentially the village versus the milk-sellers (cliques B1, B2, H, FG vs. A1, A2).

During and after the trial, relations between the disputants and their respective supporters deteriorated. An outside merchant was brought in when the suit began, so that villagers would not have to buy from the only village-run shop, owned and operated by the milk-sellers' family. These two shops have remained in the village, in full view of one another, jealous of one another's patronage, and a constant reminder of the dispute. A member of the milk-selling family was replaced as village tax collector under pressure occasioned by animosity resulting from this case. Villagers blame subsequent lack of village unity largely on the case. Attempts to improve the water supply have failed, and money granted by the government to repair the school and to build a community center has gone unused. Villagers say that animosities kindled and fanned by the old dispute prevent agreement and coöperation on the new projects and lead individuals to purposely subvert plans that are made. Even the lineage that won the case has been split because one member family (A2) could not pay its full share of the heavy legal expenses and so was given none of the lands it had been promised for its support. It therefore broke completely away from the rest of the lineage.

CASE II

A Rajput woman, who lived with her husband in a chan, fell in love with a relative of her husband who lived in a neighboring chan. When the husband came to know he moved away from the chan to the village, whereupon his wife went to her parents, refusing to return to her husband. After two years the wife wanted to rejoin her husband, but he then refused to take her. Her family insisted, but to no avail. A council meeting was suggested, but the husband's family refused in highly insulting terms. At the urging of another relative, Sohan, they wrote the woman's family a letter saying that the marriage was void and they would have nothing to do with her. This angered the girl's family because, since no money had been demanded as compensation, the divorce implied that she was immoral and worthless. They especially resented this because no public charges had been placed against the girl. Moreover, the unstated charges involved the husband's own relative; therefore, they felt, the girl was not at fault. In their anger the woman's relatives caught and beat her husband and his brother. Thereupon Sohan urged the beaten men to go to court about the beating. This they did upon the assurance that Sohan would stand as witness in their behalf. However, when the case came up, Sohan did not appear as promised. The husband's family spent a good deal of money on the case, which lasted a year and was then dropped. Meanwhile, Sohan had shifted his loyalties to the other side and helped them with advice and encouragement. When the case was dropped, the ex-wife was turned over as wife to her former lover at the chan, who had been paying part of the legal expenses on her behalf.

As a result, the disputants (and Sohan, on the side of the wife) refused to ever again attend social or ritual occasions where they would meet and especially where eating was to take place. This avoidance was practiced for over five years until a prominent and well-liked village woman died. Her husband had been in one of the two large Rajput sibs, and she was a member of the other, a daughter of the village as well as a village wife and mother. The entire village was united in love and respect for her, and yet the two disputing factions refused to attend the death ceremonies together. A council meeting was held to come to a new agreement, as it was felt by those not involved in the dispute that the estrangement should not continue with such disruptive effect. A compromise was reached which is still followed today. The two parties agreed to attend all village functions but not to eat in the kitchen area on such occasions. They eat outside and leave as soon as they have eaten. They never eat in the kitchen area of the same house on the same day.

Villagers generally admit that the husband was in the right in this case, but because of the arrogant rejection of council arbitration and the generally haughty attitude of the husband and his family, village sympathies were with the wife—to teach the husband a lesson. General dislike of the husband's family also entered in. In this case the husband's family comprised clique B_1; Sohan's family was clique A_1; the wife's family was in clique FG.

A villager commented, in reference to this case, "Village disputes are of this silly nature."

It is evident from these somewhat simplified accounts that disputes are complex, that alignments are not firm nor entirely consistent and predictable, and that ramifications may be far-reaching and disruptive. The motivations determining sympathies and alignments among non-disputants are usually based in previous grievances and are often extremely complex. Nurturing and compounding these animosities by planning revenge is a major activity among some villagers. On the other hand, in daily activities the animosities are kept under control so that they come into the open relatively infrequently in view of the amount of interpersonal contact which is inevitable in the village.

The village settlement pattern is suggestive in this regard. While it conforms in general to sib and lineage distribution, it conforms even more closely to clique alignments (see map 3, p. 25). Thus, clique B1, the most isolated and antagonistic clique, is physically isolated in a single house on the western edge of the village; clique A1 is isolated in the house nearest the Devi shrine; clique A2 is in two adjacent houses on the edge of the eastern settlement area; clique H is in the line of houses nearest the school. Clique FG, the most open of all, is in the center of the village. In general, the most congenial households are those which occupy the central portion of the village, while those harboring animosities and rivalries and those which are simply asocial are found on the peripheries, where they have built houses in recent years; for example, all houses in the southwestern settlement area of the village have been built in the past ten years. A possible earlier pattern is suggested by older houses in the village. Among them there is a general separation of the Palial sib (lineages H, FG) and Jawari lineages B, D, E (all located in the central settlement area, although clustered by sib) on the one hand, and Jawari lineages A and C and the Kukhalwal sib (located in the eastern settlement area) on the other.

Cliques have no formal organization. The elder men of the households involved tend to be the policymakers for the cliques and to enforce, when possible, loyalty and conformity within the group. The clique is an extremely loose relationship when more than one household is involved.

Clique alignments serve as barriers to communication and common action among villagers, and therefore they are divisive factors. On the other hand, they facilitate interaction among members of the same clique, thus forming a close tie that is not always coextensive with ties of kinship and caste. Insofar as they do that they help bind the community together across natural lines of cleavage. Moreover, it should be emphasized that cliques operate primarily in the community context. Outside the community they have little relevance. None of the cliques in Sirkanda has close ties in other villages which divide them against other groups in the community in intervillage disputes. In relations with other villages, caste is often a divisive force but cliques are not. An outside threat brings unity to the village unless there are conflicting caste or kin-group loyalties. Also, clique differences are largely disregarded in dealings with the urban and official worlds. In town and in relations with officials, Sirkanda villagers usually support one another regardless of clique differences in the village.

An important source of cross-clique communication which leads to a weakening of clique loyalties and a lessening of the divisiveness of cliques is that of in-village marriage. The importance of in-law relationships among village men in cutting across clique lines has already been noted. Perhaps even more important is the role of the local girl who marries in the village and is at once a wife in one clique (and sib) and a daughter or sister in another. Seventeen per cent of all marriages (20 per cent of Rajput marriages, the relevant ones in this context) occur within the village. Such marriages always occur across sib lines, all sibs are connected by such affinal ties, and nearly half of all intracaste disputes occur across sib lines. Therefore, in-village marriage is an important factor in village cohesion which is absent in exogamous villages.

COUNCILS (*Panchayats*)

The *ad hoc* councils (panchayats) which were summoned in eight of the disputes discussed above, to arbitrate in cases concerning sex, property, and status, are the locus of formalized traditional community government insofar as this exists at all (cf. Newell, 1954). These councils act primarily in cases involving traditional rules of behavior.

Atkinson notes that in Garhwal:

> Panchayats for the settlement of social disputes have long been known . . . in the hills. . . . They are now usually assembled for the settling of cases of abduction or seduction of women, or offenses against caste. Witnesses are heard on each side, and the award given is usually submitted to. A fine is often imposed and a feast given to the assembled brethren at the expense of the offending party. (Atkinson, 1886, pp. 265 f.)

Panchayats are *ad hoc* rather than permanently constituted bodies. Their membership is recruited by invitations sent out by elders of the households involved to other interested households, who then send representatives. The membership varies with circumstances, but it is traditionally confined to the high castes, and women are never council members. In intervillage disputes councils are intervillage in composition, generally with representatives from a number of neighboring villages. In an intravillage dispute they may include representatives of neighboring villages if the matter is considered to have implications which extend beyond the village, such as a breach of proper intercaste relations. For purely local matters panchayats are made up of local men, many or few depending upon interest. A case of woman-stealing will usually involve a large meeting; a mutually desired divorce will involve a council of only three persons. Since councils consist of high-caste people, Rajputs dominate them in Sirkanda. However, except in purely internal matters within a high caste, both Brahmins and Rajputs are represented in most council meetings. Such councils decide those low-caste disputes which reach a council as well as high-caste disputes and disputes between high and low castes. Within the council, discussion and decision making are quite democratic, with the expected deference to age and generation. Wealth, ability to speak and reason convincingly, and an even temper are other qualities which lend influence to a man in these situations. Clique affiliation becomes important in that those aligned with small, unpopular, hostile groups are able to wield less influence than those affiliated with large, popular groups or those who are known to be objective or little committed to any particular group.

Councils or panchayats serve mainly to coördinate and express public opinion. Usually the members of the council are well aware in advance of the facts and opinions relevant to any dispute put before them. Their decision is often a means of making official that upon which there is already general agreement. Most often they attempt to come to a mutually agreeable compromise. In more serious cases, or those in which the parties are unable or unwilling to compromise, the council can impose sanctions under threat of physical punishment, social ostracism, or legal action. It may order a man to leave the village, to make payment or some other concession to another party, to make payment to the council itself, or to refrain from certain types of social interaction. Public humiliation or a public beating may also be inflicted, usually upon flagrant sexual offenders, primarily wife-stealers. In two such disputes among those analyzed here, the offender was led through the village wearing a garland of worn-out shoes around his neck—an extremely humiliating punishment because of the defiling nature of shoes as being made of cow leather. In one case the offender was then beaten with shoes.

There is little confidence in the objectivity of councils. They are thought (quite correctly) to be heavily influenced by caste, clique, and kin-group loyalties and to be easily swayed by money and favors. As a Rajput said, "Whoever treats the council to the best feast wins the case." Low-caste people, in particular, distrust councils, because in disputes among themselves as well as those between themselves and high castes they are often victimized by the councils. Stories of such cases are numerous. An example follows:

A blacksmith girl of a neighboring village was married to an old blacksmith man. She was unhappy with this arrangement and soon returned to her parents. From there she later eloped with a blacksmith boy. None of the parties involved were concerned enough to try to alter the situation. However, Rajputs of the village found out about it. They knew (according to blacksmiths) that the boy involved had Rs. 600 in his possession. They therefore called a council meeting of Rajputs and went to the girl's father and extracted from him, by threats and promises, a complaint in the case. They then caught the boy, brought him before the council, and fined him Rs. 600. The terrified boy paid this sum willingly, glad to escape without a beating. Two hundred rupees of the fine went to the girl's father, and the remainder was "swallowed up" by the council.

Even high-caste people are occasionally victimized in this way. A council meeting is always expensive for those whose dispute is to be decided, as they are obligated to feed and house the council members and must do it well or risk losing the case.

For these reasons cases are rarely referred to councils by the disputants. People prefer to carry on private feuds, as witness the fact that well over half the cases discussed here were kept on this level although they were of quite major importance. Councils usually intervene upon the insistence of people not parties to the dispute and usually when the dispute is such that it affects others not immediately involved in it. In extreme cases, and especially in the case of a beating, woman-selling, or illegal alienation of land, when it is felt that a law has been broken, people take their grievance to the courts—again an expensive undertaking where money counts above all else, but where the decisions are firm. Informants state that in earlier days the main resort in all cases was to gods, who would punish a person's rival or bring a favorable conclusion to a dispute in response to worship and sacrifice. As education and money have increased, courts and councils have been increasingly used, often in addition to appeal to the gods.

In these hills there are still relatively few civil and criminal cases, especially the latter. Litigation in the courts is a less important activity than it is in many plains areas, while crimes of theft and violence (other than occasional retributional beatings) are very rare. Murder occurs rarely—never in the history of Sirkanda, and four or five times in the history of Bhatbair. The cases in Bhatbair were apparently carefully planned retributional killings. In each case the victim was widely known as a scoundrel. Those who had grievances against him caught him, tied him up, told him their intent and the reasons for it, and then methodically beat him to death. Less severe beatings are also sometimes administered in this way.

Suicide is virtually unknown in this area. In the past a woman occasionally immolated herself on her husband's funeral pyre. Only one such case is known for Sirkanda. Rape has never occurred in Sirkanda; villagers have difficulty imagining it in the Pahari context. Woman-selling, illegal sale of liquor, and illegal use of government forest land are the most common offenses, and they are not offenses in Pahari customary law.

LEADERSHIP AND INFLUENCE

Outside the family, in which the eldest active male is the recognized authority, there is no generally recognized leadership in the village beyond that of elder, landowning males. Individuals hold power in the village primarily to the extent that they are influential as a result of personal qualities in important cliques, or are members (especially household heads) of large and wealthy families. Wealth, verbal ability, an even temper, modesty, and simple living are virtues which win a man respect. But no man is in a position to tell others outside his family what to do. Villagers found it hard to conceive of an influential leader, and seemed opposed to the notion. They recognized a former condition when a "sayana" held rights to collect taxes and as superior "landlord" had control over those on his lands. But since all high castes now own land, they feel that none should have power over others. Their attitude parallels that reported by Baden-Powell (1892, I, p. 153), who noted the absence of a headman in "landlord" villages where "the proprietary families were too jealous of the equal rights to allow of any degree of authority residing in one head." Sirkanda villagers do not pay much attention to the official headman (council president), nor is the position sought after. They resent the powers officially invested in this office. They neither want them for themselves, nor will they grant them to others. One man summarized:

Here all [high-caste] men are the same. They do what they want without regard for others. They decide on the basis of what is best for them. If several people agree, that is good, but it will not lead others to agree unless they come independently to the same conclusion. Every man does what is best for his household without regard for what others think or want to do.

This does not mean that power and influence are evenly distributed, but it does mean that they are ideally so and that in reality they will approximate this ideal state.

At one time Sirkanda lands were included under those granted by the Raja to a Brahmin of Kanda, as discussed previously. This man, as "sayana," collected taxes and theoretically had some control over those who occupied his lands. The term "sayana" still carries strong connotations of status and power among people of the area. The first remembered formalized village government in Sirkanda was that of the hereditary mukhia or keeper of the peace, recognized by the British. He decided petty local disputes and transgressions brought before him and referred more important cases to a council of five mukhias in the vicinity. It was his responsibility to serve as the administrative link between the British government and the villagers. Above him were the courts and the district government.

The village *lambardār* or appointed tax collector was also a man of influence under the British and was considered to be a village leader much like the mukhia. Apparently the lambardar is a more recent innovation in this village.

Today there is only one paid government employee who is normally a villager. He is the village *chaukīdār* or watchman. His duties are to report births and deaths in the village and to act as a government messenger when needed. In this area it is a position of little importance and no prestige. The man who fills this position for Sirkanda and several surrounding villages is a resident of Chamba, a nearby village. He is rarely seen in Sirkanda and is dependent upon the Sirkanda village president for the information he is required to supply to the government.

FORMAL VILLAGE GOVERNMENT TODAY

Today formal village government is in the hands of the village council as specified in the U. P. Panchayat Raj Act of 1947 and as amended thereafter (Dwivedi, 1957). According to this act, a village or group of villages is under the jurisdiction of a "village government" or assembly (*Gāõn Sabhā*), consisting of all sane adults (that is, people 21 years of age or over) within the area for which it is established. Presiding over this body is a president (*pradhān*) elected from among the membership for a three-year term of office, and a vice-president (*up-pradhān*) elected for a one-year period. This body is supposed to hold two annual meetings as well as others upon request of the membership.

From among its members the village assembly elects a "village council" (*Gãõn Panchāyat*) to function as an executive committee. This, too, is presided over by the village president and vice-president. Membership in this body is for the same period as the president's term in office (now three years). The powers, duties, and functions of village councils are wide, covering all aspects of village welfare, upkeep, and control and serving as the local agency for higher governmental authority as sanctioned by that authority. Moreover, it is empowered to impose taxes and hold property. It is required to report to the village assembly at that body's semiannual meeting.

In Sirkanda these provisions are unknown to many villagers and are imperfectly understood by those who know of them. The village assembly is thought by some to consist only of men, and in practice this is apparently the case. It did not meet in 1957–1958, nor had it met since the election of the village council two years earlier. A meeting was called by the teacher and village level worker to celebrate Republic Day in 1958, but despite advance publicity, not a single individual appeared at the appointed hour. This body is significant in village government in Sirkanda only in that it is the electoral body for the council. The area which is included with Sirkanda in a common village government includes four other, smaller villages, from 1½ to 8 trail miles from Sirkanda. They have little in common beyond the fact that they are the only villages in a large, relatively unpopulated geographic area which the government has chosen, for administrative purposes, to consider a unity. Two of the villages are trading centers on the Mussoorie-Tehri trail; one (Suakholi) is very active; the other is virtually deserted. The other two villages are similar to Sirkanda. The local governmental seat for this area is Sirkanda.

The village council is composed of 16 members at present. Eleven of these are from Sirkanda (including one low-caste man in a seat reserved for "scheduled castes"); two are from the largest of the other villages, a trading center; and one is from each of the other three villages. The president and vice-president are Sirkanda men, though they need not be. All are Rajputs except for the occupant of the reserved scheduled-caste seat, a blacksmith, and a Vaishya merchant from the trading center included in this area.

This system of village government was established in Sirkanda in 1951 when Sirkanda was joined, for administrative purposes, with five other villages in the immediate vicinity, all with common interests and problems. At that time a widely respected Sirkanda Rajput was elected president (for the then-prescribed five-year term) without opposition. At the end of his term, in 1956, the laws had been changed so that the term was reduced to three years and the area had been redivided administratively in its present unrealistic manner—apparently partly to reduce the population included under one village government. At that time the former president declined to run again and gave his approval to another man in the village—the wealthiest Sirkanda villager, but a man well known for his modesty, simplicity, and hard work, and one unaligned with any antagonistic clique (he is in clique H in figure 5; his predecessor was in clique FG). Against him ran the most generally disliked villager (head of clique B1), a man who apparently wanted the power and did not realize his own unpopularity. Needless to say, the latter lost the election, receiving only a few votes from some of his sib-fellows and apparently none from other sibs or castes or the other three major cliques in his own sib.

It was difficult to get enough candidates for the village council; there was, therefore, no competition. Some villagers on the village council are under the impression that the president of the village helps select the candidates for the council and that he must approve them before they take office. They evidently acquired this idea because, in the elections held thus far, the village president has had to use his influence to get people to accept nomination for that office. A factor which has discouraged candidates is that each had to pay a fee of Rs. 6 before assuming office. This appears to be the fee for membership in the Congress party, which many villagers evidently assumed to be a prerequisite to election. On this point there is confusion, as some villagers claim to have had to pay Rs. 12, Rs. 6 for nomination and 6 to become Congress members. In any case, there are now 17 villagers who joined the Congress party at the time of elections, including those who became council members and a few others. They paid Rs. 6 each to become members, while the council president reportedly had to pay Rs. 12. The villagers joined the Congress party, according to one of their number, under the impression that they would thereupon become members of a "ruling group"—the power elite of Sirkanda. They apparently gained this idea from government officials who helped set up the village government and who recruited members. One man remarked ruefully, "If I had spent that money on ghee, I could have been big and strong by now; this way it was wasted."

The defeated candidate for president of the council refused to join the Congress party, and so the election was officially a Congress party victory—grass-roots support for the party. In fact, no villager understands the Congress party or even the significance of party affiliation. Moreover, to a man, the village is opposed to the present (Congress) government of India and to virtually all its policies, as will be made clear below. Worst of all, from the party's point of view, the villagers are opposed to Independence.

VILLAGE GOVERNMENT IN ACTION

The village council of Sirkanda met once during 1957–1958, in a meeting called by the village level worker, a government employee stationed in the village. This meeting was announced well in advance and was scheduled to coincide with the annual visit of the government tax collector and the even rarer presence of the village accountant, with both of whom all landholders had to deal. The village level worker was motivated to call the meeting primarily because it was time for him to turn in certain reports, but it was announced as a meeting to discuss village improvements. No agenda was circulated in advance. The meeting was held in the open near the two village shops and beside the trail to the village water supply—a pleasant, convenient, and conspicuous location, with the shops serving as comfortable retreats for bored participants and observers. Even in these favorable circumstances attendance was poor. Most council members did their business with the government officials and left. Most of those who attended the meeting did so out of idle curiosity, drifting in as they felt inclined and away again as they tired of joining their colleagues in peering through the village accountant's spectacles, reading the tax collector's book of blank receipts, stamping one another with the official panchayat seal, gossiping with their neighbors, or making sarcastic remarks about the business of the meeting.

Three of the five outside members attended the meeting, having been summoned to Sirkanda for that purpose and having nothing else to do while there. Four Sirkanda members attended throughout most of the meeting and were a fairly attentive, if passive, group. Four others were there sporadically, and four or five nonmembers participated occasionally. One of the nonmembers was among the eight who signed the minutes—an official act which was the highlight of the meeting. Two members, including the vice-president, stopped by for this purpose only, having heard none of the prior business, and joined eagerly in the signing of the minutes (recorded by the village level worker) without having read them. In addition an occasional member and various nonmembers of all ages and both sexes stopped briefly by on their way to or from the water source, joining curious children and livestock to hear or see what might occur. Following is an account of the meeting as recorded by the author:

The tax collector and village accountant had been doing their business in one of the village shops beginning at about 10 A.M.

At 2:30 P.M. the village president and the village level worker [VLW] arrived with their record books and a tarpaulin and went to a spot near the shops to prepare for the meeting. The VLW sat down and wrote out an agenda of the meeting, which should have been circulated to members in advance. It read as follows:

All members of the Gram Panchayat, Sirkanda, are informed hereby that a meeting of the Panchayat is to take place on Sunday [in reality it was Monday], the twenty-third of December, 1957, at Sirkanda School, at 2 P.M. All members are requested to be present at that time. The following items will be considered by the members:

1. Consideration of last meeting's proceedings.
2. Consideration of doing the remaining work to improve the drinking water supply.
3. Consideration of collection of panchayat tax in arrears and of future tax.
4. Consideration of voluntary labor in the village.
5. Consideration of opening a night school for adults.
6. Consideration of sending five people to village training camp.
7. Consideration of starting a Village Credit Coöperative Society in Sirkanda.

After the above agenda had been written, the VLW asked the president to call the council members and begin the meeting. This was done and seven people came and sat for the meeting—four Sirkanda members, three outside members, and one nonmember. One additional member, who had been paying his tax, signed the agenda to indicate his presence but left at once with the excuse that he had to arrange for the tax collector's lunch. The village shopkeeper, who was within earshot, participated occasionally in discussions.

The VLW started the meeting by reading the minutes of the last meeting, over one year previous.

Then the second item on the agenda, concerning the drinking water supply, was discussed. The VLW asked the president what he thought should be done. The latter told him to request the Block Development Officer to send an overseer to Sirkanda to examine the problem and advise them how to solve it.

The third item on the agenda was read by the VLW to the members. The tax arrears were, for every household in the village, R. 1 per year from 1949 through 1955. The VLW read an official circular which said that a Tax Collection Week should be observed by every panchayat for which the president should appoint a committee of five persons and go from house to house with them to collect the tax arrears. When the president heard this, he said it was impossible. First, no one would go with him as a committee member to collect the tax. Second, even if someone would go with him, no one would pay the tax. The president said, and others agreed, that the government should send an official to collect the tax.

At this point a young village man on his way for water stopped by to hear what the discussion was about. When the president saw him, he told the VLW that he would ask this man to pay the tax. Everyone thought that the man would refuse to pay and thus they would be proved correct. But, to everyone's surprise, the man took out a ten-rupee note, threw it before the president, and said, "Now what do you think of me!" Everyone laughed. A receipt for his Rs. 6 and the change were returned to him, and he went on his way. This incident embarrassed the members, and the VLW immediately started putting down the names of the committee members—all the men present except two of the outside members.

The fourth item, consideration of voluntary labor in the village, was taken up. The VLW suggested that the villagers should repair the trail from Sirkanda to the valley (five miles) and should work for one week, beginning the first of January. Members suggested repairing local trails, but had difficulty deciding which to repair. Objection to repairing the trail to the valley was based on the fact that it is used by people of other villages who would thus be benefiting from the labor of Sirkanda without contributing to it. Members also complained that once before they had done voluntary labor on trails with the understanding that they would be paid for it and, although they worked hard, no payment was forthcoming. The VLW pointed out that this was probably a trick some official played on them to get them to work and, in any event, they should be satisfied with the achievement and not demand money. The members still objected. They claimed that the residents of a neighboring village got money for working on their own village trail once. Finally they agreed to work on two short trails used only by Sirkanda villagers (and rarely by them) for one week, starting in three days.

The fifth item, opening of a night school, was then read by the VLW. Everyone said that it was useless to have a night school, since no one would attend it. It had been tried by a teacher here once and failed. The matter was dropped.

The VLW then read the sixth item. It concerned sending five villagers to a training session on better methods of farming to be held in Sirkanda at some future date. This was met with considerable incredulity and banter. When one member, who had retired to a nearby shop for tea, was hailed and told that he would be sent to school to learn to farm, he replied that he had done that every day of his life. It was suggested that the blacksmith be sent. He objected that he had never held a plow in his life and owned not a foot of land. Finally five people, including one not present, were put down for this program.

Next the VLW turned to a discussion of work to be done according to the government's second five-year plan for the village. According to that plan, he said, the village was supposed to construct a community center during the year. He described the advantages and uses of such a building: meetings could be held indoors; it could be used for housing visitors; it could be used at weddings; the village would be entitled to a free public radio to be placed in it. At this point a member quipped that the blacksmith (one of the most avid listeners to the anthropologist's radio) would then not need to buy a radio. This brought laughter. The VLW pointed out that the government would give the village Rs. 800 for the community center, an amount constituting 40 per cent of the total cost of such a building, according to estimates submitted by this panchayat a few years before. Members requested the VLW to get them Rs. 1000 and they would construct the building with that money alone and spend nothing of their own. The VLW insisted that it would not be difficult to raise the money in the village. The members were dubious. One man commented, "If people were like that [willing to donate labor and money], would the water supply now be in bad condition, and would the village trails be so rough?" Someone asked how much the anthropologist would contribute. I replied, "As much voluntary labor as anyone else gives," a response which evoked considerable merriment. Finally the president said he would give Rs. 50. Another man said he would contribute only if the center were to be constructed in the central settlement area where it could be useful at times of marriages. An argument developed as to the best location, the local shopkeeper coming out and arguing that it should be outside the main village in view of the fact that strangers might use it sometimes. [It later developed that he had a vested interest in this suggestion. He hoped to get the panchayat to buy the other shop as a community center, thus eliminating his business competition.] Nothing could be agreed upon, and the matter was postponed to a future meeting.

Next a letter from the schoolteacher was read, stating that according to Education Department rules all children between the ages of 6 and 12 should be in school. It urged all villagers to comply with this rule. The president turned to one member and said, "Why isn't your son in school?" The reply was, "Those rules are meant for children that don't have anything else to do and spend their time idly at home; my boy herds cattle." One villager supported the teacher's letter, saying, "They didn't have such facilities in this village when we were young, so here we are signing these registers with our thumbprints. We should send the children to school so that they will be able to do better than we do."

The next matter was an announcement by the VLW that the council owed Rs. 12.50 to the Block Development Office. The amount was made up of Rs. 10 as contribution for an Extension Exhibition to be held in a town in the valley, Rs. 2 for some sort of training school held there, and half a rupee for a booklet on village councils. The president said it would be paid from funds on hand, though no one knew anything about these matters.

Next the economic coöperative supervisor, who had joined the meeting, asked the VLW to take up the seventh item on the agenda: formation of a credit coöperative society in Sirkanda. This the VLW did, explaining the advantages of such a society and of coöperatives in general. He told his listeners that a society had already been registered for Sirkanda on the basis of work done by a former government employee who had visited this area and had secured their approval of such a plan. He urged them to buy shares. He read the names of those who had been recorded by the previous officer as being interested. No one wanted to buy. Finally two shares each were recorded in the names of the president and another man, and one share each in the names of the shopkeeper and the blacksmith, over the latter's loud protests of insolvency. No payments were made on these shares. A villager who was not present was listed as president of the coöperative, and one of those present was designated its treasurer. None of the group showed any interest at all in this item.

The VLW then passed the register around for signatures, the last official act of the meeting. Two additional members had come for this event, and two of the original seven had left, and so a total of seven members and one nonmember signed. The meeting was over at 5 P.M.

As the members left, the VLW made a plea for the purchase of National Savings Certificates as part of the government's small savings program. By the time he finished he was talking to the anthropologist and his interpreter only, all others having departed.

Not one of the suggestions or decisions for positive action coming out of this meeting was ever acted upon. The lack of success of this meeting, as of village self-government and government programs in general in this area, lies in part in the fact that it did not contain much of real interest to villagers. Of the six items proposed for action, only item 2, having to do with the water supply, was of any real interest to members. Of four additional subjects discussed, only one, that concerning the community center, was of interest to villagers. Even more important is the uniformly negative attitude of villagers toward the government and everything associated with it, including the village level worker who called the meeting, the council itself, and every item on the agenda. This attitude and related matters are discussed in the following chapter.

In summary, the meeting was an utter failure at accomplishing its ostensible purpose—that of contributing to village uplift and improvement in conformance with the goals of the government's second five-year plan. In accomplishing immediate ends, which were evidently also the ultimate ends of those who called it, it was an eminent success. Every item of business was completed with some kind of action recorded or with appropriately filled-in lists of names, volunteers, or pledges of funds. It was a paper success and from the point of view of the village level worker and council president, that meant a real success. From the point of view of the villagers, it was a good meeting too because it satisfied the officials with a minimum of interference in village affairs. Only the schoolteacher considered it a farce and a failure, accurately predicting that nothing would come of any of the discussions held or decisions made. Not one of the decisions to act on matters raised at the council meeting was followed through as planned. Discussion of this phase appears on pp. 319–320. Many villagers stayed away from the meeting, convinced that it would be a meaningless waste of time, thus helping fulfill their own prophecy. The meeting was a typical example of reactions to government-sponsored local self-government and other programs in this area. In fact, there are villages in Bhatbair which are considerably more hostile to such programs than is Sirkanda—villages in which the meeting would, in all probability, have been boycotted entirely.

Some indication of the significance of the ineffectiveness of village self-government such as that reported here and elsewhere can be derived from an examination of the attitude of the government of India toward village government:

> The Planning Commission clearly acknowledges that rural progress depends entirely on the existence of an active village organization which can bring all the people, including those at the bottom of the social and economic ladder, into common programs and activities, using assistance from the Government, and their own contributions in labor, cash and kind.
>
> Further, India feels keenly that the nation's strength as a democracy depends to a most important degree on building, in hundreds of thousands of villages, effective local governments through which the people can, as responsible citizens, plan and participate in their own and the nation's progress. (Planning Commission, 1958, p. 123)

JUDICIAL COUNCIL

Above the village government is a body locally known as "judicial council" (adalat panchayat, now officially known as Nyaya Panchayat). This has jurisdiction over a number of villages. In this area one judicial council has jurisdiction over most of Bhatbair and a few neighboring villages. The functions of this council are unknown to most villagers. Many think that when its name is used the speaker is referring to the former constituency of the village council. The judicial council is made up of a total of five individuals chosen from among five (or fewer) individuals elected by each village assembly within its jurisdiction. Those elected may not also be members of a village council. The composition of the judicial council varies on a rotating basis with each meeting. This council is presided over by a headman from among its membership. One Sirkanda man has been headman of this council, and two Sirkanda men are currently members. This council has the benefit of a petty government official, the "panchayat secretary," to advise it, keep records, and so on. Five members are supposed to meet weekly at its headquarters, a good-sized village on the edge of the valley. In reality, it meets relatively infrequently because it has not enough business to warrant such frequent meetings. It has wide judicial powers in deciding disputes and breaches of law which would otherwise have to go into the law courts, or which have been referred down to it by courts of law. It is legally defined as a "court" and its members are "judges." It can fine those who appear before it, or refer their cases to higher courts. It is, therefore, a potentially powerful body. In practice it is avoided when possible by those with grievances because of their fear of the nonobjectivity of its decisions. One villager commented:

It has never solved a single case since it began. The members are mostly dishonest and unscrupulous, and any who aren't are in an ineffectual minority. They listen to the man who feeds them well or does them favors. They are not partial to caste so much as to favors. In this respect they are just like all other panchayats. Panchayats would be all right if they were honestly and impartially run, but they never are.

9 THE OUTSIDE WORLD: URBAN CONTACTS AND GOVERNMENT PROGRAMS

The Pahari village is always incomplete in the goods, services, and personnel necessary to its functioning. These are accessible, to a great extent, within a larger surrounding area which includes several villages and is characterized by cultural unity, frequent social interaction, and economic and ritual interdependence. We have seen in previous chapters that for Sirkanda this unit comprises the surrounding hill area (Bhatbair and a corresponding area to the east) within a four-air-mile or eight-trail-mile radius, a half-day's journey (see map 2). This area contains some 60 villages and settlements and around 5,000 people. It is the area within which all the castes and occupational specialists necessary to the economy are found. It is, therefore, the area over which artisans move to perform their duties and collect their payments. In it are also merchants who serve as important sources of goods from the outside and as markets for local goods. All Sirkanda lands are found in this area. Within the area all the necessary religious practitioners are to be found—Brahmins, ceremonial cooks, shamans, pujaris, exorcists, rope-sliders. It is the area within which most (83 per cent) Sirkanda marriages take place, and therefore within which consanguineal and affinal kin ties are concentrated. As a result it is the largest area within which visiting frequently occurs. It is the maximal area over which most women have traveled in their lives. Within this area castes which may number only one or a few families in a village find caste-fellows for ritual participation and moral support. In this area are found not only the formal and informal councils for local self-government and the judicial councils, but the local representatives of the state and national governments—the teachers, village level workers, economic coöperative supervisors, and forestry officers. Into this area come the land records officers, tax collectors, police, and others with whom villagers must deal. In the past local officials such as the mukhia, lambardar, and sayana had their jurisdiction within this area.

In short, while the village is a real, functional unit, the immediate culture area—that which can be reached in half a day—is the more nearly self-sufficient unit. Every village within this area relies upon other villages for many of the necessary elements of village life. It is this area within which we find most of the "extensions" of the village as discussed by Opler (1956). Here is found the "rural cosmopolitanism" among villages mentioned by Lewis (1958, p. 320). In relation to the outside there is, among the villages in this area, a corresponding "rural isolationism."

However, even this immediate cultural area is not isolated nor independent. It is in constant contact with similar neighboring areas of the hills. In fact, it is an area primarily from the point of view of those villages toward its center. Villages on the peripheries are seen by their residents as the centers of other, overlapping areas, just as they are the centers of other, overlapping marriage networks unless important cultural boundaries hem them in. Moreover, such areas, including the one surrounding Sirkanda, are in constant contact with the valley and especially with urban centers such as Dehra Dun and the hill town of Mussoorie. Many goods and services must come to these hill areas directly or indirectly from outside. Villagers often go outside to obtain goods and services rather than obtaining them through intermediaries. Sometimes, as in the licensing of firearms, they must go outside. Authority over the people of the area rests ultimately with outside law and outside government located in Dehra Dun and Mussoorie. Higher education, certain religious activities, and some kinds of diversion are available only outside the area. People who live within the area feel the effects of the outside world in the presence of outsiders in their villages, in communication with outsiders, and in their own trips to the outside.

LEVELS OF IDENTIFICATION

In discussing outside contacts it is necessary to define the "outside," for several levels of contact and identification are pertinent. Subgroups within the community—the family, sib, clan, caste, and village —have already been discussed at some length, and these are fundamental units of individual identification and orientation. In this chapter the discussion will be in broader terms. Bhatbair (including the adjoining area in Tehri Garhwal) will be considered to be the "inside" as distinguished from the "outside" world. It is the unit within which

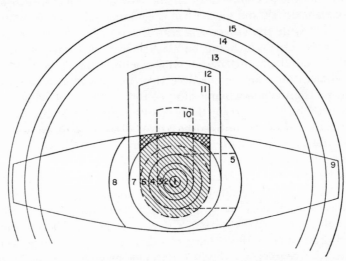

Fig. 6. Levels of identification and interaction, showing relative inclusiveness of individual's membership-identification groups. Significant groups are enclosed within numbered areas. Broken lines indicate less clearly delineated groups.

Key:
1. Ego
2. Nuclear family
3. Extended family (household)
4. Lineage (or minimal lineage)
5. Kindred (affinal kin follow a pattern similar to that of kindred but not coextensive with it)
6. Maximal lineage (where applicable)

7. Sib
8. Caste as a marriage network
9. Caste as a named group
10. Clique
11. Village
12. Bhatbair and vicinity
13. Garhwal
14. Pahari area
15. India

Clan is indicated by diagonal hatchures. Wives (and other local affiliates) of ego's sib are indicated by cross hatchures within the clan but outside the sib.

Note that cliques (10) do not divide extended families (3) nor do they extend out of the village (11), but they do divide lineage (4), kindred (5), maximal lineage (6), sib (7), and caste (8 and 9). Caste as a marriage network (8) includes all kin (1–7), and excludes some clique, village, and Bhatbair people (10–12).

Sirkanda residents feel entirely at home. Beyond it they are, to varying degrees, "outside"—in alien territory, among people different from
themselves.

Nearest to the residents of Bhatbair, in terms of cultural distance,
are the residents of adjacent Pahari areas to the east—people who speak
essentially the same dialect, dress in much the same way, share many
of the same beliefs and values. These are areas from which marriage
partners are occasionally obtained, in which distant relatives live, to
which local people are sometimes invited for ritual observances and
fairs. These are the areas to which Sirkanda people trace their own
ancestry. Rivalry and animosities occasionally crop up, as when a
council meeting was held to decide a dispute arising out of insults
exchanged between two men of the same caste, one from Bhatbair and
one from an area to the east. Each area supported its man, and the
council had wide representation from villages in each area. More
commonly, good-natured insults and banter are exchanged between the
residents of these areas. Bhatbair people used to call their neighbors in
Tehri Garhwal "slaves" because they were under the Raja's absolute
power. Now the shoe is on the other foot and the taunting goes the
other way, as the former subjects of the Raja allegedly have more
forest and land at their disposal.

More significant differences and loyalties are those associated with
more prominent cultural boundaries. The residents of Jaunpur, a hill
area north of Bhatbair (and not identical in extent to the area which
the government designates by this term), dress somewhat differently,
build houses in a slightly different style, and in general bear cultural
differences noticeable to both groups. Mutual suspicion becomes
prominent at this level. Jaunpur women are thought to be given to
witchcraft by people in Bhatbair, and, although wives are occasionally
obtained or given across this boundary, it is done with some trepidation.

Where linguistic and social traits are significantly different and distances are too great to permit accurate appraisal of the residents of
two areas, feelings are even stronger. The polyandrous people of
Jaunsar-Bawar, though recognized as fellow Paharis, are considered
immoral, treacherous, and given to evil magic and witchcraft. Wives
are not exchanged with them, travel to the area is avoided, and most
information about them is in the nature of inaccurate gossip. Residents
of a Pahari area some distance to the southeast are thought of in a
somewhat similar light. At this level dialectal differences become important. Jokes are frequently told which ridicule the alien dialect.
One probably apocryphal story concerns a man of Bhatbair who
allegedly went to a village to the southeast to see about making marriage arrangements for his nephew:

In the alien village he overheard the brother of the prospective bride make a statement to his mother which, in the dialect of that region, meant "The buffalo is ready to be milked," but to the visitor it sounded like, "I am ready to have sexual intercourse." The mother replied, "Then untie the calf," which in the visitor's dialect meant, "Then untie your loincloth." Shocked and frightened to hear a man speak in this unseemly fashion to his mother and to receive such a reply from her, the visitor ran out of the village, headed for home. The dismayed family shouted after him, "Stay, for tomorrow we will kill a goat to feast on," which only served to accelerate his departure, as in his dialect it meant, "Stay, for tomorrow we will engage in sodomy."

Despite differences in beliefs and attitudes with distance, there is recognition of cultural similarities among Paharis. A Pahari is a more congenial stranger than is a non-Pahari; he is more easily understood and can be more readily placed in terms of the relatively closed social system indigenous to this area. Common language, culture, and history result in a kind of incipient Pahari group consciousness. The fact that Paharis are considered and treated as a group by non-Paharis may also be a factor. So far this consciousness is largely in negative terms at the broader levels; the differences between Paharis and non-Paharis are more important than the similarities and common interests among Paharis. However, there is some agitation for a separate hill state in Pahari regions to the west. Among educated Paharis of Garhwal and Tehri Garhwal there is considerable pride of origin, with local societies and even publications in some urban areas stressing the heritage of Garhwal.

Paharis distinguish themselves terminologically from plains and valley people who are called *dēsī* (native). Foreigners are even farther removed and are called *pardēsī* (foreign). Representatives of either group are suspect, threatening, and somewhat baffling to Paharis. In an isolated area which stresses kin, caste, and community affiliation they are simply outside the system. To fit them into it is usually an impossible task; hence the traditional unfriendliness with which Paharis greet strangers. The usual reaction to them is avoidance. Inevitable contacts with them are kept as short and impersonal as possible. Plains people are, of course, better known and better understood than foreigners, but in their presence Paharis feel ill at ease. The plains person is considered to be sophisticated and well-off, to have a superiority complex, and to be arrogant, untrustworthy, avaricious, and immoral. These attitudes are not born of recent contacts. In 1828 Traill (1828, pp. 217 f.) noted that "all mountaineers unite in an excessive distrust of the natives of the low country, whom they regard as a race of swindlers and extortioners. . . ." One present-day Pahari who had been to Delhi commented, "I don't like Delhi or any of those places. There are too many people there and they make fun of us. I like Dehra Dun where you can always see lots of Paharis around." Sirkanda people feel that they can size up a Pahari, but a plains person or a foreigner is an unknown quantity: "You can't tell how much water they're standing in."

Concerning Europeans there are conflicting stereotypes. One set of stereotypes, based upon observation and stories of British soldiers, views them as immoral scoundrels. Another, based upon the reputation of the British civil servants, views them as stern, cold, and distant but honest and fair. A third, based upon closer observation of individuals (customers for milk, occasional hunters and hikers), views them as well-meaning but odd. One villager commented,

Englishmen [that is, "white people"] are very strange. They always coöperate with one another and never dispute among themselves, but their anger is easily aroused. Their customs are strange. If one of them comes to a village he does not enter it and ask for a place to stay, but pitches his tent alone, outside the village. They do not care what their food tastes like; they use no spices but just put a pinch of salt on it and gobble it up. They eat mostly from cans. They never take off their shoes—even if one were going to climb a tree he would do it with his shoes on. They also have immoral sexual customs.

It is usually assumed that foreigners (other than hunters) who come to the mountains are missionaries, government officials, or spies. All of these pose a threat. One foreigner came through the village several years ago riding a horse and carrying a pistol. He stopped for tea and then passed on. He is assumed to this day to have been a spy. Aside from occasional military personnel, he is said to have been the only foreigner to come to Sirkanda.

THE NON-PAHARI WORLD

The non-Pahari world impinges upon Sirkanda and the surrounding villages in many ways. Although the degree to which it does so has apparently increased since Independence, such contacts are not new. From earliest times traders, ascetics, pilgrims, and immigrants have traveled from the plains to this area. Tibetans or Bhotiyas have come from the high country to the north to pasture their sheep in the winter. There has been outside authority—the Garhwal Raja, the Nepalese, the British, the "Congress government." This authority has been represented to villagers largely by its soldiers, police, and tax collectors.

The British found the hills especially useful as a place for summer rest areas, military cantonments, encampments, and maneuvers. They established the famous "hill stations," such as Simla, Mussoorie, Naini Tal, Darjeeling, and military cantonments, such as Chakrata and Ranikhet. The "Tommy" (British soldier) gained the same reputation for arrogance and immorality that he gained over most of India and that soldiers have had from time immemorial among the civilian populations near which they have lived.

Before the beginning of World War I a small summer rest camp was set up by the army a little over a mile from Sirkanda. There small contingents of Nepalese troops and their British officers came during the hot season. Although they were rigidly segregated from all villagers except the family which sold them milk, and had no conflicts with the villagers, their presence was felt. The army bought village land, was a customer for village milk, and its presence restricted the movement of villagers, especially women, in the vicinity of the camp.

World War I found many Garhwalis, including a few from Bhatbair and one from Sirkanda, enlisting in the Garhwal Rifles to fight for the British. Sirkanda people still sing the song and proudly recount the tale of a Garhwali hero who took command of his unit when all its officers had been killed and led it to victory in a crucial battle. His widow resides in her husband's village on a comfortable pension from the government, and this too is a point of pride among Paharis of the region.

In the 1920's several Sirkanda boys attended school in nearby villages of the valley, two or three reaching the eighth class. They were the first from this area to be educated. When the army abandoned the summer encampment near Sirkanda in the early 1930's, the resulting intravillage court case over ownership of the land lasted nine years. It necessitated extended trips by several villagers to courts as far away as Allahabad. During this period a merchant from the valley was called in to run a competing shop in the village, and he has remained to the present.

Throughout these times adult male villagers occasionally went on pilgrimages to the shrines of the high Himalayas, to Hardwar or to distant Gaya in Bihar. Boys and young men, then as now, occasionally left home to seek adventure in the plains, usually returning after a few months.

World War II brought further army recruitment, with two Sirkanda men among half a dozen Bhatbair volunteers. The Sirkanda volunteers saw much of northern India in their service but did not go outside India.

Independence affected Sirkanda relatively slightly. The partition of India which accompanied it brought bands of fleeing Muslims and pursuing Hindus through these hills, but for the most part Sirkanda was not involved. Bhatbair residents refused sanctuary to Muslims of the valley out of fear of the marauding Sikhs who were pursuing them. However, they withheld information from the Sikhs about Muslim movements and helped the Bhatbair Muslim family to remain unmolested. In nearby Pahari areas fleeing Muslims were looted and occasionally killed as they passed. One Sirkanda family became wealthy overnight from money apparently looted from a Muslim chan left in their care.

After Independence the influence of the government of India was felt increasingly. Laws regarding use of forest lands were altered and, worse yet, enforced. A school was built in Sirkanda and various government programs had their effects locally, as will be discussed below. Government representatives in the village have become an increasingly familiar sight since Independence. A schoolteacher lives in the village most of the year; two other officers are there much of the time. Government survey parties on training exercises have often camped near the village during the hot season, providing a source of outside companionship for some of the younger men. The postal service now reaches Sirkanda with a postman coming through about once every two months, while letters can be mailed whenever a villager or passer-by goes to the valley.

Throughout this time outside markets have increased in importance. Milk has long been a cash product to be sold in Dehra Dun, Mussoorie, and the smaller, intermediate markets such as Nagal, Rajpur, Sahas Dhara, and Suakholi. Mussoorie has been a market for over 100 years, Dehra Dun for longer than that. Rajpur was a major market for 80 years until a motor road was built to Mussoorie in 1930 and Rajpur ceased to be an important way station en route to Mussoorie. As better trails have been built in the Bhatbair region and beyond (beginning with the pack trail past Sirkanda built by the Tehri Garhwal Raja in 1914), and as horses and mules have been acquired, agricultural products have been sold with increasing frequency. Potatoes have become an important cash crop. At the same time, more goods from the outside have come into the village—cloth and clothing, utensils and tools, corrugated iron roofing, tea, cigarettes, and so on. Trips to the valley and Mussoorie for trade have become commonplace. Dehra Dun has been increasingly frequented by villagers on official business re-

lating to the government. Dehra Dun and Mussoorie have the added
attraction of a full range of entertainment facilities.

An 85-year-old man commented:

In the old days a man wore a loincloth and had a blanket for a wrap.
Now everyone has to have a wardrobe of three coats, three shirts, three
pajamas, and shoes and many other things. We used to go to town once a
year, in a group, to buy staples, and we came home as soon as we were
through. Now someone goes almost every week. They go alone and don't
even tell others they're going. Sometimes they stay for a day or two and
waste money on the cinema or prostitutes. In my day we didn't have time,
money, nor inclination for such things.

Occasionally a Vedic doctor is consulted in town, and once a valuable horse was taken to the government veterinary. The number of
boys going to school in town has increased. Two young Sirkanda men
have taken jobs near Delhi, but their families remain in the village.
Two men from a Pahari village nearer Dehra Dun have taken jobs
in Dehra Dun, but they continue to live in their village. In all this
time no one from Bhatbair has moved permanently into Dehra Dun
or Mussoorie. When villagers go to Dehra Dun they have to stay overnight with the wholesalers to whom they sell their products, or in a
temple compound which is open to all. In Mussoorie they usually
return to chans before nightfall. There are no relatives or fellow
villagers in either place to afford them a place to stay.

Limestone quarrying operations have penetrated to the foot of the
hills, so that trucks and workers operate within five miles of Sirkanda
and are pushing farther constantly. Tourists and worshipers come increasingly to the temple and springs at Sahas Dhara five miles away
now that a dirt road enables cars to reach it. Travel to Dehra Dun is
facilitated by regular and inexpensive bus service from Rajpur to
Dehra Dun, cutting the 16-mile walk from Sirkanda to about 9 miles.
The Mussoorie-Tehri trail is being prepared for bus service so that
before many years have passed the walk to Mussoorie will be cut from
16 to 8 miles.

Therefore, outside contacts have been increasing. In view of the
changes that have come about over a long period, it is perhaps surprising that Sirkanda has not been influenced more than it has by
these contacts. A Rajput householder with an eighth-grade education
commented:

The reason most people here are so backward is that they are uneducated
and they have never been outside and gotten new ideas. You have to go
outside to learn to improve yourself. The trouble with this village is that

people aren't educated—look how few children attend school. The village is accessible enough to town that it should have improved but it hasn't, while some other Pahari areas have improved greatly. Even some government officers are Paharis, but none come from around here. Here people don't know enough to be able to improve.

Not all villagers share this attitude toward the outside. Some see it as a contaminating influence. One man remarked:

Contact with towns has been bad for Pahari villages. Farther up in the hills the people are better off. There they still wear simple clothes and practice the old customs more than we do. They are freer. Their women are not ashamed to dance and sing and drink with the men. They have more village celebrations. They are content with what they have, simple though it is, and many of them are wealthy because they have nothing to waste their money on. We are better off in this respect than are people who live near the cities, but the people farther up in the hills are better off than we are.

One reason for the relative isolation of Sirkanda is that it has nothing to attract outsiders. It is high on a ridge and is not en route to any place of interest to plains people. Unless limestone is found in its immediate vicinity, it is likely to be bypassed for a long time.

Outside influences have been felt in Sirkanda primarily as a result of direct, personal contact. Villagers who have taken extended trips outside have returned to tell their stories. Some villagers make frequent trips to market, where they learn the current news. The alien merchant and government employees have added their experience. Itinerant merchants and religious practitioners have contributed, too. From such contacts villagers have acquired some idea of what goes on in the outside world. They are familiar with Gandhi, Nehru, and the Congress party. They know of India's difficulties with Pakistan and sympathize with India (or, more accurately, they are anti-Muslim). They know something of the struggle between Russia and the United States. Certain domestic policies—land reform, Harijan uplift—are vaguely known. New developments—the launching of Sputnik, the outlawing of prostitution in Dehra Dun—cause comment and speculation. Awareness of and interest in foreign countries and other parts of India are very limited. Discussion with the anthropologist about America arose relatively infrequently. Villagers usually began with an inquiry as to how long it would take to walk there and proceeded through discussions of the price of consumer goods, productivity of land and animals, social customs, and finally sex habits.

Written materials and mass media have been of little importance. Mail, which is received rarely, consists primarily of instructions to the

council or of personal and official mail for the teacher and other outsiders in the village. Villagers who go outside communicate rarely if
at all with their relatives in Sirkanda. There are no periodicals in the
village and no books other than the school materials of the teacher and
a few largely unread religious works. The only current documents
are posters given to the village level worker or the village president,
urging public health and personal hygiene and explaining in graphic
detail the intricacies of the change to the decimal system of coinage.
There has been no functional radio in Bhatbair, although one was
once brought to a Sirkanda chan, where it failed to operate. One
brought by the anthropologist attracted an interested audience. Film
music and news programs were the favorite radio fare, in that order.
Newspapers and magazines brought to the village aroused little interest aside from their illustrations. The low level of literacy even
among those who claim to know how to read is probably largely responsible for this reception.

Contacts between villagers and representatives of urban culture and
the "new India" will probably continue to take place primarily
through villagers' trips outside and through government representatives who are attempting to initiate various programs in this and
neighboring hill villages. Governmental programs of planned change
and villagers' responses to them will be discussed below.

URBAN CONTACTS

Urban centers are important to Sirkanda villagers as they are to
all peasants. In fact, Redfield (1957, p. 31) defines peasantry with
reference to the presence of cities, stating that "there were no peasants
before the first cities."

In Sirkanda as in other peasant communities, "the account the
peasant takes of the city or town is economic, political, and moral"
(*ibid.*). That is, he carries on some trade in the city, he pays his taxes
to people from the city, he is subject to control by institutions ema-
nating from the city, he knows something of city ways, and in fact
adopts some values of urban dwellers as his own.

The sources and amounts of urban influence in Sirkanda are varied.
One of the most important kinds of contact is that of direct, personal
experience. This varies from person to person. Women have much less
urban experience than do men. While there are men who have never
been to Dehra Dun, others go every few weeks. Of 116 men in Sirkanda,
3 have never seen Dehra Dun, 62 have seen nothing beyond Dehra
Dun and Mussoorie, 20 have been as far as Hardwar or an equivalent

place within 40 miles and bordering the hills (such as Rishikesh and Kalsi), 6 have been into the plains but only as far as one of the smaller towns or cities within 60 miles of Dehra Dun (Saharanpur, Muzaffarnagar, Ambala), 15 have been as far as Delhi (150 miles), 8 have been on pilgrimage to Gaya (750 miles), 1 has been to Calcutta, and 1 has been over most of North India in the army.

Outside employment, discussed in chapter 2, has given a number of villagers firsthand experience with city life for months at a time, but no one has moved his family outside and only one man has taken a lasting job outside (another who recently joined him may be the second to do so). The general opinion of city life is that it is easy, entertaining, sinful, and expensive. For well-to-do plains people it is fine, but it is not suitable for poor Paharis. One Rajput, apparently referring to emigration, commented: "Anyone who leaves the village is a fool because here he is a king but there he is a slave." Another, referring to short-term visits, objected to this view, saying, "A person can learn and improve himself only by going away and having other experiences. In the village he can learn nothing."

The one Sirkanda man who had gone out and made a success of life on the outside was pointed to with pride by some villagers, although he had apparently not been well thought of at the time of his departure and he left as the result of a family dispute. Disputes were involved in many cases of temporary emigration from the village. Niehoff (1959, p. 501) comments that among factory workers of Kanpur, ". . . the push from the village was stronger than the pull from the city and the factory." The rise of the Sirkanda emigrant was graphically described by a villager:

> Maru used to live here. He was ignorant and dirty. He wore the worst clothes in the village. He always had manure all over his hair and clothes from carrying it to the fields, and he never had taken a bath. Even his wife didn't care for him, and she took up with his cousin. Because of that he ran off to Delhi, and no one heard from him and no one cared. Then he came back on a visit. He was clean, well-dressed, and handsome. He talked just like a sahib. He had a job at Rs. 150 per month in a spinning mill. He had had one hand mangled in a machine and got Rs. 800 for that. He brought a radio and good liquor with him. The radio did not work, but everyone was impressed. He still works there and is doing very well. It was all in his fate. It would never work for others unless that was in their fate, too. A boy from here has joined him recently. He may fail, but perhaps it is in his fate to succeed, too. We shall see.

There was considerable interest on the part of some Rajputs in Sirkanda in getting a boy into "service," that is, into a white-collar job.

So far there had been no success. Two Rajput boys had recently been sent through the eighth grade with this end in view, but they had failed. The father of one complained:

I wish one of the boys from here would get a job in service. We sent my eldest son and his cousin out to school so that they could succeed. We gave them everything they needed so that they could study and do well. When they wanted bicycles, we bought them. We got them good clothes. But all they did was waste their time going to the cinema and the like. They did not apply themselves, so they both failed the examinations at the end of the eighth grade. Now they are useless. There is plenty to be done here in the village and a good income can be made from it, but they do not want to do village work any more. They have been spoiled. My next eldest son, whom I did not educate, is content to work in the village, but not these educated boys. They are too big for that. They carry a pen and pencil in their pockets when they go to herd goats. They go off to town when they get a chance and waste their time and money. My boy says he wants a job there, but what can he do? Nothing.

I know that young men have new ideas now and I try not to stand in my boy's way. In my youth we wore only a loincloth. We ran around bare-footed. Now every young man wants an outfit of 22 clothes and goes to fetch water in boots costing Rs. 18. One has to move with the times. I cater to my boy's wants within reason. Last winter I bought wool for coats for our family. That for myself cost Rs. 8 per yard, that for my father cost Rs. 12 per yard, that for my son cost Rs. 16 per yard. But he did not even appreciate that. This fall the boy sold his coat to the schoolteacher for Rs. 10 so he could use the money for something else. He claimed the coat wasn't stylish. Now my youngest boy is in school. I hope he will do better, but I fear the same fate for him. The boys go wrong because they are not supervised in town, but how can we supervise them when we live way up here?

The son in question frequently inquired of me about jobs in town, but he had totally unrealistic goals in view of his qualifications. He spoke of wanting to be an office worker or cinema actor. He would consider no job as lowly as those for which he might have been qualified. His father commented that "Even if he made Rs. 100 per month it would not meet his expenses outside. Here in a good season we make more than that and our expenses are small." This boy's cousin was the one who ran off to join the millworker, and this boy was tempted to join him, but ties of wife and joint family were too strong to allow him to do it secretly and he was not granted permission by his father to do it. His affectations were the bane of his age-mates, who had the maximum village education (five years) or less. They, by and large, were content to remain in the village to live and work with occasional visits to town for fun. Their requirements for clothes and other possessions were patterned on his, but their concepts of what constituted "fashion" in clothing were less sophisticated than his.

The opinion of most villagers is that cultural distances are too great to permit their successful adjustment to town life. Despite their efforts to practice the proverb, "When in Nepal, eat buffalo" (do as the Nepalese do), they find it difficult to adjust to the unfamiliar way of life of the city. One young man, who had aspirations toward the bright lights of the city, explained:

People in this village are mostly content. They have the things they want, they eat enough, and many of them are well off by local standards. Sometimes they like to go to Dehra Dun. They put on their best clothes and feel proud of themselves. But when they get to town, everyone there thinks they are fools. We don't know how to dress or act in town. There even a poor untouchable puts on a shirt and pajama and looks respectable, but we can't look like that. Even if we spend Rs. 200 on the finest cloth and have the best clothes made, we still look like fools in town.

Many stories are told on themselves by villagers, illustrating this point.

Attractions in towns which draw Paharis are cinemas, "hotels" (shops which sell sweets, meals, and tea to the accompaniment of loud radio music), drinking establishments, and prostitutes. Although these are rarely the sole reason for going to town, they are the side attractions of trips intended primarily for trade or official business with government offices. A Sirkanda blacksmith is often teased about his affinity for these pleasures. He protests, "It is true, no doubt, but why must you advertise the matter? There is no act of valor in it." Two examples of his experiences, as told by himself, will serve to illustrate the adventures of Paharis in town. The first of these concerns his first visit to a prostitute in Dehra Dun.

I had a little money and nothing to do, so I decided to go to a prostitute. I had never been before and I didn't know the times when they are available, but I knew the compound where their houses are. About 12 at night I went there and entered the gate of the large compound containing the houses of prostitutes. Just after I went in and was looking around to decide my next move, the Muslim gatekeeper closed and locked the gate I had just come through. I was frightened—I wondered how I could ever get out again. Then I saw the gatekeeper hitting people who tried to leave [apparently people who wanted to sneak out without paying]. I wanted to get away. I walked around the compound, keeping to the shadows, but saw no way to escape. Finally I climbed a stairway to one of the balconies. The girl there asked me what I would pay. I had Rs. 20, so I gave her that [actually Rs. 2 to 5 would have been plenty]. She took me into her room and brought out betel nuts and a cuspidor. She called the musicians and they played and she sang for me. I sat and watched and listened. I never knew what would happen next, but I didn't want to go out and be beaten by the gatekeeper. The girl asked me several times if I was ready but I always said no, thinking that would cost extra and I had no more money. Finally, much later, the girl grew disgusted and demanded, "Why have you come here and paid all this money and not wanted intercourse? What do you want?" Then I felt foolish and realized that this was included in the price. After that I went back many times.

Another occasion was that upon which this man decided to attend a Western-type restaurant just as he had seen the important towns-people do.

I went to the Nilam Bar where I had seen the big people go in their fancy cars—the same people who drive back and forth past the prostitutes' compound waiting until there are not many people around, and then send a servant in to make sure there is no one like me with their favorite girl, before coming in themselves.

I bought a newspaper to take in with me so that they might not know I am illiterate. I went in and sat down. Soon a waiter came, all dressed in white, and handed me the menu, but I just said I would have tea and cakes. The waiter asked if I wanted single or double. I thought single would be a cup and double a tumblerful, so I ordered a double. I was amazed when he brought a great glass pitcher full of tea—enough for an army. The sugar and milk were in separate containers rather than cooked in the tea—a surprise to me. However, I drank some tea in a very blasé manner and ate some cakes. I left some of each uneaten to show that I am well-bred. The big people never eat all that is put before them as we villagers do. If I had eaten all that was served they would have known I was a bumpkin. After I was through I looked at my paper and the waiter soon brought my bill on a plate. I then realized that I did not know the cost of my refreshment and could not read the bill, but I did not want to admit this. Therefore, I got up absent-mindedly and walked to the door. There I asked the man at the desk where my bill was, and he told me it was on my table. I said I hadn't noticed it and now didn't have time to go back to get it as my car was waiting for me outside, and I asked him to tell me the amount. He did —it was Rs. 6, which I paid him. That is the most expensive tea I ever had [normally tea and cakes would cost not over R. 1 at the fanciest of eating places].

The city is an exciting, but in many ways a mysterious and dangerous, place for most Paharis. Even the cinemas are not clearly understood by many of those who attend them. One man, having recently seen one, was asked about it. Being illiterate, he knew neither the title nor the cast. The only actor he recognized, he said, was Dr. Rajendra

Prasad (President of India), who appeared near the beginning of the film. He had evidently failed to differentiate the preceding newsreel from the featured film. He was vague about the plot but agreed vigorously when it was suggested that it was about a boy and girl in love who, in spite of great obstacles, finally came together (the plot of 90 per cent of the films shown). "Yes, yes, that was the one I saw," he affirmed. Occasionally a villager happens into an English-language cinema but, having paid his admission, usually stoically sits it out. He is often rewarded, according to those who have seen these British and American films, with a display of nudity and sexual aberrations—the local interpretation of some Western women's wear and love scenes, respectively.

An important feature of village-urban contacts is that of victimization of the naïve Pahari villager by urban shopkeepers and others. A foreigner in India is likely to get the impression that shopkeepers, service personnel, and officials are "out to get" him. S. J. Perelman (1947, p. 96) has summed up his impression of India in the phrase, "It's not the heat, it's the cupidity." However, this is not exploitation of the foreigner as such; it is exploitation of the ignorant, the naïve, the unwary, in short, the vulnerable. It hits the villager, and particularly the Pahari villager, hard, for he is just as vulnerable as the foreigner and much less able to afford the results of his vulnerability than are most foreigners. Such exploitation affects villagers in most contacts with outsiders, but especially in the urban areas.

The average villager is at the mercy of shopkeepers when he goes to town, and his vulnerability is advertised by his dress, speech, and manners. He is an easy mark. He is the hillbilly come to town, and everyone knows he has money with him, as otherwise he would not have made the trip. He buys inferior goods at inflated prices and is none the wiser. He pays Rs. 2 for a flashlight bulb that costs anyone else R. 0.25, and feels fortunate to have found a store which sells such an intricate mechanism. He is victim of the cheat and thief and the dishonest official as well. The only Sirkanda villager who ever tried to buy a radio had his pocket picked of the Rs. 350 in a cinema before he had had a chance to spend it. Money is extorted from Paharis regularly by corrupt inspectors, toll-tax collectors, and police who threaten a false report if no bribe is paid. It is a simple matter to produce a bottle of illicit liquor and accuse a Pahari of having sold it—better to pay a bribe than risk a heavy fine or imprisonment. The Wisers have described well the position of residents of the plains village in which they worked for several years. Paraphrasing villagers' statements they say:

In the cities they devise ways of exploiting us. . . . We are at home in the wholesale market. But when we get our money and want to take home some cloth, the shopkeepers get out the pieces which they have been unable to dispose of, and persuade us to buy them at exorbitant prices. We know that they are laughing at us. But we want cloth, and the next shopkeeper will cheat us as badly as the last. Wherever we go in the town, sharp eyes are watching to tempt our precious rupees from us. And there is no one to advise us honestly or to help us escape from fraudulent men. When we go to town to attend the courts, there are men everywhere waiting to take advantage of our ignorance and fear. Our lawyers charge fees which they know are beyond our means to pay. And then if we win a case they think that they deserve an extra large gift. Sometimes there is a sincere helper among them, but we are never sure who is what. (C. V. and W. H. Wiser, 1951, p. 163)

As has been mentioned previously, social pressure is one factor which keeps people from bringing urban or other alien traits into the village. The man who had returned to the village after being in the army in World War II, and who had enjoyed his outside experience very much, replied to an inquiry:

When I got back to the village I didn't like it at first. I was used to the comforts of army life. But I gradually became accustomed to the village again. I would have liked to bring some things home with me, especially utensils and other conveniences for the house. However, I brought only some cloth for the family, and what I brought is similar to what other people here use. I didn't bring any really nice clothes or other things because people would have laughed at me.

This attitude has not prevented acquisition of material possessions, but it has been one reason for the gradual nature of adoption of new things. Clothing styles, especially those of men, who are in contact with outsiders more frequently than are women, have changed considerably in recent years. Costume jewelry and other ornaments have been acquired by women. Household possessions have come to include more utensils procured from town bazaars. For the most part these have been relatively minor changes—better artifacts rather than new ones. A few people have gotten new items, spurred by urban example. One villager had a functioning phonograph and a few worn records, and someone else was alleged to have a similar machine, long inoperative. The only radio in Bhatbair history, brought by the man employed near Delhi, had failed to operate. When I left, mine was in great demand but the likelihood is that it was used only until its battery was exhausted. A few young men in the village had mechanical pencils or pens, and at least one owned a cheap watch. One purchased a Japanese cigarette lighter adorned with photographs of nude girls.

Many boys owned pocket knives. The village tailor had a hand-operated sewing machine and a charcoal-heated iron for use in his craft.

Tools and materials for agriculture have changed little. Corrugated iron is now often used in roofing, and one new house has a little cement in its construction. Household furnishings now include string cots and cotton quilts or rugs in addition to the traditional wool blanket used for sleeping on the floor. A few kerosene storm lanterns and one or two flashlights are in the village.

There is an accelerating demand for all these things as they become increasingly accessible and as villagers become increasingly aware of them. However, material items in the village, like behavior and beliefs, are predominantly traditional.

THE GOVERNMENT IN SIRKANDA

Sirkanda is strategically located in many respects. It is the gateway from the valley to much of Bhatbair and neighboring areas to the east. It is the most accessible of the large villages of the interior of this area. As such it has been the focus of recent attention by agencies of the state and national governments. It has been designated as the seat of the council, originally for much of Bhatbair and now for a less populous area on the western edge of Bhatbair. It is the village which serves as headquarters for the village level worker and the economic coöperative supervisor. It contains the largest of three schools in Bhatbair. On the rare occasions when tax collectors or other officials come to Bhatbair, they usually do their work in Sirkanda.

In order to understand the relationship of villagers to specific programs in the village, it is necessary first to understand attitudes toward the government in general.

The first question asked of the anthropologist in Bhatbair villages and in all other hill areas visited was invariably, "How can we get our forests back?" In Bhatbair the remark which was usually associated with this question was, "When are the British coming back into power?" These two questions sum up village attitudes toward the present government. It is felt by villagers that the British government had two outstanding qualities: (1) it did not meddle in village affairs, (2) it was an ultimately available source of impartial, if not always comprehensible, justice. Thus, it is believed, it was the antithesis of the present government. To the further credit of the British was the fact that they established the bhaichara system of land ownership in Sirkanda, giving every high-caste family the land it cultivated, elim-

inating the intermediate landlord of earlier times, and charging
relatively low taxes.

The current state and national governments (not distinguished
from one another by villagers) are thought by Sirkanda people to be
made up of corrupt troublemakers. Anything advocated by the government or its representatives is automatically suspect and is usually
opposed out of hand. Villagers' attitudes were perfectly exemplified
in their response to Republic Day ceremonies planned for the village
by the teacher, and supported by the other two governmental employees stationed in Sirkanda. This celebration was announced well
in advance. A full day of activities was scheduled, beginning with
a flag-raising ceremony at the school, followed by a procession of
school children, led through the village by the teacher and his fellow
sponsors, singing patriotic and religious songs. In the afternoon a
village assembly meeting was to be held at which patriotic speeches
would be made and some village business would be conducted. At
the conclusion of this, tea and sweets were to be distributed.

Villagers completely ignored the whole program. When the singing
group went through the village not a soul joined, acknowledged, or
even watched, the procession. Even the usual number of people who
would be expected to be in view were out of sight, consciously avoiding the display. No one came to the scheduled meeting, and only the
school children were on hand to receive sweets. This was enough to
discourage even the conscientious teacher and to convince the other
workers that their job in Sirkanda was hopeless.

Land Reform

One of the first acts by the Independent government of India
to affect Sirkanda was the nationalization of forest lands in 1953.
This affected all uncultivated and unoccupied lands surrounding the
village. In so doing, the government placed restrictions upon cultivation of new lands and upon access to the products of uncultivated
lands, apparently with a view to reducing floods, erosion, and depletion
of forest resources. By this act alone, most hill people were alienated
from the government because it hit at the basis of Pahari livelihood.
Paharis live in their none-too-hospitable environment largely by full
utilization of forest products. Forest grass and leaves are fodder for
their animals, and forest trees are made into their tools, many of
their utensils, and essential parts of their houses. Most importantly,
the forest provides wood for fuel. Without such fuel the villagers
would have to resort to the plains practice of burning dung, and they
would then be unable to fertilize their fields. Without fertilizer their

fields would be unlikely to produce a subsistence crop. Moreover, as is readily evident to any observer, such utilization of the forests does not seriously affect the forests. Where devastating depletion has occurred and is still occurring rapidly and irreparably, is where outside contractors have been given the right to cut trees in order to make and sell charcoal. In this manner whole forests go down that have been unaffected by hundreds of years of village use. Villagers would gladly see curbs put on this practice, which benefits them not in the least and depletes their own forest resources.

The government has not forbidden use of forest lands and products (especially trees) to villagers, but it has placed tighter restrictions upon such use than existed heretofore. The villagers, however, feel that the forest is their own land, and they refuse to make even a pretense at asking permission to use that which they believe to be rightly theirs. Anyway, the appropriate governmental representatives from whom permission can be obtained, the forestry officer and the land records officer, are not easily accessible and not always sympathetic, and the necessary procedures are ponderously time-consuming and complex, so that any desire to obey the law is discouraged at the outset. Local caste and factional alignments are an obstacle because applications for forest products have to be made through the local council. Therefore, disobedience of public laws is accepted practice in this sphere, a fact which may have facilitated its spread to other spheres.

The seriousness of public reaction to these regulations may be inferred from the headline of a story in a newspaper of Dehra Dun and Mussoorie in August, 1958: "CONGRESS MEN THREATEN DIRECT ACTION, Forest Rights Issue Causes Unrest" (Himachal *Times*, 1958b). The local political figures' threat came five years after the issue arose and followed a state government decision, based on a subcommittee's report, not to make any concessions on the matter. This issue has been a major factor in support of demands, farther to the west, for a separate hill state for the "suppressed and exploited" hill people (Himachal *Times*, 1958a).

Defiance of these rules (as of the government in general) takes many forms in the village. It is against the law to burn grass in the forest. Throughout the lower Himalayas from time immemorial, the forest grass has been burned every dry season just before the rains to make a better crop of new grass after the rains. In this process fires occasionally get out of hand. Occasionally a chan and the animals in it are consumed in flames. However, villagers consider this a calculated and not unduly heavy risk, inherent in the performance of a necessary task. The government, apparently worried about forest trees (which villagers insist are unaffected by the fires), has outlawed the practice with notably unimpressive results. In June the lower Himalayan grasslands are still blackened and a thick pall of smoke obscures the Himalayan view. The difference is that now the practice has become a contest to outwit and frustrate the forest guard—a contest which villagers invariably win. In 1958, when the forest guard came to fight some fires around Sirkanda, he was greeted with complete apathy. He asked for volunteers to help fight the fires and got no one to help. He was told, "You get paid Rs. 60 per month to fight fires. Why should we who earn nothing help you? Pay us Rs. 60 per month and we will gladly join you. Otherwise, leave us alone."

Wherever the forest guard went, new fires would appear over the ridge or just out of sight, usually with a few idly watching "observers" to keep the flames away from valuable property such as chans or caches of firewood. This occurred in spite of the fact that the forest guard was relatively well liked as an individual and had the villagers' welfare in mind. He felt compelled to report one particularly large and visible fire in 1957, and asked villagers to make statements as to its origin. All he wanted them to say was that it began by a public trail, probably from the cigarette of an unknown traveler. This report would have been satisfactory to the authorities and would have precluded further investigation. Instead, villagers responded with statements to the effect, "It is our forest, and we will burn it or not as we please." This would have brought further investigation and a fine to the village had it gone in the official report. Only by privately working out the report with the village council president was a sufficiently innocuous statement obtained and submitted to avoid further complications. Such cases of defiance of forest laws are commonplace in Sirkanda and throughout the hills. Recently there has been talk of assigning a forest guard to Sirkanda, making it the center of a new forest district. This plan is bitterly opposed by villagers. At present Sirkanda is at the junction of three large forest districts under the jurisdiction of three distant forest guards, a situation which facilitates evasion of the forest laws. The boundaries actually meet in the settlement area of the village, and the responsible officers are stationed in three widely separated centers.

As has been stated earlier (chap. 2), nationalization of the forest lands has made it illegal to cultivate new lands without special permission. Villagers cite nationalization as an example of governmental stupidity. "The government asked us to increase crop production for the national welfare. We were happy to comply. However, at the same time they made illegal the only means to accomplish this." The ruling means that, as fields become depleted or inadequate for increasing family size, new ones cannot be legally prepared without special permission. An understanding village accountant (probably he understood bribes) looked the other way when villagers disobeyed the law, but a later accountant, either out of respect for the law or pique at the lack of bribes or of sufficient bribes, reported the matter. Considerable rancor was aroused before a reasonably happy solution was reached in the land records office, where the offenders were assessed back taxes and allowed to keep the land. This is not a solution for the future, however. As in the use of forest products, notably trees, there is not a rigid prohibition against use of new land, but there is a procedure of application, payment of fees, and so on, which must be followed. Villagers refuse to abide by these rules just as they do the forest laws. Their attitude is not softened by the extreme difficulty they encounter, the necessity for repeated trips to distant headquarters, the arrogant and often greedy officials with whom they must deal in making such applications. It is a task to frustrate anyone, most of all a semiliterate villager. This point will be elaborated below as one element in a pattern which villagers face in dealing with the government.

Another aspect of land legislation is that of taxation. Unfortunately, when landlordism was abolished in the state in 1953, taxes were raised slightly for Sirkanda landowners. Although the increase was slight and lower taxes resulted for the majority of agriculturists in the state, it was resented in Sirkanda, where all agriculturists had long owned the land they tilled. The village comment is, "Congress promised to lower taxes and instead they raised them." Villagers are totally unaware of the larger picture on this matter.

The indiscriminate application of general programs of land reform that are inappropriate to the Pahari context has thus been an important factor in alienating these villagers from the government. In itself it would probably have been sufficient to achieve this result. However, it was not the only factor.

Agents of Authority

For villagers, one of the most frustrating aspects of their relationship to the government is their contact with its official representatives, and especially those who hold power over them. The Wisers have discussed the problem in a plains village at some length (C. V. and W. H. Wiser, 1951, pp. 130 ff.; cf. Beals, 1954, Newell, 1954). The brutality and dishonesty of the police are proverbial in Sirkanda. The maxim, "Never trust a policeman," is often quoted and religiously practiced. Specific instances of police brutality and dishonesty are legion,

ranging from simple demands for bribes upon threat of a false accusation of illegal distilling to unreasonable violence in trying to extract
confessions or information (or, alternatively, heavy bribes) from people
who obviously had no connection with a case.

Similarly, the corruption of village accountants is proverbial. These
officials today are people totally unassociated with the village or even
the area. The accountant for most of Bhatbair in 1957–1958 had not
been seen by villagers since his appointment two years previously,
until suddenly word came to him that a higher official would be coming
on an inspection tour. The accountant appeared in great haste to
prepare records in two weeks that should have been kept over the past
two years. In the process his arrogance, incompetence, and inaccuracy,
combined with his corruption, put the villagers at a disadvantage and
aroused their resentment.

Such examples are not unique to the post-Independence era. They
carry on a long-established tradition. As many examples could be cited
under British rule.

The point, as the villagers see it, is that, compared to British times,
(1) there are now more occasions upon which a person is likely to
confront officials, and (2) there is now no ultimate authority from
which justice can be obtained, and therefore officials are arrogant
to an extreme never before seen. Whether or not the comparison is
accurate, it is believed by villagers.

To take these points in order, it is readily apparent that the amount
of official activity and consequently the number of agents of authority
affecting villagers has increased greatly since Independence with the
institution of land reforms, community development plans, and other
programs. The activities of rationing authorities may be considered
as an example. Villagers often use corrugated iron for roofing. To get
it they must apply through a rationing office whose officials, being in
league with black marketeers, never authorize enough of the material
to fulfill the villagers' needs. The official procedures are such that to
obtain any legal materials at all requires several trips to town. Most
villagers would agree with one who said:

By the time you have gone to Dehra Dun two or three times [a two-day
undertaking necessitating an overnight stay in strange surroundings] and
have been insulted by the officials and then get only one-fourth of the roofing
you need, you learn that it is better to go directly to the black market and
get what you need at the higher price. That is where you will have to go in
the end anyway.

This is just one of several newly created official hazards for villagers.
The biggest complaint of villagers against the present government

is the lack of ultimate, impartial justice. As they frequently point out, under the British the police were corrupt and the accountants were corrupt, but the courts were fair. Examples are told of corrupt officials of all types who were found guilty in the courts under the British, and of false court cases exposed by the district magistrate. Officials were restrained by the knowledge that this authority existed. Tax collectors were often polite. Milk inspectors were often honest or at least refrained from pressing their authority too far. Villagers contrast that idealized (and perhaps unrealistic) picture with the realities of the present. An example of immediate importance and tangible effect was recounted by villagers as follows:

It has long been our custom to sell milk in the markets of Dehra Dun and Mussoorie. The government sometimes inspects this milk now, as it did under the British. Under the British, if we adulterated the milk with water and were caught, as sometimes happened, we were fined and were denied permission to sell for a specified period thereafter. This we knew and could count upon. Now when we carry our milk to market we may be stopped by the inspectors who, without even looking at our milk, accuse us of adulterating it. We must pay them a bribe or go to court and be fined and penalized, for what is the word of a milkman against that of an inspector. For this reason most of us have quit selling milk since Independence. We now sell instead a solidified milk product which is less profitable but which cannot be easily adulterated and which is therefore not inspected.

The courts are held in utter contempt by most villagers. Examples are given from this area of how even the most serious and flagrant crimes or civil cases are decided on the basis of bribery. "No crime is now so serious that money cannot win acquittal; no man is so innocent that an enemy cannot put him in prison or win a judgment against him if he has sufficient money for bribes." "Under the British there was justice—water for water and milk for milk. Now water and milk are one" (that is, lies were then treated as lies, truth as truth; now they are not distinguished). It is felt that now even the highest official is subject to bribes and that a poor villager has no one to whom to turn.

Comments from a range of informants of all castes indicate consistent attitudes toward the government:

Before Independence India was ruled by the British; now it is ruled by rascals. Law was then just, now anyone with money can avoid the law.

Under the British there was government by men; now it is government by money.

In days of British rule India was a subject nation, but at least there was an established law and order. Now India is like a woman with several husbands, dominated by whichever is present at the moment.

Under the British we were free—we cultivated and worked as we pleased. Now we are slaves. The government tells us what to do and what not to do.

The Congress promised to circulate gold money when freedom was won. Instead they are circulating money of alloy that is not even pure silver or copper. So it is with their promises.

The people, especially the leaders, wanted to get rid of the British. But in fact, India under British rule was better than it has been since Independence under the Congress government.

This government will be able to stay in power by force but not by the people's will.

In this context of grass-roots rejection the government has attempted to carry out various specific programs in Bhatbair.

Community Development

On October 2, 1952, the anniversary of Mahatma Gandhi's birthday, India launched a program whose purpose was no less than a rural revolution. What it proposed was to transform the social and economic life and outlook of the rural people, raise farm production and incomes, and create from stagnant backward villages a vital, progressive rural community. It proposed to do all this, not by coercion, but, as the "essence of the program," by self-help and participation of the people themselves. (Planning Commission, 1958, p. 168)

This was the Community Development Program. Its aim was to enable people to raise their standard of living by introducing schools, community centers, pure water, better seeds, tools, and techniques of acquiring a livelihood, better transportation, and better public health.

The key person in this program is the village level worker (VLW) or *Gram Sevak* (village servant).

Living in one of a "circle" of the eight to ten villages under his care, the worker goes from village to village, from farmer to farmer, using all the techniques familiar to extension work in the west—field demonstrations, individual talks and group discussions, audio-visual teaching, approach to villagers with help on felt needs in order to awaken new needs and interest in change.

Trained as a multi-purpose worker, he brings help and information on improved methods of cultivation, on health care and sanitation, on cattle diseases and their prevention, and so on. Working through village leaders, he enlists the interest and participation of the village as a whole in change and progress. (Planning Commission, 1958, p. 171)

In January, 1955, a Community Development Block was opened in Eastern Dehra Dun District which brought a total of 88 village administrative units (and a population of 62,000 people), including those

of Bhatbair, into the Community Development program. Shortly thereafter a VLW was stationed in Nagal, a large village in the valley seven
miles from Sirkanda. His area of responsibility was large, including
Bhatbair and a number of villages in the valley. In 1957 this Development Block was changed from a National Extension Block to an Intensive Development Block, the shift being intended to increase development activity. At this time additional VLW's were assigned. In
addition to the one at Nagal, who continued to have responsibility
for a number of valley villages and a few on the edge of Bhatbair, a
new VLW was assigned with Sirkanda as his headquarters and the
interior of Bhatbair as his area of responsibility. This man was in
Sirkanda a year, from the summer of 1957 until the summer of 1958.
Therefore, virtually all his official activities were observed by the
anthropologist. This period overlapped the third and fourth year of
the program in the area, the second year of India's second five-year plan.

Specific goals for Sirkanda in the second five-year plan were the
construction of a community center and repair of thirty miles of trails.
Other projects attempted were those mentioned in the council meeting
described above (chap. 8). In addition the VLW had a box of equipment for first aid and equipment for inoculating and castrating
animals, and he was supposed to encourage the villagers in self-government, patriotic fervor, equalitarianism, and other aspects of the new
national creed.

At the end of his year in Sirkanda, when he finally achieved his goal
of securing a transfer, the VLW had achieved no tangible results in
any of his areas of responsibility in Bhatbair. He had, however, turned
in satisfactory reports. The proceedings of the only council meeting
held during that year are indicative of the programs undertaken and
the way villagers reacted to them. It is relevant here to summarize
briefly the results of the items taken up and decided upon in that
meeting: No one ever came to inspect the problem of the village's
water supply, and nothing was done about it. The panchayat tax was
not collected. No voluntary labor was performed on trails or on any
other project discussed in the meeting; the agreed-upon days for this
came and went without comment from the VLW or villagers. No
attempt was made to set up a night school (but this, unlike the other
items, had been formally rejected in council meeting). No agricultural
training session was held, although the VLW had been specifically
directed to hold a session in which he would explain to villagers the
Japanese method of rice cultivation. Despite considerable talk about
the matter on his part, no such session was ever held. The Village
Credit Coöperative Society of Sirkànda got no paid-up members as a

result of the efforts of the VLW, the council, or the society itself, although later (as will be explained below) some token success was achieved on this score. No further action or discussion about a community center took place. School attendance did rise, but because of independent efforts of the teacher rather than council action. No National Savings Certificates were sold. In addition, in the entire year the interior of the VLW's first-aid kit and the veterinary equipment were never exposed to the light of day. In short, the VLW was totally ineffective in this village and throughout his area of responsibility. As will be explained in the discussion below, this was a result of several factors, including the training, motivation, and personal characteristics of this VLW; villagers' attitudes toward the government, toward change, and toward community coöperation; and inappropriateness of the program and of its manner of presentation in the village.

Credit Coöperative Program

A second civil servant assigned to the village for approximately the same period as the VLW was the economic coöperative supervisor, locally known as the "supervisor sahib," and here termed ECS. His job was to set up government-sponsored credit coöperatives in the various villages of Bhatbair on the strength of a report submitted by another officer who had previously visited the area and had secured signatures in several of these villages indicating interest in the plan. The idea was that villagers were to buy shares at Rs. 20 (payable over two and one-half years), each of which would entitle the holder to borrow Rs. 100 at 8.5 per cent annual interest. This plan met with no success in any village in the area. In the words of the ECS:

> All of these villages signed up with the agent saying that they wanted coöperatives, but they probably did it just to get rid of him. There is no real interest, and none of the people who signed up have received me cordially. In no village has anyone paid any dues, and there is no prospect of setting up coöperatives here.

In the council meeting at Sirkanda the necessary minimum of five pledges was recorded, including the most unlikely member of all, a landless blacksmith. A month later the ECS was notified that he was to lose his job for not producing results. Upon receipt of this intelligence, the teacher and he managed to round up nine people who made payments of Rs. 2 to 10 each as initial membership fees in response to a plea to save the job of the ECS. No mention of the advantages of the society was made in this hurried fund drive. The council president, who had been a steadfast foe of the plan, later commented, "We started a coöperative society so the ECS wouldn't lose his job." The factors relevant to the ineffectiveness of the ECS are precisely parallel to those relevant to the case of the VLW.

Failure of the Programs

In analyzing the lack of success of these two men and the programs they were employed to advocate, it is obvious that social and cultural factors—the relationship of the social organization and culture of the villagers to the programs presented—were crucial. It is important, therefore, to consider both social and cultural factors and the content of the programs presented. Also significant in the degree of success or failure of the programs was the manner in which they were presented and the personnel who presented them. These factors will be discussed in that order.

SOCIAL AND CULTURAL FACTORS

Dube (1956, 1958) has discussed at some length social and cultural factors in relation to change in Indian villages:

Agents of rural development projects and of programs of technical assistance are confronted with these factors at almost every step of their work. The acceptance of the agents of change as well as the effectiveness of the media through which they endeavor to communicate their innovations are largely governed by the cultural predispositions, attitudes, and social organization of the community in which they operate. The acceptance of the program itself, or of its constituent parts, is determined to a considerable extent by a variety of complex cultural factors, ranging from simple habits and accepted social practices to the intricate patterns of belief, social structure, world view, and values and attitudes. (Dube, 1956, pp. 19 f.)

Attitudes of suspicion and avoidance of outsiders seem to be characteristic of the relatively closed society of Sirkanda, where familiar ties of kinship, caste, and community are necessary if an individual is to be accepted into the group or even to be dealt with on equal terms. Lacking these, an outsider is an unknown and potentially dangerous quantity best avoided.

The Wisers have paraphrased the attitude of plains villagers toward change as follows:

To a new-comer we may seem suspicious, obstinate, intolerant, backward —all that goes with refusal to change. We did not choose qualities for ourselves. Experience forced them upon our fathers. . . . Refusal to change is the armour with which we have learned to protect ourselves. . . . We are not blind to the advantages of the new, but unless we know just where it will lead us, we prefer to let it pass us by. (C. V. and W. H. Wiser, 1951, pp. 153 f.)

In Sirkanda the unfamiliar, be it a person or a program of change, is regarded with suspicion. The reasons are readily apparent. Contacts with outsiders have been limited largely to contacts with policemen and tax collectors—two of the most unpopular forms of life in the Pahari taxonomy. Such officials are despised and feared, not only because they make trouble for villagers in the line of duty but also because they extort bribes on the threat of causing further trouble and often seem to take advantage of their official position to vent their aggressions on these vulnerable people. Since India's independence, governmental responsibilities have increased and extended to matters previously ignored, such as closer supervision of enlarged government forest lands and rationing of certain goods. The grounds for interfering in village affairs have multiplied as the variety of officials has proliferated. Any stranger, therefore, may be a government agent and as such he is potentially troublesome and even dangerous.

Villagers' fears on this score are not groundless. Aside from the unjust exploitation which such agents are reputed to employ, the villagers themselves carry on many illegal or semilegal activities which could be grounds for punishment and are easily used as an excuse for extortion. In Sirkanda, government forest lands and products have been illegally appropriated by villagers, taxable land has been under-reported, liquor is brewed and sold illicitly, women have been illegally sold, guns have gone unlicensed, adulterated milk is sold to outside merchants, marriages of children under legal age are performed, men have fled the army or escaped from jail, and property has been illegally acquired from fleeing Muslims at the time of partition. Any of these and similar real and imagined infractions may be objects of a stranger's curiosity and therefore are reasons for discouraging his presence in the village.

Paharis are thought by people of the plains to be ritually, spiritually, and morally inferior. They are suspected of witchcraft and evil magic. In addition, they are considered naïve bumpkins; the hillbilly stereotype of other cultures is shared by Indians. Paharis try to avoid interaction with those who hold these stereotypes. Alien Brahmins may seek to discredit their Pahari counterparts by finding evidence of their unorthodoxy; alien traders may seek to relieve Paharis of their hard-earned cash or produce by sharp business practices; scoundrels may seek to waylay or abduct village women; thieves may come to steal their worldly possessions; lawyers or their cohorts may seek evidence for trumped-up legal proceedings which a poor Pahari could not hope to counteract in court. Christians may hope to infringe on their religious beliefs and practices. Strangers are therefore suspected of having ulterior motives even if they are not associated with the government.

The only way to feel sure that such dangers do not inhere in a person is to know who he is, and to know this he must fit somewhere into the known social system. Only then is he subject to effective local controls so that if he transgresses, or betrays a trust, he can be brought to account. The person who is beyond control is beyond trust and is best hurried on his way.

To take a stranger's advice and change accepted practices would be foolhardy. In view of past experience with the government, government sanction of the advocate and his program merely serves to increase the distrust of villagers.

In considering cultural factors which may be relevant to the consistent failure of Sirkanda villagers to respond to programs of village self-government and coöperative efforts toward self-improvement, certain similarities may be noted to the situation found by Banfield in a village of southern Italy, ". . . the extreme poverty and backwardness of which is to be explained largely (but not entirely) by the inability of the villagers to act together for their common good or, indeed, for any end transcending the immediate, material interest of the nuclear family" (Banfield, 1958, p. 10).

This ethos is defined in terms of the hypothesis by Banfield that the villagers act according to the following implicit rule: "Maximize the material, short-run advantage of the nuclear family; assume that all others will do likewise" (*ibid.*, p. 85).

Adherence to this rule Banfield terms an ethos of "amoral familism." He presents a list of seventeen "logical implications" of this rule (*ibid.*, pp. 85–102). Many of these implications as well as other observations by Banfield are reminiscent of findings reported here and in other studies of Indian family and village life, with the qualification that in India the relevant unit is the extended rather than the nuclear family. There is a temptation to ascribe to this society a characteristic of "amoral familism" on the extended family level. However, as Banfield points out, similar observations could be made about any society.

Amoral familism is a pattern or syndrome; a society exhibiting *some* of the constituent elements of the syndrome is decisively different from one exhibiting *all* of them together. Moreover, the matter is one of degree: no matter how selfish or unscrupulous most of its members may be, a society is not amorally individualistic (or familistic) if there is somewhere a significant element of public spiritedness or even of "enlightened" self interest. (Banfield, 1958, pp. 11 f.)

In view of this rigorous requirement, Sirkanda villagers are excluded from "amoral familism" even on the extended family level. "Amoral factionalism," "amoral casteism," and so on, are also excluded; there are too many occasions upon which behavior is inconsistent with the rule of total commitment to the short-run material advantage of these groups. The symptoms do not add up to the syndrome. Perhaps elsewhere in India there are groups to which the syndrome does apply—or more nearly so. This does not mean that Banfield's conception is useless for an understanding of social behavior in Sirkanda or other Indian villages. Its real usefulness is that it points up the "moral basis" for characteristic social behavior. That is, there may be a cultural norm or world view, an ethos, a pattern of values and attitudes, which predisposes the members of a society against combined action for long-range common goals. Similarly there may be cultural bases for rejection of change or of certain kinds of change. Certainly in Sirkanda there is enough "amoral" preoccupation with, and loyalty to, the extended family that it is a serious obstacle to community action and leads to most of the ramifications which Banfield has listed as "logical implications" of amoral familism.

In Sirkanda this is a relative matter. In interlineage relations the lineage becomes the focus of self-interest; in inter-sib relations it is the sib; in intercaste relations it is the caste. In intervillage matters where caste loyalties are not at issue, there is similar preoccupation with one's own community, as witness the Sirkanda council's refusal to volunteer work on trails to be used by other villages. It might be argued that all these manifestations of group self-interest could be reduced to "familism," since the family is the unit with which the individual is most closely identified and of which he is thinking when he takes a stand on issues at any of these levels. That is, he may take his stand on the basis of the best interests of the family which, in certain circumstances, happen to coincide with sib, caste, or community interests.

"Amoral" self-interest seems especially likely to function at the level of the social unit which acts as an entity in facing insecurity. In any event, culturally sanctioned self-interest on family and other levels is a matter which might usefully be considered along with other cultural factors by anyone attempting to influence people to implement action programs in India.

One aspect of this feature of community life in Sirkanda is the absence of an effective tradition of community coöperation in any but very specific contexts. Another is the absence of village-wide acceptance of formal leadership. Everyone claims to make his own decisions, and those who advocate their viewpoints for others are viewed with suspicion. Neither is there a precedent for democratic village government.

Opler has described perhaps the most crucial obstacle to community development programs as "the social organizational difficulty of expecting a social structure which was essentially fluid, diffuse and conservative to implement programs which demand decision, dispatch, and an experimental frame of mind" (Opler, 1960, p. 197).

The controlling group in Sirkanda has always been the high-caste landowners, and they remain so today. Although they are not a coördinated body on many matters, they are coördinated in their relationship to the low castes, whom they control in almost every sphere. This leads to one of the most perplexing problems in community development in Sirkanda, the conflicting interests of high and low castes.

Sirkanda has a sharply segmented society with important privileges granted to high castes and withheld from low castes. High castes naturally have a heavy stake in maintaining the *status quo*. The Congress party and the government of India have proclaimed an equalitarian, anticaste ideal. To Sirkanda villagers this is one important characteristic of "government" and of "Congress." This alienates high-caste people from the government and its representatives, who are assumed to be dangerous radicals who threaten the traditional system. They feel that ultimately the government will force them to associate with their caste inferiors and will help low castes to independence, prosperity, and arrogance, possibly at high-caste expense and certainly to their detriment. This is an important and explicit reason why high castes refuse to coöperate with government people and programs in Sirkanda.

Low-caste people have been hopeful of improved status and livelihood on exactly these grounds. They hope to benefit from the government's attitudes and programs. The Community Development Program, as it has functioned thus far, has been designed primarily to benefit agriculturists—the high-caste, well-off landowners. This is to be expected because, as Lewis (1959, p. 536) has pointed out, the main aim of the program has been "increases in production rather than social justice" (cf. Dube, 1958, pp. 82 f.). This has become apparent to low-caste Sirkanda villagers, who note that the VLW does not talk to them or consider their problems and obviously has no interest in aiding them. He merely tries to help those who already are well-off and in control. Low castes have not benefited from the program, and there has been no action taken to implement the government's equalitarian pronouncements. Therefore, low-caste people are disillusioned about the government's stated interest in them and their welfare. As a result they are alienated from the Community Development Program and other governmental activities in the village.

High-caste people are antagonistic to the government, partly because of its alleged interest in the equalitarian ideal, which they feel will ultimately result in active championing of low-caste grievances. The government's clumsy attempts to increase agricultural production in the village have not succeeded in counteracting this antagonism, and at the same time have contributed to alienation of the low castes.

Thus, low castes want their positions improved; high castes want their positions maintained by suppression of the low castes. The government has alienated the low castes by their actions, and the high castes by their words. This is a dilemma that has not received explicit recognition but which is very real in Sirkanda and has no readily apparent solution without a choice between production and social justice.

Other reasons for the failure of programs, and for the general attitude toward the government in Sirkanda, are to be found in the nature of the programs, their manner of presentation, and the personnel who have presented them. Since these are matters directly amenable to action by those responsible for the implementation of changes, it is appropriate to consider them here.

THE PROGRAMS

In general, the programs have ignored the traditional orientations of villagers and have not been in line with the desires or "felt needs" of the people.

Dumont and Pocock (1957, p. 19; cf. Tinker, 1959) have attributed the lack of success of village government throughout Uttar Pradesh to lack of understanding of the culture of those being governed:

> They have tried to transfer the idea of the assembly or *pañcāyat* from a caste-group to the multi-caste village. The result, according to our own observations confirmed by reports from elsewhere (all in U.P.) is a standstill since the enterprise comes up against the total disinterest of the elected judges. The institution of the caste *pañcāyat* rests on the solidarity of the caste-group, which is highly sensitive to certain kinds of offenses, while the assumed solidarity of the village is simply nonexistent at that level.

This criticism would seem to be applicable in Sirkanda to a large extent, although it would have to be modified in view of the essentially one-caste nature of the Sirkanda council today and the traditional dominance of that same caste in the village.

Specific programs in Sirkanda have consistently ignored the wants of villagers themselves. Of those presented in 1957–1958, only the water supply project was felt by villagers to be really worthwhile. An earlier attempt to improve that situation had ended in an expensive fiasco at the hands of an unscrupulous contractor, so there was great reluctance to try anything new. The VLW was unable to offer good advice on the matter and no technically qualified person who could have done so was made available, although the council requested such advice. The community center evoked interest but no general agreement. Other programs informally introduced or advocated by the VLW were equally unsuccessful. Improved seed, seed potatoes, and chemical fertilizer, which the previous VLW had attempted to introduce, were rejected by villagers largely because local resources were felt to be sufficient. Adequate natural fertilizer and local seed were available, and there was a general conviction among villagers that seeds, fertilizer, and agricultural techniques which were developed or tested in the plains would be unsuccessful in the hills. Moreover, they were difficult to obtain. They had to be purchased in a distant village of the valley, and by the time they were transported to the hills they were exorbitantly expensive. The government required that the seed be returned with 25 per cent interest and that it be carefully cleaned, requirements which discouraged villagers from its use. Seed potatoes were requested by one villager, but the minimum allotment was more than twice what he could use, and so the idea was dropped.

In the case of the ECS, there was no desire among villagers for the benefits a coöperative credit society could offer. People were accustomed to borrowing from one another or to obtaining credit from a local shop when necessary. They had no desire to risk a new system, especially one which they did not understand at all.

Thus, a general lack of appropriate programs was an important factor in the failure of the VLW and the ECS. It is likely that, had the VLW been able to present the people with a useful solution to the problem of their distant water supply, he would have been well on the way to winning their confidence. Had he practiced the first aid and simple medicine (including veterinary medicine) supposedly at his command, he certainly would have won favor. Had he been sensitive to the desires of villagers, he would have increased his chances of establishing rapport and ultimately of achieving other goals. Among young men there was a real desire for organized recreation in the village; interest had been expressed in volleyball (introduced briefly by a former teacher) and evening singing and music sessions. The VLW ignored these interests—they were not in his program.

He was bound by policy to specific programs which did not lead to the general goals of winning the confidence of the people so that they might be helped to help themselves. What was needed was not rigid application of programs, but study of local conditions—cultural, ecological, agricultural—so that appropriate programs might have been formulated to satisfy some of the immediate wants of villagers. In this way their confidence and coöperation might have been won so that the improved standard of living which is the ultimate goal of community development could be obtained. The overt goal of helping or serving people was in practice subordinated, both by the VLW and by higher administrative levels, to the covert goal of getting minimal compliance, on paper, with official programs. As a result, the entire project was an empty façade. In administrative headquarters this area had achieved a record as a successful unit. In reality it was a failure.

Had specific local programs been formulated in terms of general goals of community development and had accomplishment of covert goals not been substituted for fulfillment of overt goals, success might have been achieved.

MANNER OF PRESENTATION

Even the programs which might have been successful were not presented effectively or even comprehensibly to villagers. There was no effort to discuss planned programs informally in advance with household heads or others nor to invite discussion in their formulation. The programs were invariably presented to the village president, who then relayed the information to villagers as being the VLW's plan, or they were presented through the village council without advance warning. The villagers had no chance to think over a project in advance, much less to ask questions, make suggestions, or suggest alternatives. The VLW is known by the title "village servant," but his projects were presented as governmentally decreed programs to be carried out by villagers under his supervision. Villagers were not led to feel that they were being helped to help themselves, but rather that they were being directed to meet the whims of a government which did not understand their problems and with which they were already at odds. As a result their resentment was compounded.

The government repeatedly demonstrated its ignorance of, and indifference to, the problems of the villagers by advocating programs with no apparent local relevance (chemical fertilizer, Japanese rice cultivation) and by sending as its representatives personnel with no familiarity with the way of life of people in the hills. Simple misunderstandings were also frequent, based partly on the inability of the VLW and ECS to speak or understand the Pahari language, and partly on these officials' failure to explain their plans adequately. Thus, villagers believed that their investment in a credit coöperative would be "swallowed up" by the officials of some government agency and that it could not be refunded. They were totally unaware of some of the services which a VLW was supposed to be able to provide, especially first aid and medicine.

PERSONNEL

The VLW and ECS were poorly trained and poorly motivated. They had no special preparation for work in these rugged and isolated hills. They were therefore thought of by villagers as complete outsiders and greenhorns. Villagers ridiculed their inability to get around easily on the rough mountain trails. When one of these officials made his first appearance in the village, he was guided part of the way by a small village boy. Villagers never forgot the boy's tale of how he had to encourage the man onward at narrow points on the trail and how the man inched forward on all fours, asking God's mercy as he went. These officials constantly complained of the unpleasant surroundings, the difficult terrain, and their own loneliness and boredom. Their meager salaries did not compensate for these hardships. The hill environment did not provide them with the rewards to which they felt their education and official position entitled them. They had no intense commitment or emotional involvement in their jobs, as did the schoolteacher. They were devoted to their status rather than to their responsibilities. They did not receive the prestige, public acceptance, or personal satisfaction that came to the teacher in his well-known and widely respected profession. As a result they were personally ineffective workers as well as advocates of inappropriate programs.

The ECS has been assigned to the village (perhaps as punishment) after having failed the training program for the post. Both the men spent much of their energies trying to effect a transfer to more favorable circumstances. Worst of all, from the point of view of their reception by villagers, was their lack of understanding of or interest in the people with whom they worked. They neither understood nor sympathized with the way of life and problems of the Paharis. They considered the villagers dirty, ignorant, and immoral, not capable of raising their standards and unworthy of close association. Their lack of knowledge of the Pahari language contributed to this state of affairs. They could not even communicate easily with villagers. As a result, neither of the officials talked informally with villagers or came to know, even superficially, any of them other than the shopkeeper, the council president, and one or two men who frequented the school building where these men lived. Neither of the officials was ever seen to enter the village proper nor to go to the fields where villagers worked, in the year that they lived on its outskirts. They won neither the respect nor the trust of villagers. Although the villagers were not hospitable, it might be expected that as agents of change these officials would have made a real effort to win their confidence and understand their outlook. Instead, they relied entirely upon their official positions in their attempts to initiate and carry out programs. Gandhi has commented on the fruitlessness of this approach:

When an official becomes a reformer, he must realize that his official position is not a help but a hindrance. In spite of his Herculean efforts people will suspect him and his motives, and they will scent danger where there is none. And when they do certain things, they often do them more to please the official than to please themselves. (Gandhi, 1952, p. 103)

Education: A Successful Program

The third government employee in Sirkanda is the schoolteacher. Education is not new to Sirkanda villagers, but until 1950 they had to go out of Sirkanda to get it. Usually they went to schools in one of two or three villages of the valley not far from Bhatbair. Even now anyone desiring education beyond the fifth class must go to those villages, and anyone seeking education beyond the eighth class must go into Dehra Dun. People as old as 60 years acquired some education in their childhood. Three men in their late forties have had an eighth-grade education. There are 24 local students currently enrolled in or attending classes regularly in Sirkanda, and three attend higher classes outside Sirkanda. In addition to these students, 36 villagers have attended a village or outside school in the past—33 Rajputs, 2 Brahmins, and 1 blacksmith. Thirty-three of these are men and three are girls. The girls attended school in the village after 1950. In addition, one Brahmin man received some religious training in another hill village. The average period of attendance of these 36 was three years; five went to the eighth class, and four completed five years. It is obvious that this amount of schooling cannot make for a high rate of effective literacy. While all who have gone to school and a few who have not can sign their names, many can read or write little if at all. Little reading or writing is done in the village except in the school, and so literacy is quickly lost by those who acquire it. At best perhaps half of those who have been to school are usefully literate, making a literacy rate among village men of less than 15 per cent and that for women around 1 per cent—a village rate among adults of less than 8 per cent.

Attitudes toward education in Sirkanda are generally not favorable. School is thought of as a place for children with nothing better to do. In most families only children who are not needed elsewhere are allowed to go. Most families consider education for girls to be entirely useless and actually detrimental. As a result of these attitudes, a maximum of 20 out of 35 eligible boys in Sirkanda attend the local elementary school while 4 of 31 girls do so. Most children are in agreement with their parents on this issue, but at least one small girl attended school sporadically despite her father's refusal to enroll her, and one boy requested private tutoring when his father demanded that he work during school hours. Often one or two boys of a large family are educated and others are not. The educated one is usually one who shows some liking or aptitude for school or, perhaps more often, who dislikes other work or is unable to perform it.

One of the most successful educated men of Bhatbair is a man of another village who began school at the age of 14 after an attack of pneumonia which left him weak and sickly. His father, who had previously forbidden education in his family, saw the boy's weak condition and said, "Now he's not good for work, he may as well sit in the school each day." Despite his late start this boy went on through high school, got a job on the office staff of a limestone quarrying company and quickly advanced to an excellent position. Now he is educating a younger sister although his parents insist that it is a waste to do so.

Family size and land ownership are important factors. A small family, especially if it has much land, cannot afford to let boys go to school who might otherwise be helping to farm. A family's wealth is a primary factor, especially in higher education. Sometimes a wealthy family can afford to hire a servant to do a boy's work so that he can go to school if he wishes. Education outside the village is expensive because the student must board. The only Bhatbair boy to go to college is a Brahmin from the wealthiest family of Kanda, a neighboring village. All those in Sirkanda who have gone outside the village for schooling have been from the wealthiest families, and some had relatives near the valley with whom they could live and from whose homes they could commute to school.

Establishing schools in Bhatbair was not an easy task. Three one-teacher schools were authorized in 1949, one in each of the three largest villages, with a potential enrollment of around 50 students each. Teachers were assigned by the Dehra Dun District Board in

1950. They were all well-trained, young but experienced, apparently quite highly motivated, and, most important, were from other hill areas so that the living conditions, terrain, language, and culture of the area were not strange to them. In each village where they have established schools they have come to know villagers on a personal level and have to a considerable extent been accepted by them. However, in the initial stages they were beset by many difficulties. In one of the three villages originally picked for a school (and it is a village with a long-standing reputation for inhospitality), the teacher was unable to get a single pupil to attend school. After several months he was authorized to move to a village with one-sixth of the potential student body, but one more favorably disposed toward education. It is a village made up entirely of relatives of the wealthy Brahmin who serves as the traditional Sirkanda priest. There the teacher has run a school on the veranda of a house for six years, with an average of five pupils in attendance. The other teachers did somewhat better in Kanda and Sirkanda where eight to fifteen students have attended the schools over this period.

In 1957, when a new teacher came to Sirkanda, he found an attending student body of 8 students and an official register of over 20. He found the standard of achievement extremely low. Being a conscientious person, he set about to rectify both matters and he met with remarkable success. On the point of attendance, he was faced with three alternatives: (1) continue to falsify the attendance record as his predecessor evidently had, under pressure from the District Board to increase enrollment, though this involved the risk of detection and punishment; (2) report the truth of the matter, thus provoking an investigation that would hurt either the previous teacher, himself, or both; (3) raise the enrollment to match the records, a seemingly hopeless task. This teacher elected to follow the last course and in a period of three months he had, by begging, cajoling, and threatening, managed to raise his regular daily attendance from 8 to around 20. He received no credit for this beyond his own satisfaction and peace of mind. No one in the village cared, and the increase in attendance did not show on his records to higher officials.

As to achievement, the teacher undertook to raise standards by intensive effort, discipline, and some tutoring. His success is indicated by the fact that the only candidate for the fifth-class examinations, an exceptionally backward pupil at the beginning of his fifth year, passed the district examinations in the upper third of the group examined. For this, too, the teacher received no credit from villagers, and his efforts were unknown to the school authorities.

The teacher's efforts were not unappreciated by his students. Of 31 students, roughly 20 of whom were in attendance on any particular day, there was a core of about 10 who attended consistently. That is, 10 students came regularly, while of the remaining 21 an average of about 10 appeared daily. The consistent attendees appeared to be sincerely interested in school and respectful and appreciative of the teacher. Several of the other students were equally interested but lacked the support of their families which would have enabled them to attend regularly. It was the interest displayed by these pupils which inspired the teacher in his largely thankless task. He was especially pleased when one of his students, on his own initiative, took English lessons from the anthropologist's interpreter for a period of three or four months. However, neither the schoolteacher nor any villager knew English, and the boy finally gave up the effort.

The school year in Sirkanda consisted of about a 5-hour day of classwork, 5½ days a week for approximately 10 months per year. The curriculum was similar to that in elementary schools throughout Uttar Pradesh, consisting of exercises in reading, writing, and arithmetic and occasional study of stories, religion, history, and geography, all by rote. There was no attempt to relate school studies to practical problems of village life.

Official school enrollment in Sirkanda was 25 at its maximum, and with 6 unenrolled attendees, attendance remained consistently at around 20 despite daily absentees, except in the harvest periods and heavy rains, when it dropped to around 10. Seven of these pupils (2 Bajgis, 1 Muslim, and 4 Brahmins) were boys from two other villages about three miles distant, who came daily over an extremely rough trail. Twenty-one enrolled and unenrolled Sirkanda students were Rajputs, 2 were blacksmiths and 1 a Brahmin, and only 4 (all Rajputs) were girls. Grade distribution reflects both the drop-out rate and the successful recruitment of beginners by the new teacher: first grade, 11 enrolled and 6 in informal attendance; second grade, 5 enrolled; third grade, 4 enrolled; fourth grade, 3 enrolled; fifth grade, 1 enrolled. Only one girl attended at all regularly.

Three Sirkanda boys were enrolled in high schools in 1957–1958, one each in the seventh and eighth grades in Majra, a village bordering the valley, and one in high school (ninth grade) in Dehra Dun. At the end of the year, one Sirkanda student went on to the sixth class at Majra and the eighth-grader there went on to high school in Dehra Dun.

It seems likely that when a high school is established in Majra, where the sixth, seventh, and eighth classes are currently held, more

Sirkanda boys will pursue their education. Such a school is under construction and is expected to be opened in a year or two. There, as villagers point out, the boys can live with relatives and attend school relatively inexpensively, without being exposed to the temptations of city life.

The school, then, is a government enterprise that has fared better in Sirkanda and neighboring villages than have other programs. The reasons for this success are several. The school is an institution to which villagers have become accustomed over a long period of time, first outside the village and more recently in the village. Its potential value in achieving tangible results in the form of jobs and prestige is obvious to all, though many hold that these results are not suitable or attainable for their children. The teacher's role is a familiar one to villagers, and his purposes and functions, although not always approved, are at least understood. He may be a bother and a distracting influence to children who could be better engaged elsewhere, but at least he does not pose a threat to adult villagers nor is he suspected of ulterior motives. He is not, in the conventional sense, an agent of authority. In these respects he is different from other government employees.

Teachers have been consistently effective as individuals in this area. They have been relatively well trained in teacher training schools. They are self-selected, doing what they planned to do in a well-established profession with a secure future. They have been intelligently assigned, with their own cultural background in mind. Indicative of their appropriateness for their jobs is the length of their tenure in these jobs despite isolation and frustrating working conditions: 6, 6, and 4 years for the three recent teachers, and the replacement for the last of these is beginning his second year without yet seeking transfer. They have consistently established fairly good rapport with villagers, considering the obstacles which any outsider faces in the closed society of the area. This did not come easily. One or two years were required for each to gain acceptance, but from the point of view of the program the time has probably been well spent. Rapid turnover of personnel would have precluded the possibility of achieving such rapport.

Some of the important factors which have led to failure of other programs in the village have therefore not characterized the educational program. The goals have been relatively consistent. In the context of Indian or at least district educational policy covert goals have been the same as overt goals (the principal disparity being in the emphasis upon enrollment versus actual attendance), and general goals (teaching children facts and skills as outlined in the curriculum) have been in harmony with specific goals (enabling children to pass the examinations, or at least to fail them only after a noble try).

In spite of its relative success, education has not been enthusiastically received in Sirkanda. The teacher's job is a frustrating and thankless one. This can in part be attributed to villagers' suspicion of outsiders; in part to antigovernment sentiments; in part to lack of enthusiasm about education. The last-mentioned factor is conditioned to a large extent by the lack of tangible benefits to those who have been educated in the past. To many villagers education is simply irrelevant in traditional village life, the only way of life accessible to these people. Village education is not conducive to orientation toward the outside, nor sufficient to enable people to make a success of life on the outside, nor is it of any great practical value in the village. Its demonstrated value in Sirkanda is only that it brings to the villager the advantages of a limited literacy (which villagers are coming to appreciate in the light of increasing necessity to deal with the government) and some general awareness of geography, history, and nationalism. The villager is presumably thus helped to become a more responsible citizen in a republic—an official goal of education of which villagers are unaware.

However, to the extent that education has been successful and is becoming more so, we have presumptive evidence that inherent cultural factors do not preclude success in governmental programs. Carefully planned programs presented intelligently by properly trained and motivated people can be successful in the village. If they have the further advantage of fulfilling a "felt need" and bringing a tangible benefit, their success is even more likely. With initial hard-earned successes, subsequent accomplishments might be expected to come more easily as traditional suspicions are allayed.

BALANCE OF EXTERNAL RELATIONS

Relations between Sirkanda and the outside can be summarized by saying that on the whole, intrusions from the outside into the village have far outweighed, in numbers and effect, the extensions of the village into the outside world. That is, while villagers do go out of the hill area for trade and pilgrimage, and village boys and young men not infrequently seek adventure in other areas, the excursions are short-lived and usually result in greater appreciation of the village and its familiar way of life. Those who have been outside bring back stories of their adventures and certain material goods obtained there, but they do not often bring lasting changes to the village. On the other hand, government activity in the village, and to a lesser extent outside merchants and others, have brought into the village a number of alien ideas, practices, and material goods. Although the activity of outsiders has recently increased in effect, it is not a recent thing. Under the British and before that under the Garhwal Raja, outside government impinged on Sirkanda, and traders have long frequented the village. And for fifty years schooling has been acquired by some village children.

Within the more restricted area of the "marriage network" surrounding Sirkanda—the immediate culture area—but not extending to "outside" or urban areas, it is evident that extensions of the village are many and pervasive, as with the plains village, Senapur, of which Opler (1956, p. 10) writes, "the involvement of . . . villagers with organizations, places, and events outside of the village is considerable and it seems that this has been the case for a very long time."

The fact that this village, like communities everywhere, has such relations and extensions does not make it any less a functional unit. This fact merely puts it into perspective as one unit within a larger complex of systems on several different levels.

In discussing the problem of extensions of village communities to the extra-community world, R. J. Smith (1956, p. 4) has said:

> There are three types of extensions:
> 1. Intellectual awareness
> 2. Physical mobility
> 3. Organizational affiliation (or membership).
> These are not, of course, water-tight compartments, and it is unlikely that any one activity or extension will be entirely one or the other of these.

It is evident from the discussion above that all three of these types are found, in varying degrees, in the relationship of Sirkanda to the outside world. However, a fourth type of extension was of interest in this research and appears to be crucial to community cohesion and relevant to cultural change. This is individual or group *identification* with an outside group. That is, in addition to awareness of, mobility to, or organizational affiliation with, an outside group, there is also the possibility of adoption of that group as an identification group or, as it is commonly known in the sociological literature, a reference group (Newcomb, 1950, pp. 225 f.; Turner, 1956, p. 328).

One of the aims of the research reported here was to investigate factors relevant to social cohesion and disintegration in the community.

Unfortunately, comparative data from a culturally similar community is not at hand. There is, however, some literature of a theoretical nature on the subject, and the writer has made comparable observations in a community in the Aleutian Islands of North America which provide some useful contrasts (Berreman, 1955). In the Aleutian village, it was found that individuals tended to identify consistently with an alien group, non-Aleut participants in the urban culture of the mainland. This attitude was disintegrative to the community because the norms of the alien group could not be realized in the context of the isolated community. People had to leave the community to achieve any chance of acceptance by members of the group providing the frames of reference which influence their attitudes and behavior, or even to be able to practice this behavior and satisfy their aspirations. The situation was attributable largely to the influx into the community of alien agents of socialization, who represented the source of authority and of rewards in the community and who instilled in its members values which were not realizable in the community context. As a result, people began to look outside the community for their standards of behavior and achievement. Unable to meet these standards in the village they left, or remained as frustrated "marginal men." Their plight was evident in the high emigration rate and the many types of stress experienced by individuals in the village, including stress of unprecedented kinds for which no adaptive mechanisms were readily available.

On the basis of that example it was hypothesized that "persistently attempted projection to an . . . alien context, if it cannot be achieved by community members within their community, is disintegrative to that community" (Berreman, 1955, p. 58). That is, to the extent that members of the community adopt values which cannot be realized in the community but can be realized outside the community, that community is likely to disintegrate. Such values are most often acquired from alien reference groups—groups which are the sources of authority and rewards. Such groups are especially potent when they are in key positions as agents of socialization of children (for example, teachers), as they were in the Aleutian community. To state it differently, a high positive correlation exists between the extent to which individuals' reference groups are also their membership groups and the integration of the community as evidenced by other criteria of integration.

In attempting to counteract disintegrative trends in a community, success is as likely to be achieved (and probably more realistically so) by making new values achievable within the community as by trying to prevent their acquisition or by trying to reëstablish traditional values.

Sirkanda offers a notable contrast to the Aleutian village in its state of cohesion or integration as a community. In Sirkanda there is little in the way of adoption of alien values or reference groups aside from the ritual sphere, where plains standards are adopted as a means of social mobility. Socialization remains primarily in the hands of villagers. Schooling within the village has been relatively innocuous from this point of view. It has reached relatively few villagers with any significant intensity. Moreover, teachers have been of the same general Pahari cultural background as the villagers. The curriculum has not taught an alien way of life, nor has it conflicted in many respects with traditional values of villagers. Village schooling (unlike that obtained in Dehra Dun) has not turned students' aspirations to the outside, nor has it lessened their effectiveness as villagers. This situation is in sharp contrast to that in the Aleutian village (Berreman, 1955, pp. 54 f.).

In Sirkanda there has as yet been no significant interest in movement to the outside, no significant dissatisfaction with village life. There are few signs of stress in individuals or groups that are not well within the traditional and expectable range and are therefore dealt with effectively in traditional ways. The village is, within the traditional cultural context, which includes caste and factional divisions, cohesive and well-integrated by most indexes that could be set forth. This does not mean that it will remain so. The two recent emigrants to city jobs may be straws in the new wind which is blowing in India, generated by increasing awareness of other ways of living and resulting, as with these two men, in identification with another way of life and attempts to become part of it.

Traditional ties are strong in India. Even villages near large cities remain remarkably cohesive, and people who go to cities to work generally retain close ties in their home villages. Pahari villages very close to Dehra Dun are tied culturally, socially, and religiously much more closely to the hills than to the city. Urban emigration in them is virtually unknown. Attitudes and behavior of their residents seem to differ surprisingly little from those of their fellows in more isolated villages. It is a question to what extent education may alter this situation. So far, the evidence in Sirkanda does not contradict the hypothesis regarding community cohesion derived in the Aleutian village. These are two extreme cases which follow the expected pattern. Further work in less clear-cut circumstances is needed for more substantial verification.

10 CONCLUSION—1958

The function and relative significance of ties of kinship, caste, and community in the lives of people in and around Sirkanda have been a major focus of this research. Implicit in this focus is a belief that the findings will be relevant to an understanding of other villages not only within this culture area, but throughout Northern India and to a lesser extent in India at large.

In the five chapters immediately preceding this one it has been demonstrated that each of these levels of organization is vital in the lives of Sirkanda villagers. They are the structural framework for Pahari culture and social interaction. They come into prominence in varying degrees in various situations. Of the three, kinship ties are of most immediate significance in the lives of individuals. The patrilocal extended family is the residential unit, the property-owning and work group, the group that finds wives for its sons, that participates most actively in the life-cycle rites of its members, that worships common gods together, and that applies safeguards and sanctions to its members to keep the family reputation untarnished. It is, in short, the basic economic, social, and religious unit. Above it, the lineage, clan, sib, and kindred are kin groups which function in many contexts as social and religious units of progressively less relevance to the individual. Informal organization within the caste and community tends to follow lines of kinship. Those kin ties are strongest which occur within the community.

The caste or jati is theoretically an extension of the kin group, since its members are supposed to be descended from a common ancestor. Their kin relationship is, however, sufficiently remote that it assumes little practical significance beyond that basic to caste itself, namely the ritual and social equivalence of its members. Pahari caste is the hereditary, endogamous unit, ranked with regard to other such units in terms of ritual and social status. It is associated with a traditional occupation or range of occupations. Caste is significant in its regulation of marriage and other social and ritual contacts, in its influence on the religious and economic activities of its members, and as an effective identification group for its members. It is an important tie which extends throughout the immediate culture area across community boundaries and transcends community loyalties.

The village community is made up of people identified with a particular nucleated settlement area surrounded by agricultural lands cultivated primarily by its high-caste residents. The village cannot be understood without reference to its extensions in surrounding villages, especially those which can be reached in half a day and with which its members have most of their marriage and other extravillage social, religious, and economic ties. However in most circumstances the village is a more important identification group than is the larger locality. People feel loyalty to it, keep its secrets, and rally to its support when confronted by outsiders. It is the place where property is held, where a living can be made, where one's primary emotional attachments are focused, where one feels secure at times of crisis and happy at times of rejoicing. Disputes among villagers are most often resolved within the community, usually by high-caste pressure or arbitration. Trails, water supply, and uncultivated lands are held by the village in common. It functions as an entity in the worship of village gods, its unity and identity becoming especially explicit in the important village-protection ceremony.

Interaction among villagers is far more frequent than their interaction with members of other villages, except for villagers who live elsewhere but still identify with the village. The status of nonresident villagers, who retain their traditional village affiliation although they live in outlying dwellings where they may interact more frequently with members of other villages than with members of their own village, is one of the contrasts between hill villages and those of the plains. Often nonresident hill villagers represent the first step toward creation of a new village. They usually retain their original village identification as long as they belong to joint families which own a dwelling in that village.

An individual's identification and commitment is first and always with his local kin groups. It is not so easy to determine precedence in more distant ties within the caste and in cross-caste ties in the community. The individual is closely identified with, and committed to, both. In disputes which test these loyalties he usually takes the side of his caste over that of his village, but such situations are rare. When there is no such conflict of loyalties, intercaste disputes find him siding with his caste, and intervillage disputes find him siding with his village. Village affiliation can be changed, though not easily, while caste affiliation is inherited and unalterable. If a person emigrates from his village he may seek new village affiliation, although his village of origin will not be forgotten. He cannot seek new caste affiliation. He establishes himself among members of his own caste in his new environment. Therefore, community ties, though strong, are less stable than, and in certain respects secondary to, caste ties.

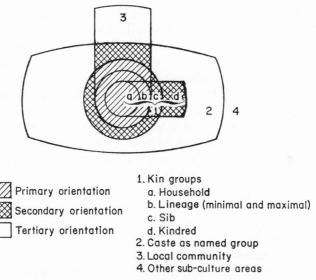

	1. Kin groups
▨ Primary orientation	a. Household
▧ Secondary orientation	b. Lineage (minimal and maximal)
	c. Sib
▢ Tertiary orientation	d. Kindred
	2. Caste as named group
	3. Local community
	4. Other sub-culture areas

Fig. 7. Kin, caste, and community orientations.

The relationship of these three levels of orientation for the individual—kin, caste, and community—can best be viewed in terms of the area in which they coincide. A portion of the diagram of "levels of identification and interaction" (fig. 6) can be adapted as a schematic way of looking at the relationships. It is intended to suggest reality rather than to define it precisely. Where kin, caste, and community ties all function at once to tie individuals to one another, we find the area of the individual's fundamental or primary identification (diagonally hatched portion of figure 7). Where two of the three coincide, there is less intense or secondary identification (crosshatched portion of the figure). Where only one of these ties is present, there is a tertiary level of identification. Of course, kinship ties always occur within the caste, a fact which assures the local kin group of its preeminent place in the orientation of the individual. In other words, kinfolk who live in the same village identify most closely with one another. Other things being equal, as they rarely are, kinfolk who reside in other villages and non-kin caste-fellows who reside in the same village are of secondary immediacy in the orientation of the individual. Non-kin caste-fellows of other villages and local villagers of other castes are of tertiary immediacy in the orientation of the individual.

These statements are applicable only within the familiar area of marriage relationships around the village, that is, Bhatbair and vicinity. To go beyond the immediate culture area is to go beyond the familiar world of villagers and hence to bring in factors of strangeness and uncertainty. Thus, a caste-fellow from another area is not comparable to a resident of Bhatbair in the minds of the people of Bhatbair. He is outside the marriage network. Here degrees of difference are crucial. A resident of a neighboring area is more easily appraised and is more likely to be acceptable in a marriage arrangement than one of a more distant and more different area. Any speaker of the Central Pahari dialect can be fitted into the system more easily than can speakers of Western and Eastern Pahari, while any Pahari is less foreign than a non-Pahari. A fourth level of identification might therefore be defined as non-kin, noncaste, noncommunity members who are of the same subcultural area.

The status of the stranger emphasizes the relatively closed nature of Sirkanda society. Ties of kinship, caste, and community are crucial. If a person has such ties in the culture area he can be incorporated into the social system. If not, he is an outsider and a stranger. Since kin and caste ties cannot be acquired, the only hope of acceptance an outsider has (shopkeeper, schoolteacher, village level worker, servant) is through community affiliation, and this comes only after continuous residence and interaction with villagers. The measure of acceptance granted the anthropologist and his interpreter came after some time, on the basis of residence in Sirkanda and interaction with its members. Redfield (1957, pp. 33 f.) says that "institutionalized forms for admitting strangers" are characteristic of peasant communities, resulting from the fact that such communities are dependent upon cities and therefore must admit representatives of necessary urban institutions into their midst. Some of these representatives have to reside in the village for extended periods, and the peasant society is prepared to allow them to do so. Redfield points out that such aliens do not participate fully in village life (indeed they would not be allowed to in Sirkanda), and cannot become village members. Like the shopkeeper and governmental employees in Sirkanda, they become instead "resident strangers," admitted upon sufferance of villagers to play their limited roles.

In this research attention has been called to the confusion which often arises between caste conceived of as an abstract, idealized system and caste viewed as behavior—as attitudes expressed by people and as interaction among people (cf. Berreman, 1960a). Both are important for an understanding of the system, but their differences and spheres of relevance have to be kept clear in the observer's mind if accurate interpretations are to result.

While this point has been made with special reference to caste, a similar point is pertinent to discussions of kin group, community, and extracommunity organization and interaction. What people say should be done is often quite different from what is done and enforced within and among these groups. Some of the confusion about the "great" and "little" religious traditions in India, with the frequent implication that these are correlated with national and local spread, respectively, is attributable in large part to failure to make the appropriate distinctions in observation and analysis or to make explicit the context in which reported religious attitudes and behavior correspond to the facts of daily life. Similar confusion is evident in much of the comment concerning the effectiveness, on the community level, of programs of community development and local self-government. Speculation about the decline, in some areas, of the village and of the extended family as effective social and economic units may also be biased by confusion on these points. Behavior, observed and analyzed in context, is necessary information upon which to base conclusions about culture and social structure.

This does not mean that such factors as private attitudes and, at the other extreme, great traditions, should be overlooked. These are important aspects of reality whose existence and relevance to those who hold them are detectable only through behavior, often verbal or other symbolic behavior. To overlook such factors would be to overlook an aspect of culture as important as any other. However, they should be analyzed in terms of their relationship to other types of behavior. When information is obtained from secondary sources or literary sources, care has to be taken to obtain the behavioral context in which it functions. Caution is especially necessary when, as in matters of caste in India, certain groups have strong vested interests in adhering to particular and often limited views of reality, particularly before an audience of outsiders.

THE PAHARI CULTURE AREA: SOURCES AND AFFINITIES

In comparisons and generalizations the Himalayan foothills from Kashmir across North India and Nepal have here been referred to as a "culture area." In some contexts smaller segments of this area as, for example, the region occupied by Central Pahari-speaking peoples (roughly between the Jumna and Kali rivers), Tehri Garhwal, or even Bhatbair and vicinity have been referred to as culture areas. This is a matter of level of generalization, since a culture area is simply an area within which the cultures are similar to one another and distinctive relative to cultures outside that area. Sirkanda residents could be legitimately described as representatives of any or all of the following culture areas: India, North India, Pahari, Central Pahari, Garhwal, Tehri Garhwal, Bhatbair and vicinity. Other areas could be delimited, including some that would crosscut these. For present purposes the Pahari culture area, an unusually distinct and sharply defined one, will be discussed.

A brief description of this culture area which has been given elsewhere can be repeated here to indicate the nature of Pahari culture:

The distinctiveness of the Paharis as a group is suggested by the fact that they share a common and distinctive linguistic stock. They also share a number of other cultural features which distinguish them from the rest of the North Indian culture area and specifically from the plains-dwellers adjacent to them. These features, like their language, are not entirely unique or divorced from those of the rest of North India, but are divergent forms grounded in a common heritage. In emphasizing differences, care must be taken not to ignore the numerous and basic similarities common to Paharis and other North Indians. Differences are, however, the primary subject of this analysis. Among distinguishing Pahari characteristics are:

(1) A somewhat distinctive caste structure wherein there is a major division between the dominant high or twice-born castes ("big castes" in local parlance), made up of Brahmins and Rajputs, and the "untouchable" (*achut*) low or "small" castes. The former are the land-owning agriculturalists; the latter comprise all of the service castes (blacksmiths, carpenters, weavers, musicians, shoemakers, and others), collectively termed Dom, and make up only about 10 percent of the population in any area. While there is hierarchical caste ranking within each of these two major categories, it is of significance primarily to those within that category. From across the high-low caste pollution barrier, it appears insignificant. The range of castes found in the hills is

smaller than in the plains. Conspicuous by their absence are indigenous Vaisya (merchants) and Sudra (clean caste artisans). On the other hand, occupational variability within castes is considerable in the hills. . . .

(2) A number of rules pertaining to marriage which would be unacceptable to many plains groups and especially to those of high caste. These include bride-price marriage with no necessity for a Sanskritic marriage ceremony, polyandry in some areas, levirate, divorce by mutual consent, remarriage of widows and divorcees, toleration of intercaste marriage within the high- or low-caste group. There is also a good deal of postmarital sexual freedom and sanctioned relations of brothers with one another's wives. Marriage is universally prohibited only in own and mother's clan [that is, sib], and village exogamy is not everywhere the rule.

(3) No seclusion of women and freer participation of women in most aspects of life than on the plains, including their participation in singing and dancing at festivals. Relatively free informal contact between the sexes is usual.

(4) A number of religious and ritual features such as absence of the requirement for a Sanskritic marriage ceremony and absence of the requirement for a sacred thread ceremony for high-caste boys, though such ceremonies are coming rapidly into vogue in some areas. Distinctive Pahari marriage and death ceremonies are performed. There is a great reliance upon mediums and diviners and in some areas the Brahmin priest is relatively less important than on the plains. Frequent and elaborate ritual purification and other religiously motivated acts common on the plains are less widespread in the hills. There are many distinctively Pahari religious beliefs and forms of worship. Animal sacrifice is a part of most Pahari ceremonies, and buffalo sacrifice is found in some areas. Paharis are widely known for their devotion to the Pandavas of *Mahabharata* fame and to Siva. The unique and spectacular rope-sliding ceremony is performed in honor of the latter. . . .

(5) Distinctive folklore, songs, dances and festivals.

(6) Consumption of meat and liquor by all castes.

(7) Greater flexibility of intercaste relations and freer intercaste interaction than on the plains. The caste hierarchy is important and caste status differences are actively enforced, but the rules allow considerably more contact and informal interaction than is usual in India.

(8) In addition to a nucleated settlement adjacent to a concentration of village lands there are temporary-cum-permanent dwellings on widely scattered and often distant agricultural and grazing lands. These are thought of as part of the village even when other villages intervene.

(9) Terrace agriculture with primary dependence on millets, wheat, and barley. Soil productivity is maintained by systematic fertilization, crop rotation, and fallowing. Water is scarce but wherever possible is used for irrigated rice cultivation.

(10) Dwellings of stone and timbers, often with slate roofs. Distinctive architecture of two stories with lower floor as barn and upper floor as living area, often with large open veranda or porch at the upper level.

(11) A number of artifacts including lathe-turned wooden utensils, elaborately carved wooden porch columns, lintels, windows, etc.; virtual absence of pottery.

(12) Distinctive women's dress and ornamentation, including full skirt, fitted jacket, and several types of gold and silver jewelry. Men's dress is not so distinctive and has rapidly become like that of men of the plains, but now includes a black or colored cap, a woolen blanket, and a cane as typical Pahari accoutrements.

This list is suggestive rather than exhaustive. Some items on it may not be as widespread in the hills as others, especially in the area east of Garhwal, for which there is little information. It serves to make the point, however, that this can for some purposes be considered a distinct culture area or subarea within the greater North Indian area. In view of its geographical and ecological isolation, its distinctiveness is not surprising; in view of its common heritage with the rest of North India, its basic similarity thereto is only what would be expected. (Berreman, 1960b, pp. 775–778)

Several explanations for these and other distinctive Pahari traits have been offered by the people themselves and by various observers. Perhaps the most frequent explanation is an environmental one. A villager commented:

We can't observe all of those rules that plains people do. Our women have to work, they can't bother with being secluded [purdah] or being out of circulation when they menstruate or for a long time after they give birth. We haven't enough water nor enough time to waste bathing all of the time like some plains people do. If a Brahmin here practiced all the observances a plains Brahmin does, his family would starve.

Some writers have set forth very explicit, and often curious environmentally deterministic, explanations. Raturi (1928, p. 207) says that "it is natural to eat meat and drink wine and wear woolen clothes to keep warm in cold countries," and Majumdar (1944, p. 128) asserts that "in cold climates dances form the most important form of recreation."

Some traits have been explained in terms of economics. Bahadur (1916, p. 135) attributes polygyny to the need for wives as agricultural laborers, and many villagers also give this explanation. Walton (1911a, p. 88) attributes fraternal polyandry, where it occurs, to pressure on the land and a desire to maintain family lands intact. Majumdar (1944, p. 127) mentions the expense of a woman's jewelry as contributing to polyandry. Several writers have attributed polygamy in this area to disparity in proportions of the sexes (Berreman, 1962a).

A frequently suggested source of the unique configuration of customs found in this hill area is in the assumed cultural origins of the hill people. They are often pictured as modern survivals of an earlier era. Briffault (1927, p. 671) says that "The highland regions of the Himalaya are but a residual cultural island which preserves social customs that had once a far more extensive distribution. The institutions which are found surviving there were once common throughout the greater part of Central Asia." Another author has called them "a fossil of the age of *Mahabharata*" (Munshi, 1955, p. i). Statements such as the latter are based on similarities between certain practices common in the area (polyandry, meat-eating, freedom of women, lack of caste rigidity) and practices recorded in classic texts of Hinduism.

As has been pointed out in chapter 1, it is frequently asserted that the high-caste Khasiyas represent a population of Indo-Aryan speaking invaders who came into this area from the northwest, either directly or via Rajasthan. These people presumably conquered or absorbed an indigenous non-Aryan population ancestral to present-day Doms. It is often assumed that the Indo-Aryans were originally of the pure high-caste stock both genetically and culturally, but that they have since degenerated as a result of isolation or adoption of the practices of the people they conquered. Grierson (1916, p. 7) states that the Khasiyas ". . . were looked upon [by the most ancient Indian authorities] as Kshatriyas of Aryan origin. . . . They were considered to have lost their claim to consideration as Aryans, and to have become . . . barbarians due to their non-observance of the rules of eating and drinking observed by the Sanskritic peoples of India."

The Himalayan area may once have been the home of the ancestors of today's plains Hindus. Basham states that "It has been reasonably suggested that the main line of Aryan penetration was not down the [Ganges] river, the banks of which were then probably thick swampy jungle, but along the Himalayan foothills" (Basham, 1953, p. 41). "While the Aryans had by now [later Vedic period, *ca.* 700 B.C.] expanded far into India their old home in the Panjab and the North-West was practically forgotten. Later Vedic literature mentions it rarely, and then usually with disparagement and contempt, as an impure land where the Vedic sacraments are not performed. It may have been once more invaded by Indo-Iranian tribes who did not follow the orthodox rites" (*ibid.*).

Majumdar believes that the social and religious life of this culture area is a result of mixture of the cultural traditions of indigenes and the Indo-Aryan invaders, and even claims to find evidence that the Doms were "matriarchal" and the Khasiyas "patriarchal." He assigns particular distinctive Pahari traits such as "the double standard of morality practiced by women" (in their home villages as contrasted to those of their husbands) to the influence of alleged matriarchal Dom culture (Majumdar, 1944, pp. 173 f.).

Saksena (1955, p. 30) notes that "it has been suggested by Mayne that the Indo-Aryans adopted their polyandrous customs from the aborigines or from a neighboring polyandrous people." Meat-eating, religious unorthodoxy including worship of household and village gods, and even worship of the god Shiva, have been attributed by some writers to the "aboriginal" culture. Saksena disagrees, on grounds that "when a superior culture imposes itself over an inferior culture, it is the latter which is affected more" (Saksena, 1955, p. 31). Instead, following Briffault, he attributes polyandry as well as most distinctive contemporary practices to survivals of the common Indo-Aryan cultural origin of the high-caste people.

The unique Pahari cultural configuration can also be attributed in part to the distinctive combination of cultural contacts to which the area has been subject since the period of settlement of Indo-Aryan speaking peoples there.

The Pahari area, a long, narrow strip following the southern face of the Himalayas, comprises the northernmost border of the Indian and North Indian culture areas, meeting throughout its length the southern edge of the Tibetan culture area. Off the western end of the Pahari area lies the Southwest Asian area—the Indus valley and Afghanistan (cf. Bacon, 1946). To the east the Pahari area seems to terminate in contact with Tibetans, Tibeto-Burman, and perhaps other "tribal" peoples (cf. Iijima, 1960), and North Indian plains groups. Paharis are to some extent physically isolated from these other areas and groups. They are separated from peoples of the Indo-Gangetic plain by the fact that they occupy rugged hills bordered by a band of talus slopes, swamps, and jungles. They are separated from the Tibetan plateau by the high Himalayas, and from Afghanistan by the mountains of the old Northwest Frontier Province. More important in separating Paharis from adjacent peoples have been cultural and ecological factors. Kawakita (1957, 1961) and Iijima (1961) have commented in some detail on ecological zones and their ethnic correlates in the Nepal Himalaya. Such barriers have contributed to Pahari isolation, but they have not proved insuperable.

The most intensive outside contact in Garhwal has been with the people of the plains of North India, who share historical ties with Paharis and are of the same racial, cultural, and linguistic stock. People from North India—the Gangetic plain, the Punjab, and Rajasthan—have come to the Pahari area frequently on pilgrimages, to trade, to seek refuge from the tribulations of their native areas, or to find new lands and subjects. Thus, the Paharis have felt directly or indirectly the effects of most of the important invasions and other upheavals of North India. Occasionally South Indians have come, especially on pilgrimage, and a few important temples in the mountains are said to have South Indian priests.

Contact with the Southwest Asian area has been extremely limited in contemporary times because of the short common boundary, the great distances, intervening mountains and desert, and political and cultural factors. However, historically this was very likely a region inhabited at least for a time by the Indo-Aryan populations which ultimately extended over all of North India including the Himalayan hills, and which are presumed to have been the source of much of today's Indian culture. The Paharis share this cultural tradition. Contact with Kashmiris, in the northwest, continues today as an indirect Southwest Asian contact.

Observers have frequently attributed Pahari polyandry to contacts with polyandrous Tibetans. This is an unlikely source in view of the distribution and functioning of Pahari polyandry. There has been, however, considerable contact and mutual influence between the two cultures. There are numerous regular trade routes over the Himalayas into Tibet including at least one (Nilang) in Tehri Garhwal. Trade is carried on in both directions. Moreover, there are peoples (the Bhotiyas) living in the higher Indian Himalayas, whose cultural affinities are with Tibet (cf. Kawakita, 1957, 1961; Iijima, 1961; Pant, 1935; Srivastava, 1958). The Bhotiyas are in frequent contact with adjacent Paharis, and they come each winter to trade and to pasture goats and sheep in Pahari areas. In fact, as was noted in chapter 1, the traditional name of the hill area in which this study was carried out, Bhatbair, means "sheep den," in reference to its yearly use by Bhotiya shepherds. Pahari culture has been influenced by contacts with Bhotiyas, especially in Almora District. As a rule in India, Bhotiyas seem to show more markedly than Paharis a cultural amalgam or syncretism brought about by a combination of Tibetan affinities and contacts and close association with Paharis of the Indian culture area. In the hill area of Nepal (the Eastern Pahari-speaking region) Tibetan influence has evidently been considerably stronger than it has in most of the Indian Himalayas and is evidenced today in the greater numbers of people and cultural traits of Tibetan affinities there (cf. Kawakita, 1957, 1961; Iijima, 1961).

The Pahari area is, therefore, a relatively isolated one whose residents share common origins, history, contacts, and environment and who interact with one another more than with outsiders. They have numerous contacts with the residents of the adjacent North Indian plains area, with whom they share origins, much history, and therefore much culture. A significant number of Paharis are relatively recent immigrants from the plains. With the Tibetan area Paharis have long had occasional contact. They have had historical ties and rare contacts with the Southwest Asian culture area as well. No attempt can be made here to outline cultural element distributions to enumerate the debts Pahari culture owes to these other areas. Comparative data are not available and their collection was beyond the scope of this research, but it is obvious that Pahari culture owes them much and has contributed to them as well.

Origins, outside contacts, cultural amalgamation, and environmental and economic adaptation are therefore all relevant to an explanation of the distinctive Pahari culture. In conjunction with such explanatory factors, the fact of isolation and the concept of cultural drift are useful in throwing light on this subject.

All cultures change through time as a result of the transmission, among those who carry them, of the results of experience—cultural variants, alternatives, and additions and deletions, derived from new conditions, relationships, contacts, and insights. Common experience resulting from common environment and from frequent, intensive interaction results in common culture. However, when two or more groups of people become isolated so that social interaction and therefore cultural transmission is decreased or cut off between them, they gradually accumulate differential experience and consequently their cultures change in divergent ways. This cultural drift accounts in large part for the differences between plains and Pahari cultures (Berreman, 1960b). Paharis have had more frequent and intensive contacts with one another than with peoples of the plains or of other culture areas. For example, marriage networks apparently interconnect throughout the Pahari area, but they end abruptly at the plains boundary. Despite their probable common origin, Paharis and plains people have long been separated by topographical and sociocultural barriers, and subjected to different contacts and environments. As a result they are culturally distinct. Language, social organization, economy, religion, and material culture all reflect their distinctiveness.

Degree of mutual isolation also explains contrasts between the degree of cultural variability found among social groups in the hills and that in the plains. Although Pahari culture displays relatively consistent differences when contrasted with plains culture, and in that context appears to be relatively homogeneous, small Pahari localities and regions show a high degree of cultural difference from one another. This variability is evidently greater over shorter distances than in the plains, just as Pahari marriage networks are smaller. This is largely a result of greater isolation between Pahari localities with consequent divergent or differential culture change, that is, cultural drift. Because of the terrain, Pahari settled areas are relatively inaccessible to one another. A fertile valley or gently sloping ridge may have a fairly dense population but may be a difficult journey from another such settled locality. It is such localities which differ culturally so conspicuously from one another. Rosser (1955) describes an extreme example of an isolated and culturally distinct Pahari locality.

Caste groups within a Pahari locality show notably less cultural difference from one another than do castes of the plains—probably also a function of isolation. Plains castes are socially more isolated from one another than are those of the hills and so have had an opportunity to become or remain culturally more distinct than if they had been in frequent, intensive, and extensive contact as are hill castes. On the plains, most intensive contacts are among caste-fellows, often across local boundaries. In the hills, most intensive contacts are within the locality, often across caste boundaries (Berreman, 1960b).

FUNCTIONAL IMPLICATIONS OF PLAINS–PAHARI CONTRASTS

Most generalizations about North Indian society and culture in the anthropological literature are in reality generalizations about the Indo-Gangetic plain. They ignore the Himalayan area either through lack of information or an impression that Paharis are unimportant marginals or possibly tribal peoples. One aim of the present research is to provide a basis for correcting such errors or oversights and to broaden the scope of available information about Indian village life and its regional variations by describing a Pahari village and its region.

Distinctive Pahari characteristics and their possible sources have been pointed out above and contrasted to those of the plains of North India. In conclusion, it is appropriate to comment on the functional implications of some of the most prominent contrasts between these two culture areas.

The nature of the Pahari local group—the village—is affected by its physical environment. Cultivable areas are often small and scattered. Travel between them is slow and difficult as compared to that in the plains. As a consequence, villages are small and isolated. They have an inward-looking, self-contained character as compared to plains villages, and the area of near self-sufficiency in economic, social, and ritual matters is relatively small. Interaction has to be within local or nearby groups if it is to occur at all.

In many Pahari areas there has always been more potentially cultivable land available than could be put into cultivation under the rigorous conditions of this sparsely populated region. Therefore, population increase has proceeded with minimal pressure on the land. Since much usable land is scattered in small amounts, a system of residence in field houses (chans) has developed. As a consequence, population increase has taken place without significant increase in the size of particular villages. New settlements have arisen instead. The chans may also have enabled growing joint families to remain intact as social, economic, and ritual units by permitting them to divide as residential units, thereby reducing interpersonal frictions which lead to dissolution of joint families.

The small, inward-looking nature of the Garhwali village is reflected in the relations among social units within it. The village is not exogamous. All members of the locally dominant Rajput caste in Sirkanda have affinal or consanguineal ties with one another. Marriage networks of all castes are small, their size varying inversely with the population of the caste in the surrounding area. Between high and low castes there is more permissiveness or flexibility in rules of interaction than on the plains, so that within the village they interact frequently and intensively. Minority castes have to interact with their fellow villagers of other castes if they are to interact at all, because caste-fellows are few, far, and difficult of access. Permissiveness of interaction as compared to plains custom does not indicate decreased importance of the pollution barrier or ambiguity as to where it lies or what it means. It merely indicates that there are different behavioral symbols of status in the hierarchy. The lines are drawn as sharply as in the plains, but in different places and in different ways.

Because Paharis have relatively little interaction with distant people, even of their own caste, regional variation in culture is a prominent feature. As a result of the nature of interaction between high and low castes, cultural homogeneity within a locality is great. Everyone knows everyone else's way of life, beliefs, and secrets. To a large extent, these are common to all groups except where particular behaviors are symbols of status differences or are the means of maintaining advantages for particular groups in the village. Freedom of association, including toleration of occasional intermarriage between Rajputs and Brahmins, seems to indicate a genuinely smaller social and ritual distance at this level than is found on the plains.

Associated with permissiveness of intercaste relations is a great amount of flexibility of occupational specialization among castes. There are few castes of occupational specialists, and few individuals in these castes. In any one village or local area, certain specialists may be lacking, or inaccessible. It is therefore important to have artisans who can adopt any of several occupations, and even to have high castes willing and able to take over in an emergency. The flexibility of rules of caste behavior makes this possible without jeopardizing caste status, but it has the effect of reducing the economic security of artisans, for they have little in the way of effective occupational monopolies. Consequently the jajmani system of traditional exchange of goods for services is less rigid, and is less effective from the artisans' point of view, than on the plains (Berreman, 1962b).

The fact that villages have been occupied primarily by owner-cultivators has contributed to self-reliance and an independent attitude among high-caste Sirkanda residents quite in contrast to the alleged *ma-bapism,* or dependence upon paternalistic agents of outside authority, reported for some peoples of India. Paharis owe allegiance to no landlord. No cultivator in the locality in recent times has been master of any other. No landholder is free of arduous agricultural labor in his fields. No one has conveniences or luxuries not available to nearly everyone else. Pahari agricultural techniques, such as fertilization of fields and crop rotation, together with ample land, regular rainfall, and large forest areas to provide fuel and fodder, have made for an economy sufficient to consistently meet subsistence needs. Famine is virtually unknown. People work hard, but economic sufficiency is the result. For the dominant high castes this means a kind of security unknown to many cultivators of the plains.

Also contributory to an independence of spirit in and around Sirkanda has been relative isolation from outside supervision and intervention. Sirkanda people seem to feel less restricted than many plains people. They have a mild kind of frontier mentality associated with freedom from authority and freedom from absence of alternatives. For high-caste Paharis there has always been more land for the taking if one could muster the labor to prepare and cultivate it. Moreover, one could move out of his family's house and out of the village to a new chan location if he wished. If worst came to worst, he could remove to an entirely new area, as did those who settled Sirkanda over 300 years ago.

Low-caste people are acutely aware of their insecure economic position and of high-caste advantage. They feel that they are virtual puppets of the agriculturists. They do not need to fear starvation as long as they remain in the good graces of the cultivating high castes.

What they fear is the rather erratic bestowal and withdrawal of those good graces. Among themselves they are more competitive and less cohesive than is usual among equivalent plains castes. They must often compete for clients because they are dependent on their craftwork for livelihood and there are others, even of other castes, who will take their place if the opportunity arises. This competition varies from place to place and time to time, depending upon the population of artisans in a particular area.

Because of their isolation from caste-fellows resulting from their small numbers and the isolation of villages, low-caste people have little opportunity to coördinate their activities to defend their interests. Perhaps, in view of factors noted above, they would not do so anyway. They have little in the way of caste government, so that their position relative to the high castes is especially weak. The high castes have maintained the situation by serving as authoritarian and ideally paternalistic overseers of the low castes, deciding among themselves all matters pertaining to low-caste people, both internal and intercaste. Low castes are controlled by being kept economically dependent through being denied the opportunity to acquire land in amounts sufficient to make a living. All castes recognize that land means independence for those who own it and control over those who depend upon the owners. This is why agrarian reform is one of the most important problems of rural India.

The nature of Pahari economic organization has ramifications in the position of women, which is one of unusual freedom compared to that of high-caste plains women. Like low-caste women of the plains, hill women participate in the economy in a way incompatible with seclusion.[1] Their work in fields and forests is essential to the well-being of their families. If anything, they do more of this kind of work than the men. Under the circumstances it would not only be difficult for them to observe the niceties of seclusion and other disabilities common on the plains, but also impossible for their menfolk to supervise them closely. This is probably a factor in the sexual freedom allowed Pahari women.

The Pahari rule of bride-price marriage is combined with easy divorce and universal remarriage for divorcees and widows. The family of the groom seeks out a bride and arranges the marriage with her family, whereas in the plains, where dowry is the rule, the bride's family performs these functions. The Pahari bride is in a sense considered the property—and valuable property—of the husband's joint family who paid for her, who derive benefit from her labor, and who will give her up only upon return of the bride price. Even after her husband's death the family's interest in her remains. Usually she becomes her husband's brother's wife by the custom of levirate. The idea of a wife as common property is undoubtedly related to the fact that brothers share their wives' sexuality and that in several Pahari areas fraternal polyandry is the rule (Berreman, 1962a).

Hindu unorthodoxy in the area is due in part to the cultural heritage of the Paharis and in part to their isolation from areas where modern Hinduism developed. It is ascribed by Paharis to poverty and their difficult environment. They have little time or money for the luxury of the elaborate rituals of the plains. They claim to lack the water for the frequent purificatory baths of plainsmen, the leisure to endure fasts and food taboos, the money to hire learned Brahmins, and the education to appreciate these things. In this, as in the freedom of women, they are like low-caste people of the plains. Their increasing awareness of this similarity, resulting from increasing contacts with plains people, leads high-caste Paharis to aspire to emulate plains behavior in order to improve their relative status.

In discussing Pahari culture, the plains have been chosen for comparison because the culture of that area is closely associated with that of the Himalayan hills. The two areas have a common cultural base upon which differences stand out in high relief. Also, it is among people of the plains that the most comparable work has been done upon which comparisons can be based. However, one familiar with the plains must guard against plains-oriented ethnocentrism, in which the plains become the yardstick by which Pahari culture is measured. It is important to bear in mind that Pahari culture is viable in its own right. The fact that it is marginal to the Indian and North Indian culture areas and that it has also apparently been influenced from Tibet does not mean that it is a hodgepodge of borrowings or a distorted reflection of other cultures. The borrowed traits have been integrated into the matrix that is Pahari culture.

The observer of Pahari culture is struck not only by the traits which bear similarities to those found in other culture areas and that have been either borrowed from them or derived from a common origin, but also by the unique traits that, so far as can be determined, were developed by the residents of this region. These range from agricultural techniques such as complex feats of terracing and irrigation, and uniquely constructed and styled houses, to the songs, dances, folklore, and religion of the area.

Moreover, the Pahari area has made important contributions to the cultures of adjacent areas. The Hindu god Shiva, for example, may have originated in Pahari culture, and it is not improbable that some cultural characteristics commonly attributed to the plains have emanated from the hills.

Perhaps more significant than particular traits and their affinities is the distinctive over-all configuration of Pahari culture. To those who live it, Pahari culture is as distinct and as internally consistent as is the culture of any other group, whether it be in an area of "culture climax" or in a "marginal" area. Marginality is relative. From the Pahari's point of view the plains of North India constitute an area as marginal to his own as do the high Himalayas to the north.

When the Pahari disparages his homeland and his way of life to outsiders, it does not mean that he thinks them inferior. It merely indicates his knowledge of outsiders' views of him and his anticipation of their remarks or thoughts. He may feel that the time is coming when the modern plains way will be the only way to success in a new world. He may envy a movie star or a well-to-do contractor or a suave lawyer, but he does not envy the plains villager or urban peon. He is embarrassed by his conspicuous rusticity when he goes to town. He resents taunts and exploitation by strangers. But as long as he is in his homeland, among his own people, he sees the Pahari way of life as superior.

The Pahari's rejection of strangers and their ideas is in part an indication of his satisfaction with his own way of life, a fact which is further indicated by the community cohesion characteristic of this area and by the fact that few have left the area. The Pahari ridicules the man of the plains who cannot easily negotiate the mountain trails, who is afraid of the terrain and its fauna, who cannot survive on its resources. He pities the people of the plains who do not dance, sing, and drink together; whose women are secluded; whose widows cannot remarry; who must drink stagnant water and breathe dusty air; who do not eat meat; who suffer extreme heat, and risk drought and famine in the hot season; who face flood and malaria in the rainy season. Paharis work hard, but they know how to enjoy their spare time together, regardless of age, sex, and caste differences, in a way that plains people might envy. Paharis are proud of their way of life and their environment, but are sensitive to ridicule of them.

While it is useful to analyze this culture in terms of contacts and outside sources of diffusion, the analysis, if it is to be complete, must consider the adjustments, innovations, and distinctive integration which make of the Pahari region a culture area in its own right. As more data become available on the way of life of the peoples of surrounding areas, it will be possible to determine more accurately the culture areas of this part of the world and to assess the mutual cultural debts and affiliations of the Paharis and their neighbors, and the kinds and directions of change they face.

In the meantime, the Himalayan hill peoples, in common with villagers all over India, are beginning to play an increasingly important role as contributors and recipients in the development of the national culture of Independent India. They live in a region which will assume increasing importance to the nation as a reservoir of rich mineral, forest, agricultural, and hydraulic resources, natural beauty, climatic attractiveness, and religious inspiration. The Paharis themselves, as the human resources, are essential to the development of this area and important in the development of the nation. They have much to offer as well as much to learn if India is to realize the potential inherent in them and in the land they occupy.

EPILOGUE :
SIRKANDA TEN YEARS LATER

THE RETURN

On Raksha Bandhan Day, August 8, 1968, ten years almost to the day since I had left Sirkanda, I made my way back up the familiar trail. Spurred by the previous day's news reports that American researchers might be barred from the strategic area—or possibly from all of India—because some had been discovered to be financed by the United States Department of Defense, I had arisen early to make at least one return visit to the village before I could be prohibited from going (although ultimately I was not, cf. Berreman, 1969a, 1971a). The trip to Sirkanda was not crucial to my research, which this time was to be a study of ethnic relations in Dehra Dun (Berreman, 1972), but it was important to me personally because of my interest in and affection for the village and its people.

The journey was not unlike those of ten years before, except that this time I was able to take a bus for the first stage of the trip, from Dehra Dun to Sahas Dhara, the temple and mineral springs at the foot of the mountains. There the tea shops had prospered, expanded and modernized in response to the increased trade provided by worshippers and picknickers. The footbridge had been replaced by one capable of supporting motor vehicles, and a rest house for traveling officials had been erected. Limestone quarrying activities had moved farther up the valley from Sahas Dhara but little closer to Sirkanda.

In Sahas Dhara I briefly renewed my acquaintance with the tea shop keeper I had known ten years before, and in whose custody I had customarily left my decrepit Jeep during the few months that I had owned it and used it to get from town to the foot of the mountains. Then I began the ascent to Sirkanda, walking quickly in the hot and humid morning, noting that it was steeper than I had remembered but hoping nevertheless to reach the village ahead of word of my arrival. Three hours, seven miles, and 3000 feet of climbing later I succeeded as I approached the two pipal trees and the village shop which announce Sirkanda to passersby. I had met not a single Sirkanda resident enroute. The shop of the Vaisya merchant, abandoned in 1958, had tumbled down, but the other remained unchanged, its proprietor, Puran Singh, sitting precisely as he had ten years before, by a cold hearth, apparently wearing the same tattered coat, and keeping an eye on the comings and goings of villagers, alert to any traffic and potential customers on the trail bypassing Sirkanda. He eyed my approach, greeted me guardedly as I sat to rest, and upon my request lit a meagre, fuel-conserving fire to prepare a barely hot cup of tea.

"Where are you from?" he asked after a few minutes.

"Dehra Dun," I answered noncommittally.

"No—where before that?"

"America."

A long pause followed as the closely-watched pot warmed slowly. Finally: "An American fellow lived here once for a couple of years" he offered.

After another pause I answered: "Yes—look at me again. Don't you recognize me, Puranji?"

He gave me a long look, a slow smile and nodded: "So, you are back."

With this, my return was accomplished. There remained the meeting, greeting, reminiscing with those I had known a decade before, the inquiries after those departed and deceased, making the acquaintance of and explanations to those too young to remember, and the discussions of experiences of the intervening years, my own and those of Sirkanda people. For me there remained the challenging but intriguing task of discovering what this decade had meant in the lives of these people: the fate of earlier plans, aspirations and trends; the emergence of new ones—in short, the changes that had occurred and what they indicate about the past and what they portend for the future. This I undertook by going to the village for a day or two, once or twice a month during the ten months I was in Dehra Dun. In addition, I frequently encountered and talked with Sirkanda men in the wholesale bazaar of the city, where they sold vegetables, or at a dairy to which they sold milk. Occasionally they visited me and my family at our house in town. One young Rajput man, Mangal—whom I had known as a 12-year old (see photograph 28)—often stayed with us, largely as an escape from the routine of village life, accompanying me in my peregrinations around the city, or sitting for hours listening to film music on my radio, smoking cigarettes and sipping tea. He ultimately became something of a pest whose arrival was dreaded by the family. I curtailed my potential resentment by reflecting on how my year in Sirkanda (now doubled or quadrupled in villagers' memories) must have seemed to some of its citizens. Other villagers came to me in town to get assistance or moral support in such tasks as seeking medical aid or dealing with petty officials. My house was a secure stopping place in a strange city. Mangal's mother, for example, a woman in her forties, stopped over with her husband on the second visit of her lifetime to town, when she came to consult a medical practitioner. Her unfamiliarity with city ways was almost concealed by the dignity and aplomb with which she dealt with whatever confronted her. But occasionally she was overcome with surprise or interest as when, upon viewing our Indian-style (floor-level) ceramic flush toilet, she clapped her hands together and said, "for washing clothes, how wonderful!"

On several occasions I timed my visits to Sirkanda to accord with ceremonial occasions or to accept invitations to special events there or in other villages of the region. I was especially interested in tape recording the music of these events, and villagers were fascinated to hear the playback. Several times I took my wife and children with me, so villagers had a chance to see all of them (I now had three children: Janet, whom villagers had known in 1957–1958 as a two-year-old, now 13; another daughter, Lynn, 9; and a son, Wayne, 7). Two American friends, anthropologists Lucile F. Newman of the University of California Medical Center, San Francisco, and J. Michael Mahar of the University of Arizona, visited the village in our company, giving villagers the opportunity to see what they perceived as part of our social milieu, and giving me a chance to compare research notes and impressions. Usually I went alone. Only in the last six weeks did an Indian friend accompany me and provide assistance.

In the intervening years, contact had been minimal between myself and the Sirkanda people. I had written several letters in the first years and thereafter conveyed occasional greetings, through my former assistant, to those villagers he met in town. He showed several of them copies of my book, summarizing and translating portions he thought would interest them. I also sent a copy to the teacher, though this was largely a gesture of friendship rather than a communication of information since he knew no English. Later I had an exchange of letters with Mangal, in which he requested help in emigrating to America and in acquiring certain medicines.

The most impressive and surprising contact, to villagers and to myself, came via my parents who, in 1964, while on a Fulbright teaching fellowship in Lahore, West Pakistan, made a vacation trip to Dehra Dun and, with the help and in the company of my old friend and assistant Mohammad, managed to spend a day in Sirkanda. It is no exaggeration to say that this astounded the Sirkanda people, and it provided familial context for me among these people to whom family is all-important. During the visit, my friend Sibba, the blacksmith, escorted them around the village, pointing out the landmarks relevant to my stay (including my humble dwelling, which he styled my "palace"), and regaling them with episodes of my life in the village. Upon my return to Sirkanda four years later, my parents' one-day visit was mentioned and discussed by everyone who met me. Nothing could have cemented my relationship with villagers more.

This, then, is some of the context of my return to Sirkanda. I set for myself the task of inquiring into change in the village without undertaking a major or detailed study, for I had more than I could handle in the urban study of Dehra Dun. In the course of the inquiry, I looked for change in each of the ethnographic spheres that have been reported in previous chapters of this book. I also watched for any insights or hindsights I could derive about the research process described in "Behind Many Masks." Ultimately, finding change to be minimal, I focused on the careers and fortunes of a few individuals in the village, primarily two young men: Kalmu, son of Sibba the blacksmith, and Mangal, son of my closest Rajput friend, Ram Singh. The former had unexpectedly become a religious phenomenon of wide repute; the latter betrayed his own aspirations and those of his family and teacher when he failed the matriculation examination, thereby ending his education at the eighth class. He returned to the village to farm, marry two wives, and dream continually of a life of urban ease and sophistication.

My purpose in this chapter is to report what I learned of change and continuity in the village in such a way as to relate directly and comprehensibly to what has gone before in this book and in time, thereby conveying some further understanding of what life is for the people of

Sirkanda (cf. Wiser and Wiser, 1963). In the process, I shall hope also to convey something of the impact this research and these people had on me and I on them. I will organize the presentation to give first some of my initial impressions of the village and of conspicuous change within it. Then I will proceed to a roughly topical account and conclude with the careers of several young men who have followed paths of change similar to those others have followed or will be likely to follow. Page references are to this book unless they refer to materials deleted from this edition, in which case they are preceded by the notation: "1st ed."

INITIAL IMPRESSIONS

As I approached Sirkanda, but before reaching the teashop, I noted a cement cistern below the trail at the point where the water pipe ends (cf. p. 33). I took this to be an indication that some further community development work had taken place, although I soon noted that people still procured water from the spring far around the hill. The tea shop appeared to be just as it had been the day I left ten years before, even to the demeanor and appearance (overlooking a few more lines and a little more grey) of the shopkeeper.

On the knoll behind the shop, approximately at the former site of the small stone enclosure which comprised the Nag Raja temple, I noticed two small but conspicuous buildings, one evidently a temple and the other surrounded by a border of flowers. Shortly, a sturdy young man emerged from the latter wearing a white garment in sari fashion. He was long haired and bare from the waist up, with a garland of flowers around his neck and he carried a transistor radio over one shoulder. He displayed a peculiar, languid manner with a benign far-away look, rather vacant smile and almost no words. I subsequently realized that, as was often his wont, he probably had been stoned on marijuana. He was addressed as "Dēvtā" (god). I was told quietly that he was a "jōgī" (ascetic, religious devotee), that he lived on the knoll, kept a temple there, and was the son of my friend Sibba the blacksmith, to whom he indeed bore a striking resemblance. The latter appeared shortly to renew our friendship enthusiastically and proudly point to his retreating son with the one English word he remembered from our association, "God."

A few minutes later, while I was still sipping Puran's weak but expensive tea, about ten men and boys appeared on the trail having ascended from Sahas Dhara behind me. Among them were several I recognized at once as having been roughly age-mates of mine a decade before. They reported that they had been on their daily early-morning trip to Sahas Dhara where a Dehra Dun milk dealer meets them in a taxi to pick up the milk they bring down. After completing their business they had returned to the nearby shops for tea and a smoke, as is their custom, when the proprietors told them I had just arrived on the bus and was headed for Sirkanda on the trail. They had immediately set out to overtake me and in fact saw me once or twice on the trail far ahead, but could not catch up—they commented that my reputation as a fast walker was still deserved. Their greeting was surprisingly enthusiastic, for some had been rather wary of me when I knew them. They said that they could hardly recognize me, which, I replied to their amusement, was because I had grown old and fat (they were in a mood to be easily amused). They also said my Hindi had improved (untrue, I think), and they then debated how long it had been since I had left, and how long my residence in the village had lasted. Estimates of the former averaged seven years. More surprisingly, the minimum estimate of my time in the village was two years and they ranged up to four, whereas in fact it was exactly a year. These disparities gave me some pause about attributing much accuracy to their estimates of past time spans—something which was confirmed by disparities in ages and dates reported in subsequently gathered data when compared to those of a decade before. The reader will have to draw his own conclusions about whether the exaggerated impression of the duration of my stay was complimentary to me or not.

After this greeting and an exchange of anecdotes from our past acquaintance, I was escorted over the nearby crest of the ridge past the school and my former house to the village. My nostalgia and the impact of the inadequately remembered beauty of the view over the immense Bandal ravine did not prevent me from noting that the village appeared virtually unchanged by time. My little house was now occupied by a small family (one of the sons of the now-deceased owner, I learned), but the adjacent room still harbored a contingent of buffalo. The school building was in disrepair, its kitchen area having caved in. In the central settlement area the Brahmins' house, almost completed when I left, was impressive, but little newer construction was evident in the village. The only discernible village improvement was the flagstone and cement paving of the path into the main settlement area of the village, which made walking easier and cleaner, especially in the rainy season. It was clear from the corn and amaranth growing lushly near the village, the pumpkin vines on several houses, and distant figures scattered in terraced fields weeding the millet crops that agriculture was much as it had been a decade before. Cows and buffalo tethered in the yards confirmed the continued emphasis on animal husbandry.

After viewing the village and its environs briefly with my many guides, I was urged to have lunch and to stay the night in the home of my Rajput friend, Ram Singh. The former I accepted gladly in lieu of the cold chapatis and hard-boiled egg I had brought from town. The overnight invitation was unexpected—no one had ever asked me to sleep in his home during my residence there a decade earlier. Although I was expected back in Dehra Dun that evening, I was persuaded by the insistence of my hosts and by the downpour which had commenced and which promised to continue throughout the afternoon. Ram Singh warned that travel was dangerous under such conditions because of slippery trails, loosened boulders, and landslips, informing me that Bhopal Singh, the prominent Rajput villager who had challenged my research when I was there before (Prologue, p. xxiv) had been killed falling from a trail north of the village under just such conditions. I acquiesced with the only slightly rueful thought that in previous years I had gone over more dangerous trails than the one back to Sahas Dhara—including the very one on which Bhopal had been subsequently killed—in worse weather than this and no one had been concerned about it then.

During the afternoon of this initial visit most of the men of the village came to see me and hear me tell of my journey from America, of my family, and to ask me again to amaze them with an account of prices, wages, and agricultural productivity in America, the size and speed of airplanes, etc. Sibba, the blacksmith, reminded them all with relish that in America there is no caste. In return, I learned of many events in the village in the decade of my absence, especially the marriages, departures, and deaths of those I had known before. Of the last there were too many, for medical care remains inaccessible and mortality is high. Several of the deceased whom I had known best and would miss most had lived full lives and died in relatively old age, however, notably the owner of my house, and Ram Singh's mother, one of the most admired people of the village—the woman who had interceded on my behalf with a pugnacious and inebriated young Brahmin at the fair ten years before so that I might photograph some young women of another village (see Prologue, p. 00). I was apprised also of the effects of rising prices and dry weather, the departure of the well-liked school teacher and the inferiority of subsequent teachers, and above all, I was told of the events surrounding the advent of Kalmu, the miracle worker and vehicle of god, now known simply as "Devta" (god). I will speak of these things again in some detail.

Three events occurred during the afternoon which, while not of great intrinsic importance, stood out, reminding me sharply of the nature of social organization in Sirkanda—a topic on which I had lectured and written for ten years, to the point that it had virtually become to me a matter of words and concepts rather than the reality of daily life from which I originally learned it. I repeat them here because they impressed me, reminding me that I had indeed returned to Sirkanda.

The first, demonstrating familial organization and sex-roles, involved Mangal, 22-year-old son of my Rajput host and the outstanding scholar of the village school ten years before (see photographs 28 and 31). When I first settled on the verandah of his family's house, he pointed out two attractive young women working in the cattle yard and said boastfully, "Those are my wives; one is from Taal (a village across the river), the other is only a girl of this village." Then he added rather selfrighteously, "I have given the Sirkanda girl to my younger brother because I think it is more fitting to have only one." I noted, nevertheless, that on subsequent occasions he was extremely possessive of both, and while he had me take his photograph with each on several occasions, he exercised his prerogative as eldest brother to prohibit his brother from being photographed (at his own request) with the wife he had presumably been given. Needless to say, the girls' wishes were not ascertained.

The second incident was a puzzled query by a twelve-year-old Rajput boy as I was invited for dinner, "But he isn't Khas, is he?" His father replied hastily that I was different—a foreigner—and that in any case I would be eating on the verandah, not in the kitchen. The son's implication had been, of course, that I was untouchable and therefore could not eat in the Rajput home.

The third incident was reminiscent of the way in which Sibba, by the force of his own personality and intelligence, so often had transcended his lowly caste status in influencing high-caste activities (cf., pp. 60–61; pp. 240–241). He had noticed that the strap on one of my sandals had broken loose on the hike to the village, and commented that it was both a discomfort and a danger. He repeated this to the Rajputs talking with me on Ram Singh's verandah from his perch on the nearby stairs. When no one responded he told the man who owned the shoe repair equipment to go home and get a hammer and shoe nails. When these were brought, he directed my host, Ram Singh, in the lowly task of repairing the shoe—never lifting a finger himself except to test the job when it was done. Knowing him, I am confident that he would have winked at me if he had dared, though few of the Rajputs would have known why. Not long afterwards, noting that I was surrounded and lionized by Rajputs, Sibba said to me in a private moment, "It is not good to be always surrounded by proud people; one cannot talk freely to old friends. Remember the good times and conversations we used to have?" He was resenting, as of old, the high-caste men's attempt to monopolize interaction and control impressions.

After much exhausting interaction, of which these incidents were a part, I was served an opulent meal by Sirkanda standards, heavy on the clarified butter and sugar. By then it was dark and late, so I was soon given the household's only bed—evidently the same string cot I had so often sat upon a decade before—and slept on the verandah, my host and two of his sons on the floor beside me, between me and the securely fastened door to the adjacent room wherein slept the women of the family. True to Ram Singh's apologetic prediction, I was virtually consumed by the fleas in the bedding, but they were somehow less disturbing to sleep in the cool night than had been the swarming flies in the hot afternoon, when I had been prevailed upon to take a welcome but impossible nap.

Up by five, an hour after those with work to do, I was fed and by seven was enroute to Sahas Dhara in the company of a dozen men taking the day's milk to market. I promised to return in a few weeks with my family for a longer stay. Then, accompanied by a couple of men with errands to do in town, I caught the bus back to Dehra Dun. There I found letters awaiting me which summoned me to Delhi to explain my research and the source of its funding to the Ministry of Internal Affairs, to enable them to determine whether I would be allowed to pursue my year's research. I went, and after a few anxious days of governmental inquiry, during which I demonstrated that I had no objectionable funding and assured officials that I would refrain from working with Tibetan refugees and from going into the interior, I was assured that I could continue. So I did.

Unmasked: Response to the Ethnographer

It was clear from my first visit, and it became clearer throughout the year, that villagers were more hospitable to me than they had been during the year of my residence in Sirkanda. This surprised me, but upon reflection, substantiated by some overheard remarks and some judicious inquiries, it seems perfectly explicable.

First, there was the fact that this time I was not living in the village, and so was always regarded as a temporary guest; therefore I did not become a burden, I was not a constant intrusion. Second, I was not usually accompanied by an assistant, with all of the problems that had raised for villagers ten years before. They were thus able to interact directly and more or less exclusively with me—or avoid me if they wished. These facts are not a sufficient explanation of the hospitality, however, because on my first return visit they were not known, and moreover, throughout the year I was, apparently genuinely, urged to return to live in Sirkanda full time. The reasons for the favorable response clearly lay deeper.

I think the most important reason was nostalgia. I had been there ten years earlier when beloved people now dead had been alive, when my informants had been ten years younger and consequently more able-bodied and perhaps more optimistic about the future. In an absolute sense, times had been perhaps somewhat better: prices were lower, there were certain benefits promised or experienced through community development, mosquito abatement, and other governmental programs, the school was in the hands of a respected and dedicated teacher and there was the prospect that some high-caste boys would be successful in education and employment outside the village. Independence was only ten years old, Nehru was Prime Minister and, despite cynicism about the government in Sirkanda, there was hope that things might improve once the trauma of Independence was overcome. More importantly, the past of even ten years ago is tinged with an aura of "the good old days," wherein hardships are forgotten and memories of good times are cherished. My stay was associated with these times and conditions.

Not unrelated to this was the fact that whatever fears had been harbored about negative consequences of my presence in the village had proved unwarranted. No missionaries had descended upon Sirkanda, no tax collectors, no thieves, policemen, or government agents. It was known that I had written a book which had not disparaged the villagers nor resulted in overt public attention to them of any kind— they had discussed this with my former assistant and the teacher long after I had left and were reassured, even gratified. In addition, my positive interest in them was verified and my credentials enhanced by the surprising visit of my parents, by occasional messages from me via the mails or indirectly through my assistant, and finally by my reappearance in the flesh, together with my enlarged family. As one old Rajput woman said upon first recognizing me, "many of us ignore even our relatives and forget those who have departed; you have returned all the way from America to this remote village. What friendship that is." The facts that I remembered many people by name, knew their relationships to one another, admired grown children and inquired after deceased elders, reminisced about common memories, and brought with me new prints of my old village photographs seemed to elicit warm responses.

Somehow I was validated by the events of that decade and by my return, and the validation was augmented by the softening haze of nostalgia. In fact, people of other villages who had only glimpsed me ten years before, or had only heard of me in the interim, came to see me. The young who could barely remember me, if at all, inquired endlessly about me. I was something of a village attraction, more on the order of a mascot than a hero, perhaps, and was in considerable demand in that role.

The hospitality upon my return came strongly and somewhat surprisingly from the Rajputs—to the extent that I found it difficult to visit freely with my low-caste friends. Whereas I had never been invited to stay overnight in a high-caste house before, I was never able to avoid doing so during 1968–1969. Twice I settled hopefully in the school building, planning to use it as a neutral headquarters while in the village, but each time I was almost bodily removed to a more suitable and restrictive environment, a Rajput home. Ultimately I quit bringing my own food and bedroll, so essential a decade earlier, because they were never used.

To spend time with low-caste people I had to excuse myself from my hosts and go to their houses under, I thought, rather disapproving eyes. On one occasion, in order to take a trip to a neighboring low-caste village, I arranged to skirt Sirkanda and meet Sibba on the trail beyond, from whence we proceeded to our destination. I incurred innumerable embarrassingly accusatory questions from my Rajput hosts upon my return the next day for not having let them know I had come.

The motives for this high-caste solicitude were doubtless a combination of concern for my welfare, genuine hospitality, and concern for high-caste prerogatives, high-caste prestige, and high-caste impression management.

Several Rajputs asked about Sharma and Mohammad, my assistants on the previous research, commenting favorably on the former and unfavorably on the latter. Low-caste people seemed almost to have forgotten Sharma, inquiring only, and favorably after Mohammed. Of course, they had only come to know me well after Sharma left. Incidentally, the widely held belief that my Hindi had improved vastly is attributable, I think, less to my proficiency than to the fact that I did not have a bilingual assistant to turn to for help, so was forced to use my Hindi to the maximum.

MATERIAL CHANGE

As I have indicated, the thing which impressed me most upon an initial view of the village, and more so on subsequent and more detailed observation and inquiry, was the lack of conspicuous evidence of change. By this I mean especially material, technological change. I had expected to see evidence of increased access to commercial manufactured goods, technological innovations, results of government programs, etc. Instead, it was as though I had been gone a year rather than a decade.

Most of the houses now look precisely as they did before, though two or three have been abandoned. None of those unused in 1958 have been reoccupied. Only two new houses have been built, while three had been built during the single year 1957–1958. One house, that of the current Pradhan, is undergoing substantial renovation. It had been the previous Pradhan who had completed the most construction ten years before. Now, as then, I learned, it is gossiped that the Pradhan has been able to build because of misuse of his office and/or village funds. Approximately the same proportions of roofs are thatch, slate and corrugated iron as before, with no notable substitution of the last of these as I had thought might happen; in fact, most of them are the very same roofs. There has been no conspicuous influx of household furniture: no chairs, no tables, little chinaware, few cupboards or string cots—all items people had professed to want a decade earlier. Sibba still has no cot; most Rajput households have only one. No new types of utensils or tools are in evidence except that aluminum milk cans have almost totally replaced the traditional wooden vessels, gourds, and kerosene tins for transporting milk to market. The older containers are still used around the village, but the wooden ones may be on their way out. There are no pressure lanterns or flashlights, despite their availability in the marketplace and the great demand for mine ten years before. Handmade leaf rain capes are still widely used, although I had thought them well on the way to being replaced by umbrellas in 1958. There are only two transistor radios in the village, one belonging to the Devta, evidently purchased from the donations of his devotees (he also has a thermos bottle, the only one in the village), and the other belonging to a well-to-do family whose son bought it while in teacher-training in Dehra Dun. Clothing styles have not altered except that western-style shoes are somewhat more common than before, and the young women of one Rajput family have plains-style saris which they wear when they go to Sahas Dhara to visit relatives (Sibba's young daughter, who subsequently married in Sahas Dhara and died there in 1968, was the only one to wear such a sari in 1958).

Farming technology remains unchanged from the previous decade. Two relics of the Community Development program remain: the unused cistern at the end of the waterpipe, and the flagstone paving of the trail through the center of the village which makes it less muddy and slightly more sanitary.

On the whole, therefore, the widely heralded changes in village India, some of which I observed on the Gangetic plain, have not reached Sirkanda or its neighboring villages.

ECONOMIC CHANGE

There has been economic change in Sirkanda, but again, not the spectacular change I had thought might occur. The greatest change is in the increased sale of milk, and to a lesser extent of vegetables, to Dehra Dun wholesalers. These are, in turn, consequences of improved transportation between Dehra Dun and Sahas Dhara, which takes the form of relatively cheap and frequent bus service (almost hourly during the day), and the taxi which picks up the milk. More than half of the households in the village take advantage of this to market milk daily. Although precise figures were not obtained, it is clear that income from this source has risen appreciably. Moreover, as a result of improved dairy techniques among buyers, all milk is now sold in its natural state rather than as the less profitable solidified milk product. In the fall and spring a few Sirkanda men are to be found on almost any day in the wholesale bazaar of Dehra Dun selling ginger, okra, potatoes, and other vegetables, a rare occurrence a decade ago. Some occasionally even bring milk or milk products that far for the higher price it brings in town. In the opposite direction, there is a daily bus each way between Mussoorie and Tehri on the Tehri Road, weather permitting and rainy season excluded. This is a precipitous, dirt road,

40 miles long, which is often in disrepair. The bus schedule is so erratic as to make it useless to Sirkanda villagers, who in any case have almost arrived in Suakholi by the time they reach the road, eight miles from Sirkanda. If the road were improved, it would make Mussoorie considerably more accessible than it is now. Some villagers walk from chans in the vicinity to Suakholi and even to Mussoorie to market their milk and other products, but most of the trade is in the opposite direction.

Two mules are still for hire in the village to transport produce to market. Puran Singh, who owned them in 1958, subsequently sold them to another family with less land and more sons. For him the profit was too small to be worth the sacrifice of agricultural labor, though, as he points out, if minerals are found in the area, mules may become profitable as a result of increased demand for transportation. Several high-caste families still own and use horses for transportation.

Puran Singh's shop still stocks almost exactly the same items as a decade ago, although his sales have, if anything, decreased because people go more frequently than before to Dehra Dun or Sahas Dhara where cigarettes, tea, salt and other items can be bought more economically.

Agricultural productivity has not changed perceptibly, and aside from an increase in vegetable-growing for market, the entire agricultural scene is as before. I visited several plains villages during the year, including Kalapur where J. Michael Mahar was doing the first restudy following the large team-research effort there in the early 1950's. There is no doubt that the dramatic increase in agricultural productivity which has been termed the "green revolution" has occurred there (although it is worth pointing out that it has not redounded noticeably to the benefit of those who do not hold land, nor have its benefits been disseminated effectively to less favored parts of India). Sirkanda's situation is not one in which the agricultural benefits Kalapur has experienced can be reaped, for as Mahar pointed out to me, the green revolution in Kalapur and similar villages results from the acquisition of irrigation through tube wells, and the use of improved seeds, chemical fertilizers and insecticides. None of these has been available in Sirkanda and, since change in agricultural output requires change in the input, agriculture has remained essentially static. The absence of dramatic increases in productivity does not mean the absence of productivity in Sirkanda, as earlier chapters in this book have demonstrated, and in any case the blessings of the green revolution may not be unmixed. Sirkanda's natural fertilizers seem to be adequate and certainly less likely than chemical ones to damage soil and crops. Both water and insects seem to be less troublesome to agriculture here than on the plains, and the dangers of massive use of insecticides are avoided where they are unused.

The two rather productive stills in Sirkanda, both operated by low-caste men, had been dismantled upon the departure and disinterest, respectively, of their proprietors. Nearby villages fill this lack, however, with only moderate inconvenience.

The jajmani system remains roughly as it was, although the departure of the tailor to a neighboring village and the failure of any young men to learn blacksmithing suggest that practitioners located in market centers and demanding cash payment will play an increasingly important role in these specialties.

In sum, neither prosperity nor substantial technical or economic change has come to Sirkanda. More cash passes through villagers' hands than did a decade ago, but drastic inflation combined with monetary devaluation has fully offset any advantage the increased cash might have been expected to produce. The few families who do, apparently, have a significant amount of cash in hand have not utilized it to explore new areas of consumption or investment. Sirkanda remains a relatively isolated, relatively backward, relatively peaceful village. This does not mean that it has been static, as following sections will demonstrate.

PLANNED CHANGE

Each of the government programs described in previous chapters has declined or disappeared in Sirkanda. People hardly remember the "economic cooperative supervisor" and no one has come to replace him or to carry on his program of establishing a village cooperative.

While the village remains under the Community Development program, no Village Level Worker has lived in the village since 1958, and there has been little contact with agents of the program since early in the decade, when the cistern was built and the trail in the central village area paved. Funds for community development have been dispersed through the village council rather than by a Block Development office, as before, and they have been sparse and used to little, if any, effect. Villagers always accuse the Pradhan, as council president, of diverting those funds to his own use, regardless of who the Pradhan may be at any given time. More generally, everyone assumes that the funds are allocated for the benefit of the powerful and well-to-do rather than the needy or the general welfare. This has been the general fate of programs depending upon locally allocated funds (cf. Berreman, 1963). To all practical purposes, therefore, there is no community development taking place in Sirkanda or its vicinity. This is not unusual; the program has been largely written off nationwide.

The school remains a viable institution—the most successful official effort in the region—but after the transfer of the teacher I knew, about a year after I left, there has not been another as successful and well-liked, and never again has the enrollment been as large as it was during his tenure. No student since has pursued education as diligently or successfully as did several of his students, six of whom went beyond the eighth grade (only one Sirkanda resident had done so previously), and several of whom went as far as the eighth grade. During 1968–1969, enrollment varied between ten and eighteen pupils in the village school, with only one girl in attendance and one untouchable—a decline on every count from ten years before (cf. pp. 330–335). Moreover, the current teacher, a Pahari himself, who had been posted in Sirkanda for four years and is considered the best teacher since the one I knew, is frequently absent, clearly disinterested in the village and its school, and is actively seeking a transfer. The school building is literally collapsing, and while villagers are ultimately responsible for its repair, the teacher has not tried to exert pressure on them to get the job done. The government has provided funds for its repair but villagers regard them as insufficient. They want a new building and they say the government will have to pay for it. So nothing has been done.

The exceptional promise of the school in 1957–1958 was largely the product of an exceptional teacher. When he was transferred to a distant school, that promise went with him. His dedication did not result in a more responsible assignment for himself or an opportunity for him to do more. I visited him to find him the lone teacher in an even smaller Pahari school, housed under a canvas canopy. For him its redeeming feature is that it is within walking distance of his own home. He remains the same dedicated teacher and loyal friend, a little more tired and discouraged by the lack of detectable effect from his efforts—either on his students or on his own career. The demand for education will no doubt increase in this area, but it will not be met until there is much more money to be put into salaries and facilities for education, which will create a more rewarding environment for teachers.

There is renewed governmental activity in the region resulting from a search for scarce mineral resources, and results have been achieved at Suakholi, but so far nothing has been found near Sirkanda. If such resources should be found in quantity in the vicinity, better transportation and a limited amount of wage labor would result and would, no doubt, affect the village, but this remains an unrealized possibility. A forestry officer has been posted about four miles from Sirkanda, on the other side of the ridge, and a forestry department bungalow and rest house built there, but it has not perceptibly affected the village. There is neither increased commercial utilization of forest products in the area nor increased surveillance of villagers' use of them, as far as I could ascertain.

Thus, official interest in Sirkanda and its surroundings, evidenced for a few years in some concerted effort to get a community development program underway and in the attempt to establish a village credit cooperative, has waned. Villagers regard those efforts as mere gestures which, as they had anticipated, resulted in nothing. They assume that the demise of the programs is a result of corruption at higher levels, but they are just as happy to be rid of the intrusions. Sirkanda has been almost forgotten now that the post-Independence flurry of interest in developing India's most remote villages has worn off. Only if the village were to have some immediately and conspicuously valuable product to offer the nation would attention be likely to be directed to it again.

THE VILLAGE COMMUNITY

In general, Sirkanda villagers' morale seems to have declined somewhat. In 1958, governmental activity in Sirkanda was novel, and while it was not welcomed by villagers, it was regarded with some interest and curiosity. The fact that official attention was being directed to the village had an invigorating effect. There was some thought that, in spite of everything, it might result in some of the advantages its advocates advertised. Now the novelty is gone, the results have not materialized, and the village is again ignored, so cynicism reigns. Villagers say that, as they expected, some officials and opportunists lined their pockets and otherwise it came to naught. The same attitudes prevail with regard to political activity in the area. The Congress party, and party politics as a whole, have not impressed Sirkanda people. Politicians are inherently corrupt, they believe, and nothing has happened to alter this belief. People vote, but they are entirely cynical

about the impact of their votes. Their attitude toward their own village panchayat is similar, and therein little different from a decade
ago. So far as they are concerned, the democratic process simply has
not worked at any level; in fact, they never even got a feeling for what
it was supposed to be or how it was supposed to work, from which they
infer that it can't work except to benefit politicians and their cohorts.

On the other hand, outside contact has resulted in greater awareness of the outside world in Sirkanda than was previously the case.
People go to town more often, they know better how to deal with officials, and they are less vulnerable to both officials and merchants.
They are better informed on events outside of the village and its
vicinity than they were before. They are, in short, somewhat more
active and capable participants in the larger society.

Minor, but to me impressive, evidence of this lay in the fact that in
1958 Sirkanda residents, together with most Indians, were just beginning to accept the new decimal coinage; now they are not only
fully at ease with it, but have also adopted quite thoroughly the recently instituted metric system of weights and measures. This is something more prosperous nations have been reluctant to undertake, yet
even gnarled old villagers talk easily of kilos, meters, and the like, and
use them daily. There is also greater familiarity with commercial (but
not Western) medicines than previously, and more frequent resort to
urban medical practitioners.

The Indian government's widely hailed, heavily financed and ex-
uberantly promoted family planning program seems to have missed
Sirkanda altogether. Most male villagers have heard of it through trips
to town, and know a little of its purposes, but they regard it as irrelevant to their situation. No one is practicing its precepts or has attempted to do so. Although I did not collect a detailed census, it was
clear from the direct and indirect data I did get that the population
of Sirkanda has not increased significantly in the past decade. The
adult and infant mortality rates (the latter probably between twenty
and fifty percent) continue as before. There simply have been no factors of change in this sphere. Extended family membership, including
children, continues to be regarded as the work force, and hence the
source of livelihood and security—the larger, the better. Family planning is not perceived to be a need as it might be if pressure on land
and houses had increased dramatically (cf. Newman, 1970).

Sirkanda, therefore, remains a village of practical, hard-working
people, acutely aware of the realities of their situation, which includes
the moderately increasing impingement of outside factors, but which

gives them few grounds for optimism and a good many grounds for anxiety and, especially for the young, feelings of relative deprivation and boredom.

SOCIAL ORGANIZATION

In the broad area of social organization there also has been little change, hardly surprising in the passage of only a decade. Family, lineage, sib, phratry, and caste persist as before. In observing the annual worship of the children's god, Lhesania, I noted as I had not before, that in a hilarious mock "war" among children (in which the missiles were mainly food offerings prepared for the god) following the worship, the adversaries were children of the Jawari Rajput sib versus those of the Palial Rajput sib. These, I learned, were the traditional adversaries in this battle. That I had not learned this in 1957–1958 represents my oversight rather than change, but indicates an area within which these social units continue to be recognized.

There has been a reported decline in bride-price marriage, but this is impossible to verify. The claim represents the persistent trend of "plainsward mobility," (cf. pp. 128–129). Polygyny, however, seems to occur with about the same incidence as before.

Caste organization and behavior related thereto also remain unchanged. Anti-untouchability legislation has had no more effect in the past ten years than in the first decade of Independence. On the trail one day I met a Bajgi from another village whom I did not know, but who had heard of me. As we walked I struck up a conversation about his occupation and the economic fortunes of his people. He spontaneously commented on the relative social positions of his caste and others:

"High-caste people think of us as something to be kicked with impunity. We just cannot stand up to them or they would tell us to leave or would threaten to burn down our houses at night. If they were men they would do it in the daytime, before our eyes, but they do it surreptitiously. They won't marry our girls nor will they take water from our hands, but they rape our girls readily and take them as mistresses, and we cannot do anything about it. These things happen. They treat us very badly."

He also commented on caste and politics:

"Last election no low-caste people voted in my village, because the politicians don't do anything for us. Also, it is the fault of the Pradhan, who takes no interest in us. Congress (government) gave money for helping the poor, but the panchayat drank it all up themselves and we didn't get it. We applied for corrugated iron roofing, but the Pradhan did some skulduggery and we didn't get any. That's the way it is here."

Ritual pollution is of as much concern as ever among high castes. I noted that my host shared his hooka (water pipe) with a Hindu friend of mine who was a stranger to him, but he would not let him pass the pipe to me. He gave the Hindu's uneaten *popper* and *pakora* (types of fried bread) to children, while mine were quietly disposed of behind a stone, probably to be fed later to animals. I also noted that a Rajput's water pot, left unattended and overflowing at the spring, prevented the Devta, a blacksmith by caste, from getting a drink despite his religious role, and a Rajput man who normally would not avoid touching me, recoiled to avoid doing so when carrying drinking water. Potential ritual pollution was in each case the basis for the behavior.

The caste distribution of Sirkanda has changed somewhat in the last decade, through the departure of several Bajgis. This is hardly evident on ceremonial or festival occasions, because those who perform as drummers have moved only to a nearby village and continued to fulfill their roles in the jajmani system, but it is noticeable in daily activities in Sirkanda. The most noticeable move has been that of the village tailor who moved to a neighboring village to live with his mistress, now become wife (cf. p. 166), and to be in a village comprised mostly of fellow Bajgis where he would be largely unmolested by high-caste demands. The most sociable, active young Bajgi man in Sirkanda, and its sole tailor, his departure was keenly felt. His father remains in the village but cannot fill his son's role. His father's brother has died, the old Bajgi basketmaker and distiller has moved to a relative's village, and the elderly Bajgi exorciser, who came to the village to live in about 1935, has moved on. This leaves the Bajgi population—and in fact the low-caste population—of Sirkanda drastically depleted. To a large extent, I think, the exodus was a response to the heavy domination of the village by high castes and the continual repression they visited on the low castes, combined with increased sophistication and perceived opportunities for emigration among Bajgis.

When I met Bajgis under 40 years of age from surrounding villages, and especially from one nearby, largely Bajgi village, I was impressed with the apparent sophistication in dress and life-style compared to other people of Bhatbair. They are poor, but their clothing styles and accoutrements are more urban than one sees among others. Trousers, bush shirts, and sport jackets are more prevalent, and there is a taste for sunglasses, which I have never seen worn by any other Pahari (see photograph 32). This probably is a combined result of their sartorial sophistication as tailors, who frequent the cloth bazaars of Dehra Dun to purchase their raw materials, and of the flamboyance of a depressed group seeking distinctiveness and self-esteem. Combined with these conspicuous evidences of rejection of their traditional status, they also exhibit the exuberance, informality and openness in relations with one another, with strangers, and between the sexes for which Doms of all castes are noted and upon which I have commented in other chapters. Bajgis in the vicinity of Sirkanda have an advantage over other Doms of the region because most of them live in a village where they are numerically dominant. In addition, they monopolize two vital occupations, one secular (tailoring), and one ritual (drumming). They thus have an adequate and assured income. Blacksmiths, by contrast, are not well off. They are few in number, widely scattered, and their traditional occupation is being infringed upon heavily by commercial products and marketplace entrepreneurs. The same is true for shoemakers. Increasing numbers of both of these groups are migrating to urban centers where they practice their crafts for cash. As I shall point out, no Sirkanda blacksmith has done so, largely because the young men have not learned the traditional trade, seeking other means of escape instead.

RELIGION

Religion has been an area of fundamental stability—a point which I will not belabor. I had the opportunity to be present on several ceremonial occasions and to observe that there has not been conspicuous change since 1957–1958. The most impressive ceremony I attended, for example, was the infrequent Mundkile (village protection) rite, in the village of Taal, directly across the Bandal River from Sirkanda, a village many of whose residents are affinal relatives of Sirkanda men. I had attended this ceremony in somewhat attenuated form in another, smaller village near Sirkanda in 1958 (cf. p. 102 and 1st. ed., Appendix IB). In Taal it was an elaborate affair, prepared for many months in advance at considerable expense, with several Brahmins hired as cooks and priests, numerous animal sacrifices, much music and night-long dancing, and a high incidence of spiritual possession during the dancing. A large crowd came from many villages, mostly in the last two days, to watch and participate. The ceremony culminated in the sacrifice of a full-grown male buffalo which, after being blessed at the Pandava shrine in the village, and having there been given an initial blow sufficient to draw blood, was driven to an open field of four or five acres where crowds, grouped by villages, watched from the terraces which formed a kind of natural amphitheater. The buffalo was chased repeatedly around the field by a group of a dozen high-caste male Taal villagers, led by their Pradhan, brandishing heavy knives and swords and hacking at it as opportunity permitted (see photograph 30). Ultimately the weakened, bleeding animal sought refuge in a small ravine several hundred yards away, where it died under a rain of blows. The sacrificing group returned triumphant and blood-smeared to the edge of the village where they and others danced, the audience gradually dispersed, and the ceremonial days were concluded. Some Sirkanda residents professed disgust at the sacrifice and its method, reminding me that on their side of the river buffalos are not sacrificed. But this may have been largely an effort to convince me, as one who knows sophisticated Hindus, of their own sophistication. For most it was obviously an exhilarating experience, uniting them in a spectacular event of transcendent importance and deep religious significance, confirming and assuring their rapport with the ever-present, all-powerful supernatural, and displaying and validating their common Pahari identity and their continuity with the past and future. No evidence of secularization or Sanskritization was to be seen in the event. To me it exemplified the stability, vitality and distinctiveness of the Pahari version of Hinduism, despite considerable outside pressure and increasing pressure from within to Sanskritize in the manner of the people of the Gangetic plain.

Within the stable context of Sirkanda religion an astounding event took place several years after my initial visit: the appearance of the Devta in a manner miraculous yet entirely in accord with tradition. It is worthwhile to describe the circumstances in some detail.

ADVENT OF THE MIRACLE-WORKER

The miraculous advent of the Devta (god) was the most widely remarked event to have occurred in Sirkanda in the decade of my absence and for many years previous. He appeared in the person of the lowly Kalmu, who soon came to be addressed and referred to as "Devta," though he also calls himself "*jōgī*" (religious devotee). His role, characteristics and capabilities include those common to the category of supernatural functionaries which Paharis call *baki*, and I, as an anthropologist, call *shamans* (*cf.* pp. 89–90, 133–136). At first, therefore, I was puzzled that he was not referred to as a baki. Subsequently I concluded that the reason for this is that his supernatural power, prestige and rapport exceed those possessed by bakis. Proof of his special divinity is to be found in the fact that he was chosen as human vehicle by a village god (one fast becoming a regional god) rather than merely a personal or household god as in the case of bakis (cf. pp. 98–103). To have as his familiar spirit a god of such power and importance is truly remarkable, putting Kalmu beyond the usual category of those who possess, and are possessed by, familiar spirits. Evidently, then, there is an upper limit beyond which one's supernatural power and rapport are too great to be designated the power of a baki. This distinction, I think, explains Kalmu's unusual fame and status. I infer it with some confidence on the basis of usage and behavior, although it is not explained in these terms by the people. The distinction does not appear in earlier chapters because in 1957–1958 it had not occurred in the Pahari world I knew—there was no such person as the Devta—an indication that my ethnographic report, like any other, is inevitably incomplete.

Although the god has not revealed his name to Kalmu or others, and perhaps never will, the fact that he demanded and was awarded a village temple, now a regional temple, and commands the respect of people of all castes over a wide area, is ample evidence that he is of a different order than the lesser gods which speak through bakis. His powers, as revealed by his miraculous feats, far exceed those of the familiar spirits of bakis. Also, his arrival was spectacular and public, as are his frequent reappearances, in contrast to the more mundane manifestations of bakis' gods. Just as the god is more magnificent than bakis' gods, so his human vehicle is more honored than a baki. To have a village god—or better yet, a regional god—as one's familiar spirit, as does Kalmu, is indeed to be graced, and therefore to be honored by men and to be powerful among men.

I know of no comparably spectacular appearance of a god in this region save, perhaps, that of *Memendia,* a village god who came to Sirkanda during an epidemic some 40 or 50 years ago, possessing temporarily almost the entire village population, demanding and getting a village temple, curing the ill, but choosing no individual as his vehicle and thereafter relatively rarely reappearing (cf. 1st ed., Appendix IB, pp. 374–75).

Having made a study of the roles of supernatural practitioners in Pahari society and in Indian society generally (Berreman, 1964), and inspired by the unique opportunity before me, I decided to make it a point to get to know the Devta, to learn how he had come to be what he is, and to make of his experiences and the beliefs and impressions of others about him, a principal research topic on my visits to the village. Through my friendship with his father, and as a result of his own childhood memories of me, I had an unusually solid basis for rapport. There is not space here to give the details of what I learned, but some of the main features will be recorded in order that their implications for an understanding of religion and social processes in Sirkanda can be assessed.

Advent of the Devta

Kalmu, son of Sibba the blacksmith, was thirteen years old in 1958 when I first knew him, a third-grade dropout from the village school, and uninterested in learning from his father his hereditary trade; he occupied his time raising goats from a few which his understanding father had given him; he was not particularly interested in or challenged by life. His activities and interests had not changed until, at 18, with something of a reputation as a ne'er-do-well, he was married to an attractive Kholi (weaver) girl of Taal village. Then a conspicuous change came over him. In love with his wife, he settled down and took an interest in making a living. Within two years, two children were born. Then tragedy struck, in the form of an illness which afflicted all four members of the young family, and from which only Kalmu survived. Grief-stricken, he tried to immolate himself on his wife's funeral pyre but was prevented from doing so by bystanders. He brooded for some time thereafter, drifting aimlessly from place to place and spending considerable time in worship and meditation on other-worldly matters. Then one day, while meditating and worshipping in his father's house, and in the company of several other people, there was a sudden commotion in the semidarkness, and a silver coin, a brass coin and a small smooth, oblong stone (described as a "bindī" and regarded as a Shiva lingam) dropped from nowhere into a brass tray he had been holding. He then grasped a pumpkin from nearby, stood up, and as he held it over his head, an unseen being ate half of it before the onlookers' amazed eyes. Then Kalmu began to be "played upon" or possessed by a supernatural being. He showed the typical symptoms: his head moving in circles, hands and body trembling, speaking incoherently. Outside was heard the roar of a tiger, the mount of Devi, goddess of the region (cf. p. 381). People recognized at once that he was possessed by a deity (dēvtā) of great power (shāktī), and all of the villagers gathered to watch in awe and amazement. Drums were played so that the devta could dance in Kalmu's body. Finally the devta spoke through Kalmu's mouth without identifying himself (something it has never done), requiring that a temple be built for him by villagers on the hillock where the Nag Raja shrine stands.

Shortly thereafter a very small but substantial house was built there for Kalmu, with a small temple beside it. Kalmu lived in the house and worshipped in the temple, abstaining from worldly pleasures and from all contact with women and other sources of defilement, eating only food cooked with his own hands or by one of several village boys who served as his helpers. He let his hair grow long and adopted costumes appropriate to a jogi or ascetic religious devotee. He held twice-daily worship, during which he became possessed by the unnamed god who had chosen him as its vehicle. At various times, but especially while possessed, he performed miracles, many of which were described to me by witnesses, others by hearsay. The ability to perform miraculous feats became his hallmark, and his reputation as a miracle-worker spread with surprising rapidity not only in the surrounding hills, but to the cities of Dehra Dun and Mussoorie and thence to farther reaches of the Punjab and Uttar Pradesh. The village became well known within a period of weeks, and for several months it is said to have had the appearance of a fairground; nearly a dozen shops were set up to accommodate the various needs of the pilgrims, some of whom are said to have journeyed hundreds of miles and covered the whole hillside with their camps. People came to see him, to witness the miracles and derive the benefit of being in his presence (*darshan*), to worship the deity which possessed him, make offerings, receive the deity's blessing, get advice and predictions from it and, so they believed, be cured or have their other troubles solved by it. Although Kalmu denied any healing powers and refused to listen to de scriptions of problems and ailments, the deity speaking through him responded to supplicants, describing for them the problems which had brought them to him, predicting their outcome, or prescribing solutions and cures. People claimed to have been given remarkable insights, infallible predictions and miraculous cures. Considerable amounts of money, grain and other offerings were accumulated by Kalmu.

The miracles performed were various. Ganges water and milk had spouted from Kalmu's forehead when he was possessed. When he blew the conch shell, blood spewed from it. He could turn water into milk, milk into curds and curds into ghee (clarified butter). He could close his hand over a handful of uncooked rice and when he reopened his hand, it had become *khir* (rice cooked in milk and sugar); a handful of flour would similarly emerge as *halwā* (sugared porridge). He could make a fruit disappear into thin air. When he cut up a cucumber and distributed it to onlookers, it tasted like banana to one, apple to another, orange to a third, mango to a fourth, etc. The Pradhan reported seeing him create a flow of cocoanuts in his temple, the Pradhan himself having collected a bagful for ceremonial use. He could bring water out of the earth at will, and stop it with equal ease. He frequently disappeared for short periods, to reappear with the report that he had been to some holy spot (Hardwar, Badrinath, etc.), and would show a relic of the visit as proof. On several occasions he disappeared only to be discovered singing and drumming inside his temple, which was padlocked from the outside. Once he asked the Pradhan's permission to be buried for meditation, and when it was denied some young men helped him to dig a hole a meter deep, as large as a man, and after he had crawled in they covered him up. Twenty-four hours later, villagers heard drumming and playing of the conch in his temple, but found it empty. Then he was heard to call that he had been underground long enough. They dug him up and he was alright.

Frequently Kalmu performed feats of strength—such as breaking flagstones against his chest—and feats of daring—such as handling fire and inflicting wounds upon himself with chains, axes, swords, etc. He demonstrated detachment from worldly things by repudiating his family ties. When someone described a man in Taal as his father-in-law, he said testily, "It isn't a matter of father-in-law; I have no relatives, I am Devta." When I asked him something about his father, he gave a similar response. His detachment was also manifest by his refusal to accept food cooked by others, by refusing meat, liquor and tobacco, and by burning money given to him—all things he did sporadically rather than consistently. Villagers asserted that he spoke several languages, including Sanskrit and English, when posessed, and that he quoted the Vedas at length. I do not maintain that he did all of these things; only that villagers believe he did.

There was no clear distinction between the person and the god who possessed him. The person was addressed and referred to as Devta, never Kalmu. He attributed all of his powers to the god, but he was treated with deference at all times as God's vehicle, frequently displaying his other-worldly powers when not possessed.

The Devta's fame and popularity began to wane after about six months, and the curiosity seekers, devotees and supplicants began to decrease in numbers. But two and three years later, during my stay, he was still addressed as Devta, villagers still regarded him with considerable awe, he still was in demand throughout the area as a participant in ceremonial events, he still was consulted for supernatural advice and help, he still was able to collect gifts and offerings both in Sirkanda and in his peregrinations to other villages, and occasionally people still came to see him, even from non-Pahari areas. He continued to live in his little house next to the temple, and he had hired a carpenter-mason to rebuild the temple into a more permanent structure, mortared with cement and topped with a pyramidal spire in the style of temples of the adjacent plains. He remained aloof from other villagers both by choice and by the status accorded him by others, sacred at the same time that his caste heritage made him polluting. This last point is an important one, for it is clear that while his religious role insulated him from many consequences of his caste status, it did not alter that inborn state of pollution. When I saw him honored yet excluded from sitting on a Rajput verandah, and thirsty yet unable to get a drink from a spring where a Rajput's water pot had been left, I recognized shades of my own ambiguous status as an honored but inherently defiling personage.

The Devta talked to me about himself a great deal, partly, I think, because I subtly encouraged him to do so, partly because he was eager to convince me of his powers. Extracts from my notes taken after talking to him for the first time in his own house, and only slightly edited, will give an idea of the view of himself he presented to me.

Devta saw me arrive in the village and called loudly to me as I passed below his house. He insisted that I come and eat some vegetables he had cooked, and some chapatis. When I came to his house, he seated me, offered me food and asked if I had any liquor I could give him. Previously he had denied that he drank it because he is an ascetic; this time he pointed out that he could drink it without untoward effect because of his supernatural powers. During my visit he acted very erratic, sitting and talking quietly, then suddenly breathing hard and shouting, then jumping up and running outside excitedly, then back inside, then calm again, then suddenly saying irrelevant or incomprehensible things, then rational again. In the course of our conversation he had the following things to say:

"I sit in puja twice a day. morning and evening, at about 5 AM and 5 PM. I take a bath before each puja and put on clean clothes. If I don't I bleed from the mouth. For puja I blow this conch [demonstrated], beat this drum, burn incense, control my breath in yogic fashion [demonstrated], and sit very still, concentrating [demonstrated]. Then Devta comes. When I am possessed I don't know what happens. You will have to ask others what I do then.

"Sometimes I take off my clothes during puja, even in the cold. In summer when it is hot, I put on a lot of clothes. I do the opposite of what the weather requires. People ask me questions when I am possessed. I don't know what I answer, the god answers. I do not have much education, but with the kindness of God I understand several languages. When people want to tell me their problems, I do not allow it. I tell them to wait; God will tell both the problems and the solutions, and he does. I cannot know or answer questions of that sort if God is not with me. Most people ask not out of devotion but out of selfish desires. People came from Punjab, Delhi and other places, including foreign countries, to see me. I collected 15,000 rupees, but burned most of it and used the rest to build this little house and temple. People of the village don't much believe in me any more. I go hungry for days, but I don't need to eat. I didn't make these chapatis. They just appeared [he offered me some to eat]. I do not eat things cooked by others. I haven't had any liquor for a long time. I don't have any tobacco, so I'm smoking marijuana [offered me some]. These are poisonous things, but I am powerful so they don't hurt me. See these scars [all over abdomen and chest]? This axe did it. When the Devta comes to me I forget all about myself and just run around for an hour or so. I run away and then come back. I hurt myself. But that is the Devta's work, not my own. My heart isn't stable—it races— varies from fast to slow, erratically.

"Sometimes I let my father come to see me and sometimes I tell him to leave me alone. Nobody has anything to do with a jogi. not even his relatives.

"Here are the things I use in my puja [a brass tray holding two brass bells. a conch shell (which he blew loudly again by way of demonstration), a small oil lamp, several drums including especially a large hour-glass-shaped one, a small book with the Bhagavad Gita in Sanskrit in it, a small elongated smooth stone (the bindi), a stalactite kept in a tin can (another lingam), some yellow rice]. I also have this big iron trisul [trident, five feet long].

"When my wife and children died, I loved my wife so much I felt like cremating myself with her, but someone prevented me. I wanted to jump into the ravine and kill myself, but again God stopped me and then turned my thoughts in another direction. I don't know how I became a jogi, it just happened.

"People gave me money, fruit, bedding. I destroyed it all because I was angry with the people. They were asking for too much, thinking only of themselves when they came to see me. Some strangers claimed I was doing magic. They called the police and government officers. They came. I said 'Where is the magic here? It is God's will!' They saw and believed. I once stopped a train I was on with my power. [Some children had gathered and he sought and received confirmation of the last statement from them.] Children serve me—they help with errands. They sleep here and are my students and devotees.

"I have been many places: Kedarnath, Badrinath, Hardwar—all over. But mostly I travel around to villages in these hills. I am in great demand. The

Forestry Department has said I may go anywhere and they will welcome me.
The Forestry Officer of this district likes me. He frequently has me do puja
for him.

"Now I am having a new temple built. It will have a slab roof and a pyramid on top. God is building it—he provides the money for it. A carpenter-
mason does the work. If people do not treat me properly, I will leave this
place. Then what will they do? [This was a frequently repeated threat.] I
will leave no shred of cloth for anyone if I leave."

As Others See Him

It is clear that the Devta's fame has declined and that villagers
themselves hold him in less esteem than formerly was the case. The
decline in fame is not surprising. People came, saw, and their curiosity was satisfied. Moreover, the miracles became less impressive, the
predictions less accurate, the cures less effective than originally reported. Familiarity and closer inspection have bred a kind of contempt.

Several explanations of his partial fall from grace are offered, differing in accord with the caste perspectives of the informants. All high-
caste people attribute it to his failure to live up to the ascetic, meditative, other-worldly existence required in the role. The reasons given
for his failure to maintain appropriate behavior vary from informant
to informant.

Puran Singh, the shopkeeper, said, "If Devta had conducted himself
properly he could have built a temple of gold. People gave him money,
but it is gone; he wasted it and threw it away. A person cannot change
his nature: an elephant remains an elephant, a horse remains a horse,
a dog remains a dog." By this he meant that because Kalmu is an untouchable, he inevitably reverts to the ways of his caste, unable to
transcend them to live a life of purity and meditation, so his power
has diminished.

The Pradhan attributed the decline not to caste, but to youth. "The
Devta is a boy, young, without much wisdom. If he had had the wisdom of age he could have kept the faith of the people by acting properly." Presumably that faith would have assured God's grace.

My Rajput host, Ram Singh, cited as the cause Kalmu's personality
and the behavior associated with it, without reference to caste or age.
"He left his pious ways and reverted to his former ways. Always before
he was unreliable, lazy and given to self-indulgence. He has now reverted and become too worldly. Now again he drinks liquor, eats
things cooked by women or anyone else, talks with women, listens to
his radio, smokes tobacco and marijuana, so he has lost his powers and
no one pays much attention to him any more."

Low-caste people tend to blame the decline on high-caste villagers. Kalmu's father exemplified this when he said, "If they would believe, the power would remain. The Devta is still there, hiding, waiting. If villagers would unite in respect for the Devta, and sing and drum and pray, he would come back in full power. But they do not, and he stays in hiding. And because there are fewer offerings, the boy doesn't get enough to eat. When they honored him, the Devta came frequently to him and he lived well. Now as a consequence of his decline he has turned to drinking too much."

A washerman and a Sikh merchant from the town of Mussoorie who had made the difficult journey to Sirkanda to see the Devta two years previously when he was in his prime, were unimpressed in retrospect. The washerman had had a sick child whom he hoped would be cured, but although promised by the Devta, it did not occur and he was disillusioned. The Sikh claimed to have doubted from the first, having gone merely out of curiosity, and he now regarded Kalmu as a clever charlatan, possibly put up to it by the villagers in order to bring attention and business to the village.

Nevertheless, Kalmu is regarded with respect, even awe, by virtually everyone who comes into his presence. People criticize and deprecate him behind his back, but not in his presence. Individuals continue to seek the Devta's blessing and to bring him offerings—even those who derogate him privately. People also fear him, both for his supernatural powers and for his unpredictable behavior. When he visits another village, passes a teashop or chaan, or attends a public event, his arrival is the occasion for hushed comment. When he becomes possessed to the accompaniment of the inevitable drumming at any ceremonial occasion, the audience is electrified and a murmur goes around, "God will dance." His importance as a religious figure was revealed on the several ceremonial occasions which I observed. At the Diwali celebration in Sirkanda, for example, he was the central figure when he became possessed during the evening's dancing, as everyone had expected he would. At the Mundkile ceremony in Taal, where there were many participants from many places, the Devta was the principal sacred personage during the evening and night of ceremonial activities preceding the buffalo sacrifice. He blessed the sacrificial pig, kid, cock and pumpkin before they were sacrificed at the four corners of the village—a crucial function usually performed by Brahmin priests. His dancing—wild, energetic, acrobatic and protracted—in a state of possession by his god, to the accompaniment of the Bajgis' insistent drumming, was the focal point of the night's activities.

It seems unlikely that Kalmu will lose his supernatural aura and influence. Unless he leaves or deliberately forsakes his role, he will probably remain the significant religious figure he now is, albeit without
the spectacular success of his initial year.

*Transcendental Impression Management; Presentation of Super-
natural Self*

How has Kalmu sustained the respect, and more importantly, the
belief, of villagers despite his continual close contact with them? Ad-
mittedly he has slipped, but he has not fallen completely—or even
dangerously—from grace, and this is an impressive fact which I sought
to understand.

First, of course, there is the legacy of his original reputation as a
miracle-worker. It is clear that he is believed to have performed a
variety of miracles while possessed by a very powerful and flamboyant
god. The memory of this assures his reputation. As an outsider and
non-believer, I frankly doubt the supernatural explanation of the phenomena reported, but I do not know how these miracles came about.
No doubt some are mythical, others rumored or imagined, others elaborated from actual or reported events, still others matters of sleight-of-
hand and ventriloquism aided by the half-light of Pahari interiors and
the noise and confusion of worship and dancing, as well as exaggerated
by exhaustion, liquor, and marijuana. It is entirely possible, given his
father's intelligence, wit and interest in the supernatural, that there
was some clever, purposeful stage-management, especially of the initial
appearance of the Devta, reported to have occurred in Sibba's house.
Beyond these possibilities I simply cannot account for all of the miracles in pragmatic terms. Sirkanda villagers do not try to account for
them—from their point of view the explanation is supernatural. Kalmu
himself is not talking. If he did, I think he would affirm that many
(but not all) were managed, not in order to deceive but only to draw
attention and to convince, so that the god could communicate with
the people (such communication requiring worship by them and the
granting of favors in return by the god). I think it entirely likely that
Kalmu is convinced that he is the chosen vehicle of a powerful yet
puzzling god.

Another important factor is the Sirkanda villagers' predisposition to
believe. Their world includes an abundance of supernatural beings,
events, intermediaries and practitioners. Spiritual possession is a commonplace occurrence. People know that miracles occur, they believe in
them and the powers which create them, they hope to witness them

and feel blessed if they have done so. They feel blessed even to be in the vicinity of a miracle or to behold one who performed it. Yet, like all people, they have doubts, and doubts feed on the failure of beliefs to be confirmed in experience.

The appearance of the Devta as a miracle-worker, and as an intermediary between themselves and the supernatural, validates villagers' religious beliefs and alleviates their doubts. If their version of Hinduism is correct, the arrival of such a miracle-worker is an expectable and vastly auspicious phenomenon. It confirms their understandings about the supernatural, provides them a direct means of contact with it, and gives them a degree of control over it. Not only that, it is a mark of distinction and blessing for the entire village that the Devta should have appeared there. It is both a sacred distinction that this impressive god should have chosen Sirkanda as his home and a Sirkanda villager as his vehicle, and a secular distinction in the fame he has brought the village.

After the initial period of miracles, by what means has Kalmu sustained the respect and belief of others on a day-to-day basis? Partly, and perhaps crucially, it has been done by occasionally laying claim to a new miracle. Most consistently, however, it has been accomplished by maintaining an image, albeit an imperfect one, of other-worldliness; by fostering a reputation for abnormal behavior which is interpreted as evidence of supernaturalism. This seems to me to be the basis for the continued awe, fear and respect in which the Devta is held and the thing which keeps doubts about him in abeyance. Kalmu's abnormalities are minor but conspicuous, and they are frequently remarked upon and are endowed with great significance in the view of others. For example, he does things which are painful without evincing pain. In the rugged life of Paharis, pain is commonplace but response to it is expressed freely; there is no cult of manliness to prevent crying out, groaning, gasping, weeping. Kalmu, however, walks barefoot through hot coals, picks up red-hot iron, falls among rocks, inflicts minor wounds on himself, beats himself with chains, wears clothing inappropriate to the weather—all without flinching or complaint. Once when walking with me he exemplified this characteristic by stripping the leaves from one of the large and incredibly painful nettle plants which abound in the area, holding them in his hand and asking me with a straight face what kind of plant this was, then dropping them with a smile, thereby validating his powers by pretending to feel no pain. That he felt pain is suggested by the fact that I saw him inconspicuously rubbing his palm on his shirt for the next mile or so. Another time, while possessed, he fell, knocking himself unconscious on a stone wall. When he came to, he came to me, put my hand over the gash on his head and claimed the blood came from God (evidently unaware that he had fallen, or assuming I had not seen). He later claimed the wound not only was not painful, but had disappeared in twenty-four hours without scab or scar. On yet another occasion I remarked on a large blister on his hand after he had handled fire, asking if he would like medication. He closed his hand and denied that the blister existed, saying fire did not affect him because of his power. He claims that this power is such that he does not tire or even perspire on arduous treks over the rugged mountain trails, and that he is strong and quick even though he eats very little. His intellectual and verbal accomplishments are an important part of his image. His very real linguistic virtuosity (he speaks excellent Hindi, several styles of Pahari, as well as an unintelligible "language," and he knows several words of Sanskrit and of English and is an excellent mimic), his ability to read Hindi and to sight-read passages of Sanskrit, his ability to memorize complex ritual passages, and his knowledge of religious lore and folklore—all are inconsistent with his caste status and lack of schooling, suggesting supernatural origin.

Another feature of his presentation of an atypical self is his erratic behavior. He may be carrying on a normal conversation when suddenly he begins to sway rhythmically, or to speak in a peculiar cadence, to breathe heavily, to look intently at his companions while widening and narrowing his eyes hypnotically, or he will leap up shouting and run about, pick up his sword or trident and flail about dangerously with it, then return to normal interaction, or perhaps break it off abruptly. He often displays an exaggerated version of the euphoric, idiosyncratic behavior and discourse which villagers associate with heavy use of marijuana, something they generally avoid. It is small wonder that he is feared and regarded with awe—emotions I have shared on occasion, although I soon learned that he would not physically harm me, no matter how vehement his actions.

Similarly, he shows a disregard for property which would be incomprehensible in a normal villager. He has burned the scarcest of commodities, money; he rejects gifts; he destroys food. When I gave him two enlarged, glass-framed copies of photographs of himself which he had requested, he precipitously flung them across the room of his house, eliciting a gasp from several onlookers who had shared his elation at receiving them. The fact that the pictures landed unharmed on his bed seemed to me no accident. He had preserved his reputation for superhuman detachment from property, and at the same time he had preserved the pictures by throwing them carefully.

In his dress he is also consistently unique. I never saw him in standard attire. He affects either a white sari-like garment, remaining bare from the waist up except for a garland of flowers, or he wears white fitted pajamas, a loose white shirt, a red feather necklace, and a long white turban, often with a bright sprig of red and green plastic flowers in it (nowhere else in the mountains have I ever seen a plastic flower). He always wears his hair uncut, flowing over his shoulders in clear announcement of his renunciation of the role of male householder, and his devotion to the other-worldly life.

All of these things, together with his nonparticipation in the daily round and in conventional family life and economic pursuits, assure him of the special status of deviant, a minimal requisite for a full-time mystic.

Nothing brought home to me more clearly the contrast between Kalmu's religious and secular roles, and the divergent rewards of each, than his activities at the Mundkile ceremony in Taal. There, on the penultimate day, Kalmu was the center of ritual activities, followed by an admiring crowd as he moved from place to place, watched with a hush as he performed his sacred duties. He carried with him the conch which was his badge of office, blowing it at intervals in mighty blasts. During the evening he became wildly possessed, to the accompaniment of frenetic drumming by the Bajgis. He danced through the bonfire, scattered hot coals in the audience, flailed himself with chains and sliced the air with his sword in front of the entranced crowd, whose children had been put safely out of his reach lest they be incorporated, as was his wont, in his gyrations. Later still, as I have indicated, it was he who blessed the sacrifices to protect the village boundaries. Then he continued his ecstatic performance through the night. This climaxed a day in which his rapport with the supernatural and his personal prowess as an intermediary between that world and the world of daily life were prevailed upon to the benefit of all the people of Taal for the next 10–15 years, an important profession of their faith in him and his god. His personal charisma was crucial; his performance innovative and convincing. His reward was the approbation and respect of all.

The following day a transformation had taken place. Kalmu appeared calm, restrained and secular as Brahmin priests took over the supernatural preparations for the climactic sacrifice of the buffalo. They drew the sacred *mandāla* on which the animal would be offered to the

Pandavas, doing so in accord with precise Sanskritic prescriptions, and they performed the pujas which surrounded the offering and the sacrifice. Kalmu had no role in it, for this day and its activities were the province of the Brahmins with their scripturally prescribed duties— they depended for their effectiveness upon exact replication of prescribed rituals. Here was no place for innovation, no place for personal charisma, no place for direct supernatural intercession (cf. Berreman, 1964). That had been the order of the day before, and that was the sphere in which Kalmu, the blacksmith miracle-worker, excelled. Today Kalmu put away his conch, symbol of his religious role. In its place he carried his new transistor radio, symbol of his secular life. It emitted sounds of popular film music, in contrast to the commanding blare of the sacred conch. The radio attracted almost as many admirers as his conch, but, while keeping a little distance, they tended to be boisterous rather than reverent in their response. Whereas Kalmu had forbidden photographs the day before while he was in his supernatural role, he sought them today. On both days, incidentally, he made a concession to practicality which was as unique as his plastic flower: he carried with him at all times a thermos bottle filled with hot tea, liberally laced with milk and sugar—a ready source of energy and sustenance during his exhausting routines when suitable food is often unavailable (although he claims such sustenance is unnecessary). No other Sirkanda villager owned or had any clear idea of the utility of such an item. It was Kalmu, the Devta, who had seen one in the bazaar, learned its characteristics, recognized its potentialities for his rigorous, itinerant, and often lonely life, and purchased and used it—another clue to the qualities it takes to be a successful shaman: originality, intelligence, and style, all of which Kalmu has in abundance.

The Pragmatic Pay-off

Kalmu's role is unique in Sirkanda, but it is recurrent in the Pahari area, with varying degrees of eminence achieved by the individuals who fill it. It therefore is well within the tradition of the religious system. As I suggested in an earlier paper, long before Kalmu became a vehicle of God and a super shaman, "Shamanism affords people [of low caste] who would otherwise spend their lives deferring to others, a role in which they can hope to acquire not only prestige and economic well being, but a large measure of influence in the lives of others, and especially in the lives of their caste superiors who otherwise exert authority over them. . . . Religious roles, such as that of shaman . . . which exempt those who play them from the full implications of their caste status, often attract those who most resent their status." (Berreman, 1964, p. 62). The implications of the status of low-caste people, who most often occupy these roles, include continual denigration, economic insufficiency, and the difficult, tedious, defiling work that is theirs by heredity. There can be little doubt that escape from these things is an important reward for Kalmu. As he said to me, alone in his temple late one night, "they feed me and clothe me and honor me, and I do no work at all. And I am young—most of my life lies before me" (cf. Lewis, 1971).

Kalmu shares with most of his caste-fellows resentment of the bigotry and repression by the high castes. Most people have to content themselves with some kind of compromise, some kind of accommodation to repression. He has taken this route more readily than others because circumstances thrust it upon him—and perhaps because, like his father, he is unusually resentful of caste discrimination and, like his cousin (see below), he is unusually disinterested in blacksmithing. More importantly, also like his father, he is unusually intelligent, insightful, socially adept, self-confident, independent, original and courageous. These are the requisites for the religious status he has attained so successfully—virtually the only honorable status for which the rank and wealth society denies him are not prerequisites. That status carries with it the prestige, influence and independence which would normally be precluded by his untouchability; it is an escape from all that he despises. The cost, which many would find prohibitive, is the loss of conventional family life (which fate, in any case, took from him), and a kind of loneliness and vulnerability from which a conventional life within the family and caste usually provides insulation. He is forced to live by his wits and by his god (in my opinion, his god *is* his wits), a risk for which he evidently finds adequate compensation.

MEDIUM WITHOUT A MESSAGE

Kalmu is reputed and believed to have worked miracles which demonstrate his intimate relationship with an unusually powerful god. He has derived remarkable charisma and fame as a result, yet although many people believe in his powers, he has not established a body of devotees or disciples. If one looks to his future, and if one compares him with the minor and major miracle-workers who appear from time to time in other societies, it is clear that his impact is destined to be very limited. It is unlikely that during his lifetime he will achieve a greater reputation or have greater impact than has already occurred.

More likely, they will diminish. It is also unlikely that his capabilities
or religious functions will undergo qualitative change. It seems that he
is now all that he is destined to be.

The reason is, I think, that he has exploited to their limit the potentialities inherent in his role as intermediary for a deity. He is not
a prophet, he has not the potential for being a messiah, nor has his
culture provided him with a model for such a role. He has no message for those who believe in him. He has no teachings upon which to
build a following; no program for the future or for the incorporation
of others into his activities. He advocates no social or religious action,
he envisions no millenium. He is, in short, a medium without a message. And this is the difference between a shaman, no matter how successful, and a prophet, no matter how minor. The former is simply
a medium; the latter is a medium with a message, and the message
carries with it the possibility of attracting a body of believers and followers and therefore the possibility of the establishment of a movement. Were a convincing or attractive message or plan of action, or a
utopian goal to have been injected into Kalmu's performance, he
might have attracted a lasting, coherent and even growing following.
This could still occur, but it seems unlikely because that is not in the
nature of shamans nor in the experience of Pahari supernaturalism.
Hence, the Devta's future seems to be that of charismatic miracle-
worker, religious practitioner and vehicle of his god, but not that of
prophet, leader of men or leader of a movement. He is destined to
continue to have a religious "practice" among those seeking supernatural advice, assistance and intercession—the size of the practice depending upon how ably he performs his role as judged by the impressions he conveys and the results he produces. His services will be
sought so long as, and to the extent that, he is thought to have access
to a powerful and active god. This must be continually demonstrated
and reinforced through his behavior. Kalmu's reputation for divinely
granted power is unlikely to be enhanced during his lifetime, for no
doubt its most spectacular and widely noticed manifestation occurred
with the initial miracles. They were novel, surprising and convincing,
and the demand for his services arose spontaneously from the com
munity. Familiarity, repetition and the passage of time have rendered
Kalmu and his god vulnerable to public doubt and disaffection. Perhaps in the future, after Kalmu is no longer mortal, his person no
longer familiar, his powers no longer subject to confirmation, those
powers may be exaggerated in the retelling. Then he could well become a major regional deity in his own right, worshipped in the im-

pressive little temple on the edge of Sirkanda which was built at his god's request, paid for by his god's worshippers, and used by Kalmu in his daily communion with his god.

CHANGING LIFE-STYLES

Young men of Sirkanda are increasingly dissatisfied with village life. They aspire to different fortunes and new life styles. Such aspirations and their realization comprise the most obvious and far-reaching changes underway in Sirkanda. They portend individual social and economic mobility in a cultural milieu which puts a premium on stability and on the rigidity of caste ties. Mobility striving has attracted the scholarly attention of many students of contemporary Indian society, focused primarily on group (especially caste) mobility with particular attention to ritual status (e.g., Silverberg, 1968; Srinivas, 1966). Such processes have been described for Sirkanda in earlier chapters of this book as "Sanskritization" and "Plainsward mobility." The aspirations we are discussing here tend to result in individual efforts toward escape from traditional status and role. This is a familiar trend in cities and among elites; it is less familiar in the literature on rural Indian peasants. The forms these efforts take in Sirkanda are significant well beyond this village and its region, for the pattern recurs and increases as education, mass media and consumer goods are disseminated to formerly isolated communities. To understand the aspirations and strivings of Sirkanda's young people and the avenues they find or forge to accomplish them, is to anticipate the directions and processes of change in other rural areas of India. It is therefore worthwhile to look into individual mobility striving in Sirkanda.

The case of Kalmu has been presented in detail because of its intrinsic interest. Obviously it is far from typical, but it is consistent with important features of low-caste people's responses to the deprivations and inadequacies of village life as they experience it. High-caste people are dissatisfied in different ways, and find different remedies. I turn briefly now to a characterization, and some examples, of these caste-specific responses.

ALTERNATIVES UNDER OPPRESSION

All low-caste people resent their status and feel deprived by it. They find it economically, as well as psychically, damaging, and there are as yet no new avenues available in Sirkanda by which to escape from the implications of their status. For blacksmiths it is perhaps worse than for other Doms. Money is lacking, schooling is for the few and well-to-do, and these are the requisites if one is to escape the village context. The religious life, in that situation, becomes one of the few ways out. For Kalmu, his beloved wife and children would probably have kept him from it, but without them, it became a viable alternative as I have pointed out above. It is not the only alternative, however.

One day in Sahas Dhara I noticed an exceptionally ragged, unkempt young man with matted hair and beard who was covertly watching me. He looked like the most dissolute of beggars, quite out of place in this rural environment. Upon a closer look, I thought I recognized the unusually pale grey eyes and aquiline nose, but could not place them, so I walked over and asked, "Do you know me?" He replied that he did. Then I remembered the person, but not the name, from 10 years before, and asked, "Are you the nephew of Sibba the blacksmith?" He smiled and said that he was, Bishnu by name. I remembered his father, Sibba's brother, who had retreated into a continual haze of marijuana, and perhaps opium, quite in contrast to Sibba, who was outgoing and gregarious, regarding life as something of a game and something of a joke, negotiating it and manipulating it by his wit and social agility. Bishnu, Kalmu's cousin and senior by two years, during my previous visit repeatedly had run away from home, refused to learn blacksmithing and imitated urban dress and ways learned during his brief sojourns as a dishwasher in Dehra Dun teashops. It turned out that he had been unable to make a go of it outside the village, and was unwilling to do so in the village. As an alternative worked out during the decade of my absence, he had adopted the role of a wanderer who lives by collecting firewood in the forests and selling it to whomever he can. He is regarded by all as insane, but both I and an Indian friend talked with him and came to the conclusion that he was mentally whole and healthy, however socially deviant. Like his cousin, he had opted out of oppression in a situation with few options: both had adopted roles in which they were exempt from the requirements and consequences of their caste status, unaccountable for much of their behavior. Unlike his cousin, Bishnu had done so without adopting a respectable alternative role, and without a religious rationale—he was a kind of secular "conscientious objector" to untouchability. That way is difficult in India, as in most societies, because only divine authority can adequately sanction radical nonconformity in the minds of those in power. One can be called from on high to deviate, because the call is involuntary and rare, and therefore no threat to the system. To choose to deviate without divine sanction is a threat to the system if to do so is rewarding, because it might easily become commonplace. It is therefore made dangerous, painful or costly as indeed the role of mindless wanderer is. Evidently for Bishnu the cost is less than that of the role of untouchable blacksmith villager.

Several Bajgis, a caste whose numbers are greater and whose life is economically more rewarding than that of blacksmiths but whose social position is lower, have also sought escape from the normal repressions of untouchability, but they have done so in a different way—by moving to a nearby village populated predominately by their peers. This village is a haven for members of the Bajgi caste in which they pursue agriculture as well as their caste occupations. There they are relatively free of highcaste interaction and consequently of domination and bigotry. The Sirkanda tailor's emigration is a case in point. A similar escape from an oppressive social situation is one followed by shoemakers throughout Bhatbair (cf. p. 233). Although they, like blacksmiths, have no such village refuge, they make it on their own, living in isolated chaans where they farm or along roads where passersby comprise their clientele.

For low castes, then, escape from the unpleasant aspects of village life is escape from the usual consequences of their traditional status. The routes followed, thus far, have been difficult but traditional ones. If escape has been increasingly sought, it may be a result of an increase in perceived opportunities for change, which is the result of a degree of economic independence generated by increased use of cash for services, and perhaps more importantly, a changed definition of their situation stemming from the equalitarian rhetoric of Independence and from exposure to schooling and outside contacts. They increasingly think of escape from their status not only as possible, but even appropriate, as a result of such changes. To achieve it they make the best of a bad situation, using whatever escape routes are open to them, costly though those may be.

THE PASSPORT OF PRIVILEGE

For high castes the situation is quite different. Their young men have been exposed fairly systematically and intensively to education, and their economic situation makes aspirations for a more sophisticated style of life seem realistic to them—the kind of life depicted in books, magazines, movies and on the radio, described in the school, and observed on trips to the city. Increasing numbers of them no longer want to farm the rocky terraces of Bhatbair when well-paid and esteemed white-collar jobs are thought to be in the offing in the cities. This was not new in 1968–1969; it had been present in 1957–1958 (cf. pp. 305–311), but in the intervening decade it had had time to be realized in the careers of several young men. I was surprised to find that it had not motivated a greater number of emigrations than had in fact occurred. Four young Rajputs during that decade had undertaken teacher training, a fifth was undergoing technical training (to become an auto mechanic) after having unsuccessfully applied for teacher training, and two had joined the army during the intensive recruiting following the border incidents with China in 1962. The impact of the village school teacher in the preparation and career choices of potential emigrants was obvious: all had gone through the village school under him. In addition, all but the two army recruits had passed the eighth grade in order to gain entrance into training programs, which means they had spent three years at the high school in Majra, near Dehra Dun, and thereafter commenced a training period of at least two years in Dehra Dun. Of those training to be teachers, one had finished and is teaching in a distant Pahari school, two had almost completed their training, and the other—the only fifth grade pupil when I was in the village before—died in 1969 during his training. The technical trainee was almost ready to graduate and take a job in his new profession. It is unlikely that any of these men will earn a higher income than if they had farmed in the village, but they will lead a more varied and sophisticated life and, as Puran Singh commented, "They will bring honor to the village." Another young man, the most ambitious one of a decade ago, failed to pass the eighth grade examination, but secured a position as part-time postmaster in the small market town from which Sirkanda gets its mail. He commutes frequently to the village. His office provides him with a small cash income, prestige, and an excuse to spend most of his time in the town. It gives him some power and generates both envy and resentment. On the other hand, he resents the fact that he has not attained a more exalted white-collar position. His age-mates claim that he has intercepted and destroyed or delayed crucial letters in response to their applications for entry into training programs or for coveted jobs. Specifically, the man who has become a teacher says that after he had failed to receive two successive notices of appointment to a teaching position, the third and final one was found accidentally by an old man in an abandoned water mill where it had been thrown by the postmaster. It was then delivered to him on the date of its expiry. He rushed to Dehra Dun and got the appointment in the nick of time. Mangal claims to have lost a factory job because the notice of appointment was destroyed in the mails. The technical trainee says he lost the opportunity to enter teacher training by the postman's sabotage. There is a long history of mutual jealousy behind these allegations, and their truth cannot be assessed. There is no doubt that the part-time postmaster deeply resents those who have opportunities he has missed. (There is also no doubt that he opens interesting incoming mail.) The allegations indicate the importance attached by young high-caste men to scarce opportunities to escape the village for a more modern, urban life, and they reveal the anxieties and jealousies these create. They also indicate the suspicion directed toward those in pivotal positions of power, and the ways such positions can be used for selfish purposes.

It is clear that the numbers of men who move out of Sirkanda and find a new way of life are small. The individual career choices and the qualifications of those who have succeeded in achieving them no doubt reflect the influence of Sirkanda's outstanding, but now departed, school teacher. One would expect now, however, as I did also in 1958, that the trend to education and outside employment will continue if economic and political conditions permit.

WOMEN: THE UNLIBERATED

In writing of social mobility I have thus far mentioned only men because opportunities for change or escape from traditional roles and statuses are not available to women in Sirkanda except through the avenue of marriage (arranged by their male relatives), illicit elopement, or acquiescence in "abduction." Exceedingly few go to school, none beyond the village school. The one who received the most schooling in the village (the only one to have gone the full five years) was married to a prosperous resident of a village near Dehra Dun, where she lives a semi-urban life. The combination of schooling and a well-to-do father made her a suitable bride. Two other women had made similar, though less prosperous matches, in the decade of my absence. All three are now housewives, but in houses where their activities more nearly resemble those of the women of the plains than the hard-working outdoor life of the Pahari woman.

This does not mean that women in India cannot escape their roles as housewives and mothers whose status depends upon their menfolk. On the contrary, as I have pointed out in detail elsewhere (Berreman, 1969b, first published 1966), women's political participation is far greater in India than in the United States, and I there analyzed the reasons for this. But this aspect of women's roles in India does not affect their lives in Sirkanda or in other relatively isolated rural areas, because the mechanisms for escape from the circumscriptions of their assigned status have been denied to women there—mechanisms such as education, employment outside the family, freedom from household responsibilities, wealth, adoption of atraditional standards of female conduct. As I have pointed out in earlier chapters, Pahari women have considerably more personal freedom than do women in most of traditional Hindu India, but their horizons are limited to the village context. Change will come to women in Sirkanda and elsewhere in rural India only when there is change in values, social organization and opportunity structure—changes presaged in contemporary urban India.

FINAL IMPRESSION

I last saw Sirkanda and its environs on a warm evening and a long night in May, 1969. In response to my request to record music and singing in which women participate, Sibba took me without advance warning to the home of relatives (Rajputs regard such activity by women as inconsistent with their high caste status). There, in a lonely chaan several miles from the village, a small group of blacksmith men and women served their uninvited guests supper and then sang and danced through the night, exhilarated by the unexpected celebration after a long day of hard work. Inhibitions were cast aside, liquor flowed freely and exuberant good humor rang from the verandah of the tiny house. The pulse of the drums carried in the starry darkness over the terraced fields which step down to the deep-cut river and to the mountainside beyond, with its palely silhouetted peaks and the faint pinpoint lights of its scattered villages, whose residents must have wondered at the inexplicable festivity. Occasionally an energetic outburst would rouse the tethered livestock or elicit the bark of a jackal. An elderly Brahmin from a nearby chaan came, drank, watched with quiet enjoyment, slept and went home. Other high-caste people stayed away, for the evening was not theirs. Kalmu the Devta was an honored but aloof guest who ostentatiously refused food and drink as inappropriate to his role, and spent much of the evening satisfying his curiosity and ego by taking innumerable badly-aimed pictures with my flash camera. His father, Sibba, insisted on taking over operation of my tape recorder so I might dance, justifying my estimate of his aptitude and powers of observation by handling this absolutely strange and delicate instrument carefully, ably and at the same time gleefully. Tape and film were exhausted long before the human participants were, until finally, as dawn broke, we put aside the drums and slept. An hour later my hosts and hostesses were busy with their early-morning routine tending the animals, preparing food, and beginning another day of work on the land, in the house, and over the anvil.

On the day of my initial return to Sirkanda I had been reminded, after a decade, of the fundamental human reward of being an anthropologist. On that last long night, in the frenetic camaraderie of music, drink and laughter, a stranger caught up in the moment and taking it for granted, I came perhaps as close as I ever had or ever will to knowing what life is about for these people—and that is a step on the way to understanding not only Paharis and their India, but a whole world where people seek fulfillment in their diverse ways, and often find it even as they are caught and ground down in the mill of social existence. That understanding is, in large part, the aim of anthropology.

I understood, as I watched and participated, that fulfillment for most people is wherever they can find it rather than the product of careful planning; that it is sought and grasped where and when it is available rather than being assured by benevolent arrangements of society or the altruism of the privileged. The fact that it is found at all by many peo ple is an incredible tribute to the irrepressibility of the human spirit. For vast numbers of oppressed people it is grasped fleetingly through temporary diversions such as that evening of companionship; for some it is found in the escape provided by liquor, drugs and other fantasies; for some, like Sibba, it is found through wily manipulation of one's place in society—through discovering and exploiting the cultural loopholes and social interstices which pervade any social system; for some, like Kalmu and several of his age-mates in Sirkanda, it is found through single-minded efforts toward individual escape from the conventional requirements of one's society; for still others it is sought through sober attention to social uplift of an entire caste or ethnic group.

In the haze and noise, I reflected on the hard, brief and monotonous lives (yes, the celebrants themselves would define them as such), from which the evening was a momentary but eagerly welcomed respite. I recognized that in the long run, the full realization of the humanity of these people and their fellows throughout India will be achieved, if at all, not through risky manipulation and dodging within the *status quo*, nor through grasping at transitory moments of escape, nor through emulating rare individual or group successes in social mobility. Rather, that humanity will only be achieved through fundamental changes in the social, economic and political arrangements which comprise the deadly, disheartening *status quo*. Only a social revolution will suffice; one not simply talked about, but one acted out. (If words had been enough it would have been achieved by now, because India's leaders have been talking about that revolution for fifty years.) Sibba, the illiterate but uncommonly perceptive Pahari blacksmith, knows this as clearly as does Indira Gandhi, the Prime Minister. Those who know this face the task of communicating their understanding of the problem and its solutions to one another and widely in the society. Their knowledge must be translated into commitment to concerted action in pursuit of the common goal—action taken in opposition to traditional arrangements which have benefited the few and reassured the timid at the expense of the many. It is a difficult and dangerous undertaking, but neither as difficult nor as dangerous as maintaining the *status quo*.

Obviously these thoughts did not come to me anew that evening, for they were the result of many experiences in Sirkanda and elsewhere, but they did come together vividly as I felt the imminence of my own departure from Sirkanda and as I sensed, not wholly rationally, that I was abandoning these people I knew, liked, empathized with, more or less understood, and (not unaccountably) feared for.

As I can never know fully what life in Sirkanda means to its people, so also there is no way I can adequately describe the impact of Sirkanda and its people on me. The attempt could easily become maudlin, for it is a sentimental, emotional thing as well as an intellectual one. But the fact of that impact, at least, I have wanted to record, for it would be a denigration of this ethnographic experience and of the purpose and method of this study to obliterate it in the summary descriptions and analyses which are the conventional contents of scholarly books. What I have said in the rest of this account is true, so far as I could discover and tell the truth, but the experience which led to it is another order of truth which is the origin of the rest, colors the rest, and hence is crucial to an understanding of it. I have tried to convey some of this richer, more personal truth explicitly in the prologue, "Behind Many Masks," and in this epilogue.

CONCLUSION

Upon my unexpected return to Sirkanda, a decade after my year of intensive research there, I was touched by the warmth of my reception; surprised at the lack of conspicuous material change; disappointed at the absence of increased economic well-being and the absence of greater social equality; intrigued by the appearance and career of Kalmu the miracle-worker; empathetic with those seeking a new life, high and low castes, each in their own ways; sympathetic with those clinging to the tried and true. Above all, I was reimpressed with the humanity and fundamental courage of these people as they strive for fulfillment in their hard, repetitive lives, and by their cautious loyalty to our improbable friendship.

Sirkanda residents are not typical of their countrymen—no one is—but they are representative people of India who share in its problems and its destiny. India is faced with unimaginably difficult problems of poverty, economic disparities, population growth, political controversy, religious and ethnic conflict, and social injustice, all of which are experienced as hardship in the lives of its people; all of which are reflected to varying degrees in Sirkanda and in every other village and city of India. One can only hope that as the nation grapples with these problems, the people of all segments of the society and every reach of the nation will be uppermost in the minds and consciences of those making fateful decisions on their behalf, for it is they—the 384 people I have written about here and the 500 million like them—who are India, rather than some abstract ideal; and India, like any nation, will stand or fall by its people. I hope that, in the immense diversity of Indian culture and society, the people, including their leaders, will regard one another with respect and consideration in recognition that their foibles and conflicts of interest are human ones, their perceptions comprehensible ones, their aspirations legitimate ones, their fears and anxieties real ones. Hard choices will have to be made because the problems people face and the conflicts and sufferings those problems engender and reflect are profound, urgent and often unamenable to solution through compromise. I hope those choices will be made with humanity and will be pursued with courage. If these hopes seem overly modest, it is well to remember that their realization would be more than has been granted most peoples of the world by those who rule, those who conquer, and those who exploit.

The right to democratic self-determination free of alien intervention is one upon which India has steadfastly insisted and acted since Independence. It is a right too few in southern Asia have been permitted to exercise in peace. Whatever else happens, I hope the people of Sirkanda together with the rest of the people of India will be allowed to seek their common destiny in their own way.

Bibliography

Atkinson, Edwin T.

   1882, 1884a, 1886 *The Himalayan Districts of the North-Western Provinces of India.* Vol. I (1882); Vol. II (1884); Vol. III (1886), comprising Vols. X–XII of the Gazetteer of the North-Western Provinces and Oudh. Allahabad: North-Western Provinces and Oudh Press.

   1884b, 1885 "Notes on the History of Religion in the Himalaya of the N. W. Provinces." *Journal of the Asiatic Society of Bengal,* Vol. 53 (1884), 39–103; Vol. 54 (1885), 1–16.

Bacon, Elizabeth

   1946 "A Preliminary Attempt to Determine the Culture Areas of Asia." *Southwestern Journal of Anthropology,* Vol. 2, pp. 117–132.

Baden-Powell, B. H.

   1892 *The Land-System of British India,* 3 vols. Oxford: Clarendon Press.

Bahadur, Rai Pati Ram

   1916 *Garhwal, Ancient and Modern.* Simla: Army Press.

Bailey, F. G.

   1957 *Caste and the Economic Frontier.* Manchester: University Press.

   1959 "For a Sociology of India?" *Contributions to Indian Sociology,* Vol. 3, pp. 88–101.

Banfield, Edward C.

   1958 *The Moral Basis of a Backward Society.* Glencoe, Ill.: Free Press.

Basham, A. L.

   1954 *The Wonder That Was India,* Evergreen edition. New York: Grove Press.

Beals, Alan

   1954 "The Government and the Indian Village." *Economic Development and Cultural Change,* Vol. 2, pp. 397–407.

Beidelman, Thomas O.
 1959   *A Comparative Analysis of the Jajmani System.* Locust Valley, N.Y.:
         J. J. Augustin.
Berreman, Gerald D.
 1955   "Inquiry into Community Integration in an Aleutian Village."
         American Anthropologist, Vol. 57, pp. 49–59.
 1959   "Kin, Caste and Community in a Himalayan Hill Village." Ph.D.
         dissertation, Department of Sociology and Anthropology, Cornell
         University. Ann Arbor: University Microfilms.
 1960a   "Caste in India and the United States." *American Journal of Soci-
         ology,* Vol. 66, pp. 120–127.
 1960b   "Cultural Variability and Drift in the Himalayan Hills." *American
         Anthropologist,* Vol. 62, pp. 774–794.
 1961   "Himalayan Rope Sliding and Village Hinduism: An Analysis."
         Southwestern Journal of Anthropology, Vol. 17, pp. 326–342.
 1962a   "Pahari Polyandry: A Comparison." *American Anthropologist,*
         Vol. 64, pp. 60–75.
 1962b   "Caste and Economy in the Himalayas." *Economic Development
         and Cultural Change,* Vol. 10, pp. 386–394.
 1962c   *Behind Many Masks: Ethnography and Impression Management in
         a Himalayan Village.* Monograph 4, Ithaca, N. Y.: Society for Ap-
         plied Anthropology.
 1962d   "Village Exogamy in Northernmost India." *Southwestern Journal
         of Anthropology,* Vol. 18, pp. 55–58.
 1962e   "Sib and Clan Among the Pahari of North India." *Ethnology,* Vol.
         1, pp. 524–528.
 1964   "Brahmins and Shamans in Pahari Religion." *Journal of Asian
         Studies,* Vol. 23 (June, Supplement), pp. 53–69. *Also in Religion
         in South Asia* (E. Harper, ed.). Seattle: University of Washington
         Press. Pp. 53–69.
Blunt, E. A. H.
 1931   *The Caste System of Northern India.* London: H. Milford, Oxford
         University Press.
Bose, N. K.
 1958   "Some Aspects of Caste in Bengal." *American Journal of Folklore,*
         Vol. 71, pp. 397–412.
Bouglé, C.
 1908   *Essais sur le Régime des castes.* Paris: Librairies Félix Alcan et
         Guillaumin Réunies.
Bowen, Elenore Smith (pseud.)
 1954   *Return to Laughter.* New York: Harper & Row.
Briffault, Robert
 1927   *The Mothers,* Vol. I. New York: The Macmillan Company.
Brown, W. Norman
 1953   *The United States and India and Pakistan.* Cambridge, Mass.:
         Harvard University Press.

Census of India, 1931
  1933 *Bengal and Sikkim,* Vol. 5. Calcutta: Central Publication Branch.
  1933 *Punjab,* Vol. 17 (Parts I and II). Lahore: Civil and Military Gazette Press.
  1933 *United Provinces of Agra and Oudh,* Vol. 18 (Parts I and II). Allahabad: Superintendent, Printing and Stationery, United Provinces.
  n.d. *Jammu and Kashmir State,* Vol. 24. Jammu: Ranbir Government Press.
Census of India, 1941
  1943 *Jammu and Kashmir,* Vol. 22. Ranbir: Ranbir Government Press.
Census of India, 1951
  1952a *Paper No. 2, Population Zones, Natural Regions, Sub-Regions and Divisions.* New Delhi: Government of India Photo-Litho Press.
  1952b *District Population Statistics, Uttar Pradesh: I. Dehra Dun District.* Allahabad: Superintendent, Printing and Stationery, Uttar Pradesh.
  1952c *Volume II, Uttar Pradesh, Part IIa, General Population Tables.* Allahabad: Superintendent, Printing and Stationery, Uttar Pradesh.
  1953 *District Population Statistics, Uttar Pradesh: XXXIX. Tehri-Garhwal District.* Allahabad: Superintendent, Printing and Stationery, Uttar Pradesh.
  1954 *District Census Handbook, Uttar Pradesh: I. Dehra Dun District.* Allahabad: Superintendent, Printing and Stationery, Uttar Pradesh.
  1955 *District Census Handbook, Uttar Pradesh: XXXIX. Tehri-Garhwal District.* Allahabad: Superintendent, Printing and Stationery, Uttar Pradesh.
Cohn, Bernard S.
  1954 "The Camars of Senapur: A Study of the Changing Status of a Depressed Caste." Ph.D. dissertation, Department of Sociology and Anthropology, Cornell University. Ann Arbor: University Microfilms.
  1955 "The Changing Status of a Depressed Caste," in *Village India,* ed. by McKim Marriott. Memoir 83, American Anthropological Association, Vol. 57, pp. 53–77.
Cohn, Bernard S., and McKim Marriott
  1958 "Networks and Centres in the Integration of Indian Civilization." *Journal of Social Research* (Bihar University), Vol. 1, pp. 1–9.
Corbett, Jim
  1946 *Man-Eaters of Kumaon.* New York: Oxford University Press.
Crooke, William
  1926 *Religion and Folklore of Northern India.* London: Oxford University Press.
Davis, Kingsley
  1949 *Human Society.* New York: The Macmillan Company.
Dollard, John
  1957 *Caste and Class in a Southern Town,* 3rd edition. Garden City, N. Y.: Doubleday.

Dube, S. C.
1955   *Indian Village*. Ithaca, N. Y.: Cornell University Press.
1956   "Cultural Factors in Rural Community Development." *Journal of Asian Studies*, Vol. 16, pp. 19–30.
1958   *India's Changing Villages*. London: Routledge and Kegan Paul.

Dumont, Louis, and D. Pocock, eds.
1957   *Contributions to Indian Sociology*, No. 1. Paris: Mouton.
1958   *Contributions to Indian Sociology*, No. 2. Paris: Mouton.

Dwivedi, J. N.
1957(?) *Practice and Digest of U. P. Panchayat Raj*, 2nd edition. Allahabad: Allahabad Law Agency.

Fraser, James B.
1820   *Journal of a Tour Through Part of the Snowy Range of the Himala Mountains and to the Sources of the Rivers Jumna and Ganges*. London: Rodwell and Martin.

Gadgil, D. R.
1952   *Poona, A Socio-Economic Survey*, Part II. Poona: Gokhale Institute of Politics and Economics.

Gandhi, M. K.
1952   *Rebuilding Our Villages*. Ahmedabad: Navajivan Publishing House.

Ghurye, G. S.
1952   *Caste and Class in India*. New York: Philosophical Library.

Gilbert, William H.
1948   "Caste in India, a Bibliography." Washington, D.C.: Library of Congress. (Mimeographed.)

Goffman, Erving
1959   *The Presentation of Self in Everyday Life*. Garden City, N.Y.: Doubleday.

Gorer, Geoffrey
1938   *Himalayan Village*. London: Michael Joseph.

Gough (Aberle), Kathleen
1959   "Criteria of Caste Ranking in South India." *Man in India*, Vol. 39, pp. 115–126.

Gould, Harold A.
1960   "The Micro-Demography of Marriages in a North Indian Area." *Southwestern Journal of Anthropology*, Vol. 16, pp. 476–491.
1961a   "Sanskritization and Westernization: A Dynamic View." *Economic Weekly*, Vol. 13 (No. 25), pp. 945–950.
1961b   "A Further Note on Village Exogamy in North India." *Southwestern Journal of Anthropology*, Vol. 17, pp. 297–300.

Grierson, George A.
1916   *Linguistic Survey of India*, Vol. IX, Part IV. Calcutta: Superintendent of Government Printing.

Harper, Edward B.
1957   "Shamanism in South India." *Southwestern Journal of Anthropology*, Vol. 13, pp. 267–287.

Himachal *Times*

1958a "Demand for Separate Hill State." Himachal *Times*, Mussoorie-Dehra Dun, Vol. X, No. 21 (June 5, 1958), 1.

1958b "Congress Men Threaten Direct Action." Himachal *Times*. Mussoorie-Dehra Dun, Vol. X, No. 31 (August 8, 1958), 1.

Hitchcock, John T.

1956 "The Rajputs of Khaalaapur: A Study of Kinship, Social Stratification, and Politics." Ph.D. dissertation, Department of Sociology and Anthropology, Cornell University. Ann Arbor: University Microfilms.

Hocart, A. M.

1950 *Caste, A Comparative Study.* London: Methuen.

Hutton, J. H.

1946 *Caste in India.* Cambridge, England: Cambridge University Press.

Iijima, Shigeru

1960 "The Thakali—A Central Himalayan Tribe" (Torbo Ethnography No. 2). *Japanese Journal of Ethnology,* Vol. 24, No. 3, pp. 1–22. (In Japanese.)

1961 *Agriculture and Land System in Nepal* (Research Series 18). Tokyo: Institute of Asian Economics. (In Japanese.)

Jain, S. C.

1948 "Some Features of Fraternal Polyandry in Jaunsar Bawar." *Eastern Anthropologist,* Vol. 1, No. 2, pp. 27–33.

Joshi, L. D.

1929 *The Khasa Family Law in the Himalayan Districts of the United Provinces of India.* Allahabad: Superintendent, Government Press, U. P.

Karve, Irawati

1953 *Kinship Organization in India.* Deccan College Monograph Series 11. Poona: Deccan College Postgraduate and Research Institute.

Kawakita, Jiro

1957 "Ethno-Geographical Observations on the Nepal Himalaya," in *Scientific Results of the Japanese Expeditions to Nepal Himalaya, 1952–53,* Vol. 3 (Peoples of Nepal Himalaya), ed. by Hitoshi Kihara. Kyoto: Fauna and Flora Research Society. Pp. 1–362.

1961 "Some Ecological Observations in Nepal Himalaya" (Torbo Ethnography No. 3). *Japanese Journal of Ethnology,* Vol. 25, No. 4, pp. 1–42. (In Japanese.)

Kroeber, Alfred L.

1930 "Caste," in *Encyclopedia of the Social Sciences,* Vol. 3, ed. by E. R. A. Seligman and Alvin Johnson. New York: The Macmillan Company. Pp. 254–256.

1948 *Anthropology.* New York: Harcourt, Brace.

Leach, E. R.

1960 "Introduction: What Should We Mean by Caste," in *Aspects of Caste in South India, Ceylon and North-west Pakistan,* ed. by E. R.

Leach. Cambridge Papers in Social Anthropology, No. 2, pp. 1–10. Cambridge, England: Cambridge University Press.

Lewis, Oscar
  1958   *Village Life in Northern India.* Urbana: University of Illinois Press.
  1959   "Review of *Pilot Project, India,* by Albert Mayer *et al.*" *American Anthropologist,* Vol. 61, pp. 534–536.

Lipset, Seymour M., and Reinhard Bendix
  1960   *Social Mobility in Industrial Society.* Berkeley and Los Angeles: University of California Press.

Lowie, R. H.
  1947   *Primitive Society.* New York: Liveright.

Mahar, James M.
  1958   "Occupational Adjustment in a Caste Society." Paper read before the 57th annual meeting of the American Anthropological Association, Washington, D.C., November 20, 1958.

Mahar, Pauline Moller
  1957   "The Functional Relations of a Hindu Cult." Paper read before the meeting of the Society for Scientific Study of Religion, Cambridge, Mass., November 2, 1957.
  1958   "Changing Caste Ideology in a North Indian Village." *Journal of Social Issues,* Vol. 14, No. 4, pp. 51–65.
  1959   "A Multiple Scaling Technique for Caste Ranking." *Man in India,* Vol. 39, pp. 115–126.
  1960   "Changing Religious Practices of an Untouchable Caste." *Economic Development and Cultural Change,* Vol. 8, pp. 279–287.

Majumdar, D. N.
  1944   *The Fortunes of Primitive Tribes.* Lucknow: Universal Publishers.
  1955   "Demographic Structure in a Polyandrous Village." *Eastern Anthropologist,* Vol. 8, pp. 161–172.

Mandelbaum, David G.
  1955   "The World and the World View of the *Kota,*" in *Village India,* ed. by McKim Marriott. Memoir 83, American Anthropological Association, Vol. 57, pp. 223–254.

Marriott, McKim
  1955a "Little Communities in an Indigenous Civilization," in *Village India,* ed. by McKim Marriott. Memoir 83, American Anthropological Association, Vol. 57, pp. 171–222.
  1959   "Interactional and Attributional Theories of Caste Ranking." *Man in India,* Vol. 39, pp. 92–107.
  1960   *Caste Ranking and Community Structure in Five Regions of India and Pakistan.* Deccan College Monograph Series 23, Poona: Deccan College Postgraduate and Research Institute.

Marriott, McKim, ed.
  1955b *Village India,* Memoir 83, American Anthropological Association, Vol. 57, No. 3, Part 2.

Mayer, Adrian C.

1958 "The Dominant Caste in a Region of Central India." *Southwestern Journal of Anthropology*, Vol. 14, pp. 407–427.

Merton, Robert K., and Alice Kitt

1950 "Contributions to the Theory of Reference Group Behavior," in *Continuities in Social Research*, ed. by R. K. Merton and P. F. Lazarsfeld. Glencoe, Ill.: Free Press. Pp. 40–105.

Morgan, Kenneth W., ed.

1953 *The Religion of the Hindus*. New York: Ronald Press.

"Mountaineer" [Mr. Wilson of Mussoorie]

1860 *A Summer Ramble in the Himalayas*. London: Hurst and Blackett.

Munshi, K. M.

1955 "Forward," in *Social Economy of a Polyandrous People*, ed. by R. N. Saksena. Agra: Agra University Press. Pp. i–viii.

Murdock, George P.

1949 *Social Structure*. New York: The Macmillan Company.

Nadel, S. F.

1954 "Caste and Government in Primitive Society." *Journal of the Anthropological Society of Bombay*, Vol. 8, pp. 9–22.

Nevill, H. R.

1904 *Naini Tal: A Gazetteer*, comprising Vol. XXXIV of the District Gazetteers of the United Provinces of Agra and Oudh. Allahabad: Government Press.

Newcomb, Theodore M.

1950 *Social Psychology*. New York: Dryden Press.

Newell, William H.

1954 "A Note on Village Government in the Indian Northern Hill States Since Indian Independence." *Economic Development and Cultural Change*, Vol. 2, pp. 416–419.

1955 "Goshen, a Gaddi Village in the Himalayas," in *India's Villages*, Development Department, West Bengal Government. Calcutta: West Bengal Government Press. Pp. 51–61.

Niehoff, Arthur

1959 "Caste and Industrial Organization in North India," *Administrative Science Quarterly*, Vol. 3, pp. 494–508.

Oakley, E. S.

1905 *Holy Himalaya*. Edinburgh: Oliphant Anderson and Ferrier.

Olcott, Mason

1944 "The Caste System of India." *American Sociological Review*, Vol. 9, pp. 648–657.

O'Malley, L. S. S.

1932 *Indian Caste Customs*. New York: Cambridge University Press.

Opler, Morris E.

1956 "The Extensions of an Indian Village." *Journal of Asian Studies*, Vol. 16, pp. 5–10.

1958   "Spiritual Possession in a Rural Area of Northern India," in
         Reader in Comparative Religion, ed. by W. A. Lessa and E. Z. Vogt.
         Evanston: Row, Peterson. Pp. 553–566.

1959a   "Family, Anxiety and Religion in a Community of North India,"
         in *Culture and Mental Health: Cross-Cultural Studies,* ed. by Mar-
         vin K. Opler. New York: The Macmillan Company. Pp. 273–289.

1959b   "The Place of Religion in a North Indian Village." *Southwestern
         Journal of Anthropology,* Vol. 15, pp. 219–226.

1960   "Political Organization and Economic Growth, the Case of Village
         India." *International Review of Community Development,* No. 5,
         pp. 187–197.

Opler, Morris E., and R. D. Singh

1948   "The Division of Labor in an Indian Village," in *A Reader in Gen-
         eral Anthropology,* ed. by C. S. Coon. New York: Henry Holt and
         Company. Pp. 464–496.

Pant, S. D.

1935   *The Social Economy of the Himalayans.* London: George Allen and
         Unwin.

Pargiter, F. E.

1922   *Ancient Indian Historical Tradition.* London: Oxford University
         Press.

Passin, Herbert

1955   "Untouchability in the Far East." *Monumenta Nipponica,* Vol. 11,
         pp. 27–47.

Perelman, S. J.

1947   *Westward Ha!* New York: Simon and Schuster.

Planalp, Jack M.

1956   "Religious Life and Values in a North Indian Village." Ph.D. dis-
         sertation, Department of Sociology and Anthropology, Cornell Uni-
         versity. Ann Arbor: University Microfilms.

Planning Commission, Government of India

1958   *The New India: Progress Through Democracy.* New York: The
         Macmillan Company.

Raturi, Pundit Hari Krishnan

1928   *Garhwal ka Ityhas* (History of Garhwal). Dehra Dun: Garhwali Press.
         (In Hindi.)

Redfield, Robert

1955   "The Social Organization of Tradition." *Far Eastern Quarterly,*
         Vol. 15, pp. 13–22.

1957   *The Primitive World and Its Transformations,* Great Seal Books.
         Ithaca: Cornell University Press.

Rosser, Collin

1955   "A 'Hermit' Village in Kulu," in *India's Villages,* Development De-
         partment, West Bengal Government. Calcutta: West Bengal Gov-
         ernment Press. Pp. 70–81.

Rowe, William L.
1960a "Social and Economic Mobility in a Low-Caste North Indian Community." Ph.D. dissertation, Department of Sociology and Anthropology, Cornell University. Ann Arbor: University Microfilms.
1960b "The Marriage Network and Structural Change in a North Indian Community," *Southwestern Journal of Anthropology*, Vol. 16, pp. 299–311.

Ryan, Bryce
1953 *Caste in Modern Ceylon*. New Brunswick, N. J.: Rutgers University Press.

Saksena, R. N.
1955 *Social Economy of a Polyandrous People*. Agra: Agra University Institute of Social Sciences.

Sankrityayana, Rahul
1958 *Kumaon*. Banaras: Jana Mandal. (In Hindi.)

Sharma, K. N.
1961 "Occupational Mobility of Castes in a North Indian Village." *Southwestern Journal of Anthropology*, Vol. 17, pp. 146–164.

Singer, Milton
1955 "The Cultural Pattern of Indian Civilization." *Far Eastern Quarterly*, Vol. 15, pp. 23–36.

Singh, K. K.
1967 *Patterns of Caste Tension*. Bombay: Asia Publishing House.

Sivananda, Swami
1947 *Hindu Fasts and Festivals and Their Philosophy*. Rikhikesh: Sivananda Publication League.

Smith, Robert J.
1956 "The Problem of Extensions of a Community." Cornell University Studies in Culture and Applied Science, Cornell University. (Mimeographed.)

Srinivas, M. N.
1952 *Religion and Society Among the Coorgs of South India*. Oxford: Clarendon Press.
1955a "Castes: Can They Exist in India of Tomorrow?" *Economic Weekly* (Bombay), Vol. 7, pp. 1230–1232.
1955b "The Social System of a Mysore Village," in *Village India*, ed. by McKim Marriott. Memoir 83, American Anthropological Association, Vol. 57, pp. 1–35.
1956 "A Note on Sanskritization and Westernization." *Far Eastern Quarterly*, Vol. 15, pp. 481–496.
1957 "Caste in Modern India." *Journal of Asian Studies*, Vol. 16, pp. 529–548.
1959 "The Dominant Caste in Rampura." *American Anthropologist*, Vol. 61, pp. 1–16.

Srivastava, R. P.
　1958　"The Bhotia Nomads and Their Indo-Tibetan Trade." *Journal of the University of Saugar,* Vol. 7, Part 1, Sec. A, pp. 1–22.

Stevenson, H. N. C.
　1954　"Status Evaluation in the Hindu Caste System." *Journal of the Royal Anthropological Institute of Great Britain and Ireland,* Vol. 84, pp. 45–65.

Stowell, V. A.
　1907　*A Manual of the Land Tenures of the Kumaun Division.* Allahabad: United Provinces Government Press.

Tinker, Hugh
　1959　"Authority and Community in Village India." *Pacific Affairs,* Vol. 32, pp. 354–375.

Tod, James
　1829–1832　*Annals and Antiquities of Rajast'han,* 2 vols. London: Smith, Elder.

Traill, G. W.
　1828　"Statistical Sketch of Kamaon." *Asiatic Researches,* Vol. 16, pp. 137–234.

Turner, Ralph
　1956　"Role-Taking, Role Standpoint, and Reference-Group Behavior." *American Journal of Sociology,* Vol. 61, pp. 316–328.

Upreti, Pandit Ganga Datt
　1894　*Proverbs and Folklore of Kumaun and Garhwal.* Lodiana: Lodiana Mission Press.

Walton, H. G.
　1910　*British Garhwal: A Gazetteer,* comprising Vol. XXXVI of the District Gazetteer of the United Provinces of Agra and Oudh. Allahabad: Government Press.

　1911a　*Dehra Dun: A Gazetteer,* comprising Vol. I of the District Gazetteer of the United Provinces of Agra and Oudh. Allahabad: Government Press.

　1911b　*Almora: A Gazetteer,* comprising Vol. XXXV of the District Gazetteer of the United Provinces of Agra and Oudh. Allahabad: Government Press.

Weber, Max
　1958　*The Religion of India,* tr. and ed. by H. H. Gerth and D. Martindale. Glencoe, Ill.: Free Press.

Williams, G. R. C.
　1874　*Historical and Statistical Memoir of Dehra Doon.* Roorkee: Thomason Civil Engineering College Press.

Wiser, Charlotte V., and William H.
　1951　*Behind Mud Walls,* 3rd printing. New York: Agricultural Missions.

Wiser, William H.
　1936　*The Hindu Jajmani System.* Lucknow: Lucknow Publishing House.

CHAPTER BIBLIOGRAPHIES, 1971

PROLOGUE: BEHIND MANY MASKS

Berreman, Gerald D.
  1966 "Anemic and Emetic Analyses in Social Anthropology" *American Anthropologist*, Vol. 68, pp. 346–354.
  1968 "Ethnography: Method and Product" in *Introduction to Cultural Anthropology: Essays in the Scope and Methods of the Science of Man* (James A. Clifton, ed.). Boston: Houghton Mifflin Co. Pp. 337–373, (with photographs of the research in Sirkanda). See also *Anthropology Today*, CRM Books: Del Mar, California, 1971, pp. 76–87, 338, 341. 344, for photographs of Sirkanda in color.

Blumer, Herbert
  1969 *Symbolic Interactionism.* Englewood Cliffs, N. J.: Prentice–Hall.

Cicourel, Aaron V.
  1964 *Method and Measurement in Sociology.* New York: The Free Press of Glencoe.
  1968 "Preliminary Issues of Theory and Method" in *The Social Organization of Juvenile Justice.* N. Y.: John Wiley and Sons. Pp. 1–21.

Goffman, Erving
  1967 *Interaction Ritual: Essays on Face-To-Face Behavior.* Garden City, N. Y.: Doubleday (Anchor Book).
  1969 *Strategic Interaction.* Philadelphia: University of Pennsylvania Press.

INTRODUCTION (Village Studies and General Works), PP. 1–8

Ahmed, Zahir
  1965 *Dusk and Dawn in Village India.* New York: Frederick A. Praeger.

Bailey, F. G.
   1960   *Tribe, Caste and Nation.* Manchester: Manchester University Press.

Beals, Alan
   1962   *Gopalpur.* New York: Holt, Rinehart and Winston.

Berreman, Gerald D.
   1969   "Urgent Anthropology in India" in *Urgent Research in Social An-*
           thropology (B. L. Abbi and S. Saberwal, eds.). Simla, India: Indian
           Institute of Advanced Study. Pp. 41–53.

Hiebert, Paul G.
   1971   *Konduru: Structure and Integration in a South Indian Village.* Min-
           neapolis: University of Minnesota Press.

Ishwaran, K. (editor)
   1970   *Change and Continuity in India's Villages.* New York: Columbia
           University Press.

Karve, Irawati
   1961   *Hindu Society, an Interpretation.* Poona, Deccan College.

Majumdar, D. N.
   1958   *Caste and Communication in an Indian Village.* Bombay: Asia
           Publishing

Mandelbaum, David G.
   1970   *Society in India* (2 Vols.). Berkeley: University of California Press.

Mathur, K. S.
   1964   *Caste and Ritual in a Malwa Village.* Bombay: Asia Publishing
           House.

Mayer, Adrian C.
   1960   *Caste and Kinship in Central India.* Berkeley: University of Cal-
           ifornia Press.

Opler, Morris E.
   1968   "The Themal Approach in Cultural Anthropology and Its Ap-
           plication to North Indian Data." *Southwestern Journal of Anthro-*
           pology, Vol. 24, pp. 215–227.

Orenstein, Henry
   1965   *Gaon: Conflict and Cohesion in an Indian Village.* Princeton, N. J.:
           Princeton University Press.

Ratnam, Bala (editor)
   1963   *Anthropology on the March.* Madras: The Book Centre.

Singer, Milton, and B. S. Cohn
    1968   *Structure and Change in Indian Society*. Chicago: Aldine Publishing Company.

1. THE SETTING (The Mountain Area), PP. 9–37

Ballard, R. E. H.
    1969   "Land, Caste and Kin: A Study of a Village in Himachal Pradesh" [Sirmur District]. Unpublished Ph. D. thesis, Department of Sociology, University of Delhi, Delhi, India.

Berreman, Gerald D.
    1963   "Peoples and Cultures of the Himalayas." *Asian Survey*, Vol. 3, pp. 289–304.

Hitchcock, John T.
    1966   *The Magars of Banyan Hill*. New York: Holt, Rinehart and Winston.

Newell, William H.
    1965   *Himachal Pradesh: Report on Scheduled Castes and Scheduled Tribes (A Study of Gaddi)*. Census of India, 1961, Vol. 20, Part 5–B.
    1970   "An Upper Rāvi Village: The Process of Social Change in Himāchal Pradesh" in *Change and Continuity in India's Villages* (K. Ishwaran, ed.). New York: Columbia University Press. Pp. 37–56.

Nitzberg, Frances L.
    1970   "Land, Labor and Status: The Social Implications of Ecologic Adaptation in a Region of the Western Himalayas of India" [Chamba District, Himachal Pradesh]. Unpublished Ph. D. thesis, Department of Social Relations, Harvard University, Cambridge, Massachusetts.

Sebring, James M.
    1968   "Caste Ranking and Caste Interaction in a North Indian Village" [Almora District, Uttar Pradesh]. Unpublished Ph. D. dissertation, Department of Anthropology, University of California, Berkeley, California.

Sen, Biswajit
    1970   "Social Changes in the Himalayan Villages: A Case Study of Three Villages in Kinnaur District" [Himachal Pradesh]. Unpublished D. Phil. thesis, Calcutta University, Calcutta, India.

von Fürer–Haimendorf, Christoph
    1962   "Moral Concepts in Three Himalayan Societies" in *Indian Anthro-*

pology: Essays in Memory of D. N. Majumdar (T. N. Madan and
G. Sarana, eds.). Bombay: Asia Publishing House. Pp. 279-309.

2. THE ECONOMIC CONTEXT, PP. 38-79.

Andress, Joel M.
1966   "Culture and Habitat in the Central Himalayas" [Dehra Dun and
        Tehri Garhwal Districts, Uttar Pradesh]. Unpublished Ph. D. dis-
        sertation, Department of Geography, University of California,
        Berkeley, California.

Etienne, Gilbert
1968   *Studies in Indian Agriculture.* Berkeley: The University of Califor-
        nia Press.

Gould, Harold A.
1964   "A Jajmani System of North India: Its Structure, Magnitude and
        Meaning." *Ethnology,* Vol. 3, pp. 12-41.

Jinha, Padam Singh
1961   *Agriculture in the Hill Regions of North India.* New Delhi: Direc-
        torate of Extension, Ministry of Food and Agriculture.

Kolenda, Pauline M.
1963   "Toward a Model of the Hindu Jajmani System." *Human Organ-
        ization,* Vol. 22, pp. 11-31.

McDougal, Charles
1968   *Village and Household Economy in Far Western Nepal.* Kirtipur,
        Nepal: Tribhuvan University.

Neale, Walter C.
1962   *Economic Change in Rural India, Land Tenure and Reform in
        Uttar Pradesh, 1800-1955.* New Haven, Conn.: Yale University
        Press.

Omvedt, Gail
1969   "Imperialism and Rural Modernization." *Berkeley Journal of So-
        ciology,* Vol. 14, pp. 130-151.

Orans, Martin
1968   "Maximizing in Jajmaniland: a Model of Caste Relations." *Amer-
        ican Anthropologist,* Vol. 70, pp. 875-897.

Rowe, William L.
1963   "Changing Rural Class Structure and the Jajmani System." *Human
        Organization,* Vol. 22, pp. 41-44.

3. THE RELIGIOUS CONTEXT: THE SUPERNATURAL, PP. 80–120

Berreman, Gerald D.
1963   "Gods Worshipped in Sirkanda" (Appendix I) in *Hindus of the Himalayas* (1st Edition). Berkeley: University of California Press. Pp. 369–387.

Gumperz, John J.
1964   "Religion and Communication in Village North India." *Journal of Asian Studies*, Vol. 23 (June, Supplement), pp. 89–97. Also *Religion in South Asia* (E. Harper, ed.). Seattle: University of Washington Press. Pp. 89–97.

Harper, Edward B.
1963   "Spirit Possession and Social Structure" in *Anthropology on the March* (B. Ratnam, ed.). Madras: The Book Center. Pp. 165–197.

Harper, Edward B. (editor)
1964   *Religion in South Asia*. Seattle: University of Washington Press. (Also comprising *Journal of Asia Studies*, Vol. 23 [June, Supplement], 1964.

Kolenda, Pauline M.
1964   Religious Anxiety and Hindu Fate." *The Journal of Asian Studies*. Vol. 23, pp. 71–82.

Mandelbaum, David G.
1966   "Transcendental and Pragmatic Aspects of Religion." *American Anthropologist*, Vol. 68, pp. 1174–1191.

Sharma, K. N.
1961   "Hindu Sects and Food Patterns in North India." *Journal of Social Research* (Prof. Majumdar Memorial Volume: Aspects of Religion in Indian Society), Vol. IV, No. 1–2, pp. 45–58.

Srivastava, S. K.
1963   "The Process of Desanskritization in Village India" in *Anthropology on the March* (B. Ratnam, ed.). Madras: The Book Centre. Pp. 263–267.

4. THE RELIGIOUS CONTEXT: CALENDRICAL AND LIFE-CYCLE CEREMONIES, PP. 121–142

Berreman, Gerald D.
1963   "Calendrical Rites in Sirkanda" (Appendix II) in *Hindus of the Himalayas* (1st Edition). Berkeley: University of California Press. Pp. 388–394.

1963	"Life-Cycle Rites in Sirkanda" (Appendix III) in *Hindus of the Himalayas* (1st Edition). Berkeley: University of California Press. Pp. 395-409.

5. Kin Groups and Kinship, pp. 143-196

Berreman, Gerald D.
1963	"Sirkanda Kin Terms" (Appendix IV) in *Hindus of the Himalayas* (1st Edition). Berkeley, University of California Press. Pp. 410-414.
1969	"Women's Roles and Politics: India and the United States" in *Readings in General Sociology* (4th Edition, R. W. O'Brien, C. C. Schrag, and W. T. Martin, eds.). Boston: Houghton Mifflin. Pp. 68-71.

Ishwaran, K.
1965	"Kinship and Distance in Rural India." *International Journal of Comparative Sociology*, Vol. 6, pp. 81-94.

Karve, Irawati
1963	"A Family Through Six Generations" in *Anthropology on the March* (B. Ratnam, ed.). Madras: The Book Centre. Pp. 241-263.

Kolenda, Pauline M.
1968	"Region, Caste and Family Structure: A Comparative Study of the Indian 'Joint' Family" in (Singer and Cohn, eds.) *Structure and Change in Indian Society*. Chicago: Aldine Publishing Company. Pp. 339-396.

Luschinsky, Mildred Stroop
1962	*The Life of Women in a Village of North India: A Study of Role and Status* (2 Vols.). Unpublished Ph. D. Dissertation, Dept. of Sociology and Anthropology, Cornell University, Ithaca, N. Y.

Mahar, J. Michael
1966	*Marriage Networks in the Northern Gangetic Plain*. Unpublished Ph. D. Dissertation, Cornell University, Department of Anthropology.

Madan, T. N.
1965	Family and Kinship: *A Study of the Pandits of Rural Kashmir*. Bombay: Asia Publishing House.

Majumdar, D. N.
1962	*Himalayan Polyandry*. New York: Asia Publishing House.

Minturn, Leigh, and John T. Hitchcock
1966	*"The Rājpūts of Khalapur, India"* (Six Cultures, Vol. III). New

York: John Wiley & Sons. Part I Ethnographic Background; Part II Child Training.

Sharma, K. N.
1969 "Resource Networks and Resource Groups in the Social Structure." *The Eastern Anthropologist*, Vol. XXII (1), pp. 13-17.

Vatuk, Sylvia
1969 "Reference, Address and Fictive Kinship in Urban North India." *Ethnology*, Vol. 8, pp. 255-272.

6. CASTE, PP. 197-228

Bailey, F. G.
1963 "Closed Social Stratification in India." *Archives of European Sociology*, Vol. 4, pp. 107-124.

Berreman, Gerald D.
1965 "The Study of Caste Ranking in India." *Southwestern Journal of Anthropology*, Vol. 21, pp. 115-129.
1966 "Caste in Cross-Cultural Perspective" in *Japan's Invisible Race: Caste in Culture and Personality* (G. DeVos and H. Wagatsuma, eds.). Berkeley: University of California Press. Pp. 275-324.
1967a "Stratification, Pluralism and Interaction: A Comparative Analysis of Caste" in *Caste and Race* (deReuck and Knight, eds.). London: J. and A. Churchill, Ltd. Pp. 45-91.
1967b "Caste as Social Process." *Southwestern Journal of Anthropology*, Vol. 23, pp. 351-370.
1968 "Caste: The Concept of Caste" in *International Encyclopedia of the Social Sciences* (D. Sills, ed.). New York: Macmillan and Free Press. Vol. 2, pp. 333-339.

1972 "Race, Caste and other Invidious Distinctions in Social Stratification," *Race* Vol. 13, No. 4 (In Press).
n.d. "Social Mobility and Change in a Caste Society" in *Response to Change: Adjustment and Adaptation in Personality and Culture* (tentative title, George A. DeVos, ed.) Forthcoming.

Béteille, André
1965 *Caste, Class and Power.* Berkeley: University of California, Berkeley.
1969 *Castes Old and New.* Bombay: Asia Publishing House.

de Reuck, Anthony, and Julie Knight (eds.)
1967 *Caste and Race: Comparative Approaches.* London: J. and A. Churchill, Ltd.

Dumont, Louis
1970 *Homo Hierarchicus: The Caste System and Its Implications* (M. Sainsbury, Trans.). London: Weidenfeld and Nicolson.

Dumont, Louis, and D. F. Pocock
1959 "Pure and Impure." *Contributions to Indian Sociology,* Vol. 3, pp. 9–39.

Freed, Stanley A.
1963 "An Objective Method for Determining the Collective Caste Hierarchy of an Indian Village." *American Anthropologist,* Vol. 65, pp. 879–891.

Galanter, Marc
1968 "Changing Legal Conceptions of Caste" in *Structure and Change in Indian Society* (M. Singer and B. Cohn, eds.). Chicago: Aldine Publishing Company. Pp. 299–336.
1969 "Untouchability and the Law." *Economic and Political Weekly, Annual Number* (January, 1969). Bombay. Pp. 131–170.

Gumperz, John J.
1958 "Dialect Differences and Social Stratification in a North Indian Village." *American Anthropologist,* Vol. 60, pp. 668–682.

Hsu, Francis L. K.
1963 *Clan, Caste and Club.* Princeton, N. J.: D. Van Nostrand Co.

Lynch, Owen M.
1969 *The Politics of Untouchability.* New York, Columbia University Press.

Marriott, McKim
1968 "Caste Ranking and Food Transactions: A Matrix Analysis" in *Structure and Change in Indian Society* (Singer and Cohn, eds.). Chicago: Aldine Publishing Company. Pp. 133–171.

Mayer, Adrian C.
1968 "Caste: The Indian Caste System" in *International Encyclopedia of the Social Sciences* (D. Sills, ed.). New York: MacMillan and Free Press. Vol. 2, pp. 339–344.

Sebring, James A.
1969 "Caste Indicators and Caste Identification of Strangers." *Human Organization,* Vol. 28, pp. 199–207.

Silverberg, James (ed.)
1968 *Social Mobility in the Caste System in India* (Comparative Studies in Society and History, Supplement III). The Hague: Mouton.

7. INTERCASTE RELATIONS, PP. 229–258

Anant, Santokh S.
  1970   "Self- and Mutual Perception of Salient Personality Traits of Different Caste Groups." *Journal of Cross-Cultural Psychology*, Vol. 1, no. 1, pp. 41–52.

Atal, Yogesh
  1968   *The Changing Frontiers of Caste.* Delhi: National Publishing House.

Isaacs, Harold R.
  1965   *India's Ex-Untouchables.* New York: The John Day Co.

8. THE VILLAGE COMMUNITY, PP. 259–293

Doctor, Adi H.
  1965   "India's Experiment in Democratic Decentralization" in *Studies in Indian Democracy* (S. P. Aiyar and R. Srinivasan, eds.). Bombay: Allied Publishers. Pp. 373–389.

Maddick, Henry
  1962   "Panchayat Raj: Rural Local Government in India." *Journal of Local Administration Overseas* (London), Vol. 1, pp. 201–212.

Nicholas, Ralph
  1965   "Factions: A Comparative Analysis" in *Political Systems and the Distribution of Power* (M. Gluckman and F. Eggan, eds.). New York: Frederick A. Praeger (ASA Monograph No. 2). Pp. 21–61.

Retzlaff, Ralph H.
  1962   *Village Government in India: A Case Study.* Bombay: Asia Publishing House.

9. THE OUTSIDE WORLD: URBAN CONTACTS AND GOVERNMENT PROGRAMS, PP. 294–338

Berreman, Gerald D.
  1963   "Caste and Community Development." *Human Organization*, Vol. 22, pp. 90–94.
  1964   "Aleut Reference Group Alienation, Mobility and Acculturation." *American Anthropologist*, Vol. 66, pp. 231–250.

Epstein, T. S.
  1962   *Economic Development and Social Change in South India.* Manchester: Manchester University Press.

Fox, Richard G.
  1969   *From Zamindar to Ballot Box.* Ithaca, N. Y.: Cornell University Press.

Lambert, Richard D.
  1962   "The Impact of Urban Society Upon Village Life" in *India's Urban Future* (Roy Turner, ed.). Berkeley: University of California Press. Pp. 117–140.

Mayer, Albert, M. Marriott, R. L. Park
  1959   *Pilot Project India.* Berkeley: University of California Press.

Nair, Kusum
  1961   *Blossoms in the Dust: The Human Factor in Indian Development.* New York: Frederick A. Praeger.

Orans, Martin
  1965   *The Santal: A Tribe in Search of a Great Tradition.* Detroit: Wayne University Press.

Rowe, William L. (ed.)
  1963   *Contours of Culture Change in South Asia (Special Issue). Human Organization,* Vol. 22, No. 1, Ithaca, N. Y., Society for Applied Anthropology.

Srinivas, M. N.
  1962   *Caste in Modern India and Other Essays.* Bombay: Asia Publishing House.
  1966   *Social Change in Modern India.* Berkeley: University of California Press.

Weiner, Myron
  1962   *The Politics of Scarcity.* Chicago: University of Chicago Press.

10. CONCLUSION—1958, PP. 339–357

Berreman, Gerald D.
  1970   "Pahāri Culture: Diversity and Change in the Lower Himalayas" in *Change and Continuity in India's Villages* (K. Ishwaran, ed.). New York: Columbia University Press. Pp. 73–103.

11. SIRKANDA TEN YEARS LATER, PP. 358–404

Berreman, Gerald D.
  1963   "Caste and Community Development." *Human Organization,* Vol. 22, pp. 90–94.

1964   "Brahmins and Shamans in Pahari Religion." *Journal of Asian Studies*, Vol. 23 (June, Supplement), pp. 53–69, and *Religion in South Asia* (E. Harper, ed.). Seattle: University of Washington Press. Pp. 53–69.

1969a "Academic Colonialism: Not So Innocent Abroad." *The Nation,* Nov. 10, 1969, pp. 505–508.

1969b "Women's Roles and Politics: India and the United States" in *Readings in General Sociology* (R. O'Brien, C. Schrag, W. Martin, eds.), 4th Edition. Boston: Houghton Mifflin Co. Pp. 68–71. (First published, 1966.)

1971   "Ethics, Responsibility and the Funding of Asian Research." *Journal of Asian Studies,* Vol. 30, pp. 390–399.

1972   "Social Categories and Social Interaction in Urban India." *American Anthropologist.* Vol. 74, No. 3, in press.

Lewis, I. M.
1971   *Ecstatic Religion: An Anthropological Study of Spirit Possession and Shamanism.* Middlesex, England: Penguin Books.

Newman, Lucile F.
1970   "Cultural Factors in Family Planning" in *The Impact of Fertility Limitation on Women's Life, Career and Personality* (E. Milner, ed.). *Annals of the New York Academy of Sciences,* Vol. 175, Art. 3 (Oct. 30, 1970), pp. 833–840.

Silverberg, James M. (ed.)
1968   *Social Mobility in the Caste System of India* (Comparative Studies in Society and History, Supplement III). The Hague: Mouton.

Srinivas, M. N.
1966   *Social Change in Modern India.* Berkeley: University of California Press.

Wiser, William and Charlotte
1963   *Behind Mud Walls. 1930–1960.* Berkeley: University of California Press.

PROLOGUE

* The author would like to thank Aaron V. Cicourel, Erving Goffman, Dell Hymes and William L. Rowe for their helpful comments on the manuscript of this section. It appeared originally, in slightly different form, as Monograph Number 4 of the Society for Applied Anthropology, in 1962.

1 This is partly attributable to the substitution, soon afterwards, of a low-status assistant in place of Sharma, a circumstance to be described below.

2 An effective appeal for accurate responses from villagers was to picture my academic examining committee in America as made up of relentless and omniscient task-masters who would unerringly detect any inadequacies or inaccuracies in my report and perhaps fail me on that basis so that I could not pursue my chosen profession. This evoked sympathy and cooperation from several informants, one of whom said he would assume personal responsibility for the accuracy of all information obtained from or checked through him.

3 The pressures which commitment to a team performance may exert to prevent a person from behaving spontaneously, or from freely choosing the kind of impression he will strive to make, are exemplified in an insightful description by George Orwell: "Shooting an Elephant," in *Shooting an Elephant and Other Essays,* Harcourt, Brace and Company, New York, 1950, pp. 3-12. As a police officer in Burma, Orwell once shot an elephant against his better judgment, solely in order to sustain the image of himself as a "sahib" before an expectant crowd. "For it is the condition of his rule that the sahib shall spend his life trying to impress the 'natives,' and so in every crisis he has got to do what the 'natives' expect of him. He wears a mask, and his face grows to fit it" (p. 8).

4 I am indebted to Thomas S. Chambers for calling my attention to the following apt definition by Ambrose Bierce; a definition which might serve as a motto for this monograph: "Interpreter, *n.* One who enables two persons of different languages to understand each other by repeating to each what it would have been to the interpreter's advantage for the other to have said" (Ambrose Bierce, *The Devil's Dictionary,* Dover Publications, Inc., New York, 1958, p. 69).

Notes

[1] As was explained in the "Note on Hindi Terms," "Sirkanda" is a pseudonym, as are the names used for other villages in the vicinity, and for all individuals mentioned hereafter.

CHAPTER 1 THE SETTING

[1] The western boundary of the Himalaya West is the Tons River (a tributary of the Jumna), and the eastern is the Kali or Sarda River the boundary with Nepal. The Himalaya West comprises the present districts of Almora, Garhwal, Tehri Garhwal, and the hill sections of Naini Tal and Dehra Dun districts.

[2] Following Lowie (1947, p. 111) and Murdock (1949, p. 47), the Pahari *sib* can be defined as an exogamous, patrilineal, consanguineal kin group whose members claim common descent but are often unable to trace the lines of descent accurately. In much of the anthropological literature, including some of my own writings, this group has been referred to as the *clan* (cf. chapter 5).

[3] Even the most ethnocentric foreigners find Paharis to have admirable traits. J. B. Fraser, referring to a Western Pahari group whose polyandry he found shocking, had this to say:

> It is remarkable, that a people so degraded in morals, and many of whose customs are of so revolting a nature, should in other respects evince a much higher advancement in civilisation, than we discover among other nations, whose manners are more engaging and whose moral character ranks infinitely higher. Their persons are better clad and more decent; their approach more polite and

unembarrassed; and their address is better than that of most of the inhabitants of the remote Highlands of Scotland; . . . and their houses, in point of construction, comfort and internal cleanliness, are beyond comparison superior to Scottish Highland dwellings. (Fraser, 1820, p. 209)

CHAPTER 2 THE ECONOMIC CONTEXT

[1] This figure is the one used in official accounting. It includes the 176 acres around Sirkanda plus 29 acres in other areas included with Sirkanda for accounting purposes, and excludes 93 acres which in the accounts are included with other villages. These 205 acres represent less than one-fourth of all lands within the official boundaries of Sirkanda. The remainder is uncultivated.

[2] Rs. is the abbreviation for *rupee,* the monetary unit worth about 21¢ in United States currency in 1957–1958 (Rs. 4.75 = $1.00). In buying power in India, a rupee is approximately equal to a dollar in America.

[3] Scientific names of plants are obtained from Atkinson (1882), who provides complete listings by scientific and "vernacular" names of both domestic and wild plants of the hills.

[4] A maund is about 80 pounds. A maund of wheat was worth about Rs. 15 in this area at this time. Wheat is a standard medium of exchange. A common way to report income is to estimate its value in wheat. If a man gets Rs. 100 in cash it is often reported as "seven maunds of wheat."

[5] Estimates of yearly cash expenditures per family averaged roughly as follows: *gūr* (brown sugar) Rs. 100, salt Rs. 25, kerosene Rs. 20, cooking oil Rs. 150, molasses Rs. 8, tobacco and cigarettes Rs. 15, cloth and bedding Rs. 110, utensils Rs. 15, ceremonies Rs. 80, taxes Rs. 12, meat and drink Rs. 70, sweets, trinkets, and entertainment Rs. 50, proportional year's expenditures on house construction Rs. 50 (figuring the life of a house at forty years at Rs. 2,000), livestock Rs. 150. Medical expenses are included in the total for ceremonies, as medical treatment almost always takes the form of a ceremony. Education is not a significant extra expense, amounting to only a rupee or so for school supplies to those families with school-going children.

Low-caste expenditures are significantly less than those reported above— perhaps half as much. The low castes buy fewer and less expensive clothes and utensils, eat less sugar, own fewer livestock. Their weddings are inexpensive, their houses are cheap, and they depend for tobacco, sweets, entertainment, meat, drink, and so on largely on handouts from the high castes.

[6] In 1958 he withdrew from the village because his servant left and he could find no suitable substitute. He was gone for several months, and the chances of his returning were slim because he was ready to retire and his sons did not want to work in this isolated spot, preferring instead to operate the profitable family shop in Rajpur.

[7] The occurrence in the village of a house belonging to a member of the Palial sib of Rajputs in a line of houses owned by Jawari sib members is due to such a case, which also involved a chan at the southwest end of the village

(see map 3). Two other village houses whose occupant-owners are isolated from their sib fellows can probably be accounted for in the same way.

CHAPTER 3   THE SUPERNATURAL

[1] There are Pahari Muslims who are, except for religion, indistinguishable from other Paharis. One such family lives in Bhatbair, and a boy of that family attends the Sirkanda school. Other Pahari Muslims live in Tehri Garhwal. There have also been a few Pahari converts to Christianity among the Doms of Tehri Garhwal. However, no missionary has ever come to Sirkanda or, so far as I could determine, to Bhatbair.

[2] The term "pujari" also refers to individuals who are the keepers of particular temples and who supervise worship and receive offerings to the deities of such temples. In this account they will be called "temple keepers" to avoid confusion. Temple keepers are usually of high-caste, and, though they preside over the pujas to a particular god, their functions are entirely distinct from those of the specialists described in the text.

[3] For a description of these gods and their worship see Appendix IA, first ed.

[4] For a description of the characteristics and manner of worship of these gods see Appendix IB, first ed.

CHAPTER 4   CALENDRICAL AND LIFE-CYCLE CEREMONIES

[1] For further description of these ceremonies see Appendix IIIA, first ed.

[2] For a description of each of these types of marriage see Appendix IIIB, first ed.

[3] Karve notes, "All over India there is the custom of giving bride-price among the poorer castes and of receiving dowry among the higher castes" (Karve, 1953, p. 132).

[4] M. E. Opler (1959a) has discussed in some detail the religious functions of the family in Senapur. The situation he described is parallel to that in Sirkanda.

[5] Of course "local Hinduism" can be used to denote local practices regardless of their origins and affinities, but the implication of local origin or local spread must be avoided.

CHAPTER 5   KIN GROUPS AND KINSHIP

[1] In Sirkanda the word "jat" or "jati" refers to either the endogamous caste or to the exogamous sib. Since it literally means "birth" or "lineage," this is not surprising. Both caste and sib are determined by birth. Hocart (1950, pp. 32 f.) has discussed the word "jati," pointing out that it "has much wider and looser a meaning than we have put upon the Portuguese creation 'caste.' It does not refer to any particular kind of division or grouping, but simply to hereditary status."

As was noted in note 2 of chap. 1, in much of the anthropological literature the group here referred to as the sib is called the *clan*. I have decided to follow Murdock's usage because his distinction between sib and clan is relevant to an understanding of Pahari social organization, for reasons to be explained below. Villagers of the plains often refer to the sib as *gōtrā*.

2 The differences between these figures are attributable to records of marriages of now-deceased men or men no longer identified with Sirkanda. The 471 figure includes marriages of Sirkanda women, most of whom have gone elsewhere at marriage.

3 One of these marriages is the three-wife family, in which two wives occupy one dwelling and the third another.

4 Perhaps in certain other Pahari areas there is greater laxity, especially between Rajputs and Brahmins. Saksena states, for Jaunsar-Bawar, "As intermarriage between Brahmans and Rajputs is easily possible, but not outside, they constitute a single endogamous group. . ." (Saksena, 1955, p. 28; cf. Majumdar, 1944, pp. 115, 138).

5 The 53 Rajput marriages include several with people of these sibs who come from houses in the immediate vicinity of Sirkanda but who are not identified as members of the village. Since these cases added to the size of the sample and brought in no extraneous factors, they have been included in the discussion.

6 This means that 77 Sirkanda people found mates within the village. The number represents approximately half as many marital unions, since it takes two to make a marriage, although polygynous and sequential marriages bring the total up somewhat. In addition, one barber woman lived as wife of a weaver man who resided in Sirkanda temporarily.

7 Majumdar found, in an exogamous Pahari village in Jaunsar-Bawar, that 35 per cent of the Rajput marriages were contracted within three miles and only 8 per cent were contracted over 12 miles away. He found similar proportions among the low castes of the village (Majumdar, 1955, p. 172).

8 The barber caste, being nonindigenous to this area, must go outside to seek mates or, as is often done, take them from other low castes.

Only two Sirkanda marriages were contracted more than 18 miles distant. These were of the women sold to outsiders. One of the two women went to Delhi, the other to the Punjab, each some 150 miles distant.

9 Jain (1948) reports that of 605 women interviewed in Jaunsar-Bawar, nearly half had been divorced one or more times, and 145 of those undivorced were still young enough that he felt they still might become divorced. Majumdar reports that in a village of Jaunsar-Bawar 62 per cent of the Rajput women, and 55 per cent of the low-caste (Kolta) women, had been divorced one or more times. In each case almost as many had been divorced two or more times as had been divorced once (Majumdar, 1955, p. 172).

10 Some of this material, including fig. 4, has appeared in Berreman, 1962e.

11 If a married daughter happens to be visiting her parents at the time of a funeral or other ceremony in which her natal family participates, she joins them, even though she would not participate if she were at that time living in her husband's house. Her sib affiliation obligates her to participate when

she is in the local sib group, even if only temporarily; that is, sib affiliation in such a case overrides clan affiliation. Clan affiliation might be explained as entirely a matter of place of residence—however temporary—among those affiliated by consanguinity or affinity with the core sib of the clan. That is, it may not be inaccurate to say that whether a woman is considered a member of her parents' or her husband's clan depends upon whose house she is staying in at the moment.

[12] "Descent, in fine, does not necessarily involve any belief that certain genealogical ties are closer than others, much less a recognition of kinship with one parent to the exclusion of the other. . . . It merely refers to a cultural rule which affiliates an individual with a particular selected group of kinsmen for certain social purposes such as mutual assistance or the regulation of marriage" (Murdock, 1949, p. 16). In Sirkanda maternal ties are recognized and prominent. This is made explicit in the kindred or sapinda rules of marriage regulation, in kindred participation in marriage and other life-cycle rites, and in kinship terminology.

CHAPTER 6 CASTE

[1] Blunt, 1931, p. 5; Bouglé, 1908, pp. 1 ff.; Brown, 1953, p. 30; Davis, 1949, pp. 378 f.; Dumont and Pocock, 1958, pp. 7 ff.; Ghurye, 1952, pp. 2 ff.; Hocart, 1950, pp. 3 ff.; Hutton, 1946, pp. 42, 44; Kroeber, 1930, p. 254; Leach, 1960; Nadel, 1954; O'Malley, 1932, pp. 1 f.; Ryan, 1953, p. 19; and Srinivas, 1952, pp. 24 ff. Gilbert (1948) lists over 5,000 references on caste and gives 17 sample definitions as well as one of his own.

[2] This definition incorporates the elements most frequently included in definitions of caste in the literature. See, for example, Blunt, 1931, p. 5; Brown, 1953, p. 30; Davis, 1949, pp. 378 f.; Ghurye, 1952, pp. 2–30; and Kroeber, 1930, p. 254. In a survey of definitions of twelve authors, it was found that in addition to the criteria listed in this minimal definition, only "distinct occupational and / or ethnic tradition," and "restrictions on eating (commensality)" were mentioned with comparable frequency.

[3] In this area kachchā food is that cooked in water, pakkā food that cooked in oil or parched. Kachcha food is easily polluted and can be eaten only if cooked and handled by one's own caste or a higher caste. Pakka food is much less vulnerable to pollution and can be eaten by a wider range of castes. In Sirkanda foods cooked in oil are considered less immune to pollution than parched foods.

[4] If a Dom is greeting a non-landowning Brahmin, he may say "Samani Pundit." The derivation of the word "samani" is not definitely known. One writer thinks it derives from "Shivaman," made up of the words "Shiva" (the god) and manāna (to honor). He interprets the greeting as an entreaty by indigenous Doms for their Indo-Aryan conquerors to honor or worship the Doms' deity, Shiva (Bahadur, 1916, pp. 73 f.). A. C. Chandola suggests more plausibly, in a personal communication, that it derives from the word samnyān, meaning to bow properly. As a greeting, "samani" is used among

all castes and is always given first by the person of inferior status. If two people are of the same caste, then it is given first by the person of junior generation or relationship, and if these are equivalent, then by the younger of the two. Only low castes addressing high castes use the honorific title in conjunction with the greeting.

5 In such statements the terms "high caste" and "low caste" are literally translatable as "big caste" and "little caste," that is, big and small in the sense of important and unimportant, as a "big man" (district magistrate) and a "small man" (peasant).

6 There is one family of Muslims in Bhatbair. They came from Tehri Garhwal about three generations ago and bought land from a Brahmin. They are Pahari agriculturists and are indistinguishable from other Paharis except in their religion. Their status position is ambiguous. All castes claim superiority to them and practice ritual avoidance of them. In social relations, however, they rank about equivalent to weavers who are their neighbors. They are not really incorporated into the local caste hierarchy, and they marry exclusively with Muslims in Tehri Garhwal or the valley.

7 William Rowe (in a personal communication) has pointed out that a similar mechanism for resolution of the low-caste dilemma of mobility aspirations and dharma is to blame one's own unalterable fate for failure to attempt to move up. There may simply be no use trying to improve one's condition if it is determined by fate.

CHAPTER 7   INTERCASTE RELATIONS

1 At the Bhatbair fair most of the women in attendance were of low castes while many of the men were of high castes, and the sexual activities among them were a prominent feature of the fair. There is also the well-known fact that Pahari girls who become prostitutes are usually of low castes, as are all of the traditionally available singing and dancing girls.

CHAPTER 8   THE VILLAGE COMMUNITY

1 In the context of informal village social interaction, clans and sibs are almost synonymous, the sib forming the core and including wives of sib members. The named groups are sibs, and the corresponding interacting groups are thought of as sibs by villagers but are usually clans. This should be borne in mind throughout the chapter.

CHAPTER 10   CONCLUSION

1 The history of Pahari contacts may also be a factor. Seclusion of women in India is attributable in large part to Moghul rule. Apparently people of the hills escaped most of this influence, and those plains people who came to the hills in Moghul times were among the ones who resisted Moghul influence most strongly.

Index

Language. *See* Pahari
Law. *See* Crime; Disputes; Government; Inheritance; Judicial council; Village government; *Panchayat*
Leach, E. R., 197, 431 n. 1
Leadership, 281, 283–284, 324–325
Levirate, 79, 152–153
Lewis, I. M., 393
Lewis, O., 81, 110, 122, 127, 187, 247, 249, 258, 264, 265, 295, 325
Life-cycle ceremonies, 126–131
Lineage, 176, 177 (figure), 178–179
Lingra, 185
Lipset, S., 223
Liquor: consumption of, 94, 227, 239, 240, 242; manufacture of, 64, 66, 73–74, 372
Literature on Paharis, 6–8
Litigation. *See* Courts
Little tradition of Hinduism, 82
Livestock. *See* Animal husbandry
Lohar. *See* Blacksmith
Low castes, 14–15, 20–21, 63–68; accommodation of, to status, 236–237, 254–256, 392–393, 395–397; compensatory gains of, 253; disadvantages of status of, 242–254; discrimination against, 226, 236, 237–238; place of, in economy, 41, 59–61, 63–71; rank of, 211–217; rationale and resentment of status among, 84–86, 220–226, 392–393, 395–397; relations among, xlii–xlv, 232–233; relations of, with high castes, 233–242, 255–256; social organization of, 181–182, 190–191
Lower Himalayas. *See* Kumaon
Lowie, R. H., 149, 427 n. 2

Madan (maidān), 92, 102
Mahabharata, 8, 12, 15, 104
Mahadev. *See* Mahasu; Shiva
Mahar, J. M., 70, 360
Mahar, P. M., 81, 109, 136, 199, 210, 247
Mahasu, 102, 107–109
Majumdar, D. N., 8, 18, 19, 20, 21, 80, 81, 143, 160, 169, 200, 201, 249, 346, 347, 348, 430 nn. 4, 7, 9
Mandelbaum, D. G., 210
Mandir. See Temple
Mantra, 89
Manu, 19, 138
Marijuana, 74
Markets. *See* Trade and Markets

Marriage: age at, 153; ceremonies, 127–130; cross-caste, 154–157, 229; kin groups in, 184–185, 188–190; matrilocal, 78–79, 183–187; networks, 24 (map), 159–160, 350; regulations, xlv–xlvi, 148–150; second, 129–130, 160–163
Marriott, M., 81, 82, 103, 110, 122, 123, 124, 138, 199, 202
Mass media, 303–304
Material culture, 32–33, 310–311, 345–346, 369. *See also* Clothing and ornament; Houses
Matri, 98
Matris. See Sprites
Mayer, A. C., 208
Mayne, H., 348
Medicine, 69, 89, 116–117. *See also* Curers; Illness
Mememdia, 380
Merchants. *See* Shops in Sirkanda; Trade and markets; Vaishya
Merton, R. K., 140
Methods. *See* Research methods and conditions
Milk products, 50–51, 317, 363
Miracles, 381–386, 388–392; *See also Devta*
Missionaries, 429 chap. 3 n. 1
Mistri, 213, 216
Mobility, 397–398; *See also* Caste, mobility; Plainsward mobility; Reference groups; Sanskritization
Moiety, 188, 189
Morgan, K. W., 81, 82, 124
Mortality, infant, 164
Mother goddess. *See* Devi; Matri
"Mountaineer" [Mr. Wilson of Mussoorie], 6–7
Mourning. *See* Death ceremonies
Mukhia, 78
Mundkile ceremony, 102, 133, 378, 387, 391–392
Munshi, K. M., 8, 347
Murder, 282–283
Murdock, G. P., 148, 149, 176, 179, 183, 184, 188, 189, 191, 193, 427 n. 2, 429–430 n. 1, 431 n. 12
Music, 400. *See also* songs
Muslims, 209, 224, 301, 429 chap. 3 n. 1, 432 n. 6
Mussoorie, 9, 13, 24 (map), 31, 295, 301–302

Nadel, S. F., 431 n. 1
Nai. *See* Barber